The
PRAYER BOOK
HYMNAL

A Supplement of Hymns & Propers for the Book of Common Prayer

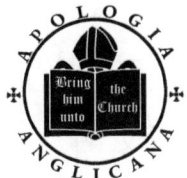

APOLOGIA ANGLICANA
BOSTON, MASSACHUSETTS
A. D. MMXXV

Table of Contents

Copyright i

Editor's Preface ix

Ferial Hymns 1
    Invitatory Hymns 2
    Summer Hymns 14
    Winter Hymns 32

Liturgical Hymns 51
    Ordinary of the Office 52
    Office Service 60
    Great Litany 77
    Communion Services 78
    Creeds 98
    Sequences 102
    Paraliturgical Hymns 108

Devotional Hymns 117

Propers of the Church Year 307
    Proper of Season 308
    Proper of Saints 419

Commons of the Saints 671
    Commons for the Apostles 672
    Commons for a Martyr Bishop 682
    Commons for a Martyr 688
    Commons for Many Martyrs 692
    Commons for Martyrs in Eastertide 705
    Commons for a Confessor Bishop 715
    Commons for a Confessor 725
    Commons for Virgin Martyresses 733
    Commons for a Virgin 742
    Commons for Holy Women not Virgins 746
    Commons Dear to Christ 753

Hymn Index 769

Copyright

The Prayer Book Hymnal (© 2025 Apologia Anglicana, LLC) is licenced under CC BY-SA 4.0. To view a copy of this license, visit https://creativecommons.org/licenses/by-sa/4.0/

ISBN: 978-1-969461-02-6 (Hardcover)

Library of Congress Control Number: 2025918495

Edited by J. P. 'Augustine' Watson (Augustine@ApologiaAnglicana.org), with the irreplaceable assistance of Ryan May.

We are thankful to have such great giants upon whose shoulders we stand. These works are used in this Book according to fair use, where their content is not already in the public domain. What was used from each book, or in what way it was consulted, is described under the citation.

Davis, C. Lance, ed. *The Anglican Office Book*. 2nd edition. Chester: Whithorn Press, 2023.
The adapted Office portions of the Feasts of Our Lady of Walsingham and St. Joseph of Arimathea.

The English Missal for the Laity. London: W. Knott & Sons Limited, 1933.
Mass Prayers for Feast Days, and Rubrics.

Monastic Breviary Matins. Tymawr: Society of the Holy Cross, 1961.
Invitatory Hymn for the Feasts of St. Scholastica, St. Benedict, the Precious Blood, St. Mary Magdalene, the Chains of St. Peter, and the Seven Sorrows.

And a special thanks must be given to GregoBase (https://gregobase.selapa.net/), without whose Public Domain notation files for the Invitatory and Office Hymns this Book simply would not be possible. I am especially thankful to the transcribers Albert Bloomfield, Benedictine monk, BruceL, Mateusz Ciesiółka, Dominique CROCHU, pcouderc, Pierre François, Harpa Dei, HdP, Andrew Hinkley, Nguyễn Thiện Tuấn Hoàng, Joerg Hudelmaier, Jakub Jelínek, MarkM, marteo, Br Michael, Br Michael OSB, rcarey, and Christopher Tatum.

Copyright

Devotional Hymn Copyright

¶ The copyright for each hymn is Public Domain, unless otherwise noted. Great thanks must be given to the Open Hymnal Project.

A Mighty Fortress is Our God
Words: Martin Luther, 1529. Translation Frederic Henry Hedge, 1853.
Music: 'Ein Feste Burg (Isorhythmic)' Martin Luther, 1529. Setting: "Common Service Book" (ULCA), 1917, alt.
Music source: 'Common Service Book with Hymnal', ULCA 1918 Hymn 195, alt. to match syncopation of Hedge translation
Lyric source: Presbyterian Hymnal, Revised, 1911 Hymn 122.

Alleluia, Sing to Jesus!
Words: William Chatterton Dix, 1867.
Music: 'HyFrydol' Rowland H. Prichard, 1830. Setting: "The English Hymnal", 1906.
Arrangement: English hymnal, 1906 assumes RV Williams.
Music source: 'The English Hymnal' 1906, Hymn 563.

All Creatures of Our God and King
Words: Francis of Assisi circa 1225. Translated by William H. Draper, 1919.
Music: 'Lasst Uns Erfreuen' from Geistliche Kirchengesäng, Köln, 1623. Setting: Ralph Vaughan Williams, 1906.
Music source: 'Lutheran Worship' Hymnal, 1982 Hymn 436.

Amazing Grace
Words: John Newton, 1779. last verse author unknown, before 1829.
Music: 'New Britain' James P. Carrell and David L. Clayton, 1831. Setting: Edwin Othello Excell, 1900.
Music source: "Joy to the World", 1915, Hymn 209 Ed. E. O. Excell explicit about arrangement. Christian Classics Ethereal Library (ccel.org) Hymnary Think setting from "Make His praise glorious", 1900. Ed. Edwin Othello Excell.

And did those feet in ancient time
Words: First (Original) Verse, William Blake, c. 1804. Second Verse, Kenneth G.H. Bryant, 2017.
Music: Jerusalem (Parry) Charles H. H. Parry, 1916.
Arrangement: Augustine Watson, 2025.
Copyright: CC0 Public Domain Dedication (Bryant dedicated his words to the public domain).

Be Thou My Vision
Words: Attr. Dallan Forgaill, 8th Century. Translated by Mary Byrne, 1905 and Eleanor Hull, 1912.
Music: 'Slane' Traditional Irish. Setting: Mark Hamilton Dewey, 2007.
All portions of the setting that were not already public domain were released to the public domain by the arranger on 27 July 2007. He already had released the parts and the versification (except for a few changes in the third verse, which he released to the public domain in 2007) to the public domain in 2006.

Come Thou Fount of Every Blessing
Words: Robert Robinson, 1758. Music: 'Nettleton' Asahel Nettleton, 1812.
Setting: "The Evangelical Hymnal", 1921.
Music source: The Evangelical Hymnal, 1921, Hymn 256. Almost the same as The Presbyterian Hymnal, 1874 Hymn 94.

Crown Him with Many Crowns
Words: Verses 1, 4, 5, 6, & 9: Matthew Bridges, The Passion of Jesus, 1852. Verses 2 & 3: Godfrey Thring, Hymns and Sacred Lyrics, 1874.
Music: 'Diademata' George J. Elvey, 1868. Setting: "Appendix to Hymns Ancient and Modern", 1869.
Music source: "Appendix to Hymns Ancient and Modern", 1869 Hymn 318. Ed. William H. Monk. Unknown if the arrangement is Elvey's or Monk's.

Dear Christians, One and All Rejoice
Words: Martin Luther, 1523. Translated by Richard Massie, 1854, alt.
Music: 'Nun Freut Euch' attr. Martin Luther from Etlich Christlich Lider, Wittenberg, 1524. Setting: Johann Hermann Schein, 1627.
Music source: "The Hymns of Martin Luther" by Bacon, 1883. Setting originally from "Cantional oder Gesangbuch Augburgischer Konfession" by Johann Hermann Schein.

Faith of Our Fathers
Words: Frederick W. Faber, 1849. Refrain by James G. Walton, 1874.
Music: 'St. Catherine' Henri F. Hemy (1818-1888). Setting: James G. Walton, 1874.
Music source: The Evangelical Hymnal, 1921 Hymn 408.

I Need Thee Every Hour
Words: Annie Sherwood Hawks, 1872.
Music: 'I Need Thee Every Hour' Robert Lowry, 1872. Setting: "Pentecostal Hymns, No. 2", 1898.
Music source: "Pentecostal Hymns, No. 2" 1898 page 155. ABC file contributed to the Open Hymnal by Samuel Cantrell, 18 Jan 2012.

Copyright

I Sing the Mighty Power of God
Words: Isaac Watts, 1709.
Music: 'Ellacombe' from Gesangbuch der Herzogl. Hofkapelle, Wurttemberg, 1784. Setting: "Amore Dei", 1897.
Music and Lyrics source: Hymnal "Amore Dei" (published 1897) Hymn 115. ABC file contributed to the Open Hymnal by Tobin Strong, 09 Jan 2014.

I Vow to Thee My Country
Words: Cecil Spring-Rice, 1859-1918.
Music: 'Thaxted' Gustav Holst, 1918.
Arrangement: Augustine Watson, 2025, based on "The Winchester Hymn Supplement: with Tunes", 1928, in consultation with the arrangement by Paul Hayward, 2011.
Copyright: CC0 Public Domain Dedication.
Music source: "The Winchester Hymn Supplement: with Tunes", 1928.

If God Had Not Been on Our Side
Words: Martin Luther, 1524. Translation composite.
Music: 'Wär Gott nicht mit uns diese Zeit (1537)' from Walter's Hymnal, 1537.
Setting: "Evangelical Lutheran Hymn-Book", 1931.

Immaculate Mary
Words: "Catholic Church Hymnal", 1905. Verses added by Augustine Watson, 2025 (put into public domain).
Music: Traditional tune.
Setting: "Catholic Church Hymnal", 1905.
Copyright: CC0 Public Domain Dedication.

Immortal, Invisible, God Only Wise
Words: Walter Chalmers Smith, 1876.
Music: 'St. Denio' or 'Joanna' or 'Palestrina' traditional Welsh found in "Caniadau y Cyssegr" by John Roberts, 1839.
Setting: "Caniadau y Cyssegr a'r Teulu", 1878, alt.
Music source: Episcopal Hymnal, 1940, Hymn 301. Also in English Hymnal, 1906 Hymn 407 (page missing in my copy). Setting from "Caniadau y Cyssegr a'r Teulu", 1878 hymn 442, alt.

It Is Well with My Soul
Words: Horatio G. Spafford, 1873.
Music and Setting: 'It Is Well' or 'Ville Du Havre' Philip P. Bliss, 1876.
Music source: The Evangelical Hymnal, 1921 Hymn 208.

Joyful, Joyful, We Adore Thee
Words: Henry J. van Dyke, 1907.
Music: 'Ode to Joy' Ludwig van Beethoven; Adapted by Edward Hodges, 1824.
Setting: "The Methodist Hymnal", 1905.
Music source: The Methodist Hymnal, 1905 Hymn 160.

Let All Mortal Flesh Keep Silence
Words: from Liturgy of St. James, 4th Century. Translated by Gerard Moultrie, 1864.
Music: 'Picardy' traditional French. Setting: "The English Hymnal", 1906, alt.
Music source: The Episcopal Hymnal, 191x Hymn 339 and English Hymnal 1906 Hymn 318.

Lift High the Cross
Words: George W. Kitchin (1827-1912). Modified by Michael R. Newbolt, 1916.
Music: 'Crucifier' Sydney H. Nicholson, 1916. Setting: "Hymns Ancient and Modern", 1922.
Music source: 'Lutheran Worship' Hymnal, 1982 Hymn 311. From "Hymns Ancient and Modern", Standard Edition Hymn 745, 1922.

Look Down, O Lord, from Heaven Behold
Words: Martin Luther, 1524. Translated by Frances Elizabeth Cox, 1864.
Music: 'Ach Gott vom Himmel' from Erfurt Enchiridion, 1524. Setting: Karl August Haupt, 1869. This tune is also used in Klug's 1543 hymnal, and that hymnal is sometimes incorrectly referenced as the source
Music source: "The Hymns of Martin Luther" by Bacon, 1883.

Lord, Keep Us Steadfast in Thy Word
Words: Martin Luther, 1541. Translated by Catherine Winkworth, 1863.
Music: 'Erhalt Uns, Herr, bei deinem Wort' from Klug's "Geistliche Lieder auffs new gebessert", 1543.
Setting: Hans Leo Hassler, unknown date.
Music source: Evangelical Lutheran Hymn Book (LCMS), Edition of 1931 Hymn 274.

Now Thank We All Our God
Words: Martin Rinkart, c.1636. Translated Catherine Winkworth, 1856. Music: 'Nun Danket' Johann Crüger, 1647.
Setting: "The New Hymnal", 1924.
Music source: "The New Hymnal", 1924.

Our God, Our Help in Ages Past
Words: Isaac Watts, 1719. Music: 'St. Anne' William Croft, 1708.
Setting: composite found in "The Lutheran Hymnary", 1913.
Music source: 'The Lutheran Hymnary', 1913, Hymn 261. Arrangement is composite, first half from "Hymns Ancient and Modern", 1869, Hymn 231. ed William Henry Monk. Second half is from "The Hymnal Companion to the Book of Common Prayer", 1890, Hymn 279. ed. Charles Vincent, D.J. Wood, John Stainer

Out of the Deep I Cry to Thee
Words: Martin Luther, 1524. Translated by Arthur Tozer Russell (1806-1874).

Copyright

Music: 'Aus Tiefer Not (Luther)' or 'Af Dybsens Nød' Martin Luther from Erfurt Enchiridion, 1524.
Setting: Johann Sebastian Bach, 1725.
Music source: "The Hymns of Martin Luther" by Bacon, 1883.

Praise God from Whom All Blessing Flow
Words: Thomas Ken, 1674. Music: 'Old 100th' Genevan Psalter, attr. Louis Bourgeois, c. 1551.
Setting: Sternhold and Hopkins' Psalter, 1561.
Music source: ccel from Sternhold and Hopkins' Psalter 1561.

Praise My Soul the King of Heaven
Words: Henry F. Lyte, 1834.
Music: 'Praise My Soul' or 'Lauda Anima' or 'St. Paul' John Goss, 1869. Setting: "The Choral Hymnal", 1888.
Music Source: "The Plymouth Hymnal", 1894 Hymn 219. "The Choral Hymnal", 1888 page 54.

Praise to the Lord, the Almighty
Words: Joachim Neander, 1680. Translated by Catherine Winkworth, 1863.
Music: 'Lobe den Herren' from Ander Theil des Erneuerten Gesangbuch, 1665.
Setting: William Sterndale Bennett, 1863, alt.
Music source: "The Chorale Book for England", 1863 Hymn 9. Ed. Winkworth (words) and Bennett (music)., slightly alt. per "Evangelical Lutheran Hymn-Book", 1931.

That Men a Godly Life Might Live
Words: Martin Luther, 1524. Translated by Richard Massie, 1854, alt.
Music: 'Dies sind die heil'gen zehu Gebot' or 'In Gottes Namen fahren wir' circa 1200s found in Erfurt Enchiridion, 1524. Setting: Michael Praetorius, 1609.

The Church's One Foundation
Words: Samuel John Stone, 1866. Music: 'Aurelia' Samuel Sebastian Wesley, 1864. Verse 4 modified by Augustine Watson, 2025.
Setting: "Order of worship for the Reformed Church in the United States", 1866.
Copyright: CC0 Public Domain Dedication.
Music source: 'Lutheran Worship' Hymnal, 1982 Hymn 289. Almost the same as "Order of worship for the Reformed Church in the United States", 1866 Hymn 441

The King of Love
Words: Henry W. Baker, 1868.
Music: Irish Melody, harm. from "The English Hymnal", 1906.
Arrangement: Augustine Watson, 2025.
Copyright: CC0 Public Domain Dedication.
Music source: Hymnary.org

The Mouth of Fools Doth God Confess
Words: Martin Luther, 1524. Translated by Richard Massie, 1854, alt.
Music: 'Es spricht der Unweisen Mund' from Walter's Geistliche Gesangbüchlein, 1524. Setting: Michael Praetorius, 1610.

Though in the Midst of Life We Be
Words: v.1 Medieval sequence, vs 2,3 Martin Luther, 1524. Translated by Richard Massie, 1854, alt.
Music: 'Mitten wir im Leben Sind' Medieval sequence altered by Martin Luther. Found in Walter's Geistliche Gesangbüchlein, 1524. Setting: Erythraeus, 1608.

To Avert from Men God's Wrath
Words: Latin c. 1400, sometimes attr. John Hus. Translated Christian Ignatius Latrobe, 1789.
Music: 'Gethsemane' or 'Petra' Richard Redhead, 1853.
Setting: "The Church Hymnal, Revised and Enlarged" (Episcopal), 1896.
Music source: "The Church Hymnal, Revised and Enlarged" (Episcopal), 1896 Ed. Charles Hutchins Hymn 93.
Lyrics source: "Hymnal and Liturgies of the Moravian Church", 1920.

Ye Watchers and Ye Holy Ones
Words: John Athelstan Laurie Riley, 1906.
Music: Geistliche Kirchengesäng, 1623; harm. Ralph Vaughan Williams, 1906.
Arrangement: Augustine Watson, 2025.
Copyright: CC0 Public Domain Dedication.
Music source: Hymnary.org

Come, Thou Long Expected Jesus
Words: Charles Wesley, 1745.
Music and Setting: 'Jefferson' from "Southern Harmony", 1835, alt.
Music source: Southern Harmony, 1835, Hymn 42. Setting heavily altered for congregational use.

O Come O Come Emmanuel
Words: various, combined by unknown author approx 12th Century, Translated by John Mason Neale, 1851. Second and seventh verses translated by H. S. Coffin (modified by Augustine Watson), 1916. Last verses by Augustine Watson, 2025.
Music: 'Veni Emmanuel' 15th Century French processional.
Setting: "Common Service Book" (ULCA), 1917.
Arrangement: Augustine Watson, 2025.
Copyright: CC0 Public Domain Dedication.
Music source: ULCA Hymnal, 1917 Hymn 1. PECUSA Hymnal (1920), Hymn 44.

On Jordan's Bank the Baptist's Cry
Words: Charles Coffin, 1736. st. 1-3 translated by John Chandler, 1837; st 4-5 translator unknown.
Music: 'Puer Nobis Nascitur' Michael Praetorius, 1609.

Copyright

Setting: George Ratcliffe Woodward for "The English Hymnal", 1906.
Music source: 'The English Hymnal', 1906 Hymn 14.

Saviour of the Nations Come
Words: Ambrose of Milan, c. 397. Translated to German by Martin Luther, 1524. Translated from German to English by William M. Reynolds, 1851.
Music: 'Nun Komm, Der Heiden Heiland' from Walter's Geistliche Gesangbüchlein, 1524.
Setting: "Mehrstimmiges ChoralBuch", 1906.
Music source: "Mehrstimmiges ChoralBuch", 1906 Hymn #135, page 109 Ed. Karl Brauer. slightly altered. The Evangelical Lutheran Hymn Book, 1931, Hymn 141.

A Great and Mighty Wonder
Words: Germanus of Constantinople (634-734). Translated by John Mason Neale, 1862.
Music: 'Es Ist Ein Ros Entsprungen (Rhythmic)' German from Köln, 1599. Setting: Michael Praetorius, 1609.
Music source: The English Hymnal, 1906. Hymn 19

All Praise to Jesus' Hallowed Name
Words: verse 1, ancient German. verses 2-7, Martin Luther, 1524. Translated by Richard Massie, 1854, alt.
Music: 'Gelobet Seist Du' ancient German found in Walter's Geistliche Gesangbüchlein, 1524.
Setting: Karl August Haupt, 1869.
Music source: "The Hymns of Martin Luther by Leonard Woolsey Bacon 1883, p. 20.

Angels We Have Heard on High
Words: French Carol; Translated by James Chadwick, 1862.
Music: 'Gloria' French carol melody. Setting: Edward (or Edwin) S. Barnes, before 1916.
Music source: 'Lutheran Worship' Hymnal, 1982 Hymn 55. "Carols Old And Carols New", 1916 Carol 181.

Away in a Manger
Words: stanzas 1,2 anonymous published Philadelphia, 1885. stanza 3 John T. MacFarland (1851-1913).
Music: 'Mueller' James R. Murray, 1887. Setting: "Hymnal for American Youth", 1919.
Music source: "Hymnal for American Youth", Hymn 84 1919 ed. H. Augustine Smith. Music reputed to be first published in "Dainty Songs for Little Lads and Lasses" by James R. Murray, 1887, hymn 8.

God Rest Ye Merry Gentlemen
Words: Traditional English.
Music: 'God Rest Ye Merry Gentlemen' Traditional English. Setting: "Carols Old And Carols New", 1918.

Music source: 'Carols Old And Carols New', 1918 carol 722.

Good King Wenceslas
Words: John M. Neale, 1853.
Music: 'Tempus Adest Floridum' 13th Century spring carol; first published in the Swedish Piae Cantones, 1582.
Setting: Carols Old And Carols New, 1916.

Hark! The Herald Angels Sing
Words: Charles Wesley, 1739, alt.
Music: 'Mendelssohn' from 'Festgesang' Felix Mendelssohn, 1840. Setting: William H. Cummings, 1857.
Music source: 'Lutheran Worship' Hymnal, 1982 Hymn 49.

In the Bleak Mid-Winter
Words: Christina Georgina Rossetti, 1872, alt.
Music and Setting: 'Cranham' Gustav Theodore Holst, 1906, alt.
Music source: "The English Hymnal, 1906.

It Came upon a Midnight Clear
Words: Edmund H. Sears, 1849. Music: 'Carol' Richard S. Willis, 1861.
Setting: "Order of worship for the Reformed Church in the United States", 1866.
Music source: "Order of worship for the Reformed Church in the United States", 1866 Hymn 63. Supposed to be found in "Church Corals and Choir Studies" 1850 by Willis, but I don't see it in that book. Some sources say 1850, some 1859, some 1861. Willis was editor for "The Musical World" magazine. Probably first appeared there.

Joy to the World
Words: Isaac Watts, 1719.
Music: 'Antioch' pieced together from "Messiah" George F. Handel, 1741. Setting: Lowell Mason, 1836.
Music source: 'Lutheran Worship' Hymnal, 1982 Hymn 53.

Lo, How A Rose E'er Blooming
Words: verses 1-2, 15th Century German. Translated by Theodore Baker, 1894. Verses 3,4 Fridrich Layriz (1808-1859). Translated by Harriet Reynolds Krauth, 1875. Verse 5, 15th Century German. Translated by John C. Mattes, 1914.
Music: 'Es Ist Ein Ros Entsprungen (Rhythmic)' German from Köln, 1599. Setting: Michael Praetorius, 1609.
Music source: The English Hymnal, 1906. Hymn 19

O Come, All Ye Faithful
Words: John F. Wade, circa 1743. v.1-3, 6 Translated by Frederick Oakeley, 1841; v. 4, 5 Translated by William T. Brooke (1848-1917).
Music: 'Adeste Fideles' or 'Portuguese Hymn'

Copyright

John F. Wade, 1743. Setting: "A Hymnal" (Episcopal), 1916.
Music source: "A Hymnal" (Episcopal), 1916 Hymn 72, alt.

O Word of God the Father
Words: Bradford Littlejohn.
Music: 'Thaxted', Holst, 1921.
Arrangement: Augustine Watson, 2025.
Copyright: 2024 Bradford Littlejohn. Permission received for use in this hymnal. All Rights Reserved.

Silent Night
Words: Josef Mohr, 1818. stanzas 1,3 Translated by John Freeman Young, 1863. Stanzas 2,4 translator anonymous.
Music: 'Stille Nacht' Franz Xaver Gruber, 1818.
Setting: "Concordia Kinderchöre", 1908.
Music source: 'Lutheran Worship' Hymnal, 1982 Hymn 68.
Music source: "Concordia Kinderchöre", 1908 Hymn 42 page 54.

The First Noel
Words: Traditional English carol, possibly dating from as early as the 13th Century.
Music: 'The First Noel' Traditional English carol, possibly dating from as early as the 13th Century.
Setting: "The Methodist Sunday School Hymnal", 1911.
Music source: The Methodist Sunday School Hymnal, 1911 Hymn 66.

To Shepherds as They Watched by Night
Words: Martin Luther, 1543. translated by Richard Massie, 1854.
Music: 'Vom Himmel Hoch' traditional German from Schumann's Geistliche Lieder, Leipzig, 1539.
Setting: "Common Service Book" (ULCA), 1917.
Music source: 'Common Service Book with Hymnal', ULCA 1918 Hymn 19.

What Child is This?
Words: William Chatterton Dix, 1865.
Music: 'Greensleeves' 16th Century English Traditional.
Setting: traditional from "The Sunday School Hymnal and Service Book", 1871.
Music source: 'Lutheran Worship' Hymnal, 1982 Hymn 61. very tiny changes from "The Sunday school hymnal and service book", 1871 edited by Charles Lewis Hutchins Carol 9 (after hymns).

As with Gladness Men of Old
Words: William Chatterton Dix, 1860.
Music: 'Dix' or 'Treuer Heiland, Wir Sind Heir' Conrad Kocher, 1838. Abridged by William Henry Monk, 1861.
Setting: Conrad Kocher, 1838, alt. by William Henry Monk, 1861, alt. for "The English Hymnal", 1906.

Music source: The English Hymnal, 1906 Hymn 39. Music from "Stimmen aus dem Reiche Gottes", 1838 by Kocher, Hymn 201 page 250. Adapted by William Henry Monk from the original (removed two measures and changed parts of the arrangement) for "Hymns Ancient and Modern, 1861. Also almost just like the Bristol Tune Book of 1863, Hymn 172.

Brightest and Best of the Sons of Morning
Words: James P. Harding, 1892.
Music: Morning Star.
Music source: The English Hymnal, 1940 Hymn 46.

Lord, Who at Cana's Wedding Feast
Words: Adelaide Thrupp, 1853. Music: 'St. Ursula' Frederick Westlake, 1863.
Setting: "The Church Hymnal, Revised and Enlarged" (Episcopal), 1896.
Music source: "The Church Hymnal, Revised and Enlarged" (Episcopal), 1896 Ed. Charles Hutchins Hymn 237. Words compared against "The Church Hymnal, Revised and Enlarged", 1896.

We Three Kings
Words: John Henry Hopkins, Jr., 1857.
Music: John Henry Hopkins, Jr., 1857, alt.
Setting: "Cyber Hymnal".
Arrangement: Augustine Watson, 2025.
Copyright: CC0 Public Domain Dedication.
Music source: "Cyber Hymnal".

Maker of Earth, To Thee Alone
Words: Laeta mundi, conditor. C. Coffin. Translated by J. M. Neale.
Music: Dunfermline. "Scottish Psalter", 1615.
Arrangement: Augustine Watson, 2025.
Copyright: CC0 Public Domain Dedication.
Music source: "The English Hymnal: with tunes", 1906, Hymn 64.

O Love, How Deep, How Broad
Words: O Amor quam ecstaticus. 15th century. Translated by B. Webb.
Music: Eisenach. J. H. Schein. J. S. Bach.
Arrangement: Augustine Watson, 2025.
Copyright: CC0 Public Domain Dedication.
Music source: "The English Hymnal: with tunes", 1906, Hymn 459.

Praise to the Holiest in the Height
Words: J. H. Newman.
Music: Richmond. Adapted from T. Haweis by S. Webbe (the younger).
Arrangement: Augustine Watson, 2025.
Copyright: CC0 Public Domain Dedication.
Music source: "The English Hymnal: with tunes", 1906, Hymn 471.

There is a Book Who Runs May Read
Words: J. Keble.

Copyright

Music: St. Flavian. Adapted from Psalm 132 in 'Day's Psalter', 1563.
Arrangement: Augustine Watson, 2025.
Copyright: CC0 Public Domain Dedication.
Music source: "The English Hymnal: with tunes", 1906, Hymn 497.

All Glory, Laud, and Honour
Words: Theodulf of Orleans, circa 820. Translated by John Mason Neale, 1851.
Music: 'Valet Will Ich Dir Geben' or 'St. Theodulph' Melchior Teschner, 1615.
Setting: Presbyterian Hymnal, 1911.
Music source: Presbyterian Hymnal, Revised, 1911 Hymn 216.

Lord Who Throughout These Forty Days
Words: Claudia F. Hernaman, 1873. Music: 'St. Flavian' Day's Psalter, 1563.
Setting: "The Church Hymnal, Revised and Enlarged" (Episcopal), 1905.
Music source: Episcopal Hymnal, 1905 Hymn 78.

O Jesu Christ From Thee Began
Words: 9th century text.
Music: Plaistow.
Arrangement: Augustine Watson, 2025.
Copyright: CC0 Public Domain Dedication.
Music source: "The English Hymnal: with tunes", 1906, Hymn 69.

O Sacred Head, Now Wounded
Words: Bernard of Clairvaux, 1153. Translated by James W. Alexander, 1830.
Music: 'Passion Chorale' or 'Herzlich Tut Mich Verlangen' Hans Leo Hassler, 1601. Adapted by J.S. Bach, 1729.
Setting: Johann Sebastian Bach, 1729.
Music source: The Episcopal Hymnal, 1916, Hymn 158.

When I Survey the Wondrous Cross
Words: Isaac Watts, 1707.
Music: 'Duke Street' John Hatton, 1793. Setting: "Finest of the Wheat No. 3" Hymnal, 1904.
Music source: "Finest of the Wheat No. 3" Hymnal, 1904 Hymn 257. ABC file contributed to the Open Hymnal by Tobin Strong, 20 Dec 2013. Composite from "The Anglican hymn Book", 1871 hymn 127 and "Hymns Ancient and Modern", 1869 Hymn 101.

At the Lamb's High Feast
Words: Latin, circa 6th Century. Translated by Robert Campbell, 1849.
Music: 'Sonne der Gerechtigkeit' Czech, Kirchengeseng, 1566. Setting: Brian J. Dumont, 31 Dec 2009.
Copyright: Words and Music, public domain. Setting: Copyright 2009 Brian J. Dumont. This setting may be freely reproduced or published for Christian worship, provided it is not altered, and this notice is on each copy. All other rights reserved.
Music source: tune found in many places, arrangement by BJD

Christ the Lord Is Risen Today
Words: Stanzas 1-7, Charles Wesley, 1739. Stanzas 8-10, 14th Century; translated in Lyra Davidica.
Music: 'Llanfair' Robert Williams, 1817. Setting: John Roberts, 1837.
Music source: Lutheran Worship, 1982, Hymn 137 (later modified to more closely match John Robert's original setting).

Hail Thee, Festival Day
Words: Venantius Honorius Fotunatus; translation from 'The English Hymnal', 1906, alt.
Music: Ralph Vaughan Williams, 1906.
Music source: 'Songs of Praise', 1925, Hymn 445. PECUSA Hymnal, 1940, Hymn 86.

The Strife is O'er, the Battle Done
Words: from Symphonia Sirenum Selectarum, Kʻln, 1695; translated by Francis Pott, 1861.
Music: 'Victory' or 'Palestrina' Giovanni P. da Palestrina, 1591.
Setting: William Henry Monk, 1861.
Music source: "Hymns Ancient and Modern", 1861 Hymn 114. Words checked against the same source.

See, The Lord Ascends in Triumph
Words: Christopher Wordsworth, 1862, alt.
Music: 'Rex Gloriae' Henry Thomas Smart, 1868.
Setting: "Appendix to Hymns Ancient and Modern", 1869.
Music source: "Appendix to Hymns Ancient and Modern", 1869 Hymn 293. Text is the same as "Appendix to Hymns Ancient and Modern" with the exception of the title.

Sing We Triumphant Hymns of Praise
Words: St. Bede the Venerable. Translated by B. Webb.
Music: Tugwood. Nicholas Gatty.
Arrangement: Augustine Watson, 2025.
Copyright: CC0 Public Domain Dedication.
Music source: "The English Hymnal: with tunes", 1906, Hymn 146.

Blest Joys for Mighty Wonders Wrought
Words: Beata nobis gaudia. St. Hilary of Poitiers, 4th century. Translated by Neale.
Music: T. B. Southgate.
Arrangement: Augustine Watson, 2025.
Music source: "The Armagh Hymnal", 1915, Hymn 46.

Let the Holy Spirit's Grace
Words: Nobis Sancti Spiritus. Benedict XII, 14th century. Translated by Neale.
Music: Regina Clementiae. Harleian MS. 978. Mode I.

Copyright

Arrangement: Augustine Watson, 2025.
Copyright: CC0 Public Domain Dedication
Music source: "The Armagh Hymnal", 1915, Hymn 47.

God the Father Be Our Stay
Words: 15th Century Litany, adapted by Martin Luther, 1524. Translated by Richard Massie, 1854, alt.
Music: 'Gott Der Vater, Wohn Uns Bei' from Walter's Geistliche Gesangbüchlein, 1524.
Setting: composite from Landgraf Moritz, 1612 and "Evangelical Lutheran Hymn-Book", 1931.

Holy God, We Praise Thy Name
Words: attr. Ignaz Franz, 1774. Translated by Clarence A. Walworth, 1858.
Music: 'Te Deum' or 'Hursley' or 'Grosser Gott, wir Loben Dich' from Katholisches Gesangbuch, Maria Theresa, 1774. Setting: "Hymns Ancient and Modern", 1869, alt.
Music source: "Hymns Ancient and Modern", 1869 Hymn 11

Holy, Holy, Holy
Words: Reginald Heber, 1826.
Music: 'Nicaea' John Bacchus Dykes, 1861. Setting: "Hymns Ancient and Modern", 1869.
Music source: Hymns Ancient and Modern, 1869 hymn 135. Tune from Hymns Ancient and Modern, 1861.

I Bind unto Myself Today
Words: attributed to St. Patrick of Ireland (circa 387-466). Paraphrased by Cecil F. Alexander, 1889.
Music: 'St. Patricks Breastplate' Charles V. Stanford, 1902. Setting: "The English Hymnal", 1906.
Music source: 'The English Hymnal', 1906 Hymn 212.

Isaiah, Mighty Seer, in Days of Old
Words: Martin Luther, 1526 as the Sanctus of the German Mass, after Is 6:1-4. Translation composite.
Music: 'Jesaia Dem Propheten das Geschah' Martin Luther, 1526 in the German Mass. Setting: Erythraeus, 1608.

We All Believe in One True God
Words: Medieval text expanded by Martin Luther, 1524. Translation composite.
Music: 'Wir Glauben all an Einen Gott, Schoepfer' or 'Apostolic Creed' Medieval tune altered by Martin Luther. Found in Walter's Geistliche Gesangbüchlein, 1524.
Setting: "Eisenach Kirchenconserenz", G.v. Tucher et. al., Stuttgart, 1854.

O Wondrous Type, O Vision Fair
Words: From the "Sarum Breviary", 1495. Translated by John Mason Neale, 1851.
Music: 'Deo Gracias' or 'Agincourt' traditional English, circa 1415. Setting: Charles Winfred Douglas, 1918, alt.
Music source: "A Hymnal" (Episcopal), 1918 Hymn 439, alt by BJD 21 Mar 2011. Translation found in Hymns Ancient & Modern, 1861.

Tis Good, Lord, to Be Here
Words: Joseph Armitage Robinson, 1888.
Music: 'Potsdam' adapted from Johann Sebastian Bach, 1750, by John Goss, 1854. Setting: John Goss, 1854.
Music source: "The Church Psalter and Hymn Book", 1863 hymns 212-214 (rev. from 1854 edition). Mus. Dir and arrangements by John Goss. Words match those in "Hymns Ancient And Modern", 1904, Hymn 251

Editor's Preface

> O God, my heart is ready, my heart is ready : I will sing and give praise with the best member that I have. Awake, thou lute and harp : I myself will awake right early. —Psalm 108:1-2

We are blessed to finally be able to publish the *Prayer Book Hymnal*. Together with the 2025 Proposed Book of Common Prayer (or the Office book), it completes everything necessary for a full recitation of the Daily Office within the English Orthodox tradition. It provides not only the Office propers for the Seasons and Festivals—taken almost always from the Benedictine tradition—but also the Ordinary and even devotional hymns, which are especially helpful in a parish context.

The devotional hymns hold a special place in our hearts, for it is truly an amazing display of local piety. Our goal was to provide a selection of the best of the hymnal tradition. American Anglican hymns were given pride of place, without excluding the beautiful and well-known hymns of other traditions. We trust that it will enrich not only individual Christians but also Congregations, especially smaller ones with limited choirs.

In addition to the Daily Office, it was our concern that also the Holy Sacrifice of the Mass could be celebrated with the BCP when a Minor Festival needs to be celebrated or commemorated. For everything a parish may need to celebrate, Holy Week excluded for practical reasons, the BCP and the *Prayer Book Hymnal* provide everything necessary.

As the Prayer Book Tradition matured, two kinds of 'two-book' solutions developed. On the one hand, many followed the Roman tradition of dividing the Daily Office and the Holy Mass into separate books—the Missal and the Breviary (along with a Hymnal in parish contexts). On the other hand, however, due to the centrality of the Book of Common Prayer, a second 'two-book' solution developed, retaining the BCP as the core and then providing supplements. It is within this tradition that the *Prayer Book Hymnal* has been formed and exists.

While time will tell which arrangement of liturgical books will be favoured and become dominant within the English Orthodox tradition, we are confident this Book holds an important place and unique benefit for all those committed to the daily recitation of the Office and the reverent offering of the Holy Sacrifice of the Mass.

We hope this *Prayer Book Hymnal* assists you in your prayers. Please pray for us as we pray for you and the salvation of all men.

Pax Christi,
Mr. Augustine Watson, MSt
Chief Editor, Apologia Anglicana

Ferial Hymns

Invitatory # Ferial Hymns Summer Sunday

Invitatory Hymns

Sunday Invitatory Hymn in Summer

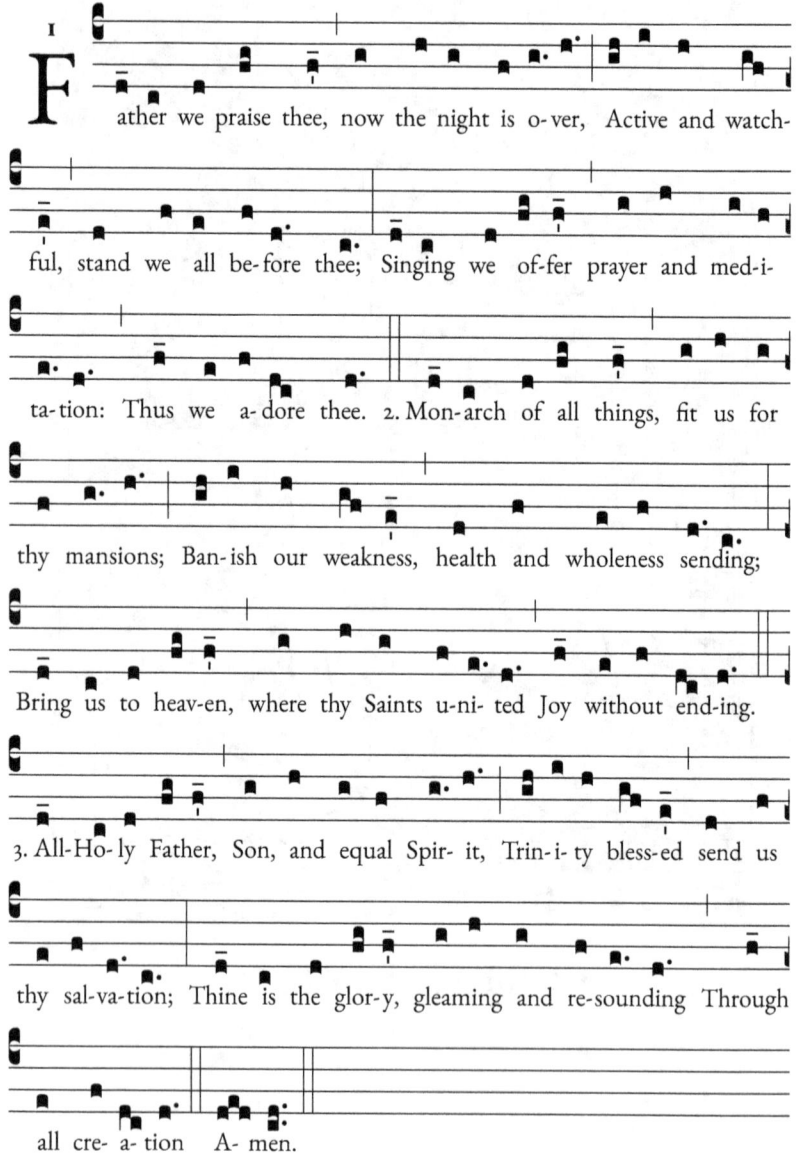

1. Father we praise thee, now the night is o-ver, Active and watch-ful, stand we all be-fore thee; Singing we of-fer prayer and med-i-ta-tion: Thus we a-dore thee. 2. Mon-arch of all things, fit us for thy mansions; Ban-ish our weakness, health and wholeness sending; Bring us to heav-en, where thy Saints u-ni-ted Joy without end-ing. 3. All-Ho-ly Father, Son, and equal Spir-it, Trin-i-ty bless-ed send us thy sal-va-tion; Thine is the glor-y, gleaming and re-sounding Through all cre-a-tion A-men.

Winter Sunday   **Ferial Hymns**   *Invitatory*

SUNDAY INVITATORY HYMN IN WINTER

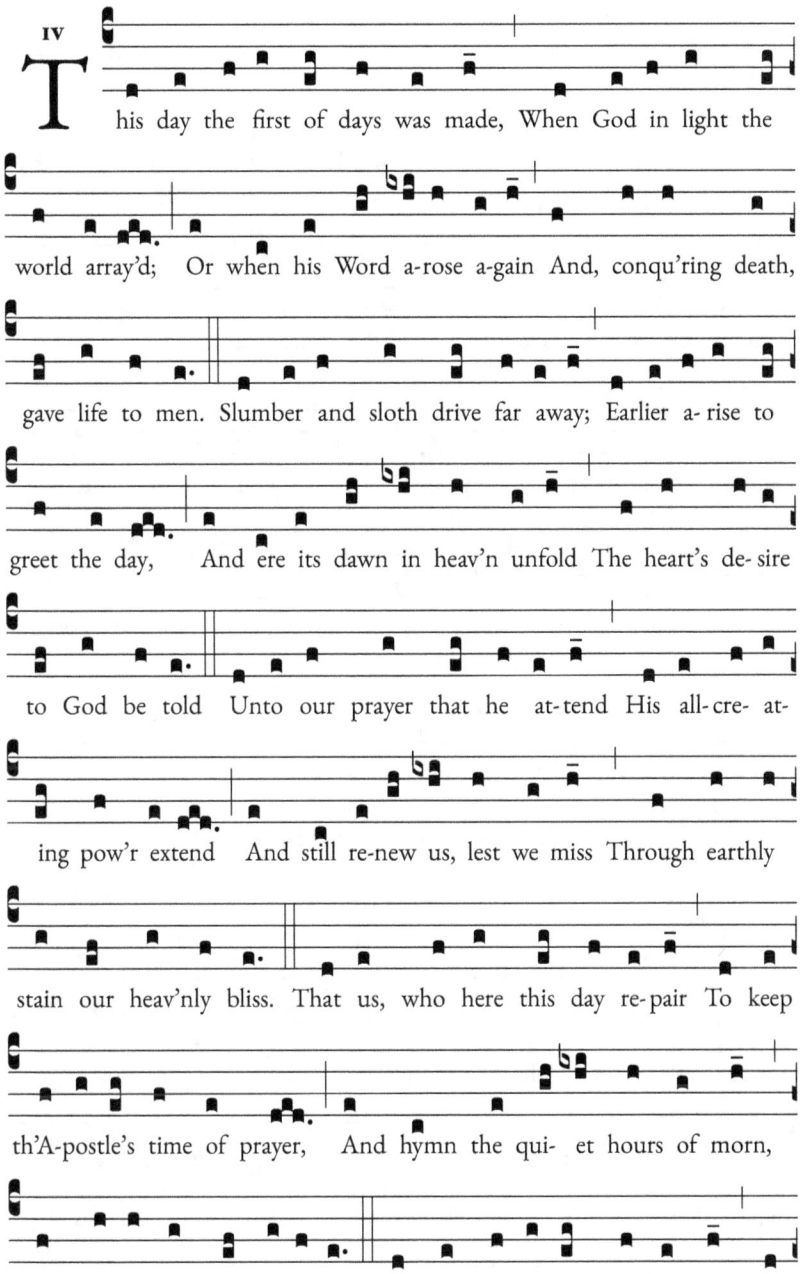

This day the first of days was made, When God in light the world array'd; Or when his Word a-rose a-gain And, conqu'ring death, gave life to men. Slumber and sloth drive far away; Earlier a-rise to greet the day, And ere its dawn in heav'n unfold The heart's de-sire to God be told Unto our prayer that he at-tend His all-cre-at-ing pow'r extend And still re-new us, lest we miss Through earthly stain our heav'nly bliss. That us, who here this day re-pair To keep th'A-postle's time of prayer, And hymn the qui-et hours of morn, With bless-ed gifts he may a-dorn. For this, Re-deemer, thee we pray That

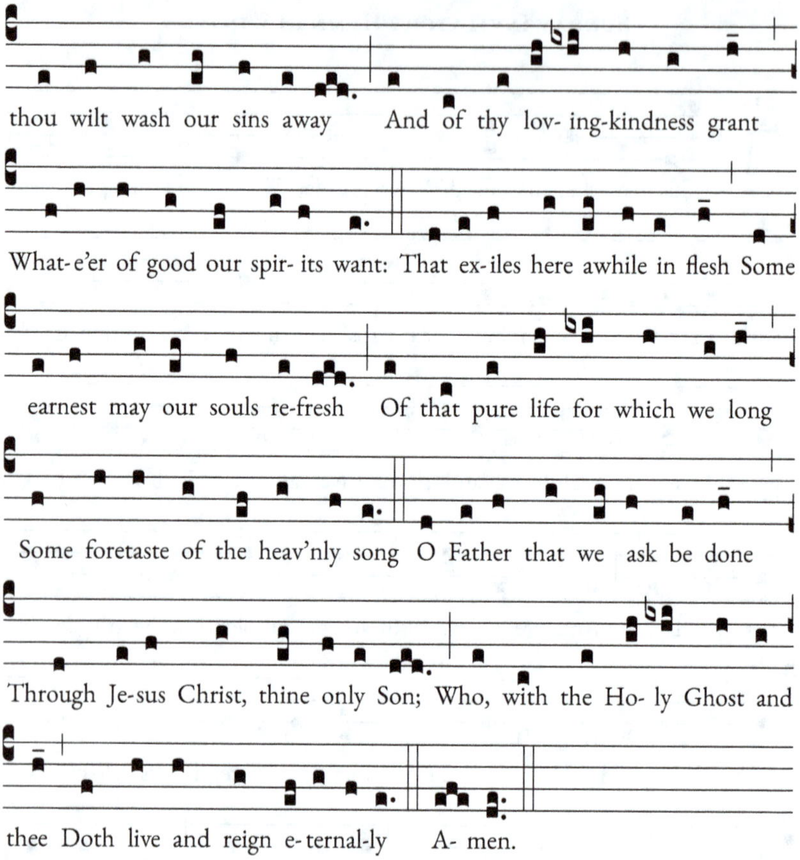

Invitatory   **Ferial Hymns**   Weekday

thou wilt wash our sins away   And of thy lov- ing-kindness grant

What-e'er of good our spir- its want: That ex-iles here awhile in flesh Some

earnest may our souls re-fresh   Of that pure life for which we long

Some foretaste of the heav'nly song   O Father that we ask be done

Through Je-sus Christ, thine only Son; Who, with the Ho- ly Ghost and

thee Doth live and reign e- ternal-ly   A- men.

WEEKDAY INVITATORY HYMN

℣ The following Invitatory Hymn is said on weekdays when Mattins is anticipated the evening prior.

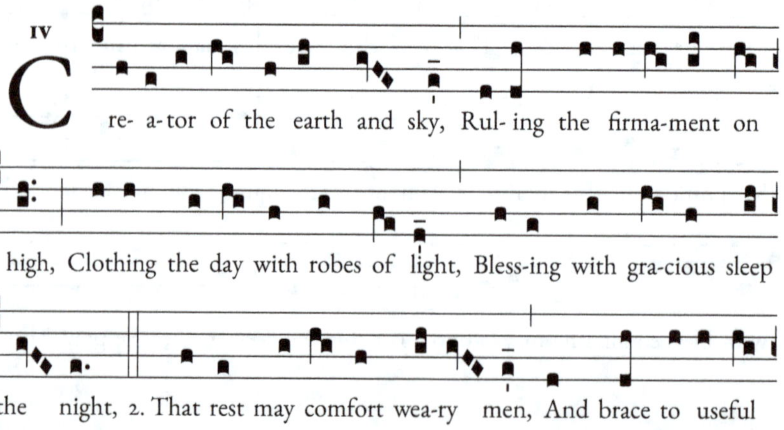

IV

Cre- a-tor of the earth and sky, Rul- ing the firma-ment on

high, Clothing the day with robes of light, Bless-ing with gra-cious sleep

the night, 2. That rest may comfort wea-ry men, And brace to useful

Weekday · **Ferial Hymns** · *Invitatory*

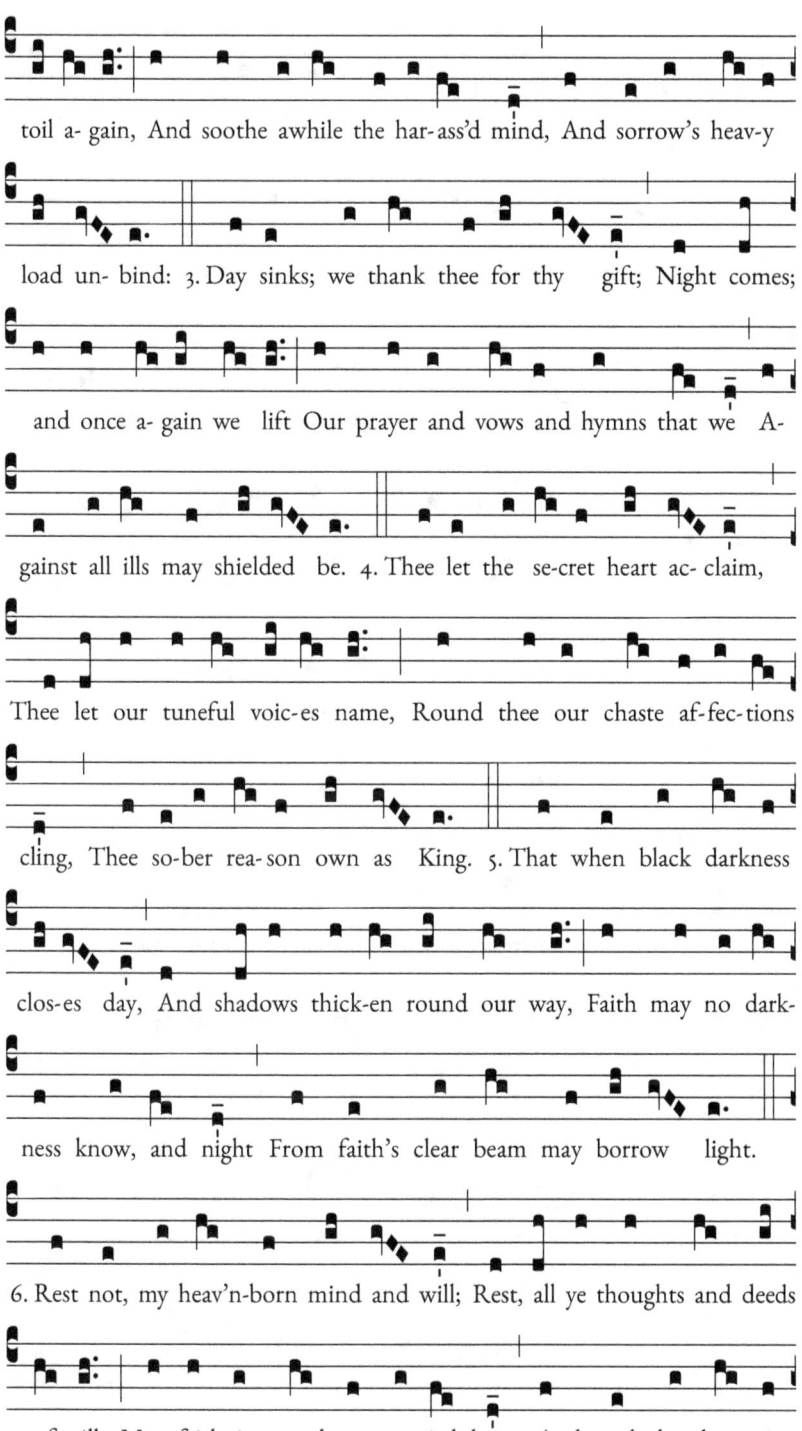

toil a-gain, And soothe awhile the har-ass'd mind, And sorrow's heav-y load un-bind: 3. Day sinks; we thank thee for thy gift; Night comes; and once a-gain we lift Our prayer and vows and hymns that we A-gainst all ills may shielded be. 4. Thee let the se-cret heart ac-claim, Thee let our tuneful voic-es name, Round thee our chaste af-fec-tions cling, Thee so-ber rea-son own as King. 5. That when black darkness clos-es day, And shadows thick-en round our way, Faith may no dark-ness know, and night From faith's clear beam may borrow light. 6. Rest not, my heav'n-born mind and will; Rest, all ye thoughts and deeds of ill; May faith its watch unwear-ied keep, And cool the dream-ing

Invitatory   **Ferial Hymns**   Monday

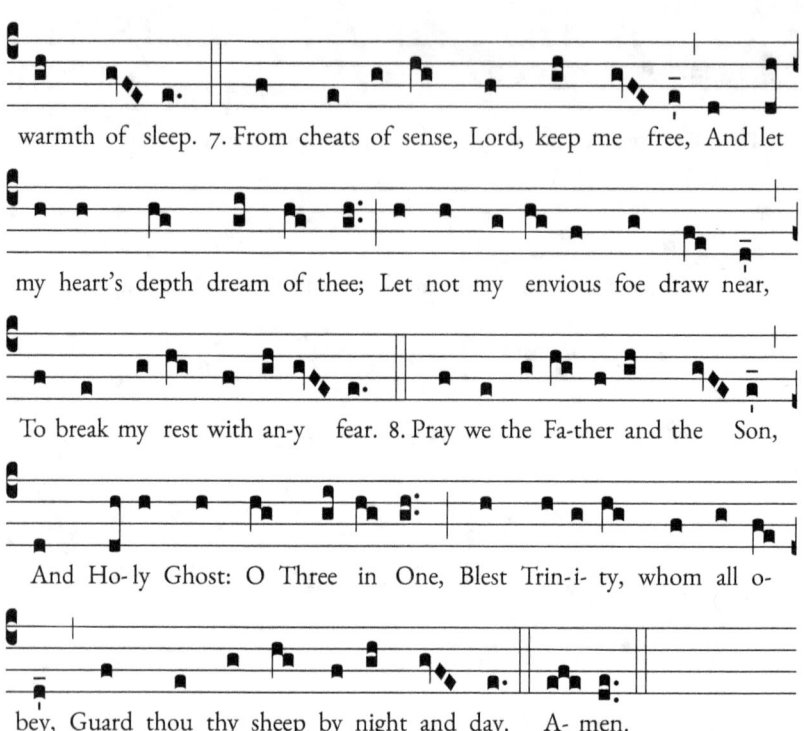

warmth of sleep. 7. From cheats of sense, Lord, keep me free, And let my heart's depth dream of thee; Let not my envious foe draw near, To break my rest with an-y fear. 8. Pray we the Fa-ther and the Son, And Ho-ly Ghost: O Three in One, Blest Trin-i-ty, whom all o-bey, Guard thou thy sheep by night and day. A-men.

Monday Invitatory Hymn

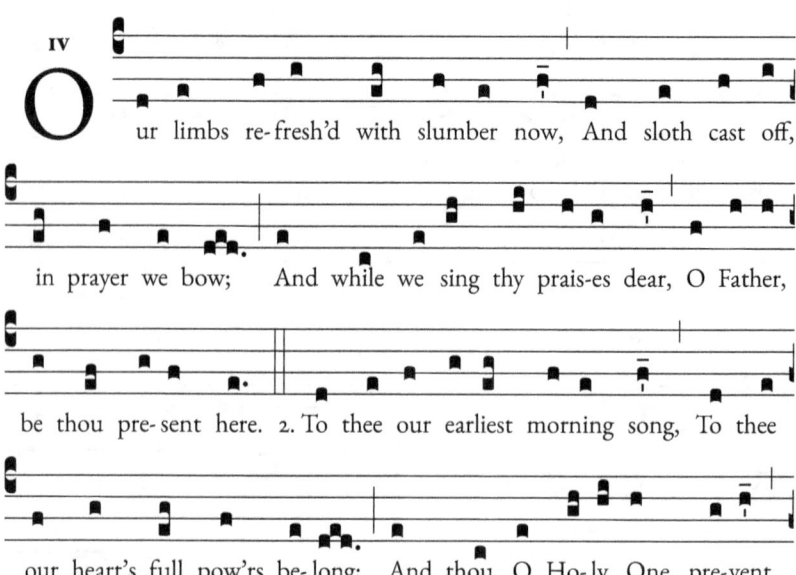

Our limbs re-fresh'd with slumber now, And sloth cast off, in prayer we bow; And while we sing thy prais-es dear, O Father, be thou pre-sent here. 2. To thee our earliest morning song, To thee our heart's full pow'rs be-long; And thou, O Ho-ly One, pre-vent

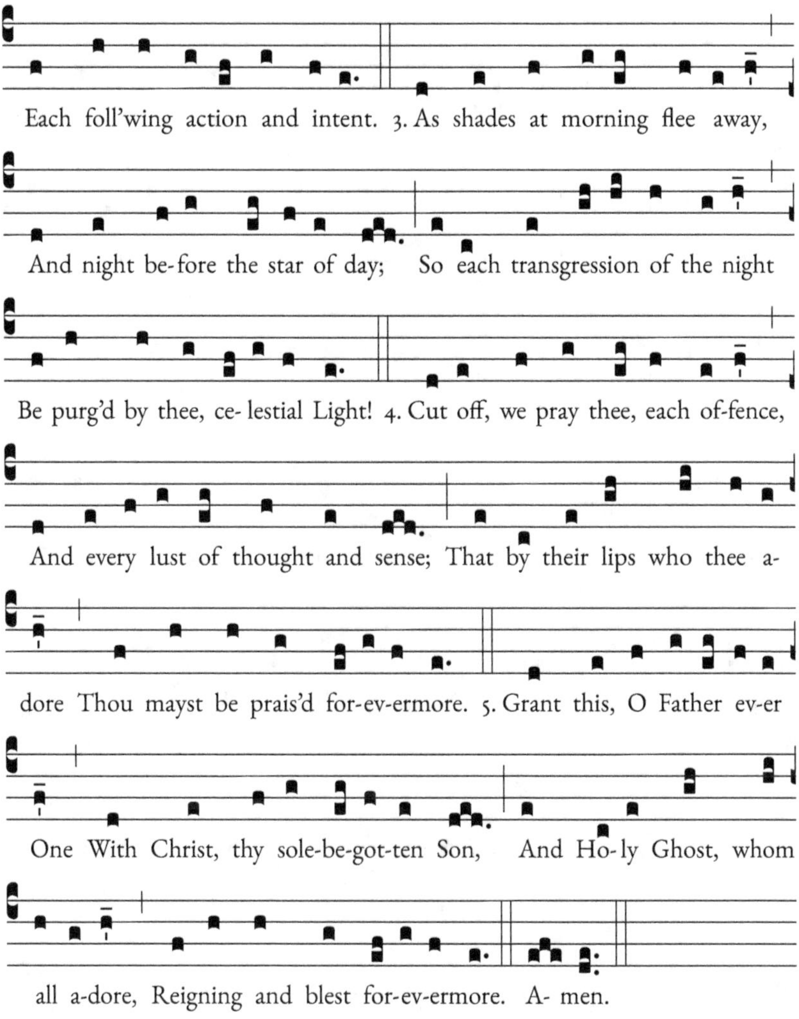

Tuesday   **Ferial Hymns**   *Invitatory*

Each foll'wing action and intent. 3. As shades at morning flee away,

And night be-fore the star of day; So each transgression of the night

Be purg'd by thee, ce-lestial Light! 4. Cut off, we pray thee, each of-fence,

And every lust of thought and sense; That by their lips who thee a-

dore Thou mayst be prais'd for-ev-ermore. 5. Grant this, O Father ev-er

One With Christ, thy sole-be-got-ten Son, And Ho-ly Ghost, whom

all a-dore, Reigning and blest for-ev-ermore. A-men.

Tuesday Invitatory Hymn

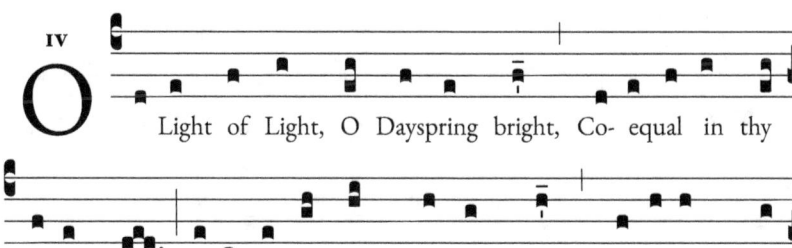

O Light of Light, O Dayspring bright, Co-equal in thy

Father's Light: Assist us, as with prayer and psalm Thy servants break

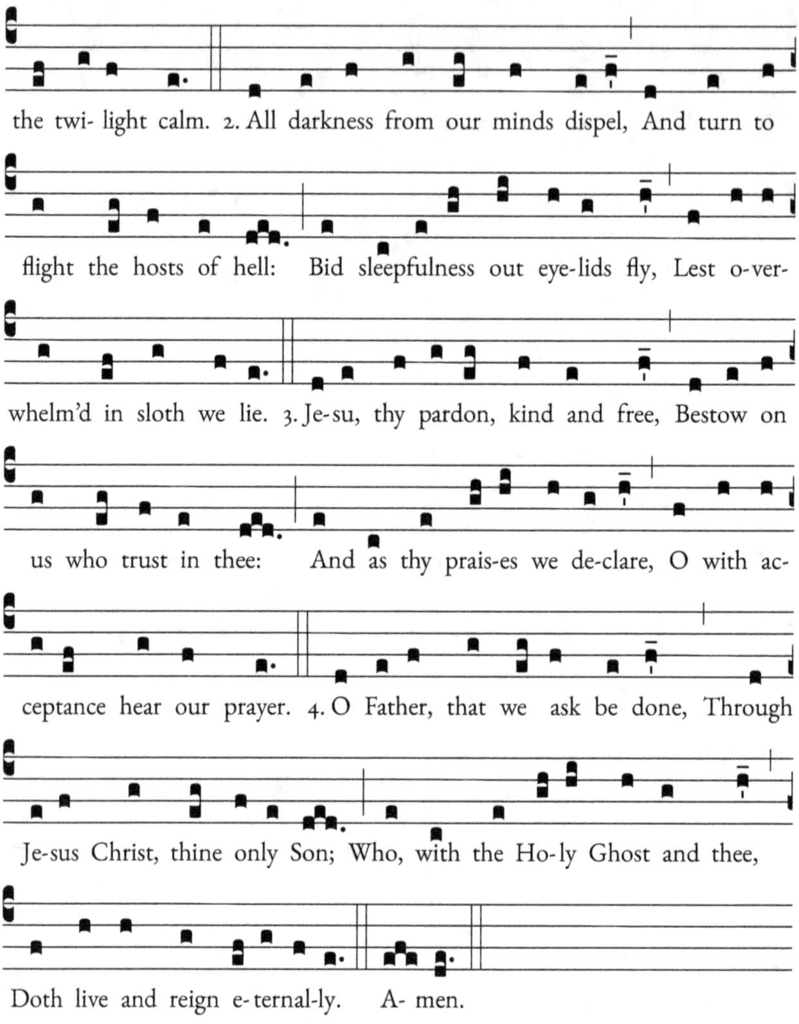

Invitatory   **Ferial Hymns**   Wednesday

the twi- light calm. 2. All darkness from our minds dispel, And turn to flight the hosts of hell: Bid sleepfulness out eye-lids fly, Lest o-ver-whelm'd in sloth we lie. 3. Je-su, thy pardon, kind and free, Bestow on us who trust in thee: And as thy prais-es we de-clare, O with ac-ceptance hear our prayer. 4. O Father, that we ask be done, Through Je-sus Christ, thine only Son; Who, with the Ho-ly Ghost and thee, Doth live and reign e-ternal-ly. A-men.

Wednesday Invitatory Hymn

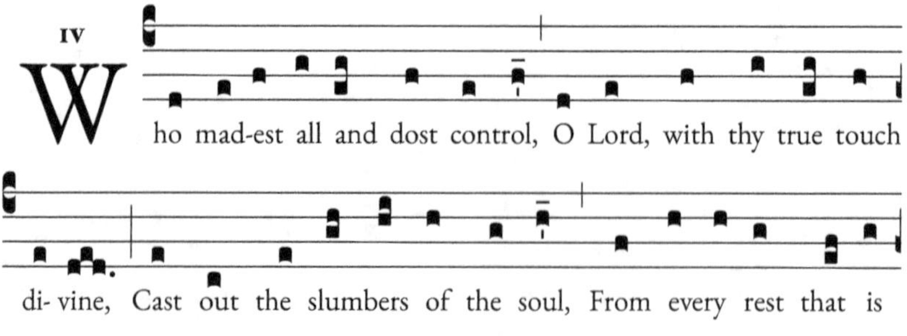

IV

Who mad-est all and dost control, O Lord, with thy true touch di-vine, Cast out the slumbers of the soul, From every rest that is

Wednesday — **Ferial Hymns** — *Invitatory*

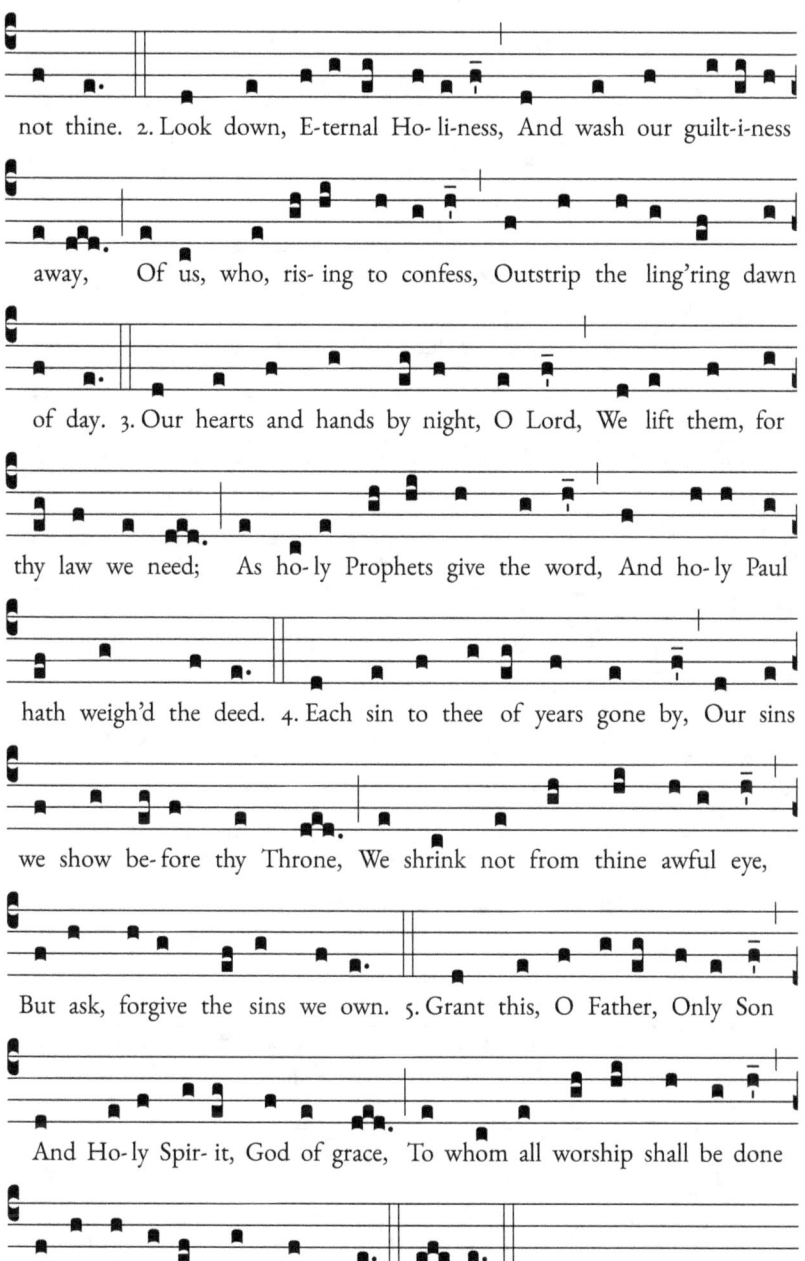

not thine. 2. Look down, E-ternal Ho-li-ness, And wash our guilt-i-ness away, Of us, who, ris-ing to confess, Outstrip the ling'ring dawn of day. 3. Our hearts and hands by night, O Lord, We lift them, for thy law we need; As ho-ly Prophets give the word, And ho-ly Paul hath weigh'd the deed. 4. Each sin to thee of years gone by, Our sins we show be-fore thy Throne, We shrink not from thine awful eye, But ask, forgive the sins we own. 5. Grant this, O Father, Only Son And Ho-ly Spir-it, God of grace, To whom all worship shall be done In every na-tion, time, and place. A-men.

Invitatory   **Ferial Hymns**   Thursday

THURSDAY INVITATORY HYMN

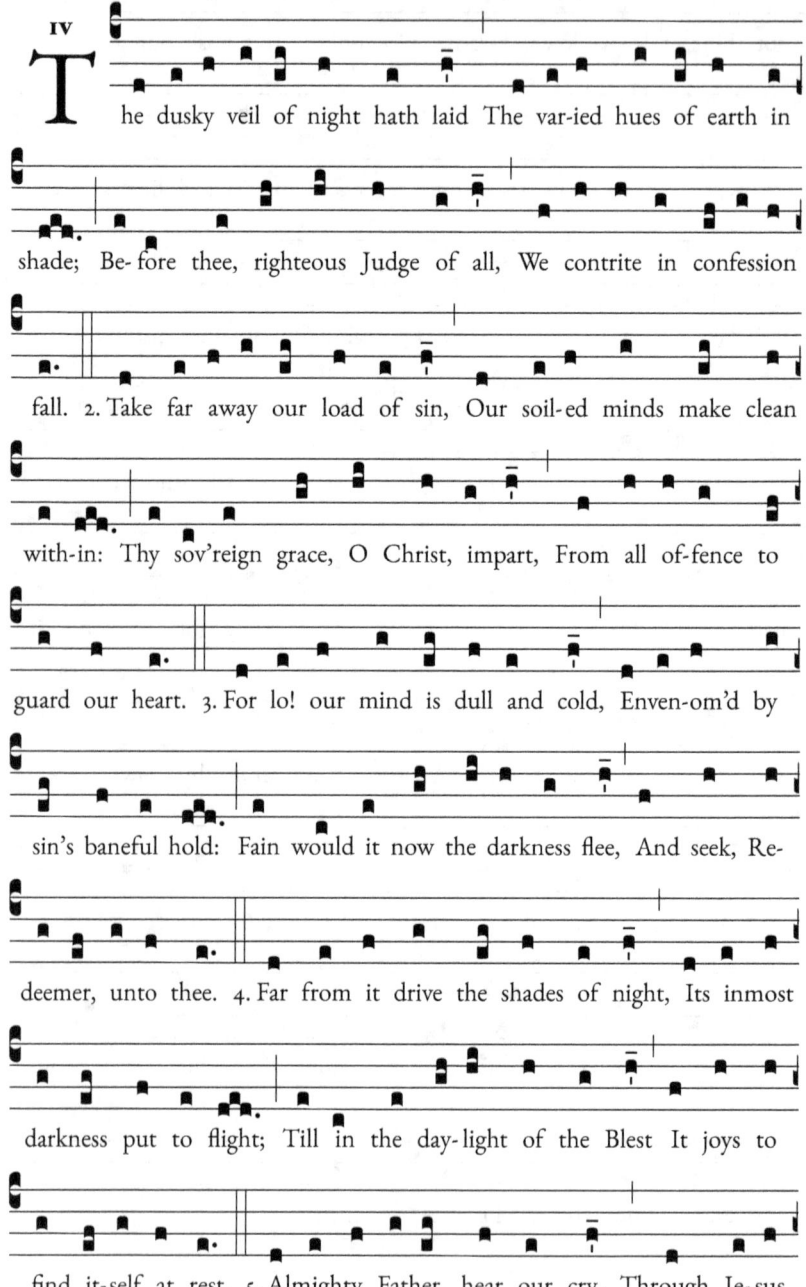

The dusky veil of night hath laid The var-ied hues of earth in shade; Be-fore thee, righteous Judge of all, We contrite in confession fall. 2. Take far away our load of sin, Our soil-ed minds make clean with-in: Thy sov'reign grace, O Christ, impart, From all of-fence to guard our heart. 3. For lo! our mind is dull and cold, Enven-om'd by sin's baneful hold: Fain would it now the darkness flee, And seek, Re-deemer, unto thee. 4. Far from it drive the shades of night, Its inmost darkness put to flight; Till in the day-light of the Blest It joys to find it-self at rest. 5. Almighty Father, hear our cry, Through Je-sus

Ferial Hymns

Friday — *Invitatory*

Christ, our Lord most High, Who, with the Ho-ly Ghost and thee, Doth live and reign e-ternal-ly. A-men.

FRIDAY INVITATORY HYMN

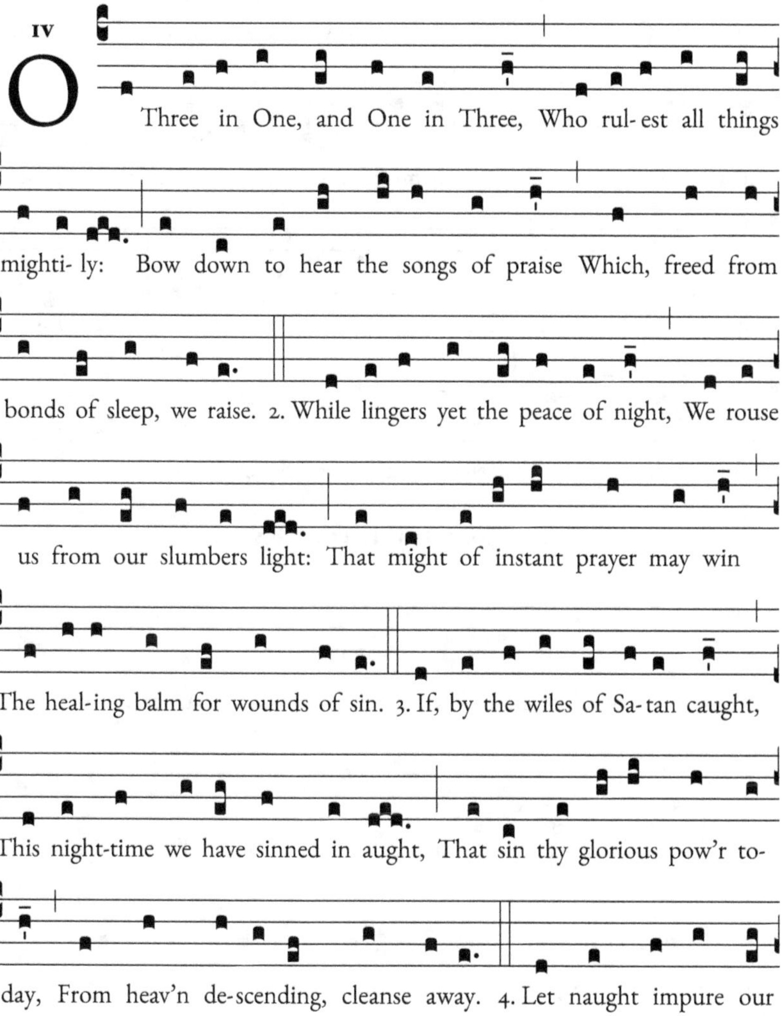

IV. O Three in One, and One in Three, Who rul-est all things mighti-ly: Bow down to hear the songs of praise Which, freed from bonds of sleep, we raise. 2. While lingers yet the peace of night, We rouse us from our slumbers light: That might of instant prayer may win The heal-ing balm for wounds of sin. 3. If, by the wiles of Sa-tan caught, This night-time we have sinned in aught, That sin thy glorious pow'r to-day, From heav'n de-scending, cleanse away. 4. Let naught impure our

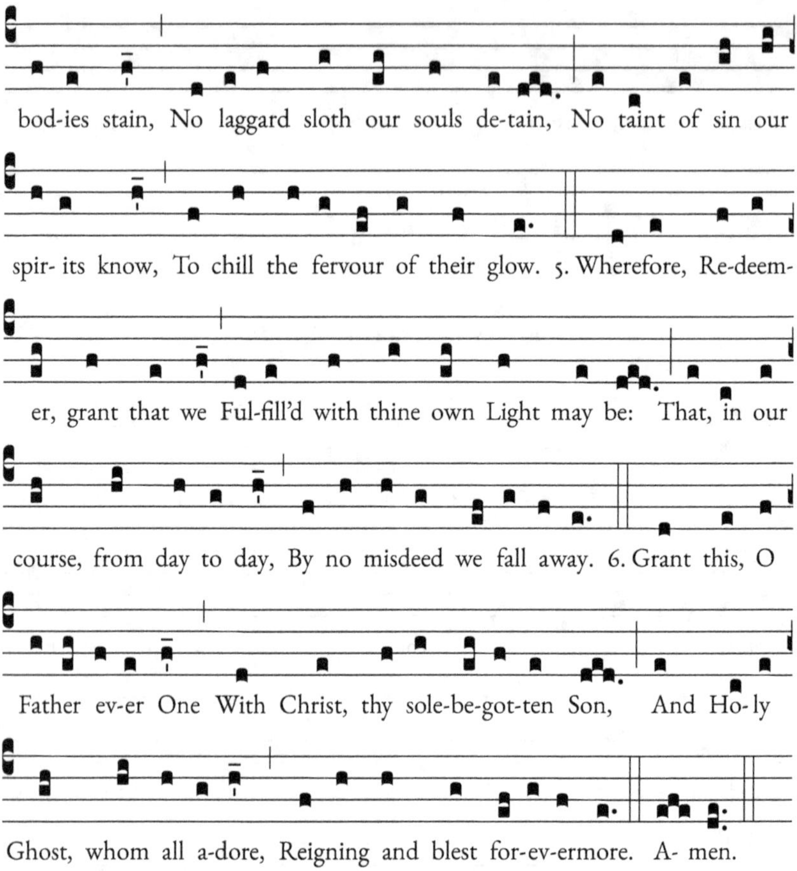

Invitatory — **Ferial Hymns** — Saturday

bod-ies stain, No laggard sloth our souls de-tain, No taint of sin our spir-its know, To chill the fervour of their glow. 5. Wherefore, Redeem-er, grant that we Ful-fill'd with thine own Light may be: That, in our course, from day to day, By no misdeed we fall away. 6. Grant this, O Father ev-er One With Christ, thy sole-be-got-ten Son, And Ho-ly Ghost, whom all a-dore, Reigning and blest for-ev-ermore. A-men.

Saturday Invitatory Hymn

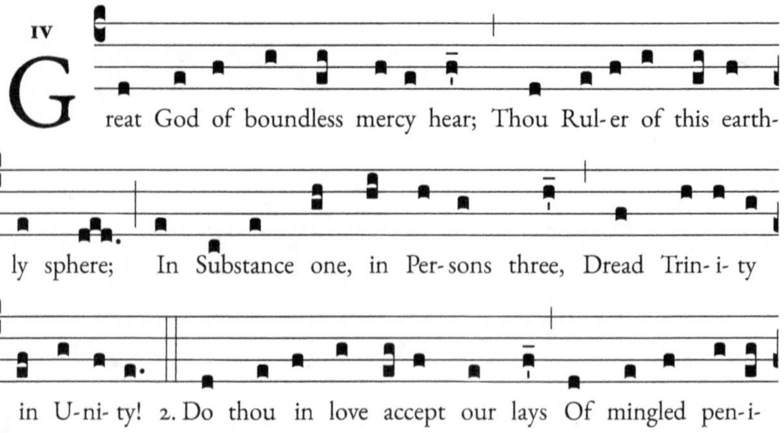

IV. Great God of boundless mercy hear; Thou Rul-er of this earth-ly sphere; In Substance one, in Per-sons three, Dread Trin-i-ty in U-ni-ty! 2. Do thou in love accept our lays Of mingled pen-i-

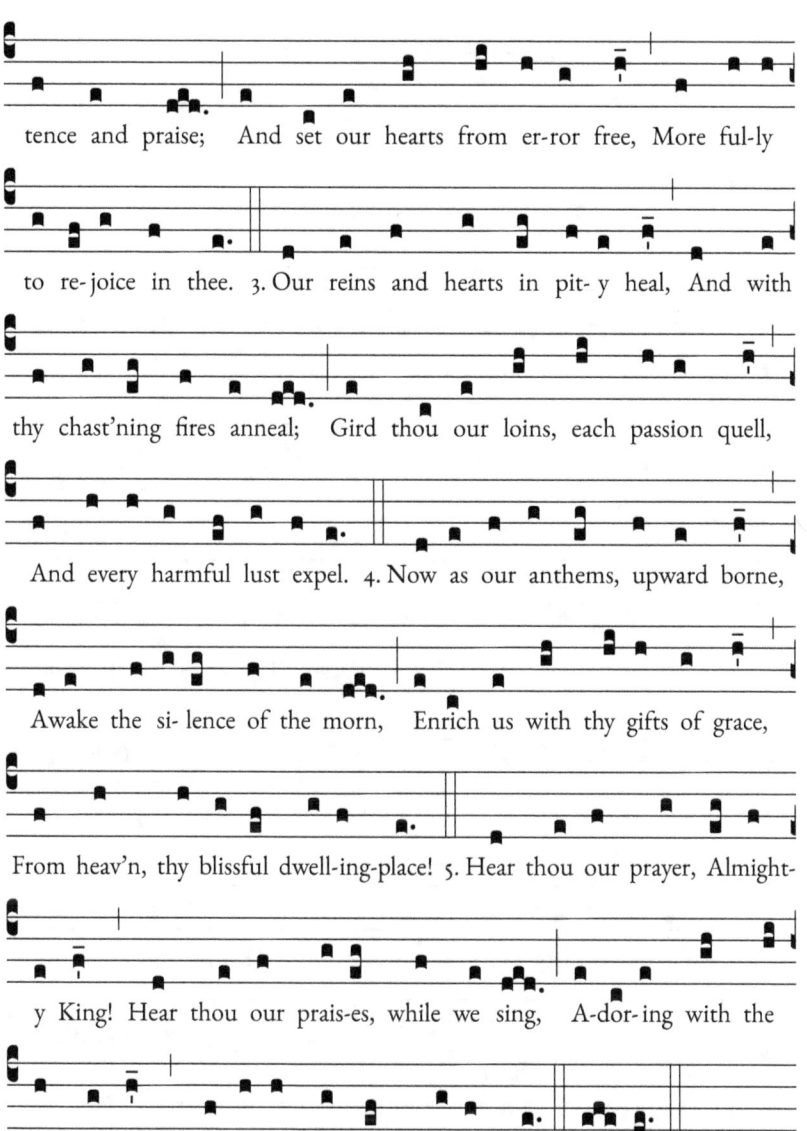

Summer Sunday — **Ferial Hymns** — Mattins

Summer Hymns

¶ The Summer Hymns are said from the Second Sunday after Trinity until the Sunday within 28 September - 4 October, exclusive.

SUNDAY MATTINS OFFICE HYMN

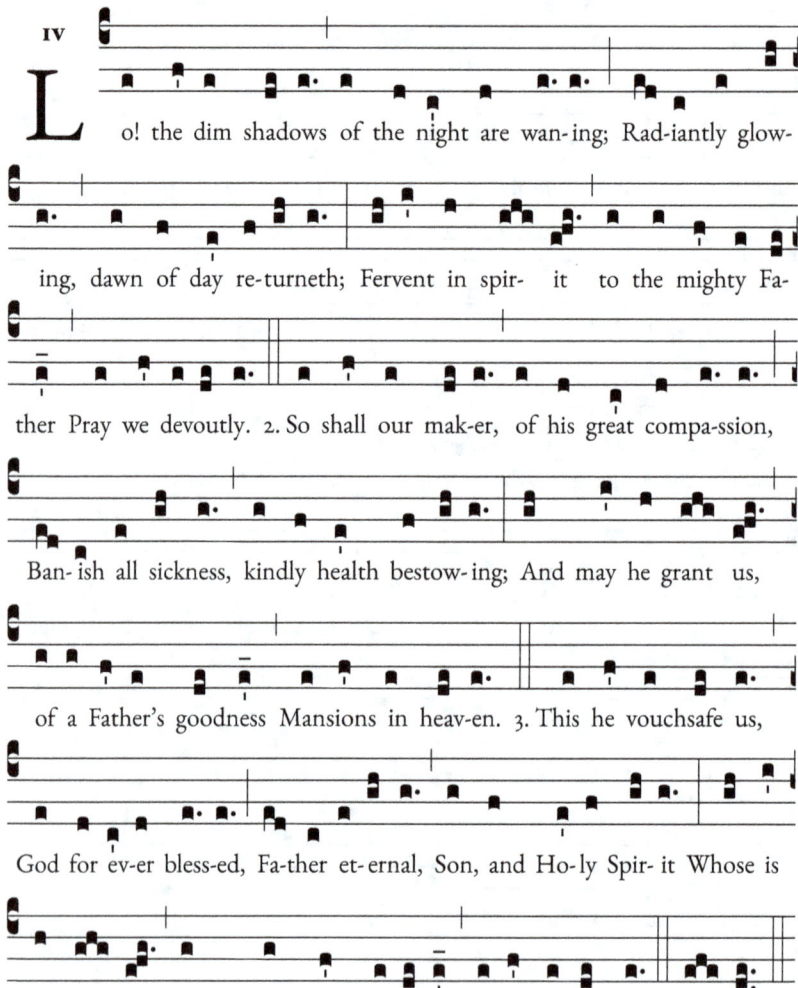

Lo! the dim shadows of the night are wan-ing; Rad-iantly glow-ing, dawn of day re-turneth; Fervent in spir- it to the mighty Fa-ther Pray we devoutly. 2. So shall our mak-er, of his great compa-ssion, Ban-ish all sickness, kindly health bestow-ing; And may he grant us, of a Father's goodness Mansions in heav-en. 3. This he vouchsafe us, God for ev-er bless-ed, Fa-ther et-ernal, Son, and Ho-ly Spir- it Whose is the glor- y which through all cre- a-tion Ev-er res-oundeth. A- men.

℣. The Lord is King, and hath put on glorious apparel.
℟. The Lord hath put on his apparel, and girded himself with strength.

Evensong   **Ferial Hymns**   *Summer Sunday*

Sunday Evensong Office Hymn

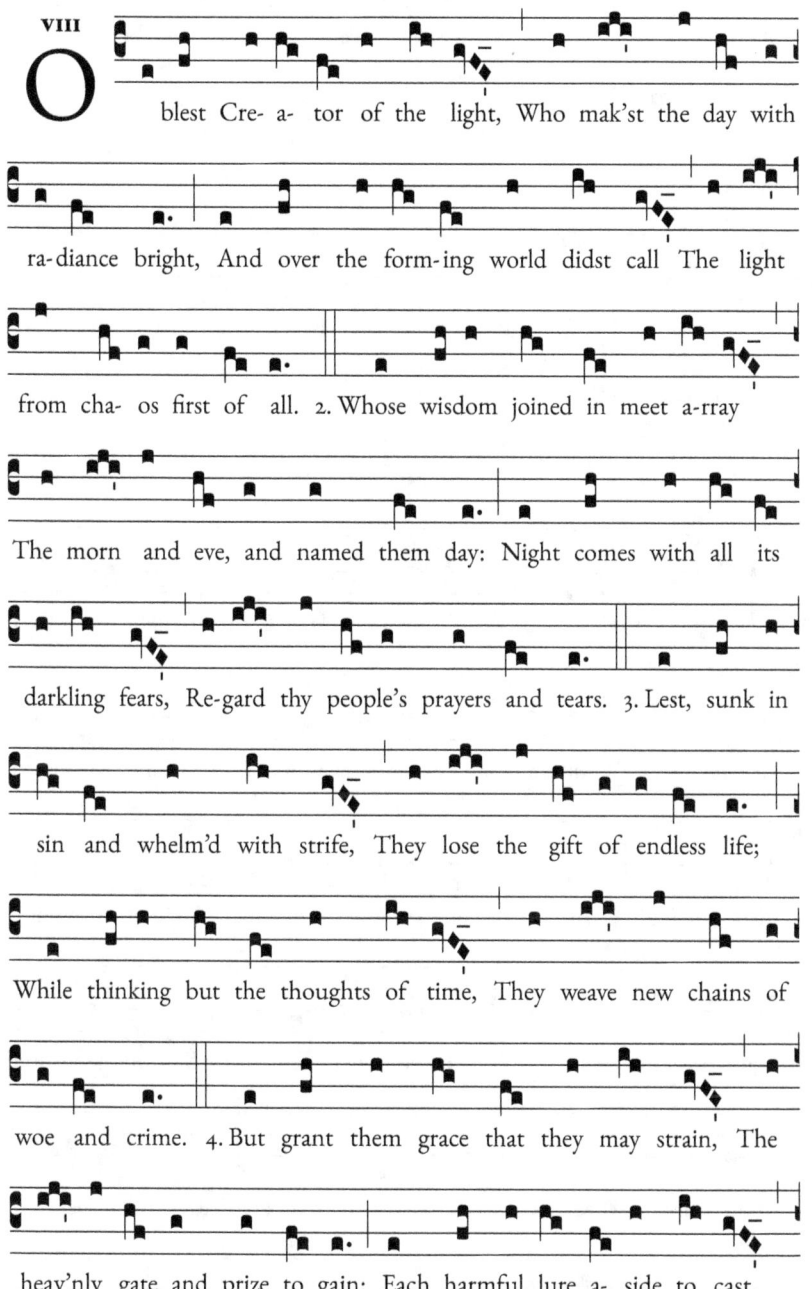

VIII

O blest Cre- a- tor of the light, Who mak'st the day with ra-diance bright, And over the form-ing world didst call The light from cha- os first of all. 2. Whose wisdom joined in meet a-rray The morn and eve, and named them day: Night comes with all its darkling fears, Re-gard thy people's prayers and tears. 3. Lest, sunk in sin and whelm'd with strife, They lose the gift of endless life; While thinking but the thoughts of time, They weave new chains of woe and crime. 4. But grant them grace that they may strain, The heav'nly gate and prize to gain: Each harmful lure a- side to cast,

Summer Monday   **Ferial Hymns**   Mattins

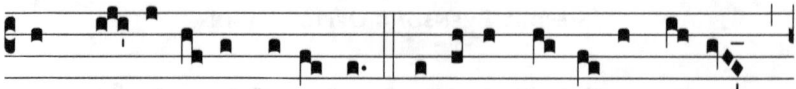
And purge away each error past. 5. O Father, that we ask be done

Through Jesus Christ, thine only Son, Who, with the Holy Ghost

and thee, Shall live and reign eternally. Amen.

℣. Lord, let my prayer be set forth
℟. In thy sight as the incense.

MONDAY MATTINS OFFICE HYMN

IV

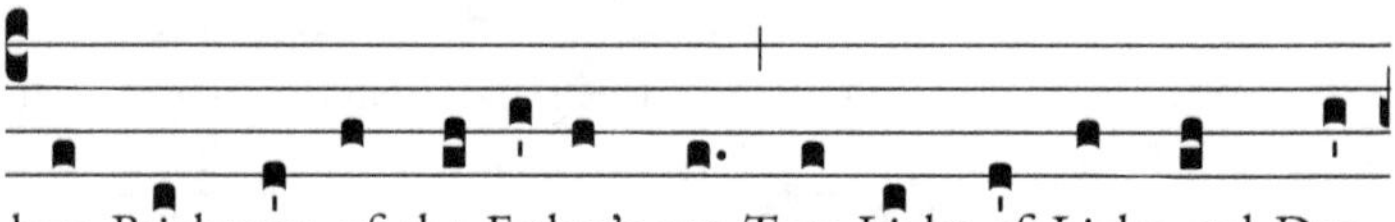

Thou Brightness of the Father's ray True Light of Light and Day of Day Light's fountain and eternal spring, Thou Morn, the morn illumining! 2. Glide in, thou very Sun divine; With everlasting brightness shine: And shed abroad on every sense The Spirit's light and influence. 3. Thee, Father, let us seek aright The Father of perpetual light, The Father of almighty grace, Each wile of sin away to chase

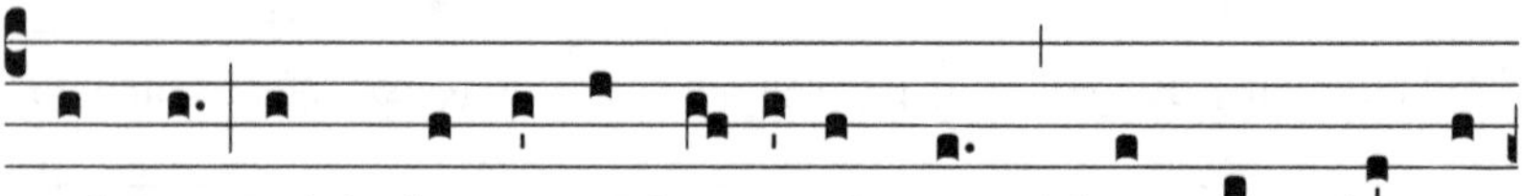

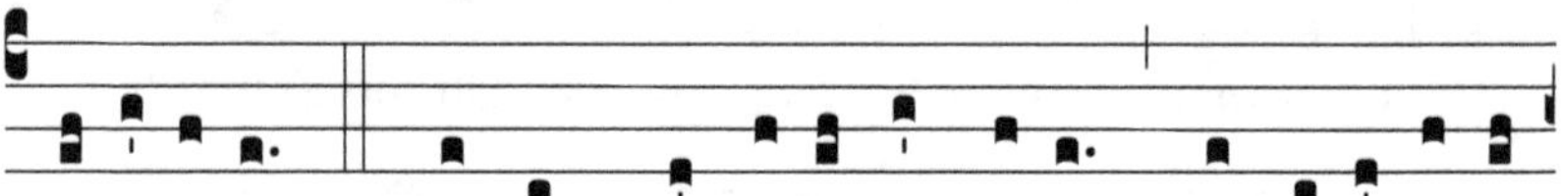

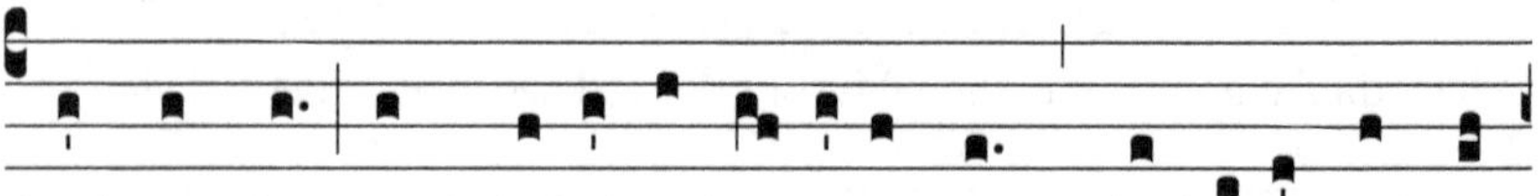

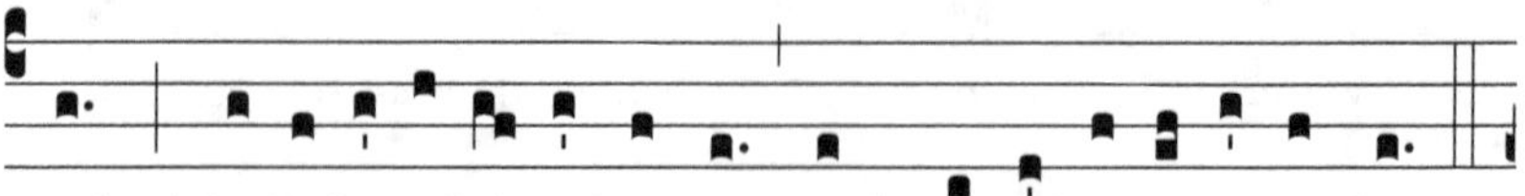

Mattins **Ferial Hymns** *Summer Monday*

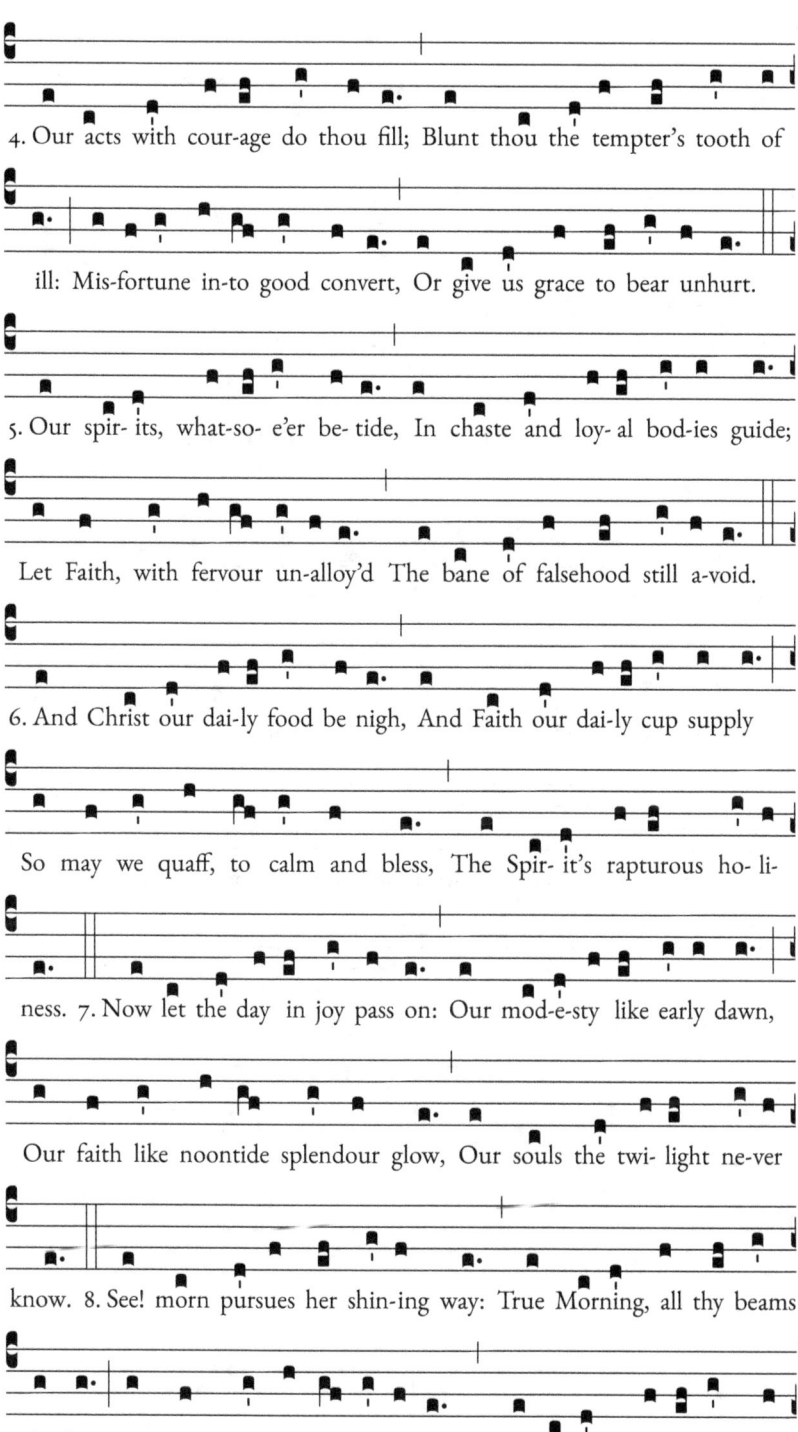

4. Our acts with cour-age do thou fill; Blunt thou the tempter's tooth of ill: Mis-fortune in-to good convert, Or give us grace to bear unhurt.

5. Our spir-its, what-so- e'er be- tide, In chaste and loy-al bod-ies guide; Let Faith, with fervour un-alloy'd The bane of falsehood still a-void.

6. And Christ our dai-ly food be nigh, And Faith our dai-ly cup supply So may we quaff, to calm and bless, The Spir-it's rapturous ho-li-ness.

7. Now let the day in joy pass on: Our mod-e-sty like early dawn, Our faith like noontide splendour glow, Our souls the twi-light ne-ver know.

8. See! morn pursues her shin-ing way: True Morning, all thy beams display! Son with the mighty Father one, The Father wholl-y in the

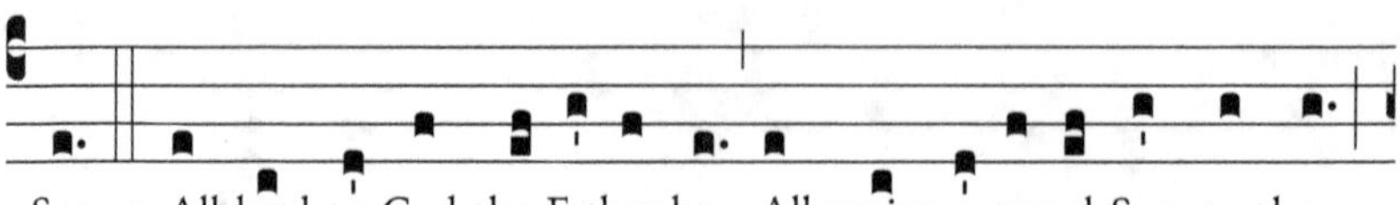

Summer Monday   **Ferial Hymns**   Evensong

Son. 9. All laud to God the Father be; All praise, e-ternal Son, to thee; All glor-y, as is ev-er meet, To God the Ho-ly Par-a-clete. A-men.

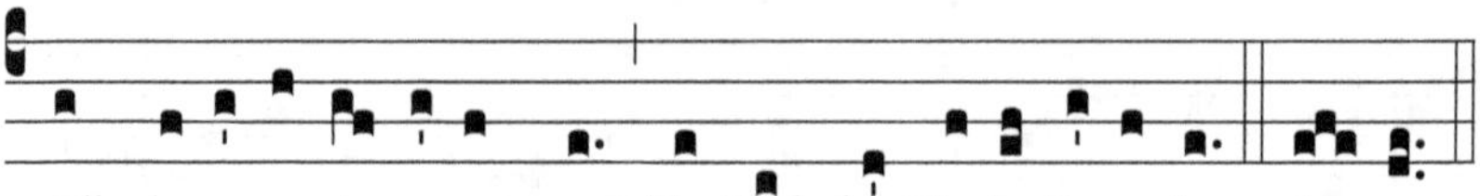

℣. O satisfy us with thy mercy, and that soon.
℞. So shall we rejoice and be glad all the days of our life.
Ben. Ant. Blessed † be the Lord God of Israel.

Monday Evensong Office Hymn

1. O great Cre-a-tor of the sky, Who wouldest not the floods 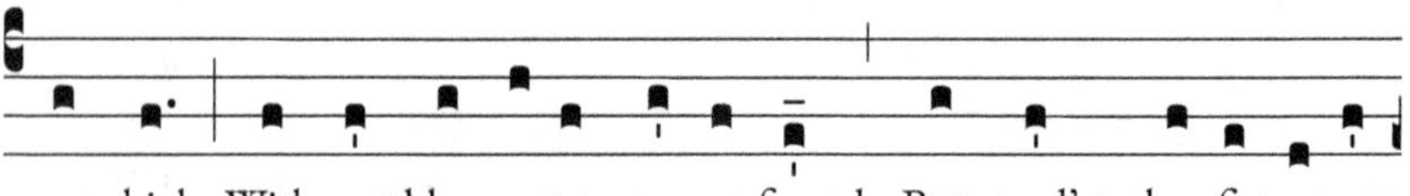 on high With earthly wa-ters to confound, But mad'st the firmament their bound: 2. The floods a-bove thou didst ordain; The floods be-low thou didst restrain: That moisture might at-temper heat, Lest the parch'd earth should ru-in meet. 3. Upon our souls, good Lord, bestow The gift of grace in endless flow: Lest some renew'd de-ceit or wile Of former sin should us beguile. 4. Let Faith dis-cov-er heav'nly light;

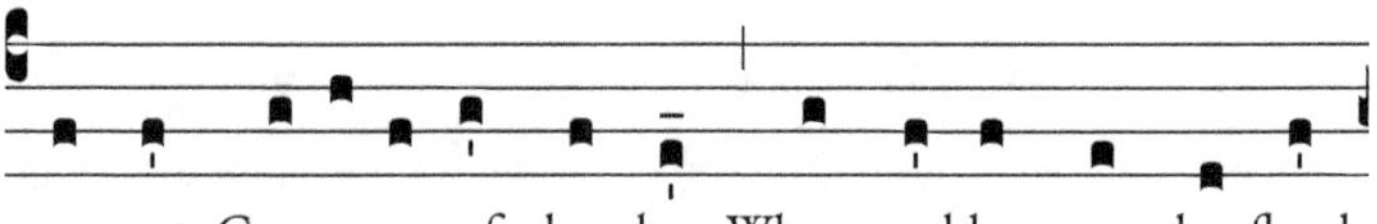

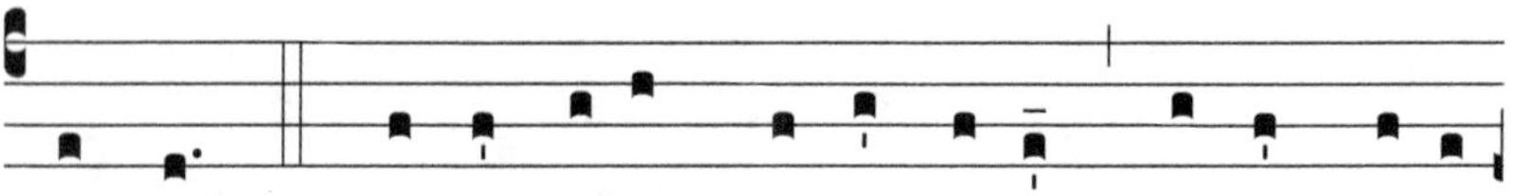

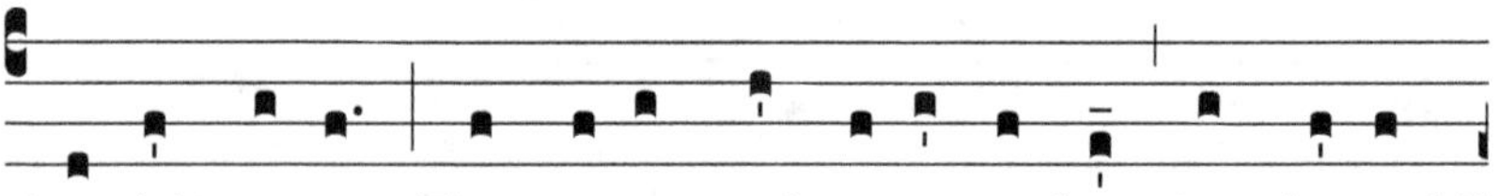

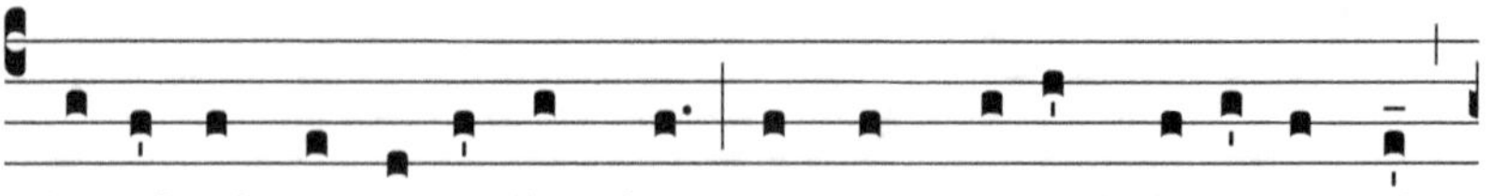

Mattins — **Ferial Hymns** — *Summer Tuesday*

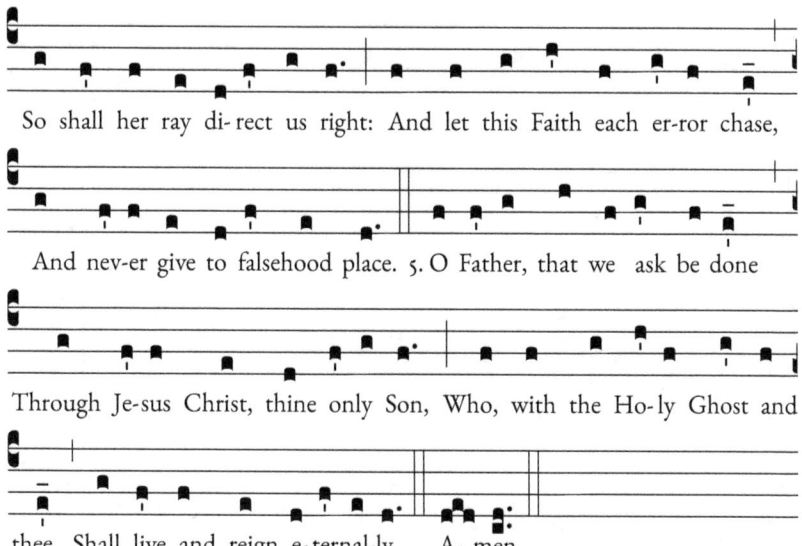

So shall her ray di-rect us right: And let this Faith each er-ror chase, And nev-er give to falsehood place. 5. O Father, that we ask be done Through Je-sus Christ, thine only Son, Who, with the Ho-ly Ghost and thee, Shall live and reign e-ternal-ly. A-men.

℣. Lord, let my prayer be set forth.
℟. In thy sight as the incense.
Mag. Ant. My soul † doth magnify the Lord, for he hath regarded my lowliness.

Tuesday Mattins Office Hymn

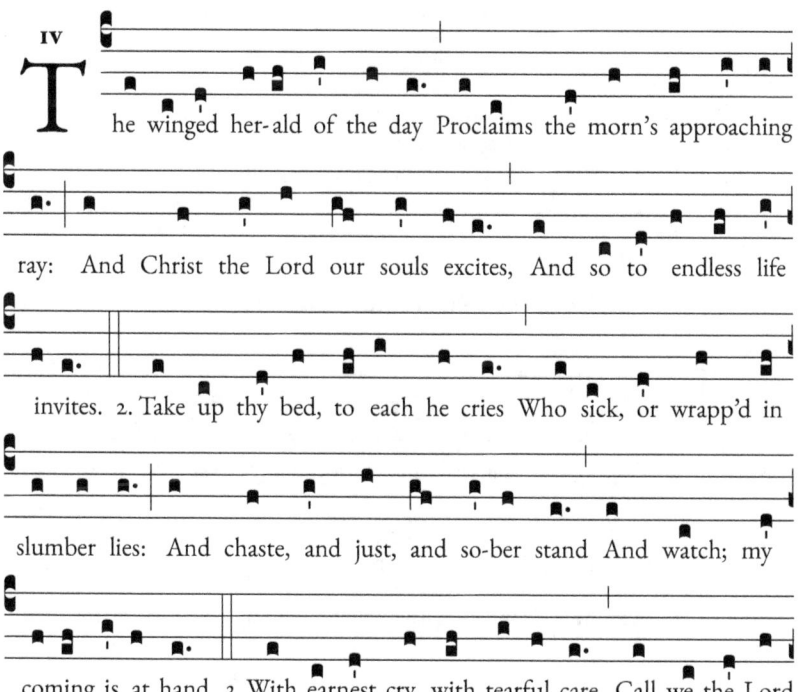

The winged her-ald of the day Proclaims the morn's approaching ray: And Christ the Lord our souls excites, And so to endless life invites. 2. Take up thy bed, to each he cries Who sick, or wrapp'd in slumber lies: And chaste, and just, and so-ber stand And watch; my coming is at hand. 3. With earnest cry, with tearful care, Call we the Lord

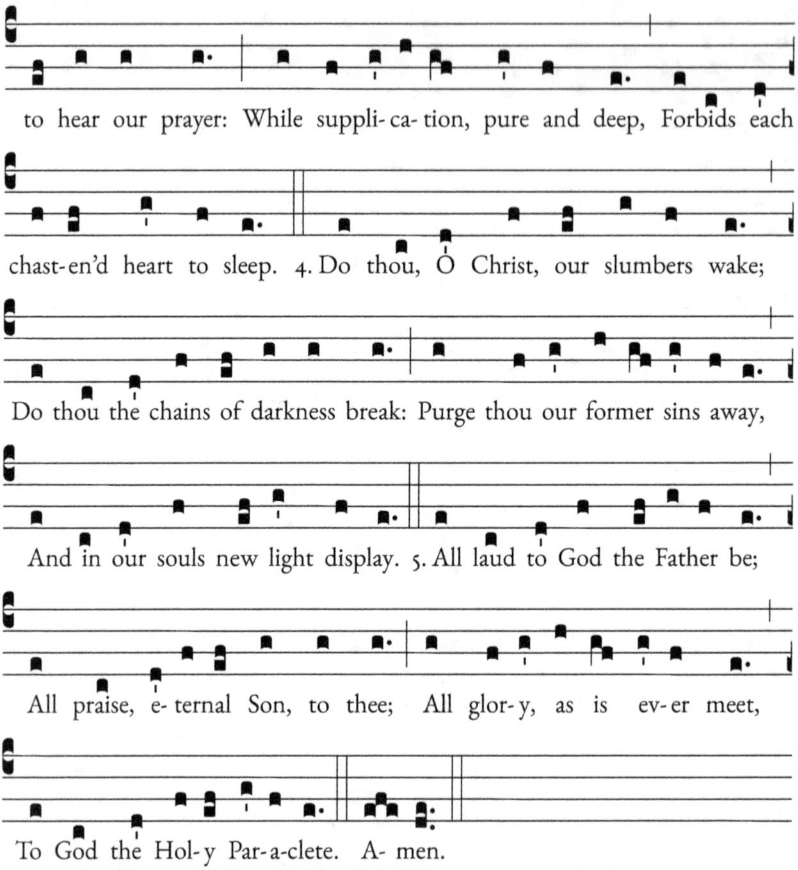

Summer Tuesday — **Ferial Hymns** — Evensong

to hear our prayer: While suppli-ca-tion, pure and deep, Forbids each chast-en'd heart to sleep. 4. Do thou, O Christ, our slumbers wake; Do thou the chains of darkness break: Purge thou our former sins away, And in our souls new light display. 5. All laud to God the Father be; All praise, e-ternal Son, to thee; All glor-y, as is ev-er meet, To God the Hol-y Par-a-clete. A-men.

℣. O satisfy us with thy mercy, and that soon.
℟. So shall we rejoice and be glad all the days of our life.
Ben. Ant. The Lord hath raised up for us † an horn of salvation in the house of his servant David.

Tuesday Evensong Office Hymn

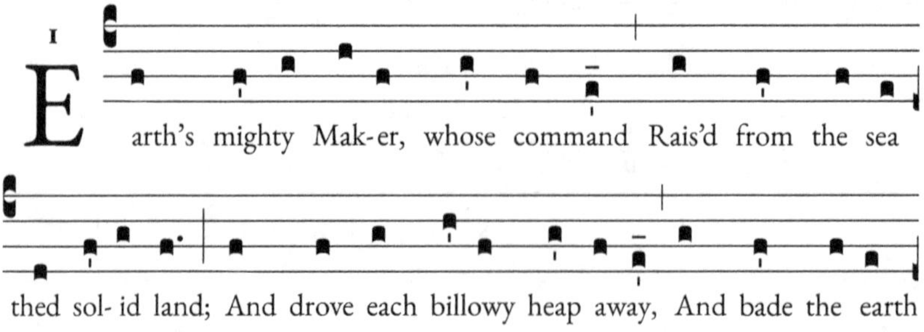

Earth's mighty Mak-er, whose command Rais'd from the sea thed sol-id land; And drove each billowy heap away, And bade the earth

Evensong — **Ferial Hymns** — *Summer Tuesday*

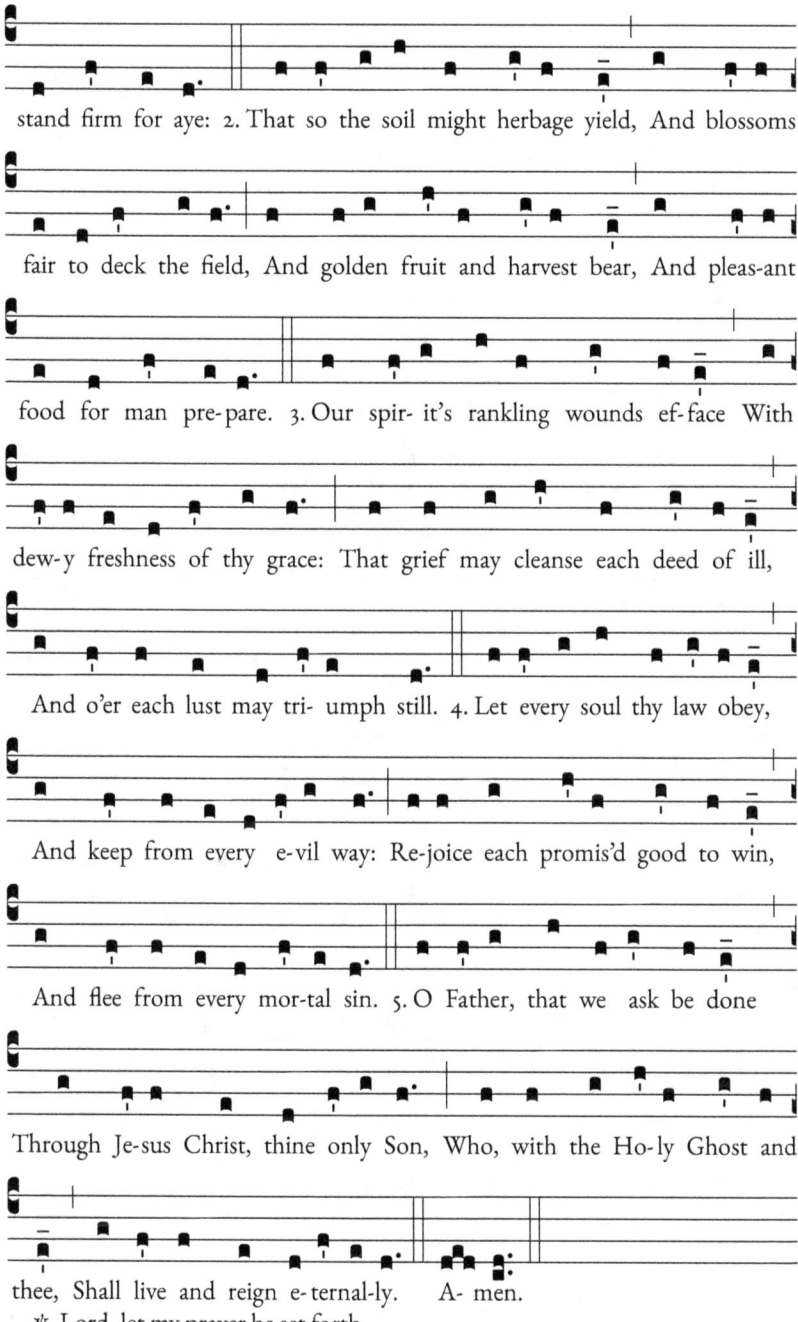

stand firm for aye: 2. That so the soil might herbage yield, And blossoms fair to deck the field, And golden fruit and harvest bear, And pleas-ant food for man pre-pare. 3. Our spir- it's rankling wounds ef-face With dew-y freshness of thy grace: That grief may cleanse each deed of ill, And o'er each lust may tri- umph still. 4. Let every soul thy law obey, And keep from every e-vil way: Re-joice each promis'd good to win, And flee from every mor-tal sin. 5. O Father, that we ask be done Through Je-sus Christ, thine only Son, Who, with the Ho-ly Ghost and thee, Shall live and reign e- ternal-ly. A- men.

℣. Lord, let my prayer be set forth.

℟. In thy sight as the incense.

Mag. Ant. Let my spirit rejoice † in God my Saviour.

Summer Wednesday   **Ferial Hymns**   Mattins

Wednesday Mattins Office Hymn

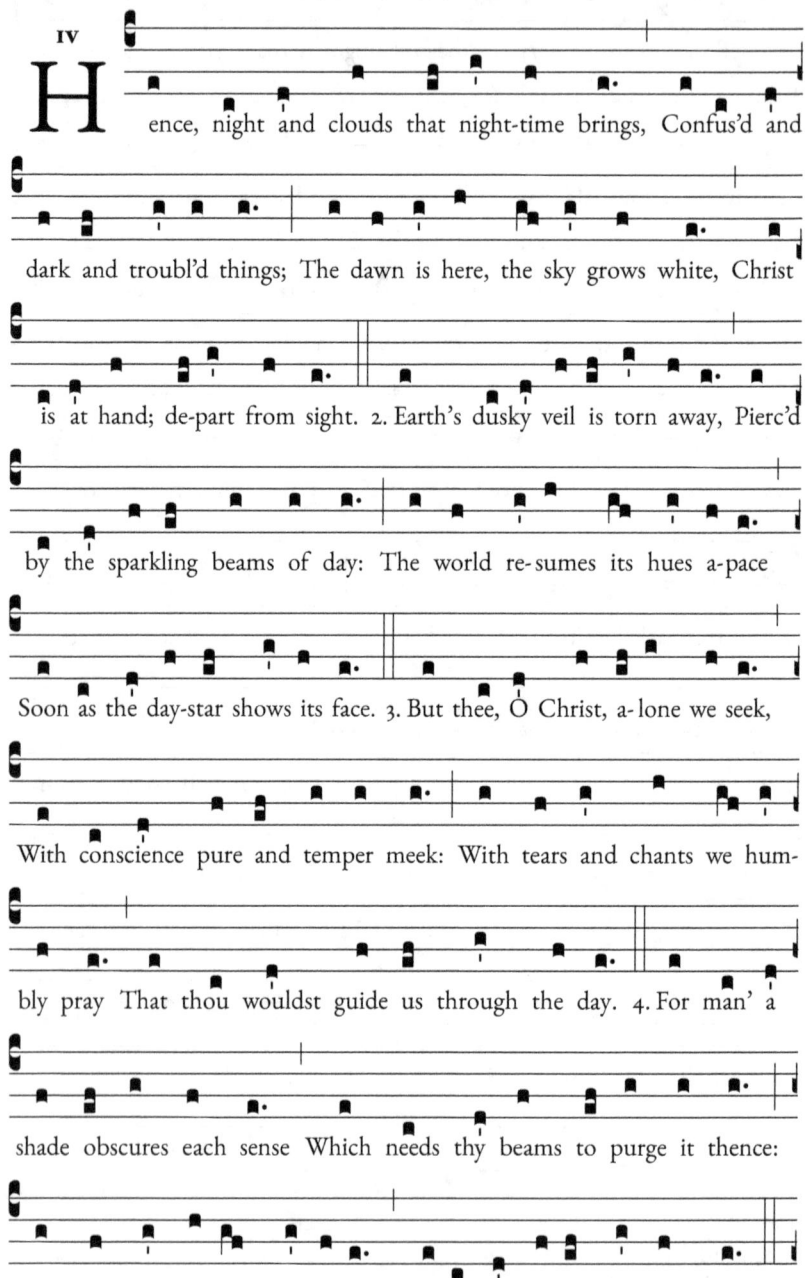

Hence, night and clouds that night-time brings, Confus'd and dark and troubl'd things; The dawn is here, the sky grows white, Christ is at hand; depart from sight. 2. Earth's dusky veil is torn away, Pierc'd by the sparkling beams of day: The world resumes its hues apace Soon as the day-star shows its face. 3. But thee, O Christ, alone we seek, With conscience pure and temper meek: With tears and chants we humbly pray That thou wouldst guide us through the day. 4. For man' a shade obscures each sense Which needs thy beams to purge it thence: Light of the Morning Star, illume, Serenely shining, all our gloom.

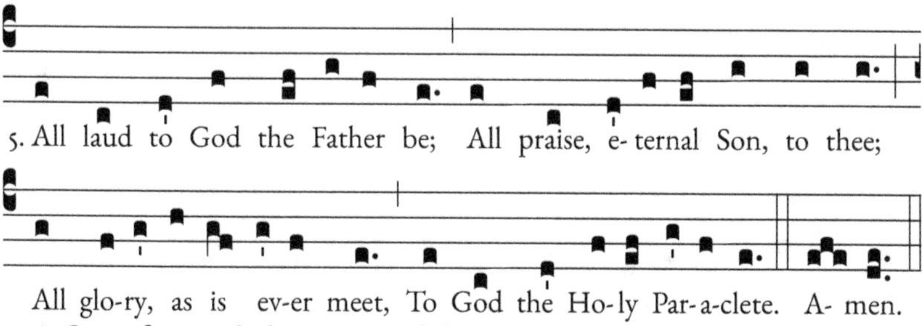

Evensong   # Ferial Hymns   *Summer Wednesday*

5. All laud to God the Father be; All praise, e-ternal Son, to thee; All glo-ry, as is ev-er meet, To God the Ho-ly Par-a-clete. A-men.

℣. O satisfy us with thy mercy, and that soon.
℟. So shall we rejoice and be glad all the days of our life.
Ben. Ant. From the hand of all † that hate us, the Lord hath delivered us.

WEDNESDAY EVENSONG OFFICE HYMN

1. O God, whose hand hath spread the sky, And all its shin-ing hosts on high, And, painting it with fier-y light, Made it so beauteous and so bright: 2. Thou, when the fourth day was be-gun, Didst frame the circle of the sun, And set the moon for order'd change, And plan-ets for their wid-er range: 3. To night and day, by certain line, Their var-ying bounds thou didst as-sign: And gav'st a signal, known and meet, For months be-gun and months complete. 4. Enlighten thou the hearts of

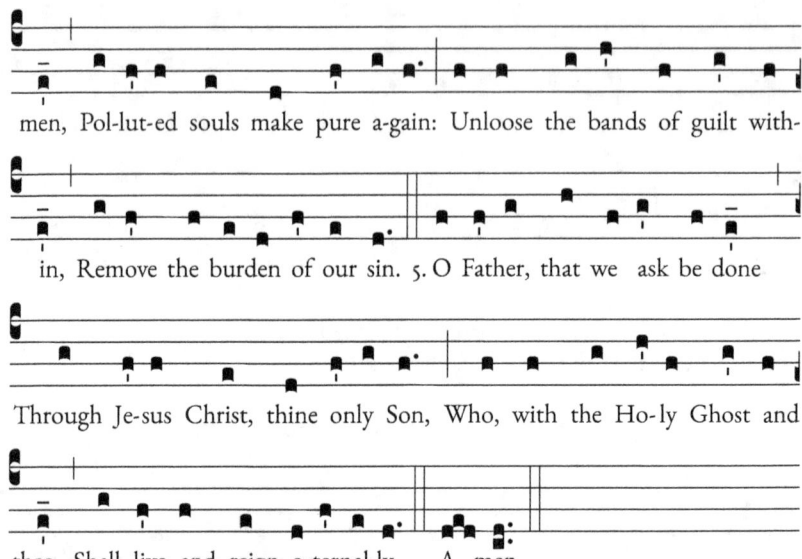

men, Pol-lut-ed souls make pure a-gain: Unloose the bands of guilt with-in, Remove the burden of our sin. 5. O Father, that we ask be done Through Je-sus Christ, thine only Son, Who, with the Ho-ly Ghost and thee, Shall live and reign e-ternal-ly. A-men.

℣. Lord, let my prayer be set forth.

℟. In thy sight as the incense.

Mag. Ant. The Lord † hath regarded my lowliness: and he that is mighty hath done in me great things.

THURSDAY MATTINS OFFICE HYMN

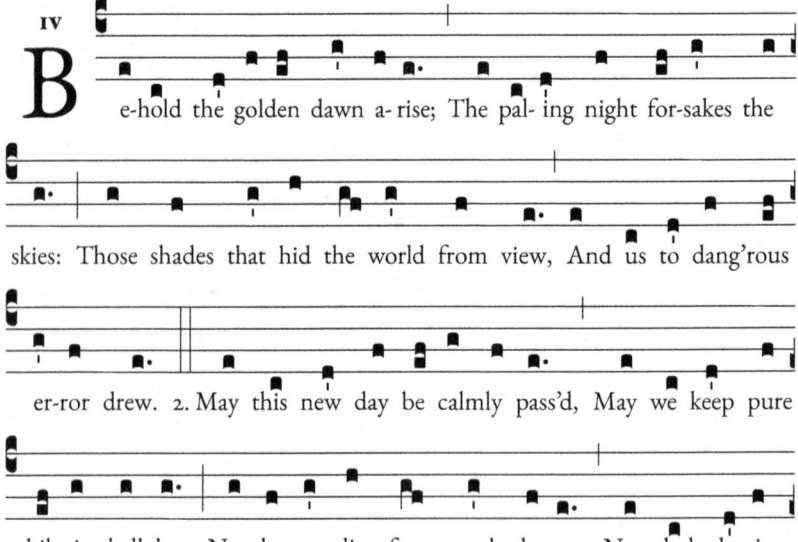

Be-hold the golden dawn a-rise; The pal-ing night for-sakes the skies: Those shades that hid the world from view, And us to dang'rous er-ror drew. 2. May this new day be calmly pass'd, May we keep pure while it shall last: Nor let our lips from truth de-part, Nor dark de-signs

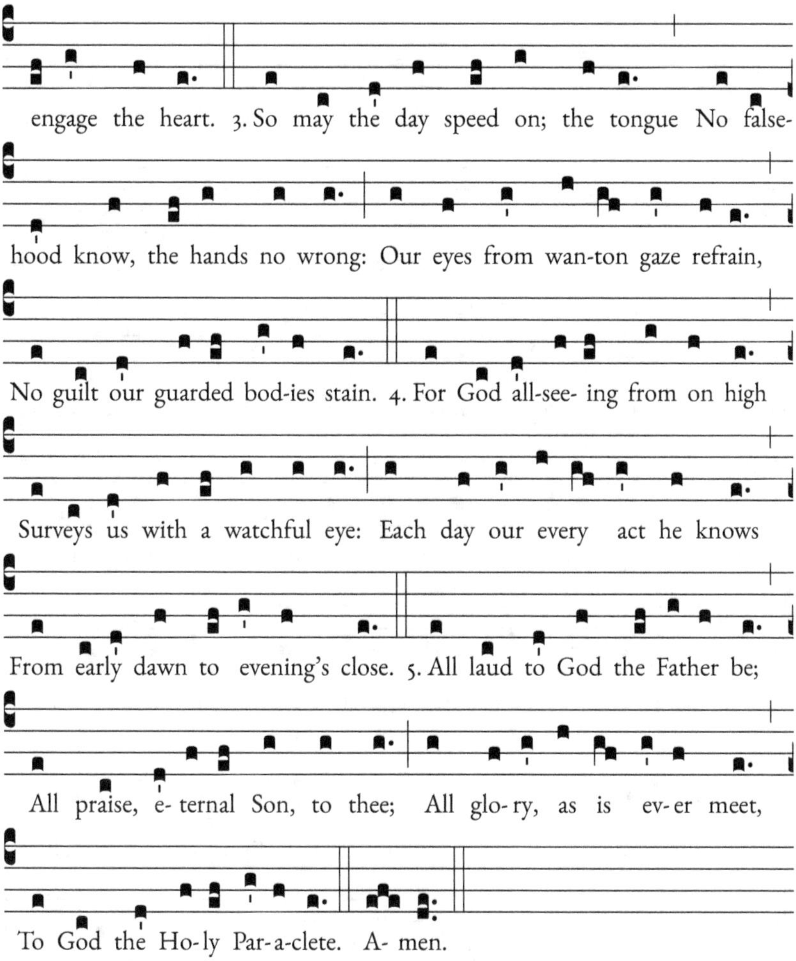

Evensong   **Ferial Hymns**   *Summer Thursday*

engage the heart. 3. So may the day speed on; the tongue No falsehood know, the hands no wrong: Our eyes from wan-ton gaze refrain, No guilt our guarded bod-ies stain. 4. For God all-see-ing from on high Surveys us with a watchful eye: Each day our every act he knows From early dawn to evening's close. 5. All laud to God the Father be; All praise, e-ternal Son, to thee; All glo-ry, as is ev-er meet, To God the Ho-ly Par-a-clete. A-men.

℣. O satisfy us with thy mercy, and that soon.
℟. So shall we rejoice and be glad all the days of our life.

Ben. Ant. Let us serve † the Lord in holiness, and he will deliver us from the hand of our enemies.

Thursday Evensong Office Hymn

Al-mighty God, whose will supreme Made oc-ean's flood with life to teem; Part in the firmament to fly, And part in o-cean depths

Summer Thursday — **Ferial Hymns** — Evensong

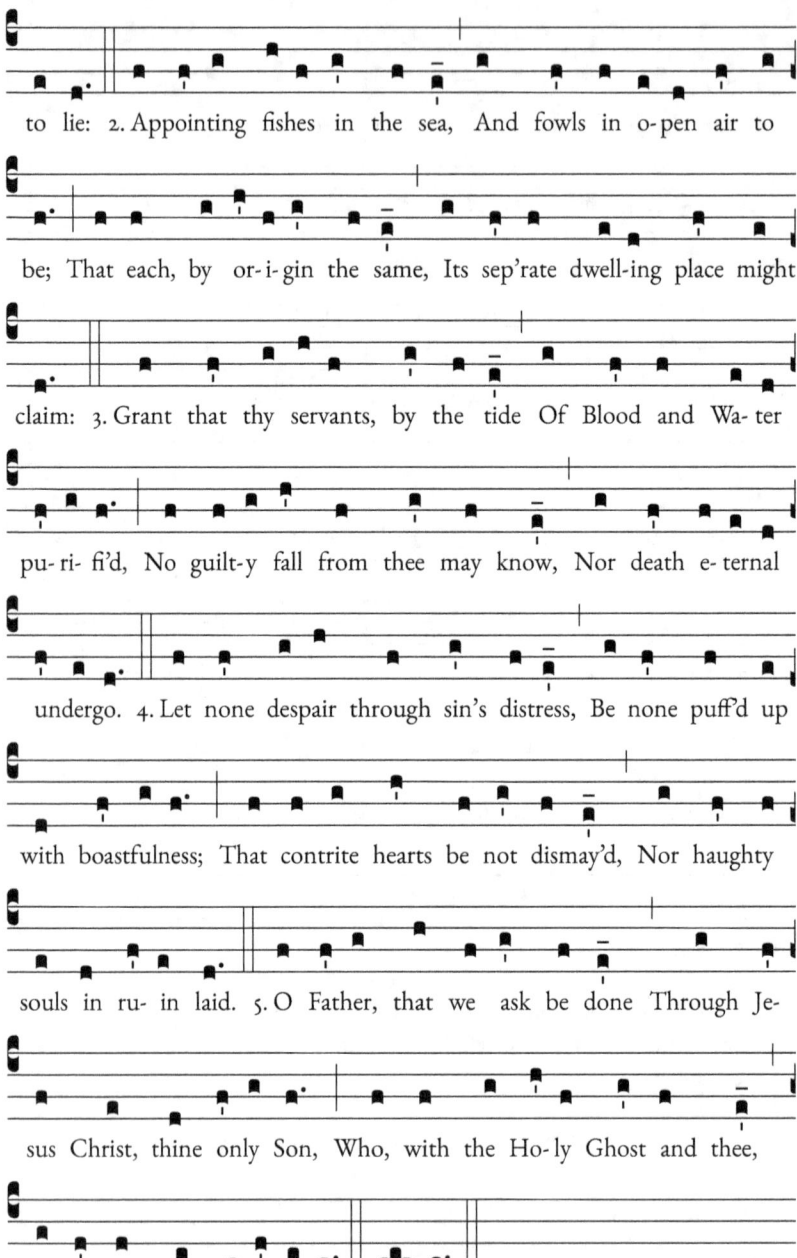

to lie: 2. Appointing fishes in the sea, And fowls in o-pen air to be; That each, by or-i-gin the same, Its sep'rate dwell-ing place might claim: 3. Grant that thy servants, by the tide Of Blood and Wa-ter pu-ri-fi'd, No guilt-y fall from thee may know, Nor death e-ternal undergo. 4. Let none despair through sin's distress, Be none puff'd up with boastfulness; That contrite hearts be not dismay'd, Nor haughty souls in ru-in laid. 5. O Father, that we ask be done Through Je-sus Christ, thine only Son, Who, with the Ho-ly Ghost and thee, Shall live and reign e-ternal-ly. A-men.

℣. Lord, let my prayer be set forth.

℟. In thy sight as the incense.

Mag. Ant. Show strength, O God, † with thine arm: scatter the proud, and exalt the humble.

Ferial Hymns

Mattins — *Summer Friday*

Friday Mattins Office Hymn

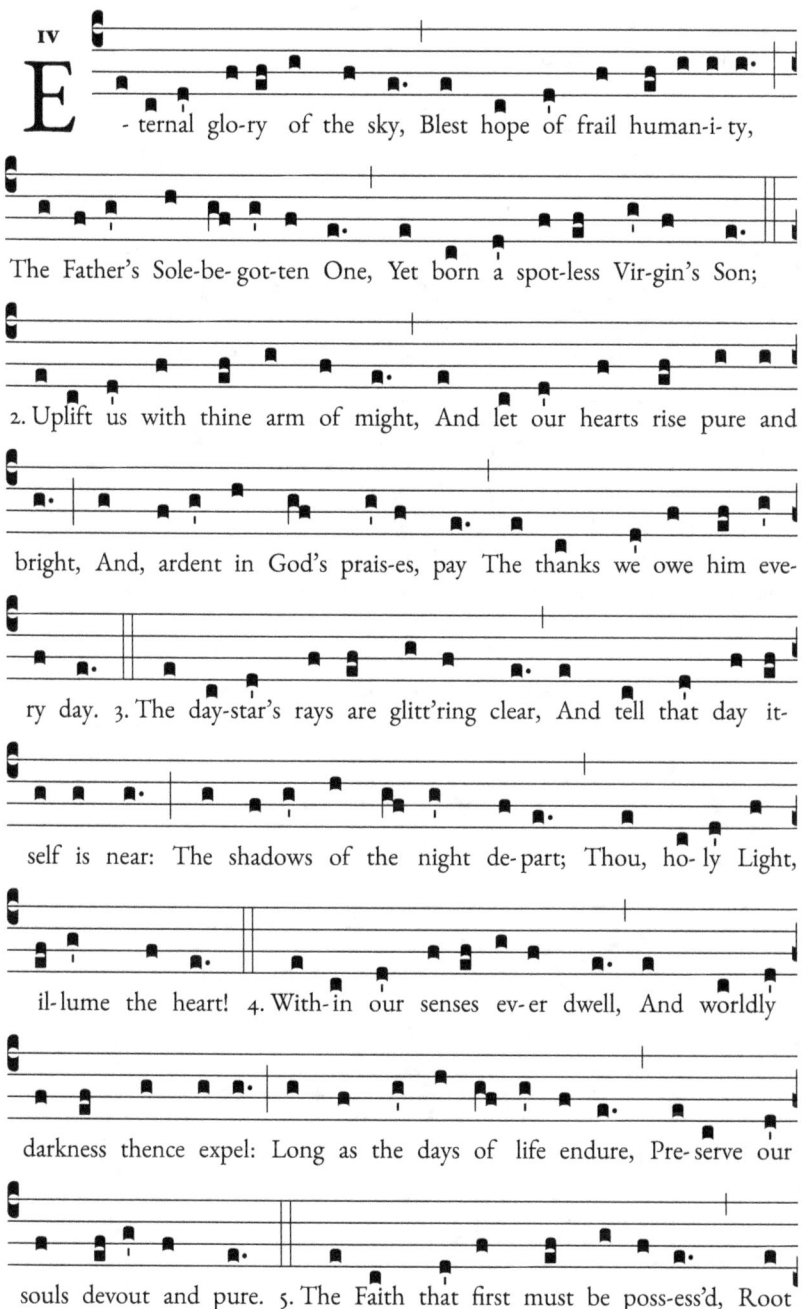

E - ternal glo-ry of the sky, Blest hope of frail human-i-ty,
The Father's Sole-be-got-ten One, Yet born a spot-less Vir-gin's Son;
2. Uplift us with thine arm of might, And let our hearts rise pure and bright, And, ardent in God's prais-es, pay The thanks we owe him eve-ry day. 3. The day-star's rays are glitt'ring clear, And tell that day it-self is near: The shadows of the night de-part; Thou, ho-ly Light, il-lume the heart! 4. With-in our senses ev-er dwell, And worldly darkness thence expel: Long as the days of life endure, Pre-serve our souls devout and pure. 5. The Faith that first must be poss-ess'd, Root

Summer Friday — **Ferial Hymns** — Evensong

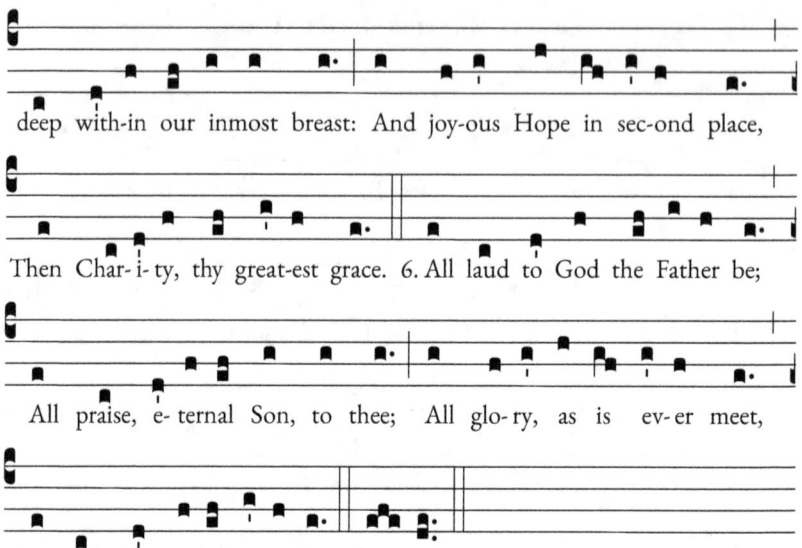

deep with-in our inmost breast: And joy-ous Hope in sec-ond place, Then Char-i-ty, thy great-est grace. 6. All laud to God the Father be; All praise, e-ternal Son, to thee; All glo-ry, as is ev-er meet, To God the Ho-ly Par-a-clete. A-men.

℣. O satisfy us with thy mercy, and that soon.
℟. So shall we rejoice and be glad all the days of our life.
Ben. Ant. Through the tender mercy † of our God: whereby the day-spring from on high hath visited us.

Friday Evensong Office Hymn

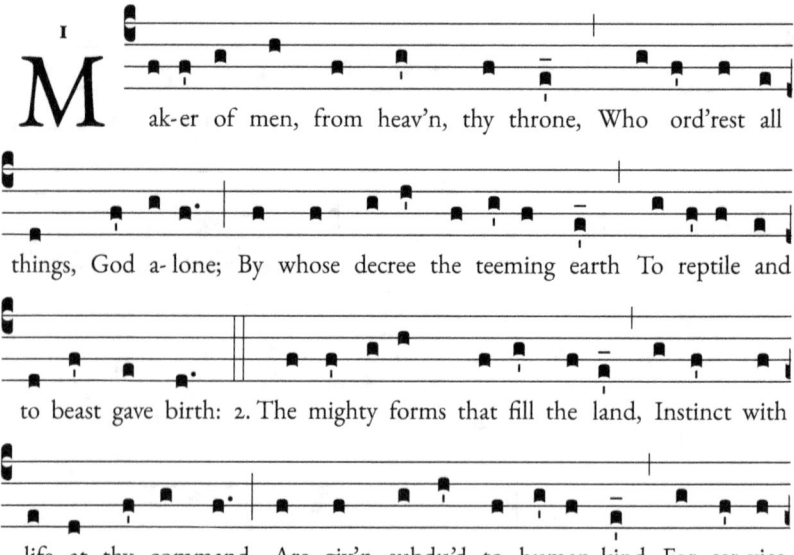

Mak-er of men, from heav'n, thy throne, Who ord'rest all things, God a-lone; By whose decree the teeming earth To reptile and to beast gave birth: 2. The mighty forms that fill the land, Instinct with life at thy command, Are giv'n subdu'd to human-kind For ser-vice

Evensong   **Ferial Hymns**   *Summer Friday*

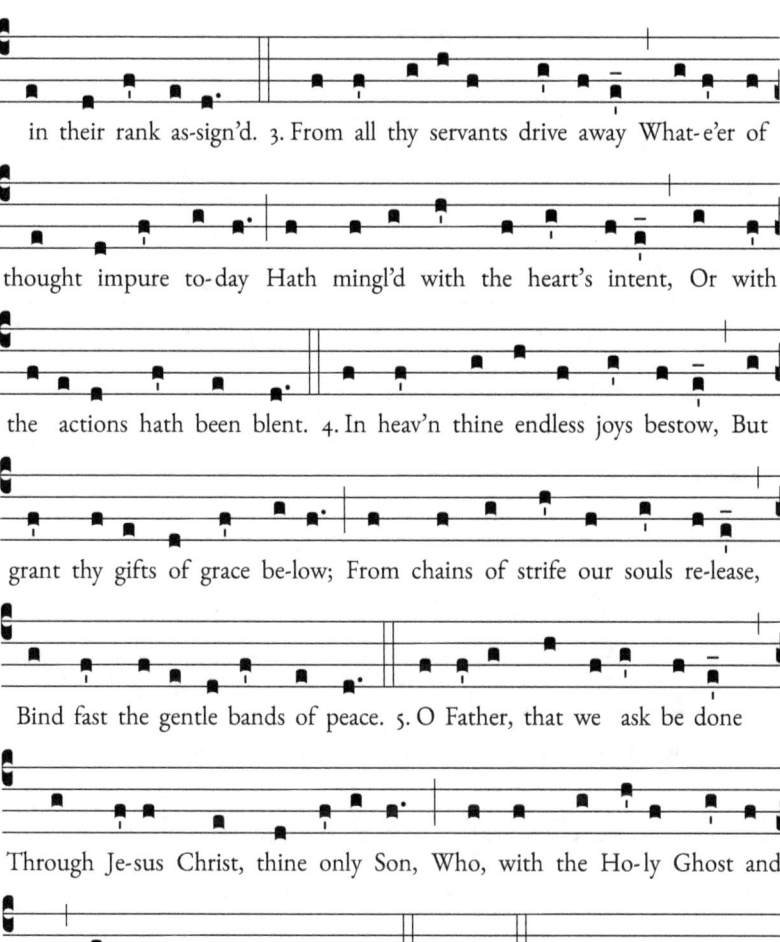

in their rank as-sign'd. 3. From all thy servants drive away What-e'er of thought impure to-day Hath mingl'd with the heart's intent, Or with the actions hath been blent. 4. In heav'n thine endless joys bestow, But grant thy gifts of grace be-low; From chains of strife our souls re-lease, Bind fast the gentle bands of peace. 5. O Father, that we ask be done Through Je-sus Christ, thine only Son, Who, with the Ho-ly Ghost and thee, Shall live and reign e-ternal-ly. A-men.

℣. Lord, let my prayer be set forth.

℟. In thy sight as the incense.

Mag. Ant. He hath put down the mighty † that persecute the holy; and hath exalted the humble that confess his Christ.

Summer Saturday — Ferial Hymns — Mattins

SATURDAY MATTINS OFFICE HYMN

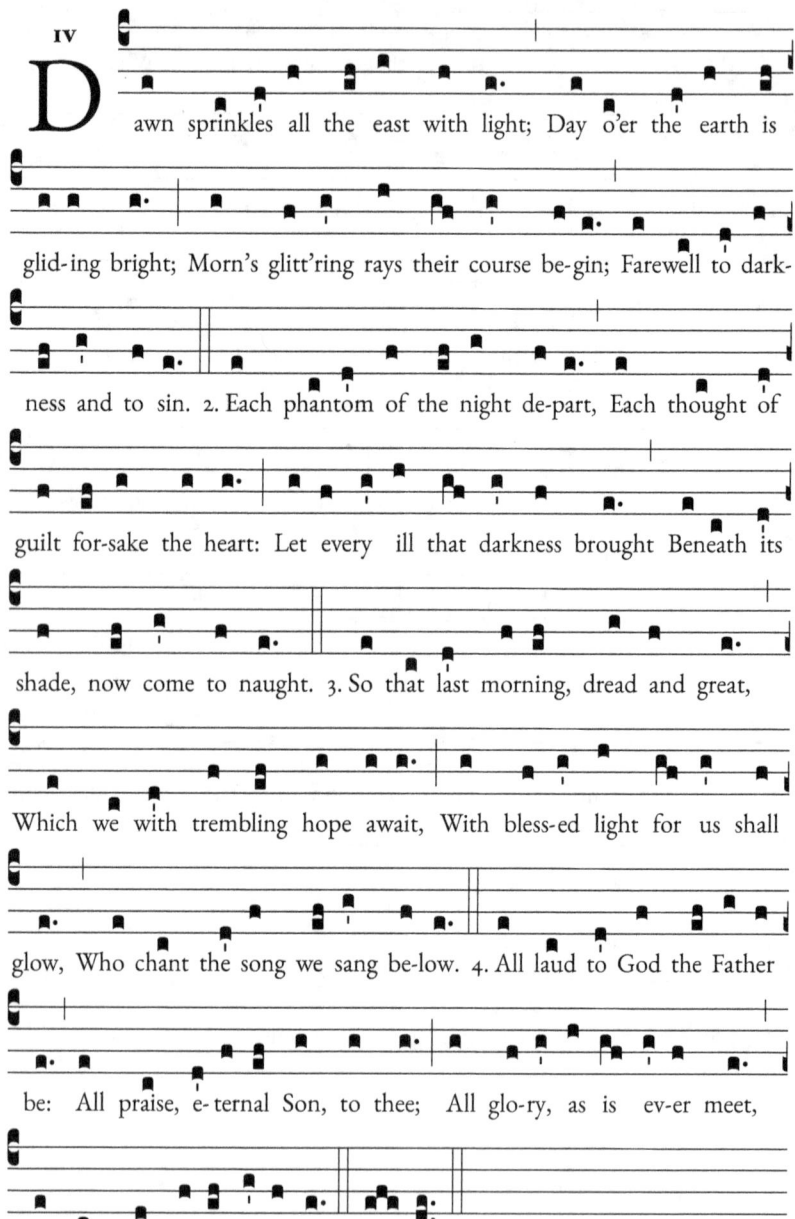

IV

Dawn sprinkles all the east with light; Day o'er the earth is glid-ing bright; Morn's glitt'ring rays their course be-gin; Farewell to dark-ness and to sin. 2. Each phantom of the night de-part, Each thought of guilt for-sake the heart: Let every ill that darkness brought Beneath its shade, now come to naught. 3. So that last morning, dread and great, Which we with trembling hope await, With bless-ed light for us shall glow, Who chant the song we sang be-low. 4. All laud to God the Father be: All praise, e-ternal Son, to thee; All glo-ry, as is ev-er meet, To God the Ho-ly Par-a-clete. A-men.

℣. O satisfy us with thy mercy, and that soon.

℟. So shall we rejoice and be glad all the days of our life.

Ben. Ant. Give light, O Lord, † to them that sit in darkness: and guide our feet into the way of peace, thou God of Israel.

Evensong | **Ferial Hymns** | *Summer Saturday*

SATURDAY EVENSONG OFFICE HYMN

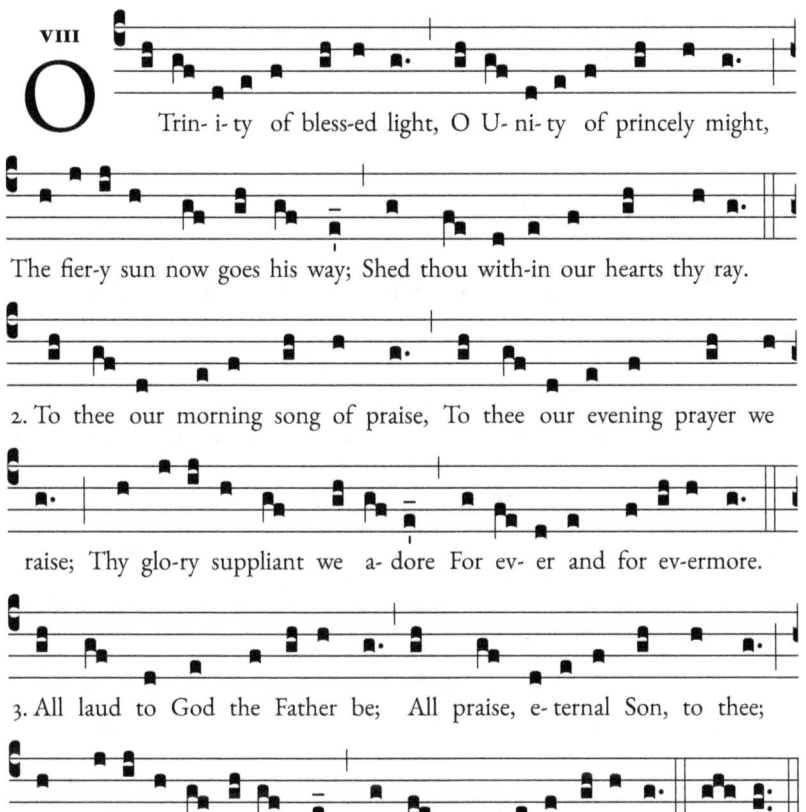

O Trin-i-ty of bless-ed light, O U-ni-ty of princely might,
The fier-y sun now goes his way; Shed thou with-in our hearts thy ray.

2. To thee our morning song of praise, To thee our evening prayer we raise; Thy glo-ry suppliant we a-dore For ev-er and for ev-ermore.

3. All laud to God the Father be; All praise, e-ternal Son, to thee; All glo-ry, as is ev-er meet, To God the Ho-ly Par-a-clete. A-men.

℣. Let our evening prayer come up before thee, O Lord.
℟. And let thy mercy come down on us.

Winter Sunday   **Ferial Hymns**   Mattins

Winter Hymns

℟ The Winter Hymns are said from the Octave of Epiphany through Quinquagesima Sunday, inclusive, and from the Sunday within 28 September - 4 October until Advent, exclusive.

Sunday Mattins Office Hymn

1. Maker of all, eternal King, Who day and night about dost bring: Who weary mortals to relieve Dost in their turn the seasons give: 2. Now chanticleer proclaims the day, And calls the sun's a-wak'ning ray, The wand'ring pilgrim's guiding light, That marks the watches night by night. 3. Rous'd at the note, the morning star Heav'n's dusky veil uplifts afar: Night's vagrant bands no longer roam, But from their dark ways hie them home. 4. Th'encourag'd sailor's fears are o'er, The foaming billows rage no more: Lo! even the very Church's Rock

Winter Sunday   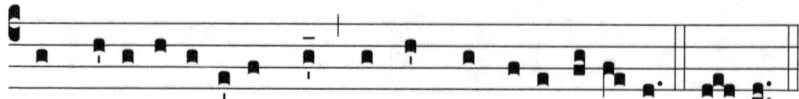   Evensong

All glor-y, as is ev-er meet, To God the Ho-ly Par-a-clete. A-men.
℣. The Lord is King, and hath put on glorious apparel.
℟. The Lord hath put on his apparel, and girded himself with strength.

SUNDAY EVENSONG OFFICE HYMN

O blest Cre-a-tor of the light, Who mak'st the day with  rad-iance bright, And o'er the form-ing world didst call The light from cha-os first of all: 2. Whose wisdom joined in meet ar-ray The morn and eve, and nam'd them day: Night comes with all its darkling fears, Re-gard thy people's prayers and tears. 3. Lest, sunk in sin and whelm'd with strife, They lose the gift of endless life; While thinking but the thoughts of time, They weave new chains of woe and crime. 4. But grant them grace that they may strain The heav'nly gate and prize to gain:

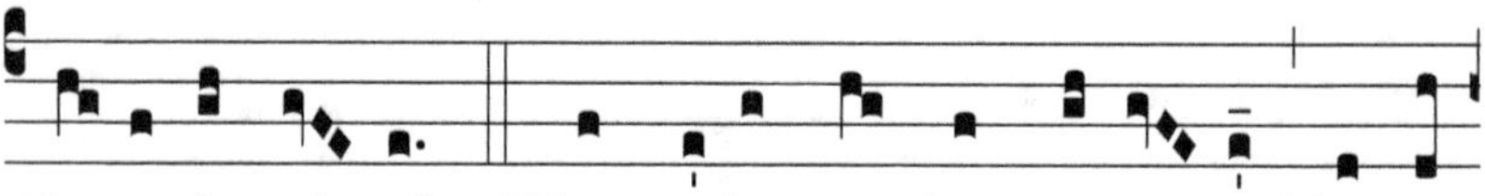

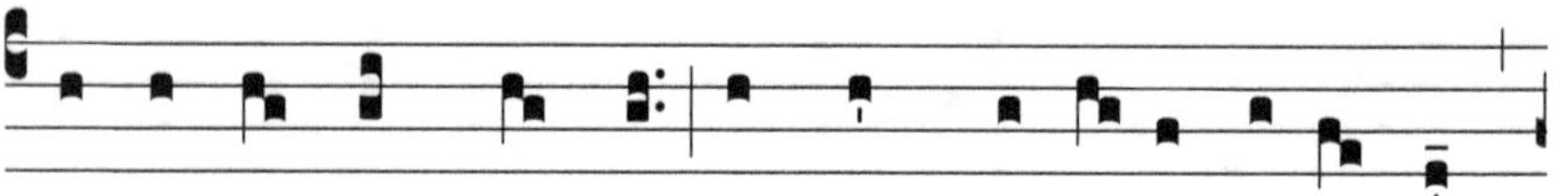

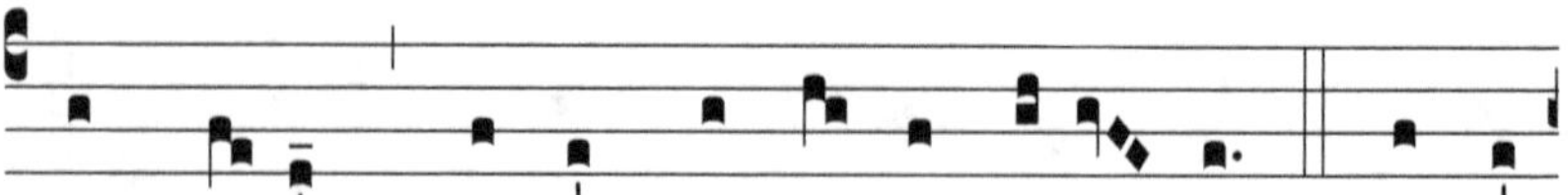

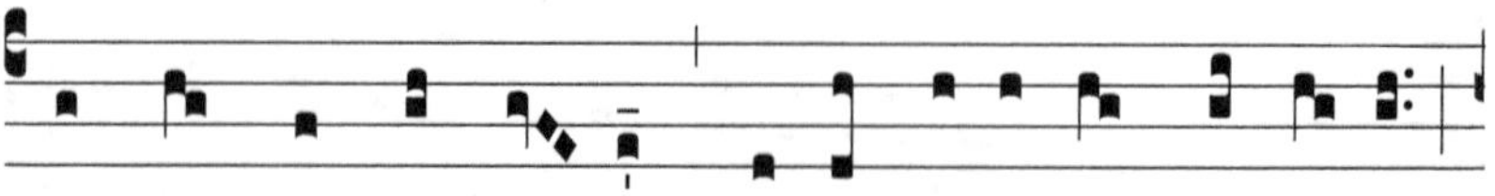

Mattins — Ferial Hymns — *Winter Monday*

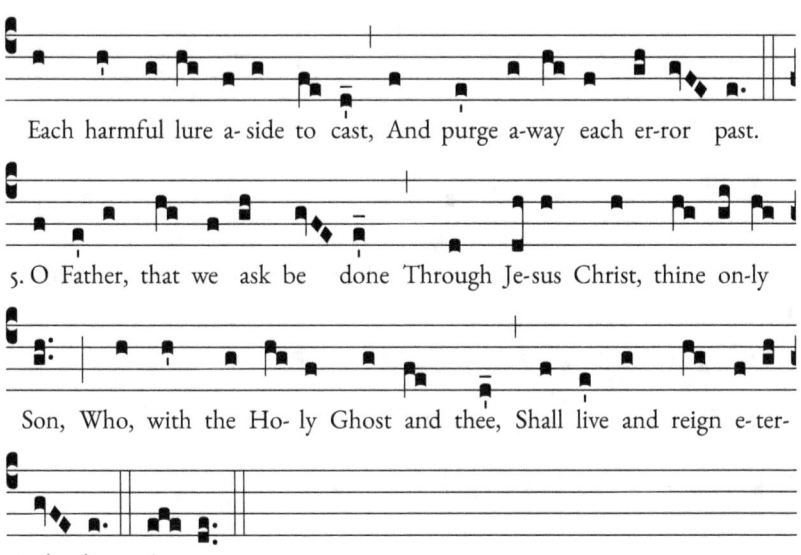

Each harmful lure a-side to cast, And purge a-way each er-ror past.

5. O Father, that we ask be done Through Je-sus Christ, thine on-ly Son, Who, with the Ho-ly Ghost and thee, Shall live and reign e-ter-nal-ly. A-men.

℣. Lord, let my prayer be set forth
℟. In thy sight as the incense.

Monday Mattins Office Hymn

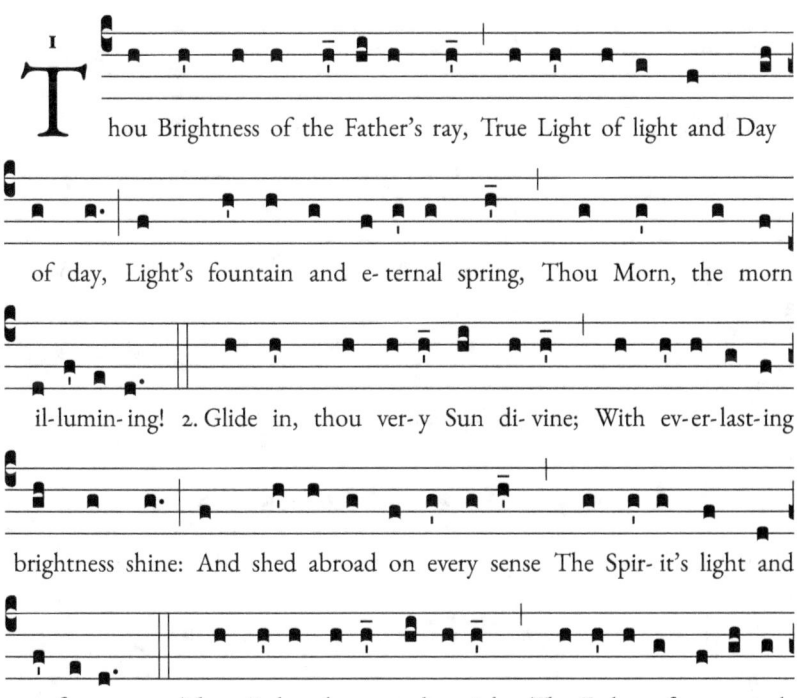

Thou Brightness of the Father's ray, True Light of light and Day of day, Light's fountain and e-ternal spring, Thou Morn, the morn il-lumin-ing! 2. Glide in, thou ver-y Sun di-vine; With ev-er-last-ing brightness shine: And shed abroad on every sense The Spir-it's light and influ-ence. 3. Thee, Father, let us seek a-right, The Father of perpet-ual

Winter Monday — Ferial Hymns — Mattins

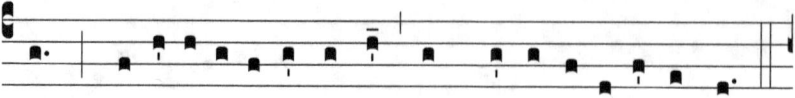
light, The Father of almighty grace, Each wile of sin away to chase.

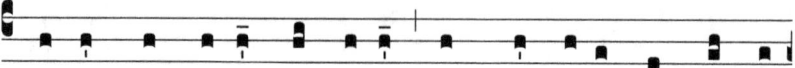
4. Our acts with cour-age do thou fill; Blunt thou the tempter's tooth of

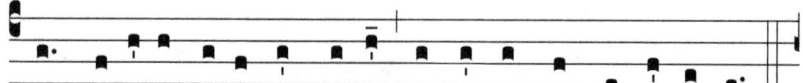
ill: Mis-fortune into good convert, Or give us grace to bear unhurt.

5. Our spir-its, what-so- e'er be- tide, In chaste and loy- al bod-ies guide;

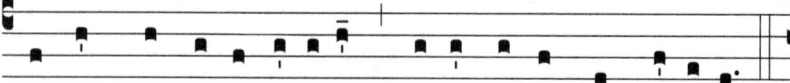
Let Faith, with fervour un-alloy'd The bane of falsehood still a-void.

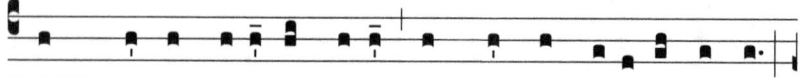
6. And Christ our dai-ly food be nigh, And Faith our dai-ly cup supply:

So may we quaff, to calm and bless, The Spir- it's rapturous ho- li-

ness. 7. Now let the day in joy pass on: Our mod-es-ty like early dawn,

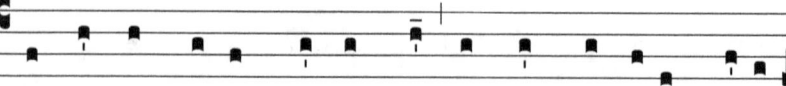
Our faith like noontide splendour glow, Our souls the twi- light nev-er

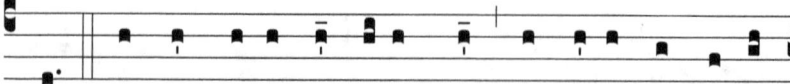
know. 8. See! morn pursues her shin-ing way: True Morning, all thy beams

Evensong   **Ferial Hymns**   *Winter Monday*

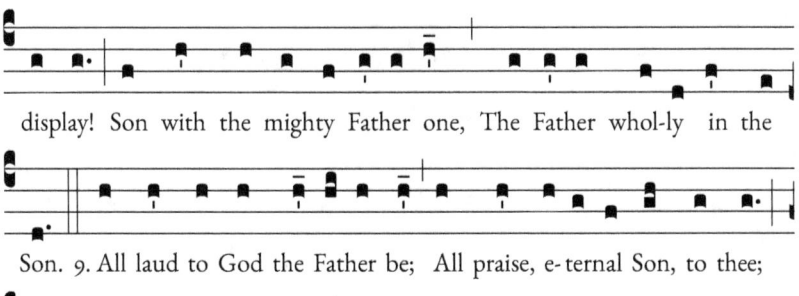

display! Son with the mighty Father one, The Father whol-ly in the

Son. 9. All laud to God the Father be; All praise, e-ternal Son, to thee;

All glo-ry, as is ev-er meet, To God the Ho-ly Par-a-clete. A-men.
℣. O satisfy us with thy mercy, and that soon.
℟. So shall we rejoice and be glad all the days of our life.
Ben. Ant. Blessed † be the Lord God of Israel.

Monday Evensong Office Hymn

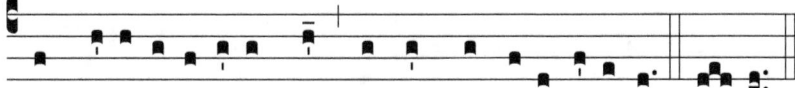

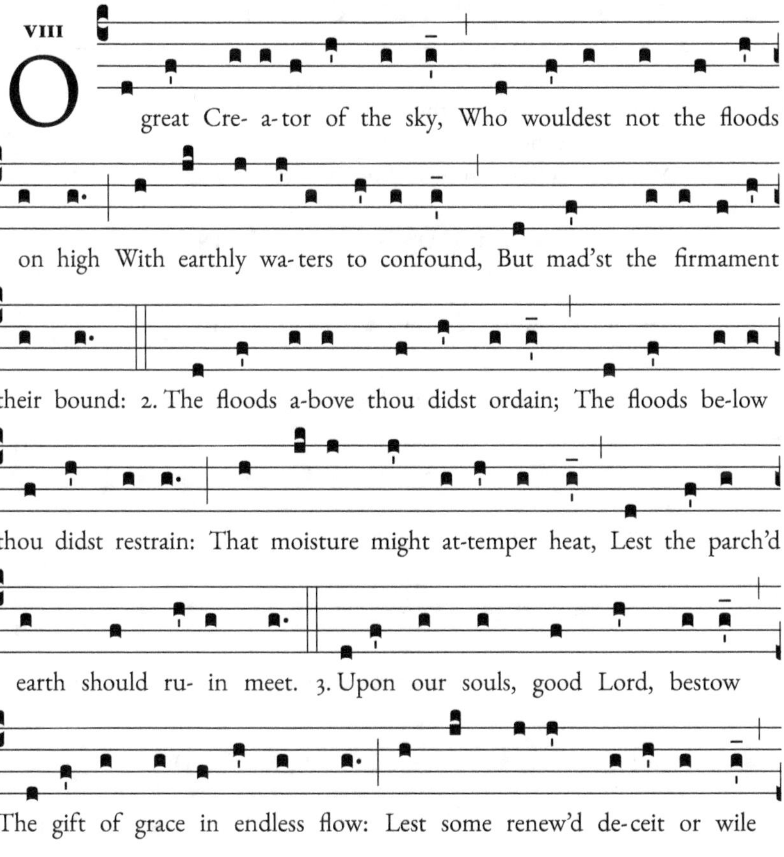

VIII

O great Cre-a-tor of the sky, Who wouldest not the floods

on high With earthly wa-ters to confound, But mad'st the firmament

their bound: 2. The floods a-bove thou didst ordain; The floods be-low

thou didst restrain: That moisture might at-temper heat, Lest the parch'd

earth should ru-in meet. 3. Upon our souls, good Lord, bestow

The gift of grace in endless flow: Lest some renew'd de-ceit or wile

Winter Tuesday — Ferial Hymns — Mattins

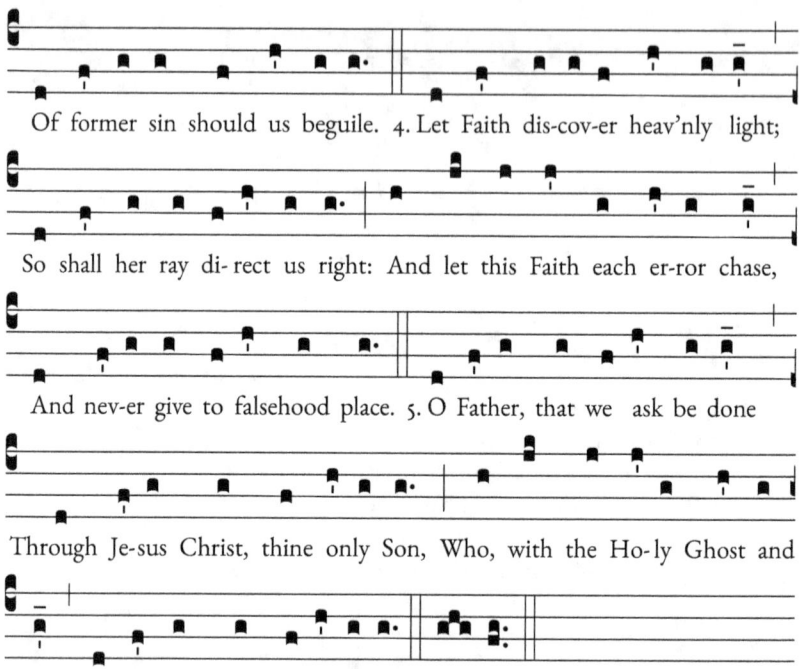

Of former sin should us beguile. 4. Let Faith dis-cov-er heav'nly light; So shall her ray di-rect us right: And let this Faith each er-ror chase, And nev-er give to falsehood place. 5. O Father, that we ask be done Through Je-sus Christ, thine only Son, Who, with the Ho-ly Ghost and thee, Shall live and reign e-ternal-ly. A-men.

℣. Lord, let my prayer be set forth.
℟. In thy sight as the incense.
Mag. Ant. My soul † doth magnify the Lord, for he hath regarded my lowliness.

TUESDAY MATTINS OFFICE HYMN

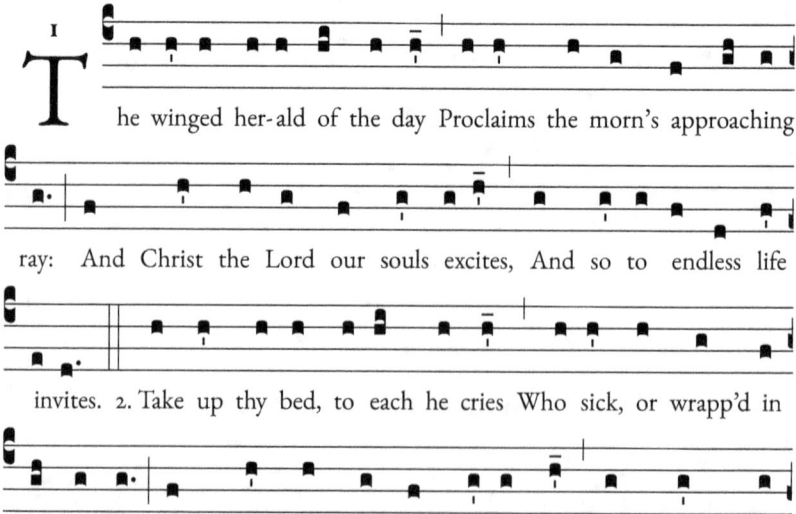

The winged her-ald of the day Proclaims the morn's approaching ray: And Christ the Lord our souls excites, And so to endless life invites. 2. Take up thy bed, to each he cries Who sick, or wrapp'd in slumber lies: And chaste, and just, and so-ber stand And watch; my

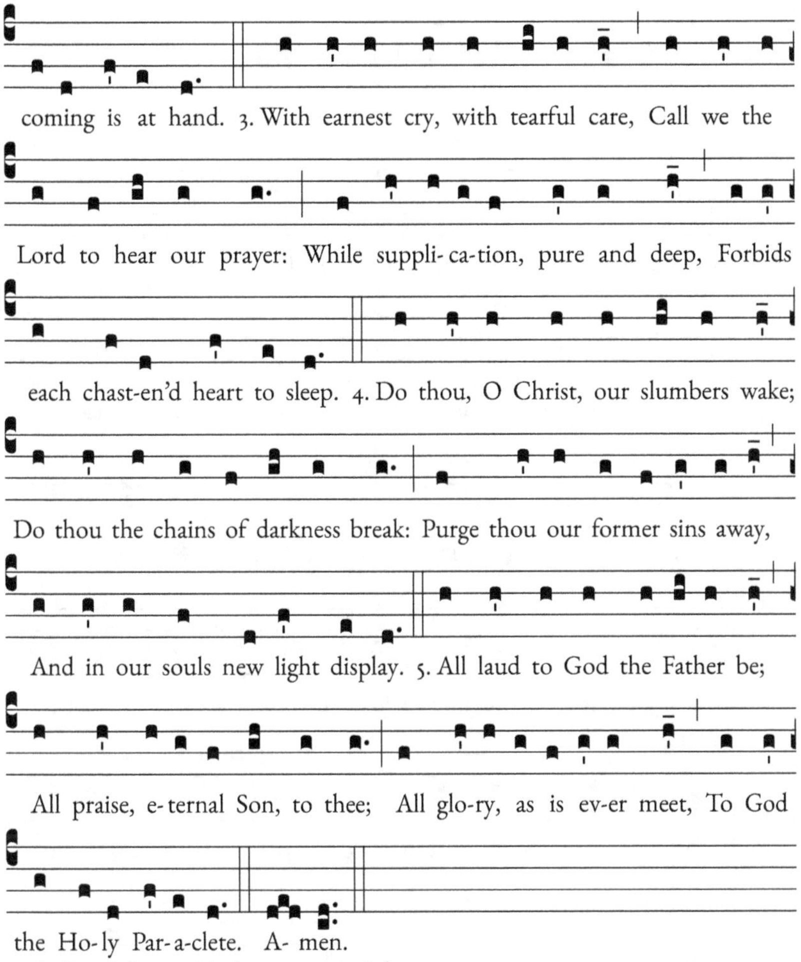

Evensong — **Ferial Hymns** — *Winter Tuesday*

coming is at hand. 3. With earnest cry, with tearful care, Call we the

Lord to hear our prayer: While suppli-ca-tion, pure and deep, Forbids

each chast-en'd heart to sleep. 4. Do thou, O Christ, our slumbers wake;

Do thou the chains of darkness break: Purge thou our former sins away,

And in our souls new light display. 5. All laud to God the Father be;

All praise, e-ternal Son, to thee; All glo-ry, as is ev-er meet, To God

the Ho-ly Par-a-clete. A-men.

℣. O satisfy us with thy mercy, and that soon.

℟. So shall we rejoice and be glad all the days of our life.

Ben. Ant. The Lord hath raised up for us † an horn of salvation in the house of his servant David.

Tuesday Evensong Office Hymn

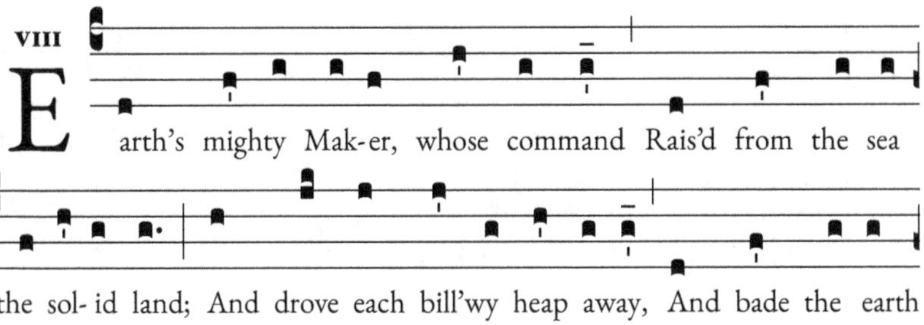

VIII

Earth's mighty Mak-er, whose command Rais'd from the sea

the sol-id land; And drove each bill'wy heap away, And bade the earth

Winter Tuesday — **Ferial Hymns** — Evensong

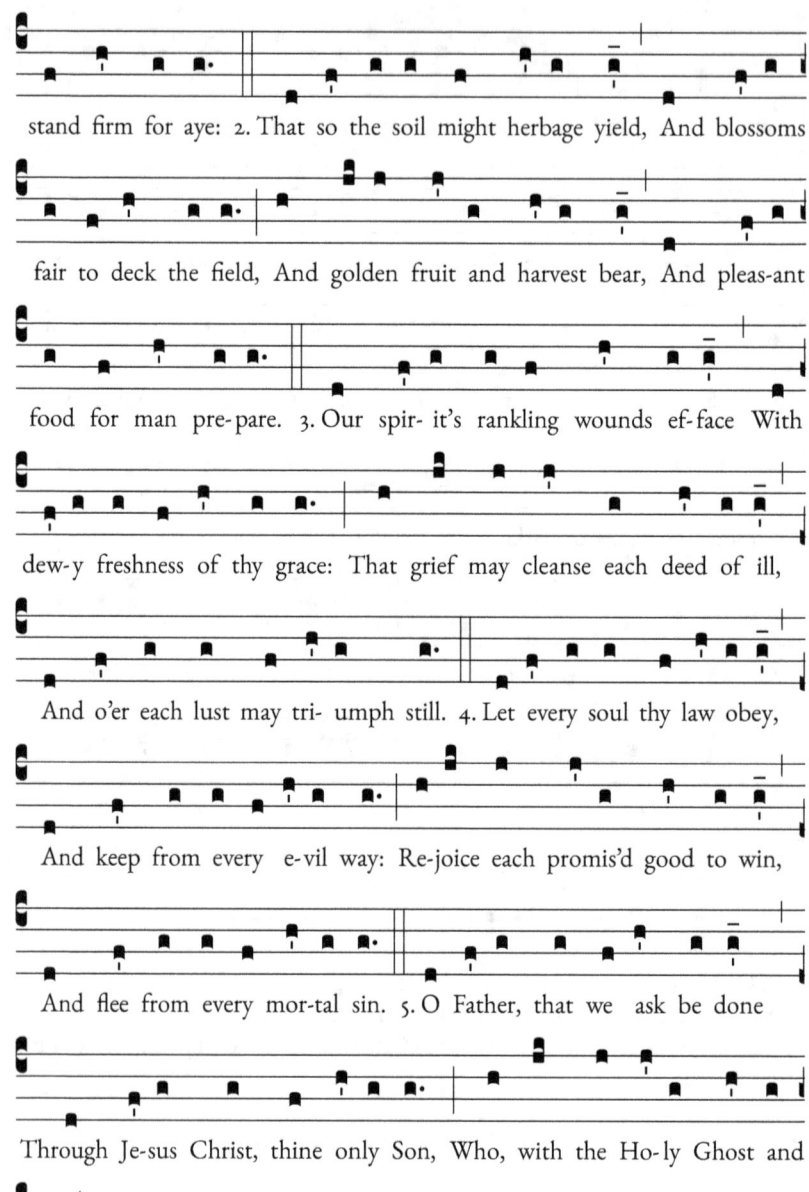

stand firm for aye: 2. That so the soil might herbage yield, And blossoms fair to deck the field, And golden fruit and harvest bear, And pleasant food for man prepare. 3. Our spirit's rankling wounds efface With dewy freshness of thy grace: That grief may cleanse each deed of ill, And o'er each lust may triumph still. 4. Let every soul thy law obey, And keep from every evil way: Rejoice each promis'd good to win, And flee from every mortal sin. 5. O Father, that we ask be done Through Jesus Christ, thine only Son, Who, with the Holy Ghost and thee, Shall live and reign eternally. Amen.

℣. Lord, let my prayer be set forth.

℟. In thy sight as the incense.

Mag. Ant. Let my spirit rejoice † in God my Saviour.

Wednesday Mattins Office Hymn

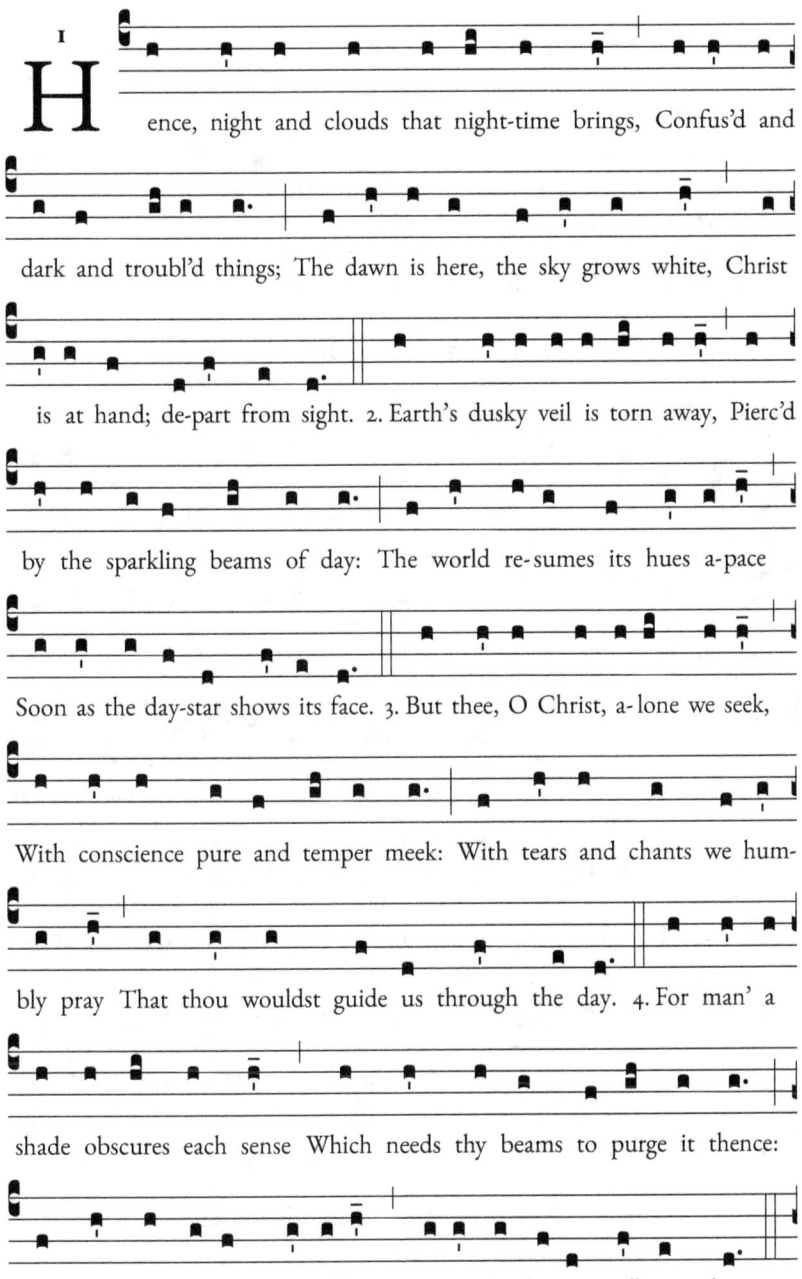

Hence, night and clouds that night-time brings, Confus'd and dark and troubl'd things; The dawn is here, the sky grows white, Christ is at hand; depart from sight. 2. Earth's dusky veil is torn away, Pierc'd by the sparkling beams of day: The world resumes its hues apace Soon as the day-star shows its face. 3. But thee, O Christ, alone we seek, With conscience pure and temper meek: With tears and chants we humbly pray That thou wouldst guide us through the day. 4. For man' a shade obscures each sense Which needs thy beams to purge it thence: Light of the Morning Star, illume, Serenely shining, all our gloom.

Winter Wednesday   **Ferial Hymns**   Evensong

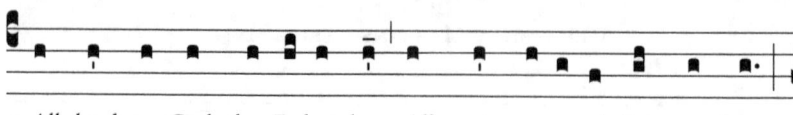

5. All laud to God the Father be; All praise, e-ternal Son, to thee;

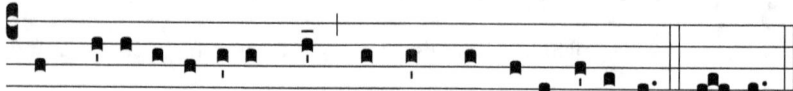

All glo-ry, as is ev-er meet, To God the Ho-ly Par-a-clete. A-men.

℣. O satisfy us with thy mercy, and that soon.

℞. So shall we rejoice and be glad all the days of our life.

Ben. Ant. From the hand of all † that hate us, the Lord hath delivered us.

Wednesday Evensong Office Hymn

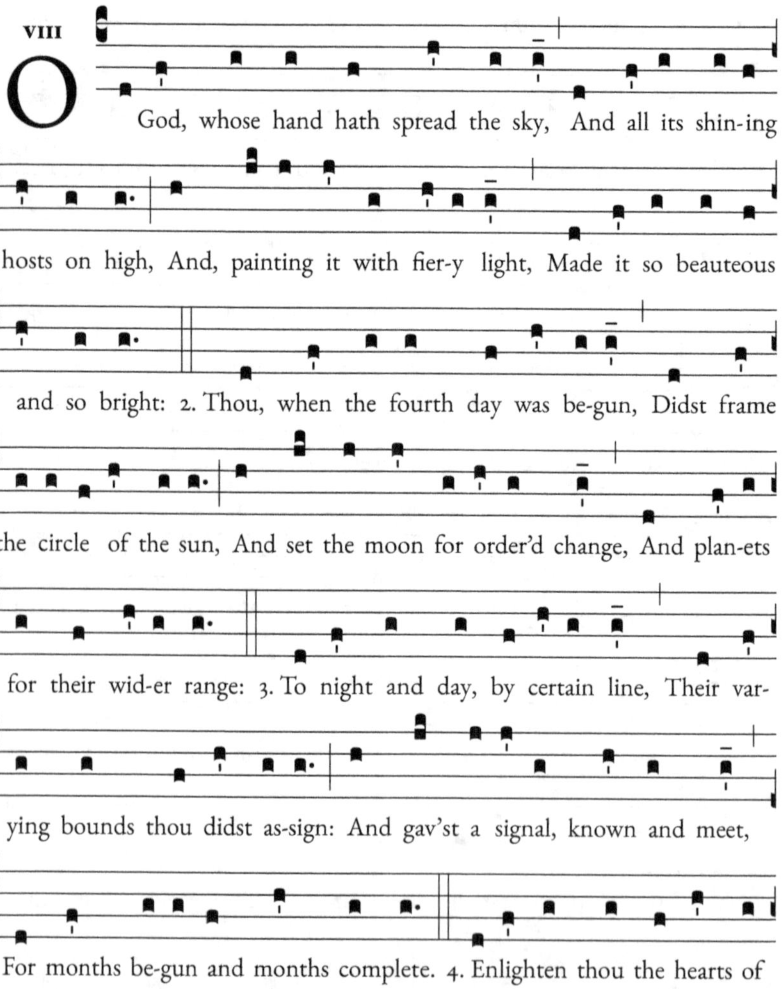

O God, whose hand hath spread the sky, And all its shin-ing hosts on high, And, painting it with fier-y light, Made it so beauteous and so bright: 2. Thou, when the fourth day was be-gun, Didst frame the circle of the sun, And set the moon for order'd change, And plan-ets for their wid-er range: 3. To night and day, by certain line, Their var-ying bounds thou didst as-sign: And gav'st a signal, known and meet, For months be-gun and months complete. 4. Enlighten thou the hearts of

Mattins   **Ferial Hymns**   *Winter Thursday*

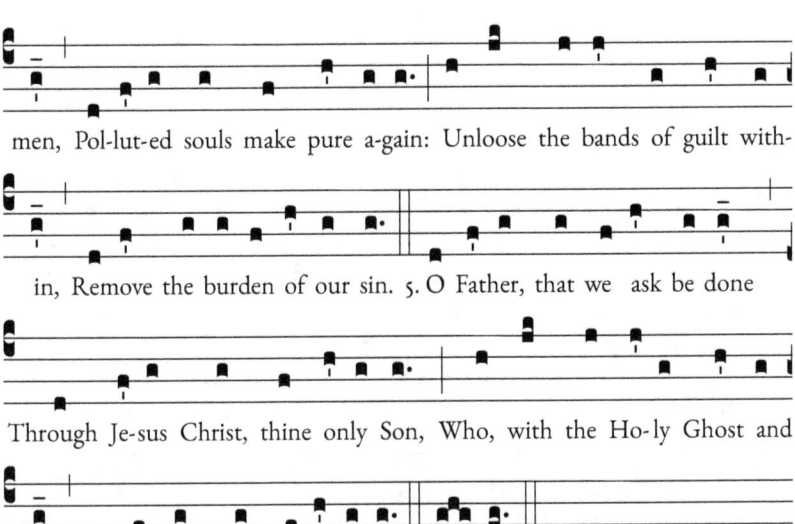

men, Pol-lut-ed souls make pure a-gain: Unloose the bands of guilt within, Remove the burden of our sin. 5. O Father, that we ask be done Through Jesus Christ, thine only Son, Who, with the Holy Ghost and thee, Shall live and reign e-ternal-ly. A-men.

℣. Lord, let my prayer be set forth.
℟. In thy sight as the incense.

Mag. Ant. The Lord † hath regarded my lowliness: and he that is mighty hath done in me great things.

Thursday Mattins Office Hymn

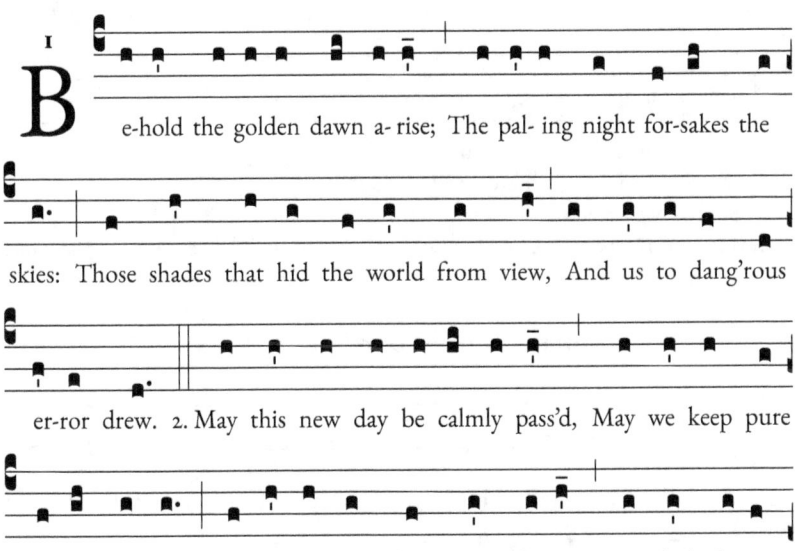

Behold the golden dawn a-rise; The pal-ing night forsakes the skies: Those shades that hid the world from view, And us to dang'rous er-ror drew. 2. May this new day be calmly pass'd, May we keep pure while it shall last: Nor let our lips from truth depart, Nor dark designs

Winter Thursday   **Ferial Hymns**   Evensong

engage the heart. 3. So may the day speed on; the tongue No falsehood know, the hands no wrong: Our eyes from wanton gaze refrain, No guilt our guarded bod-ies stain. 4. For God all-see-ing from on high Surveys us with a watchful eye: Each day our every act he knows From early dawn to evening's close. 5. All laud to God the Father be; All praise, e-ternal Son, to thee; All glo-ry, as is ev-er meet, To God the Ho-ly Par-a-clete. A-men.

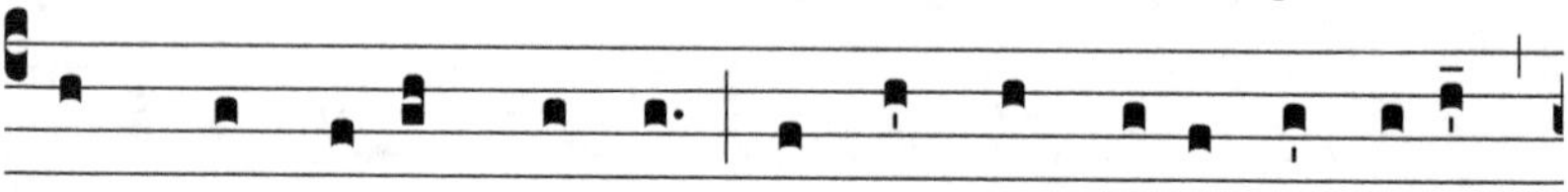

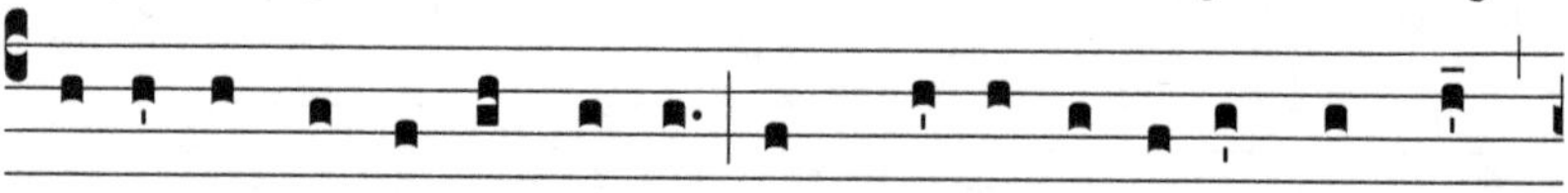

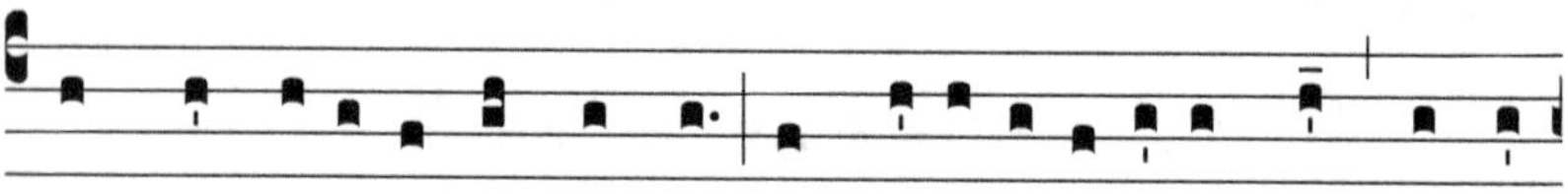

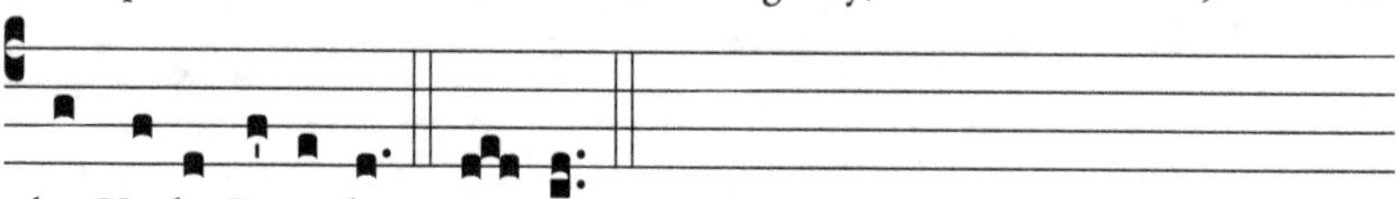

℣. O satisfy us with thy mercy, and that soon.

℟. So shall we rejoice and be glad all the days of our life.

Ben. Ant. Let us serve † the Lord in holiness, and he will deliver us from the hand of our enemies.

Thursday Evensong Office Hymn

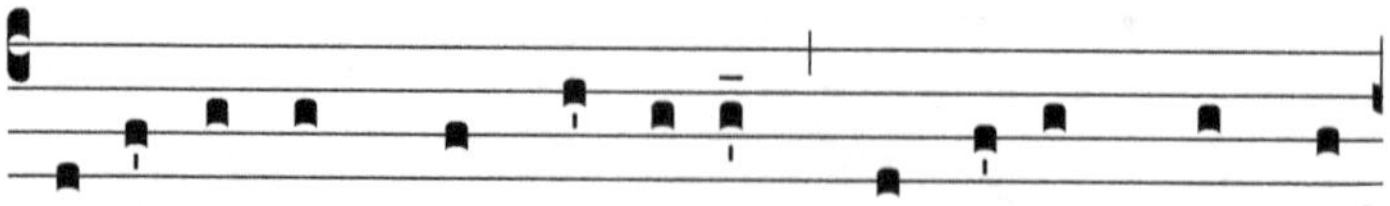

Al-mighty God, whose will supreme Made o-cean's flood with  life to teem; Part in the firmament to fly, And part in o-cean depths

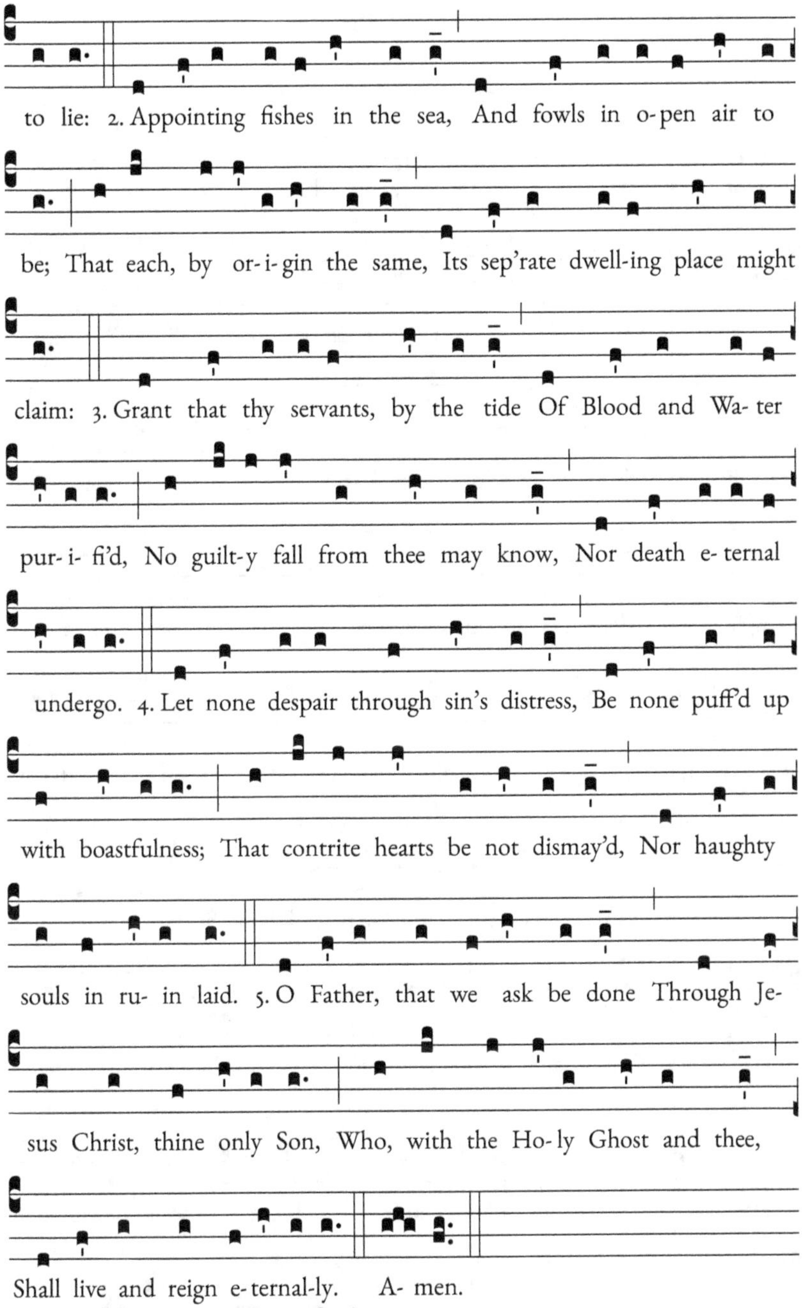

Evensong   **Ferial Hymns**   *Winter Thursday*

to lie: 2. Appointing fishes in the sea, And fowls in o-pen air to

be; That each, by or-i-gin the same, Its sep'rate dwell-ing place might

claim: 3. Grant that thy servants, by the tide Of Blood and Wa-ter

pur-i-fi'd, No guilt-y fall from thee may know, Nor death e-ternal

undergo. 4. Let none despair through sin's distress, Be none puff'd up

with boastfulness; That contrite hearts be not dismay'd, Nor haughty

souls in ru-in laid. 5. O Father, that we ask be done Through Je-

sus Christ, thine only Son, Who, with the Ho-ly Ghost and thee,

Shall live and reign e-ternal-ly.   A-men.

℣. Lord, let my prayer be set forth.

℟. In thy sight as the incense.

Mag. Ant. Show strength, O God, † with thine arm: scatter the proud, and exalt the humble.

Winter Friday   **Ferial Hymns**   Mattins

Friday Mattins Office Hymn

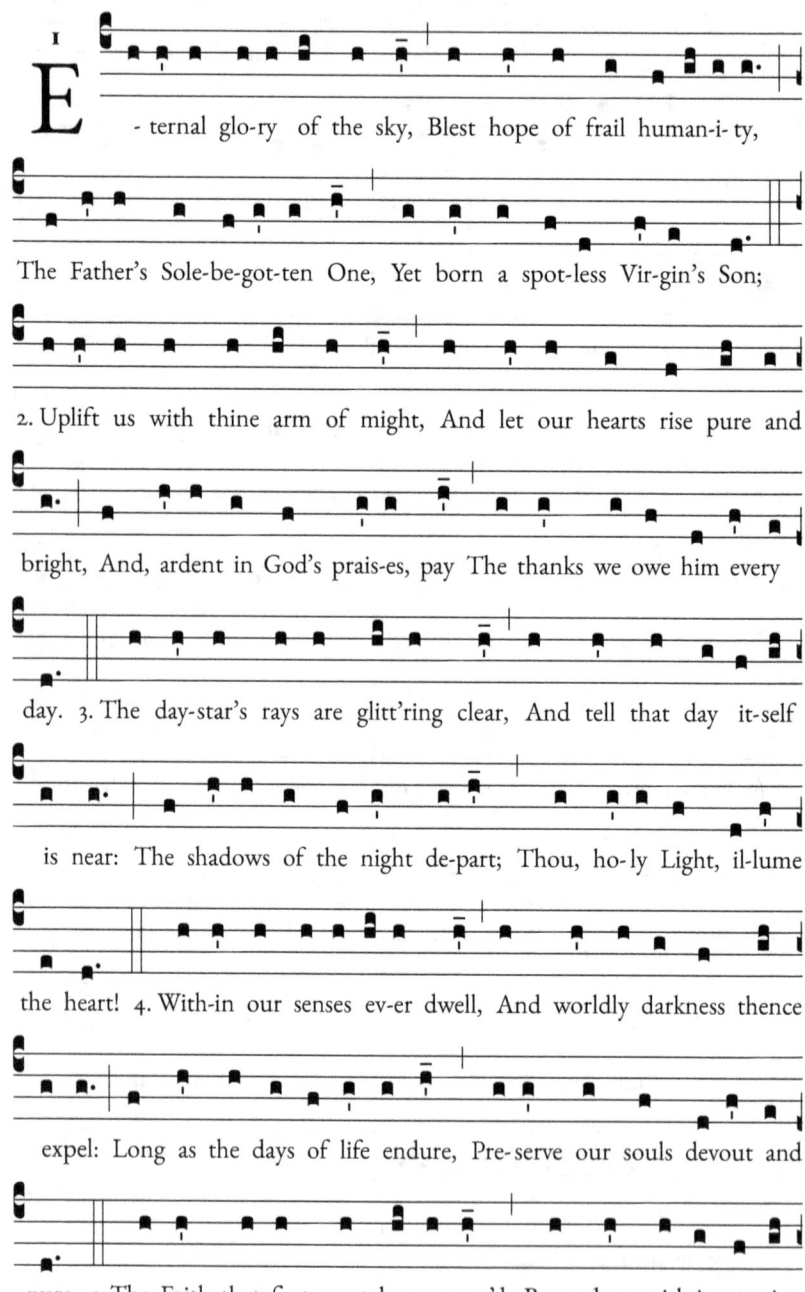

E- ternal glo-ry of the sky, Blest hope of frail human-i-ty,

The Father's Sole-be-got-ten One, Yet born a spot-less Vir-gin's Son;

2. Uplift us with thine arm of might, And let our hearts rise pure and bright, And, ardent in God's prais-es, pay The thanks we owe him every day. 3. The day-star's rays are glitt'ring clear, And tell that day it-self is near: The shadows of the night de-part; Thou, ho-ly Light, il-lume the heart! 4. With-in our senses ev-er dwell, And worldly darkness thence expel: Long as the days of life endure, Pre-serve our souls devout and pure. 5. The Faith that first must be poss-ess'd, Root deep with-in our in-

Evensong

Ferial Hymns

 *Winter Friday*

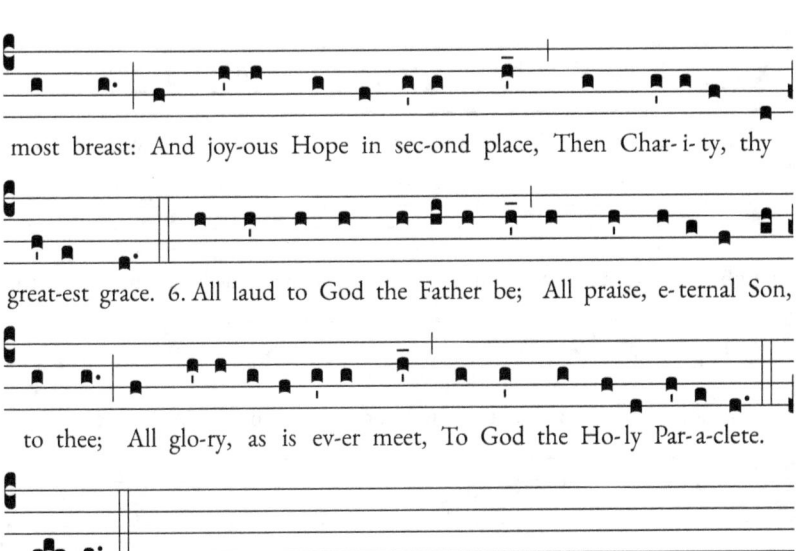

most breast: And joy-ous Hope in sec-ond place, Then Char-i-ty, thy great-est grace. 6. All laud to God the Father be; All praise, e-ternal Son, to thee; All glo-ry, as is ev-er meet, To God the Ho-ly Par-a-clete. A-men.

℣. O satisfy us with thy mercy, and that soon.
℟. So shall we rejoice and be glad all the days of our life.

Ben. Ant. Through the tender mercy † of our God: whereby the day-spring from on high hath visited us.

Friday Evensong Office Hymn

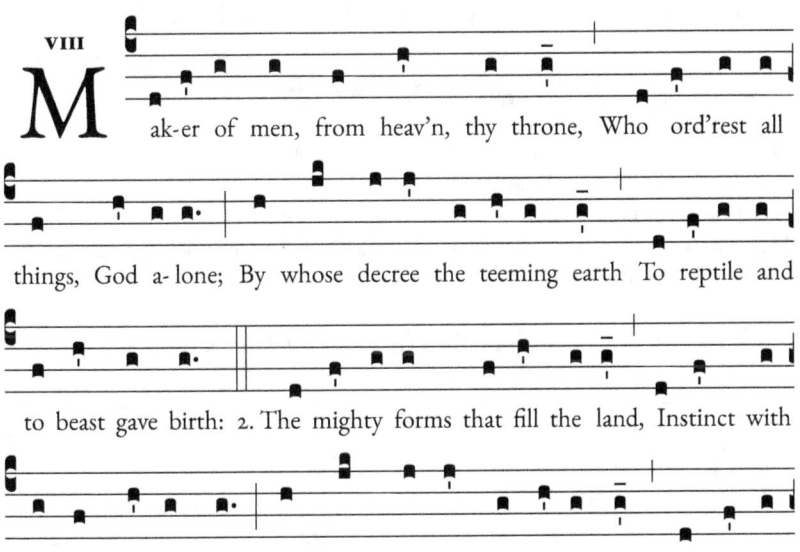

Maker of men, from heav'n, thy throne, Who ord'rest all things, God a-lone; By whose decree the teeming earth To reptile and to beast gave birth: 2. The mighty forms that fill the land, Instinct with life at thy command, Are giv'n subdu'd to human-kind For ser-vice

Winter Saturday — **Ferial Hymns** — Mattins

in their rank as-sign'd. 3. From all thy servants drive away What-e'er of thought impure to-day Hath mingl'd with the heart's intent, Or with the actions hath been blent. 4. In heav'n thine endless joys bestow, But grant thy gifts of grace be-low; From chains of strife our souls re-lease, Bind fast the gentle bands of peace. 5. O Father, that we ask be done Through Je-sus Christ, thine only Son, Who, with the Ho-ly Ghost and thee, Shall live and reign e-ternal-ly.   A-men.

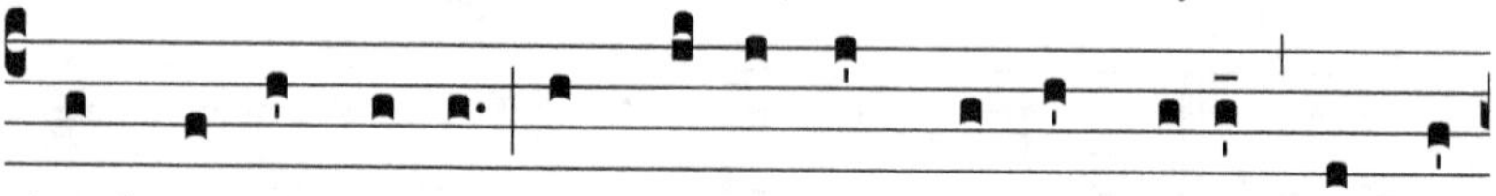

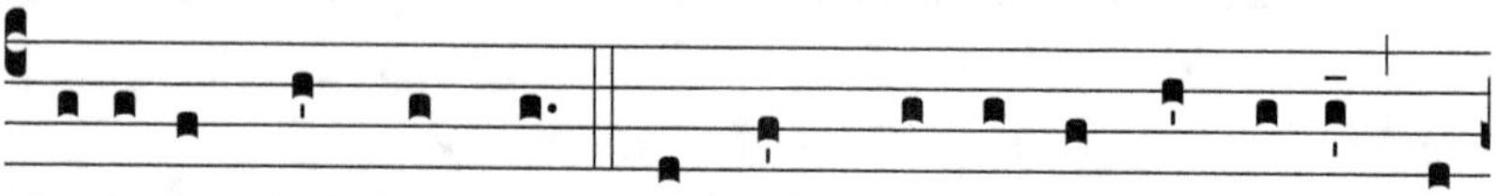

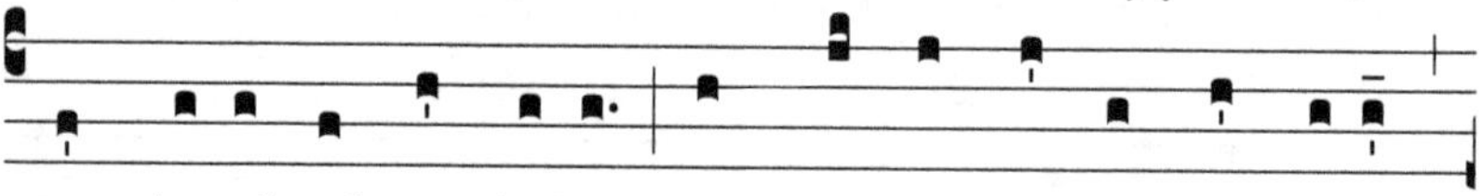

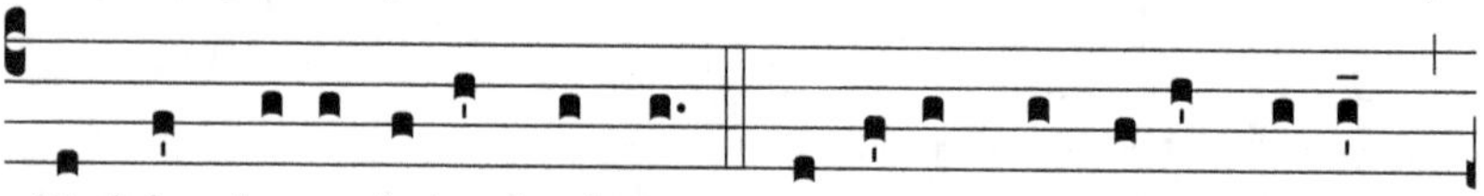

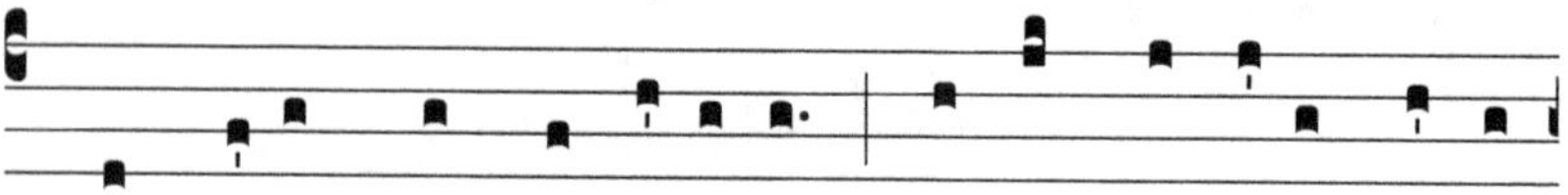

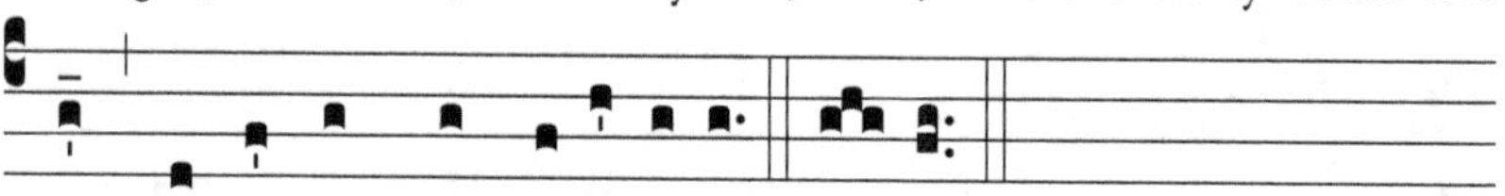

℣. Lord, let my prayer be set forth.

℟. In thy sight as the incense.

Mag. Ant. He hath put down the mighty † that persecute the holy; and hath exalted the humble that confess his Christ.

SATURDAY MATTINS OFFICE HYMN

IV

Dawn sprinkles all the east with light; Day o'er the earth is glid-ing bright; Morn's glitt'ring rays their course be-gin; Farewell to dark-

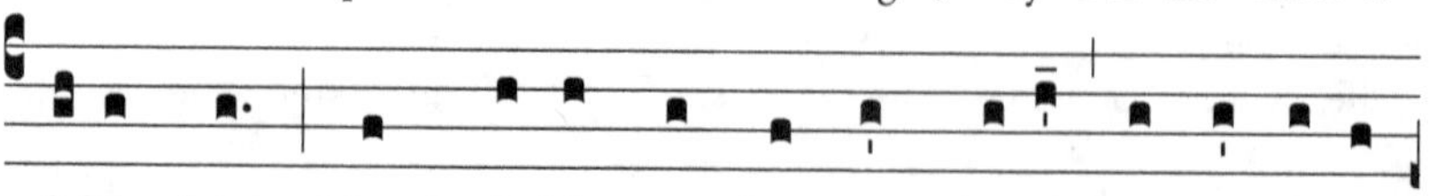

Mattins — **Ferial Hymns** — *Winter Saturday*

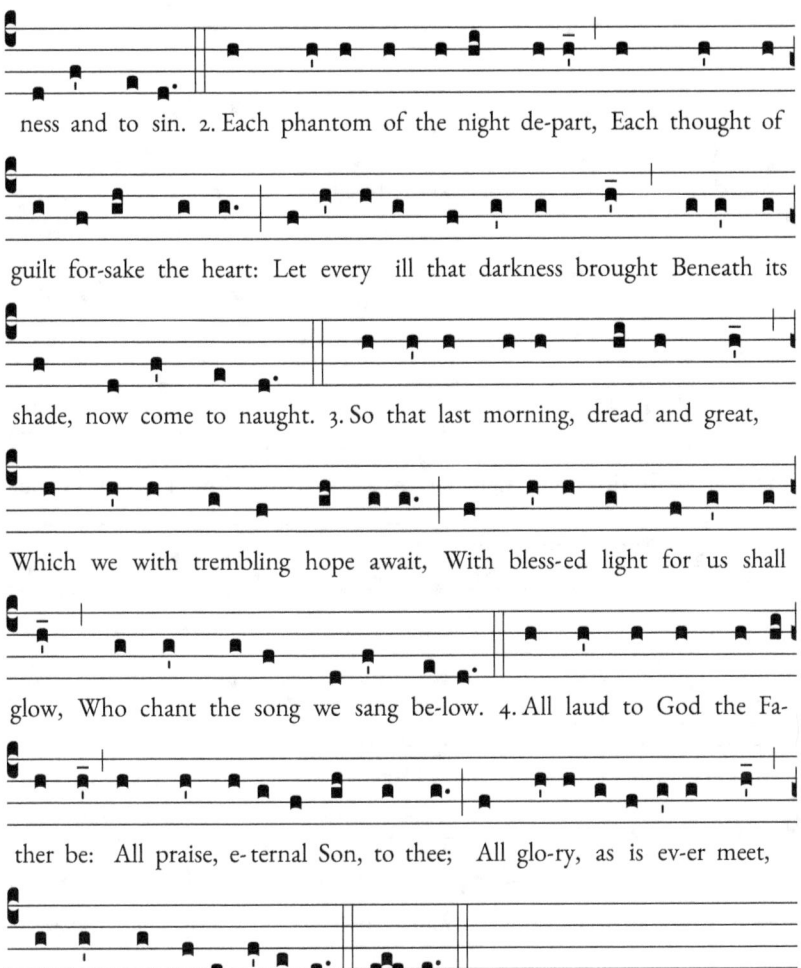

ness and to sin. 2. Each phantom of the night de-part, Each thought of guilt for-sake the heart: Let every ill that darkness brought Beneath its shade, now come to naught. 3. So that last morning, dread and great, Which we with trembling hope await, With bless-ed light for us shall glow, Who chant the song we sang be-low. 4. All laud to God the Fa-ther be: All praise, e-ternal Son, to thee; All glo-ry, as is ev-er meet, To God the Ho-ly Par-a-clete. A-men.

℣. O satisfy us with thy mercy, and that soon.

℞. So shall we rejoice and be glad all the days of our life.

Ben. Ant. Give light, O Lord, † to them that sit in darkness: and guide our feet into the way of peace, thou God of Israel.

Winter Saturday   **Ferial Hymns**   Evensong

Saturday Evensong Office Hymn

O Trin-i-ty of bless-ed light, O U-ni-ty of princely might, The fier-y sun now goes his way; Shed thou with-in our hearts thy ray. 2. To thee our morn-ing song of praise, To thee our evening prayer we raise; Thy glo-ry suppliant we a-dore For ev-er and for ev-ermore. 3. All laud to God the Father be; All praise, e-ternal Son, to thee; All glo-ry, as is ev-er meet, To God the Ho-ly Par-a-clete.

A-men.

℣. Let our evening prayer come up before thee, O Lord.
℟. And let thy mercy come down on us.

Liturgical Hymns

Office Ordinary   # Liturgical Hymns   Introduction

Ordinary of the Office

INTRODUCTION

Simple

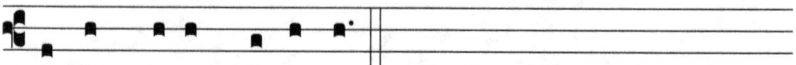

℣. O Lord, † o-pen thou our lips.

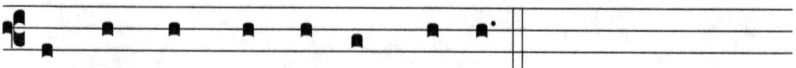

℟. And our mouth shall show forth thy praise.

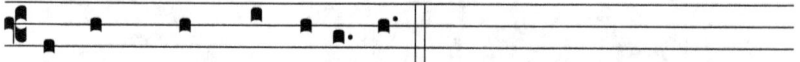

℣. O God, ✠ make speed to save us.

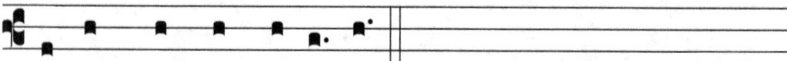

℟. O Lord, make haste to help us.

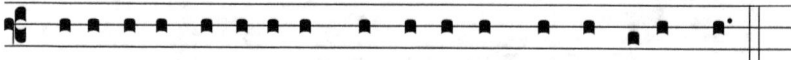

℣. Glo-ry be to the Father and to the Son and to the Ho-ly Ghost.

℟. As it was in the be-ginning, is now, and ev-er shall be, world without

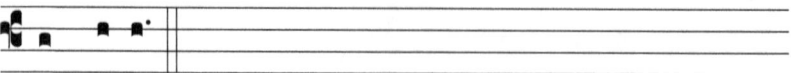

end. Amen.

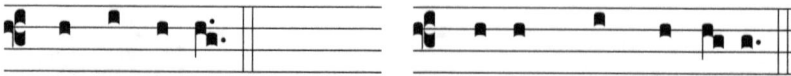

℣. Praise ye the Lord.   ℟. The Lord's Name be prais- ed.

Introduction   **Liturgical Hymns**   *Office Ordinary*

Solemn

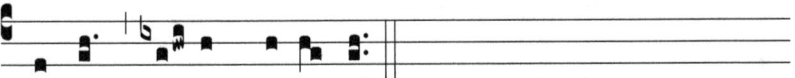

℣. O Lord, † o-pen thou our lips.

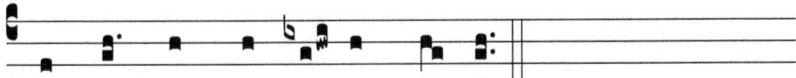

℟. And our mouth shall show forth thy praise.

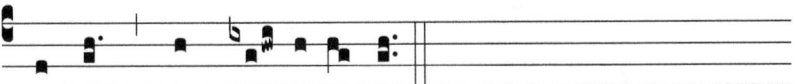

℣. O God, ✠ make speed to save us.

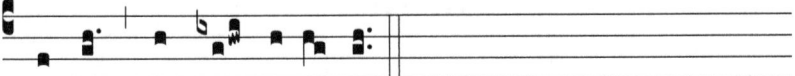

℟. O Lord, make haste to help us.

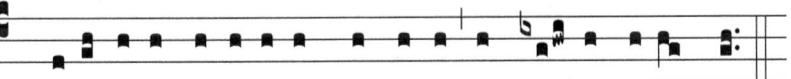

℣. Glo-ry be to the Father and to the Son and to the Ho-ly Ghost:

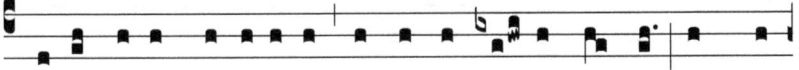

℟. As it was in the be-ginning, is now and ev-er shall be, world with-

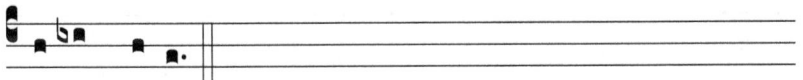

out end. Amen.

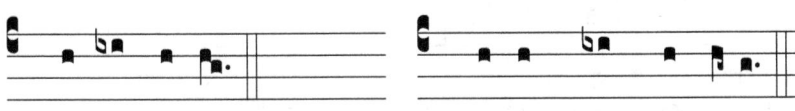

℣. Praise ye the Lord.   ℟. The Lord's Name be prais-ed.

Office Ordinary   # Liturgical Hymns   Kyrie

Apostles' Creed

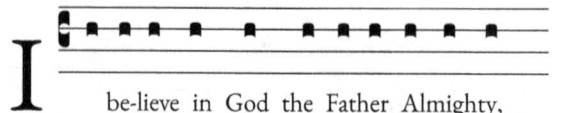

I be-lieve in God the Father Almighty, Maker of heaven and earth: And in Jesus Christ his only Son our Lord: Who was conceived by the Holy Ghost, Born of the Virgin Mary: Suffered under Pontius Pilate, Was crucified, dead, and buried: He descended into hell; The third day he rose again from the dead: He ascended into heaven, And sitteth on the right hand of God the Father Almighty: From thence he shall come to judge the quick and the dead.

I believe in the Holy Ghost: The holy Catholic Church; The Communion of Saints: The Forgiveness of sins: The Resurrection of the body: ✠ And the Life everlasting.

A -men.

Salutation

℣. The Lord be with you. ℟. And with thy spir-it. ℣. Let us pray.

or,

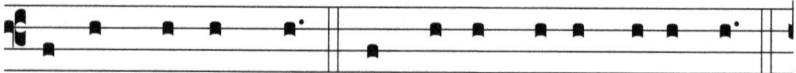

℣. O Lord, hear our prayer. ℟. And let our cry come unto thee.

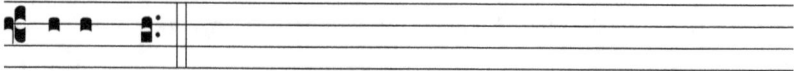

℣. Let us pray.

Kyrie

   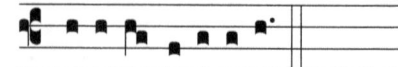

℣. Lord, have mercy up-on us.   ℣. Ký-ri- e, e-lé- i-son.
℟. Christ, have mercy upon us.   ℟. Christe, eléison.
℣. Lord, have mercy upon us.   ℣. Kýrie, eléison.

Preces **Liturgical Hymns** *Office Ordinary*

Lord's Prayer

Our Father, who art in heav-en, Hal-low-ed be thy Name.

Thy kingdom come. Thy will be done on earth, As it is in heav-en.

Give us this day our dai-ly bread. And forgive us our trespass-es,

As we forgive those who trespass a-gainst us. And lead us not into

tempta-tion; But de-liv-er us from e-vil. Amen.

Preces

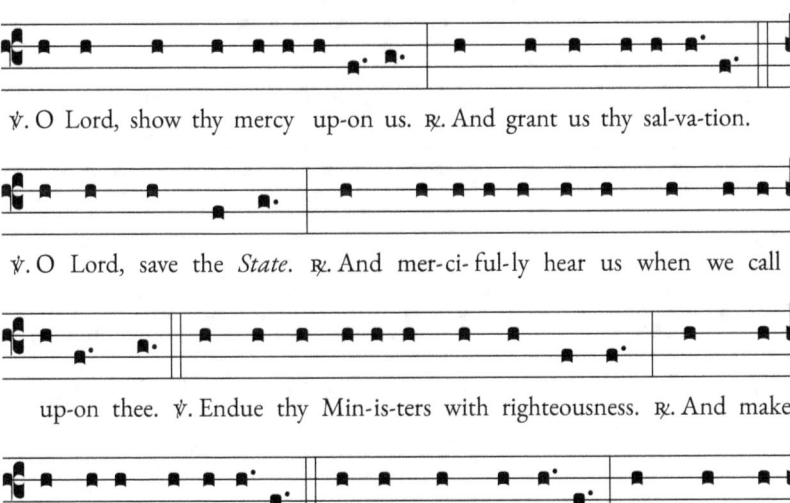

℣. O Lord, show thy mercy up-on us. ℟. And grant us thy sal-va-tion.

℣. O Lord, save the *State*. ℟. And mer-ci-ful-ly hear us when we call

up-on thee. ℣. Endue thy Min-is-ters with righteousness. ℟. And make

thy cho-sen people joy-ful. ℣. O Lord, save thy people. ℟. And bless thine

inher-it-ance. ℣. Give peace in our time, O Lord. ℞. For it is thou,

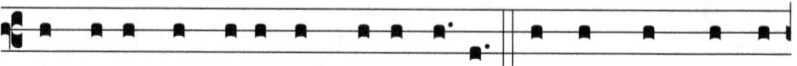

Lord, only, that mak-est us dwell in safety. ℣. O God, make clean our

hearts with-in us. ℞. And take not thy Ho-ly Spir-it from us.

Mattins Collects

A Collect for Peace

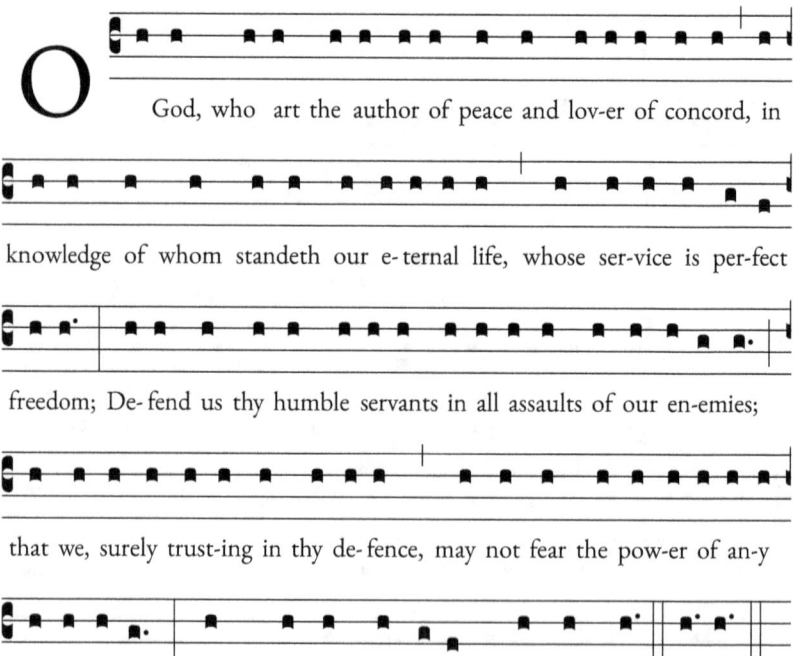

O God, who art the author of peace and lov-er of concord, in knowledge of whom standeth our e-ternal life, whose ser-vice is per-fect freedom; De-fend us thy humble servants in all assaults of our en-emies; that we, surely trust-ing in thy de-fence, may not fear the pow-er of an-y adver-sar-ies, through the might of Je-sus Christ our Lord. Amen.

Collects   **Liturgical Hymns**   *Office Ordinary*

A Collect for Grace

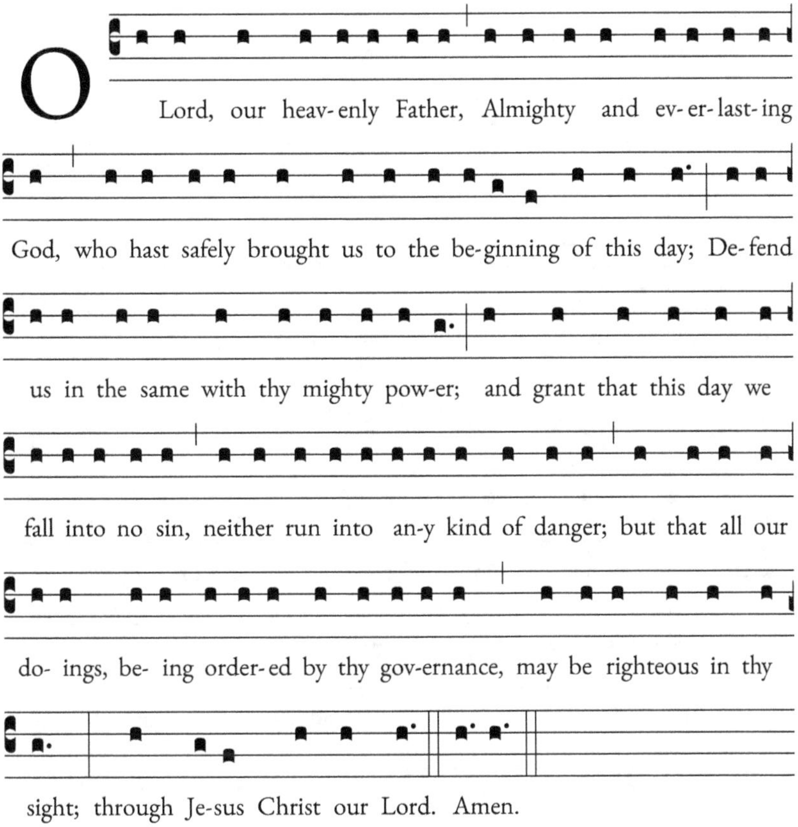

O Lord, our heav-enly Father, Almighty and ev-er-last-ing God, who hast safely brought us to the be-ginning of this day; De-fend us in the same with thy mighty pow-er; and grant that this day we fall into no sin, neither run into an-y kind of danger; but that all our do-ings, be-ing order-ed by thy gov-ernance, may be righteous in thy sight; through Je-sus Christ our Lord. Amen.

Evensong Collects

A Collect for Peace

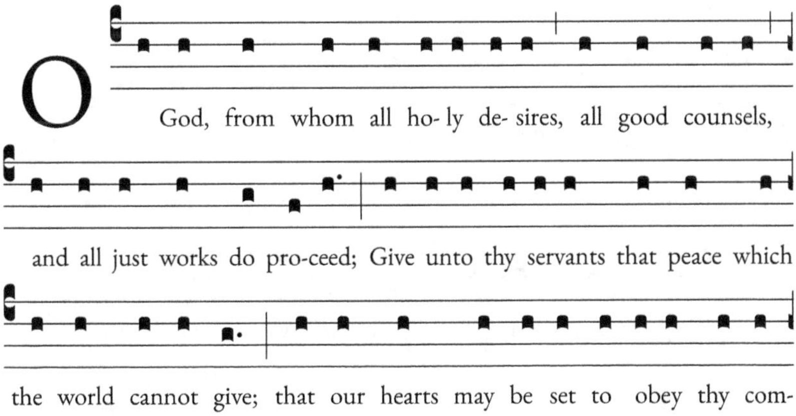

O God, from whom all ho-ly de-sires, all good counsels, and all just works do pro-ceed; Give unto thy servants that peace which the world cannot give; that our hearts may be set to obey thy com-

Office Ordinary — **Liturgical Hymns** — Conclusion

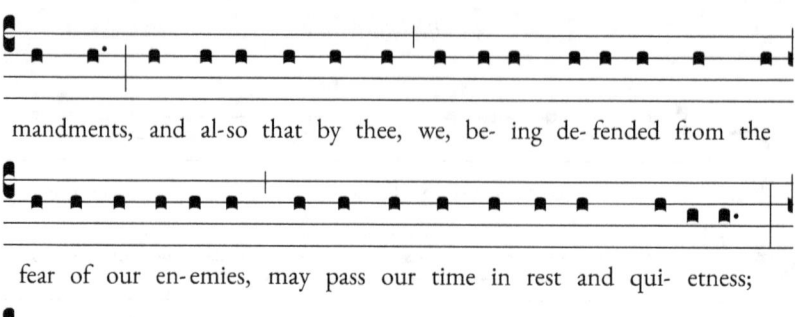

mandments, and al-so that by thee, we, be-ing de-fended from the fear of our en-emies, may pass our time in rest and qui-etness; through the mer-its of Je-sus Christ our Saviour. Amen.

A Collect for Aid against Perils

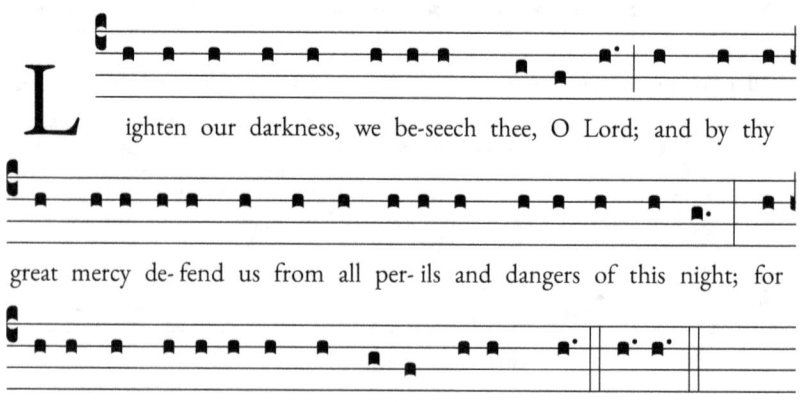

Lighten our darkness, we be-seech thee, O Lord; and by thy great mercy de-fend us from all per-ils and dangers of this night; for the love of thy only Son, our Saviour, Je-sus Christ. Amen.

CONCLUSION

℣. The Lord be with you. ℟. And with thy spir-it.

or,

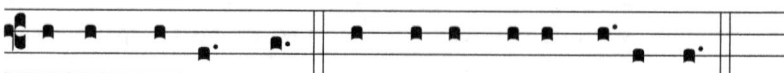

℣. O Lord, hear our prayer. ℟. And let our cry come unto thee.

Conclusion   Liturgical Hymns   *Office Ordinary*

℣ On Ferial Days,

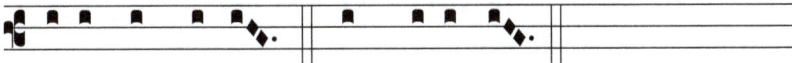

℣. Let us bless the Lord. ℟. Thanks be to God.

℣ On Feast Days,

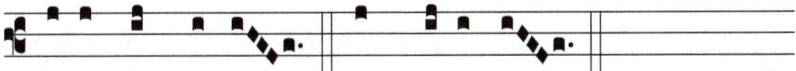

℣. Let us bless the Lord. ℟. Thanks be to God.

℣ During Eastertide,

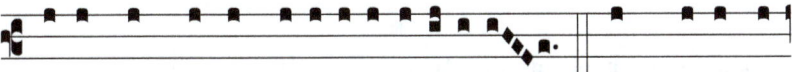

℣. Let us bless the Lord, al-le-lu-ia, al-le-lu-ia.   ℟. Thanks be to God,

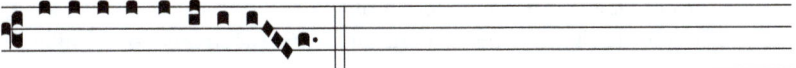

al-le-lu-ia, al-le-lu-ia.

℣ In a low voice,

℣. May the souls of the faithful de-part-ed, through the mercy of God,

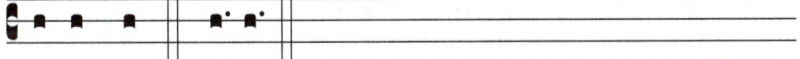

rest in peace. ℟. Amen.

Liturgical Hymns

Office Service

**OUR WORSHIP, PRAISE, AND THANKSGIVING
UNTO THE GLORY OF GOD ALONE**

Mattins

Venite, exultemus Domino

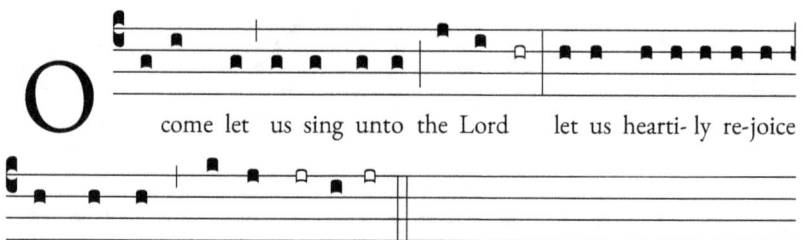

O come let us sing unto the Lord · let us hearti- ly re-joice in the strength of our sal-va-tion.

2 Let us come before his presence with • thanksgiving : and shew ourselves • glad in him with psalms.

3 For the Lord is a • great God : and a great • King above all gods.

4 In his hand are all the corners • of the earth : and the strength of the hills is • his also.

5 The sea is his, and • he made it : and his hands prepared • the dry land.

6 O come, let us worship and • fall down : and kneel before the • Lord our Maker.

7 For he is the • Lord our God : and we are the people of his pasture, and the • sheep of his hand.

8 To-day if ye will hear his voice, harden • not your hearts : as in the provocation, and as in the day of temptation • in the wilderness.

9 When your fathers • tempted me : proved me, • and saw my works.

10 Forty years long was I grieved with this generation, • and said : It is a people that do err in their hearts, for they • have not known my ways;

11 Unto whom I sware • in my wrath : that they should not enter • into my rest.

℣. Glory be to the Father, and • to the Son * and • to the Holy Ghost.

℟. As it was in the beginning, is now, and ever • shall be * world without • end. Amen.

Liturgical Hymns

Pascha Nostrum

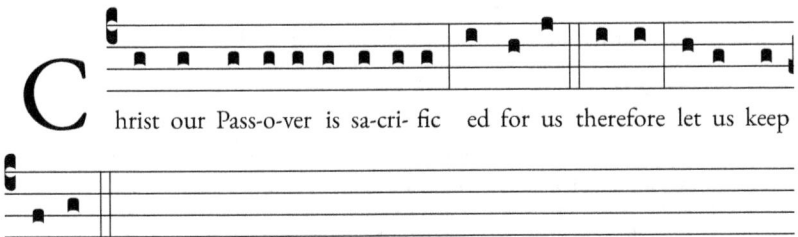

hrist our Passover is sacrificed for us therefore let us keep the feast,

Not with old leaven, neither with the leaven of malice and • wickedness * but with the unleavened bread of sin • cerity and truth.

Christ being raised from the dead dieth • no more * death hath no more do • minion over him.

For in that he died, he died unto • sin once * but in that he liveth, he • liveth unto God.

Likewise reckon ye also yourselves to be dead indeed • unto sin * but alive unto God through • Jesus Christ our Lord.

Christ is risen • from the dead * and become the first • fruits of them that slept.

For since by • man came death * by man came also the resur • rection of the dead.

For as in Adam • all die : even so in Christ shall • all be made alive.

℣. Glory be to the Father, and • to the Son * and • to the Holy Ghost;

℟. As it was in the beginning, is now, and ever • shall be * world • without end. Amen.

Te Deum laudamus

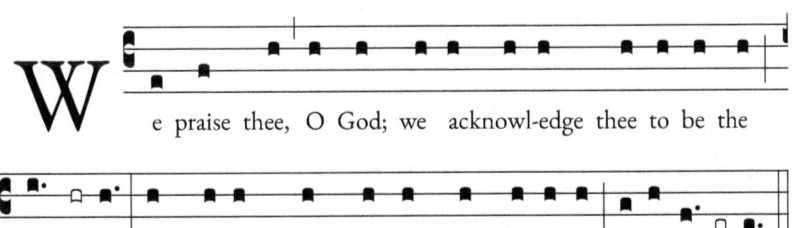

e praise thee, O God; we acknowledge thee to be the Lord.   All the earth doth worship thee, the Father everlasting.

To thee all Angels cry aloud; the Heavens, and all the • Pow'rs therein; * To thee Cherubim and Seraphim contin • ually do cry,

Holy, Holy, Holy, Lord God of • Sabaoth; * Heaven and earth are full of the Majesty • of thy glory.

The glorious company of the Apostles • praise thee. * The goodly fellowship of the • Prophets praise thee.

The noble army of Martyrs • praise thee. * The holy Church throughout all the world • doth acknowledge thee;

Office Service   **Liturgical Hymns**   Te Deum

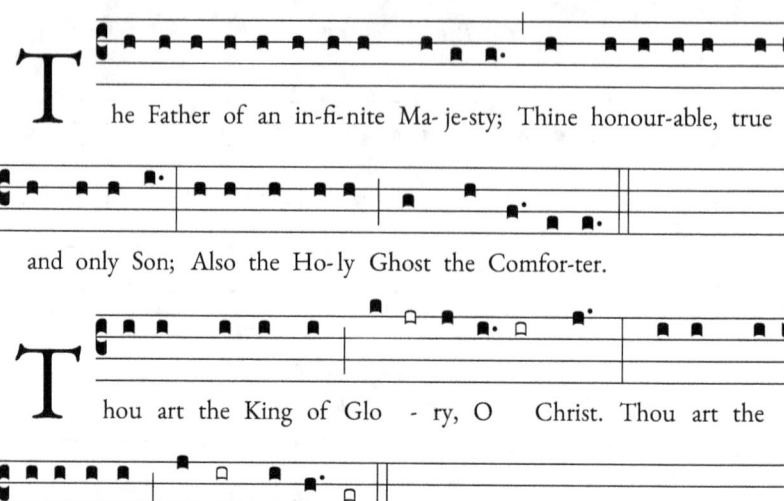

The Father of an in-fi-nite Ma-je-sty; Thine honour-able, true and only Son; Also the Ho-ly Ghost the Comfor-ter.

Thou art the King of Glo - ry, O Christ. Thou art the ev-er-last-ing Son of the Fa-ther.

When thou tookest upon thee • to deliver man, * thou didst not ab • hor the Virgin's womb.

When thou hadst overcome the • sharpness of death, * thou didst open the Kingdom of Heaven to • all believers.

Thou sittest at the • right hand of God, * in the glory • of the Father.

We believe that thou shalt • come to be our Judge. * We therefore pray thee, help thy servants, whom thou hast redeemed • with thy precious blood.

Make them to be • numbered with thy Saints, * in glory • everlasting.

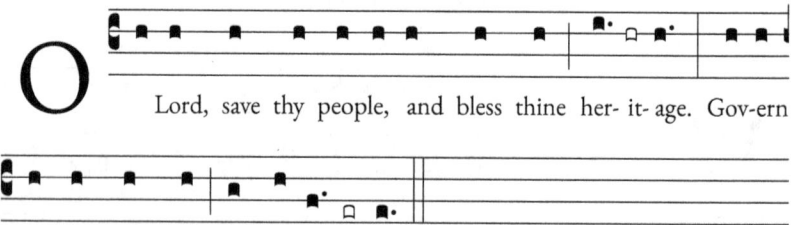

O Lord, save thy people, and bless thine her-it-age. Gov-ern them and lift them up for ev - er.

Day by day we magnify • thee; * And we worship thy Name ever, • world without end.

Vouchsafe, O Lord, to keep us this day without • sin. * O Lord, have mercy upon us, have mer • cy upon us.

O Lord, let thy mercy lighten upon us, as our trust is in • thee. * O Lord, in thee have I trusted; let me never • be confounded.

Liturgical Hymns

Benedicite   *Office Service*

Benedicite, omnia opera Domini

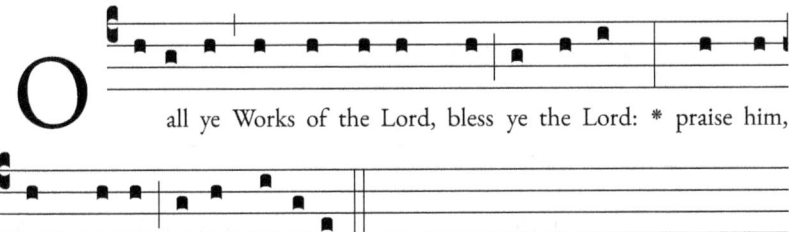

O all ye Works of the Lord, bless ye the Lord: * praise him, and magni fy him for ev-er.

O ye Angels of the Lord, bless • ye the Lord: * praise him, and magni • fy him for ever.

O YE Heavens, bless • ye the Lord: * praise him, and magni • fy him for ever.

O ye Waters that be above the firmament, bless • ye the Lord: * praise him, and magni • fy him for ever.

O all ye Powers of the Lord, bless • ye the Lord: * praise him, and magni • fy him for ever.

O ye Sun and Moon, bless • ye the Lord: * praise him, and magni • fy him for ever.

O ye Stars of heaven, bless • ye the Lord: * praise him, and magni • fy him for ever.

O ye Showers and Dew, bless • ye the Lord: * praise him, and magni • fy him for ever.

O ye winds of God, bless • ye the Lord: * praise him, and magni • fy him for ever.

O ye Fire and Heat, bless • ye the Lord: * praise him, and magni • fy him for ever.

O ye Winter and Summer, bless • ye the Lord: * praise him, and magni • fy him for ever.

O ye Dews and Frosts, bless • ye the Lord: * praise him, and magni • fy him for ever.

O ye Frost and Cold, bless • ye the Lord: * praise him, and magni • fy him for ever.

O ye Ice and Snow, bless ye the Lord * praise him, and magni • fy him for ever.

O ye Nights and Days, bless • ye the Lord: * praise him, and magni • fy him for ever.

O ye Light and Darkness, bless • ye the Lord: * praise him, and magni • fy him for ever.

O ye Lightnings and Clouds, bless ye the Lord * praise him, and magni • fy him for ever.

Office Service   # Liturgical Hymns   Benedicite

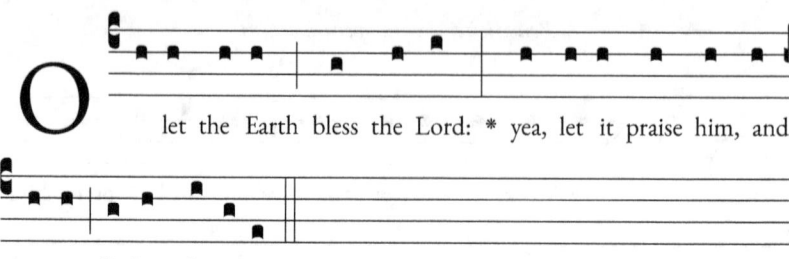

O let the Earth bless the Lord: * yea, let it praise him, and magni fy him for ev-er.

O ye Mountains and Hills, bless • ye the Lord: * praise him, and magni • fy him for ever.

O all ye Green Things upon the earth, bless • ye the Lord: * praise him, and magni • fy him for ever. O ye Wells, bless • ye the Lord: * praise him, and magni • fy him for ever.

O ye Seas and Floods, bless • ye the Lord: * praise him, and magni • fy him for ever.

O ye Whales, and all that move in the waters, bless • ye the Lord: * praise him, and magni • fy him for ever.

O all ye Fowls of the air, bless • ye the Lord: * praise him, and magni • fy him for ever.

O all ye Beasts and Cattle, bless • ye the Lord: * praise him, and magni • fy him for ever.

O ye Children of Men, bless • ye the Lord: * praise him, and magni • fy him for ever.

LET Israel • bless the Lord: * praise him, and magni • fy him for ever.

O ye Priests of the Lord, bless • ye the Lord: * praise him, and magni • fy him for ever.

O ye Servants of the Lord, bless • ye the Lord: * praise him, and magni • fy him for ever.

O ye Spirits and Souls of the Righteous, bless • ye the Lord: * praise him, and magni • fy him for ever.

O ye holy and humble Men of heart, bless • ye the Lord: * praise him, and magni • fy him for ever.

ET us bless the Father, and the Son, and the • Holy Ghost: * praise him, and magnif • y him for ever.

Liturgical Hymns

Benedictus

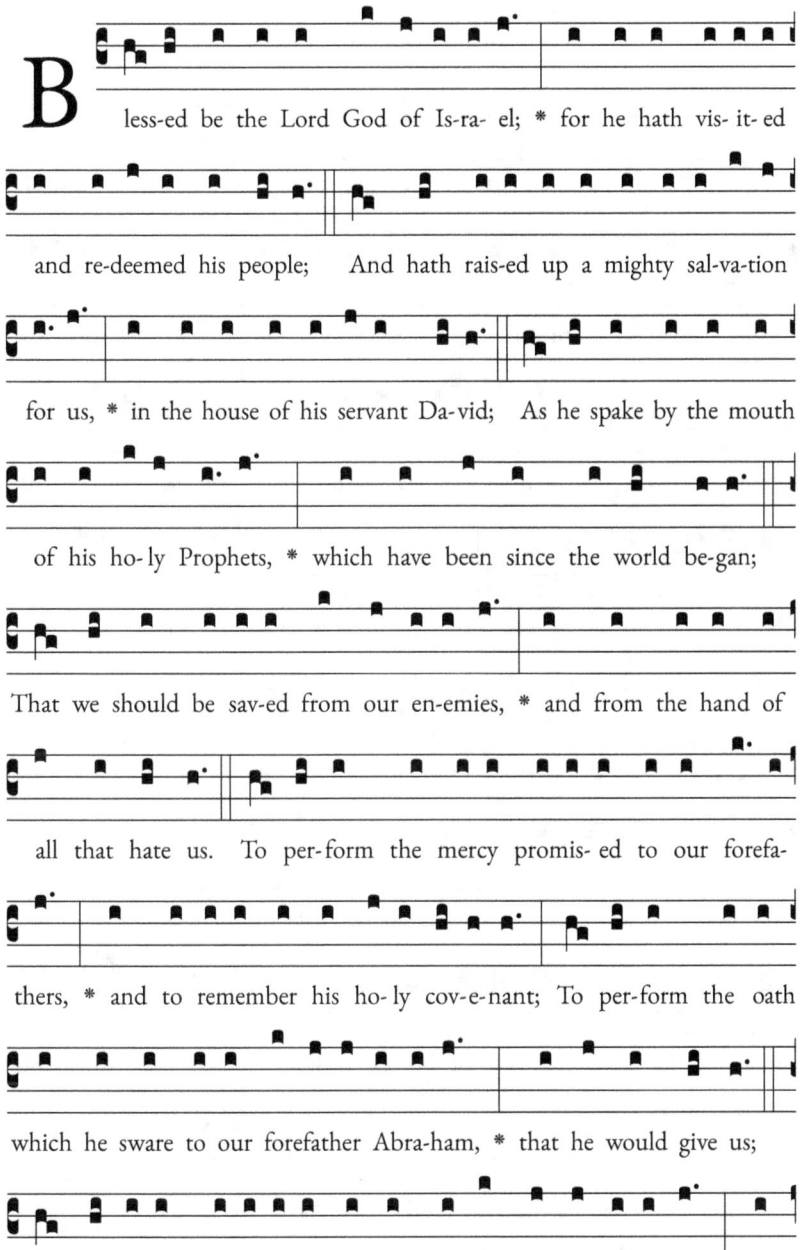

Bless-ed be the Lord God of Is-ra-el; * for he hath vis-it-ed and re-deemed his people; And hath rais-ed up a mighty sal-va-tion for us, * in the house of his servant Da-vid; As he spake by the mouth of his ho-ly Prophets, * which have been since the world be-gan; That we should be sav-ed from our en-emies, * and from the hand of all that hate us. To per-form the mercy promis-ed to our forefa-thers, * and to remember his ho-ly cov-e-nant; To per-form the oath which he sware to our forefather Abra-ham, * that he would give us; That we be-ing de-liv-er-ed out of the hand of our en-emies * might

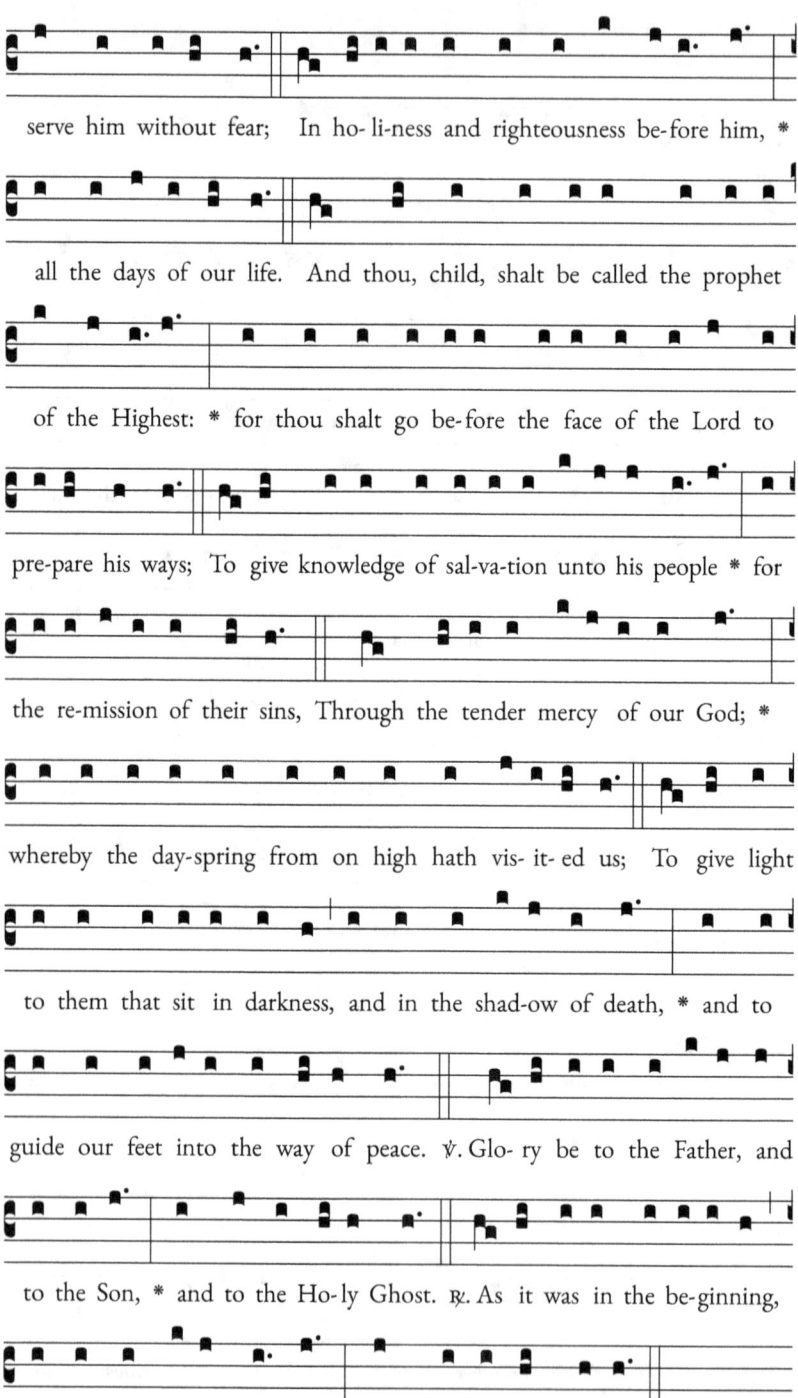

Liturgical Hymns

Athanasian Creed

Who-so-e-ver would be sa - ved * ne-e-deth be-fo-re all things to hold fast the Catho-lick Faith.

2 Which Faith except a man keep whole • and undefiled : without doubt he will perish • eternally.

3 Now the • Catholick Faith is this : that we worship one God in Trinity, and the Trinity • in Unity;

4 Neither • confusing the Persons : nor divid • ing the substance.

5 For there is one Person of the Father, • another of the Son : another • of the Holy Ghost;

6 But the Godhead of the Father, and of the Son, and of the • Holy Ghost is all one : the glory equal, the majesty • co-eternal.

7 Such as the Father is, • such is the Son : and such • is the Holy Ghost.

8 The Father uncreated, the Son • uncreated : the Holy Ghost • uncreated;

9 The Father infinite, • the Son infinite : the Holy • Ghost infinite;

10 The Father eternal, the • Son eternal : the Holy • Ghost eternal.

11 And yet there are not • three eternals : • but one eternal

12 As also there are not three uncreated, nor • three infinites : but one infinite, and one • uncreated.

13 So likewise the Father is almighty, • the Son almighty : the Holy • Ghost almighty;

14 And yet there are not • three almighties : • but one almighty.

15 So the Father • is God, the Son God : • the Holy Ghost God;

16 And yet there • are not three Gods : • but one God.

17 So the Father is • Lord, the Son Lord : • the Holy Ghost Lord;

18 And yet there • are not three Lords : • but one Lord.

19 For like as we are compelled by the • Christian verity : to confess each Person by himself to • be both God and Lord;

20 So are we forbidden by the • Catholick religion : to speak of • three Gods or three Lords.

21 The Father • is made of none : nor created, • nor begotten.

22 The Son is • of the Father : not made, nor created, • but begotten.

23 The Holy Ghost is • of the Father : not made, nor created, nor begotten, • but proceeding.

24 There is therefore one Father, not three Fathers; • one Son, not three Sons : one Holy Ghost, • not three Holy Ghosts.

Office Service   **Liturgical Hymns**   Athanasian Creed

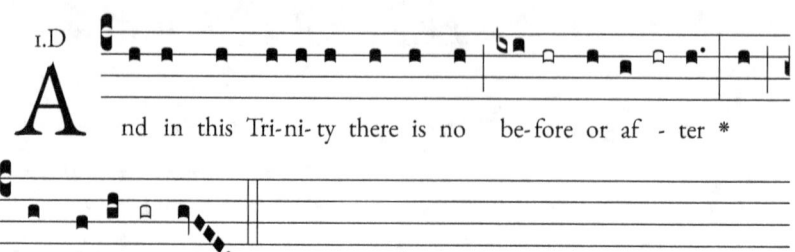

A nd in this Tri-ni-ty there is no be-fore or af - ter *

no great-er or less.

26 But all three Persons are co • eternal together : • and co-equal.

27 So that in all ways, • as is aforesaid : both the Trinity is to be worshipped in Unity, and the Unity • in Trinity.

28 He therefore that • would be saved : let him thus think • of the Trinity.

Furthermore it is necessary to • eternal salvation : that he also believe faithfully the Incarnation of • our Lord Jesus Christ.

30 Now the right faith is that we • believe and confess : that our Lord Jesus Christ, the Son of God, • is both God and man.

31 He is God, of the substance of the Father, begotten • before the worlds : and he is man, of the substance of his Mother, • born in the world;

32 Perfect • God perfect man : of reasoning soul and human • flesh subsisting;

33 Equal to the Father as • touching his Godhead : less than the Father as • touching his manhood.

34 Who although • he be God and man : yet he is not two, • but is one Christ;

35 One however, not by conversion of • Godhead into flesh : but by taking • manhood into God;

36 One • altogether : not by confusion of substance, but by unit • y of person.

37 For as reasoning soul and • flesh is one man : so God and • man is one Christ;

38 Who suffered for • our salvation : descended into hell, rose • again from the dead;

39 Ascended into heaven, sat down at the • right hand of the Father : from whence he shall come to judge • the quick and the dead.

40 At whose coming all men must rise again • with their bodies : and shall give account • for their own deeds.

41 And they that have done good will go into • life eternal : they that have done evil into • eternal fire.

This is the • Catholick Faith : which except a man do faithfully and steadfastly believe, he • cannot be saved.

℣. Glory be to the Father, • and to the Son : and • to the Holy Ghost;

℟. As it was in the beginning, is now, and • ever shall be : world • without end. Amen.

Liturgical Hymns

Gloria in excelsis — Office Service

Evensong

Gloria in excelsis

Glo- ry be to God on high, and on earth peace, good will towards men. We praise thee, we bless thee, we worship thee, we glo- ri- fy thee, we give thanks to thee for thy great glo- ry, O Lord God, heav'nly King, God the Father Almight- y. O Lord, the only-be-got- ten Son, Je-sus Christ; O Lord God, Lamb of God, Son of the Fa- ther, that tak-est away the sins of the world, have mercy up-on us. Thou that tak-est away the sins of the world, re-ceive our prayer. Thou that sitt-est at the right hand of God the Father, have mercy up-on us. For thou only art ho- ly; thou on-ly art the Lord;

Office Service　　　　**Liturgical Hymns**　　　　Gloria in excelsis

thou only, O Christ, with the Ho-ly Ghost,　art most high in the

glo-ry of God the Fa-ther.　Amen.

Magnificat   **Liturgical Hymns**   *Office Service*

Magnificat

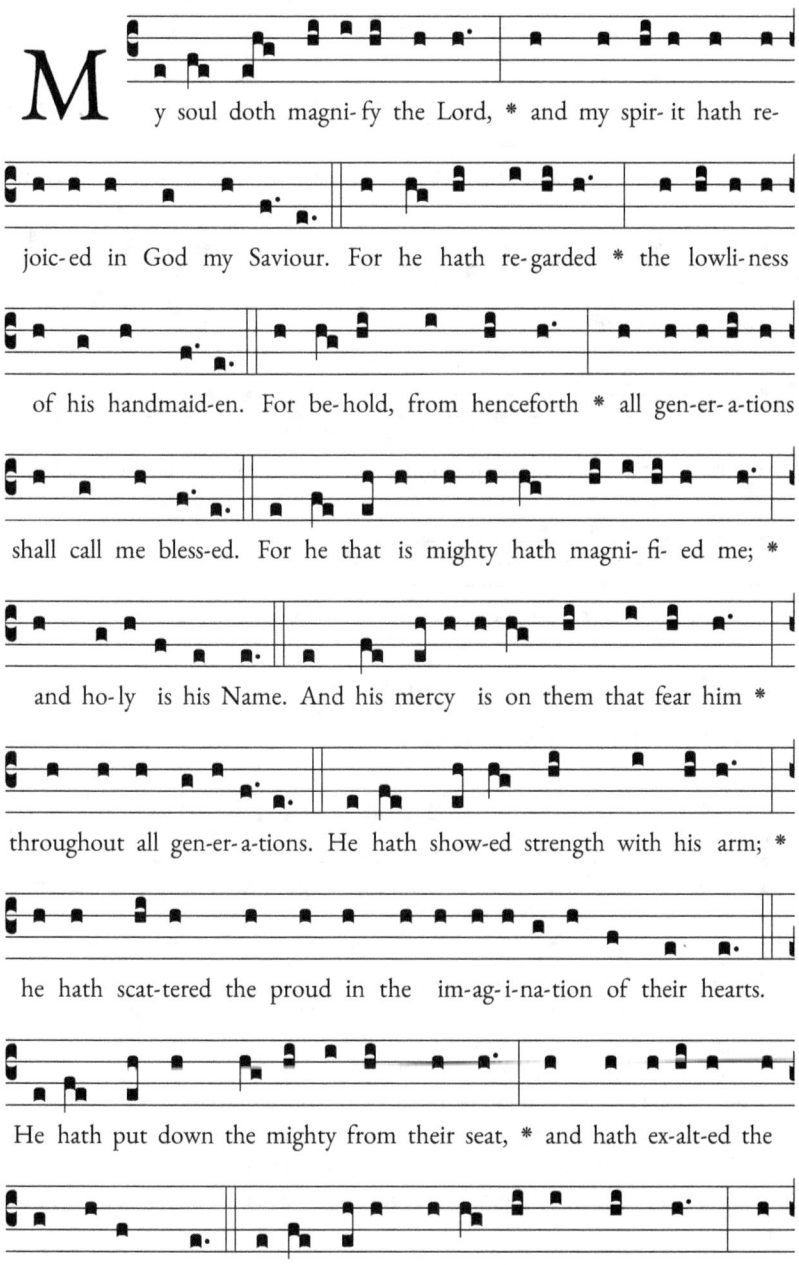

My soul doth magni- fy the Lord, * and my spir- it hath re-

joic- ed in God my Saviour. For he hath re- garded * the lowli- ness

of his handmaid- en. For be- hold, from henceforth * all gen- er- a- tions

shall call me bless- ed. For he that is mighty hath magni- fi- ed me; *

and ho- ly is his Name. And his mercy is on them that fear him *

throughout all gen- er- a- tions. He hath show- ed strength with his arm; *

he hath scat- tered the proud in the im- ag- i- na- tion of their hearts.

He hath put down the mighty from their seat, * and hath ex- alt- ed the

humble and meek. He hath fill- ed the hungry with good things; * and

Office Service   **Liturgical Hymns**   Nunc dimittis

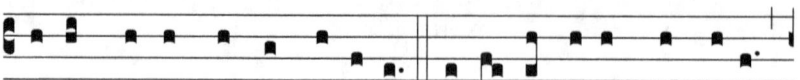

the rich he hath sent empty away. He re-member-ing his mercy

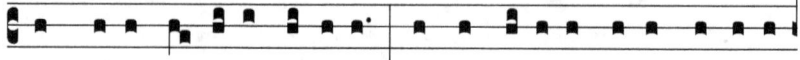

hath holpen his servant Is-ra-el; * as he promi-sed to our forefathers,

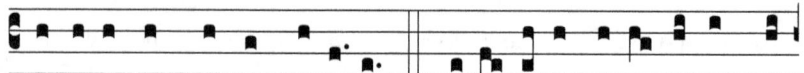

Abra-ham and his seed, for ev-er. ℣. Glo-ry be to the Fa-ther, and to

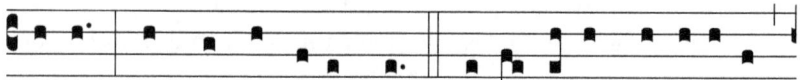

the Son, * and to the Ho-ly Ghost. ℟. As it was in the be-ginning,

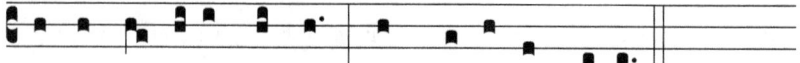

is now, and ev-er shall be, * world without end. Amen.

Nunc dimittis

¶ The intonation is sung at the beginning of every verse.

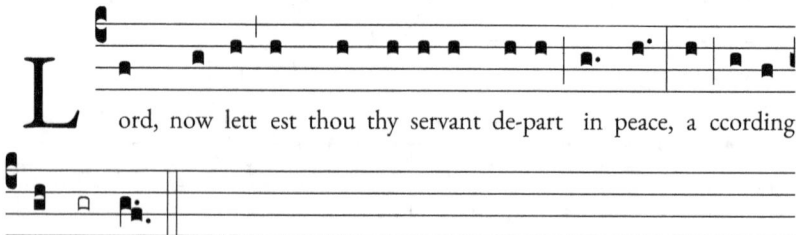

L ord, now lett est thou thy servant de-part in peace, a ccording

to thy word.
For mine eyes • have seen * • thy salvation,
Which thou hast pre • pared * before the face • of all people;
To be a light to lighten the • Gentiles, * and to be the glory of thy • people Israel.
℣. Glory be to the Father, and to • the Son, * and • to the Holy Ghost.
℟. As it was in the beginning, † is now, and ever • shall be, * world • without end. Amen.

Alma Redemptoris   **Liturgical Hymns**   *Office Service*

MARIAN ANTHEMS

Alma Redemptoris Mater

From I Evensong of Advent I until II Evensong of the Purification, inclusive.

Gra- cious Mother of our Re-deemer, for ev-er a-bid-ing, Heav- en's gateway, and star of o-cean, O succour the people, who, though fall-ing, strive to rise a-gain. Thou Maid-en who bar-est thy ho-ly Cre- a-tor, to the wonder of all na-ture; Ev-er Vir-gin, af-ter, as be-fore thou re-ceiv-edst that A-ve From the mouth of Gabri- el; have compas-sion on us sinners.

Office Service   **Liturgical Hymns**   Regina Cæli

Ave, Regina Cælorum

From Compline of the Purification until Compline of Holy Wednesday, inclusive.

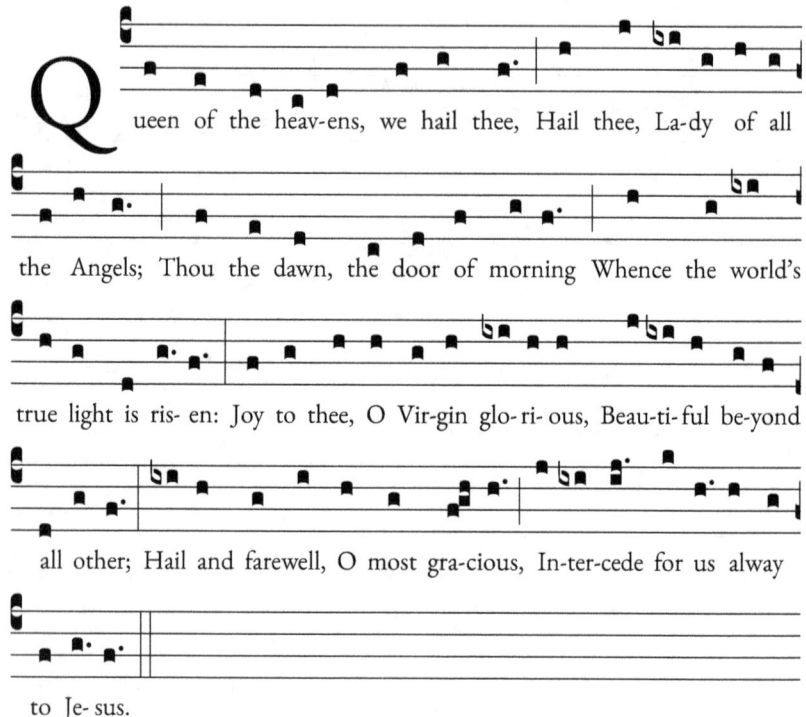

Queen of the heav-ens, we hail thee, Hail thee, La-dy of all the Angels; Thou the dawn, the door of morning Whence the world's true light is ris- en: Joy to thee, O Vir-gin glo- ri- ous, Beau-ti- ful be-yond all other; Hail and farewell, O most gra-cious, In-ter-cede for us alway to Je- sus.

Regina Cæli

From Compline of Holy Saturday until I Evensong of Trinity Sunday, exclusive.

O Queen of heav-en, be joy-ful, al-le-lu- ia; Be-cause he whom so meetly thou bar- est, al-le- lu- ia, Hath a- ris- en, as he promised, al-le- lu- ia: Pray for us to the Father, al-le- lu- ia.

Salve Regina, Simple # Liturgical Hymns *Office Service*

Salve Regina, Simple Tone

From I Evensong of Trinity Sunday until I Evensong of Advent I, exclusive.

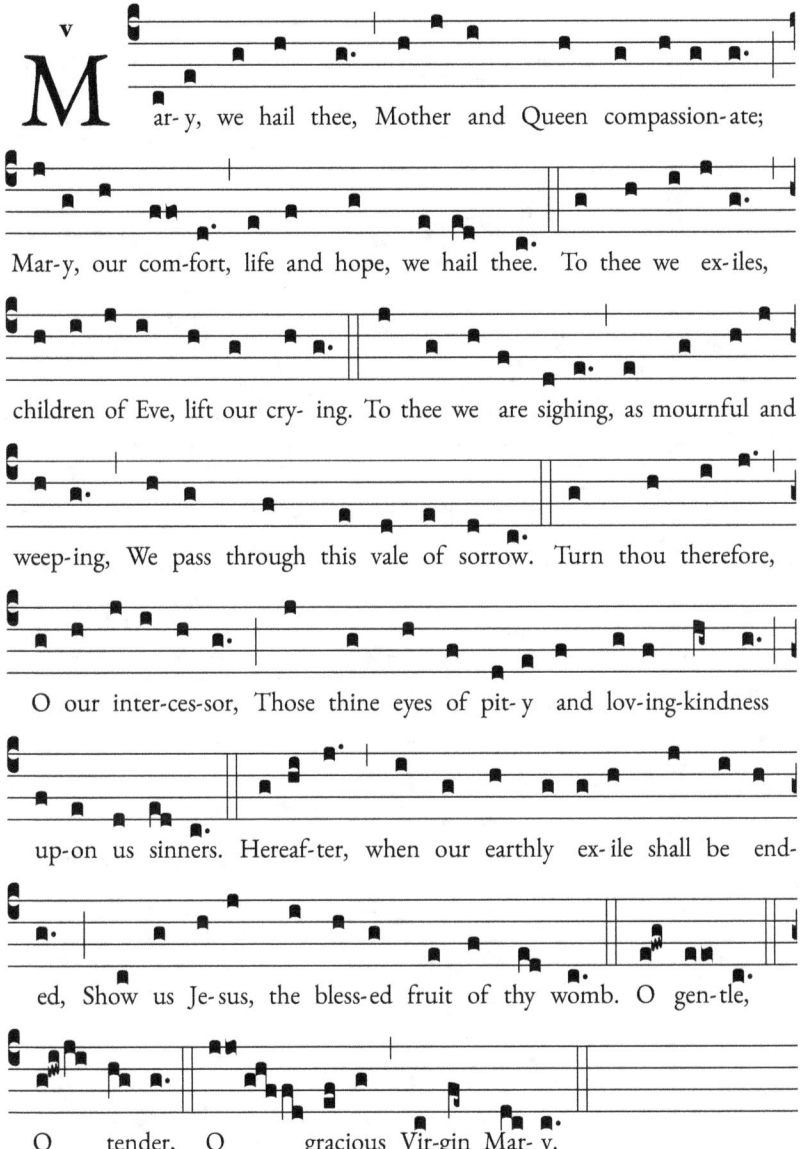

Mary, we hail thee, Mother and Queen compassionate; Mary, our comfort, life and hope, we hail thee. To thee we exiles, children of Eve, lift our crying. To thee we are sighing, as mournful and weeping, We pass through this vale of sorrow. Turn thou therefore, O our intercessor, Those thine eyes of pity and loving-kindness upon us sinners. Hereafter, when our earthly exile shall be ended, Show us Jesus, the blessed fruit of thy womb. O gentle, O tender, O gracious Virgin Mary.

Office Service   **Liturgical Hymns**   Salve Regina, Solemn

Salve Regina, Solemn Tone

From I Evensong of Trinity Sunday until I Evensong of Advent I, exclusive.

Ma-ry, we hail thee, Mother and Queen compassion-ate; Ma-ry, our com-fort, life and hope, we hail thee. To thee we e-xiles, children of Eve, lift our cry-ing. To thee we are sigh-ing, as mournful and weep-ing, We pass through this vale of so-rrow. Turn thou therefore, O our in-ter-ce-ssor, Those thine eyes of pi-ty and lov-ing-kindness u-pon us si-nners. Hereaf-ter, when our earth-ly e-xile shall be end-ed, Show us Je-sus, the ble-ssed fruit of thy womb. O gen-tle, O tender, O gracious Vir-gin Ma-ry.

Liturgical Hymns

Communion Services

COMMUNION SERVICE ONE - MASS OF THE GRACE OF GOD

Ten Commandments

¶ In response to the first nine Commandments, the following is sung.

Lord, have mercy up-on us, and incline our hearts to keep this law.

¶ In response to the final Commandment, the following is sung.

Lord, have mercy up-on us, and write all these thy laws in our hearts, we be-seech thee.

Kyrie

Lord, have mercy up-on us. *iij.* Christ, have mercy up-on us. *iij.* Lord, have mercy up-on us. *iij.*

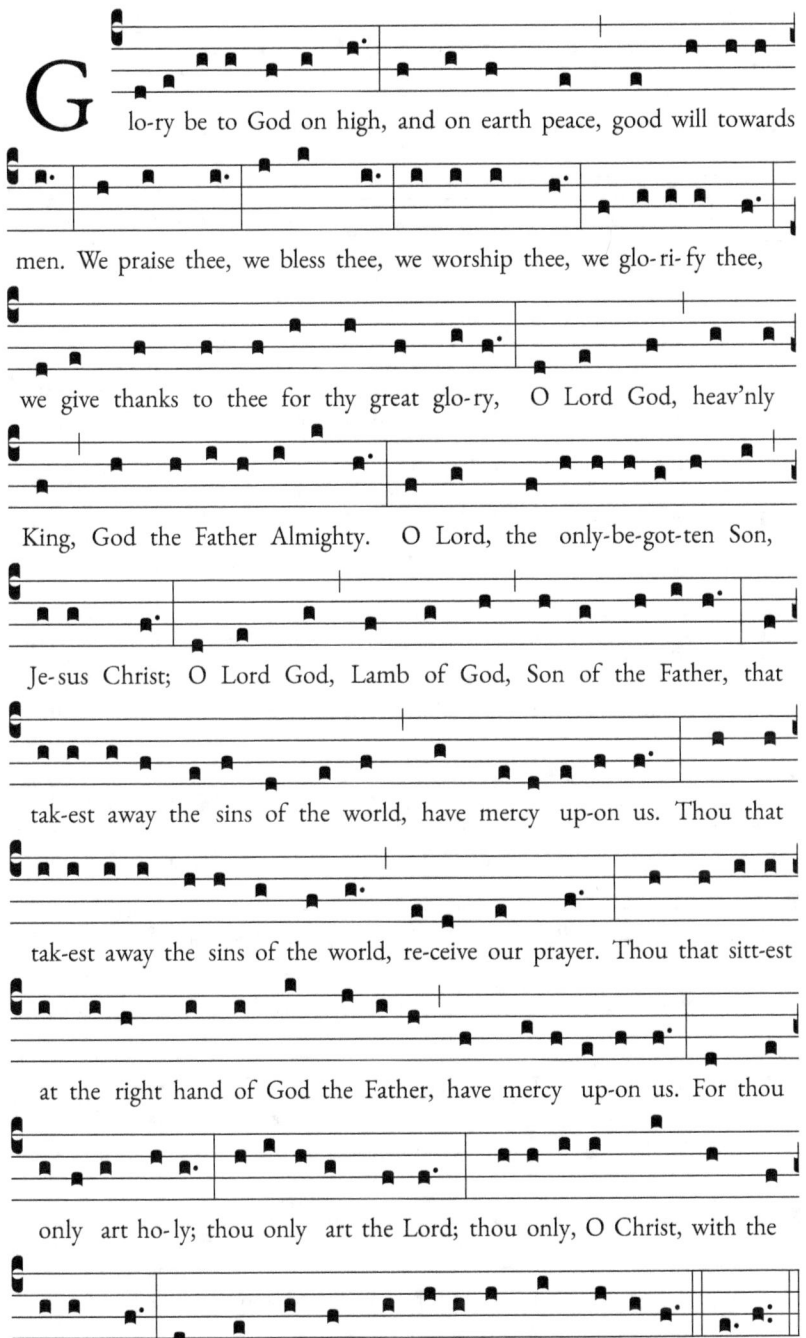

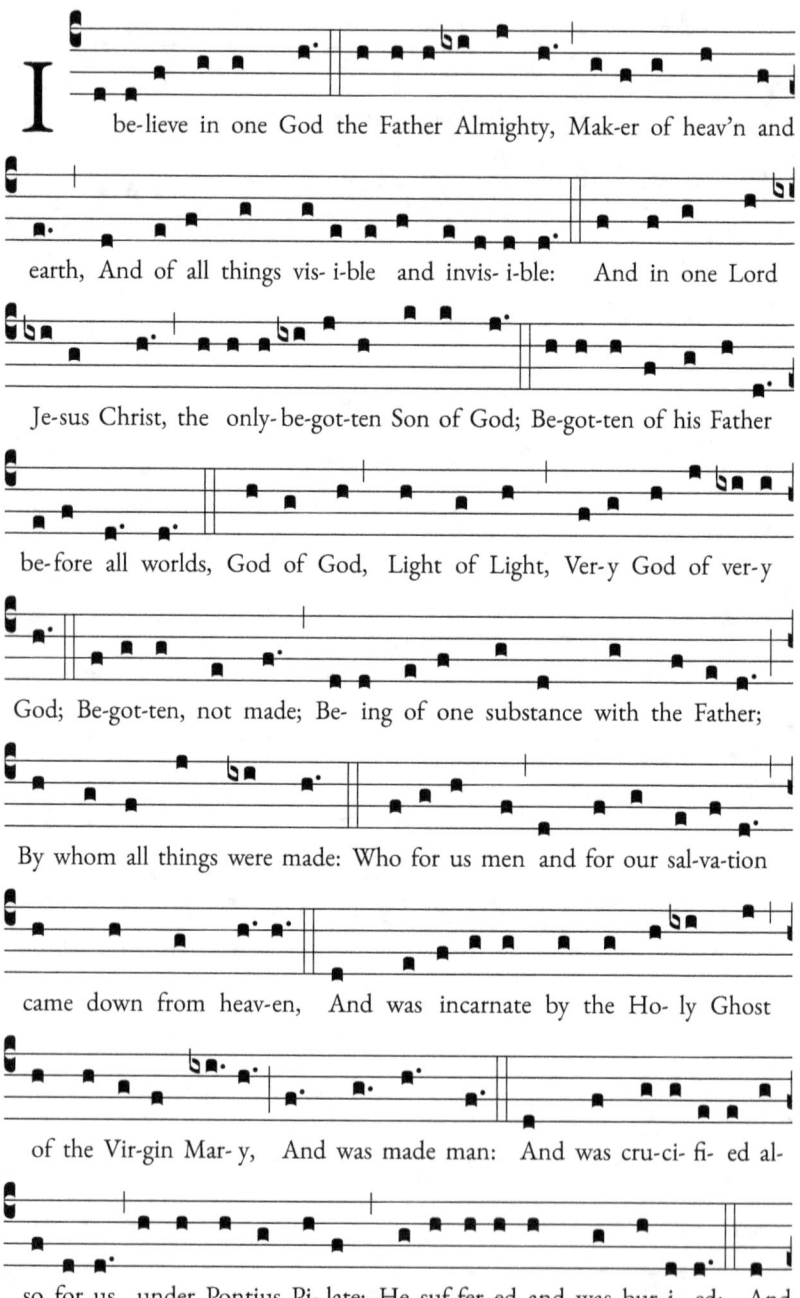

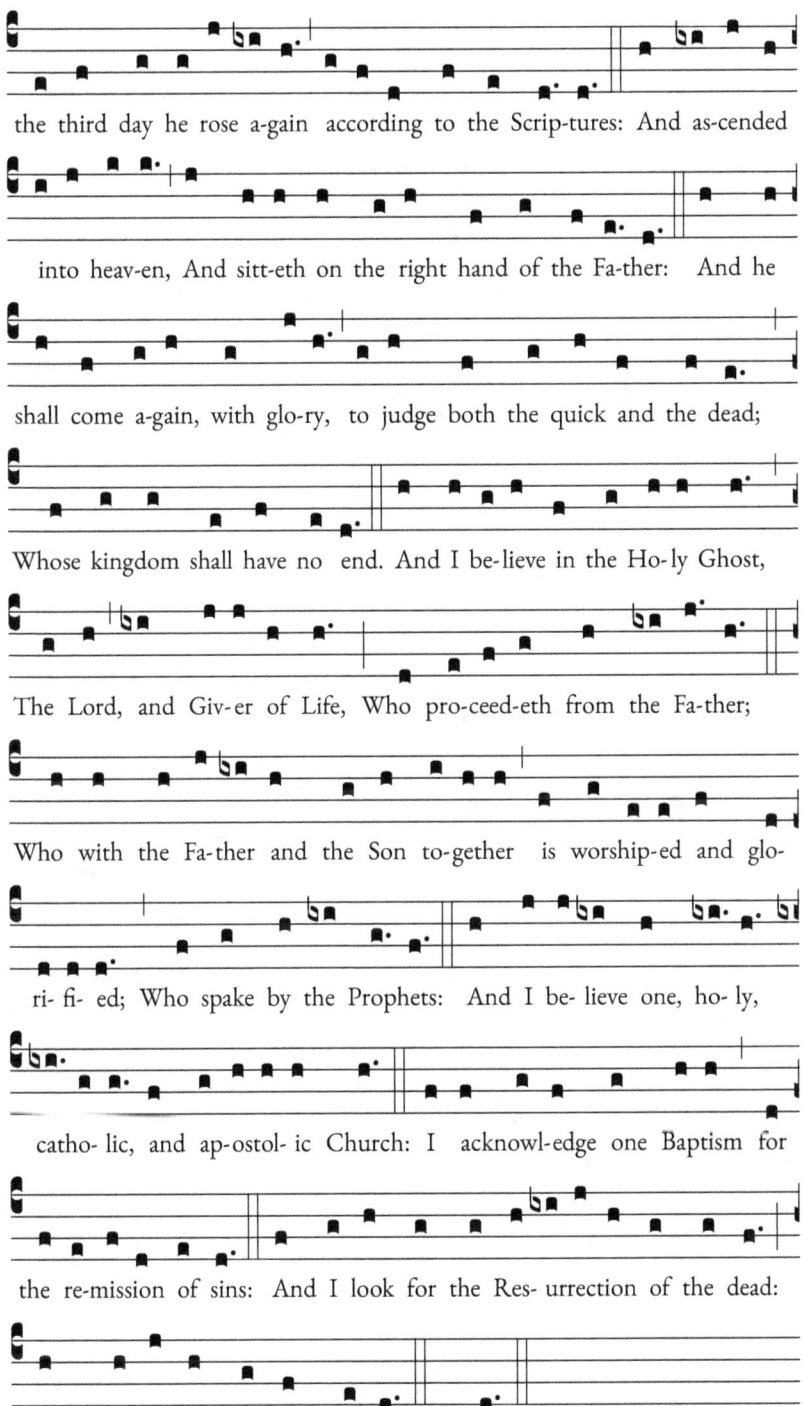

Communion I   **Liturgical Hymns**   Agnus Dei

Sanctus

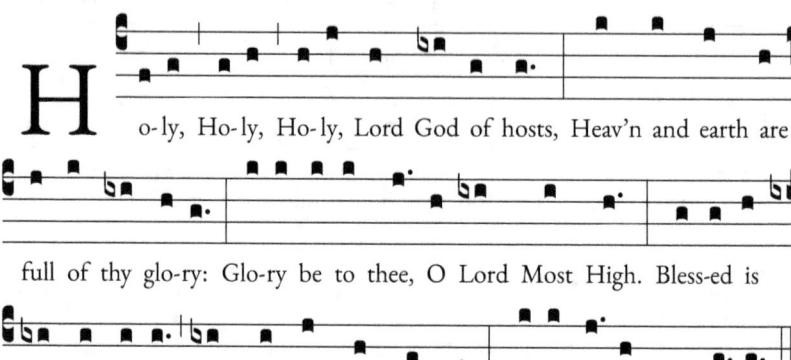

Ho-ly, Ho-ly, Ho-ly, Lord God of hosts, Heav'n and earth are full of thy glo-ry: Glo-ry be to thee, O Lord Most High. Bless-ed is he that cometh in the Name of the Lord. Ho-sanna in the Highest.

Agnus Dei

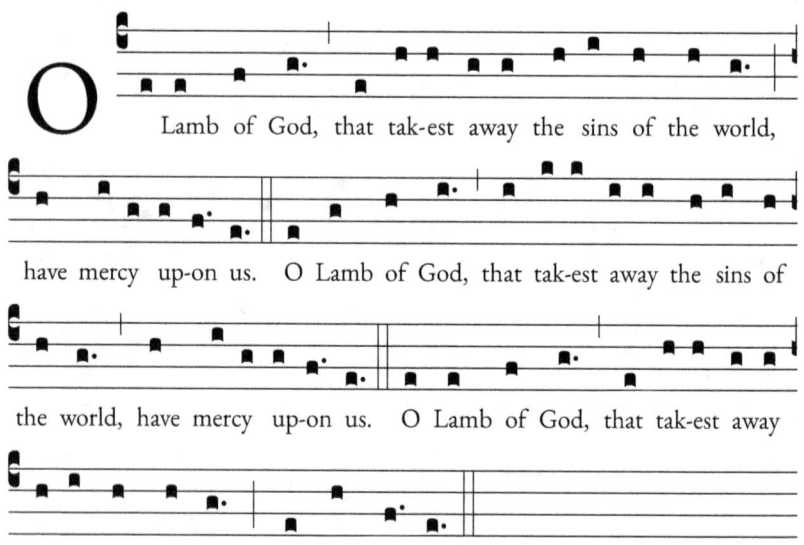

O Lamb of God, that tak-est away the sins of the world, have mercy up-on us. O Lamb of God, that tak-est away the sins of the world, have mercy up-on us. O Lamb of God, that tak-est away the sins of the world, grant us thy peace.

Liturgical Hymns

COMMUNION SERVICE TWO - MASS OF OUR LADY

Ten Commandments

¶ In response to the first nine Commandments, the following is sung.

Lord, have mercy up-on us, and incline our hearts to keep this law.

¶ In response to the final Commandment, the following is sung.

Lord, have mercy up-on us, and write all these thy laws in our hearts, we be-seech thee.

Communion II   **Liturgical Hymns**   Gloria in excelsis

Kyrie

Lord, have mer-cy up-on us. Lord, have mer-cy up-on us. Lord, have mer-cy up-on us. Christ, have mer-cy up-on us. Christ, have mer-cy up-on us. Christ, have mer-cy up-on us. Lord, have mer-cy up-on us. Lord, have mer-cy up-on us. Lord, have mer-cy up-on us.

Gloria in excelsis

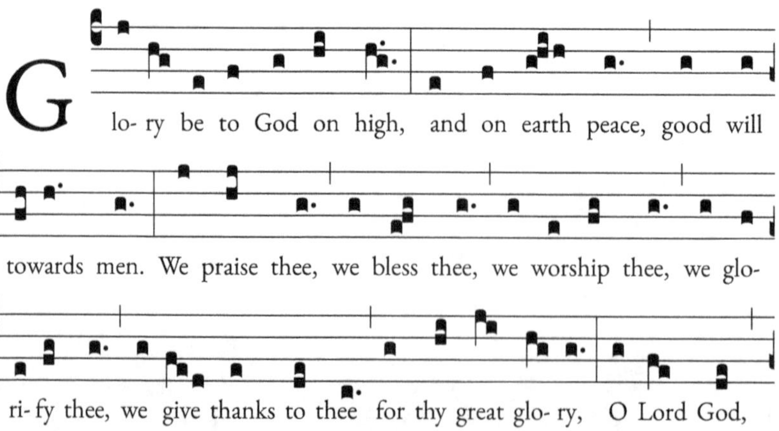

Glo-ry be to God on high, and on earth peace, good will towards men. We praise thee, we bless thee, we worship thee, we glo-ri-fy thee, we give thanks to thee for thy great glo-ry, O Lord God,

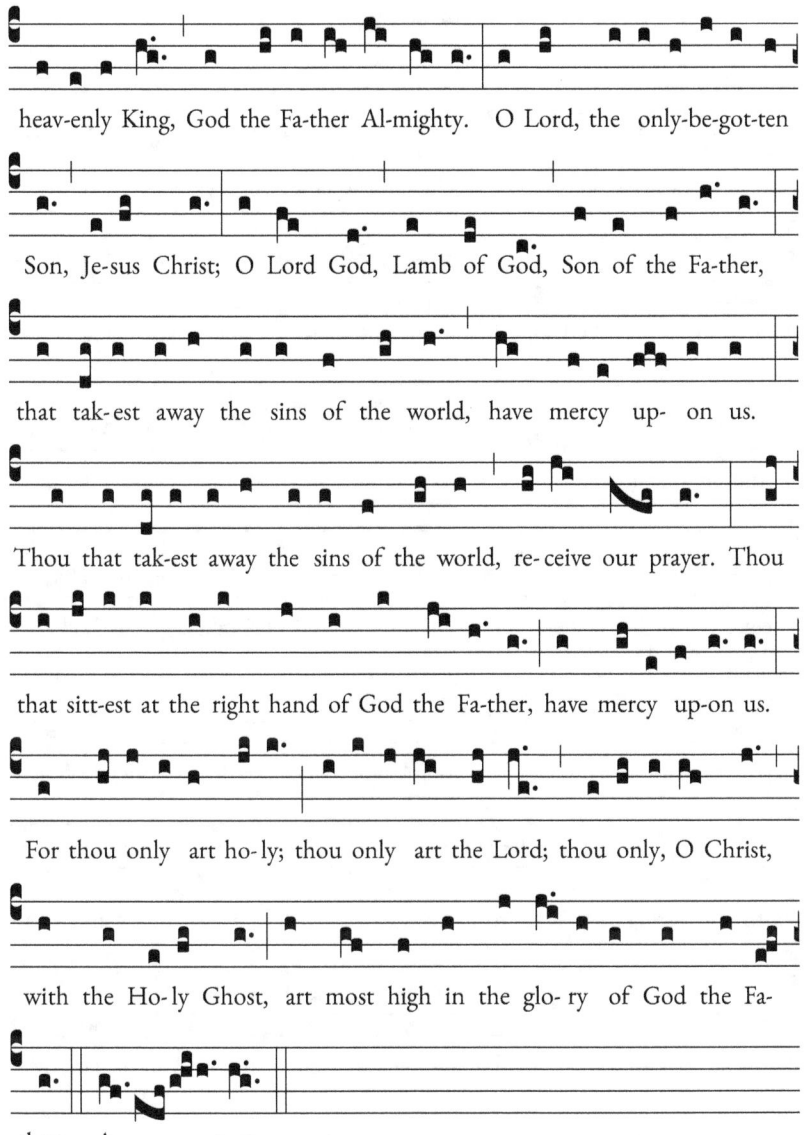

Communion II # Liturgical Hymns Nicene Creed

Nicene Creed

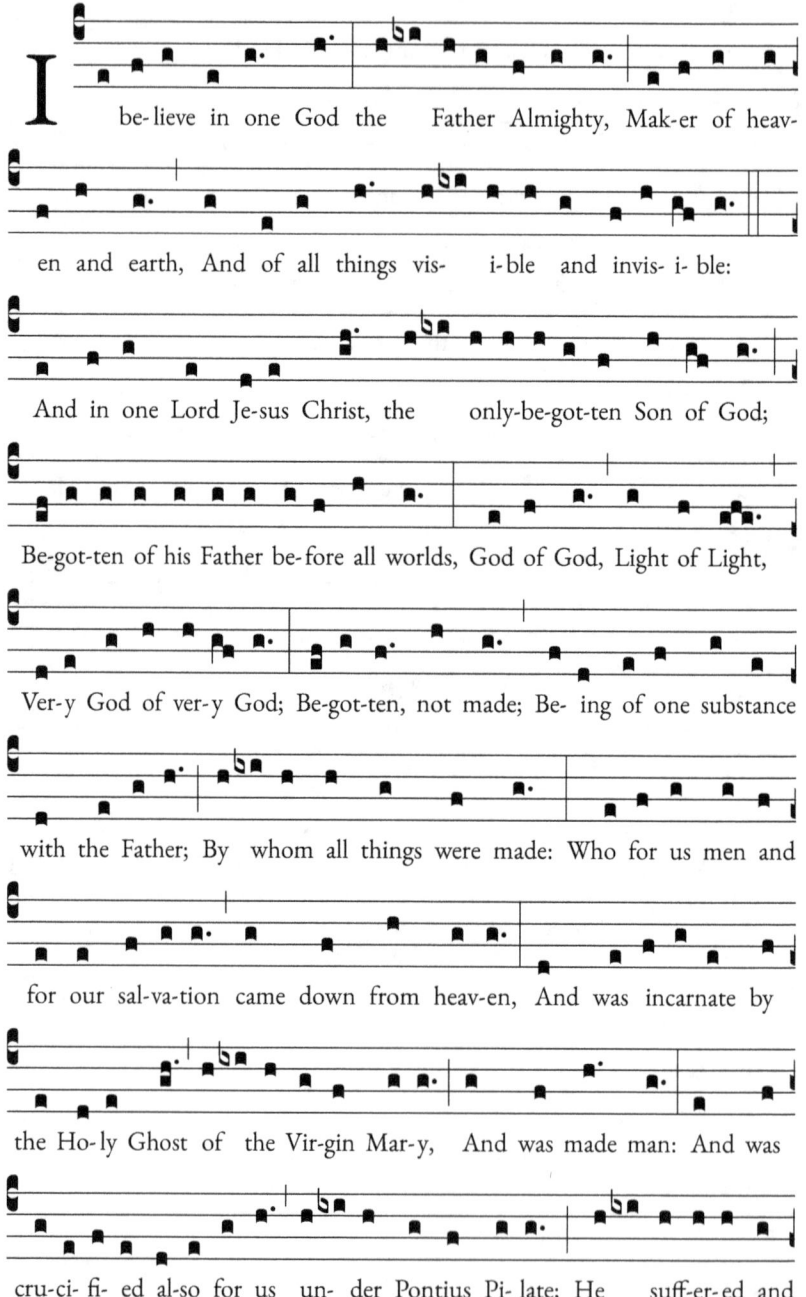

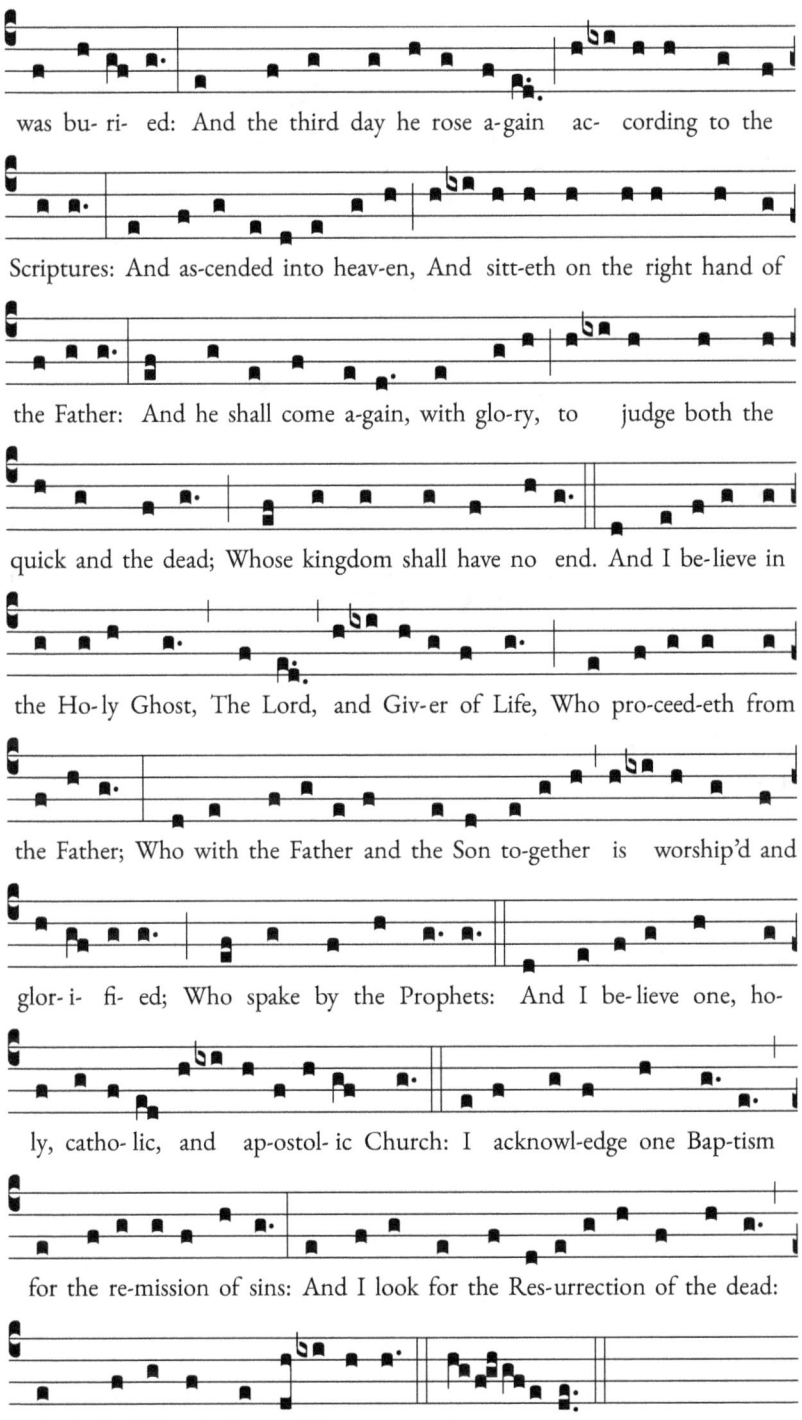

Agnus Dei # Liturgical Hymns *Communion II*

Agnus Dei

Communion III **Liturgical Hymns** Gloria in excelsis

**COMMUNION SERVICE THREE -
MASS OF THE ANGELS**

Kyrie

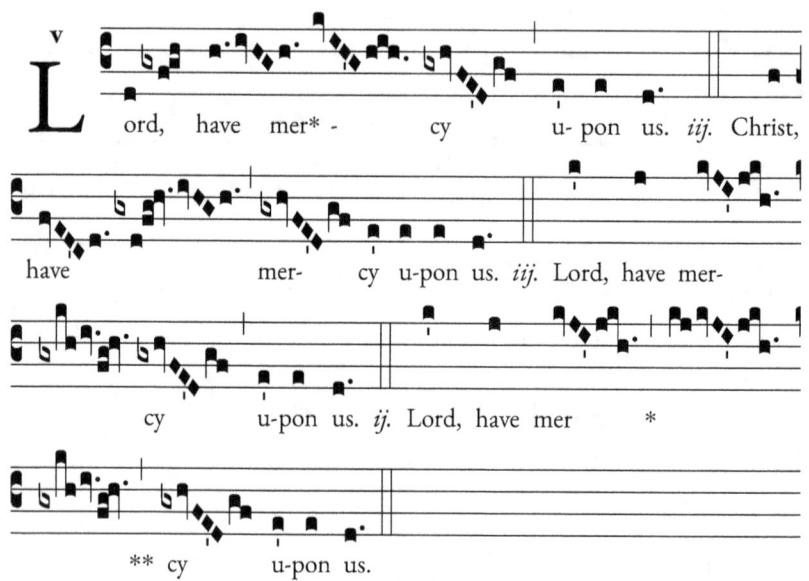

Lord, have mer* - cy u- pon us. *iij.* Christ, have mer- cy u-pon us. *iij.* Lord, have mer- cy u-pon us. *ij.* Lord, have mer * ** cy u-pon us.

Gloria in excelsis

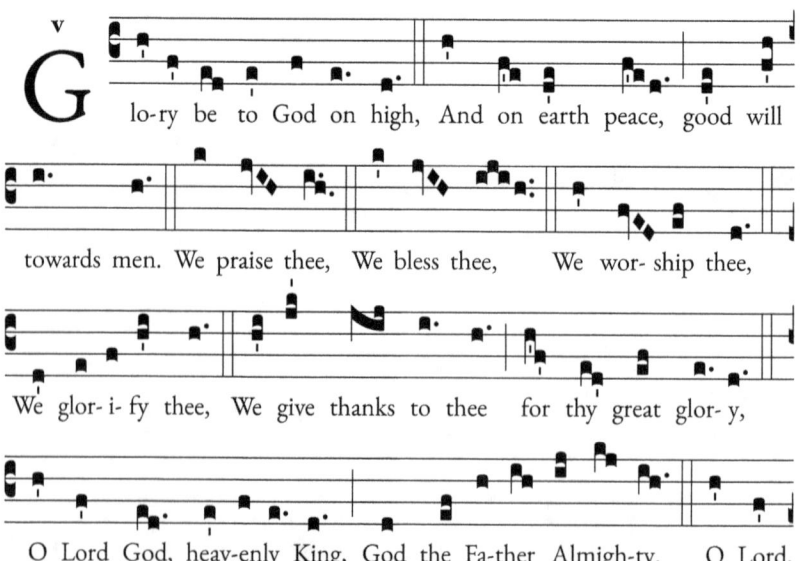

Glo-ry be to God on high, And on earth peace, good will towards men. We praise thee, We bless thee, We wor- ship thee, We glor- i- fy thee, We give thanks to thee for thy great glor- y, O Lord God, heav-enly King, God the Fa-ther Almigh-ty. O Lord,

Gloria in excelsis **Liturgical Hymns** *Communion III*

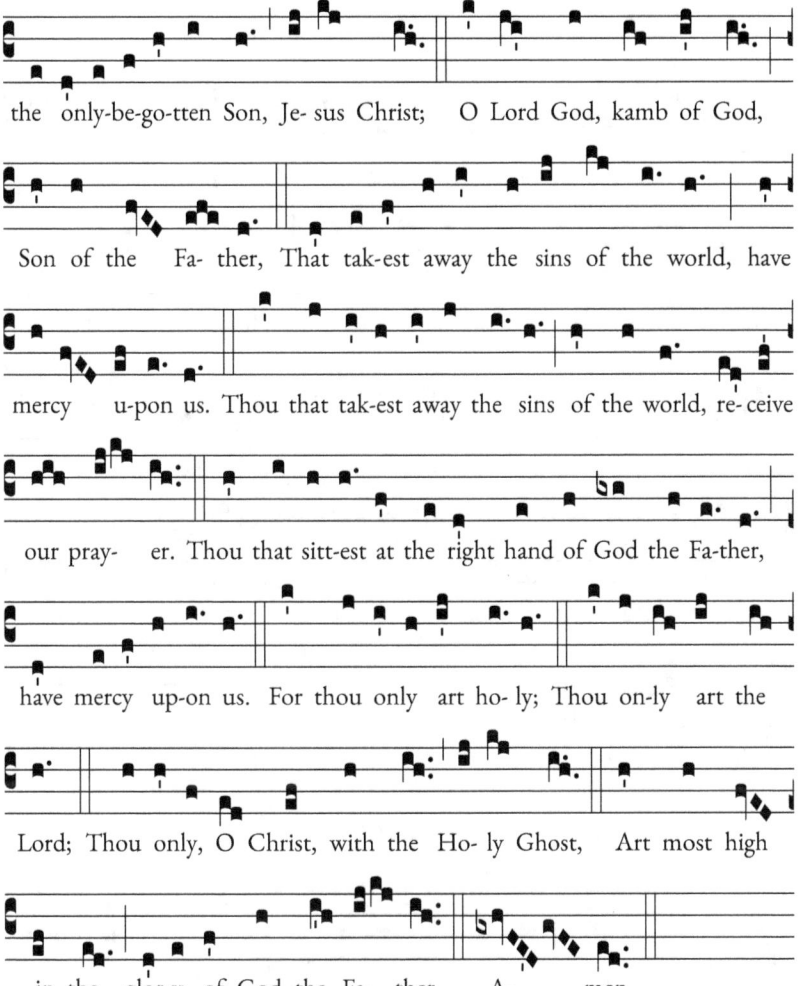

the only-be-go-tten Son, Je-sus Christ; O Lord God, Lamb of God, Son of the Fa-ther, That tak-est away the sins of the world, have mercy u-pon us. Thou that tak-est away the sins of the world, re-ceive our pray-er. Thou that sitt-est at the right hand of God the Fa-ther, have mercy up-on us. For thou only art ho-ly; Thou on-ly art the Lord; Thou only, O Christ, with the Ho-ly Ghost, Art most high in the glor-y of God the Fa-ther. A-men.

Communion III — **Liturgical Hymns** — Agnus Dei

Sanctus

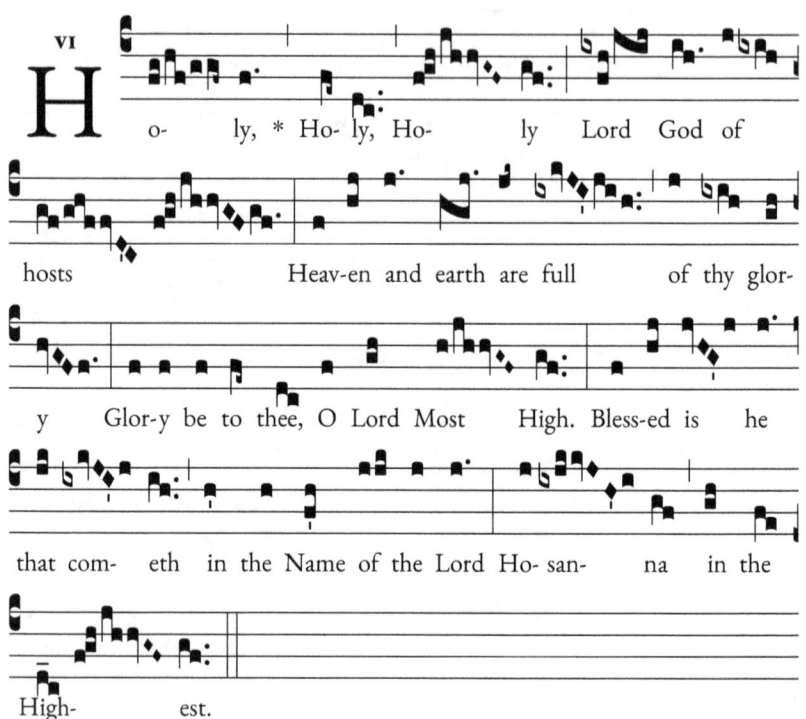

Agnus Dei

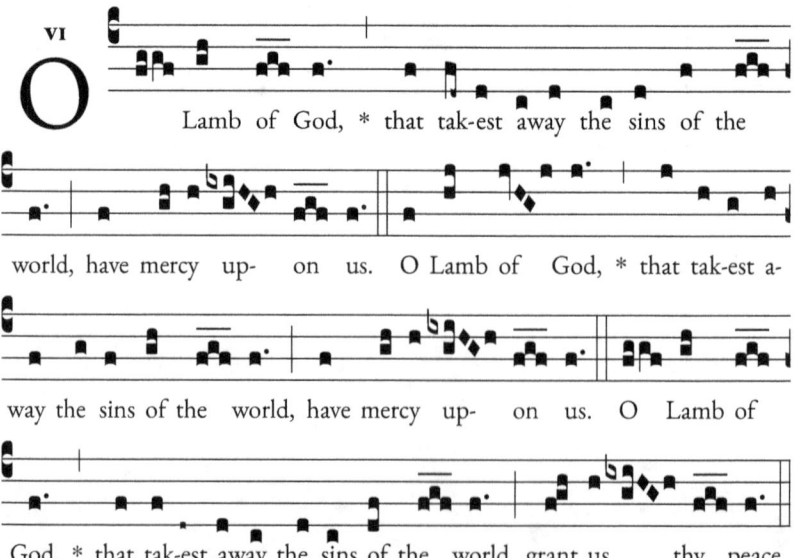

Liturgical Hymns

**COMMUNION SERVICE FOUR -
MASS OF THE MAKER OF THE WORLD**

Kyrie

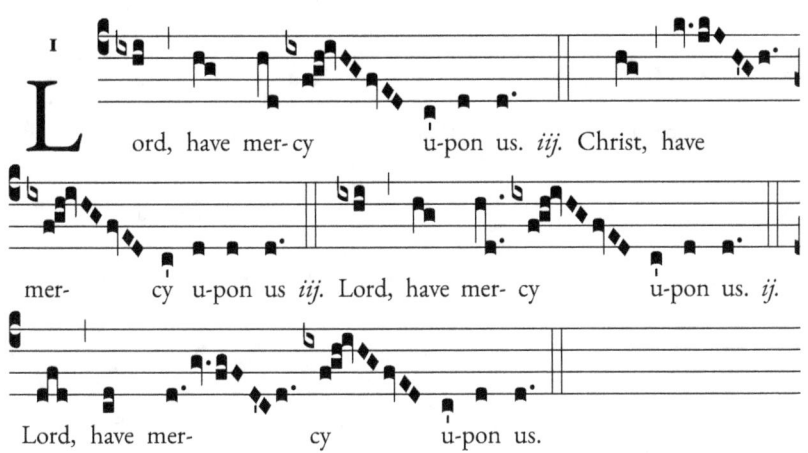

Lord, have mer-cy u-pon us. *iij.* Christ, have mer-cy u-pon us *iij.* Lord, have mer-cy u-pon us. *ij.* Lord, have mer-cy u-pon us.

Gloria in excelsis

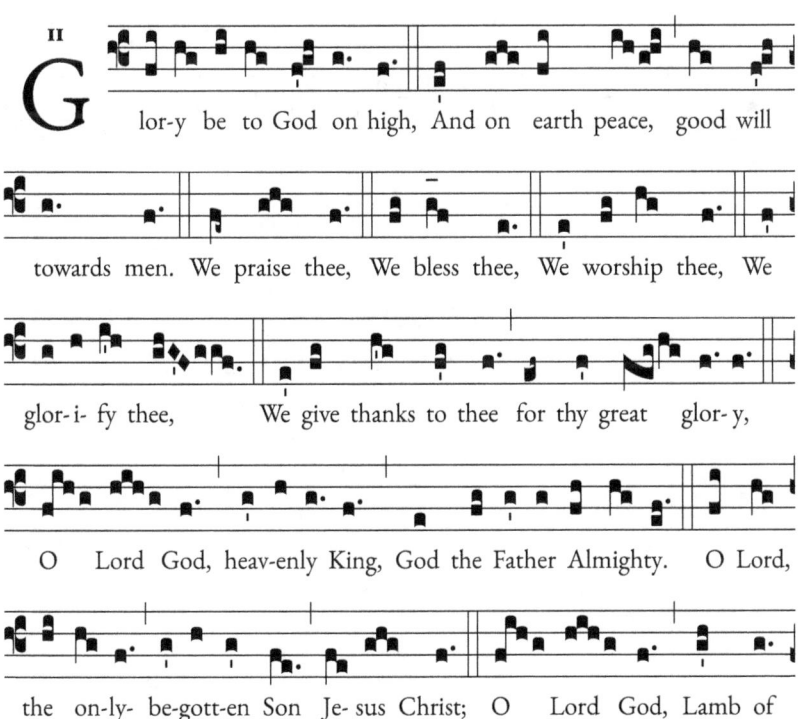

Glor-y be to God on high, And on earth peace, good will towards men. We praise thee, We bless thee, We worship thee, We glor-i-fy thee, We give thanks to thee for thy great glor-y, O Lord God, heav-enly King, God the Father Almighty. O Lord, the on-ly-be-gott-en Son Je-sus Christ; O Lord God, Lamb of

Communion IV — **Liturgical Hymns** — Gloria in excelsis

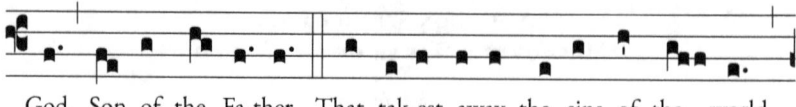
God, Son of the Father, That takest away the sins of the world,

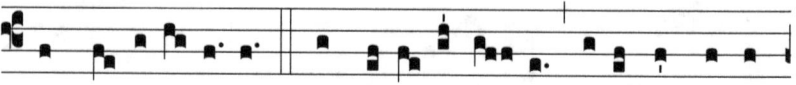
have mercy upon us. Thou that takest away, the sins of the world,

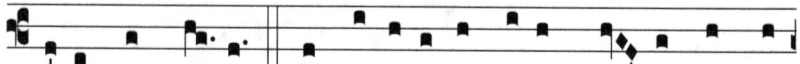
receive our prayer. Thou that sittest at the right hand of God the

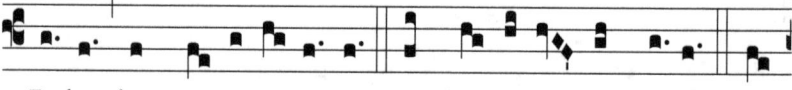
Father, have mercy upon us. For thou only art holy; Thou

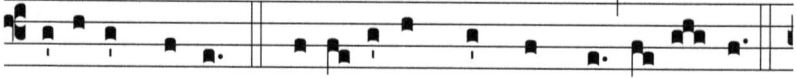
only art the Lord; Thou only, O Christ, with the Holy Ghost,

Art most high in the glory of God the Father. Amen.

Agnus Dei **Liturgical Hymns** *Communion IV*

Sanctus

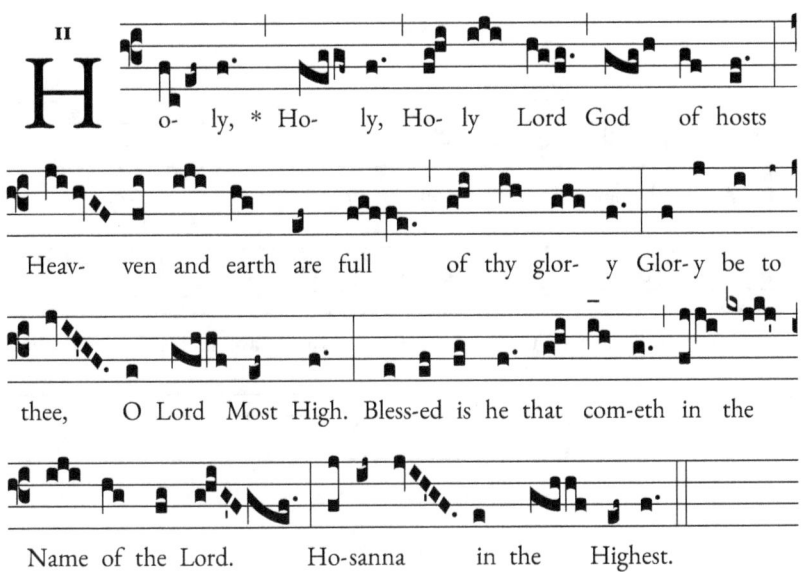

Agnus Dei

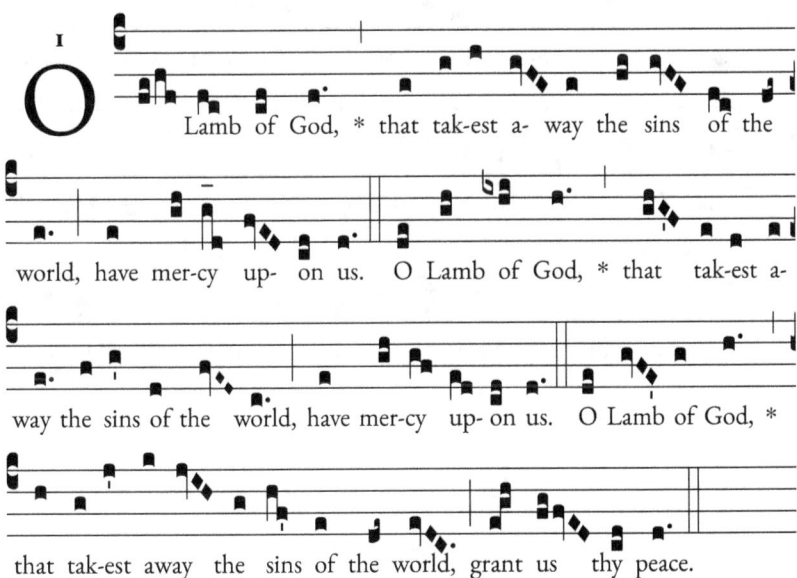

Liturgical Hymns

**COMMUNION SERVICE FIVE -
MASS OF GOD OUR SWEET FATHER**

Kyrie

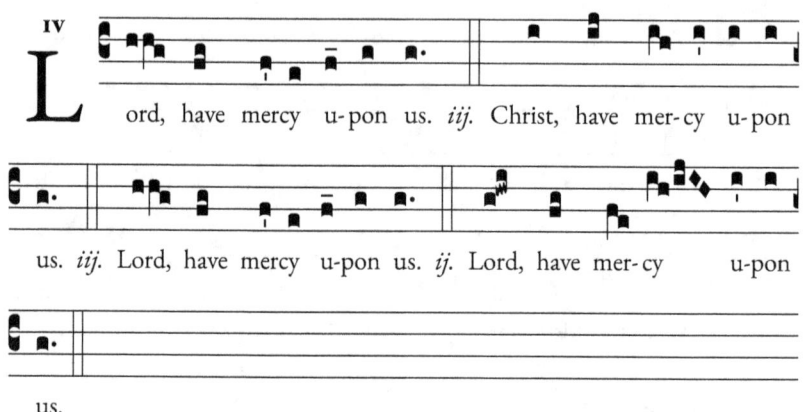

Lord, have mercy u-pon us. *iij.* Christ, have mer-cy u-pon us. *iij.* Lord, have mercy u-pon us. *ij.* Lord, have mer-cy u-pon us.

Sanctus

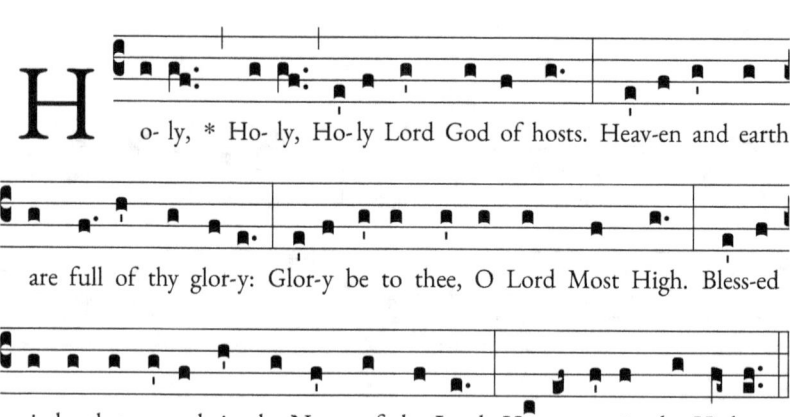

Ho- ly, * Ho- ly, Ho-ly Lord God of hosts. Heav-en and earth are full of thy glor-y: Glor-y be to thee, O Lord Most High. Bless-ed is he that cometh in the Name of the Lord. Ho-sanna in the Highest.

Agnus Dei   # Liturgical Hymns   *Communion V*

Agnus Dei

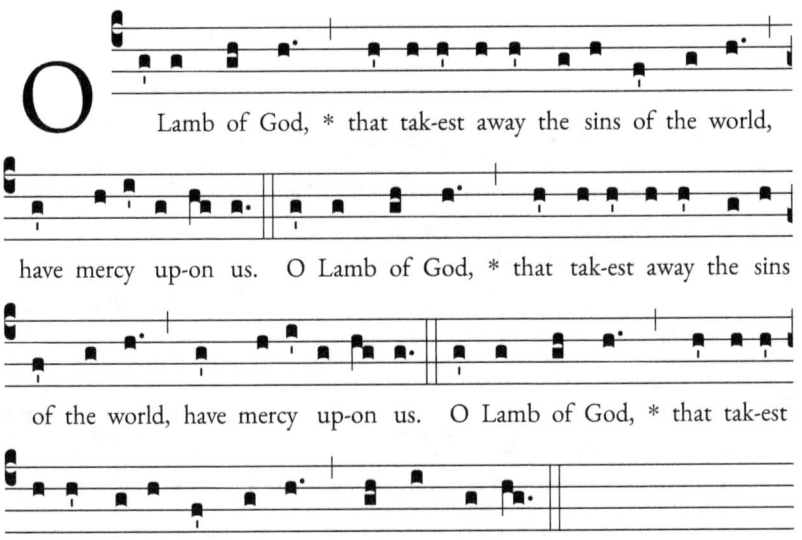

O Lamb of God, * that tak-est away the sins of the world, have mercy up-on us. O Lamb of God, * that tak-est away the sins of the world, have mercy up-on us. O Lamb of God, * that tak-est away the sins of the world, grant us thy peace

Creeds | Liturgical Hymns | Creed III

Creeds

CREED III

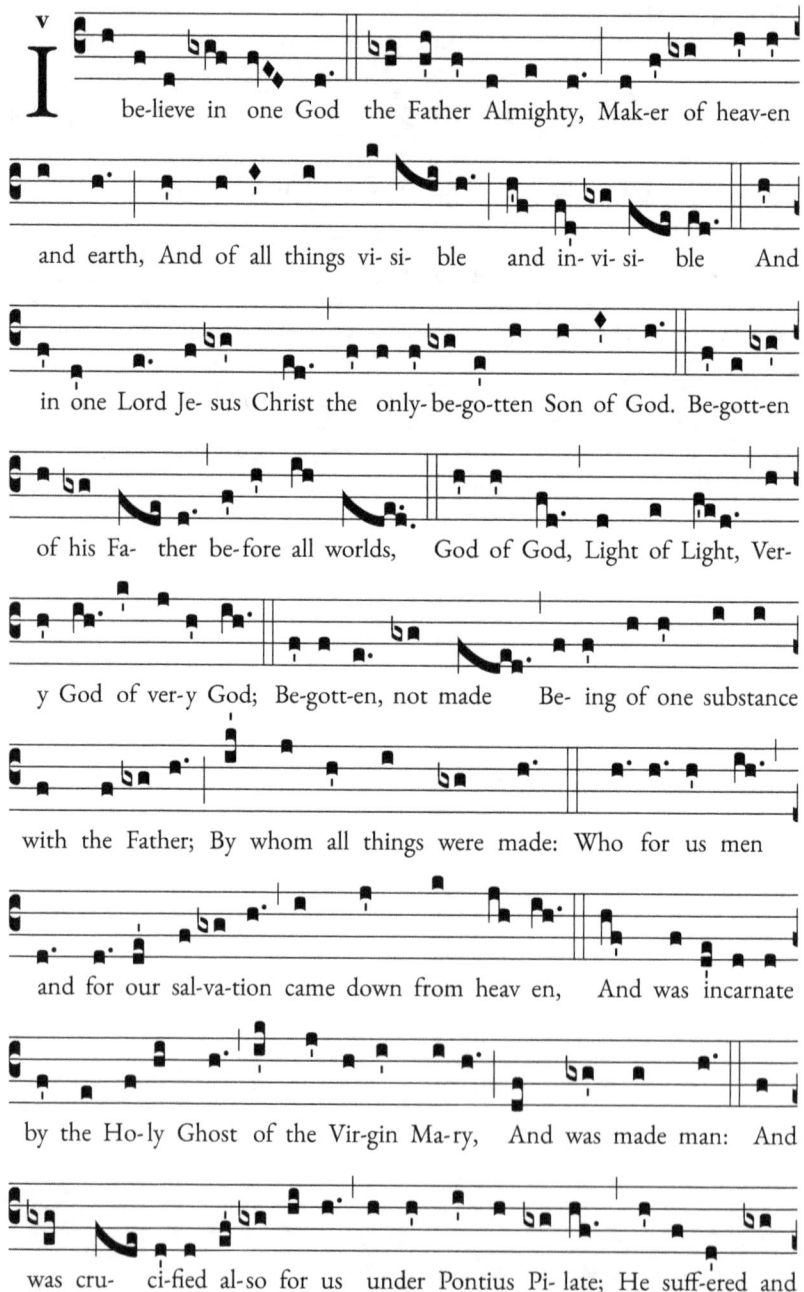

I believe in one God the Father Almighty, Maker of heaven and earth, And of all things visible and invisible And in one Lord Jesus Christ the only-begotten Son of God. Begotten of his Father before all worlds, God of God, Light of Light, Very God of very God; Begotten, not made Being of one substance with the Father; By whom all things were made: Who for us men and for our salvation came down from heaven, And was incarnate by the Holy Ghost of the Virgin Mary, And was made man: And was crucified also for us under Pontius Pilate; He suffered and

Liturgical Hymns

CREDO III

Credo in unum Deum, Patrem omnipoténtem, factórem caeli et terrae, visibílium ómnium, et invisibílium. Et in unum Dóminum Jesum Christum, Fílium Dei unigénitum. Et ex Patre natum ante ómnia saécula. Deum de Deo, lumen de lúmine, Deum verum de Deo vero. Génitum, non factum, consubstantiálem Patri: per quem ómnia facta sunt. Qui propter nos hómines, et propter nostram salútem descéndit de caelis. Et incarnátus est de Spíritu Sancto ex María Vírgine: Et homo factus est. Crucifíxus étiam pro no-

Credo III — Liturgical Hymns — Creeds

Liturgical Hymns

Sequences

Victimae Paschali Laudes

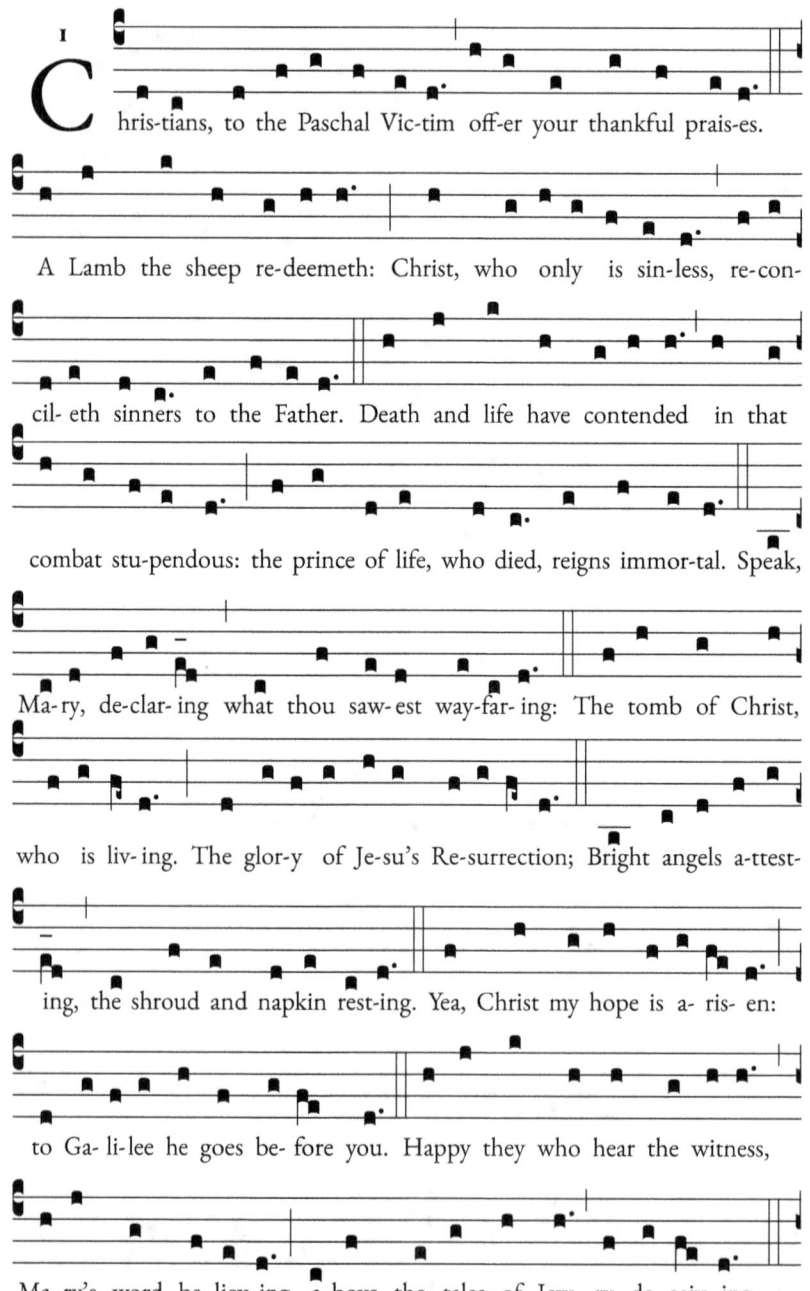

Christians, to the Paschal Victim offer your thankful praises.

A Lamb the sheep redeemeth: Christ, who only is sinless, reconcileth sinners to the Father. Death and life have contended in that combat stupendous: the prince of life, who died, reigns immortal. Speak, Mary, declaring what thou sawest wayfaring: The tomb of Christ, who is living. The glory of Jesu's Resurrection; Bright angels attesting, the shroud and napkin resting. Yea, Christ my hope is arisen: to Galilee he goes before you. Happy they who hear the witness, Mary's word believing above the tales of Jewry deceiving.

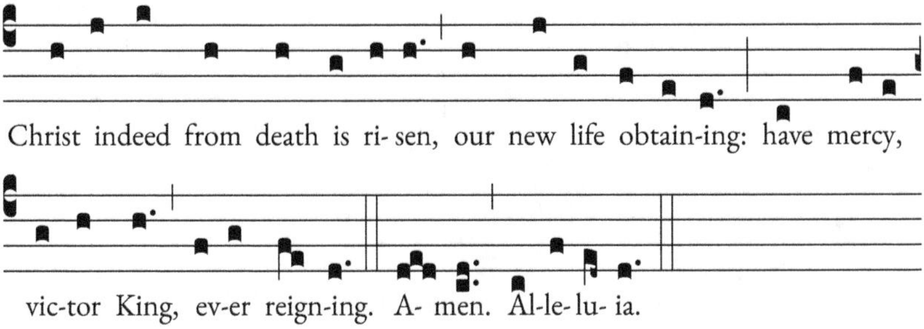

Christ indeed from death is ri-sen, our new life obtain-ing: have mercy, vic-tor King, ev-er reign-ing. A-men. Al-le-lu-ia.

Veni, Sancte Spiritus

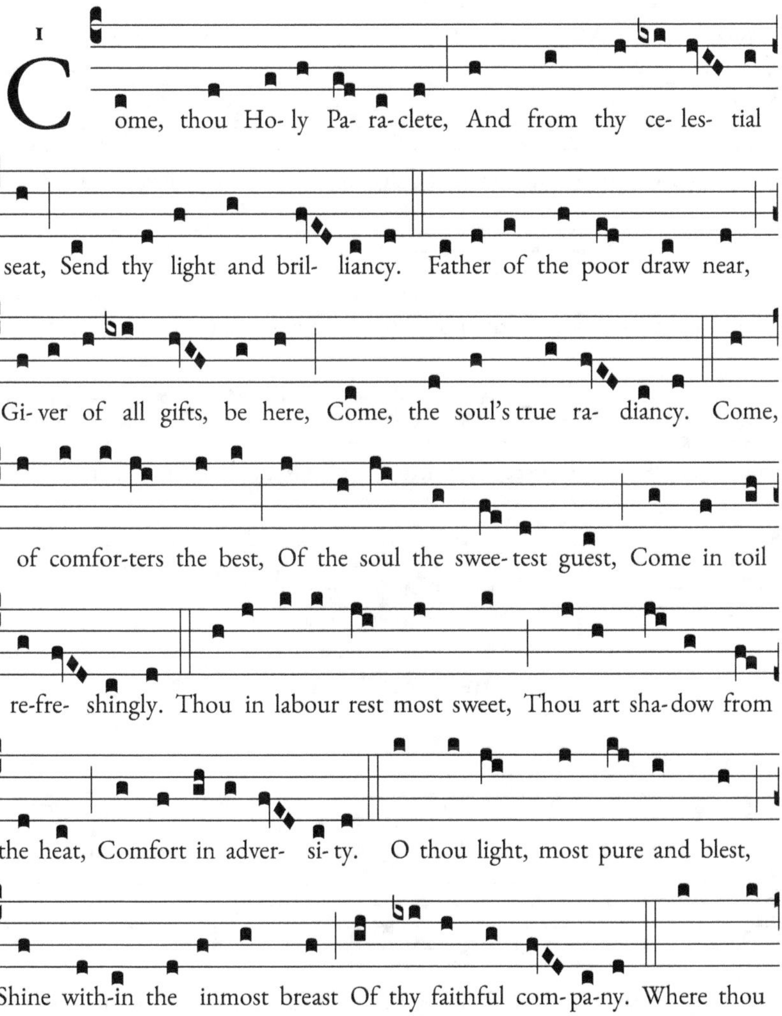

Come, thou Ho-ly Pa-ra-clete, And from thy ce-les-tial seat, Send thy light and bril-liancy. Father of the poor draw near, Gi-ver of all gifts, be here, Come, the soul's true ra-diancy. Come, of comfor-ters the best, Of the soul the swee-test guest, Come in toil re-fre-shingly. Thou in labour rest most sweet, Thou art sha-dow from the heat, Comfort in adver-si-ty. O thou light, most pure and blest, Shine with-in the inmost breast Of thy faithful com-pa-ny. Where thou

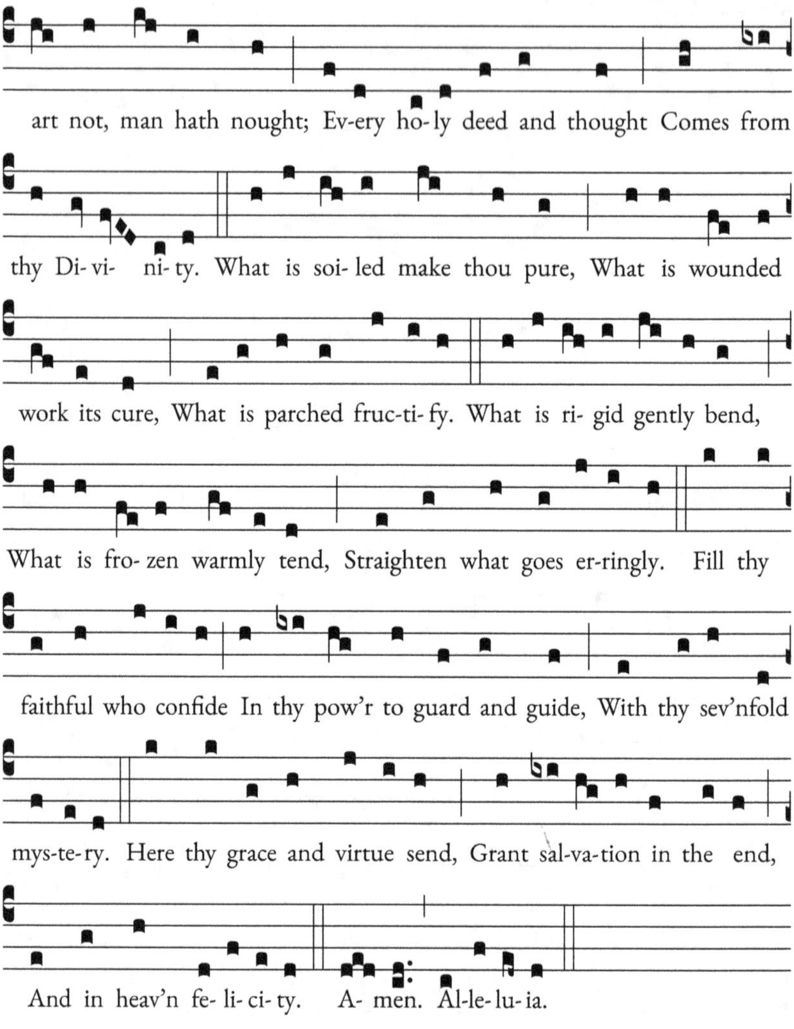

Sequences   **Liturgical Hymns**   Dies Irae, Dies Illa

art not, man hath nought; Ev-ery ho-ly deed and thought Comes from thy Di-vi-ni-ty. What is soi-led make thou pure, What is wounded work its cure, What is parched fruc-ti-fy. What is ri-gid gently bend, What is fro-zen warmly tend, Straighten what goes er-ringly. Fill thy faithful who confide In thy pow'r to guard and guide, With thy sev'nfold mys-te-ry. Here thy grace and virtue send, Grant sal-va-tion in the end, And in heav'n fe-li-ci-ty. A-men. Al-le-lu-ia.

DIES IRAE, DIES ILLA

Day of wrath and doom impending, Da-vid's word with Si-byl's blending: Heav'n and earth in ashes ending. Oh, what fear man's bo-

Dies Irae, Dies Illa — **Liturgical Hymns** — *Sequences*

som rendeth When from heav'n the judge de-scendeth, On whose sen-tence all de-pendeth! Wondrous sound the trum-pet flingeth, Through earth's se-pulchres it ringeth, All be-fore the throne it bringeth.

Death is struck, and na-ture qua-king, All cre-a-tion is a-wak-ing, To its judge an answer ma-king. Lo! the book, ex-act-ly worded, Where-in all hath been re-corded, Thence shall judgement be a-warded.

When the judge his seat attain-eth, And each hidden deed arraigneth, Nothing un-a-veng'd remain-eth. What shall I, frail man, be plead-ing? Who for me be inter-ced-ing, When the just are mercy need-ing?

King of ma-jest-y tremendous, Who dost free sal-va-tion send us,

Sequences **Liturgical Hymns** Dies Irae, Dies Illa

Dies Irae, Dies Illa — **Liturgical Hymns** — *Sequences*

With thy sheep a place pro-vide me, From the goats a-far di-vide me, To thy right hand do thou guide me. When the wicked are con-founded, Doom'd to flames of woe unbounded: Call me, with thy Saints surrounded. Low I kneel, with heart submission, See, like ash-es, my contri-tion: Help me in my last condi-tion. Ah! that day of tears and mourning, From the dust of earth re-turning, Man for judgement must pre-pare him. Spare, O God, in mer-cy spare him: Lord, all-pit-ying, Je-su blest, Grant them thine e-ternal rest. A-men.

Paraliturgical Hymns

THEREFORE, WE BEFORE HIM BENDING

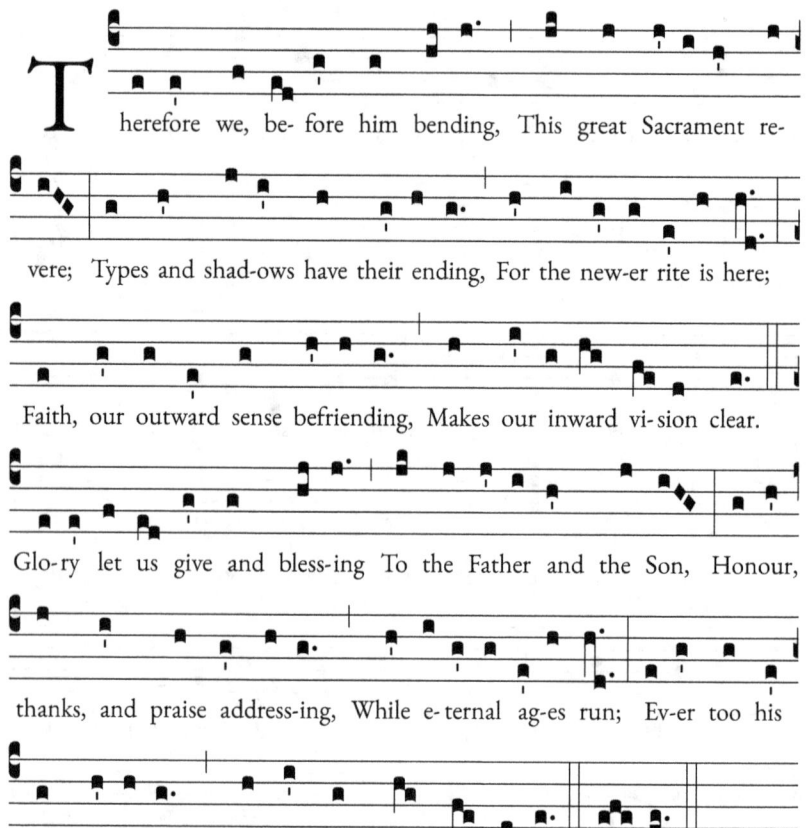

Therefore we, be-fore him bending, This great Sacrament revere; Types and shad-ows have their ending, For the new-er rite is here; Faith, our outward sense befriending, Makes our inward vi-sion clear. Glo-ry let us give and bless-ing To the Father and the Son, Honour, thanks, and praise address-ing, While e-ternal ag-es run; Ev-er too his love confess-ing Who from One with Both is One. A-men.

Liturgical Hymns

Tantum Ergo Sacramentum

Tantum ergo Sacraméntum Ve-ne-rémur cérnu-i: Et antíquum do-cuméntum No-vo ce-dat rí-tu-i: Praestet fi-des suppleméntum Sénsu-um de- fé-ctu-i. 2. Ge-ni-tó-ri, Ge-ni-tóque Laus et ju-bi-lá-ti-o, Sa-lus, ho-nor, vir-tus quoque Sit et be-ne-dí-cti-o: Pro-ce-dénti ab u-nóque Compar sit lau-dá-ti-o. A-men.

Paraliturgical Hymns # Liturgical Hymns O Salutaris

O Saving Victim Opening Wide

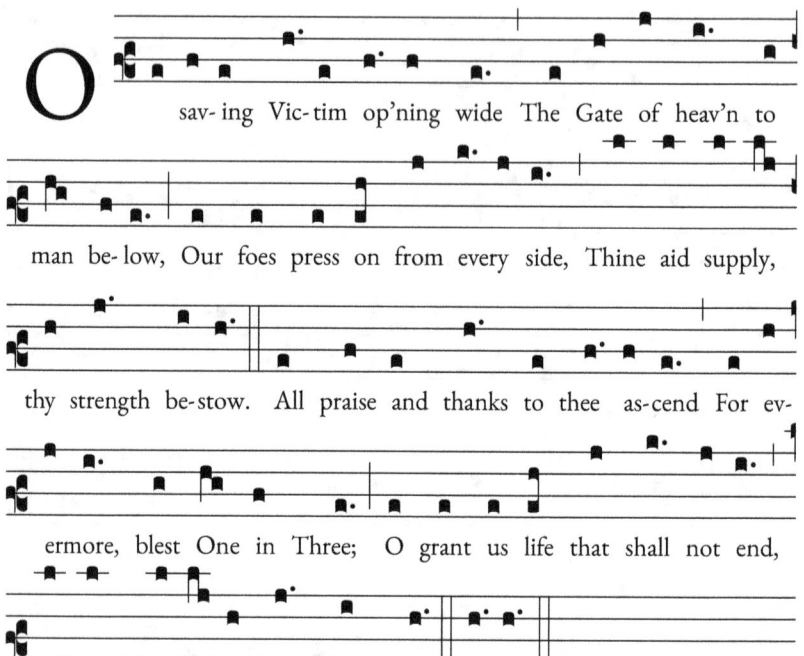

O sav-ing Vic-tim op'ning wide The Gate of heav'n to man be-low, Our foes press on from every side, Thine aid supply, thy strength be-stow. All praise and thanks to thee as-cend For ev-ermore, blest One in Three; O grant us life that shall not end, In our true na-tive land with thee. Amen.

O Salutaris Hostia

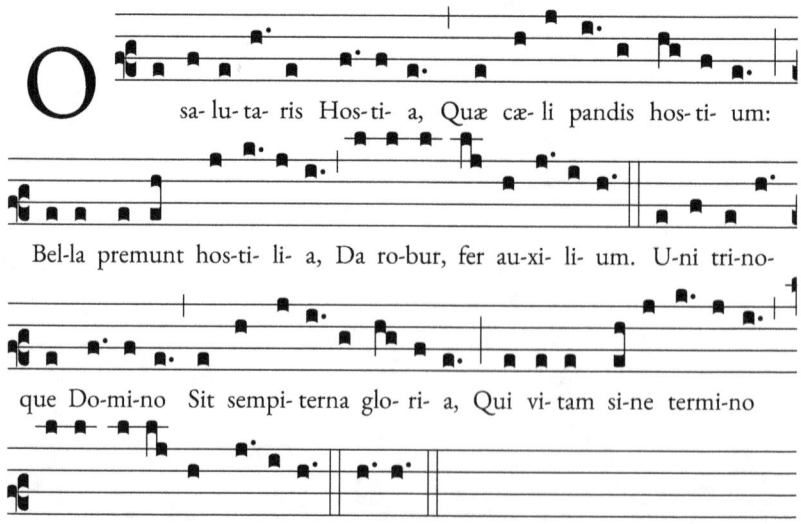

O sa-lu-ta-ris Hos-ti-a, Quæ cæ-li pandis hos-ti-um: Bel-la premunt hos-ti-li-a, Da ro-bur, fer au-xi-li-um. U-ni tri-no-que Do-mi-no Sit sempi-terna glo-ri-a, Qui vi-tam si-ne termi-no No-bis do-net in pa-tri-a. Amen.

Prostrate I Adore **Liturgical Hymns** *Paraliturgical Hymns*

PROSTRATE, I ADORE THEE

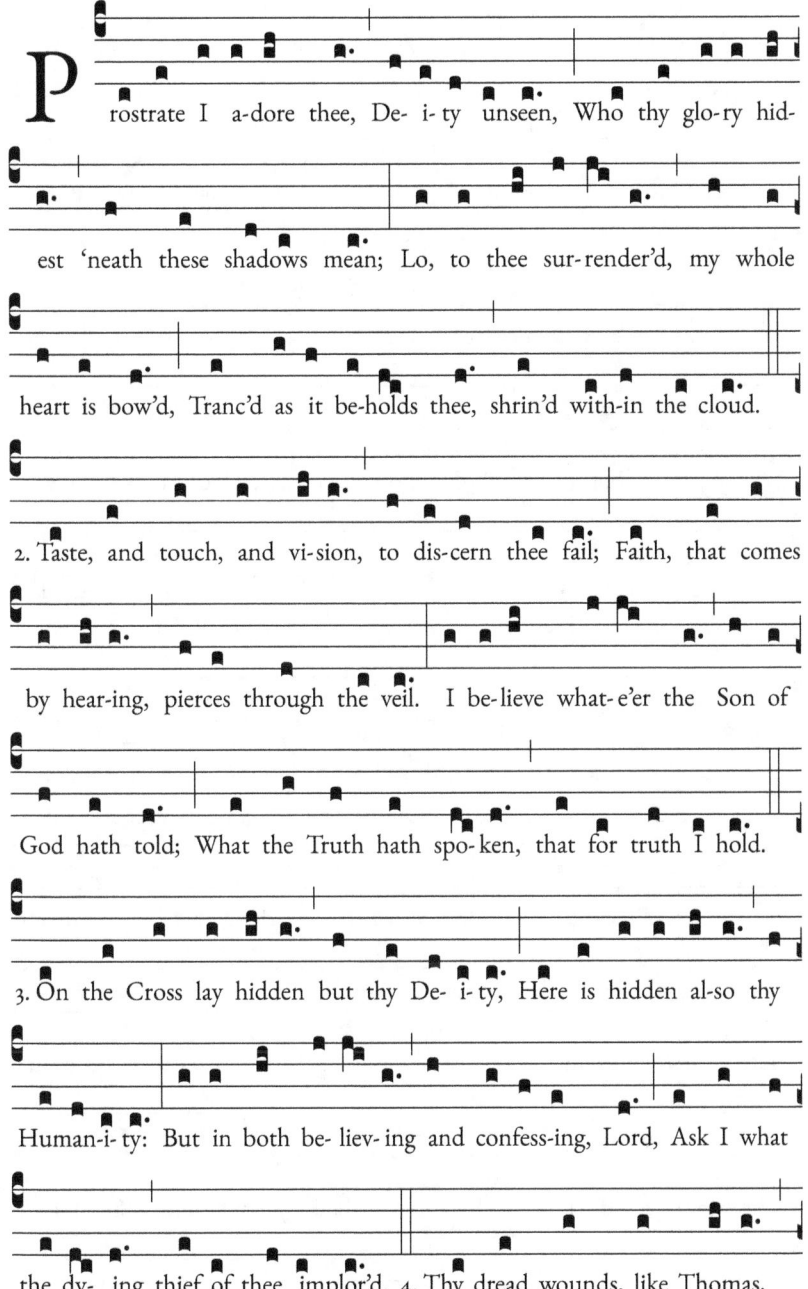

Prostrate I adore thee, Deity unseen, Who thy glory hidest 'neath these shadows mean; Lo, to thee surrender'd, my whole heart is bow'd, Tranc'd as it beholds thee, shrin'd within the cloud.

2. Taste, and touch, and vision, to discern thee fail; Faith, that comes by hearing, pierces through the veil. I believe what-e'er the Son of God hath told; What the Truth hath spoken, that for truth I hold.

3. On the Cross lay hidden but thy Deity, Here is hidden also thy Humanity: But in both believing and confessing, Lord, Ask I what the dying thief of thee implor'd. 4. Thy dread wounds, like Thomas,

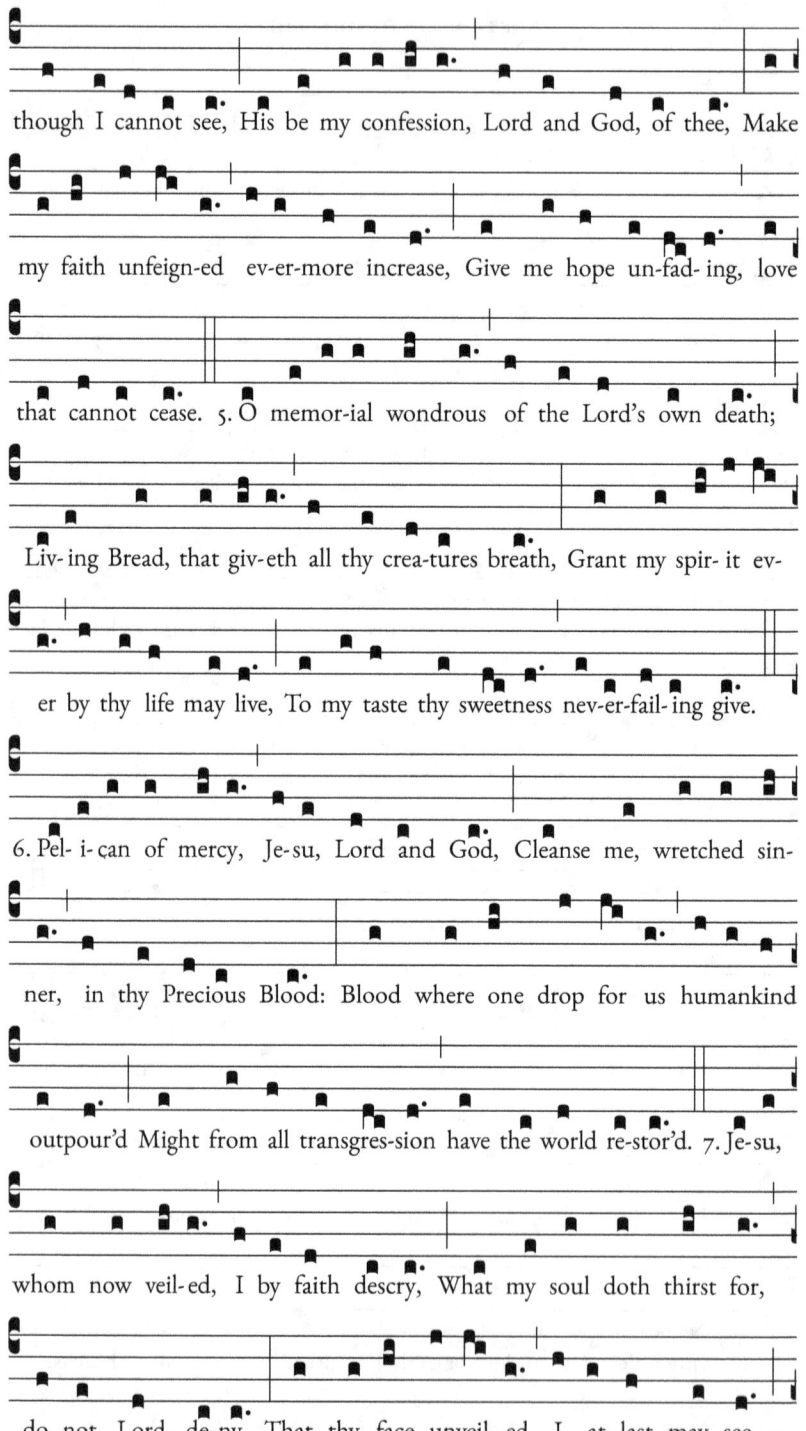

Adoro Te Devote # Liturgical Hymns *Paraliturgical Hymns*

With the blissful vision blest, my God, of thee. A- men.

Adoro Te Devote

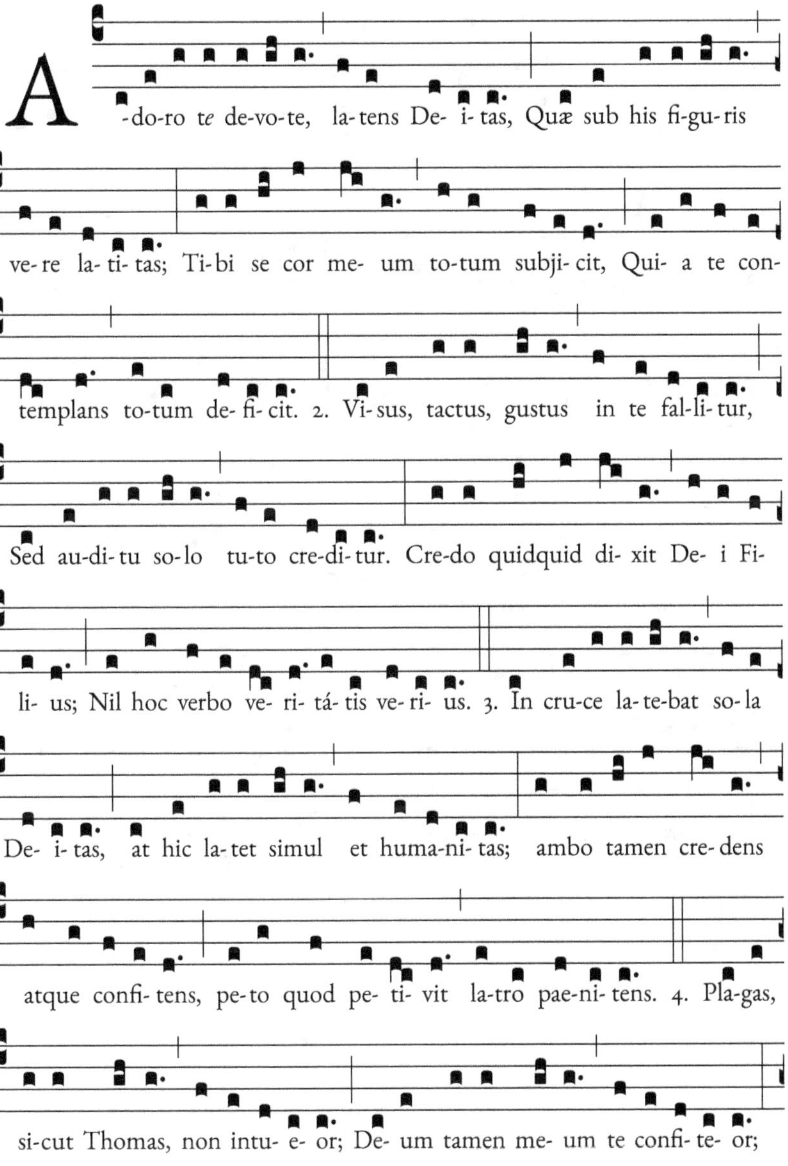

A-doro te devote, latens Deitas, Quæ sub his figuris vere latitas; Tibi se cor meum totum subjicit, Quia te contemplans totum deficit. 2. Visus, tactus, gustus in te fallitur, Sed auditu solo tuto creditur. Credo quidquid dixit Dei Filius; Nil hoc verbo veritátis verius. 3. In cruce latebat sola Deitas, at hic latet simul et humanitas; ambo tamen credens atque confitens, peto quod petivit latro paenitens. 4. Plagas, sicut Thomas, non intueor; Deum tamen meum te confiteor;

Paraliturgical Hymns **Liturgical Hymns** Adoro Te Devote

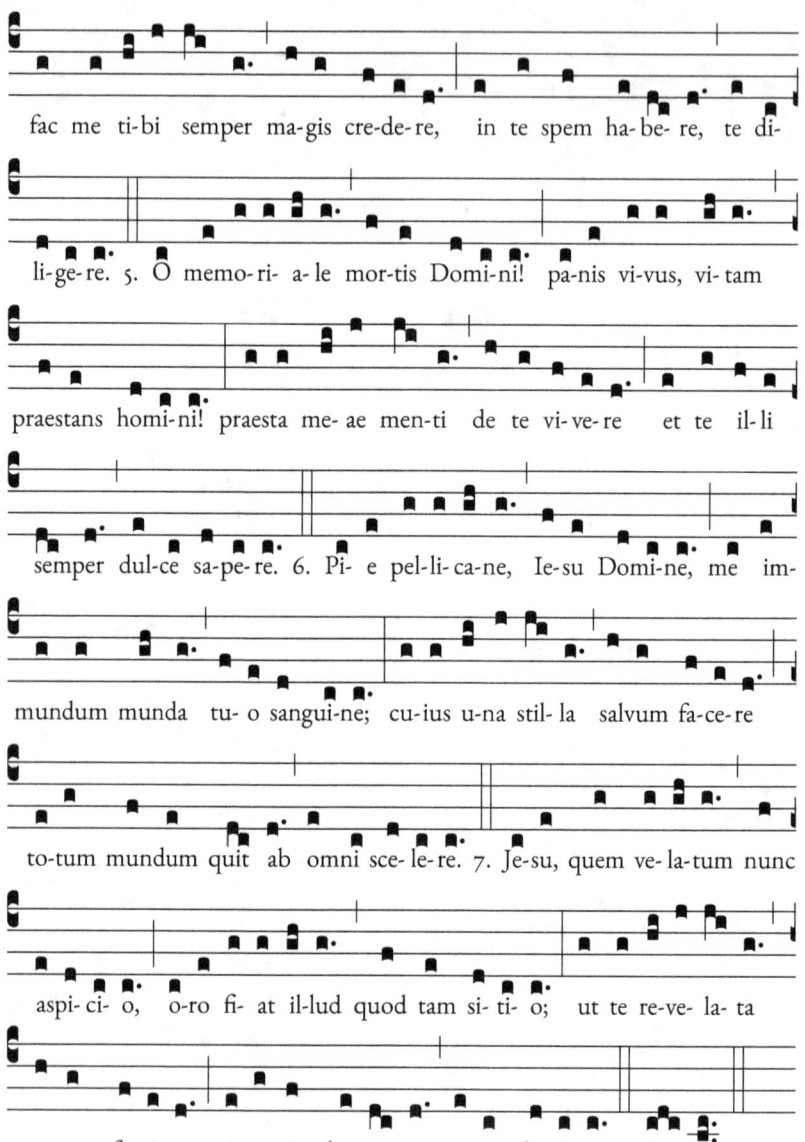

fac me ti-bi semper ma-gis cre-de-re, in te spem ha-be-re, te di-li-ge-re. 5. O memo-ri-a-le mor-tis Domi-ni! pa-nis vi-vus, vi-tam praestans homi-ni! praesta me-ae men-ti de te vi-ve-re et te il-li semper dul-ce sa-pe-re. 6. Pi- e pel-li-ca-ne, Ie-su Domi-ne, me im-mundum munda tu- o sangui-ne; cu-ius u-na stil- la salvum fa-ce-re to-tum mundum quit ab omni sce-le-re. 7. Je-su, quem ve-la-tum nunc aspi-ci- o, o-ro fi- at il-lud quod tam si-ti- o; ut te re-ve- la-ta cernens fa-ci- e, vi-su sim be- a- tus tu- ae glo-ri- ae. A- men.

Liturgical Hymns

ADVENT PROSE

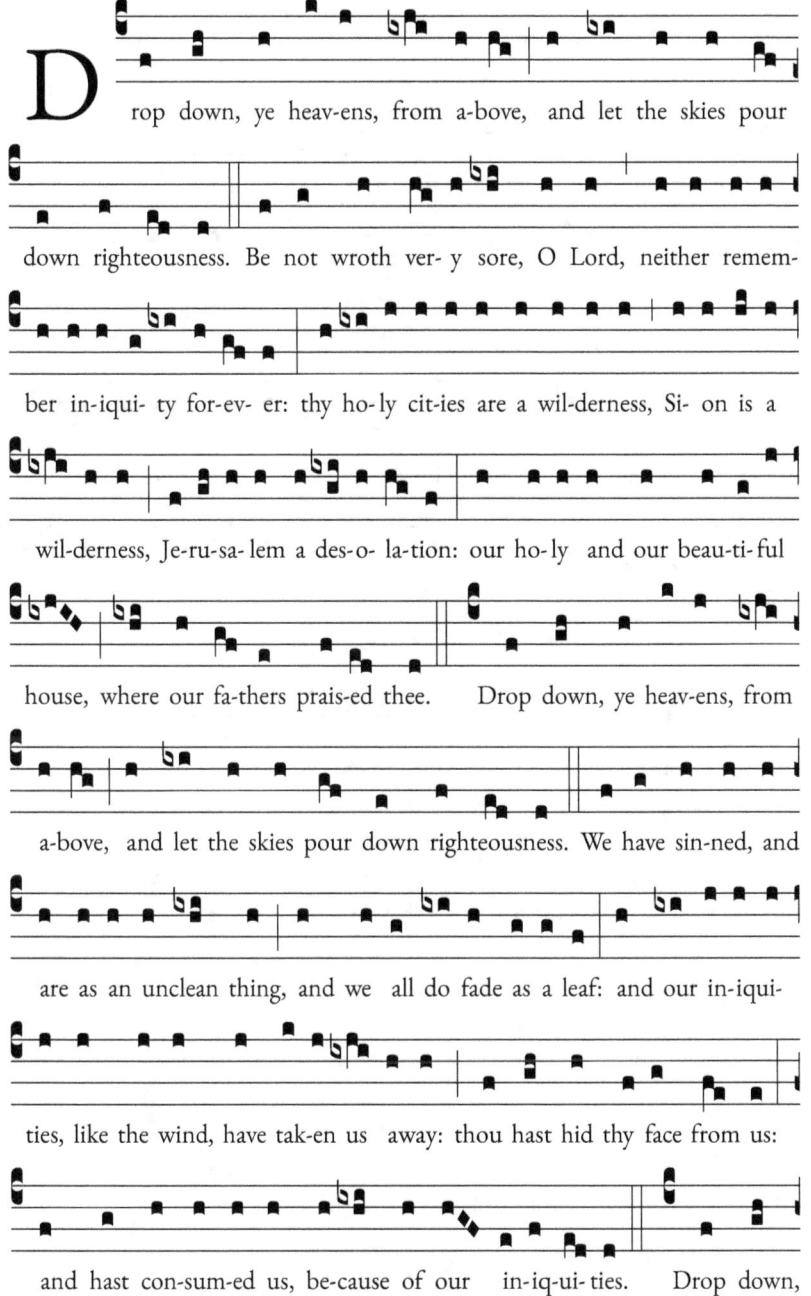

Drop down, ye heav-ens, from a-bove, and let the skies pour down righteousness. Be not wroth ver- y sore, O Lord, neither remem- ber in-iqui- ty for-ev- er: thy ho- ly cit-ies are a wil-derness, Si- on is a wil-derness, Je-ru-sa- lem a des-o- la-tion: our ho- ly and our beau-ti- ful house, where our fa-thers prais-ed thee. Drop down, ye heav-ens, from a-bove, and let the skies pour down righteousness. We have sin-ned, and are as an unclean thing, and we all do fade as a leaf: and our in-iqui- ties, like the wind, have tak-en us away: thou hast hid thy face from us: and hast con-sum-ed us, be-cause of our in-iq-ui- ties. Drop down,

Paraliturgical Hymns **Liturgical Hymns** Advent Prose

ye heav-ens, from a-bove, and let the skies pour down righteousness.

Ye are my witness-es, saith the Lord, and my servant whom I have cho-

sen: that ye may know me and be-lieve me: I, e-ven I, am the Lord,

and be-side me there is no Saviour: and there is none that can de-liv-

er out of my hand. Drop down, ye heav-ens, from a-bove, and let

the skies pour down righteousness. Comfort ye, comfort ye my people,

my sal-va-tion shall not tar-ry: I have blot-ted out as a thick cloud

thy transgressions: Fear not, for I will save thee: For I am the Lord

thy God, the Ho-ly One of Is-ra-el, thy Re-deemer. Drop down,

ye heav-ens, from a-bove, and let the skies pour down righteousness.

Devotional Hymns

1   A Mighty Fortress Is Our God   General

6. And thou most kind and gentle Death,
   Waiting to hush our latest breath,
   O praise him! Alleluia!
   Thou leadest home the child of God,
   And Christ our Lord the way hath trod.

7. Let all things their Creator bless,
   And worship him in humbleness,
   O praise him! Alleluia!
   Praise, praise the Father, praise the Son,
   And praise the Spirit, Three in One!

4 Amazing Grace — General

6. The earth shall soon dissolve like snow,
   The sun forbear to shine;
   But God, who called me here below,
   Shall be forever mine.

7. When we've been there ten thousand years,
   Bright shining as the sun,
   We've no less days to sing God's praise
   Than when we'd first begun.

Be Thou My Vision

General — 6

♩ = 100

1. Be thou my Vi - sion, O Lord of my heart;
2. Be thou my Wis - dom, and thou my true Word;
3. Be thou my ba - ttle Shield, Sword for the fight;
4. Rich - es I heed not, nor man's em - pty praise,
5. High King of Hea - ven, my vic - tor - y won,

Naught be all else to me, save that thou art.
I ev - er with thee and thou with me, Lord;
Be thou my Dig - ni - ty, thou my De - light;
Thou mine In - her - i - tance, now and al - ways:
May I reach Heav'ns joys, O bright Hea - ven's Sun!

Thou my best Thought, by day or by night,
Thou my great Fa - ther, and I thy true son;
Thou my soul's Shel - ter, thou my high To - wer:
Thou and thou on - ly, be first in my heart,
Heart of my own heart, what - ev - er be - fall,

Wa - king or sleep - ing, thy pre - sence my light.
Thou in me dwell - ing, and I with thee one.
Raise thou me heav'n - ward, O Pow'r of my pow'r.
High King of Hea - ven, my Trea - sure thou art.
Still be my Vi - sion, O Rul - er of all.

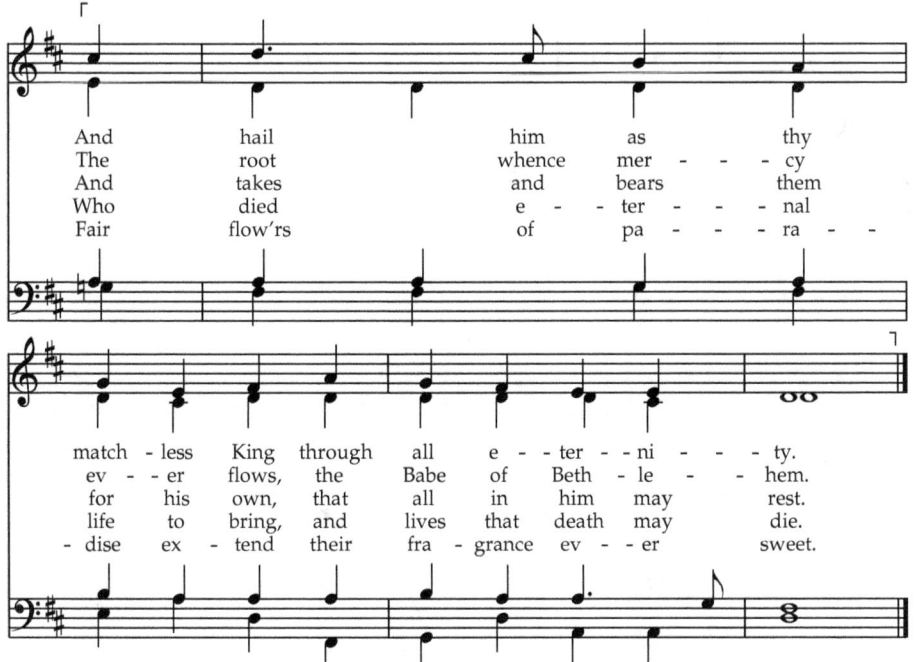

6. Crown him the Lord of love, behold his hands and side,
   Those wounds, yet visible above, in beauty glorified.
   No angel in the sky can fully bear that sight,
   But downward bends his burning eye at mysteries so bright.

7. Crown him the Lord of Heaven, enthroned in worlds above,
   Crown him the King to whom is given the wondrous name of Love.
   Crown him with many crowns, as thrones before him fall;
   Crown him, ye kings, with many crowns, for he is King of all.

8. Crown him the Lord of lords, who over all doth reign,
   Who once on earth, the incarnate Word, for ransomed sinners slain,
   Now lives in realms of light, where saints with angels sing
   Their songs before him day and night, their God, Redeemer, King.

9. Crown him the Lord of years, the Potentate of time,
   Creator of the rolling spheres, ineffably sublime.
   All hail, Redeemer, hail! For thou has died for me;
   Thy praise and glory shall not fail throughout eternity.

6. The Son delighted to obey, And born of Virgin mother,
   Awhile on this low earth did stay That he might be my brother.
   His mighty power he hidden bore,
   A servant's form like mine he wore, To bind the devil captive.

7. To me he spake : cling fast to me, thou'lt win a triumph worthy:
   I wholly give myself for thee, I strive and wrestle for thee;
   For I am thine, thou mine also;
   And where I am thou art. The foe Shall never more divide us.

8. For he shall shed my precious blood, Me of my life bereaving;
   All this I suffer for thy good; Be steadfast and believing.
   My life from death the day shall win,
   My righteousness shall bear thy sin, So art thou blest forever.

9. Now to my Father I depart, From earth to heaven ascending;
   Thence heavenly wisdom to impart, The Holy Spirit sending.
   He shall in trouble comfort thee,
   Teach thee to know and follow me, And to the truth conduct thee.

10. What I have done and taught, do thou To do and teach endeavor;
    So shall my kingdom flourish now, And God be praised forever.
    Take heed lest men with base alloy
    The heavenly treasure should destroy. This counsel I bequeath thee.

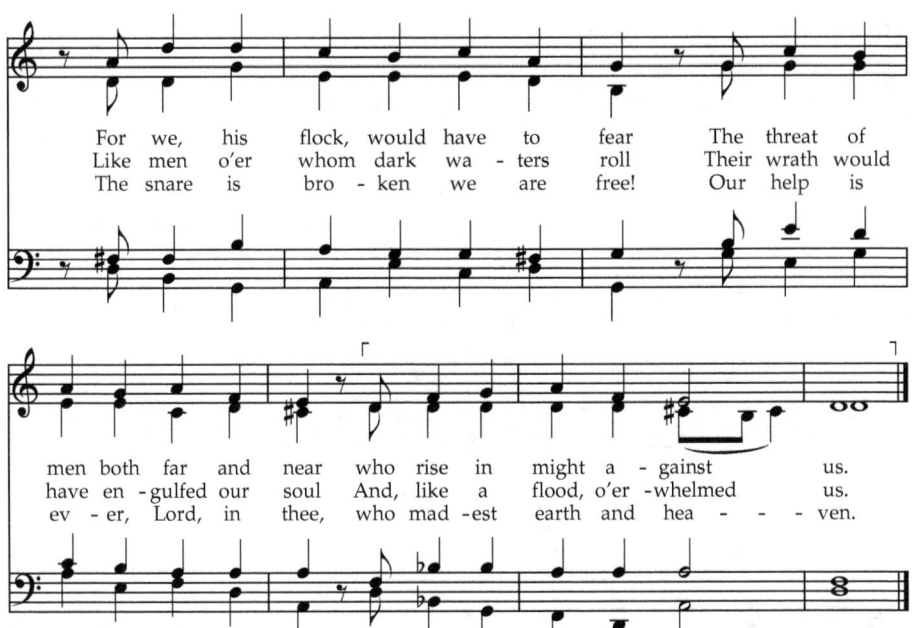

Immaculate Mary

4. We pray for all sinners,
   And souls that now stray
   From Jesus and Mary
   In heresy's way.

5. We pray for our fellows
   Who are bound in Rome
   Cut off from thy dear Son,
   Please bring them back home!

6. O Mother of the Light,
   Shine upon all men,
   Bound up in the darkness,
   Please make them all kin.

7. For poor, sick, afflicted,
   Thy mercy we crave;
   And comfort the dying,
   Thou light of the grave!

8. There is no need, Mary,
    Nor ever hath been,
    Which thou canst not succour,
    Immaculate Queen.

9. In grief and temptation,
    In joy, or in pain,
    We'll seek thee, our Mother,
    Nor seek thee in vain.

10. O bless us, dear Lady,
    With blessings from heav'n,
    And to our petitions
    Let answer be giv'n.

11. In death's solemn moment,
    Our Mother, be nigh;
    As children of Mary
    O teach us to die!

12. And crown thy sweet mercy
    With this special grace,
    To behold in heaven
    God's ravishing Face.

13. To God be all glory
    And worship for aye,
    To God's Virgin Mother
    An endless Ave.

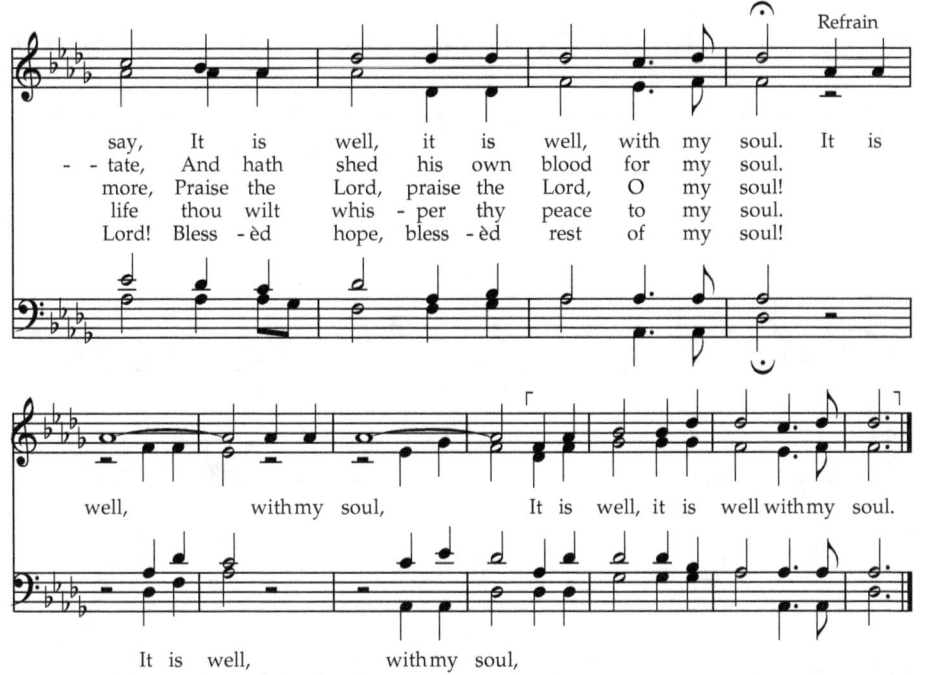

6. And Lord, haste the day when my faith shall be sight,
   The clouds be rolled back as a scroll;
   The trump shall resound, and the Lord shall descend,
   Even so, it is well with my soul.

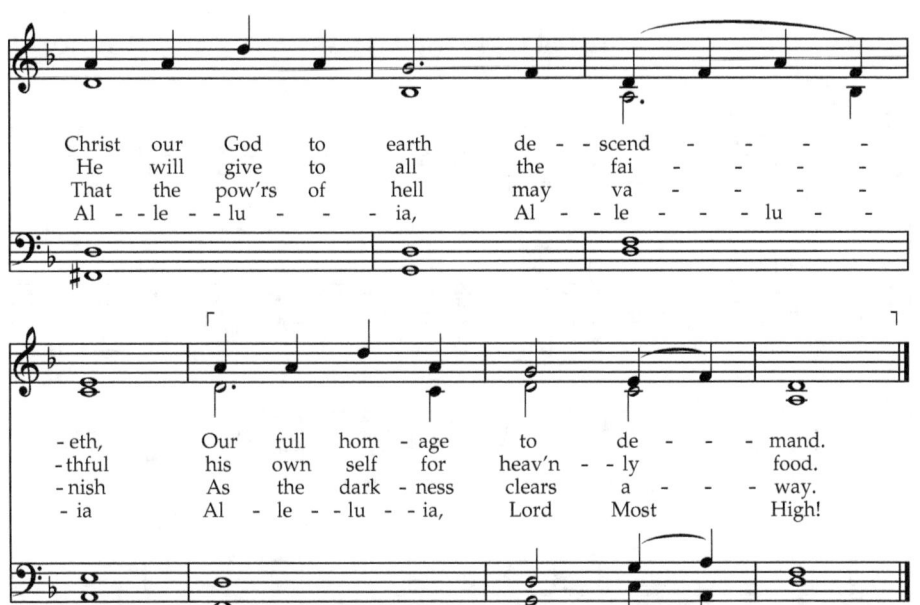

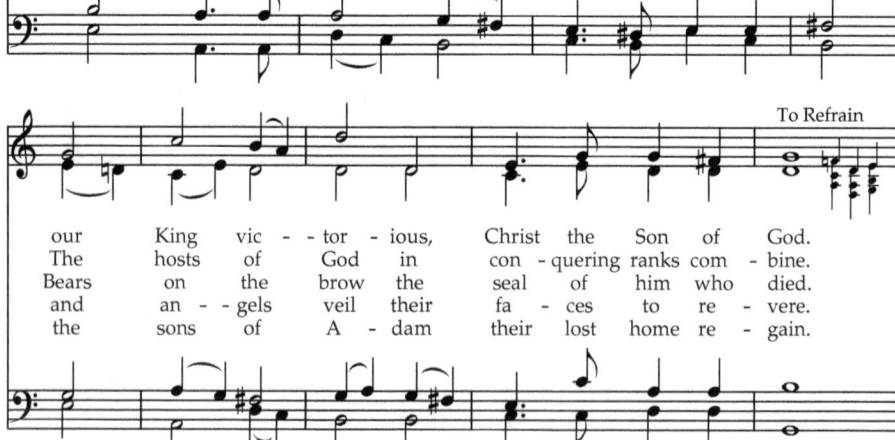

6. From north and south, from east and west they raise
   in growing unison their songs of praise. (Refrain)

7. O Lord, once lifted on the glorious tree,
   as thou hast promised, draw the world to thee. (Refrain)

8. So shall our song of triumph ever be:
   Praise to the Crucified for victory. (Refrain)

9. Let every race and every language tell
   of him who saves our souls from death and hell. (Refrain)

10. From farthest regions let their homage bring,
    and on his Cross adore their Saviour King. (Refrain)

11. Set up thy throne, that earth's despair may cease
    beneath the shadow of its healing peace. (Refrain)

12. For thy blest Cross which doth for all atone
    creation's praises rise before thy throne. (Refrain)

6. Thy truth thou wilt preserve, O Lord, From this vile generation;
Make us to lean upon thy word, With calm anticipation.
The wicked walk on every side When, 'mid thy flock, the vile abide
In pow'r and exaltation.

24 — Our God, Our Help in Ages Past — General

6. The busy tribes of flesh and blood,
With all their lives and cares,
Are carried downwards by the flood,
And lost in following years.

7. Time, like an ever rolling stream,
Bears all its sons away;
They fly, forgotten, as a dream
Dies at the opening day.

8. Like flowery fields the nations stand
Pleased with the morning light;
The flowers beneath the mower's hand
Lie withering ere 'tis night.

9. Our God, our help in ages past,
Our hope for years to come,
Be thou our guard while troubles last,
And our eternal home.

26   Praise God from Whom   General

6. Praise to the Lord, who, when darkness of sin is abounding,
   Who, when the godless do triumph, all virtue confounding,
   Sheddeth his light, chaseth the horrors of night,
   Saints with his mercy surrounding.

7. Praise to the Lord, O let all that is in me adore him!
   All that hath life and breath, come now with praises before him.
   Let the Amen sound from his people again,
   Gladly for aye we adore him.

29. That Men a Godly Life Might Live — General

6. Kill thou not out of evil will,
   Nor hate, nor render ill for ill;
   Be patient and of gentle mood,
   And to thy foe do thou good.

7. Be faithful to thy marriage vows,
   Thy heart give only to thy spouse
   Keep thy life pure, and lest thou sin
   Keep thyself with discipline.

8. Steal not; oppressive acts abhor;
   Nor wring their life-blood from the poor;
   But open wide thy loving hand
   To all the poor in the land.

9. Bear not false witness, nor belie
   Thy neighbor by foul calumny;
   Defend his innocence from blame,
   With charity hide his shame.

10. Thy neighbor's wife desire thou not,
    His house, nor aught that he hath got
    But wish that his such good may be
    As thy heart doth wish for thee.

11. God these commandments gave, therein
    To show thee, son of man, thy sin,
    And make thee also well perceive
    How man for God ought to live.

12. Help us, Lord Jesus Christ, for we
    A Mediator have in thee;
    Without thy help our works so vain
    Merit naught but endless pain.

6. Yet she on earth hath union
With God the Three in One,
And mystic sweet communion
With those whose rest is won,
With all her sons and daughters
Who, by the Master's hand
Led through the deathly waters,
Repose in Eden land.

7. O happy ones and holy!
Lord, give us grace that we
Like them, the meek and lowly,
On high may dwell with thee:
There, past the border mountains,
Where in sweet vales the Bride
With thee by living fountains
Forever shall abide!

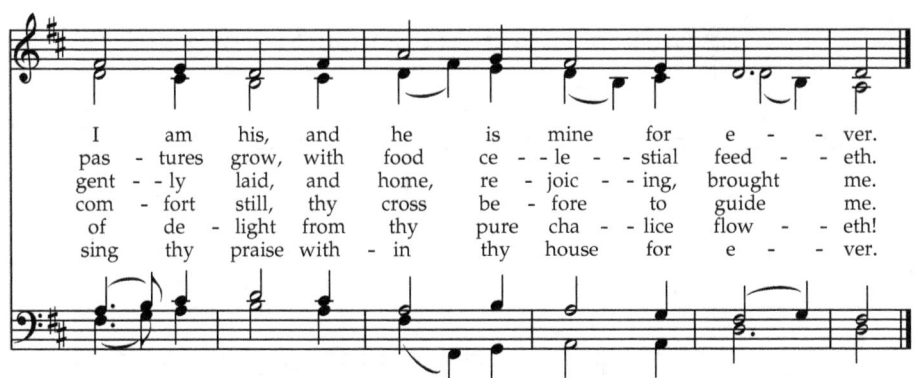

6. Who shall to Israel's outcast race From Zion bring salvation?
God will himself at length show grace, And loose the captive nation;
That will he do by Christ their King; Let Jacob then be
glad and sing, And Israel be joyful.

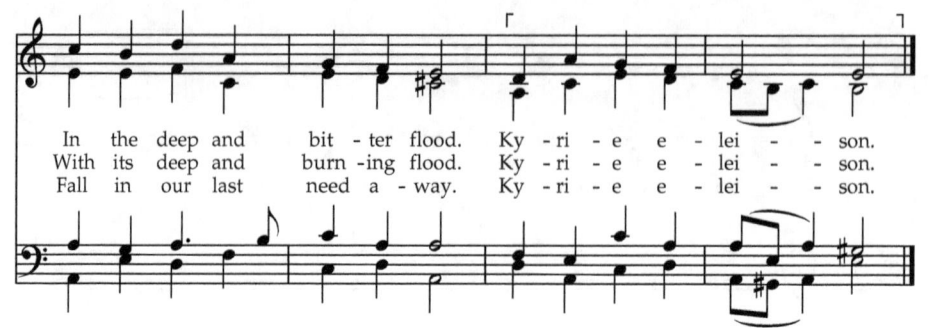

6. He who Jesus' mercy knows, Is from wrath and envy freed;
Love unto our neighbor shows That we are his flock indeed;
Thus we may in all our ways Show forth our Redeemer's praise.

37 — O Come, O Come, Emmanuel — Advent

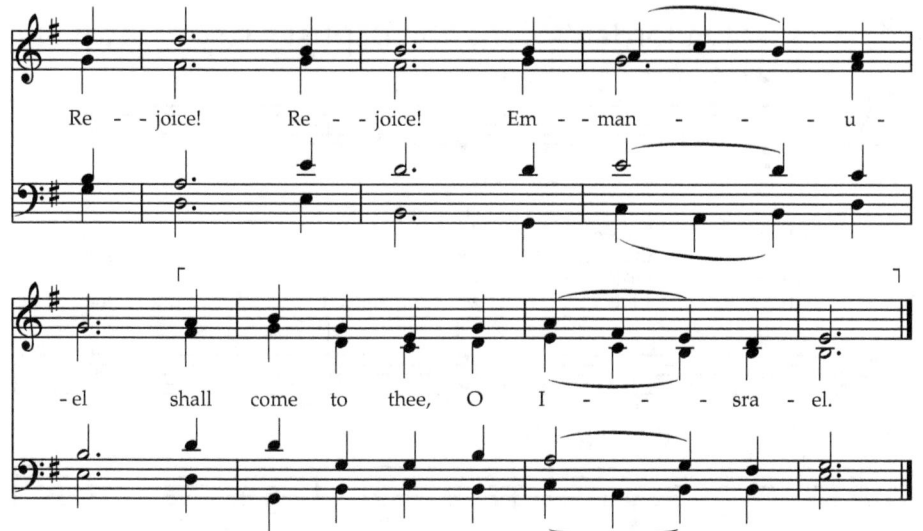

4. O come, thou Rod of Jesse, free
   Thine own from Satan's tyranny;
   From depths of hell thy people save,
   And give them victory o er the grave.

5. O come, thou Key of David, come,
   And open wide our heav'nly home;
   Make sure the way that leads on high,
   And close the path to misery.

6. O come, thou Day-spring, come and cheer
   Our spirits by thine advent here;
   Disperse the gloomy clouds of night,
   And death's dark shadows put to flight.

7. O come, thou King of nations, bind
   All peoples in one heart and mind;
   Bid envy, strife, and quarrels cease;
   Fill the whole world with heaven's peace.

8. O pure Virgin of Virgins meek
   Who humbly asks, O how shall this be?
   And angels ask, Quae Ista Est?
   The Mother of Salvation Best!

6. Brightly doth thy manger shine,
   Glorious is its light divine.
   Let not sin o'ercloud this light;
   Ever be our faith thus bright.

7. Praise to God the Father sing,
   Praise to God the Son, our King,
   Praise to God the Spirit be
   Ever and eternally.

All Praise to Jesus' Hallowed Name — Christmas

6. He came to earth so mean and poor, Man to pity and restore,
   And make us rich in heaven above, Equal with angels through his love.

7. All this he did to show his grace To our poor and sinful race;
   For this let Christendom adore And praise his name for evermore.

44. God Rest Ye Merry Gentlemen

Christmas

♩ = 160

1. God rest ye merry, gentlemen, let nothing you dismay,
   Remember Christ our Savior was born on Christmas Day;
2. In Bethlehem, in Israel, this blessèd Babe was born,
   And laid within a manger upon this blessèd morn;
3. From God our heav'nly Father a blessèd angel came;
   And unto certain shepherds brought tidings of the same;
4. "Fear not, then," said the angel, "Let nothing you affright,
   This day is born a Savior of a pure Virgin bright,
5. The shepherds at those tidings rejoicèd much in mind,
   And left their flocks a-feeding in tempest, storm and wind,

6. But when to Bethlehem they came
  where our dear Saviour lay,
  They found him in a manger
  where oxen feed on hay;
  His mother Mary kneeling
  unto the Lord did pray.

7. Now to the Lord sing praises
  all you within this place,
  And with true love and brotherhood
  each other now embrace;
  This holy tide of Christmas
  all others doth deface.

8. God bless the ruler of this house,
  and send him long to reign,
  And many a merry Christmas
  may live to see again;
  Among your friends and kindred
  that live both far and near
  That God send you a happy new year,
  happy new year,
  And God send you a happy new year.

In the Bleak Mid-Winter

Christmas

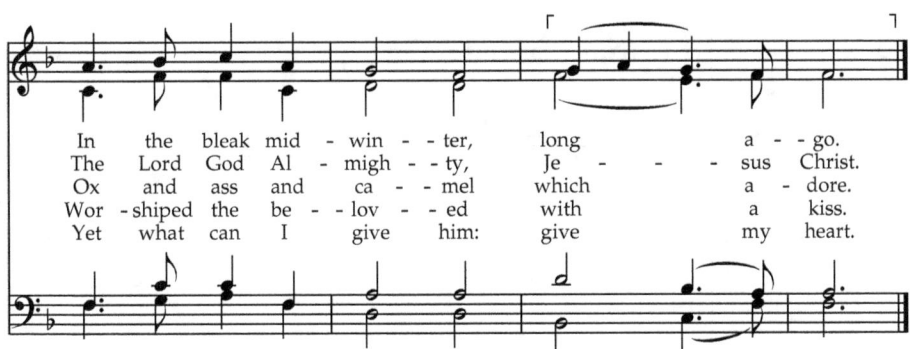

48   It Came upon a Midnight Clear   Christmas

♩ = 60

1. It came upon the midnight clear, That glorious song of old, From angels bending near the earth, To touch their harps of gold;
2. Still through the cloven skies they come With peaceful wings unfurled, And still their heavenly music floats O'er all the weary world;
3. Yet with the woes of sin and strife The world has suffered long; Beneath the angel strain have rolled Two thousand years of wrong;
4. And ye, beneath life's crushing load, Whose forms are bending low, Who toil along the climbing way With painful steps and slow,
5. For lo! the days are hast'ning on, By prophet bards foretold, When with the ever circling years Comes round the age of gold;

6. Child, for us sinners poor and in the manger,
   We would embrace thee, with love and awe;
   Who would not love thee, loving us so dearly?

7. Yea, Lord, we greet thee, born this happy morning;
   Jesus, to thee be glory given;
   Word of the Father, now in flesh appearing.

8. Adeste, fideles, laeti triumphantes;
   Venite, venite in Bethlehem.
   Natum videte Regem angelorum.
   Venite adoremus, venite adoremus,
   Venite adoremus, Dominum.

6. Ye shall and must at last prevail;
   God's own ye are, ye cannot fail.
   To God forever sing your praise
   With joy and patience all your days.

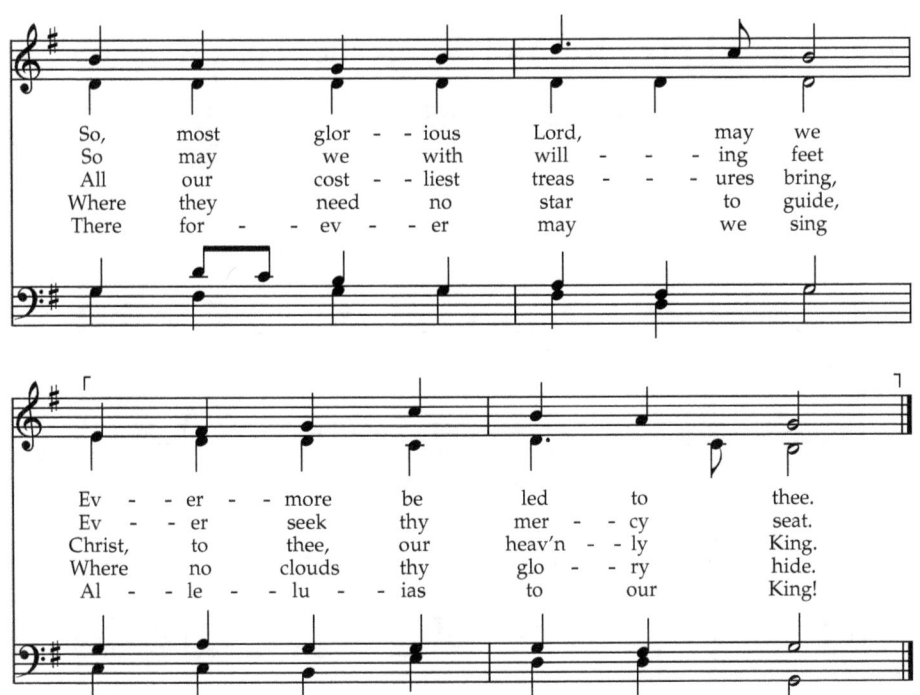

57. Brightest and Best of the Sons — Epiphany

1. Brightest and best of the sons of the morning,
   Dawn on our darkness, and lend us thine aid;
   Star of the east, the horizon adorning,
   Guide where our infant Redeemer is laid.

2. Cold on his cradle the dew-drops are shining,
   Low lies his head with the beasts of the stall;
   Angels adore him in slumber reclining,
   Maker and Monarch and Saviour of all.

3. Shall we then yield him, in costly devotion,
   Odours of Edom, and off'rings divine,
   Gems of the mountain, and pearls of the ocean,
   Myrrh from the forest, and gold from the mine?

4. Vainly we offer each ample oblation,
   Vainly with gifts would his favour secure;
   Richer by far is the heart's adoration,
   Dearer to God are the prayers of the poor.

5. Brightest and best of the sons of the morning,
   Dawn on our darkness, and lend us thine aid;
   Star of the east, the horizon adorning,
   Guide where our infant Redeemer is laid.

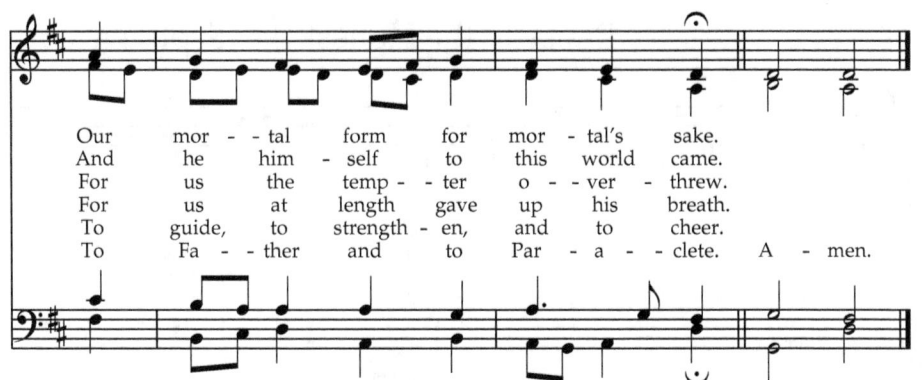

62 Praise to the Holiest — Septuagesima

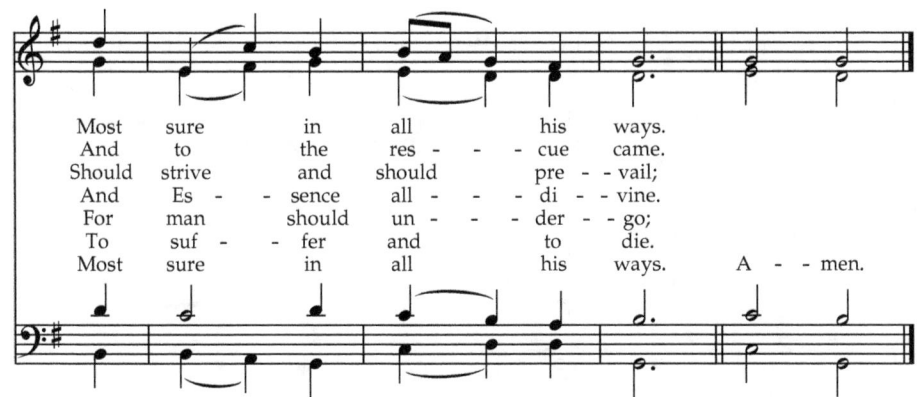

5. The Saviour lends the light and heat
   That crowns his holy hill;
   The Saints, like stars, around his seat
   Perform their courses still.

6. The Saints above are stars in heaven
   What are the saints on earth?
   Like trees they stand whom God has giv'n,
   Our Eden's happy birth.

7. Faith is their fixed unswerving root,
   Hope their unfading flower,
   Fair deeds of charity their fruit,
   The glory of their bower.

8. One name, above all glorious names,
   With its ten thousand tongues
   The everlasting sea proclaims,
   Echoing angelic songs.

9. The raging fire, the roaring wind,
   Thy boundless power display;
   But in the gentler breeze we find
   Thy Spirit's viewless way.

10. The raging fire, the roaring wind,
    Thy boundless power display;
    But in the gentler breeze we find
    Thy Spirit's viewless way.

11. Two worlds are ours: 'tis only sin
    Forbids us to descry
    The mystic heaven and earth within,
    Plain as the sea and sky.

12. Thou, who hast given me eyes to see
    And love this sight so fair,
    Give me a heart to find out thee,
    And read thee everywhere. Amen.

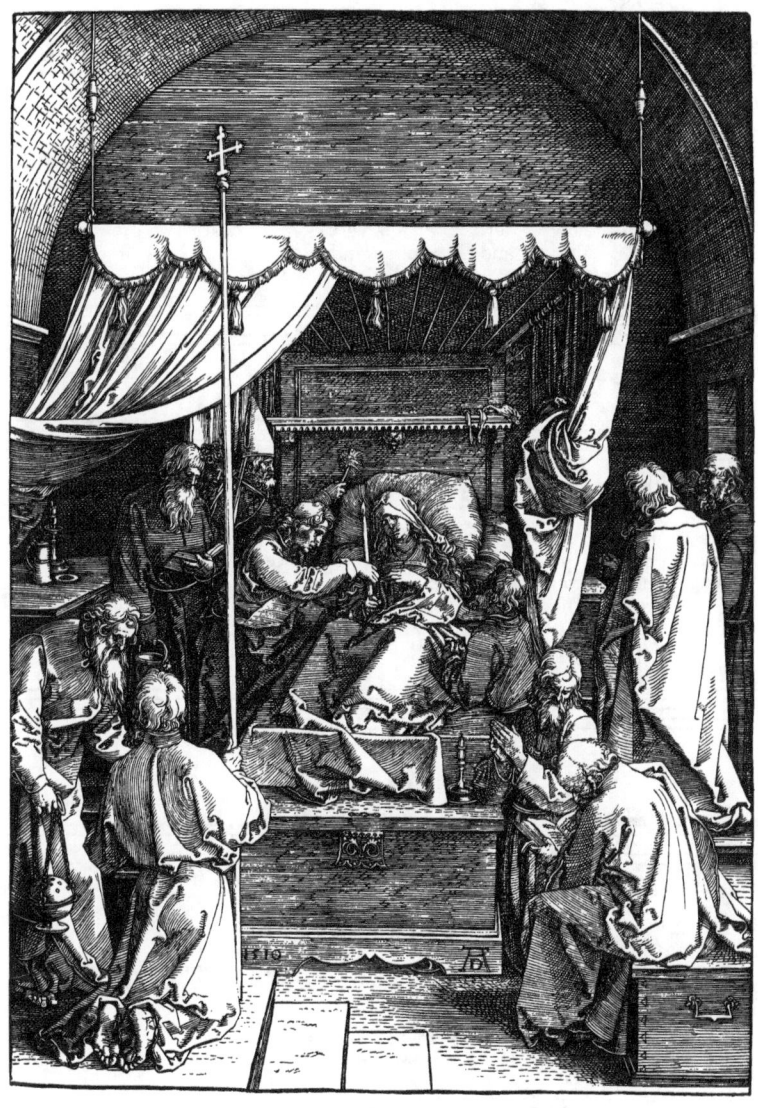

66 — O Jesu Christ From Thee Began — Lent

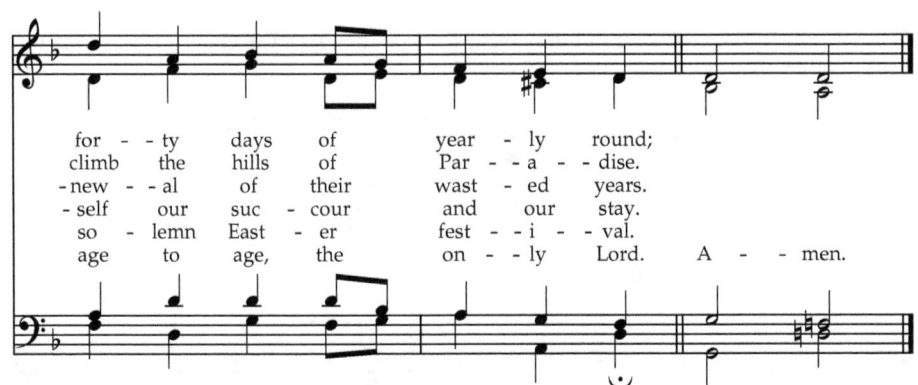

6. What language shall I borrow to thank thee, dearest friend,
For this thy dying sorrow, thy pity without end?
O make me thine forever, and should I fainting be,
Lord, let me never, never outlive my love to thee.

7. My Shepherd, now receive me; my Guardian, own me thine.
   Great blessings thou didst give me, O source of gifts divine.
   Thy lips have often fed me with words of truth and love;
   Thy Spirit oft hath led me to heavenly joys above.

8. Here I will stand beside thee, from thee I will not part;
   O Saviour, do not chide me! When breaks thy loving heart,
   When soul and body languish in death's cold, cruel grasp,
   Then, in thy deepest anguish, thee in mine arms I'll clasp.

9. The joy can never be spoken, above all joys beside,
   When in thy body broken I thus with safety hide.
   O Lord of Life, desiring thy glory now to see,
   Beside thy cross expiring, I'd breathe my soul to thee.

10. My Saviour, be thou near me when death is at my door;
    Then let thy presence cheer me, forsake me nevermore!
    When soul and body languish, oh, leave me not alone,
    But take away mine anguish by virtue of thine own!

11. Be thou my consolation, my shield when I must die;
    Remind me of thy passion when my last hour draws nigh.
    Mine eyes shall then behold thee, upon thy cross shall dwell,
    My heart by faith enfolds thee. Who dieth thus dies well.

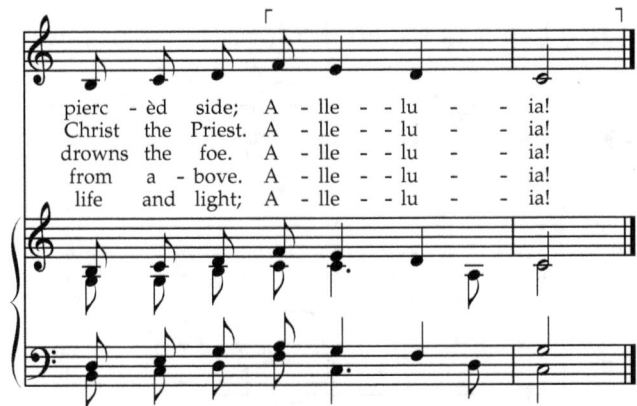

6. Now no more can death appall,
   Now no more the grave enthrall;
   Thou hast opened Paradise,
   And in thee thy saints shall rise.

7. Paschal triumph, Easter joy,
   This alone can sin destroy;
   From sin's death do thou set free
   Souls reborn, O Lord, in thee.

8. Hymns of glory and of praise,
   Father, to thee we raise;
   Risen Lord, all praise to thee,
   Ever with the Spirit be.

6. Hail, the Lord of earth and Heaven, Alleluia!
   Praise to thee by both be given, Alleluia!
   Thee we greet triumphant now, Alleluia!
   Hail, the resurrection, thou, Alleluia!

7. King of glory, Soul of bliss, Alleluia!
   Everlasting life is this, Alleluia!
   Thee to know, thy power to prove, Alleluia!
   Thus to sing and thus to love, Alleluia!

8. Hymns of praise then let us sing, Alleluia!
   Unto Christ, our heavenly King, Alleluia!
   Who endured the cross and grave, Alleluia!
   Sinners to redeem and save. Alleluia!

9. But the pains that he endured, Alleluia!
   Our salvation have procured, Alleluia!
   Now above the sky he's King, Alleluia!
   Where the angels ever sing. Alleluia!

10. Jesus Christ is risen today, Alleluia!
    Our triumphant holy day, Alleluia!
    Who did once upon the cross, Alleluia!
    Suffer to redeem our loss. Alleluia!

Hail Thee, Festival Day — Ascensiontide

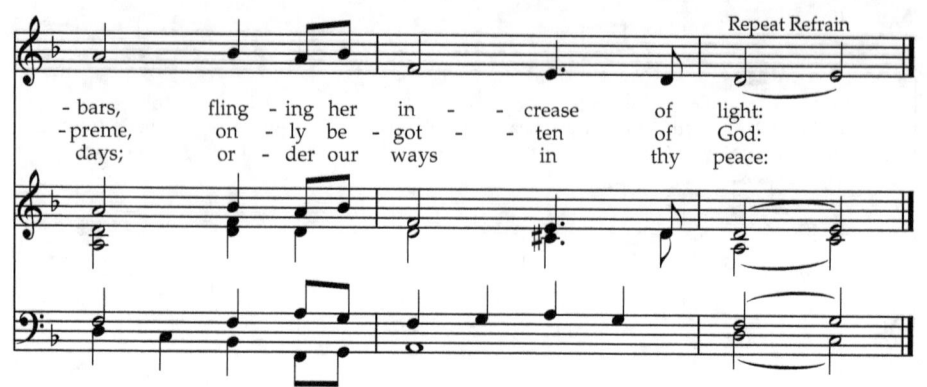

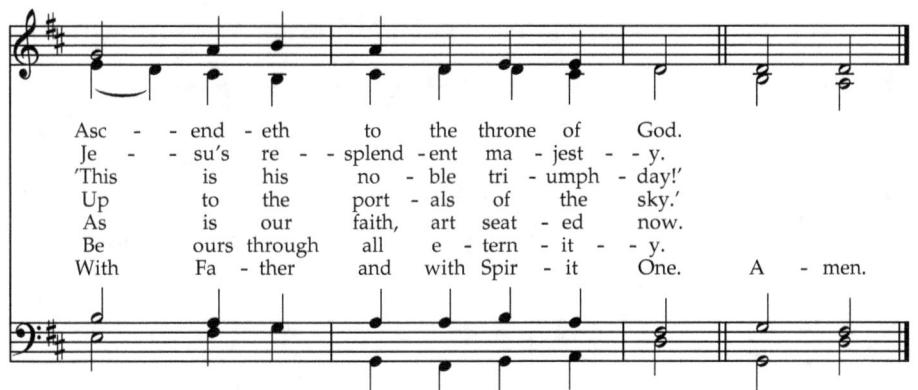

77. Let the Holy Spirit's Grace — Whitsuntide

1. Let the Ho-ly Spir-it's grace, On our souls de-scending, Guide us on our journey through, Cheer us at its ending: He that brooded o'er the deep, He whose op-er-ation In the Virgin's holy womb Wrought the Incarnation.

2. Thus God's truth can never fail, Nor his promise vary; And Incarnate was the Son, Of the Virgin Mary, Laboured, suffered, on the Cross All his Passion ended, Died, was buried, rose again, And to heav'n ascended.

3. Yet he would not leave the Twelve Orphans in their sadness; But he sent the Holy Ghost Bringing joy and gladness;

6. Against the demon snares of sin,
   The vice that gives temptation force,
   The natural lusts that war within,
   The hostile men that mar my course;
   Or few or many, far or nigh,
   In every place and in all hours,
   Against their fierce hostility
   I bind to me these holy powers.

7. Against all Satan's spells and wiles,
   Against false words of heresy,
   Against the knowledge that defiles,
   Against the heart's idolatry,
   Against the wizard's evil craft,
   Against the death wound and the burning,
   The choking wave, the poisoned shaft,
   Protect me, Christ, till thy returning.

8. Christ be with me, Christ within me,
   Christ behind me, Christ before me,
   Christ beside me, Christ to win me,
   Christ to comfort and restore me.
   Christ beneath me, Christ above me,
   Christ in quiet, Christ in danger,
   Christ in hearts of all that love me,
   Christ in mouth of friend and stranger.

9. I bind unto myself the Name,
   The strong Name of the Trinity,
   By invocation of the same,
   The Three in One and One in Three.
   By whom all nature hath creation,
   Eternal Father, Spirit, Word:
   Praise to the Lord of my salvation,
   Salvation is of Christ the Lord.

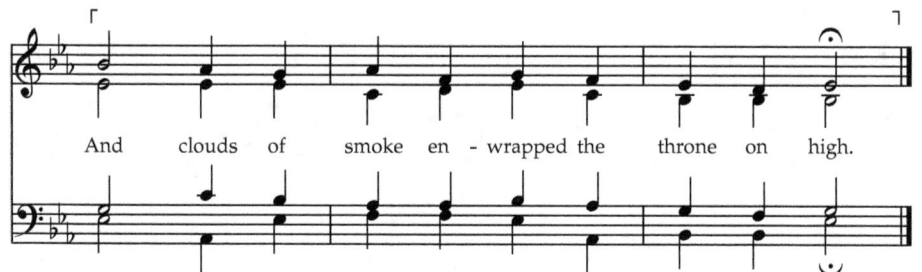

6. O Father, with th'Eternal Son,
   and Holy Spirit, ever One,
   Vouchsafe to bring us by thy grace
   to see thy glory face to face.

Transfiguration — Tis Good Lord

Propers
of the
Church Year

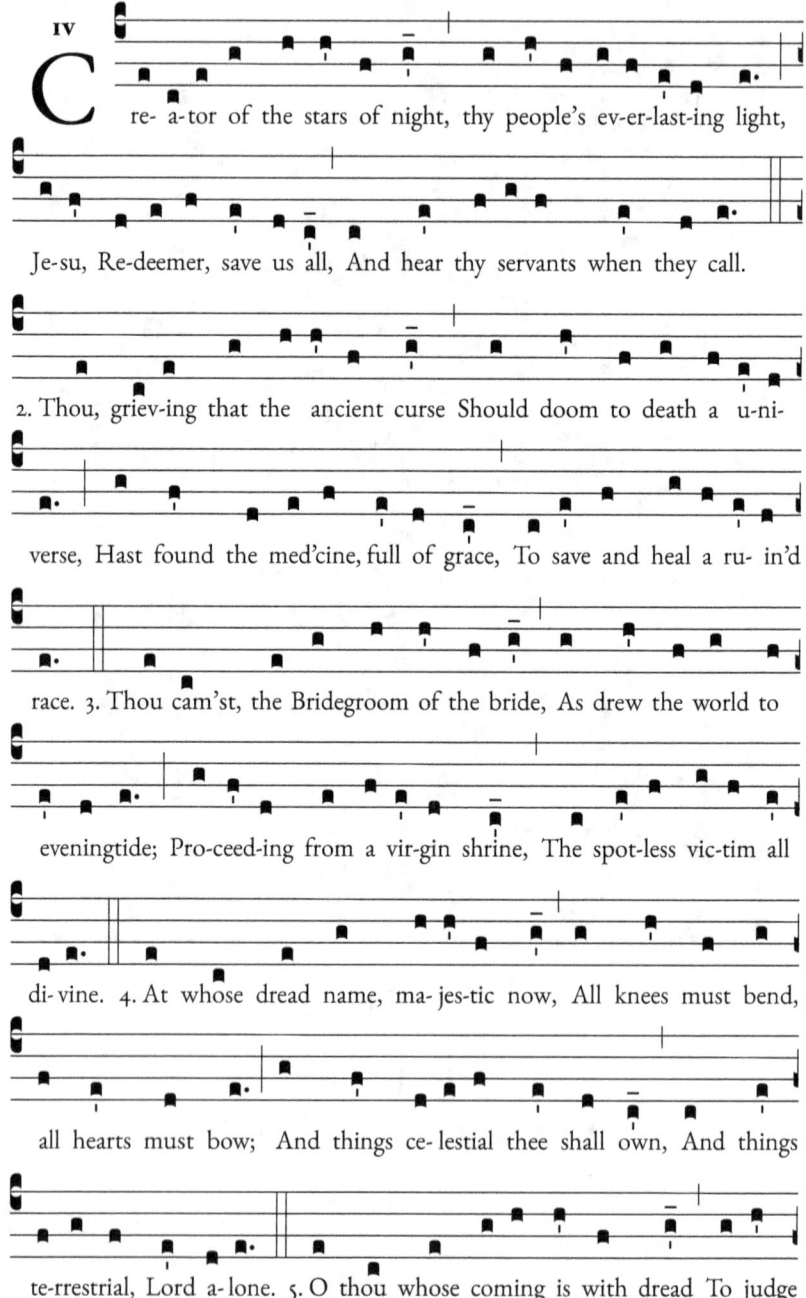

Proper of Season — Advent I

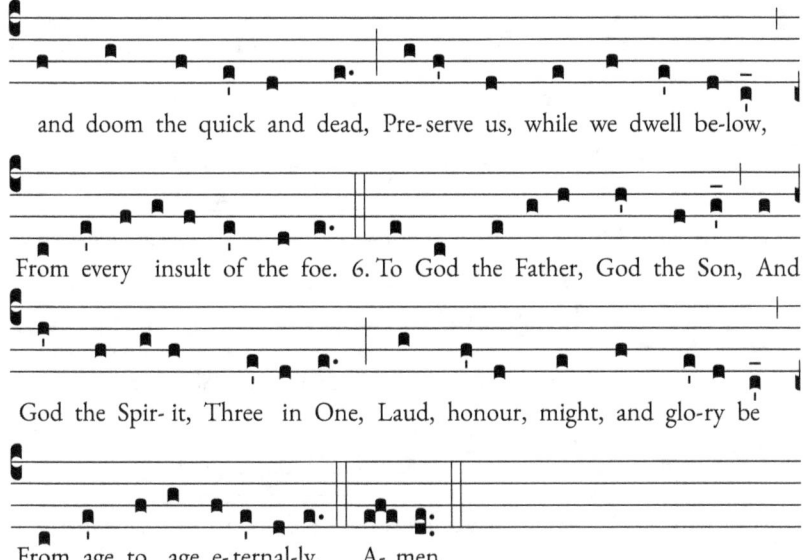

and doom the quick and dead, Pre-serve us, while we dwell be-low, From every insult of the foe. 6. To God the Father, God the Son, And God the Spir-it, Three in One, Laud, honour, might, and glo-ry be From age to age e-ternal-ly. A-men.

℣. Drop down, ye heavens, from above, and let the skies pour down righteousness.

℟. Let the earth open, and let them bring forth salvation.

Mag. Ant. Behold, the Name of the Lord † cometh from afar: and his glory filleth all the earth.

Mattins

Invitatory Hymn

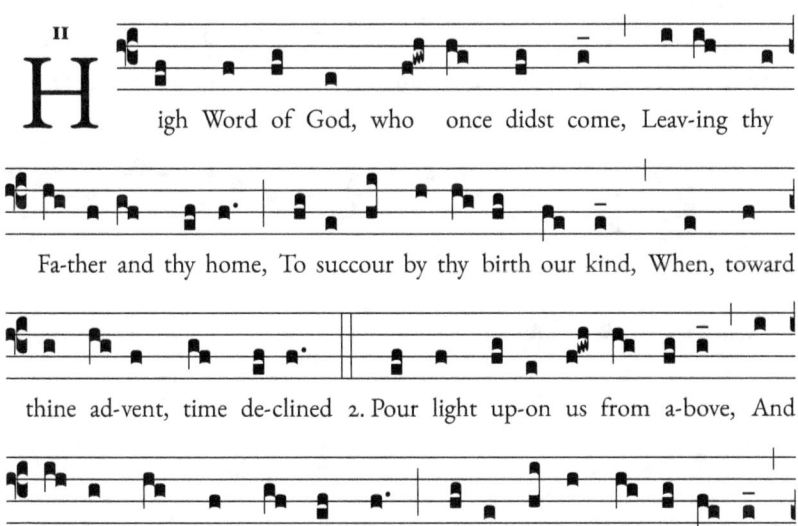

High Word of God, who once didst come, Leav-ing thy Fa-ther and thy home, To succour by thy birth our kind, When, toward thine ad-vent, time de-clined 2. Pour light up-on us from a-bove, And fire our hearts with thy strong love, That, as we hear thy Gos-pel read,

Proper of Season — Advent I

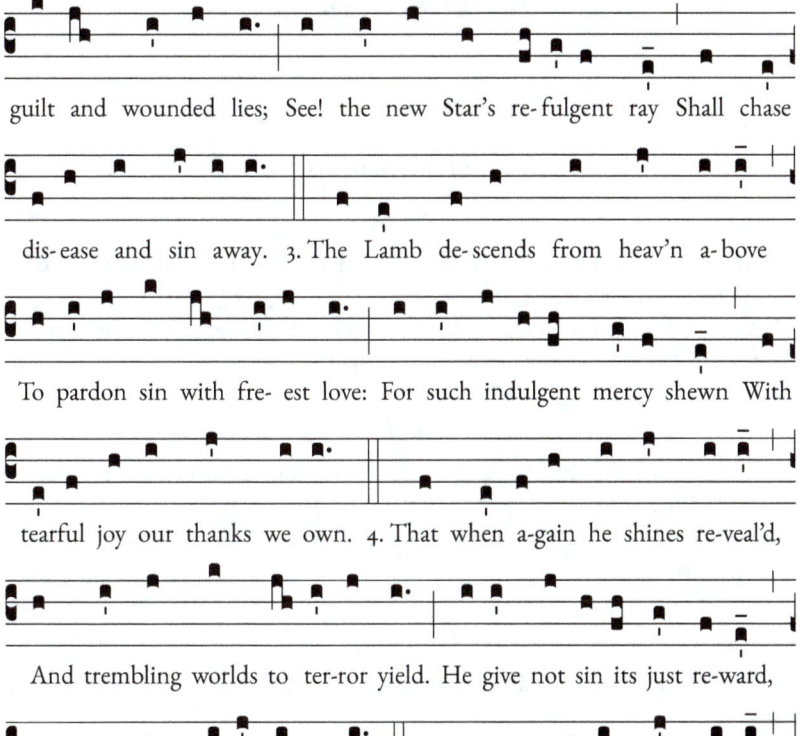

guilt and wounded lies; See! the new Star's re-fulgent ray Shall chase dis-ease and sin away. 3. The Lamb de-scends from heav'n a-bove To pardon sin with fre- est love: For such indulgent mercy shewn With tearful joy our thanks we own. 4. That when a-gain he shines re-veal'd, And trembling worlds to ter-ror yield. He give not sin its just re-ward, But in his love pro-tect and guard. 5. To God the Father, God the Son, And God the Spir-it, Three in One, Laud, honour, might, and glo-ry

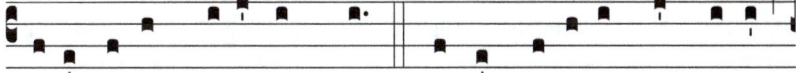

be From age to age e-ternal-ly. A-men

℣. The voice of one crying in the wilderness, Prepare ye the way of the Lord.

℟. Make his paths straight.

Ben. Ant. The Holy Ghost † shall come upon thee, Mary; fear not, thou shalt bear in thy womb the Son of God, alleluia.

II Evensong

¶ II Evensong as in I Evensong, except for the following Antiphon.

Mag. Ant. Fear not, Mary, † for thou hast found favour with the Lord: behold, thou shalt conceive, and bring forth a Son, alleluia.

Advent I Week   # Proper of Season

Advent Ferial Office

¶ On Advent Ferias, the Invitatory Hymn is of the First Sunday of Advent. The Office Hymn and Versicle is taken from Sunday (p. 32). The Antiphon is of the Day.

The First Week of Advent

Monday

Ben. Ant. The Angel of the Lord † announced unto Mary, and she conceived by the Holy Ghost, alleluia.
Mag. Ant. Lift up thine eyes, † O Jerusalem, and see the power of the King: behold, the Saviour cometh to loose thee from thy chain.

Tuesday

Ben. Ant. Before they came together † Mary was found with child of the Holy Ghost, alleluia.
Mag. Ant. Seek ye the Lord † while he may be found: call ye upon him while he is near, alleluia.

Wednesday

Ben. Ant. Out of Sion † shall go forth the law, and the word of the Lord from Jerusalem.
Mag. Ant. After me † cometh one mightier than I, the latchet of whose shoes I am not worthy to unloose.

Thursday

Ben. Ant. Blessed art thou † among women, and blessed is the fruit of thy womb.
Mag. Ant. I will wait † upon the Lord my Saviour: and I will look for him while he is near, alleluia.

Friday

Ben. Ant. Lo, there cometh one † that is both God and Man, of the house of David, to sit upon the throne, alleluia.
Mag. Ant. Out of Egypt † have I called my Son: he shall come to save his people.

Saturday

Ben. Ant. Fear not, † O Sion, behold thy God cometh, alleluia.

Proper of Season

Advent II Week

Second Sunday of Advent

❡ The Hymns & Versicles are of the First Sunday of Advent (p. 308), with the following Antiphons.

Mag. Ant. Come, O Lord, in peace; † visit us with thy salvation, that we may rejoice before thee with a perfect heart.

Ben. Ant. He shall sit upon the throne † of David, and of his kingdom there shall be no end, alleluia.

Mag. Ant. Blessed art thou, † O Mary, for thou hast believed the Lord: and there shall be a performance in thee of those things which were told thee from the Lord, alleluia.

The Second Week of Advent

Monday

Ben. Ant. From heaven there cometh † the Lord, the Ruler, and in his hand are honour and dominion.

Mag. Ant. Behold the King shall come, † the Lord of the earth, and he shall take away the yoke of our captivity.

Tuesday

Ben. Ant. The Lord shall arise upon thee, † O Jerusalem, and his glory shall be seen upon thee.

Mag. Ant. The voice of one crying † in the wilderness, Prepare ye the way of the Lord, make straight in the desert a highway for our God.

Wednesday

Ben. Ant. Behold I send my messenger, † and he shall prepare my way before thy face.

Mag. Ant. Sion, † thou shalt be renewed, and shalt see thy righteous One, he that cometh unto thee.

Thursday

Ben. Ant. Thou, O Lord, † art he that is to come, for whom we look, to save thy people.

Mag. Ant. He that cometh after me † is preferred before me, the latchet of whose shoes I am not worthy to unloose.

Friday

Ben. Ant. Say to them: † Ye that are of a fearful heart, be strong: for behold the Lord our God shall come.

Mag. Ant. Sing unto the Lord † a new song; and his praise from the end of the earth.

Advent Antiphons # Proper of Season

Saturday

Ben. Ant. The Lord shall set up an ensign † for the nations, and shall assemble the outcasts of Israel.

Magnificat Antiphons before Christmas

¶ The Magnificat Antiphon is always taken from here on these days.

16 December: O Sapientia

WISDOM, † which camest out of the mouth of the Most High, and reachest from one end to another, mightily and sweetly ordering all things: Come and teach us the way of prudence.

17 December: O Adonai

ADONAI, † and Leader of the house of Israel, who appearedst in the bush to Moses in a flame of fire, and gavest him the law in Sinai: Come and redeem us with an outstretched arm.

18 December: O Radix Jesse

ROOT OF JESSE, † which standest for an ensign of the people, at whom kings shall shut their mouths, unto whom the Gentiles shall seek: Come and deliver us, and tarry not.

19 December: O Clavis David

KEY OF DAVID, † and Sceptre of the house of Israel; that openest and no man shutteth, and shuttest and no man openeth: Come, and bring the prisoners out of the prison-house, them that sit in darkness and the shadow of death.

20 December: O Oriens

DAY-SPRING, † Brightness of the Light everlasting, and Sun of righteousness: Come and enlighten them that sit in darkness and the shadow of death.

21 December: O Rex gentium

KING OF NATIONS, † and their Desire; the Cornerstone, who makest both one: Come and save mankind, whom thou formedst of clay.

Proper of Season *Advent III Week*

22 December: O Emmanuel

EMMANUEL, † our King and Lawgiver, the Desire of all nations and their Salvation: Come and save us, O Lord our God.

23 December: O Virgo virginum

VIRGIN OF VIRGINS, † how shall this be? for neither before thee was any seen like thee, nor shall there be after. Daughters of Jerusalem, why marvel ye at me? The thing which ye behold is a divine mystery.

THIRD SUNDAY OF ADVENT

¶ The Hymns & Versicles are of the First Sunday of Advent (p. 308), with the following Antiphons.

Mag. Ant. Before me † there was no God formed, neither shall there be after me: unto me every knee shall bow, and me shall every tongue confess.
Ben. Ant. Now when John had heard † in the prison the works of Christ, he sent two of his disciples, and said unto him: Art thou he that should come, or do we look for another?
Mag. Ant. Art thou he † that should come, or do we look for another? Go and shew John those things which ye do see: the blind receive their sight, the dead are raised, and the poor have the gospel preached unto them, alleluia.

THE THIRD WEEK OF ADVENT

Monday

Ben. Ant. There shall come forth † a rod out of the stem of Jesse, and all the earth shall be filled with the glory of the Lord: and all flesh shall see the salvation of God.
Mag. Ant. All generations † shall call me blessed: for God hath regarded the lowliness of his handmaiden.

Tuesday

Ben. Ant. Thou, Bethlehem, † in the land of Juda, shalt not be the least: for out of thee shall come a Governor, that shall rule my people Israel.
Mag. Ant. Awake, awake, † arise, O Jerusalem: loose thyself from the bands of thy neck, O captive daughter of Sion.

Ember Wednesday

Ben. Ant. The Angel † Gabriel was sent to Mary, a Virgin espoused to Joseph.
Mag. Ant. Behold the handmaid of the Lord; † be it unto me according to thy word.

Advent IV Week   **Proper of Season**

Thursday

Ben. Ant. Be ye watchful † in your hearts, for the Lord our God is nigh at hand.
Mag. Ant. Rejoice ye † with Jerusalem; and be glad with her, all ye that love her, forever.

Ember Friday

Ben. Ant. For lo, as soon † as the voice of thy salutation sounded in mine ears, the babe leaped in my womb for joy, alleluia.
Mag. Ant. This is the witness † which John bare, saying: He that cometh after me is preferred before me.

Ember Saturday

Ben. Ant. How shall this be, † O Angel of God, seeing I know not a man? Hearken, O Virgin Mary: the Holy Ghost shall come upon thee, and the power of the Highest shall overshadow thee.

Fourth Sunday of Advent

¶ In the Daily Office, the Hymns & Versicles are of the First Sunday of Advent (p. 308), with the following Antiphon.
Ben. Ant. Hail, Mary, † thou that art full of grace, the Lord is with thee; blessed art thou among women, alleluia.

The Fourth Week of Advent

Monday

Ben. Ant. Thus saith the Lord † your God: Repent ye, and turn again; for the kingdom of heaven is at hand, alleluia.

Tuesday

Ben. Ant. Awake, awake, † put on strength, O arm of the Lord.

Wednesday

Ben. Ant. I will place salvation † in Sion, and in Jerusalem my glory, alleluia.

Thursday

Ben. Ant. Comfort ye, † comfort ye my people, saith your God.

Friday

Ben. Ant. Behold all things are fulfilled † which were spoken by the Angel of the Virgin Mary.

Proper of Season *Christmas*

CHRISTMAS EVE

¶ In Mattins, the Hymn is of the First Sunday of Advent (p. 308), with the following.

℣. To-morrow the iniquity of the earth shall be blotted out.
℟. And the Saviour of the world shall reign over us.
Ben. Ant. The Saviour † of the world shall arise as the sun: and shall come down into the Virgin's womb, as the showers upon the grass, alleluia.

CHRISTMAS DAY

I Evensong

Je-su, the Father's on-ly Son, Whose death for all re-demption won, Be-fore the worlds, of God Most High, Be-got-ten all in- ef-fa-bly. 2. The Father's Light and Splendour thou, Their endless Hope to thee that bow: Accept the prayers and praise to-day That through the world thy servants pay. 3. Sal-va-tion's Author, call to mind Thou took'st the form of hu- mankind, When of the Vir- gin unde- fil'd Thou in man's flesh be- cam'st a Child. 4. Thus tes-ti- fies the pre- sent day

Christmas   **Proper of Season**

Through every year in long ar-ray, That thou, sal-va-tion's source a-lone, Pro-ceed-edst from the Father's Throne. 5. Whence sky, and stars, and sea's a-byss, And earth, and all that there-in is, Shall still, with laud and car-ol meet, The Author of thine Advent greet. 6. And we who, by thy pre-cious Blood From sin re-deem'd, are mark'd for God, On this, the day that saw thy Birth, Sing the new song of ransom'd earth. 7. All honour, laud, and glo-ry be, O Je-su, Vir-gin-born, to thee; All glo-ry, as is ev-er meet, To Father and to Par-a-clete. A-men.

℣. To-morrow the iniquity of the earth shall be blotted out.

℟. And the Saviour of the world shall reign over us.

Mag. Ant. When the sun hath risen † in the heavens, ye shall see the King of kings proceeding from the Father, as a bridegroom out of his chamber.

Proper of Season *Christmas*

Mattins

Invitatory Hymn

¶ The Invitatory Hymn is as in I Evensong, with the following ending.

For that thine ad-vent glo-ry be, O Je-su, Vir-gin-born, to thee; With Father, and with Hol-y Ghost, From men and from the heav'nly host. A-men.

Office Hymn

From lands that see the sun a-rise. To earth's re-mot-est bound-a-ries, The Vir-gin-born to-day we sing, The Son of Mar-y, Christ the King. 2. Blest Author of this earthly frame, To take a ser-vant's form he came, That, lib-er-at-ing flesh by flesh, Whom he had made might live a-fresh. 3. In that chaste par-ent's ho-ly womb, Ce-lestial grace hath found its home: And she, as earthly bride unknown, Yet calls

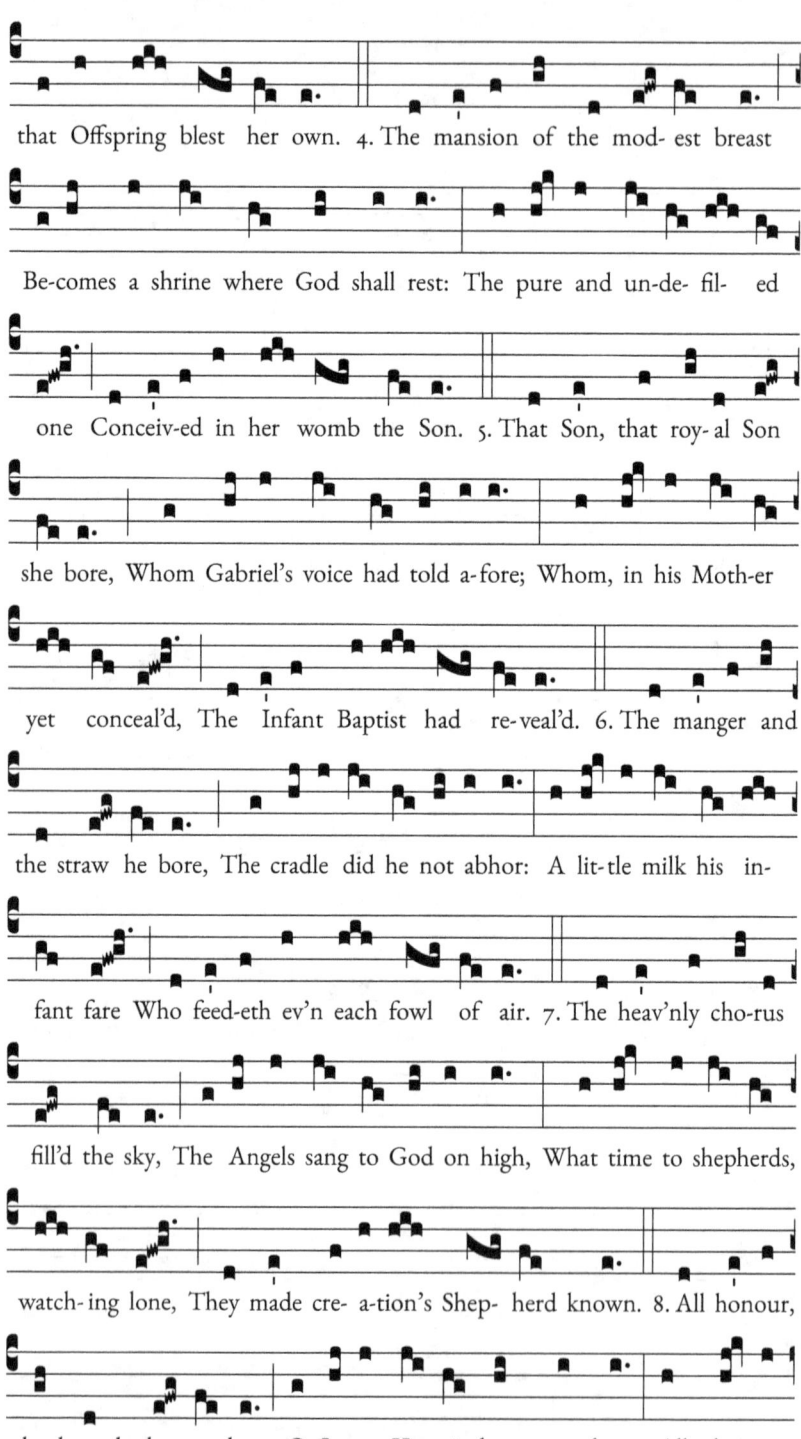

26 December   **Proper of Season**   *St. Stephen*

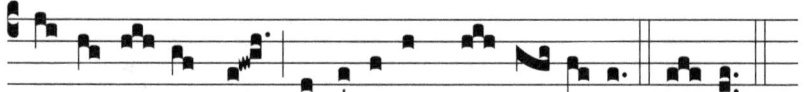

as is ev- er meet, To Father and to Par- a- clete. A- men.

℣. The Lord declared, alleluia.

℟. His salvation, alleluia.

Ben. Ant. Glory † to God in the highest, and on earth peace to men of good will, alleluia, alleluia.

II Evensong

¶ The Office Hymn is from I Evensong with the following Versicle and Antiphon.

℣. The Lord declared, alleluia.

℟. His salvation, alleluia.

Mag. Ant. To-day † the Christ is born; to-day hath a Saviour appeared: to-day on earth Angels are singing, Archangels rejoicing: today the righteous exult and say. Glory to God in the highest, alleluia.

26 December. St. Stephen

Mattins

¶ The Invitatory Hymn is from the First Common of a Martyr Bishop (p. 682).

Office Hymn

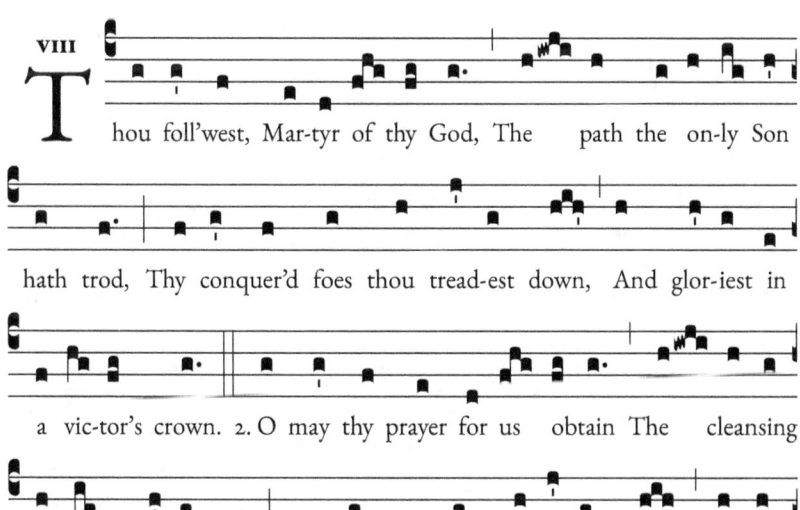

Thou foll'west, Mar-tyr of thy God, The path the on-ly Son hath trod, Thy conquer'd foes thou tread-est down, And glor-iest in a vic-tor's crown. 2. O may thy prayer for us obtain The cleansing of each guilt-y stain, Shield us from sin's contagious blight, Put life's

St. Stephen — Proper of Season — 26 December

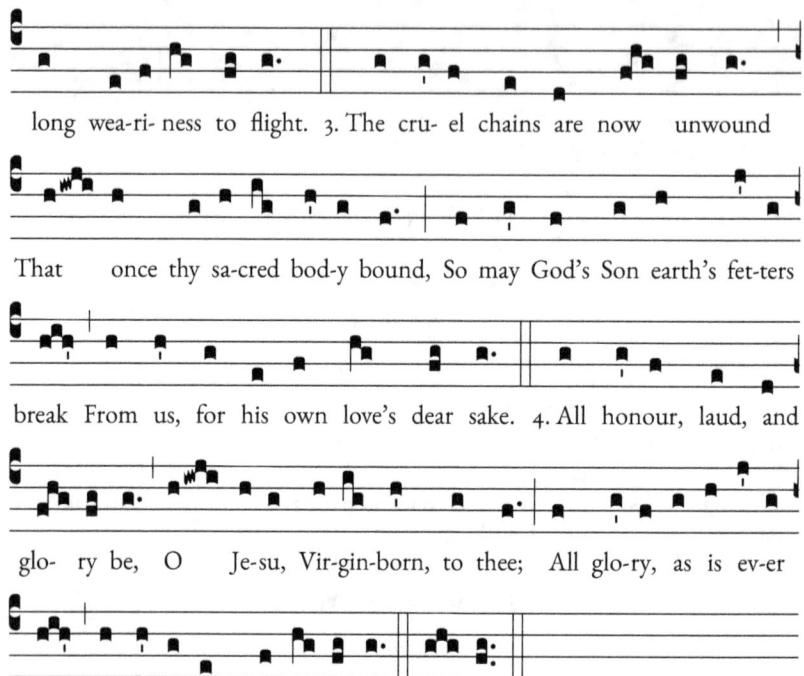

long wea-ri-ness to flight. 3. The cru-el chains are now unwound That once thy sa-cred bod-y bound, So may God's Son earth's fet-ters break From us, for his own love's dear sake. 4. All honour, laud, and glo-ry be, O Je-su, Vir-gin-born, to thee; All glo-ry, as is ev-er meet, To Father and to Par-a-clete. A-men.

℣. Devout men carried Stephen to his burial.
℟. And made great lamentation over him.

Ben. Ant. And Stephen, † full of faith and power, did great wonders and miracles among the people.

Evensong

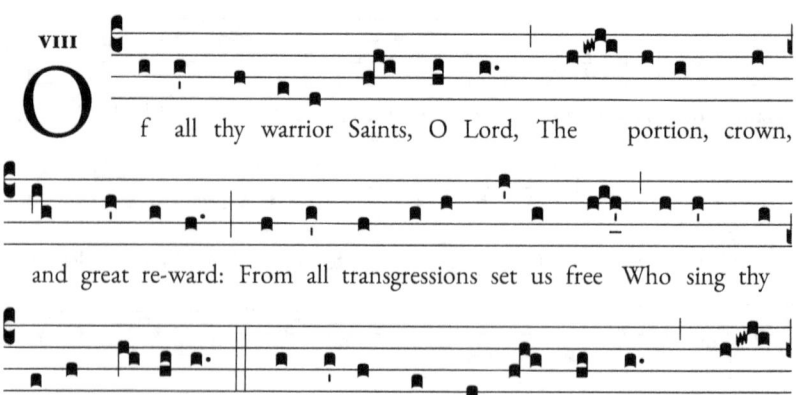

Of all thy warrior Saints, O Lord, The portion, crown, and great re-ward: From all transgressions set us free Who sing thy Mar-tyr's vic-to-ry. 2. The pleas-ures of the world he spurn'd. From

26 December — Proper of Season — St. Stephen

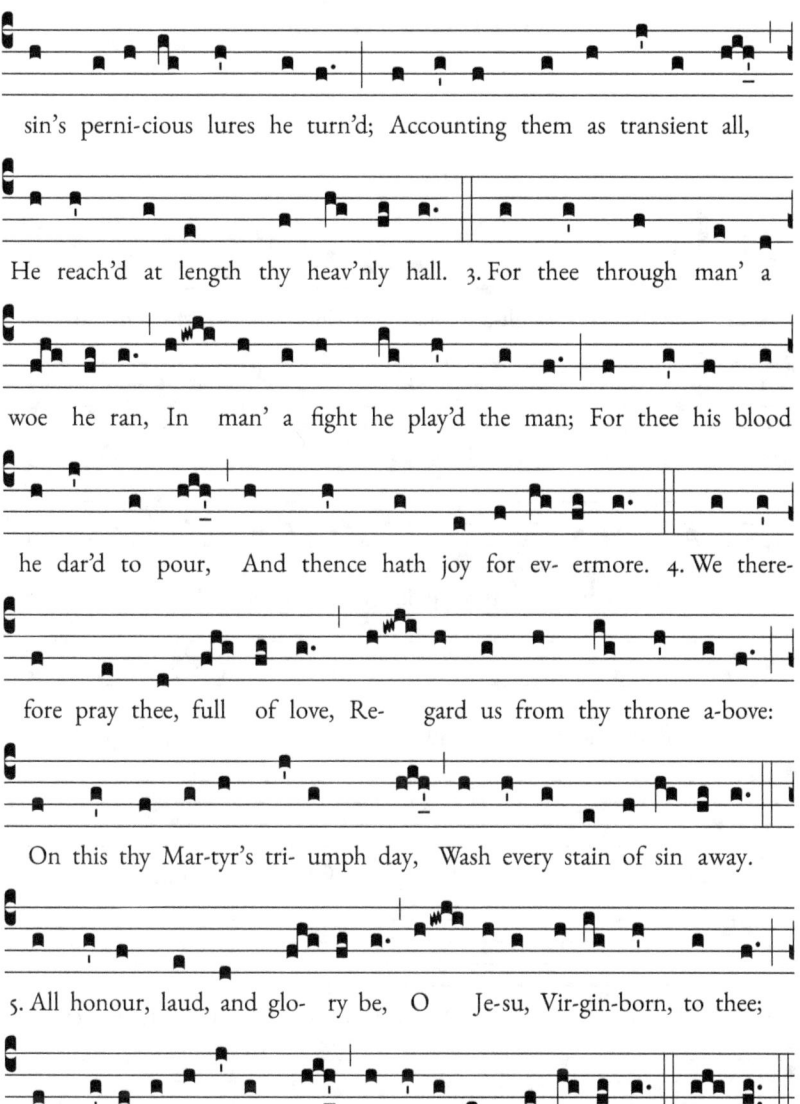

sin's pernicious lures he turn'd; Accounting them as transient all,

He reach'd at length thy heav'nly hall. 3. For thee through man' a

woe he ran, In man' a fight he play'd the man; For thee his blood

he dar'd to pour, And thence hath joy for ev- ermore. 4. We there-

fore pray thee, full of love, Re- gard us from thy throne a-bove:

On this thy Mar-tyr's tri- umph day, Wash every stain of sin away.

5. All honour, laud, and glo- ry be, O Je-su, Vir-gin-born, to thee;

All glo-ry, as is ev-er meet, To Father and to Par- a-clete. A- men.

℣. Stephen saw the heavens opened.

℞. He saw, and entered in: how blessed is the man unto whom heaven stood open!

Mag. Ant. Devout men † carried Stephen to his burial, and made great lamentation over him.

St. John **Proper of Season** 27 December

27 December. St. John

Mattins

¶ The Invitatory Hymn is from the Common of Apostles (p. 673).

Office Hymn

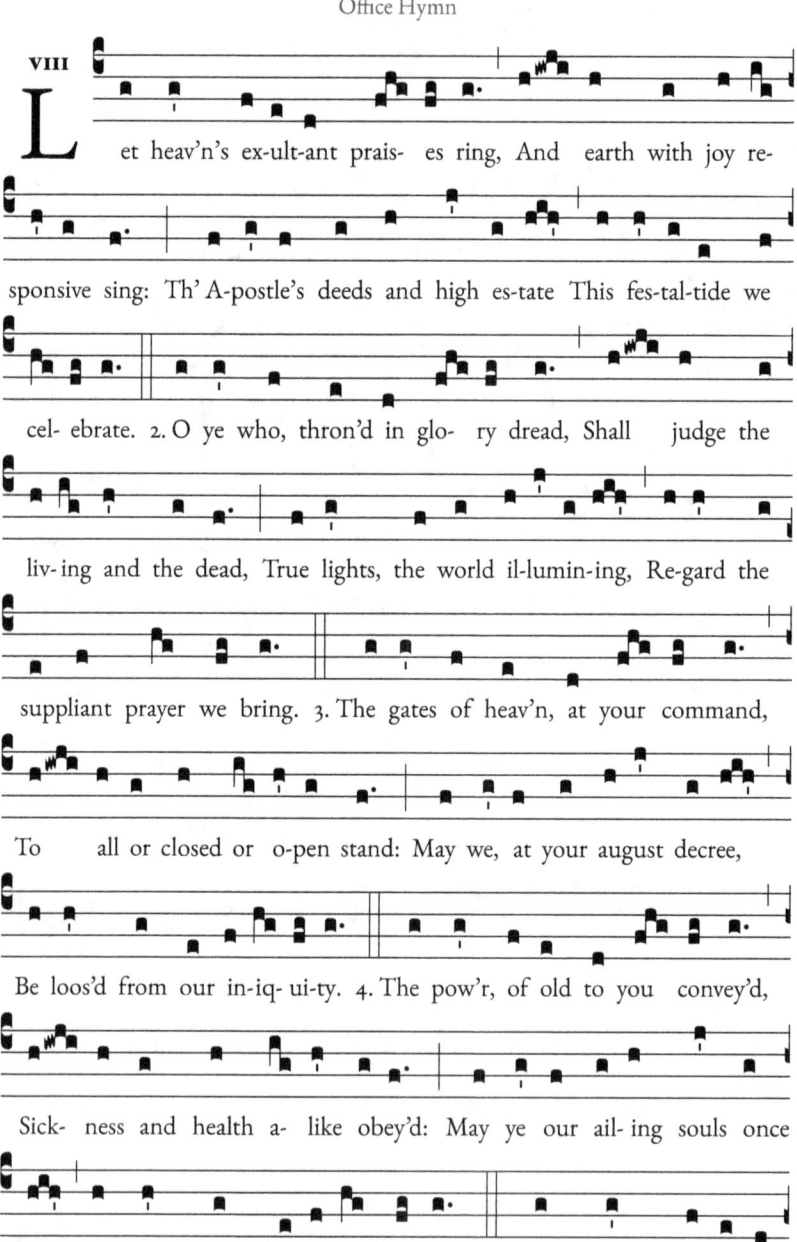

VIII Let heav'n's ex-ult-ant prais- es ring, And earth with joy re-sponsive sing: Th' A-postle's deeds and high es-tate This fes-tal-tide we cel- ebrate. 2. O ye who, thron'd in glo- ry dread, Shall judge the liv- ing and the dead, True lights, the world il-lumin-ing, Re-gard the suppliant prayer we bring. 3. The gates of heav'n, at your command, To all or closed or o-pen stand: May we, at your august decree, Be loos'd from our in-iq- ui-ty. 4. The pow'r, of old to you convey'd, Sick- ness and health a- like obey'd: May ye our ail- ing souls once more To strength and ho- li- ness re-store; 5. That Christ, th' un-err-ing

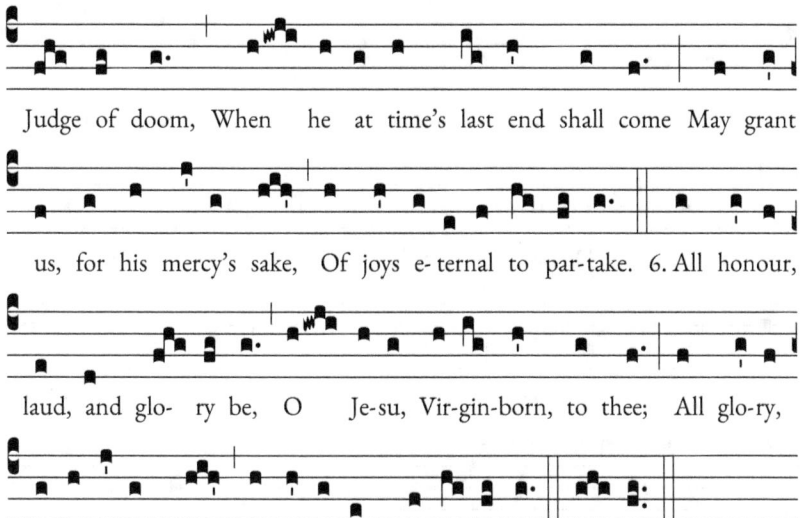

Judge of doom, When he at time's last end shall come May grant us, for his mercy's sake, Of joys e-ternal to par-take. 6. All honour, laud, and glo-ry be, O Je-su, Vir-gin-born, to thee; All glo-ry, as is ev-er meet, To Father and to Par-a-clete. A-men.

℣. This is that disciple which testifieth of these things.

℟. And we know that his testimony is true.

Ben. Ant. This is the same John, † who leaned on the Lord's bosom at the last supper: the blessed Apostle, unto whom were revealed the secret things of heaven.

Evensong

¶ The Office Hymn is of Mattins with the following Versicle & Antiphon.

℣. Right worthy of honour is blessed John the Apostle.

℟. Who leaned on the Lord's bosom at the last supper.

Mag. Ant. There went † this saying abroad among the brethren, that that disciple should not die: yet Jesus said not unto him, He shall not die; but, If I will that he tarry till I come.

28 December. Holy Innocents

Mattins

Invitatory Hymn

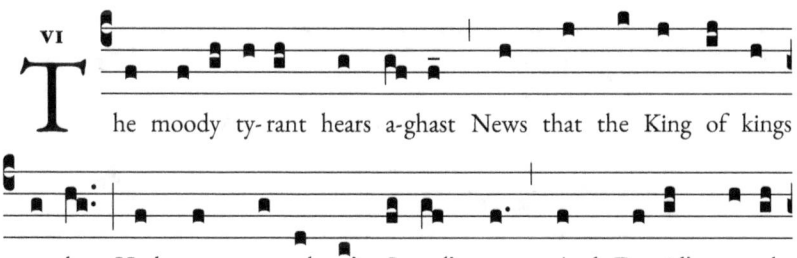

The moody ty-rant hears a-ghast News that the King of kings at last Hath come to rule o'er Is-rael's name, And Dav-id's roy-al

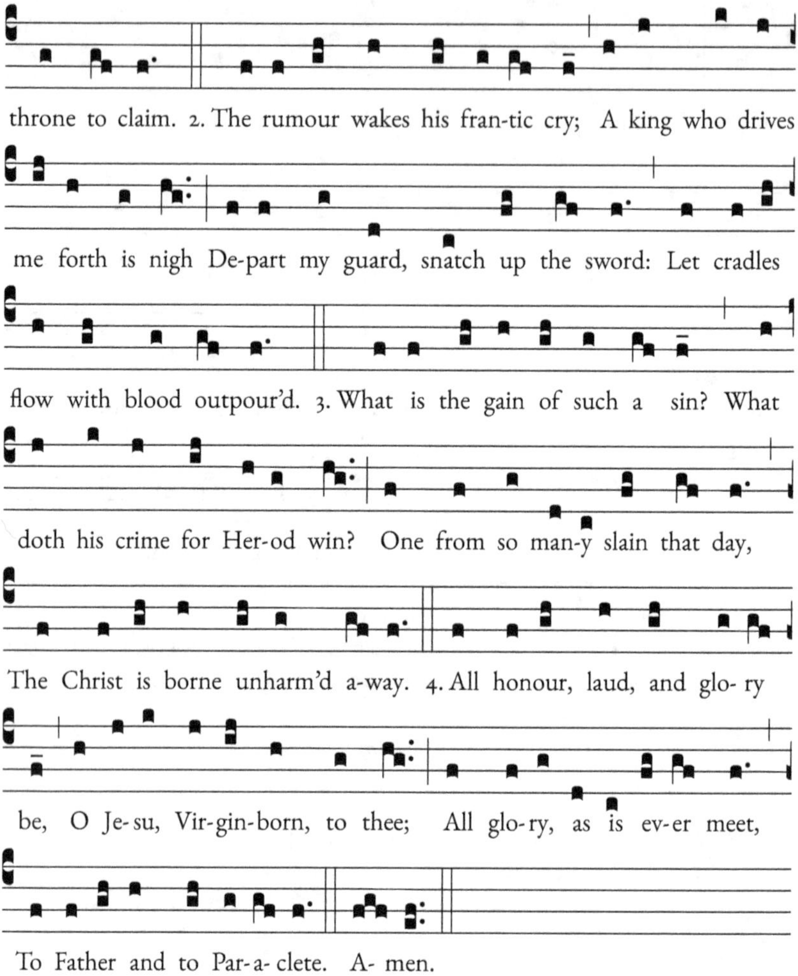

Holy Innocents — **Proper of Season** — 28 December

throne to claim. 2. The rumour wakes his fran-tic cry; A king who drives me forth is nigh De-part my guard, snatch up the sword: Let cradles flow with blood outpour'd. 3. What is the gain of such a sin? What doth his crime for Her-od win? One from so man-y slain that day, The Christ is borne unharm'd a-way. 4. All honour, laud, and glo-ry be, O Je-su, Vir-gin-born, to thee; All glo-ry, as is ev-er meet, To Father and to Par-a-clete. A-men.

Office Hymn

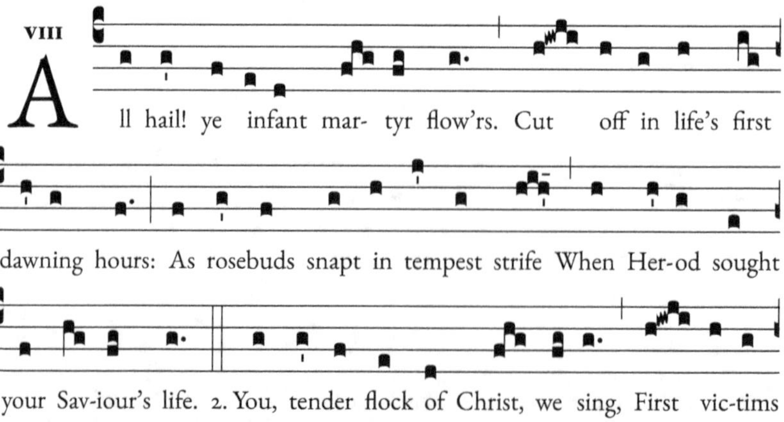

VIII

All hail! ye infant mar-tyr flow'rs. Cut off in life's first dawning hours: As rosebuds snapt in tempest strife When Her-od sought your Sav-iour's life. 2. You, tender flock of Christ, we sing, First vic-tims

Proper of Season *Christmas I*

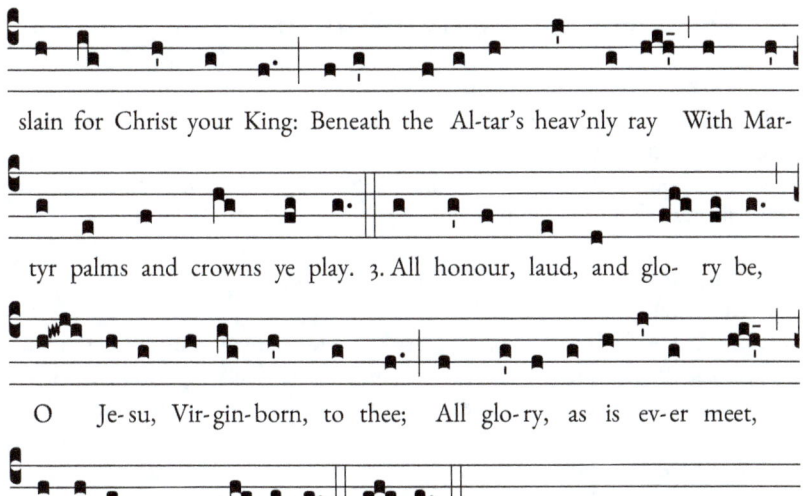

slain for Christ your King: Beneath the Al-tar's heav'nly ray With Martyr palms and crowns ye play. 3. All honour, laud, and glory be, O Jesu, Virgin-born, to thee; All glory, as is ever meet, To Father and to Paraclete. A-men.

℣. Herod was exceeding wroth, and slew many children.
℟. In Bethlehem Judah, the city of David.

Ben. Ant. These are they † which were not defiled with women; for they are virgins: and they follow the Lamb whithersoever he goeth.

Evensong

¶ The Office Hymn is of Mattins with the following Versicle & Antiphon.

℣. Beneath the altar all the Saints do cry aloud.
℟. Shall not our blood be avenged, O our God.

Mag. Ant. Then were innocent children † slain instead of Christ by a wicked ruler; the very sucklings were put to death: spotless, they follow the Lamb himself, and say for ever: Glory be to thee, O Lord.

SUNDAY WITHIN THE NATIVITY OCTAVE

¶ In the Daily Office, the Hymns are of Christmas Day (p. 317), with the following.

℣. All the ends of the world have seen, alleluia.
℟. The salvation of our God, alleluia.

Mag. & Ben. Ant. While all things † were in quiet silence, and that night was in the midst of her swift course, thine Almighty Word, O Lord, leaped down out of thy royal throne, alleluia.

Mag. Ant. The Child Jesus † increased in wisdom and stature in the sight of God and man.

Proper of Season

Most Holy Name — 2 January

1 January. Circumcision of Our Lord

¶ In the Daily Office, the Hymns are of Christmas Day (p. 317), with the following.

℣. The Lord declared, alleluia.
℟. His salvation, alleluia.

Mag. Ant. God, † for his great love wherewith he loved us, hath sent his own Son in the likeness of sinful flesh, alleluia.

℣. The Word was made flesh, alleluia.
℟. And dwelt among us, alleluia.

Ben. Ant. A great and wondrous mystery † is made known to us this day; a new thing is wrought in both natures: God is made man; that which was, remained, and that which was not, he assumed; suffering no confusion, nor yet division.

℣. The Lord declared, alleluia.
℟. His salvation, alleluia.

Mag. Ant. Great † is the mystery of the inheritance: the womb of her that knew not man is become the temple of the Godhead: by taking flesh of her, he was no way defiled: all the nations shall gather, saying: Glory be to thee, O Lord.

2 January. Most Holy Name of Jesus

I Evensong

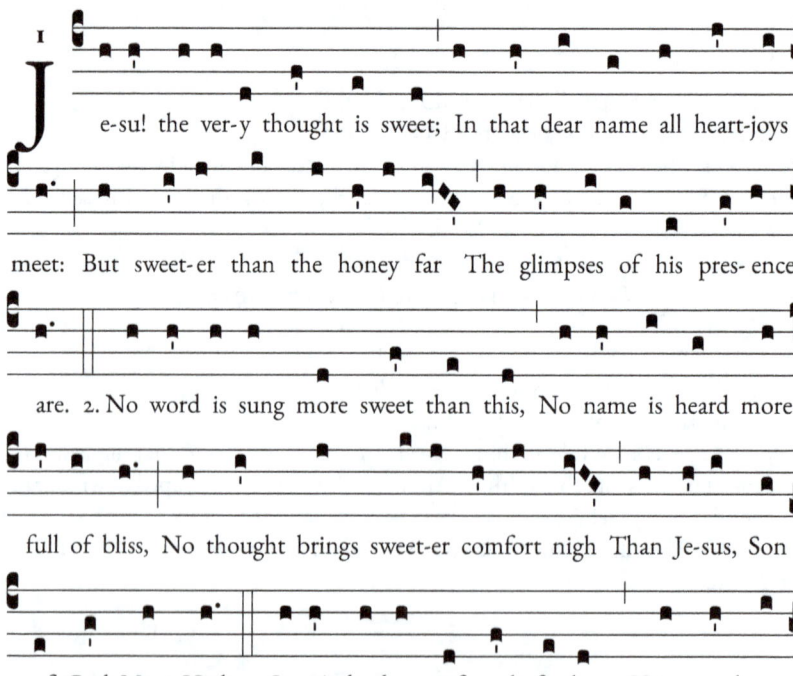

Jesu! the ver-y thought is sweet; In that dear name all heart-joys meet: But sweet-er than the honey far The glimpses of his pres-ence are. 2. No word is sung more sweet than this, No name is heard more full of bliss, No thought brings sweet-er comfort nigh Than Je-sus, Son of God Most High. 3. Je-su! the hope of souls for-lorn, How good to

2 January — **Proper of Season** — *Most Holy Name*

them for sin that mourn! To them that seek thee, O how kind! But

what art thou to them that find? 4. No tongue of mor-tal can express,

No let-ters write its bless-edness: A-lone who hath thee in his heart

Knows, love of Je-sus, what thou art. 5. Be thou our joy, and thou our

guard, Who art to be our great re-ward: Our glo-ry and our boast in

thee   For ev-er and for ev-er be.   A- men.

℣. Blessed be the Name of the Lord, alleluia.
℟. From this time forth for evermore, alleluia.
Mag. Ant. For he that is mighty † hath magnified me, and holy is his Name, alleluia.

Mattins

Invitatory Hymn

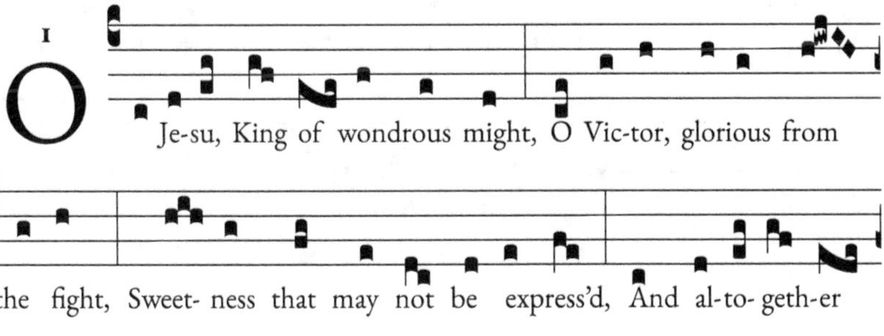

O Je-su, King of wondrous might, O Vic-tor, glorious from

the fight, Sweet- ness that may not be express'd, And al-to-geth-er

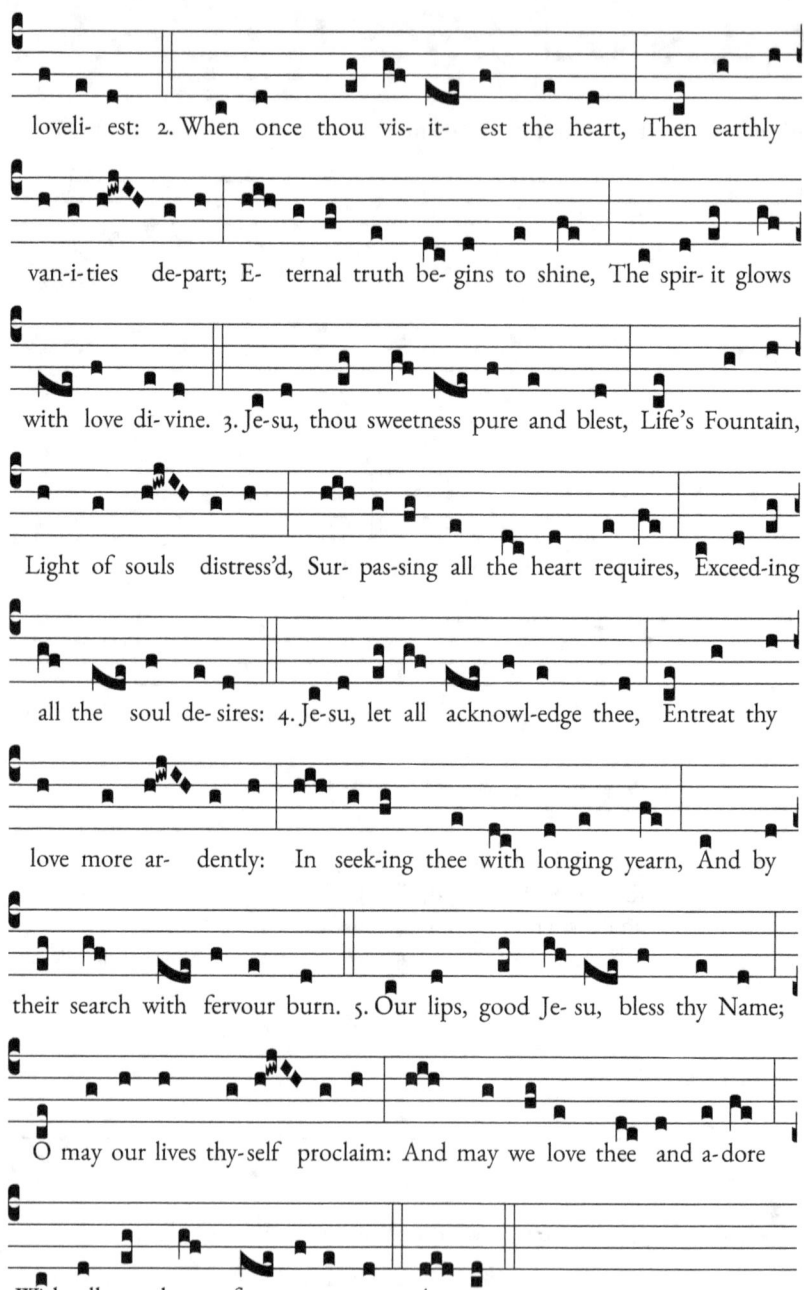

2 January — Proper of Season — *Most Holy Name*

Office Hymn

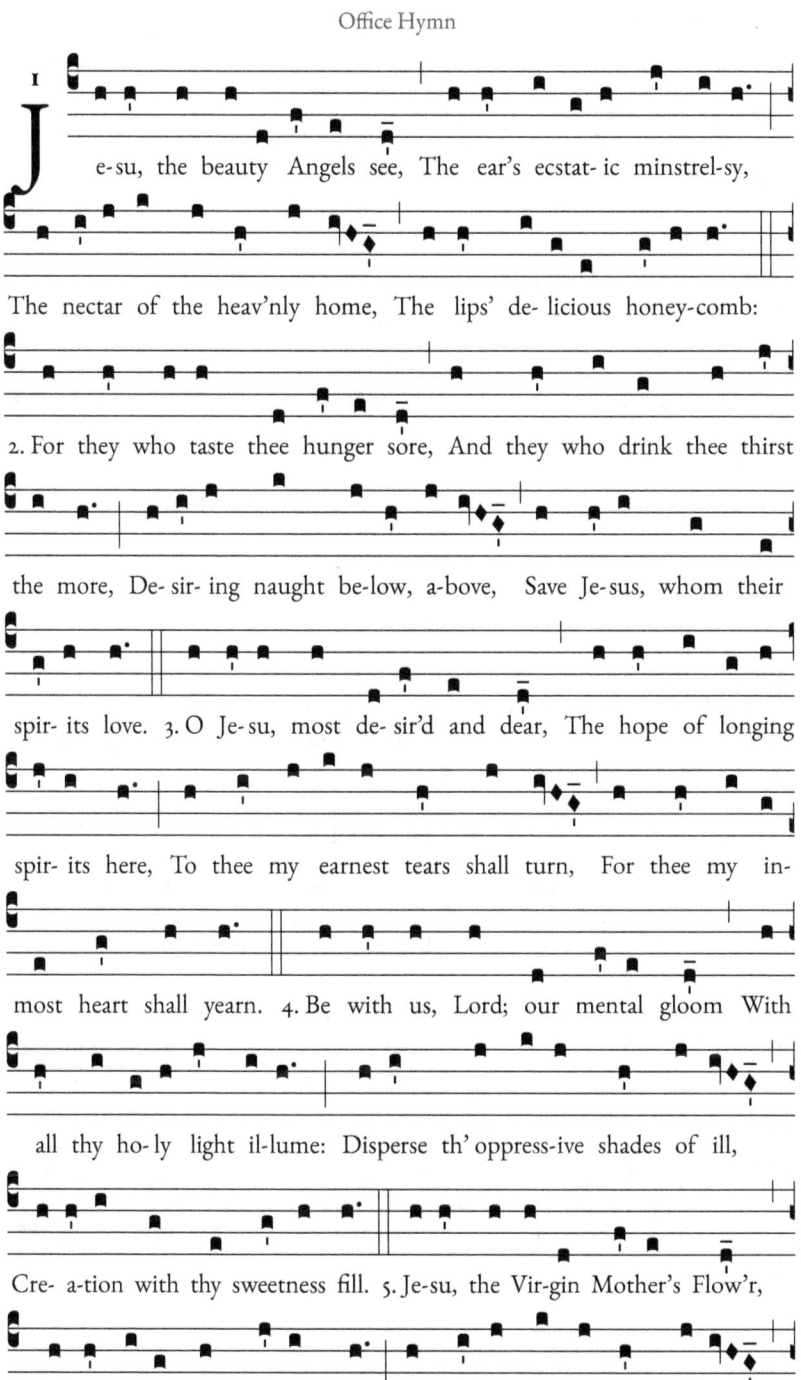

Jesu, the beauty Angels see, The ear's ecstatic minstrelsy, The nectar of the heav'nly home, The lips' delicious honey-comb:

2. For they who taste thee hunger sore, And they who drink thee thirst the more, Desiring naught below, above, Save Jesus, whom their spirits love.

3. O Jesu, most desir'd and dear, The hope of longing spirits here, To thee my earnest tears shall turn, For thee my inmost heart shall yearn.

4. Be with us, Lord; our mental gloom With all thy holy light illume: Disperse th' oppressive shades of ill, Creation with thy sweetness fill.

5. Jesu, the Virgin Mother's Flow'r, Thou love alone of sweetest pow'r, All honour to thy Name divine,

Christmas II   # Proper of Season

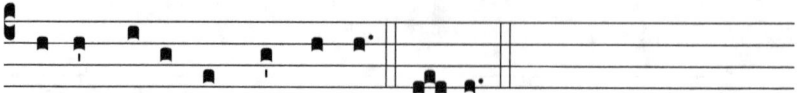

The realm of endless bliss be thine. A- men.

℣. Our help standeth in the Name of the Lord, alleluia.

℟. Who hath made heaven and earth, alleluia.

Ben. Ant. He gave himself † that he might deliver his people, and get him a perpetual Name, alleluia.

II Evensong

¶ The Office Hymn & Versicle are of I Evensong with the following Antiphon.

Mag. Ant. Thou shalt call † his Name Jesus, for he shall save his people from their sins, alleluia.

2 January. Octave Day of St. Stephen

¶ The propers are from the Feast Day, except for that which followeth.

Collect

ALMIGHTY and everlasting God, who, in the blood of the blessed Levite Stephen, didst consecrate the first-fruits of the Martyrs: grant, we beseech thee; that he may ever intercede for us, who prayed even for his persecutors to our Lord Jesus Christ, thy Son. Who with thee liveth.

Second Sunday after Nativity

Mag. Ant. Behold, the Angel of the Lord † appeareth in a dream to Joseph, saying: Arise, and take the young Child and his Mother, and flee into Egypt, and be thou there until I bring thee word; for it shall come to pass, that Herod will seek the young Child, to destroy him.

Ben. Ant. But when Herod was dead, † behold an Angel of the Lord appeareth in a dream to Joseph in Egypt, saying: Arise, and take the young Child and his Mother, and go into the land of Israel; for they are dead which sought the young Child's life.

Mag. Ant. When Joseph heard † that Archelaus did reign in Judæa in the room of his father Herod, he was afraid to go thither; and being warned in a dream, he turned aside into the parts of Galilee: and he came and dwelt in a city which was called Nazareth; that it might be fulfilled which was spoken by the prophets, He shall be called a Nazarene.

3 January. Octave Day of St. John

❡ The propers are from the Feast Day, except for that which followeth.

Mag. Ant. This is the same John † who learned on the Lord's bosom at the last supper: the blessed Apostle, unto whom were revealed the secret things of heaven.

Collect

ERCIFUL Lord, we beseech thee to cast thy bright beams of light upon thy Church: that it being enlightened by the doctrine of thy blessed Apostle and Evangelist Saint John may so walk in the light of thy truth, that it may at length attain to the light of everlasting life. Through.

Secret

ECEIVE, O Lord, the gifts which we offer unto thee on the solemnity of him, in whose advocacy we trust for deliverance. Through.

Postcommunion

GOD, who hast refreshed us with heavenly meat and drink, we humbly beseech thee: that we may be defended by the prayers of him, in whose memory we have received the same. Through.

❡ If the Postcommunion of this Mass shall have been already said for some other Saint, the Postcommunion for St. John shall be that of his Feast before the Latin Gate, 6 May, as followeth.

E beseech thee, O Lord: that we, who have been refreshed with heavenly bread, may be nourished unto life eternal. Through.

4 January. Octave Day of Holy Innocents

❡ The propers are from the Feast Day, except for that which followeth.
   NOTE, The Gloria in excelsis.
   ℣. Herod was exceeding wroth, and slew many children.
   ℟. In Bethlehem Judah, the city of David.

Mag. Ant. These are they † which were not defiled with women; for they are virgins: and they follow the Lamb whithersoever he goeth.

❡ If a Commemoration only is made of the Octave, the Prayers (of the Feast) will be as followeth.

St. Titus   **Proper of Season**   4 January

Collect

O ALMIGHTY God, who out of the mouths of babes and sucklings hast ordained strength, and madest infants to glorify thee by their deaths: mortify and kill all vices in us; and so strengthen us by thy grace, that by the innocency of our lives, and constancy of our faith even unto death, we may glorify thy holy name. Through.

¶ Commemoration is made of St. Titus (p. 334).

Secret

MAY the devout prayers of thy Saints never fail us, O Lord: that they may render our gifts acceptable unto thee, and ever obtain for us thy pardon. Through.

¶ Commemoration is made of St. Titus (p. 335).

Postcommunion

WE beseech thee, O Lord: that the gifts which we have offered and received may, through the prayers of the Saints, effectually avail for our succour both in this life, and in that which is to come. Through.

¶ Commemoration is made of St. Titus (p. 335).

¶ NOTE, In Lent, either the Ferial Day's propers or Ash Wednesday's propers may be said.

¶ The Office Hymn & Versicles of the Feast of the Epiphany of Our Lord shall be used for the foregoing Sundays and Ferial Days until I Evensong of Septuagesima, exclusive.

4 JANUARY. ST. TITUS

¶ The propers are from the First Common of a Confessor Bishop (p. 715), except for the Gospel & Prayers as followeth.

Collect

O GOD, who didst adorn blessed Titus, thy Confessor and Bishop, with apostolic virtues: grant, through his merits and intercession; that, living justly and godly in this world, we may be found worthy to attain unto the heavenly country. Through.

Gospel. Luke 10:1

AT THAT TIME: The Lord appointed seventy also: and sent them two and two before his face into every city and place, whither he himself would come. Therefore said he unto them, The harvest truly is great, but the labourers are few: pray ye therefore the Lord of the harvest, that he would send forth labourers into his harvest. Go your ways: behold, I send you forth as lambs among wolves. Carry neither purse, nor scrip, nor shoes: and salute no man by the way. And into whatsoever house ye enter, first say, Peace be to this house. And if the son of peace be there, your peace shall rest upon it: if not, it shall turn to you again. And in the same house remain, eating and drinking such things as they give: for the labourer is worthy of his hire. Go not from house to house. And into whatsoever city ye enter, and they receive you, eat such things as are set before you: And heal the sick that are therein, and say unto them, The kingdom of God is come nigh unto you.

Secret

E beseech thee, O Lord, that we remembering with gladness the merits of thy Saints, may in all places feel the succour of their intercession. Through.

Postcommunion

RANT, we beseech thee, Almighty God: that we, shewing forth our thankfulness for the gifts which we have received, may, at the intercession of blessed Titus, thy Confessor and Bishop, obtain yet more abundant mercies. Through.

5 January. Vigil of Epiphany

¶ The Daily Office propers are as on the Feast of the Circumcision, except that which followeth.

¶ Note, Commemoration is made of St. Telesphorus with the Prayers of the next Mass.

Mag. Ant. The Child Jesus † increased in wisdom and stature in the sight of God and man.
Ben. Ant. While all things † were in quiet silence, and that night was in the midst of her swift course, thine Almighty Word, O Lord, leaped down out of thy royal throne, alleluia.

Introit

HILE all things were in in quiet silence, and night was in the midst of her swift course, thine almighty Word, O Lord, leaped down from heaven out of thy royal throne. *Ps.* The Lord is King, and hath put on put glorious apparel: the Lord hath put on his apparel, and girded himself with strength.

Collect

LMIGHTY and everlasting God, direct our actions according to thy good pleasure: that in the name of thy well-beloved Son we may be made worthy to abound in good works. Who liveth and reigneth with thee.

¶ Commemoration of St. Telesphorus (p. 337) and of St. Mary after Christmas (p. BCP 541).

Epiphany Eve — **Proper of Season** — 5 January

Epistle. Galatians 4:1

BRETHREN: The heir, as long as he is a child, differeth nothing from a servant, though he be lord of all; But is under tutors and governors until the time appointed of the father. Even so we, when we were children, were in bondage under the elements of the world: But when the fulness of the time was come, God sent forth his Son, made of a woman, made under the law, To redeem them that were under the law, that we might receive the adoption of sons. And because ye are sons, God hath sent forth the Spirit of his Son into your hearts, crying, Abba, Father. Wherefore thou art no more a servant, but a son; and if a son, then an heir of God through Christ.

Gradual. Thou art fairer than the children of men: full of grace are thy lips. ℣. My heart is inditing of a good matter, I speak of the things which I have made unto the King: my tongue is the pen of a ready writer.

Alleluia. Alleluia, alleluia. ℣. The Lord is King, and hath put on glorious apparel: the Lord hath put on his apparel, and girded himself with strength. Alleluia.

Gospel. Matthew 2:19

AT THAT TIME: When Herod was dead, behold, an angel of the Lord appeareth in a dream to Joseph in Egypt, Saying, Arise, and take the young child and his mother, and go into the land of Israel: for they are dead which sought the young child's life. And he arose, and took the young child and his mother, and came into the land of Israel. But when he heard that Archelaus did reign in Judaea in the room of his father Herod, he was afraid to go thither: notwithstanding, being warned of God in a dream, he turned aside into the parts of Galilee: And he came and dwelt in a city called Nazareth: that it might be fulfilled which was spoken by the prophets, He shall be called a Nazarene.

Offertory. God hath made the round world so sure: that it cannot be moved: ever since the world began, hath thy seat, O God, been prepared, thou art from everlasting.

Secret

GRANT, we beseech thee, Almighty God: that the gift which we offer in the sight of thy Majesty, may obtain for us grace to serve thee with all godliness, and bring us in the end to everlasting felicity. Through.

¶ Commemoration of St. Telesphorus (p. 337) and of St. Mary after Christmas (p. BCP 541).

Communion. Take the young Child and his Mother and go into the land of Israel: for they are ead which sought the young Child's life.

Postcommunion

MAY the operation of this mystery, Lord, avail for the cleansing of our sins, and for the fulfilment of our godly desires. Through.

¶ Commemoration of St. Telesphorus (p. 337) and of St. Mary after Christmas (p. BCP 541).

Proper of Season *Epiphany*

5 January. St. Telesphorus

¶ The propers are from the Second Common of a Martyr Bishop (p. 686), with the Prayers below.

Collect

GOD, who makest us glad with the yearly solemnity of blessed Telesphorus, thy Martyr and Bishop: mercifully grant; that, as we now celebrate his birthday so we may likewise rejoice in his protection. (Through.)

Secret

ANCTIFY, O Lord, the gifts which we dedicate to thee: that at the intercession of blessed Telesphorus, thy Martyr and Bishop, they may obtain for us thy gracious favour. (Through.)

Postcommunion

WE beseech thee, O Lord our God, that like as we, whom thou hast refreshed by the partaking of thy sacred gift, do offer unto thee our worship: so by the intercession of blessed Telesphorus thy Martyr and Bishop, we may perceive the benefit of the same. (Through.)

6 January. Epiphany of Our Lord

I Evensong

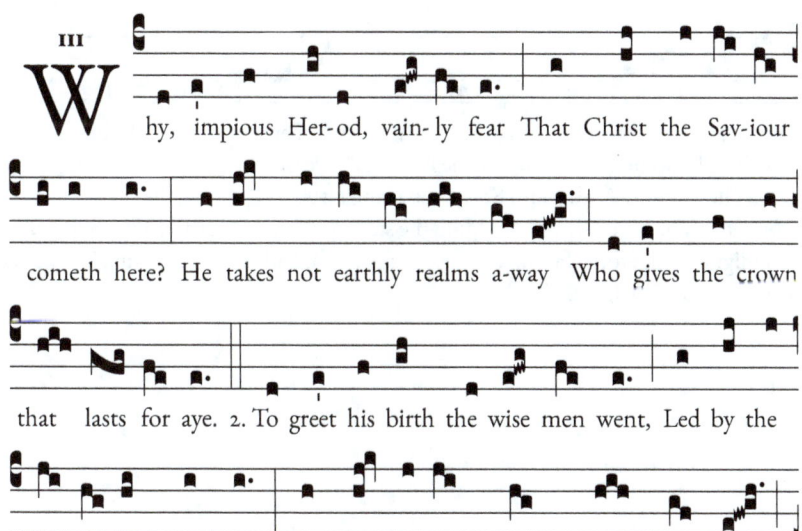

Why, impious Her-od, vain-ly fear That Christ the Sav-iour cometh here? He takes not earthly realms a-way Who gives the crown that lasts for aye. 2. To greet his birth the wise men went, Led by the star be-fore them sent; Call'd on by light, towards Light they press'd,

Epiphany

Proper of Season

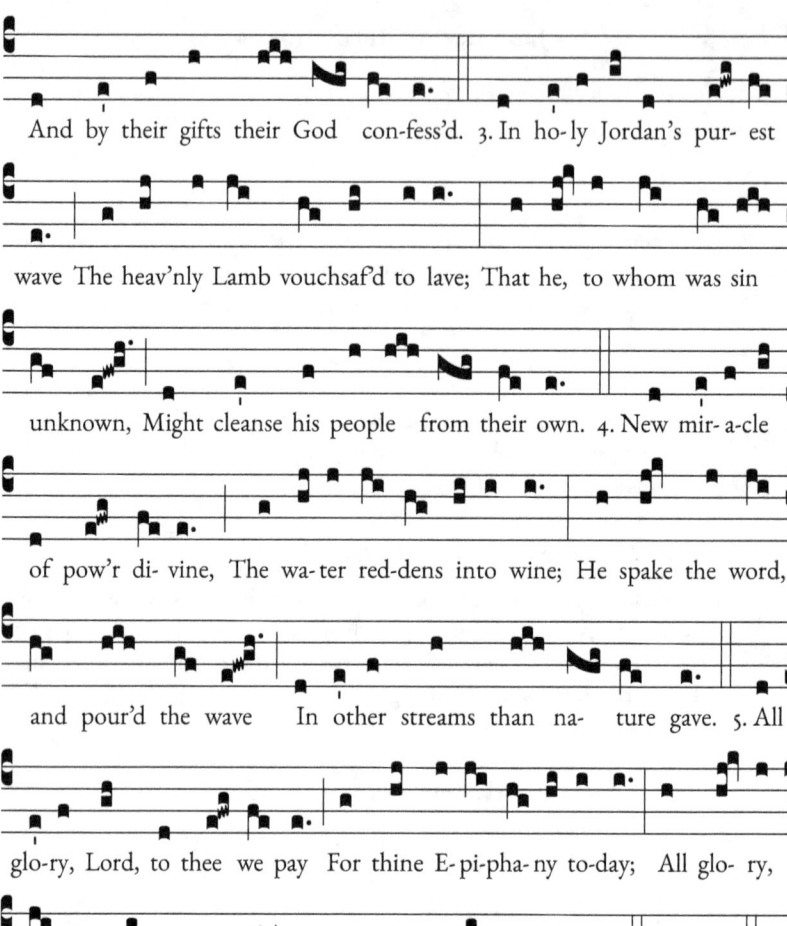

And by their gifts their God con-fess'd. 3. In ho-ly Jordan's pur-est wave The heav'nly Lamb vouchsaf'd to lave; That he, to whom was sin unknown, Might cleanse his people from their own. 4. New mir-a-cle of pow'r di-vine, The wa-ter red-dens into wine; He spake the word, and pour'd the wave In other streams than na-ture gave. 5. All glo-ry, Lord, to thee we pay For thine E-pi-pha-ny to-day; All glo-ry, as is ev-er meet, To Father and to Par-a-clete. A-men.

℣. The kings of Tharsis and of the isles shall give presents.
℞. The kings of Arabia and Saba shall bring gifts.

Mag. Ant. The wise men, † beholding the star, said one to another, This is the sign of a mighty King; forth fare we, and let us seek him: and let us offer him gifts, gold, incense, and myrrh, alleluia.

Proper of Season *Epiphany*

Mattins

¶ The Invitatory Hymn is as in I Evensong.

Office Hymn

III. O more than mighty cit- ies known, Dear Bethle-hem, in thee a-lone Sal-va- tion's Lord from heav'n took birth In human form up- on the earth. 2. And from a star that far outshone The rad-iant cir-cle of the sun In beau-ty, swift the tid- ings ran Of God on earth in flesh of man. 3. The wise men, see- ing him, so fair, Bow low be- fore him, and with prayer Their treas- ur'd or- ient gifts un-fold Of incense, myrrh, and roy- al gold. 4. The fragrant incense which they bring, The gold, pro-claim him God and King; The bit- ter spic- y dust of myrrh Foreshadows his new sep- ulchre. 5. All glo-ry, Lord,

Within Epiphany Octave **Proper of Season**

to thee we pay For thine E-pi-pha-ny today; All glo-ry, as is ev-er meet, To Father and to Par-a-clete. A-men.

℣. O worship the Lord, alleluia.

℟. All ye Angels of his, alleluia.

Ben. Ant. To-day † the Church is joined to her heavenly Bridegroom; because in Jordan Christ hath washed away her offences: the wise men with their offerings hasten to the royal marriage, and the guests are regaled with water made wine, alleluia.

II Evensong

¶ The Office Hymn & Versicle are of I Evensong, with the following Antiphon.

Mag. Ant. Now do we celebrate † a holy day adorned by three miracles: to-day a star led the wise men to the manger; to-day water was made wine at the wedding feast; to-day Christ vouchsafed to be baptized of John in Jordan that he might save us, alleluia.

¶ Within the Octave of the Epiphany, no Feast is kept except an occurrent I Double, on which Commemoration of the Octave is always made.

During the Octave all is said as on the Feast, except the Ants. on Benedictus and Magnificat appointed for each day.

The Office of Sunday within the Octave is said as set forth below, on whatever day in the Octave it may fall.

After Sunday, the days in the Octave continue according to their number, as if Sunday had not intervened. For example, if Sunday should fall on the third day in the Octave, on the following day the Ants. on Benedictus and Magnificat of the third day in the Octave are said, and so thenceforth the others.

WITHIN THE OCTAVE OF THE EPIPHANY

Day II, Semidouble

Ben. Ant. From the east † there came wise men to Bethlehem, to worship the Lord: and when they had opened their treasures, they presented unto him precious gifts: gold as to a mighty King, incense as to the true God, and myrrh to foreshew his burial, alleluia.

Mag. Ant. When the wise men saw the star † they rejoiced with exceeding great joy: and when they were come into the house, they presented unto the Lord gold, frankincense, and myrrh, alleluia.

Proper of Season *Within Epiphany Octave*

Day III, Semidouble

Ben. Ant. Three are the gifts † which the wise men presented unto the Lord: gold, frankincense, and myrrh, to the Son of God, to the mighty King, alleluia.
Mag. Ant. Light of light, † thou, O Christ, hast appeared, unto whom the wise men present their gifts, alleluia, alleluia, alleluia.

Day IV, Semidouble

Ben. Ant. We have seen his star † in the East, and are come with gifts to worship the Lord.
Mag. Ant. Herod inquired † of the wise men, What sign have ye seen, concerning him that is born King? We have seen a star shining, the brightness whereof enlightens the world.

Day V, Semidouble

Ben. Ant. Many nations † shall come from afar, bearing their gifts, alleluia.
Mag. Ant. All they from Sheba † shall come: they shall bring gold and incense, alleluia, alleluia.

Day VI, Semidouble

Ben. Ant. They that despised thee † shall come unto thee, and shall bow themselves down at the soles of thy feet.
Mag. Ant. The wise men, being warned † in dreams by an Angel, departed into their own country another way.

Saturday within the Octave

℣. We have seen his star in the east, alleluia.
℟. And are come with gifts to worship the Lord, alleluia.
Mag. Ant. The Child Jesus † tarried behind in Jerusalem; and Joseph and his mother knew not of it, supposing him to have been in the company; and they sought him among their kinsfolk and acquaintance.

¶ When the Octave Day of the Epiphany falls on Sunday, the Office of the Sunday in the Octave is said on the preceding Saturday, and I Evensong of Sunday is said on Friday with Commemoration of the preceding day in the Octave.

But if a I Double occur on this Saturday, the Office of Sunday is anticipated on the nearest day on which only the Offce of the Octave is to be said, and in the Office of the Feast Commemoration is made of the occurrent day within the Octave. In the Office of Sunday all is said as noted below.

Epiphany III # Proper of Season

Sunday within the Octave of the Epiphany

℣ The Office Hymns are from the Feast of the Epiphany (p. 337), except for the following.

℣. All they from Sheba shall come, alleluia.
℟. They shall bring gold and incense, alleluia.

Ben. Ant. The Child Jesus † tarried behind in Jerusalem; and Joseph and his mother knew not of it, supposing him to have been in the company; and they sought him among their kinsfolk and acquaintance.

℣. We have seen his star in the east, alleluia.
℟. And are come with gifts to worship the Lord, alleluia.

Mag. Ant. Son, † why hast thou thus dealt with us? behold, thy father and I have sought thee sorrowing. How is it that ye sought me? wist ye not that I must be about my Father's business?

Baptism of Our Lord

(Octave Day of the Epiphany)

℣ The Daily Office propers are as in the Feast of the Epiphany (p. 337).

℣ From the Octave of Epiphany until the Saturday before the I Sunday in Lent, when the Office is of the Feria, all is said as in the Daily Hymns except that which is appointed as Proper. The Collect is that of the preceding Sunday.

Second Sunday after Epiphany

℣ The Office Hymns & Versicles are from the Daily Hymns (p. 2), with the following Antiphons.

Mag. Ant. God hath holpen † his servant Israel, as he promised to Abraham and to his seed: and hath exalted the humble for ever and ever.

Ben. Ant. There was a marriage † in Cana of Galilee, and Jesus was there with Mary his Mother.

Mag. Ant. And when they wanted wine, † Jesus bade them to fill the water-pots with water; and it was turned into wine, alleluia.

Third Sunday after Epiphany

Mag. Ant. God hath holpen † his servant Israel, as he promised to Abraham and to his seed: and hath exalted the humble for ever and ever.

Ben. Ant. When Jesus † was come down from the mountain, behold there came a leper and worshipped him, saying, Lord, if thou wilt, thou canst make me clean. And Jesus put forth his hand and touched him, saying: I will; be thou clean.

Mag. Ant. Lord, if thou wilt, † thou canst make me clean: then saith Jesus, I will; be thou clean.

Proper of Season *Septuagesima Ferias*

Fourth Sunday after Epiphany

Mag. Ant. God hath holpen † his servant Israel, as he promised to Abraham and to his seed: and hath exalted the humble for ever and ever.
Ben. Ant. And when Jesus † was entered into a ship, behold, there arose a great tempest in the sea: and his disciples awoke him, saying: Lord, save us, we perish.
Mag. Ant. Save us, Lord, † we perish: rebuke the winds and the sea, O God, and make a great calm.

Fifth Sunday after Epiphany

Mag. Ant. God hath holpen † his servant Israel, as he promised to Abraham and to his seed: and hath exalted the humble for ever and ever.
Ben. Ant. Sir, † didst not thou sow good seed in thy field? from whence then hath it tares? He said unto them, An enemy hath done this.
Mag. Ant. Gather ye together † first the tares, and bind them in bundles to burn them: but gather the wheat into my barn, saith the Lord.

Sixth Sunday after Epiphany

Mag. Ant. God hath holpen † his servant Israel, as he promised to Abraham and to his seed: and hath exalted the humble for ever and ever.
Ben. Ant. The kingdom of heaven † is like unto a grain of mustard seed, which is the least of all seeds; but when it is grown, it is the greatest among herbs.
Mag. Ant. The kingdom of heaven † is like unto leaven, which a woman took and hid in three measures of meal, until the whole was leavened.

Septuagesima Sunday

Mag. Ant. The Lord said † unto Adam, Of the tree which is in the midst of the garden thou shalt not eat: for in the day that thou eatest thereof, thou shalt surely die.
Ben. Ant. The kingdom † of heaven is like unto a man that is an householder, which went out early in the morning to hire labourers into his vineyard, saith the Lord.
Mag. Ant. The householder † saith unto the labourers, Why stand ye here all the day idle? They say unto him, Because no man hath hired us. Go ye also into the vineyard, and whatsoever is right, I will give you.

Septuagesimatide Ferial Office

¶ On Ferias from Septuagesima Sunday until Ash Wednesday, exclusive, when the Office is not of the Feria, it is always commemorated at Mattins and Evensong on Double Feasts, even of the I Class, and on days within Octaves.

¶ The **Benedictus** Antiphons are said on Ferias as set forth in the Psalter, through Tuesday after Quinquagesima.

¶ Note, No notice is taken of an occurrent Vigil, either in the Office of a Feast, or of a day within an Octave, or of a Feria. The Office of St. Mary on Saturday is not said.

Proper of Season

ANTIPHONS WITHIN SEPTUAGESIMA WEEK

Septuagesima Monday, Feria

Mag. Ant. These last † have wrought but one hour, and thou hast made them equal unto us, which have borne the burden and heat of the day.

Septuagesima Tuesday, Feria

Mag. Ant. The householder answered and said, † Friend, I do thee no wrong: didst not thou agree with me for a penny? Take that thine is, and go thy way.

Septuagesima Wednesday, Feria

Mag. Ant. Take that thine is † and go thy way: because I am good, saith the Lord.

Septuagesima Thursday, Feria

Mag. Ant. Is it not lawful † for me to do what I will? Is thine eye evil, because I am good? saith the Lord.

Septuagesima Friday, Feria

Mag. Ant. So the last † shall be first, and the first shall be last: for many are called, but few are chosen.

SEXAGESIMA SUNDAY

Mag. Ant. The Lord † said unto Noah: The end of all flesh is come before me: make thee an ark of gopher wood, that therein the seed of all flesh may be saved.
Ben. Ant. When much people † were gathered together to Jesus, and were come to him out of every city, he spake by a parable: A sower went out to sow his seed.
Mag. Ant. Unto you it is given † to know the mysteries of the kingdom of heaven: but to others in parables, said Jesus to his disciples.

ANTIPHONS WITHIN SEXAGESIMA WEEK

Sexagesima Monday, Feria

Mag. Ant. If ye seek † the summit of true honour, hasten to yon heavenly country with what speed ye may.

Sexagesima Tuesday, Feria

Mag. Ant. The seed † is the word of God, but Christ is the Sower: every one that heareth him shall abide for ever.

Proper of Season Quinquagesima Week

Sexagesima Wednesday, Feria

Mag. Ant. But that † which fell on the good ground are they which in an honest and good heart receive the word; and bring forth fruit with patience.

Sexagesima Thursday, Feria

Mag. Ant. Some seed † fell on good ground, and brought forth fruit; some an hundred-fold, and some sixtyfold.

Sexagesima Friday, Feria

Mag. Ant. They who keep the word of God † with an honest and perfect heart bring forth fruit with patience.

QUINQUAGESIMA SUNDAY

Mag. Ant. Mighty Abraham, † the father of our faith, offered a burnt offering upon the altar, instead of his son.
Ben. Ant. Behold, we go up † to Jerusalem, and all things that are written concerning the Son of man shall be accomplished: for he shall be delivered unto the Gentiles, and shall be mocked, and spitted on; and they shall scourge him, and put him to death; and the third day he shall rise again.
Mag. Ant. And Jesus stood, † and commanded him to be brought unto him, and asked him, saying: What wilt thou that I shall do unto thee? Lord, that I may receive my sight. And Jesus said unto him, Receive thy sight, thy faith hath saved thee. And straightway he received his sight, and followed him, glorifying God.

ANTIPHONS WITHIN QUINQUAGESIMA WEEK

Quinquagesima Monday, Feria

Mag. Ant. And they which went before † rebuked him that he should hold his peace: but he cried so much the more, Have mercy on me, thou Son of David.

Quinquagesima Tuesday, Feria

Mag. Ant. Have mercy on me, † thou Son of David. What wilt thou that I shall do unto thee? Lord, that I may receive my sight.

❡ If on the following Ash Wednesday there occur a I or II Double, it is transferred to the first unhindered day. Greater and lesser Doubles and Memorials are only commemorated on the other days of Lent.

Ash Wednesday

¶ On this day all Octaves cease until Holy Sabbath. On this and other Ferias through None of the following Saturday all is said as in the Psalter throughout the Year except that which is appointed as proper.

¶ The Daily Office propers are of the Ferial Day, except the following Antiphons.

Ben. Ant. When ye fast, † be not, as the hypocrites, of a sad countenance.
Mag. Ant. Lay up for yourselves † treasures in heaven, where neither moth nor rust doth corrupt.

Thursday after Ash Wednesday

¶ The Daily Office propers are of the Ferial Day, except the following Antiphons and Collects.

Mattins

Ben. Ant. Lord, my servant † lieth at home sick of the palsy, grievously tormented. Verily I say unto thee, I will come and heal him.

GOD, who art offended by sin, and reconciled by penitence: mercifully regard the prayers of thy suppliant people, and turn away the scourge of thy wrath, which for our sins we have justly deserved. Through.

II Evensong

Mag. Ant. Lord, I am not worthy † that thou shouldest enter under my roof: but speak the word only and my servant shall be healed.

PARE us, O Lord, spare thy people: that they who are justly chastised by thy scourges, may be relieved by thy tender mercy. Through.

Introit

WHEN I called upon the Lord, he heard my voice from the battle that was against me, yea, even God, that endureth for ever, shall bring them down: O cast thy burden upon the Lord, and he shall nourish thee. *Ps.* Hear my prayer, O God, and hide not thyself from my petition: take heed unto me and hear me.

Collect

GOD, who art wroth with them that sin against thee, and sparest them that are penitent: mercifully look upon the prayers of thy people which call upon thee; and turn away the scourges of thy wrath which for our sins we justly deserve. Through.

¶ 2nd Collect is Of Saints (p. BCP 542) & 3rd Of the Living and Departed (p. BCP 544).

Thursday — **Proper of Season** — *Ash Wednesday*

Epistle. Isaiah 38:1

IN THOSE DAYS: Was Hezekiah sick unto death. And Isaiah the prophet the son of Amoz came unto him, and said unto him, Thus saith the LORD, Set thine house in order: for thou shalt die, and not live. Then Hezekiah turned his face toward the wall, and prayed unto the LORD, And said, Remember now, O LORD, I beseech thee, how I have walked before thee in truth and with a perfect heart, and have done that which is good in thy sight. And Hezekiah wept sore. Then came the word of the LORD to Isaiah, saying, Go, and say to Hezekiah, Thus saith the LORD, the God of David thy father, I have heard thy prayer, I have seen thy tears: behold, I will add unto thy days fifteen years. And I will deliver thee and this city out of the hand of the king of Assyria: and I will defend this city, saith the Lord almighty.

Gradual. O cast thy burden upon the Lord, and he shall nourish thee. ℣. When I called upon the Lord, he heard my voice from the battle that was against me.

Gospel. Matthew 8:5

AT THAT TIME: When Jesus was entered into Capernaum, there came unto him a centurion, beseeching him, And saying, Lord, my servant lieth at home sick of the palsy, grievously tormented. And Jesus saith unto him, I will come and heal him. The centurion answered and said, Lord, I am not worthy that thou shouldest come under my roof: but speak the word only, and my servant shall be healed. For I am a man under authority, having soldiers under me: and I say to this man, Go, and he goeth; and to another, Come, and he cometh; and to my servant, Do this, and he doeth it. When Jesus heard it, he marvelled, and said to them that followed, Verily I say unto you, I have not found so great faith, no, not in Israel. And I say unto you, That many shall come from the east and west, and shall sit down with Abraham, and Isaac, and Jacob, in the kingdom of heaven. But the children of the kingdom shall be cast out into outer darkness: there shall be weeping and gnashing of teeth. And Jesus said unto the centurion, Go thy way; and as thou hast believed, so be it done unto thee. And his servant was healed in the selfsame hour.

Offertory. Unto thee, O Lord, will I lift up my soul: my God, I have put my trust in thee, O let me not be confounded: neither let mine enemies triumph over me: for all they that hope in thee shall not be ashamed.

Secret

WE beseech thee, O Lord, favourably to regard these our sacrifices: that they may be profitable for our devotion and set forward our salvation. Through.

¶ 2nd Secret is Of Saints (p. BCP 542) & 3rd Of the Living and Departed (p. BCP 544).

Communion. Thou shalt be pleased with the sacrifice of righteousness, with the burnt-offerings and oblations upon thine altar, O Lord.

Postcommunion

E humbly beseech thee, Almighty God: that, as we have received the blessing of this heavenly gift; so it may be made to us thy sacrament, and avail to our salvation. Through.

¶ 2ⁿᵈ Postcommunion is Of Saints (p. BCP 542) & 3ʳᵈ Of the Living and Departed (p. BCP 544).

PRIEST. Let us pray.
DEACON. Humble your heads before God.

¶ The Priest then prays the following:

PARE, O Lord, spare thy people: that they who are justly chastised by thy scourges, may by thy mercy be relieved. Through.

FRIDAY AFTER ASH WEDNESDAY

¶ The Daily Office propers are of the Ferial Day, except the following Antiphons and Collects.

Mattins	II Evensong
Ben. Ant. When thou doest thine alms, † let not thy left hand know what thy right. hand doeth.	*Mag. Ant.* But thou, when thou prayest, † enter into thy closet, and when thou hast shut thy door, pray to thy Father.

E beseech thee, O Lord, to accompany with thy bounteous favour the fast upon which we have entered: that the observance which we shew forth in our bodies, we may be able also to practise with sincerity of heart. Through.

EFEND thy people, O Lord, and mercifully cleanse them from all their sins: for no adversity will harm them over whom iniquity hath no dominion. Through.

Introit

HE Lord heard, and had mercy upon me: the Lord became my helper. *Ps.* I will magnify thee, O Lord, for thou hast set me up: and not made my foes to triumph over me.

Collect

E beseech thee, O Lord, to further with thy gracious favour the fasts which we have begun: that as we keep this observance in the flesh, so we may have strength to perform the same in singleness of heart. Through.

¶ 2ⁿᵈ Collect is Of Saints (p. BCP 542) & 3ʳᵈ Of the Living and Departed (p. BCP 544).

Friday   **Proper of Season**   *Ash Wednesday*

Epistle. Isaiah 58:1

THUS SAITH THE LORD GOD: Cry aloud, spare not, lift up thy voice like a trumpet, and shew my people their transgression, and the house of Jacob their sins. Yet they seek me daily, and delight to know my ways, as a nation that did righteousness, and forsook not the ordinance of their God: they ask of me the ordinances of justice; they take delight in approaching to God. Wherefore have we fasted, say they, and thou seest not? wherefore have we afflicted our soul, and thou takest no knowledge? Behold, in the day of your fast ye find pleasure, and exact all your labours. Behold, ye fast for strife and debate, and to smite with the fist of wickedness: ye shall not fast as ye do this day, to make your voice to be heard on high. Is it such a fast that I have chosen? a day for a man to afflict his soul? is it to bow down his head as a bulrush, and to spread sackcloth and ashes under him? wilt thou call this a fast, and an acceptable day to the LORD? Is not this the fast that I have chosen? to loose the bands of wickedness, to undo the heavy burdens, and to let the oppressed go free, and that ye break every yoke? Is it not to deal thy bread to the hungry, and that thou bring the poor that are cast out to thy house? when thou seest the naked, that thou cover him; and that thou hide not thyself from thine own flesh? Then shall thy light break forth as the morning, and thine health shall spring forth speedily: and thy righteousness shall go before thee; the glory of the LORD shall be thy reward. Then shalt thou call, and the LORD shall answer; thou shalt cry, and he shall say, Here I am. For I the LORD thy God am merciful.

Gradual. One thing have I desired of the Lord, which I will require, even that I may dwell in the house of the Lord. ℣. To behold the fair beauty of the Lord, and to hide me in his holy temple.

Tract. O Lord, deal not with us after our sins: nor reward us according to our wickednesses. ℣. O Lord, remember not our old sins: but have mercy upon us, and that soon, for we are come to great misery. (Here genuflect.) ℣. Help us, O God of our salvation: and for the glory of thy name, O Lord, deliver us: and be merciful unto our sins, for thy name's sake.

Gospel. Matthew 5:43

AT THAT TIME: Jesus said unto his disciples: Ye have heard that it hath been said, Thou shalt love thy neighbour, and hate thine enemy. But I say unto you, Love your enemies, bless them that curse you, do good to them that hate you, and pray for them which despitefully use you, and persecute you; That ye may be the children of your Father which is in heaven: for he maketh his sun to rise on the evil and on the good, and sendeth rain on the just and on the unjust. For if ye love them which love you, what reward have ye? do not even the publicans the same? And if ye salute your brethren only, what do ye more than others? do not even the publicans so? Be ye therefore perfect, even as your Father which is in heaven is perfect. Take heed that ye do not your alms before men, to be seen of them: otherwise ye have no reward of your Father which is in heaven. Therefore when thou doest thine alms, do not sound a trumpet before thee, as the hypocrites do in the synagogues and in the streets, that they may have glory of men. Verily I say unto you, They have their reward. But when thou doest alms, let not thy left hand know what thy right hand doeth: That thine alms may be in secret: and thy Father which seeth in secret himself shall reward thee openly.

Offertory. Quicken me, O Lord, according to thy word: that I may know thy testimonies.

Secret

RANT, we beseech thee, O Lord, that this sacrifice of Lenten observance which we offer: may both render our souls acceptable unto thee, and make us more readily to serve thee in continence. Through.

¶ 2nd Secret is Of Saints (p. BCP 542) & 3rd Of the Living and Departed (p. BCP 544).

Communion. Serve the Lord in fear, and rejoice unto him with reverence: lay hold on discipline, lest ye perish from the right way.

Postcommunion

OUR forth upon us, O Lord, the Spirit of thy charity: that as thou hast fulfilled us with one heavenly bread, so of thy goodness thou wouldest make us to be of one heart and mind. Through . . . in the unity of the same.

¶ 2nd Postcommunion is Of Saints (p. BCP 542) & 3rd Of the Living and Departed (p. BCP 544).

PRIEST. Let us pray.
DEACON. Humble your heads before God.
¶ The Priest then prays the following:

EFEND, O Lord, thy people, and mercifully cleanse them from all their sins: that no adversity may harm them, over whom iniquity hath no dominion. Through.

SATURDAY AFTER ASH WEDNESDAY

¶ In the Daily Office, the propers are of the Ferial Day, except the following Antiphon.

Ben. Ant. Yet they seek me daily, † and delight to know my ways.

Introit

HE Lord heard, and had mercy upon me: the Lord became my helper. *Ps.* I will magnify thee, O Lord, for thou hast set me up: and not made my foes to triumph over me.

Saturday · **Proper of Season** · *Ash Wednesday*

Collect

ssist us, O Lord, in these our supplications: and grant; that like as this solemn fast hath been ordained for the safety and healing of our bodies and our souls, so we may with devout observance celebrate the same. Through.

¶ 2ⁿᵈ Collect is Of Saints (p. BCP 542) & 3ʳᵈ Of the Living and Departed (p. BCP 544).

Epistle. Isaiah 58:9

THUS SAITH THE LORD GOD: If thou take away from the midst of thee the yoke, the putting forth of the finger, and speaking vanity; And if thou draw out thy soul to the hungry, and satisfy the afflicted soul; then shall thy light rise in obscurity, and thy darkness be as the noonday: And the LORD shall guide thee continually, and satisfy thy soul in drought, and make fat thy bones: and thou shalt be like a watered garden, and like a spring of water, whose waters fail not. And they that shall be of thee shall build the old waste places: thou shalt raise up the foundations of many generations; and thou shalt be called, The repairer of the breach, The restorer of paths to dwell in. If thou turn away thy foot from the sabbath, from doing thy pleasure on my holy day; and call the sabbath a delight, the holy of the LORD, honourable; and shalt honour him, not doing thine own ways, nor finding thine own pleasure, nor speaking thine own words: Then shalt thou delight thyself in the LORD; and I will cause thee to ride upon the high places of the earth, and feed thee with the heritage of Jacob thy father: for the mouth of the LORD hath spoken it.

Gradual. One thing have I desired of the Lord, which I will require, even that I may dwell in the house of the Lord. ℣. To behold the fair beauty of the Lord, and to visit his temple.

Gospel. Mark 6:47

AT THAT TIME: When even was come, the ship was in the midst of the sea, and Jesus alone on the land. And he saw them toiling in rowing; for the wind was contrary unto them: and about the fourth watch of the night he cometh unto them, walking upon the sea, and would have passed by them. But when they saw him walking upon the sea, they supposed it had been a spirit, and cried out: For they all saw him, and were troubled. And immediately he talked with them, and saith unto them, Be of good cheer: it is I; be not afraid. And he went up unto them into the ship; and the wind ceased: and they were sore amazed in themselves beyond measure, and wondered. For they considered not the miracle of the loaves: for their heart was hardened. And when they had passed over, they came into the land of Gennesaret, and drew to the shore. And when they were come out of the ship, straightway they knew him, And ran through that whole region round about, and began to carry about in beds those that were sick, where they heard he was. And whithersoever he entered, into villages, or cities, or country, they laid

Lent I

Proper of Season

the sick in the streets, and besought him that they might touch if it were but the border of his garment: and as many as touched him were made whole.

Offertory. Quicken me, O Lord, according to thy word: that I may know thy testimonies.

Secret

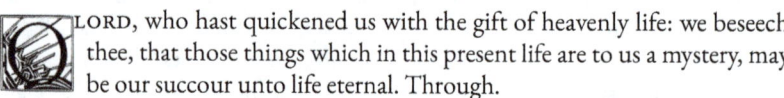CCEPT, O Lord, the sacrifice which thou hast ordained to be a worthy propitiation unto thee: and grant, we beseech thee, that we being cleansed by the operation of the same, may offer unto thee the acceptable devotion of our hearts. Through.

¶ 2nd Secret is Of Saints (p. BCP 542) & 3rd Of the Living and Departed (p. BCP 544).

Communion. Serve the Lord in fear, and rejoice unto him with reverence: lay hold on discipline, lest ye perish from the right way.

Postcommunion

LORD, who hast quickened us with the gift of heavenly life: we beseech thee, that those things which in this present life are to us a mystery, may be our succour unto life eternal. Through.

¶ 2nd Postcommunion is Of Saints (p. BCP 542) & 3rd Of the Living and Departed (p. BCP 544).

PRIEST. Let us pray.
DEACON. Humble your heads before God.
¶ The Priest then prays the following:

MAY thy faithful people, O God, be strengthened by thy gifts: that they receiving the same may seek them the more, and seeking them may obtain them everlastingly. Through.

FIRST SUNDAY OF LENT

I Evensong

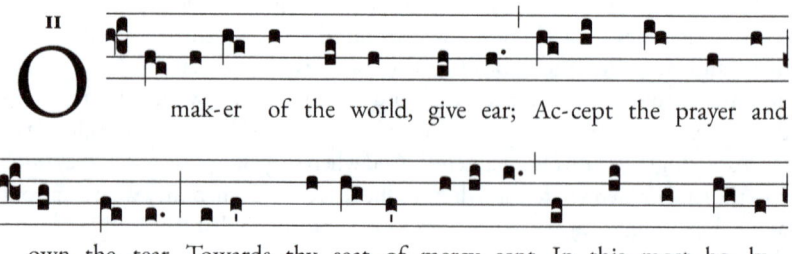

Lent I

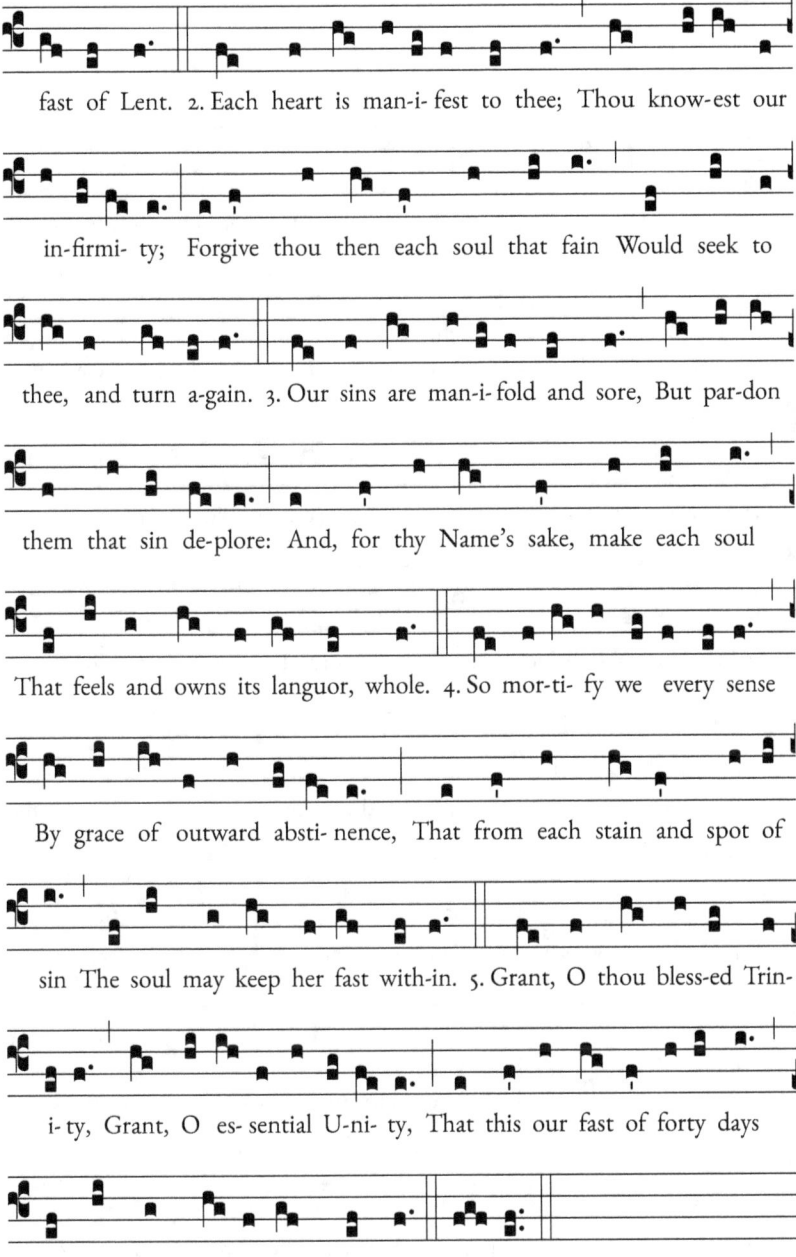

fast of Lent. 2. Each heart is man-i-fest to thee; Thou know-est our in-firmi-ty; Forgive thou then each soul that fain Would seek to thee, and turn a-gain. 3. Our sins are man-i-fold and sore, But par-don them that sin de-plore: And, for thy Name's sake, make each soul That feels and owns its languor, whole. 4. So mor-ti-fy we every sense By grace of outward absti-nence, That from each stain and spot of sin The soul may keep her fast with-in. 5. Grant, O thou bless-ed Trin-i-ty, Grant, O es-sential U-ni-ty, That this our fast of forty days May work our prof-it and thy praise. A-men.

℣. God shall give his Angels charge over thee.

℟. To keep thee in all thy ways.

Mag. Ant. Then shalt thou call, † and the Lord shall answer: thou shalt cry, and he shall say, Here am I.

Lent I # Proper of Season

Mattins

Invitatory Hymn

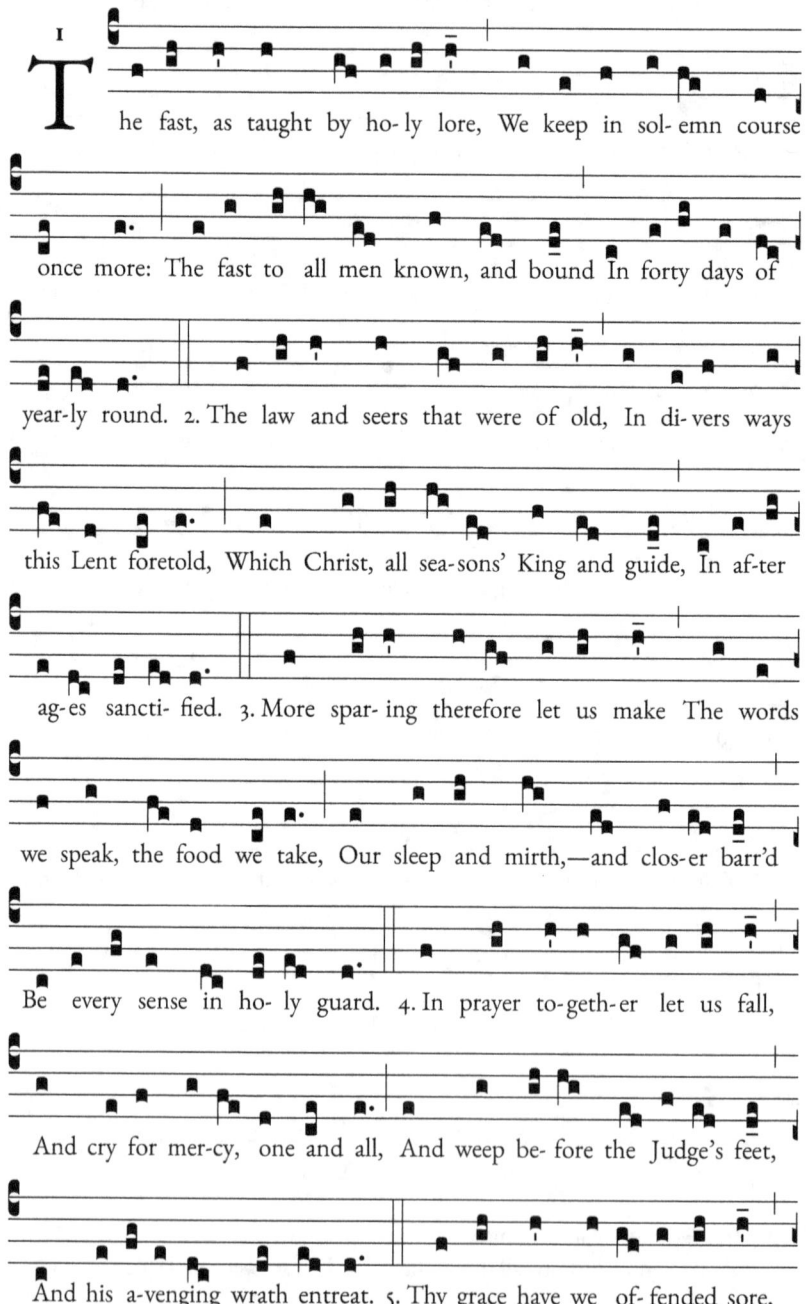

1. The fast, as taught by ho-ly lore, We keep in sol-emn course once more: The fast to all men known, and bound In forty days of year-ly round. 2. The law and seers that were of old, In di-vers ways this Lent foretold, Which Christ, all sea-sons' King and guide, In af-ter ag-es sancti-fied. 3. More spar-ing therefore let us make The words we speak, the food we take, Our sleep and mirth,—and clos-er barr'd Be every sense in ho-ly guard. 4. In prayer to-geth-er let us fall, And cry for mer-cy, one and all, And weep be-fore the Judge's feet, And his a-venging wrath entreat. 5. Thy grace have we of-fended sore,

Proper of Season *Lent I*

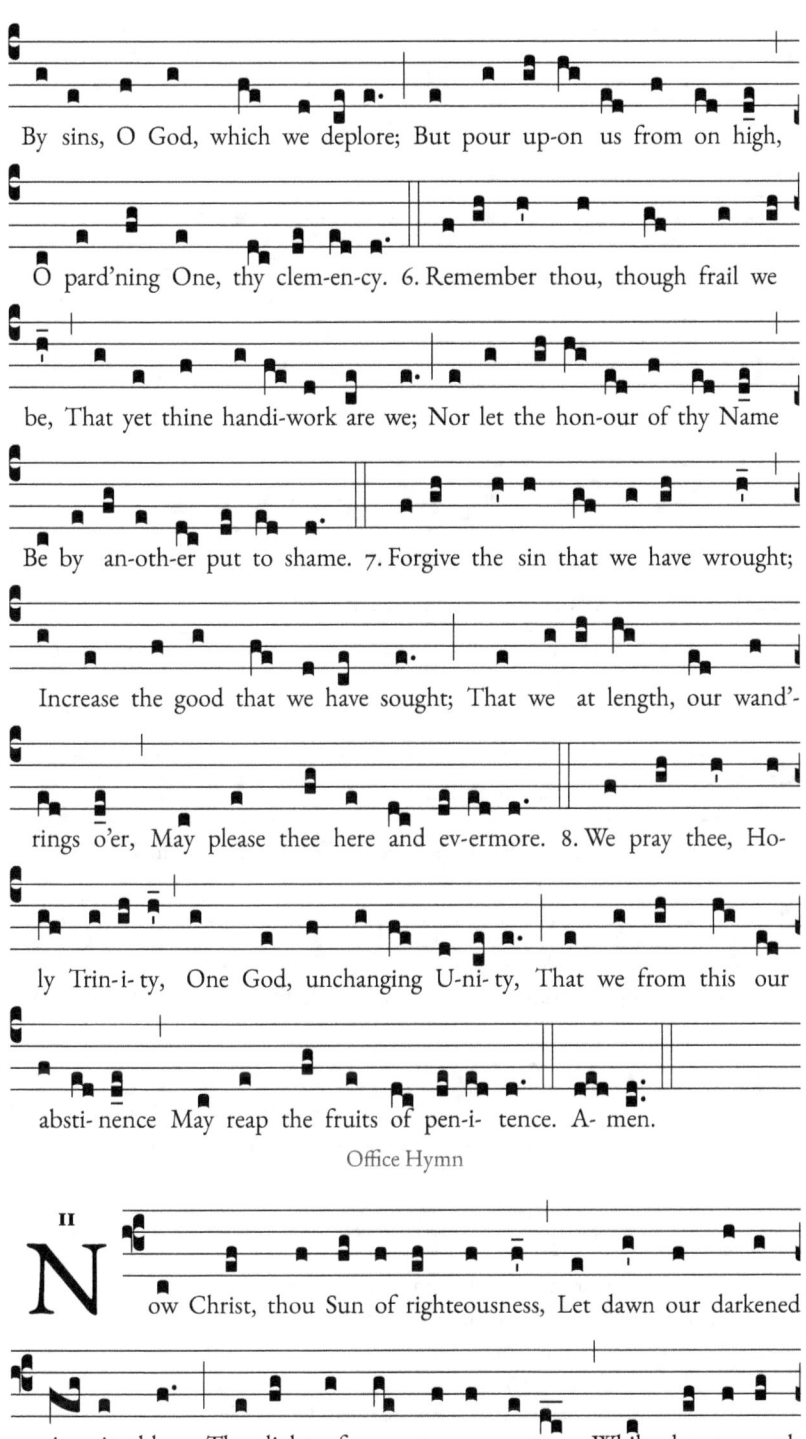

By sins, O God, which we deplore; But pour up-on us from on high, O pard'ning One, thy clem-en-cy. 6. Remember thou, though frail we be, That yet thine handi-work are we; Nor let the hon-our of thy Name Be by an-oth-er put to shame. 7. Forgive the sin that we have wrought; Increase the good that we have sought; That we at length, our wand'-rings o'er, May please thee here and ev-ermore. 8. We pray thee, Ho-ly Trin-i-ty, One God, unchanging U-ni-ty, That we from this our absti-nence May reap the fruits of pen-i-tence. A-men.

Office Hymn

Now Christ, thou Sun of righteousness, Let dawn our darkened spir-its bless: The light of grace to us re-store While day to earth

Lent I   **Proper of Season**

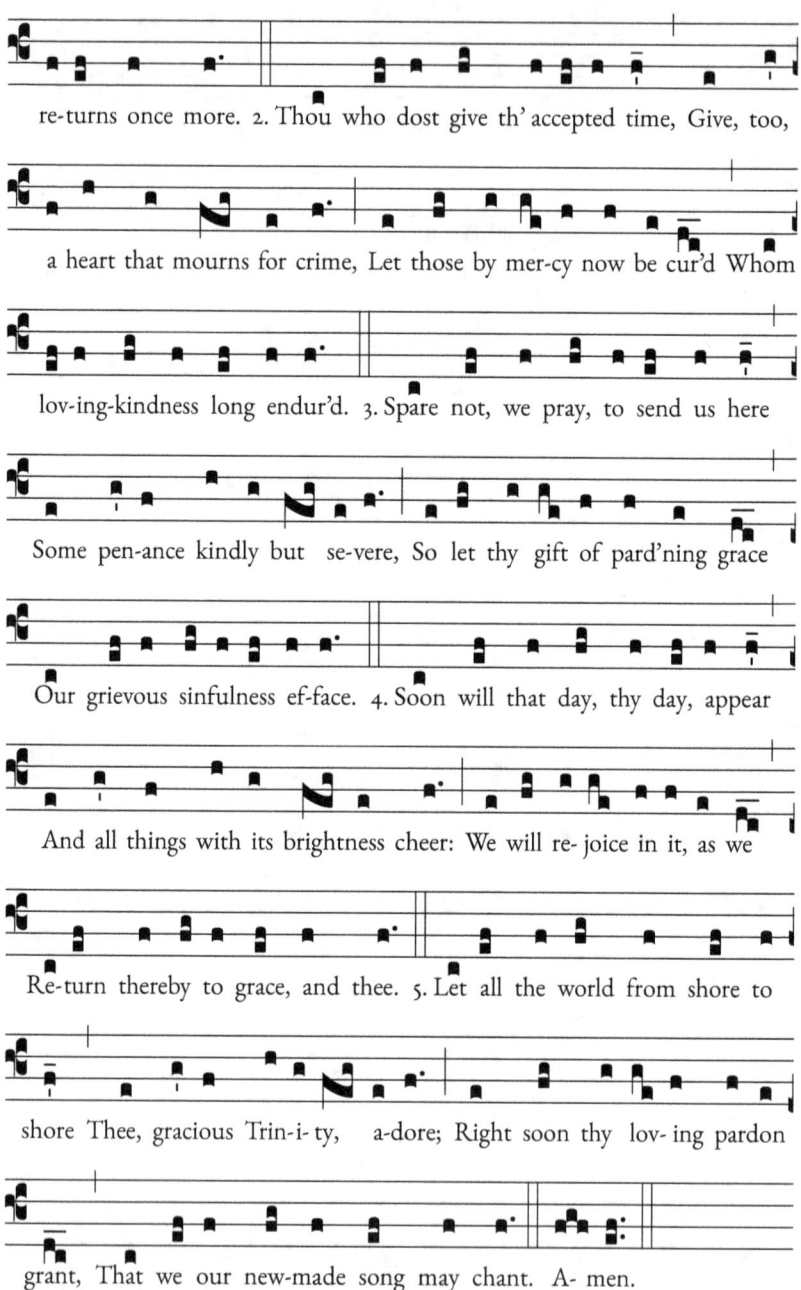

re-turns once more. 2. Thou who dost give th' accepted time, Give, too,

a heart that mourns for crime, Let those by mer-cy now be cur'd Whom

lov-ing-kindness long endur'd. 3. Spare not, we pray, to send us here

Some pen-ance kindly but se-vere, So let thy gift of pard'ning grace

Our grievous sinfulness ef-face. 4. Soon will that day, thy day, appear

And all things with its brightness cheer: We will re-joice in it, as we

Re-turn thereby to grace, and thee. 5. Let all the world from shore to

shore Thee, gracious Trin-i-ty, a-dore; Right soon thy lov-ing pardon

grant, That we our new-made song may chant. A-men.

℣. God shall give his Angels charge over thee.

℟. To keep thee in all thy ways.

Ben. Ant. Then was Jesus † led up of the Spirit into the wilderness to be tempted of the devil: and when he had fasted forty days and forty nights, he was afterward an hungred.

Proper of Season *Lent II*

II Evensong

¶ The Office Hymn & Versicle are of I Evensong, with the following Antiphon.

Mag. Ant. Behold, now † is the accepted time; behold, now is the day of salvation: let us therefore in all things approve ourselves as the ministers of God, in much patience, in watchings, in fastings, and by love unfeigned.

Lenten Ferial Office

¶ On Lenten Ferias, the Hymns and Versicles are taken from the First Sunday of Lent. The Antiphon and Collect are of the Day.

Ember Wednesday in Lent

Ben. Ant. This crooked † and perverse generation seeketh after a sign: and there shall no sign be given it, but the sign of the prophet Jonas.
Mag. Ant. For as Jonas † was three days and three nights in the whale's belly, so shall the Son of Man be in the heart of the earth.

Ember Friday in Lent

Ben. Ant. An Angel of the Lord † went down from heaven, and troubled the water, and one was healed.
Mag. Ant. He that made me whole, † the same commanded me: Take up thy bed, and walk in peace.

Ember Saturday in Lent

Ben. Ant. And Jesus taketh his disciples, † and goeth up into a mountain, and was transfigured before them.

Second Sunday of Lent

¶ The Daily Office propers are as in the First Sunday of Lent (p. 352), except for the following Antiphons.

Mag. Ant. Tell the vision † which ye have seen to no man, until the Son of Man be risen again from the dead.
Ben. Ant. Jesus went thence, † and departed into the coasts of Tyre and Sidon: and behold, a woman of Canaan came out of the same coasts, and cried, saying: Have mercy on me, thou Son of David.
Mag. Ant. Jesus said † unto the woman of Canaan, It is not meet to take the children's bread, and to cast it to dogs. Truth, Lord; yet the dogs eat of the crumbs which fall from their master's table. Then Jesus answered, O woman, great is thy faith; be it unto thee even as thou wilt.

Passion Sunday # Proper of Season

Third Sunday of Lent

❧ The Daily Office propers are as in the First Sunday of Lent (p. 352), except for the following Antiphons.

Mag. Ant. But the father † said to his servants, Bring forth the best robe and put it on him; and put a ring on his hand, and shoes on his feet.
Ben. Ant. When a strong man armed † keepeth his palace, all his goods are in peace.
Mag. Ant. A certain woman † of the company lifted up her voice and cried, Blessed is the womb that bare thee, and the paps which thou hast sucked. But Jesus answered, Yea, rather, blessed are they that hear the word of God, and keep it.

Fourth Sunday of Lent

❧ The Daily Office propers are as in the First Sunday of Lent (p. 352), except for the following Antiphons.

Mag. Ant. Woman, † hath no man condemned thee? No man, Lord. Neither do I condemn thee; go and sin no more.
Ben. Ant. When Jesus † lifted up his eyes, and saw a great company come unto him, he saith unto Philip: Whence shall we buy bread that these may eat? And this he said to prove him; for he himself knew what he would do.
Mag. Ant. And Jesus † went up into a mountain, and there he sat with his disciples.

Passion Sunday

I Evensong

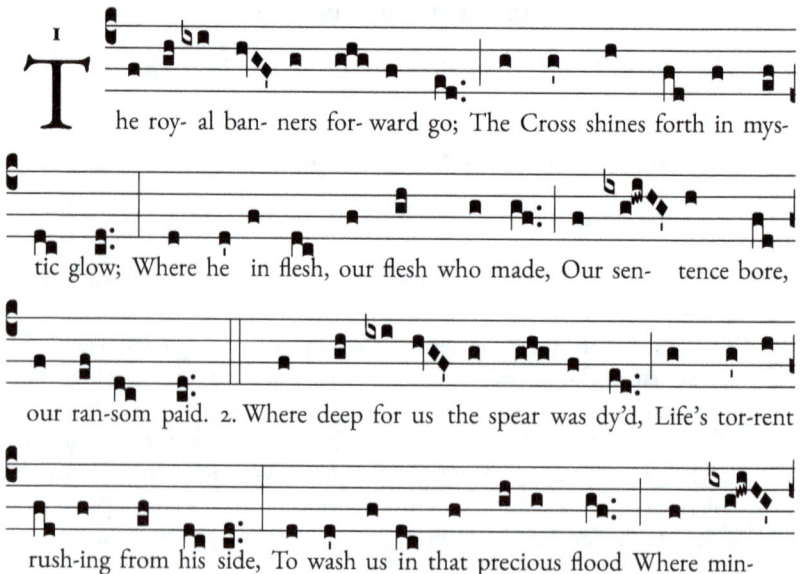

The roy-al ban-ners for-ward go; The Cross shines forth in mys-tic glow; Where he in flesh, our flesh who made, Our sen-tence bore, our ran-som paid. 2. Where deep for us the spear was dy'd, Life's tor-rent rush-ing from his side, To wash us in that precious flood Where min-

Proper of Season — *Passion Sunday*

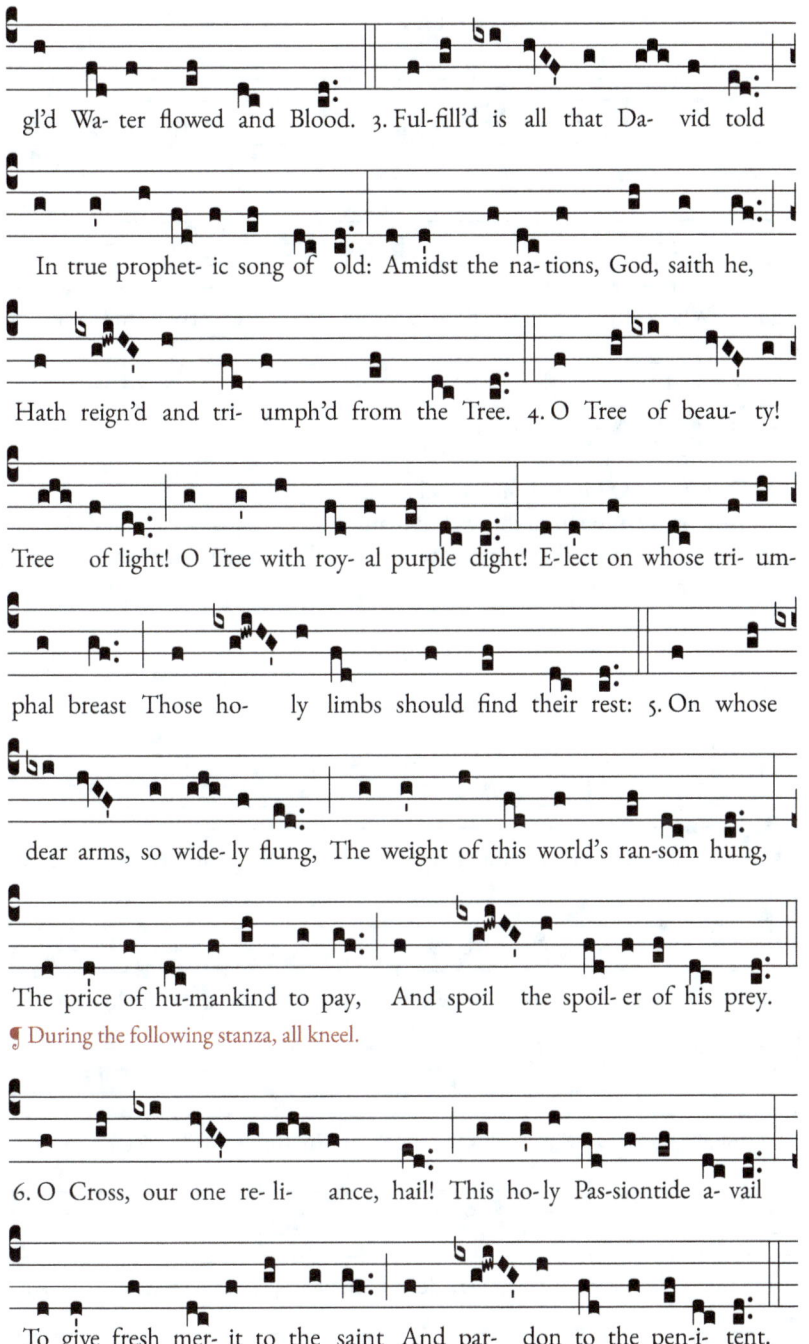

359

Passion Sunday   **Proper of Season**

¶ NOTE, The following stanza is never changed.

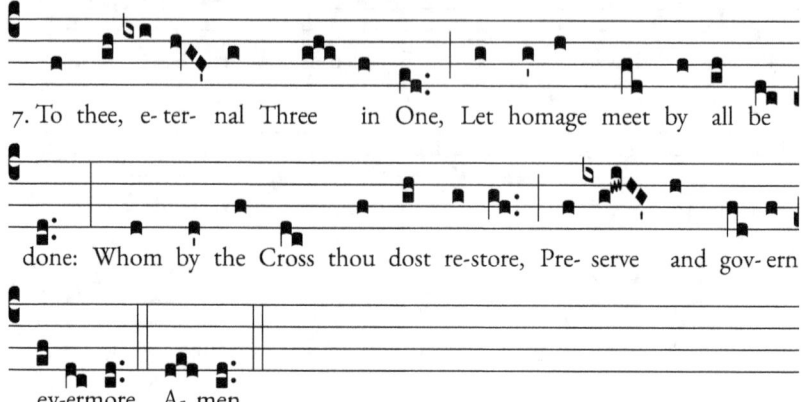

7. To thee, e- ter- nal Three in One, Let homage meet by all be done: Whom by the Cross thou dost re-store, Pre- serve and gov- ern ev-ermore. A- men.

℣. Deliver me, O Lord, from the evil man.
℟. And preserve me from the wicked man.

Mag. Ant. I am one † that bear witness of myself, and the Father that sent me beareth witness of me.

Mattins

Invitatory Hymn

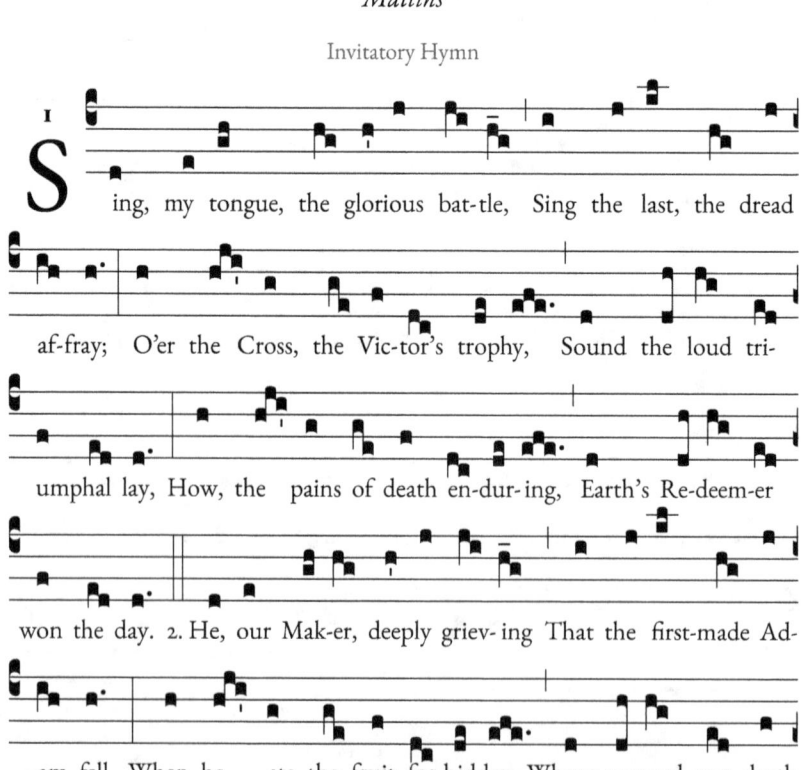

Sing, my tongue, the glorious bat-tle, Sing the last, the dread af-fray; O'er the Cross, the Vic-tor's trophy, Sound the loud tri- umphal lay, How, the pains of death en-dur-ing, Earth's Re-deem-er won the day. 2. He, our Mak-er, deeply griev- ing That the first-made Ad- am fell, When he ate the fruit for-bidden Whose re-ward was death

Proper of Season *Passion Sunday*

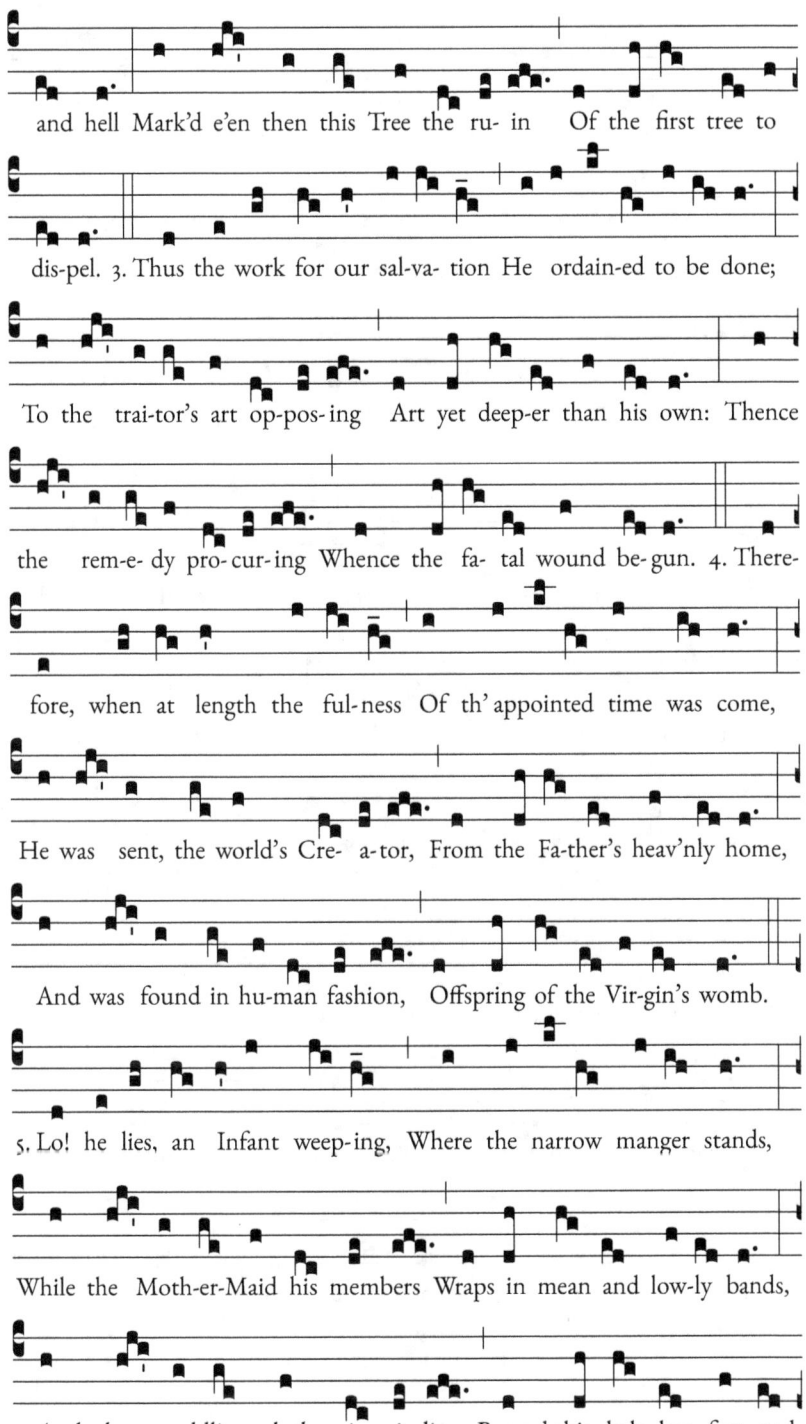

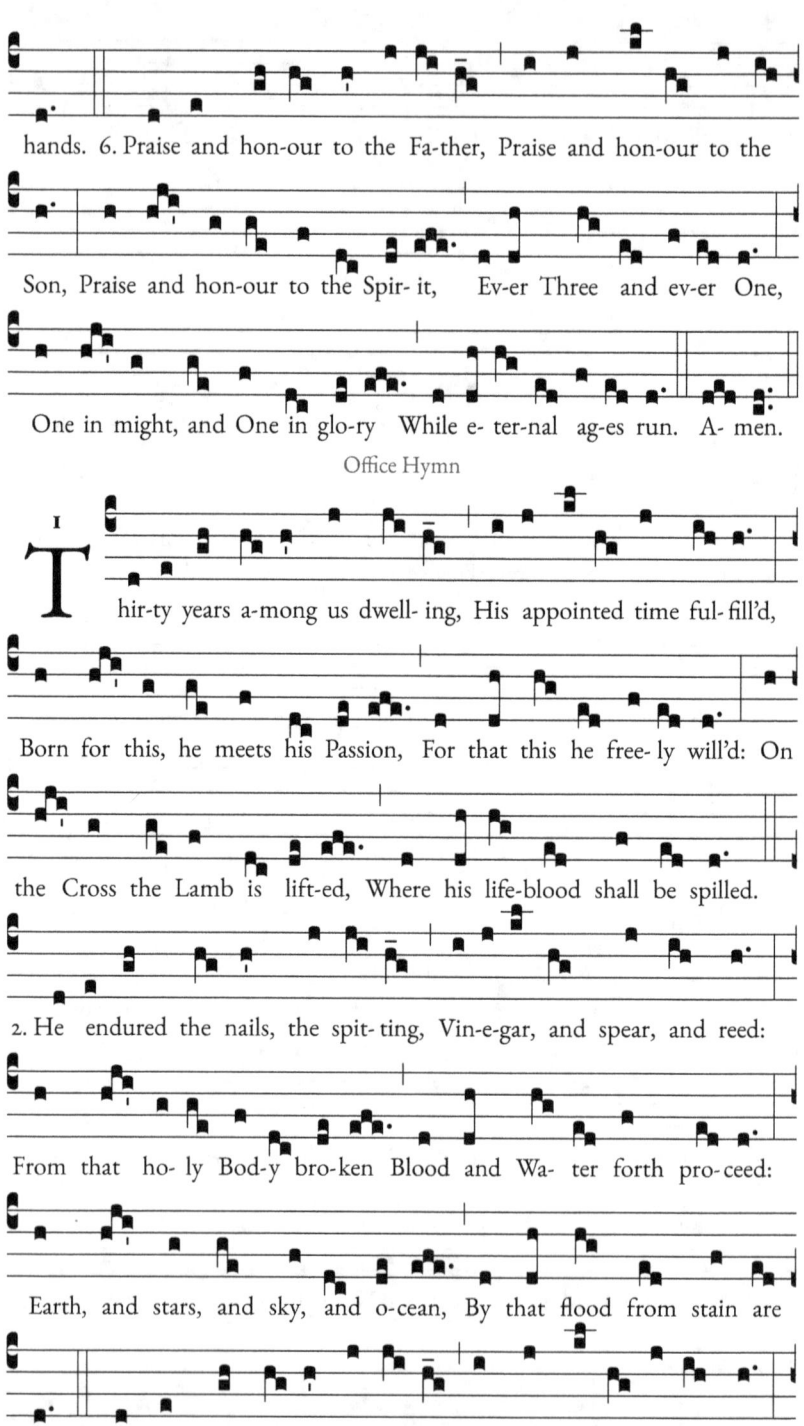

Proper of Season *Passion Sunday*

None in fol-iage, none in blossom, None in fruit thy peer may be:

Sweet-est wood, and sweet-est i-ron! Sweet-est weight is hung on thee.

4. Bend thy boughs, O Tree of glo-ry, Thy re-lax-ing sin-ews bend:

For a-while the ancient ri-gour That thy birth bestow'd, sus-pend:

And the King of heav'nly beauty On thy bos-om gently tend.

5. Thou a-lone wast counted worthy This world's ran-som to sus-tain;

That a shipwreck'd race for ev-er Might a port of ref-uge gain:

With the sa-cred Blood a-nointed Of the Lamb for sinners slain.

6. Glo-ry be to God, and hon-our In the highest, as is meet, To the

Son and to the Father, And th' e-ter-nal Par-a-clete, Whose is

Easter Day ## Proper of Season

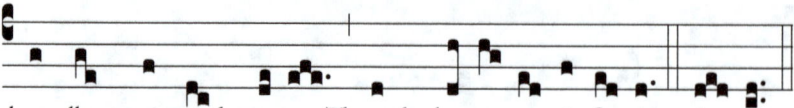

boundless praise and pow-er Through the ag- es in-fi- nite. A- men.

℣. Deliver me from mine enemies, O God.

℟. Defend me from them that rise up against me.

Ben. Ant. Jesus said † unto the multitude of the Jews, and to the chief priests: He that is of God heareth God's words; ye therefore hear them not, because ye are not of God.

II Evensong

¶ The Office Hymn & Versicle are of I Evensong, with the following Antiphon.

Mag. Ant. Your father Abraham † rejoiced to see my day: and he saw it and was glad.

PASSIONTIDE FERIAL OFFICE

¶ On Passiontide Ferias, the Hymns and Versicles are taken from Passion Sunday. The Antiphon and Collect are of the Day.

PALM SUNDAY

¶ The Daily Office propers are as in Passion Sunday, except for the following Antiphons.

Mag. Ant. Righteous Father, † the world hath not known thee: but I have known thee, because thou hast sent me.

Ben. Ant. The multitudes † which came together for the feast day cried unto the Lord: Blessed is he that cometh in the Name of the Lord. Hosanna in the highest.

Mag. Ant. For it is written, † I will smite the shepherd, and the sheep shall be scattered. But after I am risen again, I will go before you into Galilee: there shall ye see me, saith the Lord.

EASTER DAY

I Evensong

¶ If I Evensong of Easter Day be not said during the service of Easter Even, then it is said as usual with the following Antiphon, omitting the Hymn and Versicle.

Mag. Ant. In the end of the sabbath, † as it began to dawn toward the first day of the week, came Mary Magdalene and the other Mary to see the sepulchre, alleluia.

Proper of Season

Easter Day

Mattins

Invitatory Hymn

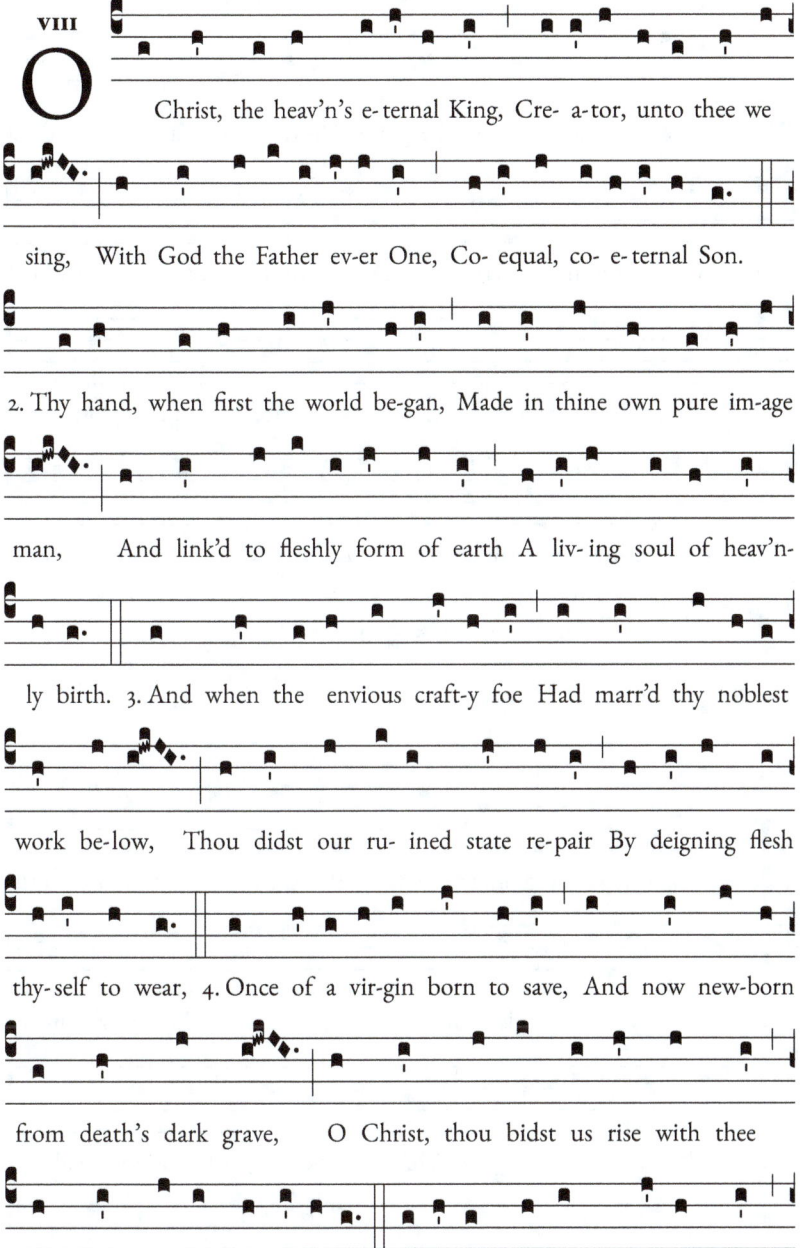

VIII O Christ, the heav'n's e-ternal King, Cre-a-tor, unto thee we sing, With God the Father ev-er One, Co-equal, co-e-ternal Son.

2. Thy hand, when first the world be-gan, Made in thine own pure im-age man, And link'd to fleshly form of earth A liv-ing soul of heav'n-ly birth. 3. And when the envious craft-y foe Had marr'd thy noblest work be-low, Thou didst our ru-ined state re-pair By deigning flesh thy-self to wear. 4. Once of a vir-gin born to save, And now new-born from death's dark grave, O Christ, thou bidst us rise with thee From death to immor-tal-i-ty. 5. E-ternal Shepherd, thou art wont

Easter Day   ## Proper of Season

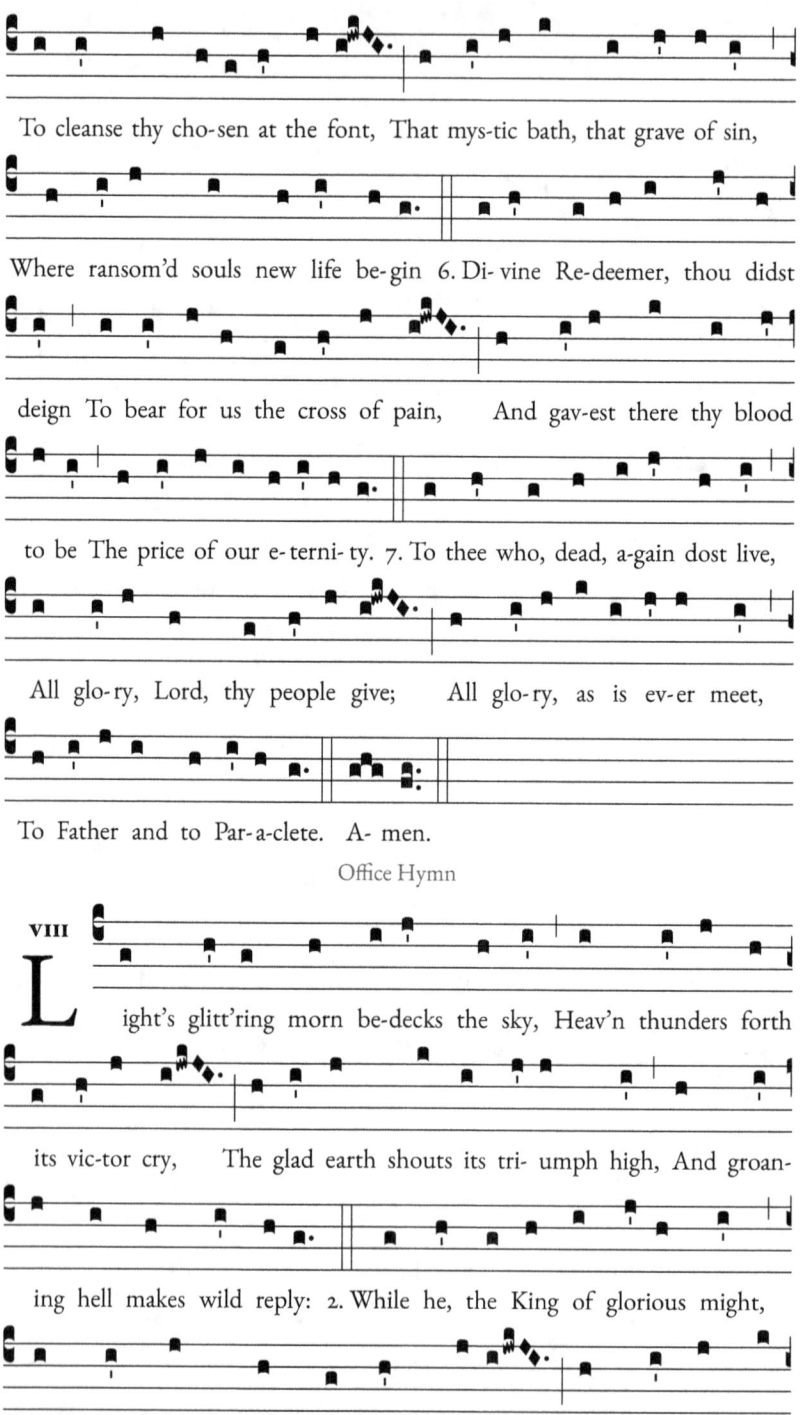

To cleanse thy cho-sen at the font, That mys-tic bath, that grave of sin,

Where ransom'd souls new life be-gin 6. Di-vine Re-deemer, thou didst

deign To bear for us the cross of pain, And gav-est there thy blood

to be The price of our e-ter-ni-ty. 7. To thee who, dead, a-gain dost live,

All glo-ry, Lord, thy people give; All glo-ry, as is ev-er meet,

To Father and to Par-a-clete. A-men.

Office Hymn

VIII

Light's glitt'ring morn be-decks the sky, Heav'n thunders forth

its vic-tor cry, The glad earth shouts its tri-umph high, And groan-

ing hell makes wild reply: 2. While he, the King of glorious might,

Treads down death's strength in death's despite, And trampling hell

Proper of Season *Easter Day*

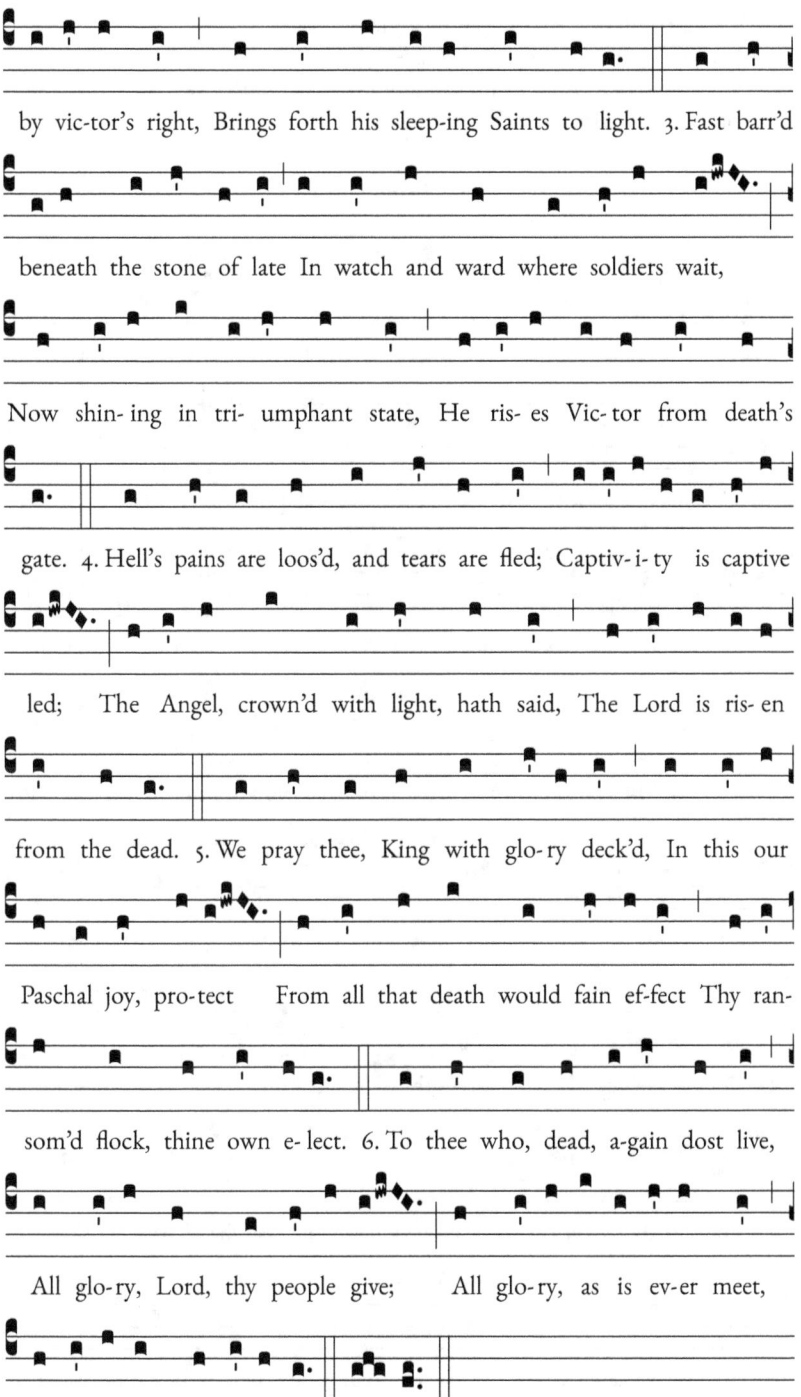

by vic-tor's right, Brings forth his sleep-ing Saints to light. 3. Fast barr'd

beneath the stone of late In watch and ward where soldiers wait,

Now shin-ing in tri-umphant state, He ris-es Vic-tor from death's

gate. 4. Hell's pains are loos'd, and tears are fled; Captiv-i-ty is captive

led; The Angel, crown'd with light, hath said, The Lord is ris-en

from the dead. 5. We pray thee, King with glo-ry deck'd, In this our

Paschal joy, pro-tect From all that death would fain ef-fect Thy ran-

som'd flock, thine own e-lect. 6. To thee who, dead, a-gain dost live,

All glo-ry, Lord, thy people give; All glo-ry, as is ev-er meet,

To Father and to Par-a-clete. A-men.

Easter Day   # Proper of Season

℣. This is the day which the Lord hath made, alleluia.
℞. We will rejoice and be glad in it, alleluia.
Ben. Ant. And very early in the morning † the first day of the week, they came unto the sepulchre at the rising of the sun, alleluia.

II Evensong

The Lamb's high banquet we await In snow-white robes of roy-al state: And now, the Red Sea's channel past, To Christ our Prince we sing at last. 2. Upon the Al-tar of the Cross His Bod-y hath re-deem'd our loss: And tast-ing of his ros-eate Blood Our life is hid with him in God. 3. That Paschal Eve God's arm was bar'd, The dev-as-ta-ting Angel spar'd: By strength of hand our hosts went free From Phar-aoh's ruthless tyr-anny. 4. Now Christ, our Paschal Lamb, is slain, The Lamb of God that knows no stain, The true Ob-la-tion of-fer'd

Easter Day

here, Our own un-leav-ened Bread sincere. 5. O thou, from whom hell's mon-arch flies, O great, O ver-y Sac-ri-fice, Thy cap-tive people are set free, And endless life re-stor'd in thee. 6. For Christ, a-ris-ing from the dead, From conquer'd hell vic-torious sped, And thrust the ty-rant down to chains, And Par-a-dise for man re-gains. 7. We pray thee, King with glo-ry deck'd, In this our Paschal joy, pro-tect From all that death would fain ef-fect Thy ransom'd flock, thine own e-lect. 8. To thee who, dead, a-gain dost live, All glo-ry, Lord, thy people give; All glo-ry, as is ev-er meet, To Fa-ther and to Par-a-clete. A-men.

℣. This is the day which the Lord hath made, alleluia.

℟. We will rejoice and be glad in it, alleluia.

Mag. Ant. And when they looked, † they saw that the stone was rolled away: for it was very great, alleluia.

¶ During Easter Week, in the Daily Office, the Office Hymns & Versicles are from Easter Day.

Proper of Season

Easter Week

ANTIPHONS WITHIN EASTER WEEK

Easter Monday

Ben. Ant. Jesus himself † drew near to his disciples in the way, and went with them: but their eyes were holden that they should not know him: and he rebuked them, saying, O fools and slow of heart to believe all that the prophets have spoken, alleluia.

Mag. Ant. What manner of communications † are these that ye have one to another, as ye walk, and are sad? alleluia, alleluia.

Easter Tuesday

Ben. Ant. Jesus stood † in the midst of his disciples and said unto them, Peace be unto you, alleluia, alleluia.

Mag. Ant. Behold my hands † and my feet, that it is I myself, alleluia.

Easter Wednesday

Ben. Ant. Cast the net † on the right side of the ship, and ye shall find, alleluia.

Mag. Ant. Jesus saith unto his disciples, † Bring of the fish which ye have now caught. Simon Peter went up, and drew the net to land, full of great fishes, alleluia.

Easter Thursday

Ben. Ant. Mary stood † at the sepulchre weeping, and seeth two Angels in white, sitting, and the napkin that was about the head of Jesus, alleluia.

Mag. Ant. They have taken † away my Lord, and I know not where they have laid him. If thou have borne him hence, tell me, alleluia: and I will take him away, alleluia.

Easter Friday

Ben. Ant. The eleven disciples, † when they saw the Lord in Galilee, worshipped him, alleluia.

Mag. Ant. All power † is given unto me in heaven and in earth, alleluia.

Easter Saturday

Ben. Ant. They ran both together, † and the other disciple did outrun Peter, and came first to the sepulchre, alleluia.

Mag. Ant. The same day † at evening, being the first day of the week, when the doors were shut where the disciples were assembled, came Jesus and stood in the midst, and saith unto them, Peace be unto you, alleluia.

Proper of Season *Easter I Week*

Low Sunday

¶ In the Daily Office, the Hymns are of Easter Day (p. 364), with the Versicles and Antiphons as followeth.

℣. Abide with us, Lord, alleluia.
℟. For it is toward evening, alleluia.

Mag. Ant. The same day † at evening, being the first day of the week, when the doors were shut where the disciples were assembled, came Jesus and stood in the midst, and saith unto them, Peace be unto you, alleluia.

℣. In thy resurrection, O Christ, alleluia.
℟. Let heaven and earth rejoice, alleluia.

Ben. Ant. The same day † at evening, being the first day of the week, when the doors were shut where the disciples were assembled, came Jesus and stood in the midst, and saith unto them, Peace be unto you, alleluia.

℣. Abide with us, Lord, alleluia.
℟. For it is toward evening, alleluia.

Mag. Ant. After eight days, † when the doors were shut, the Lord entered, and said unto them, Peace be unto you, alleluia, alleluia.

Eastertide Ferial Office

¶ On Ferias in Eastertide, the Hymns are as in Easter Day (p. 364). The Versicles are as followeth. The Antiphon is proper.

Mattins

℣. In thy resurrection, O Christ, alleluia.
℟. Let heaven and earth rejoice, alleluia.

Evensong

℣. Abide with us, Lord, alleluia.
℟. For it is toward evening, alleluia.

The First Week after the Easter Octave

Monday

Ben. Ant. When Jesus was risen † early the first day of the week, he appeared first to Mary Magdalene, out of whom he had cast seven devils, alleluia.
Mag. Ant. Peace be unto you, it is I, † alleluia: be not afraid, alleluia.

Tuesday

Ben. Ant. I go before you † into Galilee: there shall ye see me, as I said unto you, alleluia, alleluia.
Mag. Ant. Reach hither thy finger, † and examine the print of the nails, alleluia: and be not faithless, but believing, alleluia.

Easter II Week   # Proper of Season

Wednesday

Ben. Ant. I am the true vine, † alleluia: and ye are the true branches, alleluia
Mag. Ant. Because thou hast seen me, † Thomas, thou hast believed: blessed are they that have not seen, and yet have believed, alleluia.

Thursday

Ben. Ant. My heart burns † within me; I desire to behold my Lord: I seek, and find not where they have laid him, alleluia, alleluia.
Mag. Ant. I did put my finger † into the print of the nails, and thrust my hand into his side, and said, My Lord and my God, alleluia.

Friday

Ben. Ant. There came unto the tomb † Mary Magdalene and the other Mary, to see the sepulchre, alleluia.

¶ At Evensong, unless a Double Feast or some Octave occur on the following day, the Office is of Saint Mary, and this Office is said on the following Saturday. The same order is observed on the other Saturdays through the Saturday before Easter V.

Second Sunday after Easter

¶ In the Daily Office, the Hymns are of Easter Day (p. 364), with the following.

℣. Abide with us, Lord, alleluia.
℟. For it is toward evening, alleluia.
Mag. Ant. I am † the Shepherd of the sheep: I am the way, the truth, and the life: I am the Good Shepherd; and I know my sheep, and am known of mine, alleluia, alleluia.

℣. In thy resurrection, O Christ, alleluia.
℟. Let heaven and earth rejoice, alleluia.
Ben. Ant. I am † the Shepherd of the sheep: I am the way, the truth, and the life: I am the Good Shepherd; and I know my sheep, and am known of mine, alleluia, alleluia.

℣. Abide with us, Lord, alleluia.
℟. For it is toward evening, alleluia.
Mag. Ant. I am † the Good Shepherd, who feed my sheep; and I lay down my life for my sheep, alleluia.

The Second Week after the Easter Octave

Monday

Ben. Ant. Go ye into the world, † alleluia, and teach all nations, alleluia.
Mag. Ant. The Good Shepherd † layeth down his life for the sheep, alleluia.

Proper of Season — *Patronage of St. Joseph*

Tuesday

Ben. Ant. Go ye into the world † and teach all nations, baptizing them in the Name of the Father, and of the Son, and of the Holy Ghost, alleluia.

Mag. Ant. He that is an hireling, † whose own the sheep are not, seeth the wolf coming, and leaveth the sheep, and fleeth: and the wolf catcheth them, and, scattereth the sheep, alleluia.

Wednesday

Ben. Ant. Go unto my brethren † and say unto them, alleluia: that they go into Galilee, alleluia: there shall they see me, alleluia, alleluia, alleluia.

Mag. Ant. As the Father knoweth me, † even so know I the Father: and I lay down my life for the sheep, alleluia.

Thursday

Ben. Ant. Art thou only † a stranger, and hast not heard concerning Jesus, how they delivered him to be condemned to death? alleluia.

Mag. Ant. Other sheep I have, † which are not of this fold: them also I must bring, and they shall hear my voice; and there shall be one fold and one Shepherd, alleluia.

Friday

Ben. Ant. Ought not Christ † to have suffered these things, and to enter into his glory? alleluia.

PATRONAGE OF ST. JOSEPH

I Evensong

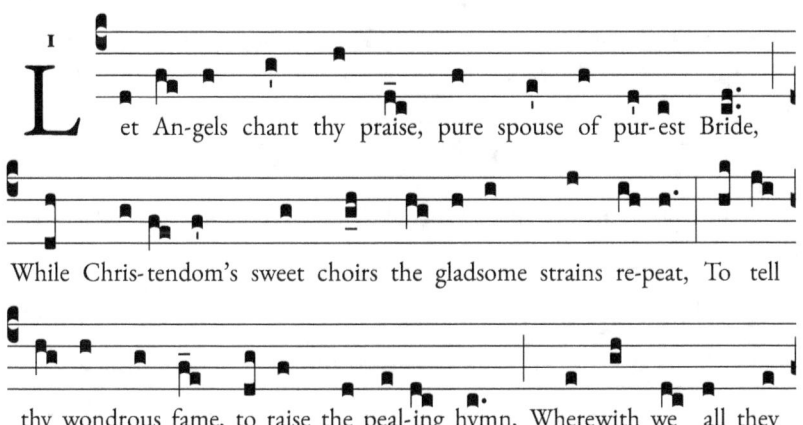

Let An-gels chant thy praise, pure spouse of pur-est Bride, While Chris-tendom's sweet choirs the gladsome strains re-peat, To tell thy wondrous fame, to raise the peal-ing hymn, Wherewith we all they

Patronage of St. Joseph Proper of Season

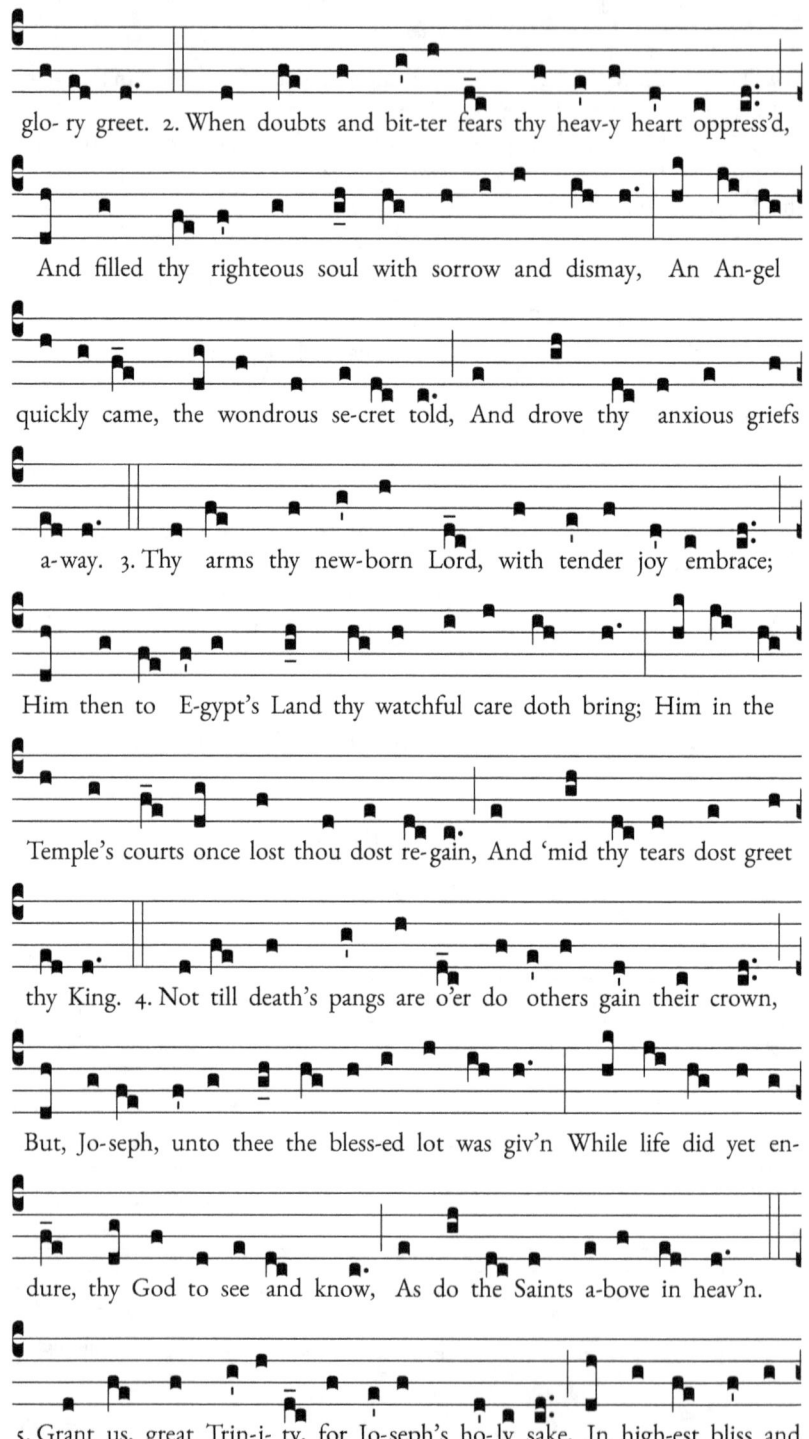

glo-ry greet. 2. When doubts and bit-ter fears thy heav-y heart oppress'd,

And filled thy righteous soul with sorrow and dismay, An An-gel

quickly came, the wondrous se-cret told, And drove thy anxious griefs

a-way. 3. Thy arms thy new-born Lord, with tender joy embrace;

Him then to E-gypt's Land thy watchful care doth bring; Him in the

Temple's courts once lost thou dost re-gain, And 'mid thy tears dost greet

thy King. 4. Not till death's pangs are o'er do others gain their crown,

But, Jo-seph, unto thee the bless-ed lot was giv'n While life did yet en-

dure, thy God to see and know, As do the Saints a-bove in heav'n.

5. Grant us, great Trin-i-ty, for Jo-seph's ho-ly sake, In high-est bliss and

Proper of Season *Patronage of St. Joseph*

love, a-bove the stars to reign, That we in joy with him may praise our lov-ing God, And sing our glad e-ter-nal strain. A-men.

℣. I do give praise unto thy name, alleluia.
℞. For thou art my defender and helper, alleluia.

Mag. Ant. When Mary † the mother of Jesus was espoused to Joseph, before they came together, she was found with child of the Holy Ghost, alleluia.

Mattins

¶ The Invitatory Hymn is of I Evensong.

Office Hymn

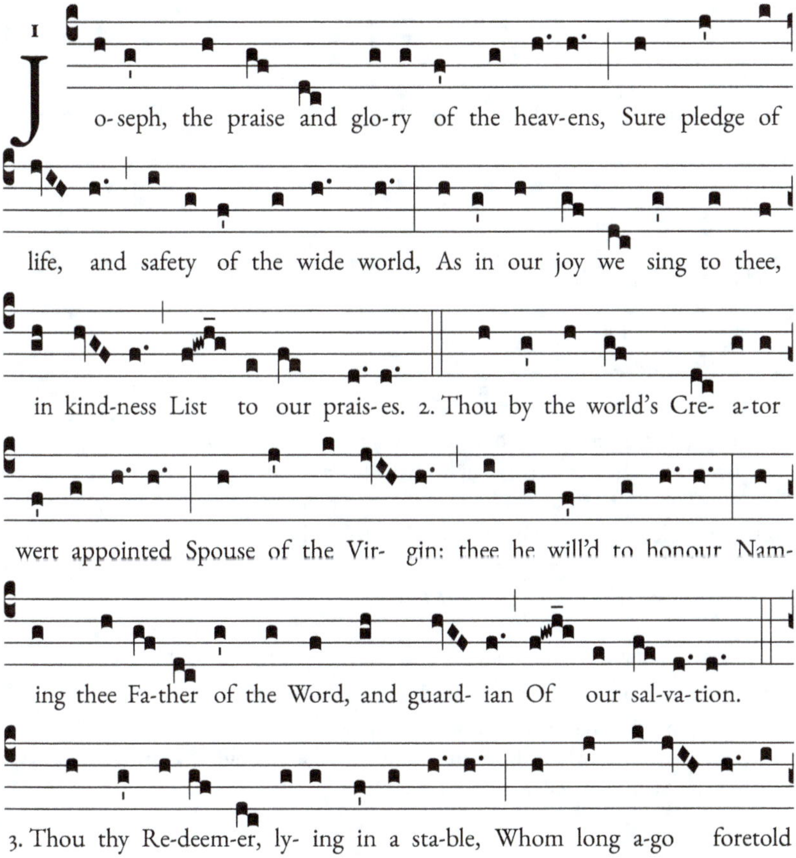

Jo-seph, the praise and glo-ry of the heav-ens, Sure pledge of life, and safety of the wide world, As in our joy we sing to thee, in kind-ness List to our prais-es. 2. Thou by the world's Cre-a-tor wert appointed Spouse of the Vir-gin: thee he will'd to honour Nam-ing thee Fa-ther of the Word, and guard-ian Of our sal-va-tion. 3. Thou thy Re-deem-er, ly-ing in a sta-ble, Whom long a-go foretold

Patronage of St. Joseph   # Proper of Season

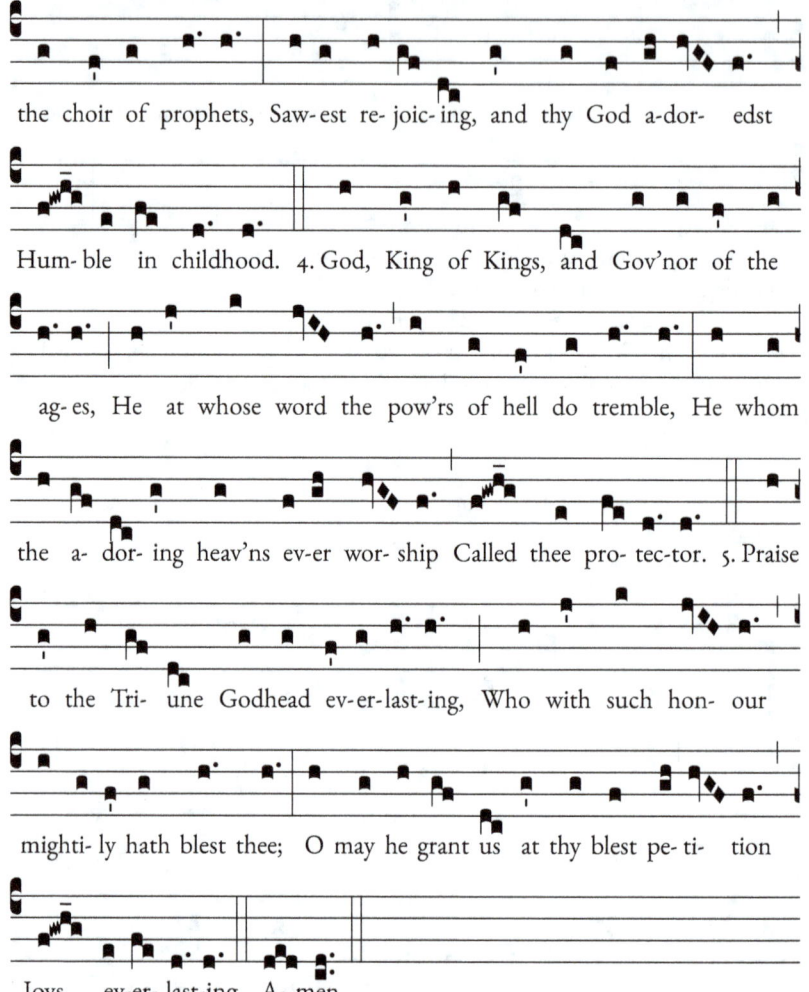

℣. Thou hast given me the defence of thy salvation, alleluia.
℟. And thy right hand also shall hold me up, alleluia.
Ben. Ant. Joseph, thou son of David, † fear not to take unto thee Mary thy wife: for that which is conceived in her is of the Holy Ghost, alleluia.

II Evensong

¶ The Office Hymn is of I Evensong, with the following Versicle & Antiphon.

℣. I sat down under his shadow with great delight, alleluia.
℟. And his fruit was sweet to my taste, alleluia.
Mag. Ant. Son, † why hast thou thus dealt with us? Behold, thy father and I have sought thee sorrowing, alleluia.

Proper of Season *Easter III Week*

Third Sunday after Easter

❡ In the Daily Office, the Hymns are of Easter Day (p. 364), with the following.

℣. Abide with us, Lord, alleluia.
℟. For it is toward evening, alleluia.

Mag. Ant. A little while, † and ye shall not see me, saith the Lord: and again, a little while, and ye shall see me, because I go to the Father, alleluia, alleluia.

℣. In thy resurrection, O Christ, alleluia.
℟. Let heaven and earth rejoice, alleluia.

Ben. Ant. A little while, † and ye shall not see me, saith the Lord: and again, a little while, and ye shall see me, because I go to the Father, alleluia, alleluia.

℣. Abide with us, Lord, alleluia.
℟. For it is toward evening, alleluia.

Mag. Ant. Verily I say unto you, † that ye shall weep and lament, but the world shall rejoice: and ye shall be sorrowful, but your sorrow shall be turned into joy, alleluia.

The Third Week after the Easter Octave

Monday

Ben. Ant. And beginning † at Moses and all the prophets, he expounded unto them the scriptures concerning himself, alleluia.
Mag. Ant. Your sorrow † shall be turned into joy, alleluia: and your joy no man taketh from you, alleluia, alleluia.

Tuesday

Ben. Ant. And they constrained him, † saying, Abide with us, O Lord, for it is toward evening, alleluia.
Mag. Ant. Sorrow † hath filled your heart: and your joy no man taketh from you, alleluia, alleluia.

Wednesday

Ben. Ant. Abide with us, † for it is toward evening, and the day is far spent, alleluia.
Mag. Ant. Your sorrow, † alleluia, shall be turned into joy, alleluia.

Thursday

Ben. Ant. And he went in † to tarry with them: and it came to pass, as he sat at meat with them, he took bread, and blessed it, and brake, and gave to them, alleluia, alleluia.
Mag. Ant. Verily, verily, I say unto you, † I will see you again, and your heart shall rejoice: and your joy no man taketh from you, alleluia.

Easter IV Week   # Proper of Season

Friday

Ben. Ant. They knew the Lord Jesus, † alleluia, in breaking of bread, alleluia.

Fourth Sunday after Easter

¶ In the Daily Office, the Hymns are of Easter Day (p. 364), with the following.

℣. Abide with us, Lord, alleluia.
℟. For it is toward evening, alleluia.

Mag. Ant. Now I go my way † to him that sent me; and none of you asketh me, Wither goest thou? alleluia, alleluia.

℣. In thy resurrection, O Christ, alleluia.
℟. Let heaven and earth rejoice, alleluia.

Ben. Ant. Now I go my way † to him that sent me; and none of you asketh me, Wither goest thou? alleluia, alleluia.

℣. Abide with us, Lord, alleluia.
℟. For it is toward evening, alleluia.

Mag. Ant. Now I go my way † to him that sent me: but because I have said these things unto you, sorrow hath filled your heart, alleluia.

The Fourth Week after the Easter Octave

Monday

Ben. Ant. Did not our heart † burn within us concerning Jesus, while he talked with us by the way? alleluia.

Mag. Ant. I tell you the truth; † it is expedient for you that I go away: for if I go not away, the Comforter will not come unto you, alleluia.

Tuesday

Ben. Ant. Peace be unto you, it is I, † alleluia: be not afraid, alleluia.

Mag. Ant. When the Comforter, † the Spirit of truth, is come, he will convince the world of sin, and of righteousness, and of judgement, alleluia.

Wednesday

Ben. Ant. A spirit † hath not flesh and bones, as ye see me have: believe ye therefore, alleluia.

Mag. Ant. I have yet † many things to say unto you, but ye cannot bear them now: howbeit, when he, the Spirit of truth, is come, he will guide you into all truth, alleluia.

Proper of Season

Thursday

Ben. Ant. The disciples † offered the Lord a piece of broiled fish, and of an honeycomb, alleluia, alleluia.
Mag. Ant. For he shall not speak of himself; † but whatsoever he shall hear, that shall he speak: and he will shew you things to come, alleluia.

Friday

Ben. Ant. These are the words † which I spake unto you, while I was yet with you, alleluia, alleluia.

ROGATION SUNDAY

¶ In the Daily Office, the Hymns are of Easter Day (p. 364), with the following.

℣. Abide with us, Lord, alleluia.
℟. For it is toward evening, alleluia.
Mag. Ant. Hitherto † have ye asked nothing in my Name ask, and ye shall receive, alleluia.

℣. In thy resurrection, O Christ, alleluia.
℟. Let heaven and earth rejoice, alleluia.
Ben. Ant. Hitherto † have ye asked nothing in my Name ask, and ye shall receive, alleluia.

℣. Abide with us, Lord, alleluia.
℟. For it is toward evening, alleluia.
Mag. Ant. Ask, † and ye shall receive, that your joy may be full: for the Father himself loveth you, because ye have loved me, and have believed, alleluia.

ROGATION MONDAY

¶ In the Daily Office, the Hymns are of Easter Day (p. 364), with the following.

℣. In thy resurrection, O Christ, alleluia.
℟. Let heaven and earth rejoice, alleluia.
Ben. Ant. Ask, † and ye shall receive; seek, and ye shall find; knock, and it shall be opened unto you, alleluia.

℣. Abide with us, Lord, alleluia.
℟. For it is toward evening, alleluia.
Mag. Ant. For the Father † himself loveth you, because you have loved me, and have believed, alleluia.

Ascension Vigil   # Proper of Season

Rogation Tuesday

¶ The Hymns of Easter Day (p. 364), with the following.

℣. In thy resurrection, O Christ, alleluia.
℟. Let heaven and earth rejoice, alleluia.
Ben. Ant. It behoved Christ to suffer, † and to rise again from the dead, alleluia.

℣. Abide with us, Lord, alleluia.
℟. For it is toward evening, alleluia.
Mag. Ant. I came forth from the Father, † and am come into the world: again I leave the world, and go to the Father, alleluia.

Vigil of Ascension

¶ The Hymns of Easter Day (p. 364), with the following.

℣. In thy resurrection, O Christ, alleluia.
℟. Let heaven and earth rejoice, alleluia.
Ben. Ant. Father, the hour is come: † glorify thy Son with the glory which I had with thee before the world was, alleluia.

Introit

WITH a voice of singing declare ye this, and let it be heard, alleluia: utter it even unto the end of the earth: the Lord hath delivered his people, alleluia, alleluia. *Ps.* O be joyful in God, all ye lands: sing praises unto his name, make his praise to be glorious.

Collect

O LORD, from whom all good things do come, grant to us thy humble servants: that by thy holy inspiration we may think those things that be good; and by thy merciful guiding may perform the same. Through.

GRANT, we beseech thee, Almighty God: that we, who in our affliction do put our trust in thy mercy; may ever be defended by thy protection against all adversities. (Through.)

GRANT, we beseech thee, O Lord God, that we thy servants may enjoy perpetual health of mind and of body: and, at the glorious intercession of blessed Mary ever Virgin, be delivered from present sadness, and rejoice in everlasting gladness. Through.

Epistle. Ephesians 4:7

BRETHREN: Unto every one of us is given grace according to the measure of the gift of Christ. Wherefore he saith, When he ascended up on high, he led captivity captive, and gave gifts unto men. (Now that he ascended, what is it but that he also descended first into the lower parts of the earth? He that

Proper of Season *Ascension Vigil*

descended is the same also that ascended up far above all heavens, that he might fill all things.) And he gave some, apostles; and some, prophets; and some, evangelists; and some, pastors and teachers; For the perfecting of the saints, for the work of the ministry, for the edifying of the body of Christ: Till we all come in the unity of the faith, and of the knowledge of the Son of God, unto a perfect man, unto the measure of the stature of the fulness of Christ.

Alleluia. Alleluia, alleluia. ℣. Christ is risen, and hath shewed light unto us, whom he hath redeemed with his blood. Alleluia. ℣. I came forth from the Father, and am come into the world: again I leave the world, and go to the Father. Alleluia.

Gospel. John 17:1

AT THAT TIME: Jesus lifted up his eyes to heaven, and said: Father, the hour is come; glorify thy Son, that thy Son also may glorify thee: As thou hast given him power over all flesh, that he should give eternal life to as many as thou hast given him. And this is life eternal, that they might know thee the only true God, and Jesus Christ, whom thou hast sent. I have glorified thee on the earth: I have finished the work which thou gavest me to do. And now, O Father, glorify thou me with thine own self with the glory which I had with thee before the world was. I have manifested thy name unto the men which thou gavest me out of the world: thine they were, and thou gavest them me; and they have kept thy word. Now they have known that all things whatsoever thou hast given me are of thee. For I have given unto them the words which thou gavest me; and they have received them, and have known surely that I came out from thee, and they have believed that thou didst send me. I pray for them: I pray not for the world, but for them which thou hast given me; for they are thine. And all mine are thine, and thine are mine; and I am glorified in them. And now I am no more in the world, but these are in the world, and I come to thee.

Offertory. O praise the Lord our God, ye people, and make the voice of his praise to be heard: who holdeth our soul in life, and suffereth not out feet to slip: praised be the Lord, who hath not cast out my prayer, nor turned his mercy from me, alleluia.

Secret

RECEIVE, O Lord, the prayers of thy faithful people, together with the offering of these sacrifices: that through these observances of our bounden devotion, we may attain unto heavenly glory. Through.

WE beseech thee, O Lord, that these our oblations may both loose the bonds of our iniquity, and obtain for us the gifts of thy loving-kindness. (Through.)

THROUGH thy mercy, O Lord, and the intercession of blessed Mary ever Virgin, may this oblation avail for our prosperity and peace both now and ever. Through.

Ascension Thursday # Proper of Season

Communion. O sing unto the Lord, alleluia: sing unto the Lord, and praise his name: be telling of his salvation from day to day, alleluia, alleluia.

Postcommunion

RANT unto us, O Lord, that we who have been fulfilled with the strength of thy heavenly table: may both desire those things which be right and obtain those things which we desire. Through.

E beseech thee, O Lord, to further with thy gracious favour these our supplications: that we, receiving thy gifts in our tribulation, may increase in thy love by the consolation of the same. (Through.)

RANT, we beseech thee, O Lord: that we who have received these aids to our salvation may at all times and in all places be protected by the advocacy of blessed Mary ever Virgin; in whose honour we have made these offerings to thy Majesty. Through.

ASCENSION OF OUR LORD

I Evensong

¶ The Office Hymn is of Mattins, with the following Versicle & Antiphon.

℣. God is gone up with a merry noise, alleluia.
℟. And the Lord with the sound of the trump, alleluia.
Mag. Ant. Father, † I have manifested thy Name unto the men which thou gavest me: and now I pray for them, not for the world, because I come to thee, alleluia.

Mattins

Invitatory Hymn

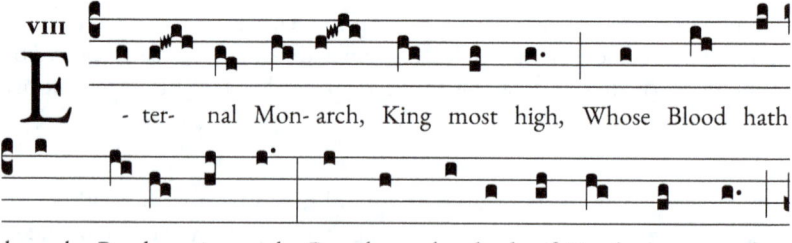

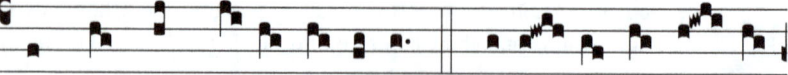

Proper of Season *Ascension Thursday*

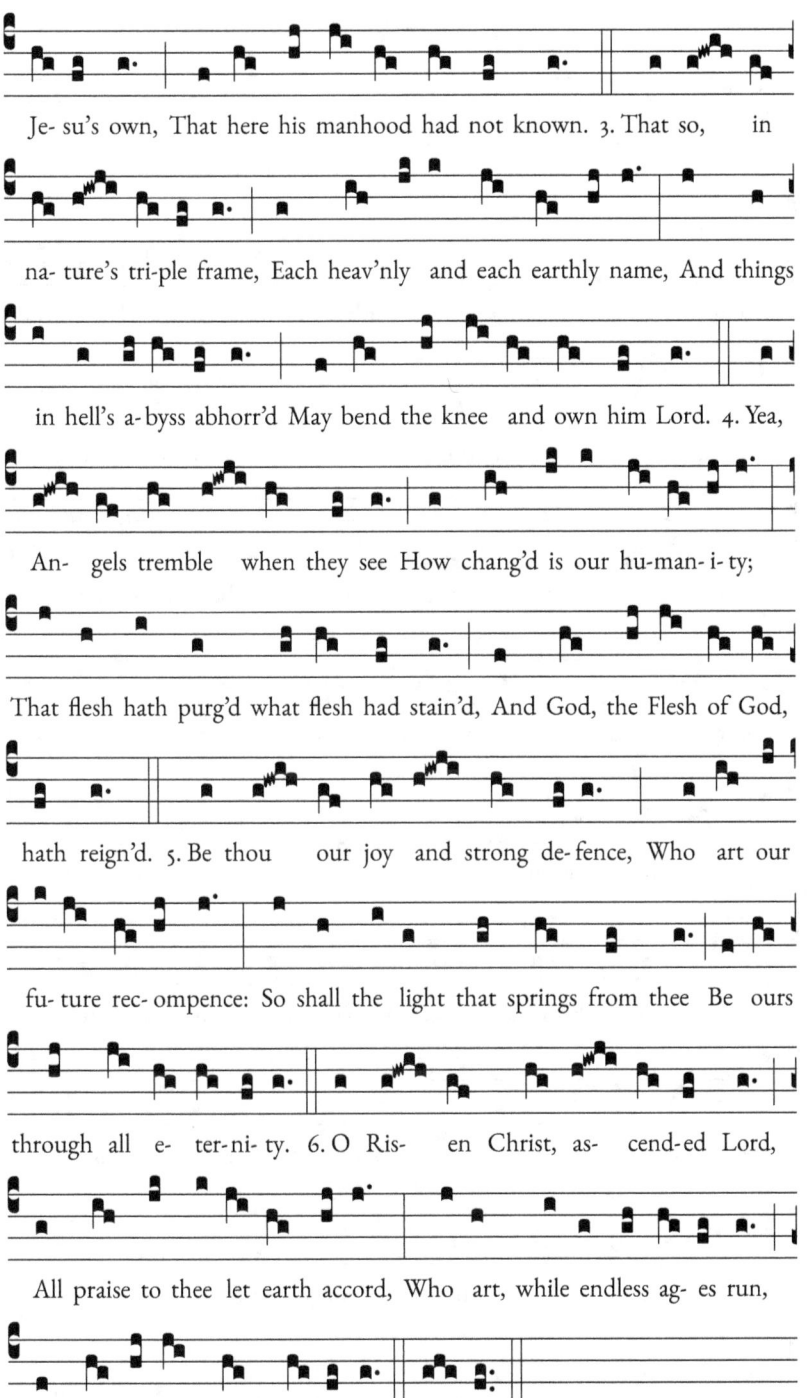

Je-sus's own, That here his manhood had not known. 3. That so, in na-ture's tri-ple frame, Each heav'nly and each earthly name, And things in hell's a-byss abhorr'd May bend the knee and own him Lord. 4. Yea, An-gels tremble when they see How chang'd is our hu-man-i-ty; That flesh hath purg'd what flesh had stain'd, And God, the Flesh of God, hath reign'd. 5. Be thou our joy and strong de-fence, Who art our fu-ture rec-ompence: So shall the light that springs from thee Be ours through all e-ter-ni-ty. 6. O Ris- en Christ, as- cend-ed Lord, All praise to thee let earth accord, Who art, while endless ag- es run, With Fa-ther and with Spir- it One. A- men.

Ascension Thursday **Proper of Season**

Office Hymn

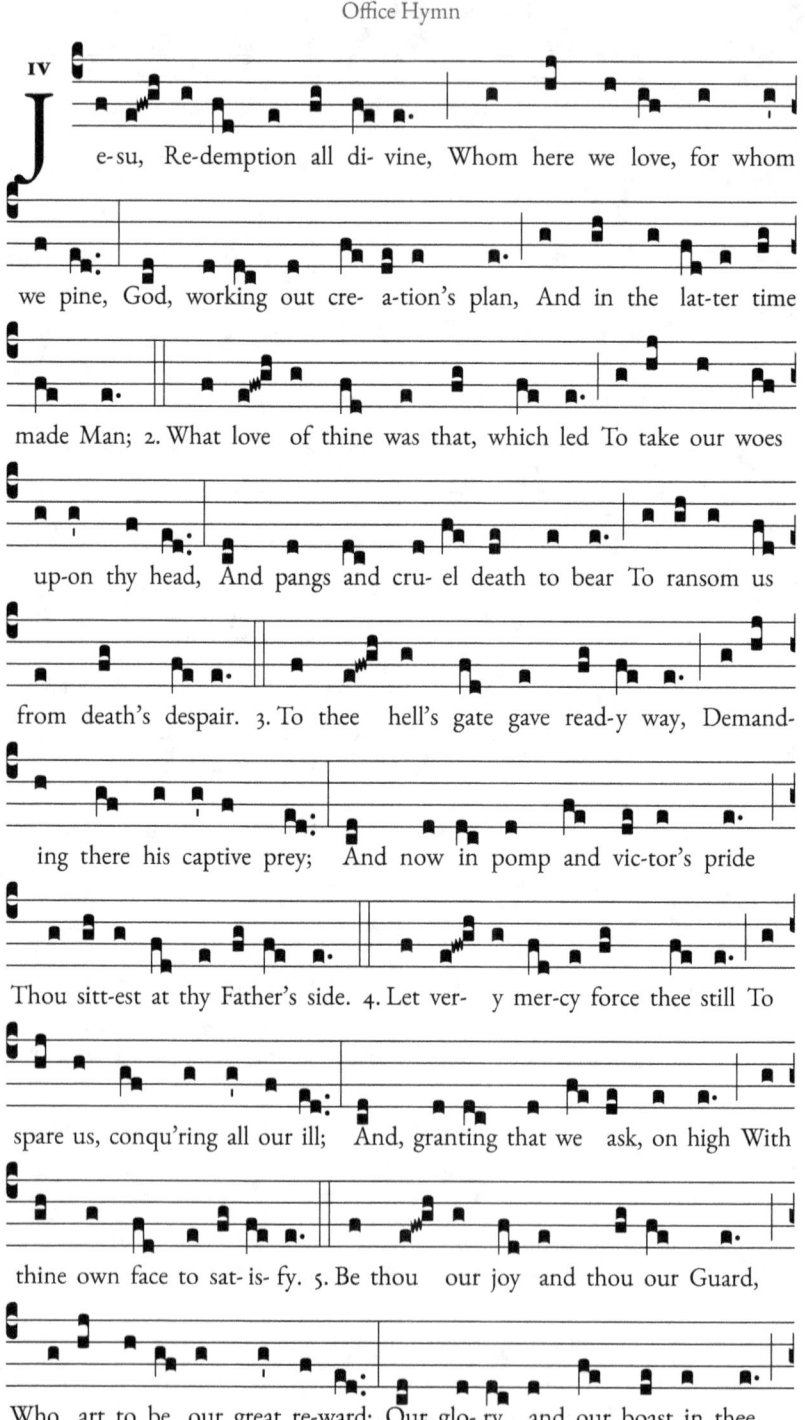

Jesu, Redemption all divine, Whom here we love, for whom we pine, God, working out creation's plan, And in the latter time made Man; 2. What love of thine was that, which led To take our woes upon thy head, And pangs and cruel death to bear To ransom us from death's despair. 3. To thee hell's gate gave ready way, Demanding there his captive prey; And now in pomp and victor's pride Thou sittest at thy Father's side. 4. Let very mercy force thee still To spare us, conqu'ring all our ill; And, granting that we ask, on high With thine own face to satisfy. 5. Be thou our joy and thou our Guard, Who art to be our great reward; Our glory and our boast in thee

Proper of Season   *Ascension Sunday*

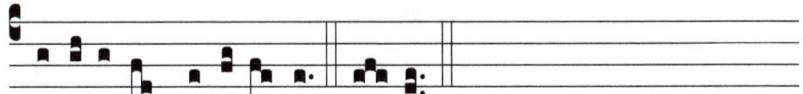

For ev-er and for ev-er be.   A- men.

℣. The Lord hath prepared, alleluia.

℟. His seat in heaven, alleluia.

Ben. Ant. I ascend † unto my Father, and your Father: and to my God, and your God, alleluia.

II Evensong

¶ The Office Hymn is of Mattins, with the following.

℣. God is gone up with a merry noise, alleluia.

℟. And the Lord with the sound of the trump, alleluia.

Mag. Ant. O King of glory, † thou Lord of Sabaoth, who triumphing to-day hast ascended above all heavens, leave us not comfortless; but send on us the promise of the Father, even the Spirit of truth, alleluia.

¶ During the Octave of the Ascension, the Office is said daily or Commemoration made. All is said as on the Feast.

SUNDAY WITHIN THE ASCENSION OCTAVE

¶ The Hymns are of Ascension Thursday (p. 382), with the following Versicles & Antiphons.

℣. The Lord hath prepared, alleluia.

℟. His seat in heaven, alleluia.

Mag. Ant. When the Comforter is come, † whom I will send unto you from the Father, even the Spirit of truth, which proceedeth from the Father, he shall testify of me, alleluia.

℣. When Christ ascended up on high, alleluia.

℟. He led captivity captive, alleluia.

Ben. Ant. When the Comforter is come, † whom I will send unto you from the Father, even the Spirit of truth, which proceedeth from the Father, he shall testify of me, alleluia.

℣. The Lord hath prepared, alleluia.

℟. His seat in heaven, alleluia.

Mag. Ant. These things have I told you, † that when the time shall come, ye may remember that I told you of them, alleluia.

Whitsun Eve # Proper of Season

Vigil of Whitsunday

¶ From this day through Trinity Sunday, if a I Double or II Double occur, it is transferred to a day after Trinity Sunday. Other Feasts and Memorials are commemorated, except during the Triduum of Whitsunday. No notice is taken of other Octaves during this time.

¶ At Mattins and the Hours, all is said as on the preceding Sunday, without Commemoration of the Ascension.

¶ Mattins (or None) having been said in Choir, the Priest and Ministers, clad in vestments of violet colour, go up to the Altar and make a reverence, and the Priest kisses it in the middle. Then the Prophecies are read without title, the candles of the Altar remaining unlighted until the beginning of the Mass, as on Holy Saturday. The Priest reads them in a low voice at the Epistle corner of the Altar. At the end of the Prophecies the Collects are said without Let us bow the knee.

Prophecy I. Genesis 22:1

IN THOSE DAYS: God did tempt Abraham, and said unto him, Abraham: and he said, Behold, here I am. And he said, Take now thy son, thine only son Isaac, whom thou lovest, and get thee into the land of Moriah; and offer him there for a burnt offering upon one of the mountains which I will tell thee of. And Abraham rose up early in the morning, and saddled his ass, and took two of his young men with him, and Isaac his son, and clave the wood for the burnt offering, and rose up, and went unto the place of which God had told him. Then on the third day Abraham lifted up his eyes, and saw the place afar off. And Abraham said unto his young men, Abide ye here with the ass; and I and the lad will go yonder and worship, and come again to you. And Abraham took the wood of the burnt offering, and laid it upon Isaac his son; and he took the fire in his hand, and a knife; and they went both of them together. And Isaac spake unto Abraham his father, and said, My father: and he said, Here am I, my son. And he said, Behold the fire and the wood: but where is the lamb for a burnt offering? And Abraham said, My son, God will provide himself a lamb for a burnt offering: so they went both of them together. And they came to the place which God had told him of; and Abraham built an altar there, and laid the wood in order, and bound Isaac his son, and laid him on the altar upon the wood. And Abraham stretched forth his hand, and took the knife to slay his son. And the angel of the LORD called unto him out of heaven, and said, Abraham, Abraham: and he said, Here am I. And he said, Lay not thine hand upon the lad, neither do thou any thing unto him: for now I know that thou fearest God, seeing thou hast not withheld thy son, thine only son from me. And Abraham lifted up his eyes, and looked, and behold behind him a ram caught in a thicket by his horns: and Abraham went and took the ram, and offered him up for a burnt offering in the stead of his son. And Abraham called the name of that place Jehovahjireh: as it is said to this day, In the mount of the LORD it shall be seen. And the angel of the LORD called unto Abraham out of heaven the second time, And said, By myself have I sworn, saith the LORD, for because thou hast done this thing, and hast not withheld thy son, thine only son: That in blessing I will

Proper of Season *Whitsun Eve*

bless thee, and in multiplying I will multiply thy seed as the stars of the heaven, and as the sand which is upon the sea shore; and thy seed shall possess the gate of his enemies; And in thy seed shall all the nations of the earth be blessed; because thou hast obeyed my voice. So Abraham returned unto his young men, and they rose up and went together to Beersheba; and Abraham dwelt at Beersheba.

¶ After this and the other Prophecies the Response **Thanks be to God** is not made: then the Priest says:

Let us pray.

GOD, who in the deed of Abraham thy servant hast given a pattern of obedience to mankind: grant us so to conquer the perversity of our desires, that we may in all things fulfil the righteousness of thy commandments. Through.

Prophecy II. Exodus 14:24

IN THOSE DAYS: It came to pass, that in the morning watch the LORD looked unto the host of the Egyptians through the pillar of fire and of the cloud, and troubled the host of the Egyptians, And took off their chariot wheels, that they drave them heavily: so that the Egyptians said, Let us flee from the face of Israel; for the LORD fighteth for them against the Egyptians. And the LORD said unto Moses, Stretch out thine hand over the sea, that the waters may come again upon the Egyptians, upon their chariots, and upon their horsemen. And Moses stretched forth his hand over the sea, and the sea returned to his strength when the morning appeared; and the Egyptians fled against it; and the LORD overthrew the Egyptians in the midst of the sea. And the waters returned, and covered the chariots, and the horsemen, and all the host of Pharaoh that came into the sea after them; there remained not so much as one of them. But the children of Israel walked upon dry land in the midst of the sea; and the waters were a wall unto them on their right hand, and on their left. Thus the LORD saved Israel that day out of the hand of the Egyptians; and Israel saw the Egyptians dead upon the sea shore. And Israel saw that great work which the LORD did upon the Egyptians: and the people feared the LORD, and believed the LORD, and his servant Moses. Then sang Moses and the children of Israel this song unto the LORD, and spake, saying:

Tract. I will sing unto the LORD, for he hath triumphed gloriously: the horse and his rider hath he thrown into the sea. The LORD is my strength and song, and he is become my salvation. ℣. He is my God, and I will prepare him an habitation; my father's God, and I will exalt him. ℣. The LORD is a man of war: the LORD is his name.

Let us pray.

GOD, who by the light of thy new Covenant hast made manifest thy wonders wrought in former times, shewing in the Red Sea a pattern of the sacred font, and in the deliverance of thy people from bondage in Egypt foreshadowing the sacraments of thy Christian people: grant that all nations, being admitted by the merit of their faith to the privilege of Israel, may be regenerated by the partaking of thy Holy Spirit. Through . . . in the unity of the same Holy Ghost.

Whitsun Eve   # Proper of Season

Prophecy III. Deuteronomy 31:22

IN THOSE DAYS: Moses wrote this song, and taught it the children of Israel. And he gave Joshua the son of Nun a charge, and said, Be strong and of a good courage: for thou shalt bring the children of Israel into the land which I sware unto them: and I will be with thee. And it came to pass, when Moses had made an end of writing the words of this law in a book, until they were finished, That Moses commanded the Levites, which bare the ark of the covenant of the LORD, saying, Take this book of the law, and put it in the side of the ark of the covenant of the LORD your God, that it may be there for a witness against thee. For I know thy rebellion, and thy stiff neck: behold, while I am yet alive with you this day, ye have been rebellious against the LORD; and how much more after my death? Gather unto me all the elders of your tribes, and your officers, that I may speak these words in their ears, and call heaven and earth to record against them. For I know that after my death ye will utterly corrupt yourselves, and turn aside from the way which I have commanded you; and evil will befall you in the latter days; because ye will do evil in the sight of the LORD, to provoke him to anger through the work of your hands. And Moses spake in the ears of all the congregation of Israel the words of this song, until they were ended.

Tract. Give ear, O ye heavens, and I will speak; and hear, O earth, the words of my mouth. ℣. My doctrine shall drop as the rain, my speech shall distil as the dew. ℣. As the small rain upon the tender herb, and as the showers upon the grass: Because I will publish the name of the LORD. ℣. Ascribe ye greatness unto our God. He is the Rock, his work is perfect: for all his ways are judgment. ℣. A God of truth and without iniquity, just and right is he.

Let us pray.

O GOD, the glory of the faithful and the life of the just, who through Moses thy servant hast instructed us also in the chanting of thy sacred song: accomplish in all nations the work of thy mercy, granting them felicity, and delivering them from terror; that those things which were uttered for punishment may be turned into an everlasting remedy. Through.

Prophecy IV. Isaiah 4:1

IN THAT DAY seven women shall take hold of one man, saying, We will eat our own bread, and wear our own apparel: only let us be called by thy name, to take away our reproach. In that day shall the branch of the LORD be beautiful and glorious, and the fruit of the earth shall be excellent and comely for them that are escaped of Israel. And it shall come to pass, that he that is left in Zion, and he that remaineth in Jerusalem, shall be called holy, even every one that is written among the living in Jerusalem: When the Lord shall have washed away the filth of the daughters of Zion, and shall have purged the blood of Jerusalem from the midst thereof by the spirit of judgment, and by the spirit of burning. And the LORD will create upon every dwelling place of mount Zion, and upon her assemblies, a cloud and smoke by day, and the shining of a flaming fire by night: for upon all the glory shall be a defence. And there shall be a tabernacle for a shadow in the daytime from the heat, and for a place of refuge, and for a covert from storm and from rain.

Tract. My wellbeloved hath a vineyard in a very fruitful hill. ℣. And he fenced it, and gathered out the stones thereof, and planted it with the choicest vine, and built a tower in the midst of it. ℣. And also made a winepress therein: for the vineyard of the LORD of hosts is the house of Israel.

Let us pray.

ALMIGHTY and everlasting God, who through thy only Son hast revealed thyself to be the husbandman of thy Church, who dost mercifully purge every branch that bringeth forth fruit in the true vine, even the same thy Christ, to the intent that it may bring forth more fruit: let not the thorns of sin prevail against thy faithful people whom by the Font of baptism thou hast brought like a vine out of Egypt; that being fortified by the sanctifying power of thy Spirit, they may be enriched with everlasting fruit. Through the same . . . in the unity of the same.

Prophecy V. Baruch 3:9

HEAR, O Israel, the commandments of life: give ear to understand wisdom. How happeneth it, O Israel, that thou art in thine enemies' land, that thou art waxen old in a strange country, that thou art defiled with the dead, that thou art counted with them that go down into the grave? Thou hast forsaken the fountain of wisdom. For if thou hadst walked in the way of God, thou shouldest have dwelled in peace for ever. Learn where is wisdom, where is strength, where is understanding; that thou mayest know also where is length of days, and life, where is the light of the eyes, and peace. Who hath found out her place? and who hath come into her treasuries? Where are the princes of the heathen, and such as ruled the beasts that are upon the earth; they that had their pastime with the fowls of the air, and they that hoarded up silver and gold, wherein men trust; and of whose getting there is no end? For they that wrought in silver, and were so careful, and whose works are past finding out, they are vanished and gone down to the grave, and others are come up in their steads. Younger men have seen the light, and dwelt upon the earth: but the way of knowledge have they not known, neither understood they the paths thereof: neither have their children laid hold of it: they are far off from their way. It hath not been heard of in Canaan, neither hath it been seen in Teman. The sons also of Agar that seek understanding, which are in the land, the merchants of Merran and Teman, and the authors of fables, and the searchers out of understanding; none of these have known the way of wisdom, or remembered her paths. O Israel, how great is the house of God! and how large is the place of his possession! great, and hath none end; high, and unmeasurable. There were the giants born that were famous of old, great of stature, and expert in war. These did not God choose, neither gave he the way of knowledge unto them: so they perished, because they had no wisdom, they perished through their own foolishness. Who hath gone up into heaven, and taken her, and brought her down from the clouds?

Proper of Season
Whitsun Eve

Who hath gone over the sea, and found her, and will bring her for choice gold? There is none that knoweth her way, nor any that comprehendeth her path. But he that knoweth all things knoweth her, he found her out with his understanding: he that prepared the earth for evermore hath filled it with fourfooted beasts: he that sendeth forth the light, and it goeth; he called it, and it obeyed him with fear: and the stars shined in their watches, and were glad: when he called them, they said, Here we be; they shined with gladness unto him that made them. This is our God, and there shall none other be accounted of in comparison of him. He hath found out all the way of knowledge, and hath given it unto Jacob his servant, and to Israel that is beloved of him. Afterward did she appear upon earth, and was conversant with men.

Let us pray.

O GOD, who by the mouths of the Prophets hast commanded us to leave things temporal, and to strive after things eternal: grant unto thy servants; that we, knowing the things which thou commandest, may by thy heavenly inspiration be enabled to perform the same. Through.

Prophecy VI. Ezekiel 37:

IN THOSE DAYS: The hand of the LORD was upon me, and carried me out in the spirit of the LORD, and set me down in the midst of the valley which was full of bones, And caused me to pass by them round about: and, behold, there were very many in the open valley; and, lo, they were very dry. And he said unto me, Son of man, can these bones live? And I answered, O Lord GOD, thou knowest. Again he said unto me, Prophesy upon these bones, and say unto them, O ye dry bones, hear the word of the LORD. Thus saith the Lord GOD unto these bones; Behold, I will cause breath to enter into you, and ye shall live: And I will lay sinews upon you, and will bring up flesh upon you, and cover you with skin, and put breath in you, and ye shall live; and ye shall know that I am the LORD. So I prophesied as I was commanded: and as I prophesied, there was a noise, and behold a shaking, and the bones came together, bone to his bone. And when I beheld, lo, the sinews and the flesh came up upon them, and the skin covered them above: but there was no breath in them. Then said he unto me, Prophesy unto the wind, prophesy, son of man, and say to the wind, Thus saith the Lord GOD; Come from the four winds, O breath, and breathe upon these slain, that they may live. So I prophesied as he commanded me, and the breath came into them, and they lived, and stood up upon their feet, an exceeding great army. Then he said unto me, Son of man, these bones are the whole house of Israel: behold, they say, Our bones are dried, and our hope is lost: we are cut off for our parts. Therefore prophesy and say unto them, Thus saith the Lord GOD; Behold, O my people, I will open your graves, and cause you to come up out of your graves, and bring you into the land of Israel. And ye shall know that I am the LORD, when I have opened your graves, O my people, and brought you up out of your graves, And shall put my spirit in you, and ye shall live, and I shall place you in your own land.

Proper of Season *Whitsun Eve*

Let us pray.

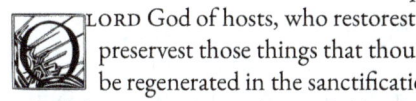LORD God of hosts, who restorest those things that are broken down, and preservest those things that thou restorest: increase the peoples that shall be regenerated in the sanctification of thy name; that all who are washed in holy baptism may ever be guided by thy inspiration. Through.

❡ These ended, the Celebrant receives a violet Cope, and, while he descends to the Font, the following is sung:

Tract. Like as the hart desireth the water-brooks: so longeth my soul after thee, O God. ℣. My soul is athirst for God, yea, even for the living God: when shall I come to appear before the presence of God? ℣. My tears have been my meat day and night, while they daily say unto me: Where is now thy God?

❡ Then the Priest, before he enters for the blessing of the Font, says near the Font:

℣. The Lord be with you.	℣. Dóminus vobíscum.
℟. And with thy spirit.	℟. Et cum spíritu tuo.
℣. Let us pray.	℣. Orémus.

RANT, we beseech thee, Almighty God: that we, who observe the solemnity of the gift of the Holy Ghost, being inflamed with heavenly desires, may thirst after the fountain of life. Through ... in the unity of the same.

❡ Then he proceeds to the blessing of the Font, as on Holy Saturday.

❡ But when there are no Fonts, the sixth Prophecy with its Collect being finished, the Celebrant lays aside the Chasuble, and prostrates himself before the Altar with the Ministers; and all kneeling, the Litany is sung by two Cantors in the middle of the choir, both choirs responding together. When they come to ℣. *We sinners beseech thee,* the Priest and Ministers rise and go to the Sacristy, where they put on red vestments, while the lights around the Altar are lighted.

❡ At the end of the Litany *Kyrie, eléison* is sung solemnly for the Mass, and repeated as usual. Meanwhile the Priest with the Ministers proceeds to the Altar, and makes the Confession, Prayer of Humble Access, and Ten Commandments (and/or Summary of the Law); then ascending, he kisses it, and censes it as usual. *Kyrie, eléison* being ended, he begins solemnly *Glory be to God on high,* and the bells are rung.

❡ Afterwards the Priest says:

℣. The Lord be with you.	℣. Dóminus vobíscum.
℟. And with thy spirit.	℟. Et cum spíritu tuo.
℣. Let us pray.	℣. Orémus.

Collect

RANT, we beseech thee, Almighty God: that the splendour of thy brightness may shine forth upon us; and that the light of thy light may, by the illumination of the Holy Spirit, strengthen the hearts of them who through thy grace are born again. Through ... in the unity of the same.

❡ This Collect only is said, even if a Commemoration has been made in the Office.

Whitsun Eve   # Proper of Season

Epistle. Acts 19:1

IN THOSE DAYS: It came to pass, that, while Apollos was at Corinth, Paul having passed through the upper coasts came to Ephesus: and finding certain disciples, He said unto them, Have ye received the Holy Ghost since ye believed? And they said unto him, We have not so much as heard whether there be any Holy Ghost. And he said unto them, Unto what then were ye baptized? And they said, Unto John's baptism. Then said Paul, John verily baptized with the baptism of repentance, saying unto the people, that they should believe on him which should come after him, that is, on Christ Jesus. When they heard this, they were baptized in the name of the Lord Jesus. And when Paul had laid his hands upon them, the Holy Ghost came on them; and they spake with tongues, and prophesied. And all the men were about twelve. And he went into the synagogue, and spake boldly for the space of three months, disputing and persuading the things concerning the kingdom of God.

Alleluia. Alleluia. ℣. O give thanks unto the Lord, for he is gracious: and his mercy endureth for ever.

¶ Alleluia is not repeated, but there immediately follows:

Tract. O praise the Lord, all ye heathen: praise him, all ye nations. ℣. For his merciful kindness is ever more and more towards us: and the truth of the Lord endureth for ever.

¶ At the Gospel, lights are not carried, but incense only.

Gospel. John 14:15

AT THAT TIME: Jesus said unto his disciples: If ye love me, keep my commandments. And I will pray the Father, and he shall give you another Comforter, that he may abide with you for ever; Even the Spirit of truth; whom the world cannot receive, because it seeth him not, neither knoweth him: but ye know him; for he dwelleth with you, and shall be in you. I will not leave you comfortless: I will come to you. Yet a little while, and the world seeth me no more; but ye see me: because I live, ye shall live also. At that day ye shall know that I am in my Father, and ye in me, and I in you. He that hath my commandments, and keepeth them, he it is that loveth me: and he that loveth me shall be loved of my Father, and I will love him, and will manifest myself to him.

Offertory. O send forth thy Spirit, and they shall be made, and thou shalt renew the face of the earth: the glorious majesty of the Lord shall endure for ever, alleluia.

Secret

SANCTIFY, we beseech thee, O Lord, the gifts which we offer: and cleanse our hearts by the enlightening of the Holy Spirit. Through ... in the unity of the same Holy Ghost.

Proper of Season *Whitsunday*

Communion. In the last day of the feast, Jesus said: He that believeth on me, out of his belly shall flow rivers of living water: but this spake he of the Spirit, which they that believe on him should receive, alleluia, alleluia.

Postcommunion

Pour thy Holy Spirit upon us, O Lord, and cleanse our hearts: that they may be made fruitful by the inward sprinkling of his dew. Through... in the unity of the same Holy Spirit.

WHITSUNDAY

I Evensong

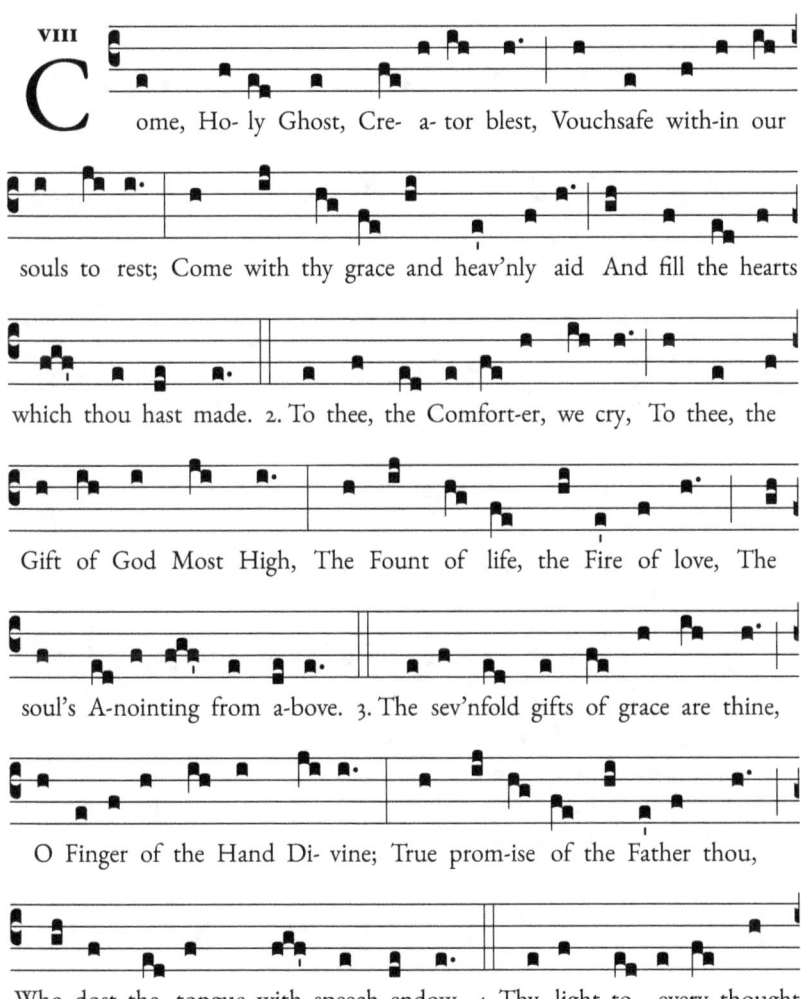

Come, Ho- ly Ghost, Cre- a- tor blest, Vouchsafe with-in our souls to rest; Come with thy grace and heav'nly aid And fill the hearts which thou hast made. 2. To thee, the Comfort-er, we cry, To thee, the Gift of God Most High, The Fount of life, the Fire of love, The soul's A-nointing from a-bove. 3. The sev'nfold gifts of grace are thine, O Finger of the Hand Di- vine; True prom-ise of the Father thou, Who dost the tongue with speech endow. 4. Thy light to every thought

Whitsunday # Proper of Season

impart And shed thy love in every heart; The weakness of our mor-tal

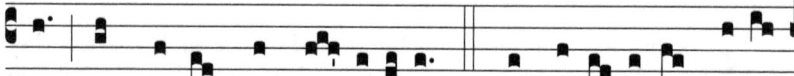
state With deathless might in-vig-or-ate. 5. Drive far a-way our wil-y

foe And thine a-bid-ing peace bestow; If thou be our pro-tect-ing

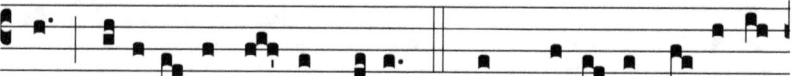
Guide, No e-vil can our steps be-tide. 6. Make thou to us the Fa-ther

known, Teach us th'e-ter-nal Son to own; And thee, whose name we

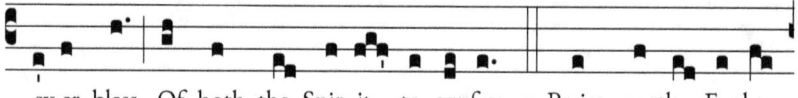
ev-er bless, Of both the Spir-it, to confess. 7. Praise we the Fa-ther

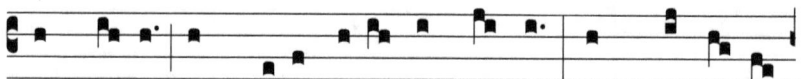
and the Son And Ho-ly Spir-it, with them One; And may the Son

on us bestow The gifts that from the Spir-it flow! A-men.

℣. They were all filled with the Holy Ghost, alleluia.

℟. And began to speak, alleluia.

Mag. Ant. I will not leave you † comfortless, alleluia: I go; but I will come to you, alleluia: and your heart shall rejoice, alleluia.

Proper of Season *Whitsunday*

Mattins

Invitatory Hymn

Now Christ, as-cending whence he came, Had mounted o'er the star-ry frame, The Ho-ly Ghost on man be-low, The Fa-ther's prom-ise, to bestow. 2. The sol-emn time was draw-ing nigh, Re-plete with heav'nly mys-ter-y, On sev'n days' sev'nfold cir-cles borne, That first and bless-ed Whit-sunmorn. 3. When the third hour shone all a-round, There came a rushing mighty sound, And told th' A- postles, while in prayer, That, as was prom-is'd, God was there. 4. Forth from the Father's light it came, That beau-ti-ful and kindly flame: To fill with fervour of his word The spir-its faith-ful to their Lord. 5. With joy th' A-post-les'

Whitsunday # Proper of Season

breasts are fir'd, By God the Ho- ly Ghost inspir'd: And straight, in di- vers kinds of speech, The wondrous works of God they preach. 6. To men of every race they speak, A- like Barbar-ian, Roman, Greek: From the same lips, with awe and fear, All men their na- tive ac- cents hear. 7. But Ju-das' sons, e'en faithless yet, With mad infur-iate rage be-set, To mock Christ's follow- ers combine, As drunk-en all with new-made wine. 8. When lo! With signs and mighty deeds, Stands Pe- ter in the midst, and pleads: Confounding their ma- lig-nant lie By Jo- el's an- cient prophe- cy. 9. To God the Fa- ther let us sing, To God the Son, our ris- en King, And equal- ly let us a- dore

Proper of Season — *Whitsunday*

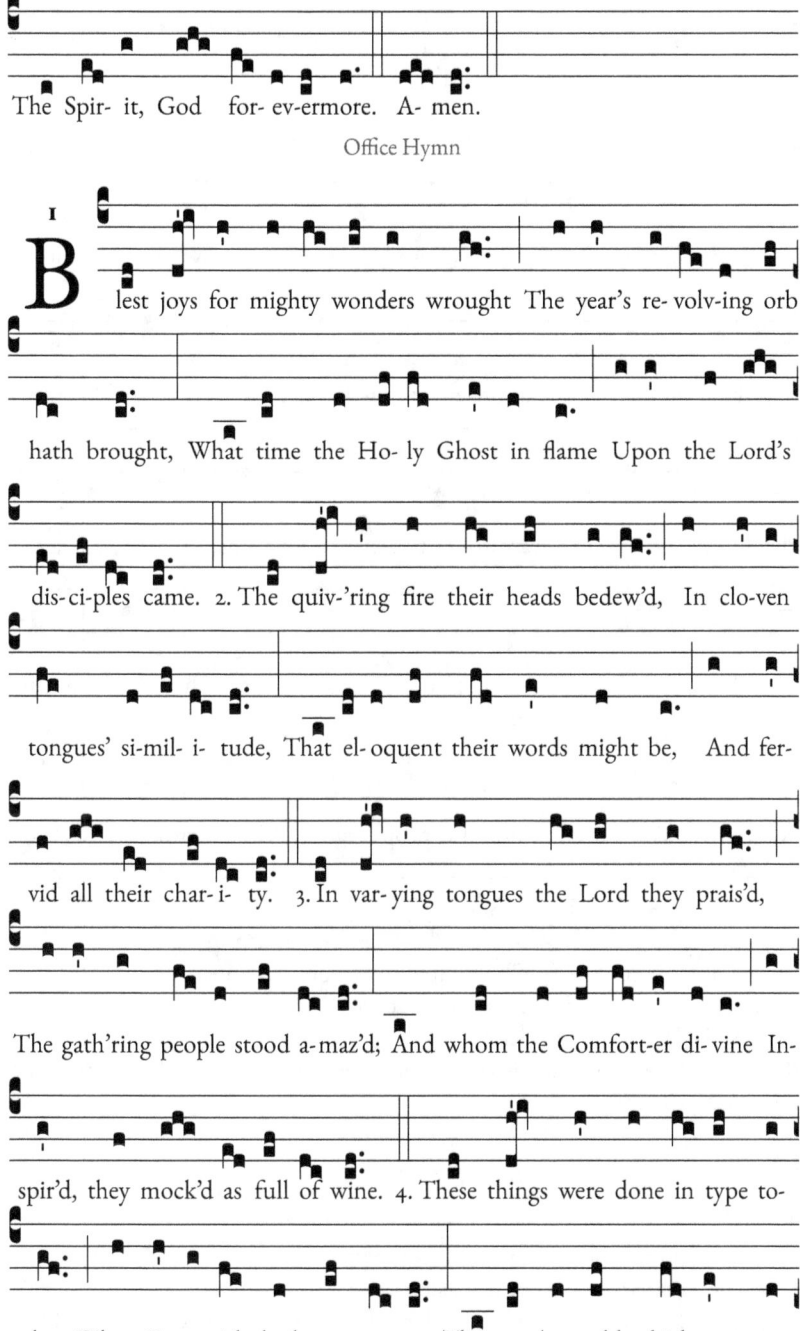

The Spir- it, God for- ev-ermore. A- men.

Office Hymn

1. Blest joys for mighty wonders wrought The year's re- volv-ing orb hath brought, What time the Ho- ly Ghost in flame Upon the Lord's dis- ci-ples came. 2. The quiv'ring fire their heads bedew'd, In cloven tongues' si-mil- i- tude, That el- oquent their words might be, And fer- vid all their char- i- ty. 3. In var- ying tongues the Lord they prais'd, The gath'ring people stood a-maz'd; And whom the Comfort-er di- vine In- spir'd, they mock'd as full of wine. 4. These things were done in type to- day, When Easter-tide had worn a-way, The number told which once set

Whitsunday ## Proper of Season

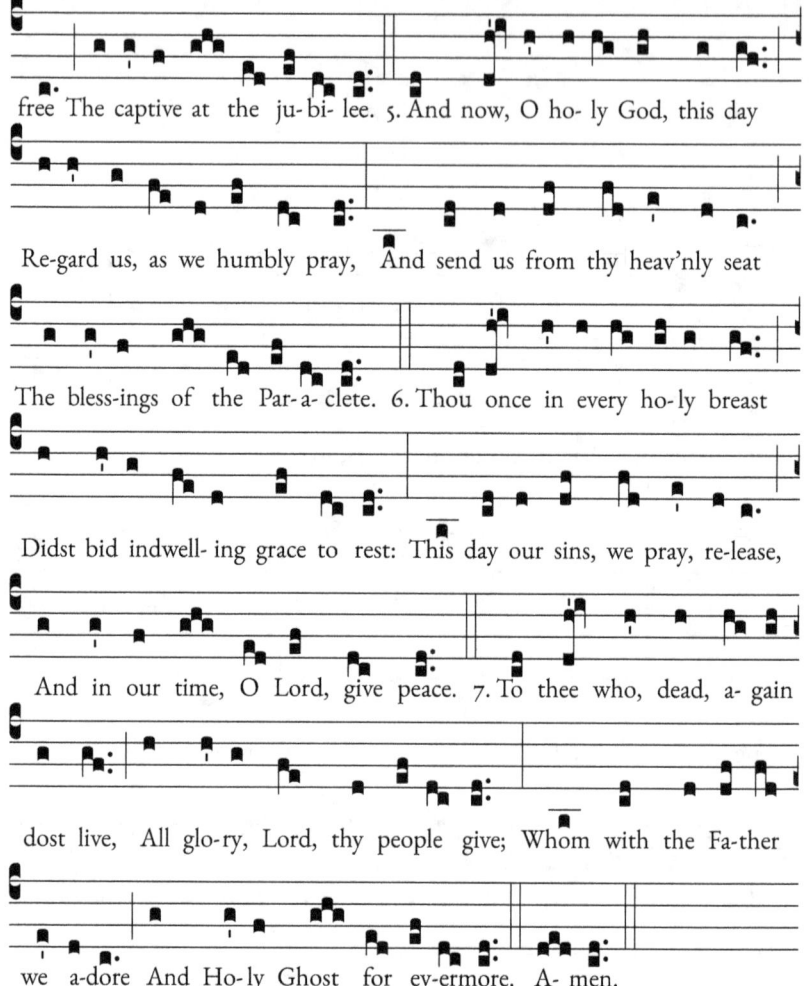

free The captive at the ju-bi-lee. 5. And now, O ho-ly God, this day
Re-gard us, as we humbly pray, And send us from thy heav'nly seat
The bless-ings of the Par-a-clete. 6. Thou once in every ho-ly breast
Didst bid indwell-ing grace to rest: This day our sins, we pray, re-lease,
And in our time, O Lord, give peace. 7. To thee who, dead, a-gain
dost live, All glo-ry, Lord, thy people give; Whom with the Fa-ther
we a-dore And Ho-ly Ghost for ev-ermore. A-men.

℣. They were all filled with the Holy Ghost, alleluia.
℟. And began to speak, alleluia.
Ben. Ant. Receive ye † the Holy Ghost: whosoever sins ye remit, they are remitted unto them, alleluia.

II Evensong

¶ The Office Hymn is of I Evensong, with the following Versicle & Antiphon.

℣. The Apostles did speak with other tongues, alleluia.
℟. The wonderful works of God, alleluia.
Mag. Ant. To-day † are fulfilled the days of Pentecost, alleluia: to-day the Holy Spirit appeared in fire to the disciples, and bestowed upon them his manifold graces: sending them into all the world, to preach the gospel, and to testify: He that believeth and is baptised shall be saved, alleluia.

Ember Friday — Proper of Season — *Whitsun Emberday*

WHIT-MONDAY

¶ In the Daily Office, the Hymns & Versicles are of Whitsunday (p. 393), with the following Antiphons.

Ben. Ant. God so loved the world, † that he gave his only-begotten Son, that whosoever believeth in him should not perish, but have everlasting life, alleluia.

Mag. Ant. If a man love me, † he will keep my saying, and my Father will love him: and we will come unto him, and make our abode with him, alleluia.

WHIT-TUESDAY

¶ In the Daily Office, the Hymns & Versicles are of Whitsunday (p. 393), with the following Antiphons.

Ben. Ant. I am the door, † saith the Lord: by me if any man enter in, he shall be saved, and shall find pasture, alleluia.

Mag. Ant. Peace † I leave with you, my peace I give unto you: not as the world giveth, give I unto you, alleluia.

EMBER WEDNESDAY IN WHITSUNTIDE

¶ In the Daily Office, the Hymns & Versicles are of Whitsunday (p. 393), with the following Antiphons.

Ben. Ant. I am the living bread, † saith the Lord, which came down from heaven, alleluia, alleluia.

Mag. Ant. I am the living bread, † which came down from heaven: if any man eat of this bread, he shall live for ever: and the bread that I will give is my flesh, which I will give for the life of the world, alleluia.

WHIT-THURSDAY

¶ In the Daily Office, the Hymns & Versicles are of Whitsunday (p. 393), with the following Antiphons.

Ben. Ant. Jesus called unto him † his twelve disciples, and gave them power and authority over all devils, and to cure diseases: and he sent them to preach the kingdom of God, and to heal the sick, alleluia.

Mag. Ant. The Spirit † which proceedeth from the Father, alleluia: he shall glorify me, alleluia, alleluia.

EMBER FRIDAY IN WHITSUNTIDE

¶ In the Daily Office, the Hymns & Versicles are of Whitsunday (p. 393), with the following Antiphons.

Ben. Ant. Jesus said: † But that ye may know that the Son of man hath power on earth to forgive sins, (he saith unto the sick of the palsy) I say unto thee, Arise, take up thy bed, and go thy way into thine house, alleluia.

Trinity Sunday

Proper of Season

Mag. Ant. But the Comforter, † which is the Holy Ghost, whom the Father will send in my Name, he will teach you all things, and bring all things to your remembrance, whatsoever I have said unto you, alleluia.

Ember Saturday in Whitsuntide

¶ In the Daily Office, the Hymns & Versicles are of Whitsunday (p. 393), with the following Antiphons.

Ben. Ant. The love of God is shed † abroad in our hearts by his Spirit which dwelleth in us, alleluia.

Trinity Sunday

I Evensong

¶ The Office Hymn is of Saturday in Winter (p. 50), with the following.

℣. Blessed art thou, O Lord, in the firmament of heaven.
℟. And to be praised, and glorified, and magnified for ever.

Mag. Ant. Thanks, O God, † be unto thee, thanks be unto thee, one and very Trinity, one and supreme Deity, holy and onely Unity.

Mattins

Invitatory Hymn

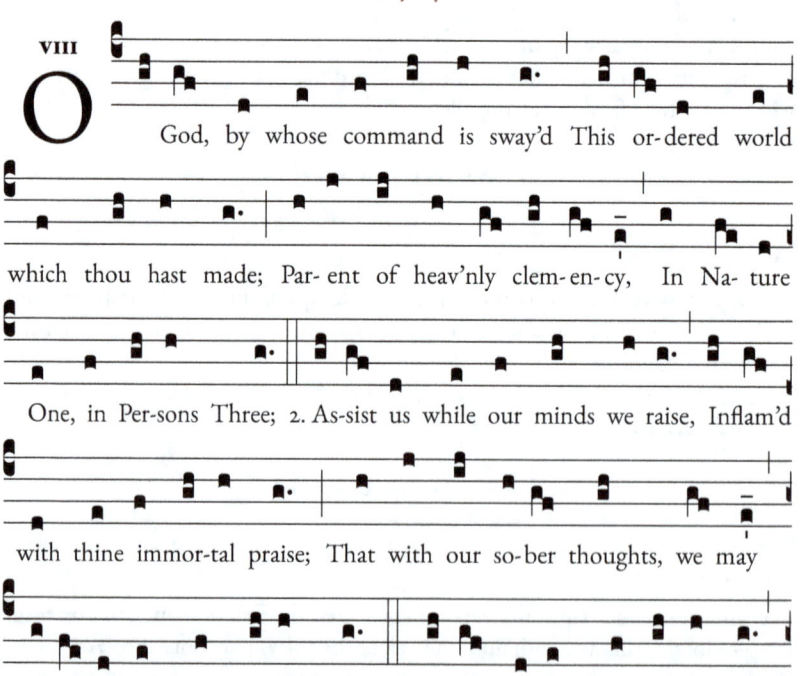

O God, by whose command is sway'd This or-dered world which thou hast made; Par-ent of heav'nly clem-en-cy, In Na-ture One, in Per-sons Three; 2. As-sist us while our minds we raise, Inflam'd with thine immor-tal praise; That with our so-ber thoughts, we may For-ev-er our thanksgiv-ing pay. 3. May age by age thy wonders tell,

Proper of Season *Trinity Sunday*

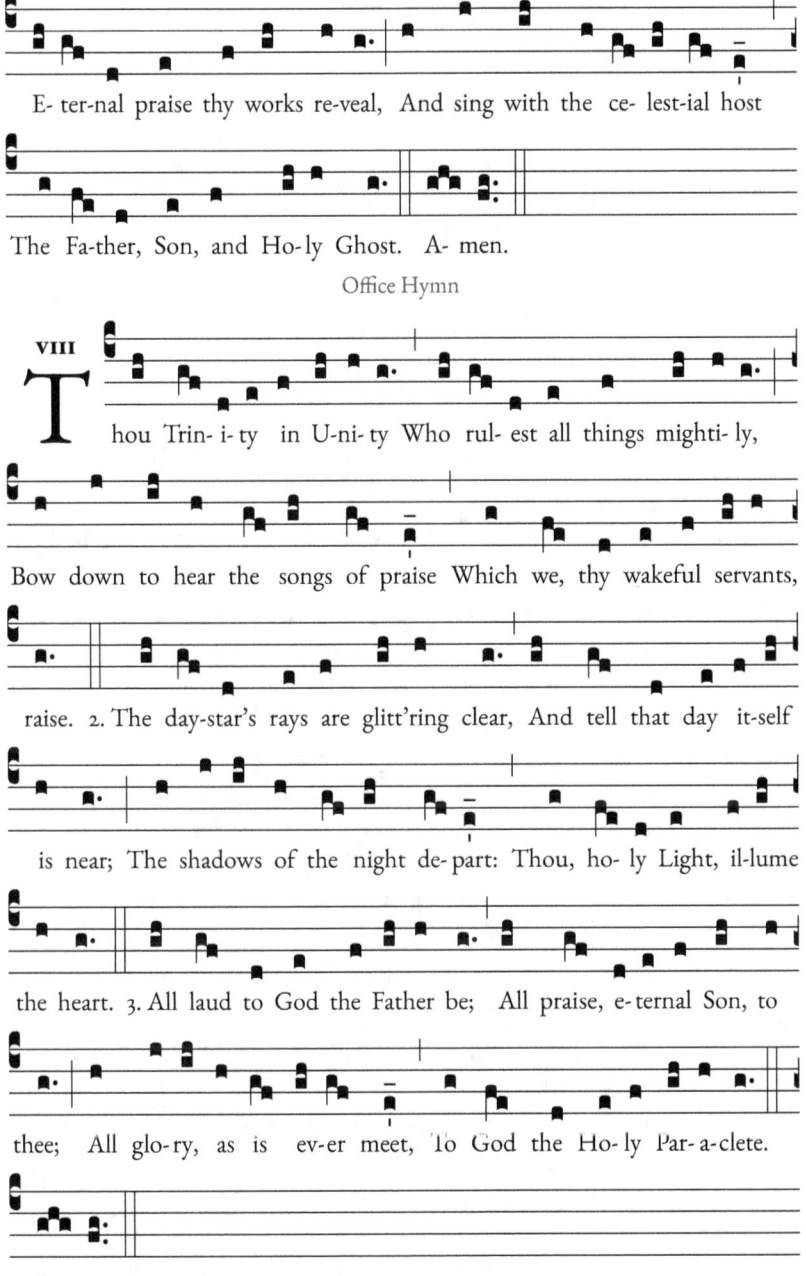

E-ter-nal praise thy works re-veal, And sing with the ce-lest-ial host The Fa-ther, Son, and Ho-ly Ghost. A-men.

Office Hymn

VIII

Thou Trin-i-ty in U-ni-ty Who rul-est all things mighti-ly, Bow down to hear the songs of praise Which we, thy wakeful servants, raise. 2. The day-star's rays are glitt'ring clear, And tell that day it-self is near; The shadows of the night de-part: Thou, ho-ly Light, il-lume the heart. 3. All laud to God the Father be; All praise, e-ternal Son, to thee; All glo-ry, as is ev-er meet, To God the Ho-ly Par-a-clete. A-men.

℣. Let us bless the Father, and the Son, and the Holy Ghost.

℞. Praise him, and magnify him for ever.

Ben. Ant. Blessed be † the holy Creator and Governor of all things, the holy and undivided Trinity, both now and ever, and to endless ages of ages.

Corpus Christi   # Proper of Season

II Evensong

¶ The Office Hymn is of Saturday in Winter (p. 50), with the following.

℣. Blessed art thou, O Lord, in the firmament of heaven.

℟. And to be praised, and glorified, and magnified for ever.

Mag. Ant. Thee, O God, † the Father unbegotten, thee, O only-begotten Son; thee, O Holy Spirit, the Paraclete; holy and undivided Trinity: with our whole heart and mouth we confess thee, we praise thee and bless thee: to thee be glory for ever and ever.

THE MOST HOLY BODY OF CHRIST

I Evensong

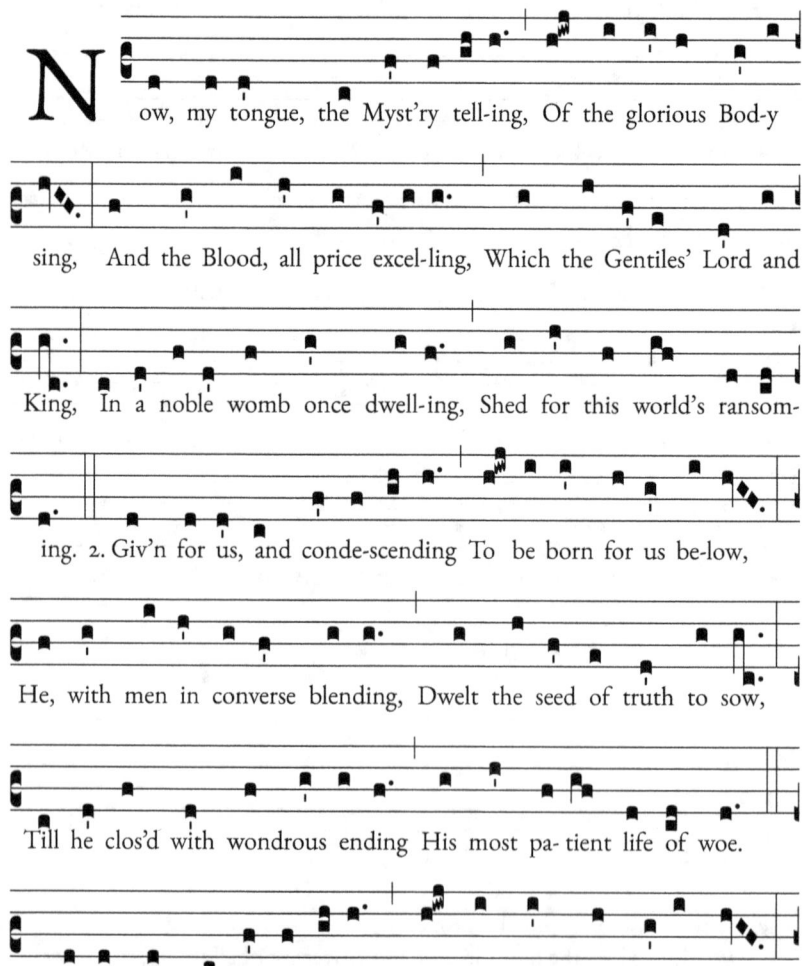

Now, my tongue, the Myst'ry tell-ing, Of the glorious Bod-y sing, And the Blood, all price excel-ling, Which the Gentiles' Lord and King, In a noble womb once dwell-ing, Shed for this world's ransom-ing. 2. Giv'n for us, and conde-scending To be born for us be-low, He, with men in converse blending, Dwelt the seed of truth to sow, Till he clos'd with wondrous ending His most pa-tient life of woe. 3. That last night, at supper ly- ing 'Mid the Twelve, his cho-sen band,

Proper of Season *Corpus Christi*

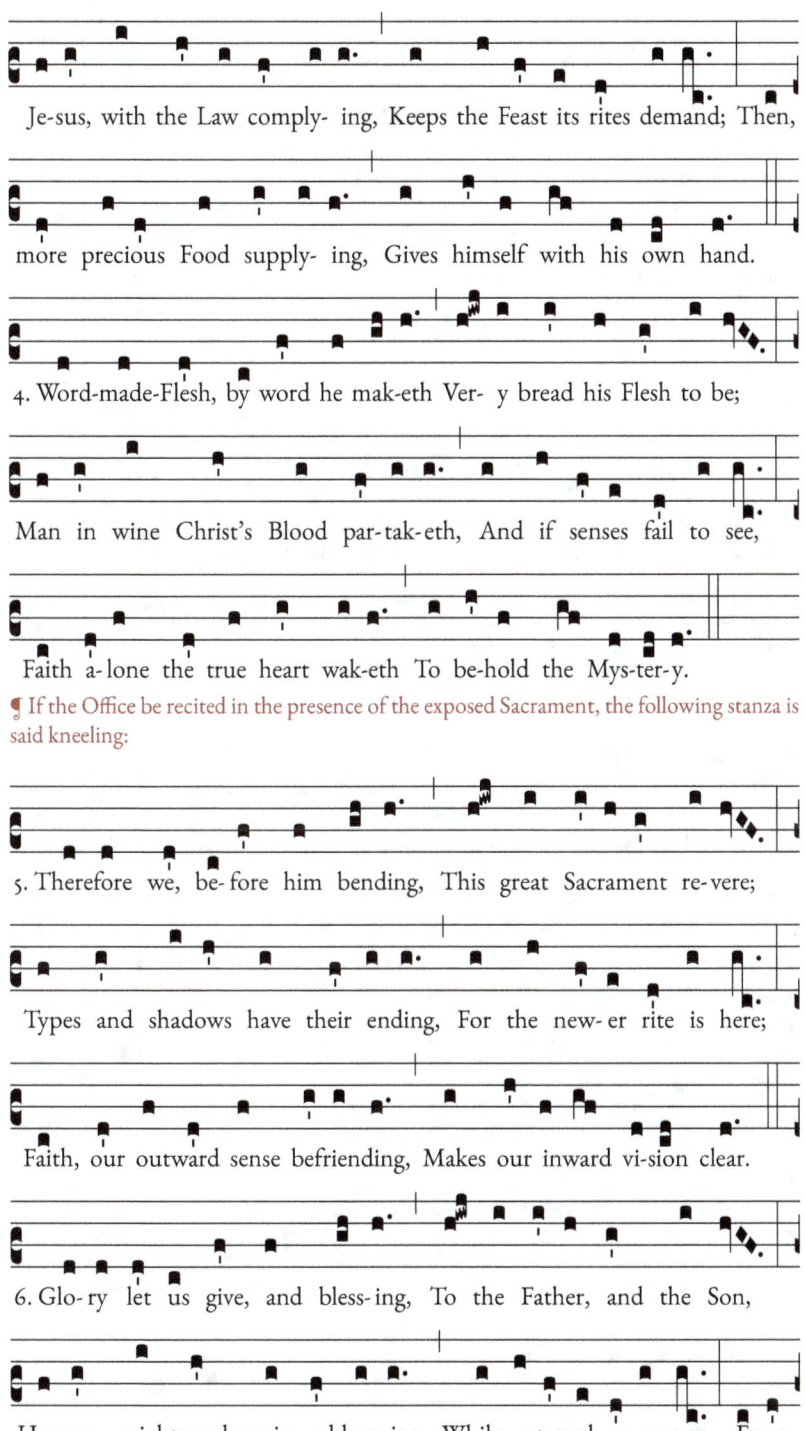

Je-sus, with the Law comply-ing, Keeps the Feast its rites demand; Then,

more precious Food supply-ing, Gives himself with his own hand.

4. Word-made-Flesh, by word he mak-eth Ver- y bread his Flesh to be;

Man in wine Christ's Blood par-tak-eth, And if senses fail to see,

Faith a-lone the true heart wak-eth To be-hold the Mys-ter-y.

¶ If the Office be recited in the presence of the exposed Sacrament, the following stanza is said kneeling:

5. Therefore we, be-fore him bending, This great Sacrament re-vere;

Types and shadows have their ending, For the new-er rite is here;

Faith, our outward sense befriending, Makes our inward vi-sion clear.

6. Glo-ry let us give, and bless-ing, To the Father, and the Son,

Honour, might and praise address-ing, While e-ternal ag-es run; Ev-er

Corpus Christi   **Proper of Season**

too his love confess-ing Who from One with Both is One. A-men.

℣. Thou gavest them bread from heaven, alleluia.

℟. Containing within itself all sweetness, alleluia.

Mag. Ant. O how sweet † is thy Spirit, O Lord, who, that thou mightest shew thy kindness unto thy children, givest them that sweetest bread from heaven, fillest the hungry with good things, and sendest the rich and scornful empty away.

Mattins

Invitatory Hymn

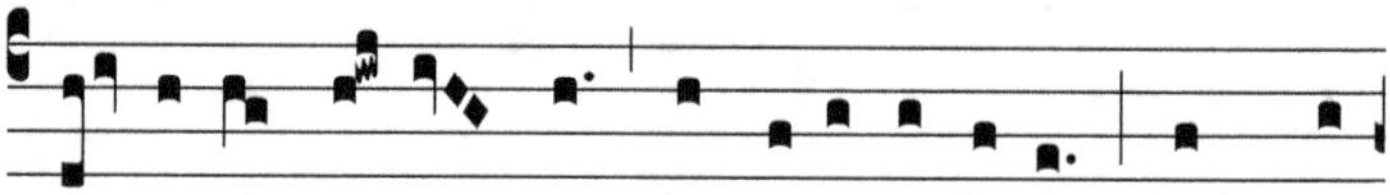

At this our sol- emn feast Let ho-ly joys abound, And from the inmost breast Let songs of praise re-sound; Let ancient rites de- part, And all be new a-round In every deed, in voice, in heart.

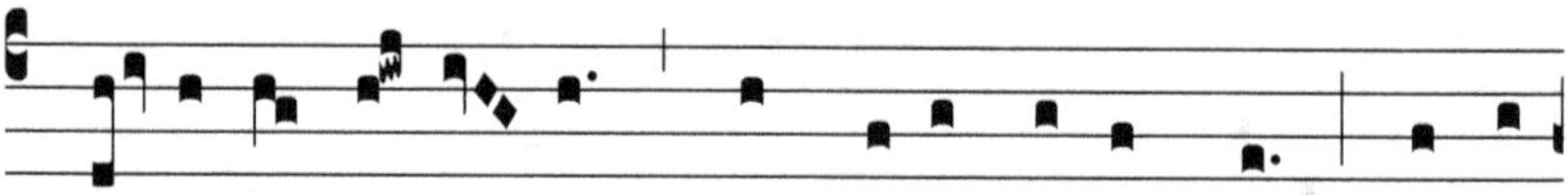

2. Re- member we that night When, the last Supper spread, Christ, as we all be-lieve, Our Lamb and leav'nless bread Amongst his brethren shar'd And thus the law obey'd, Of old un- to their sires de-clar'd.

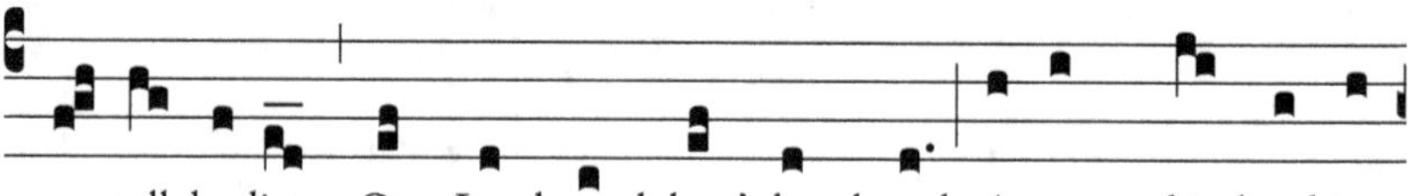

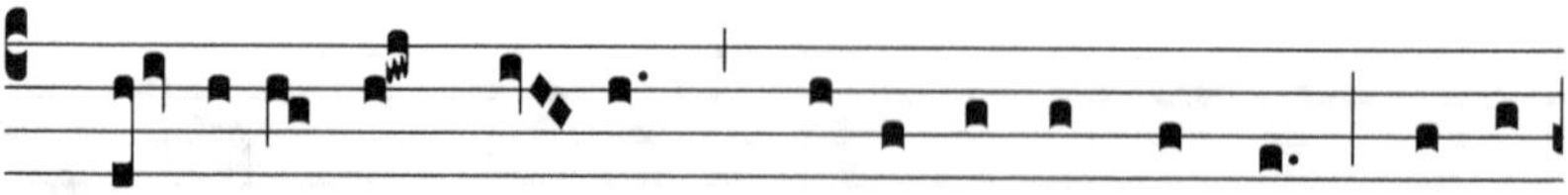

3. The ty-pick lamb con- sum'd, The Paschal feast complete, The Lord

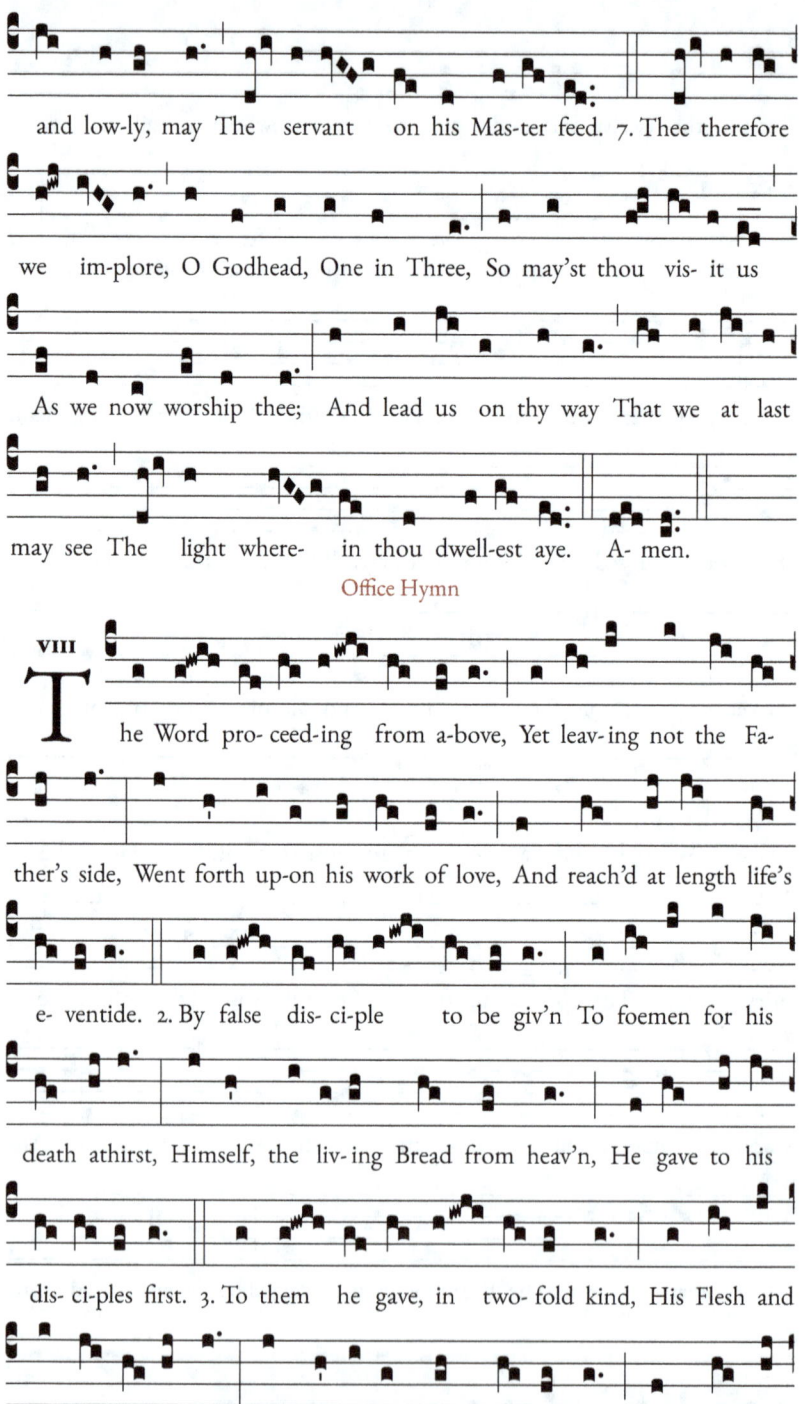

Corpus Christi — Proper of Season

and low-ly, may The servant on his Mas-ter feed. 7. Thee therefore we im-plore, O Godhead, One in Three, So may'st thou vis-it us As we now worship thee; And lead us on thy way That we at last may see The light where-in thou dwell-est aye. A-men.

Office Hymn

VIII. The Word pro-ceed-ing from a-bove, Yet leav-ing not the Fa-ther's side, Went forth up-on his work of love, And reach'd at length life's e-ventide. 2. By false dis-ci-ple to be giv'n To foemen for his death athirst, Himself, the liv-ing Bread from heav'n, He gave to his dis-ci-ples first. 3. To them he gave, in two-fold kind, His Flesh and Blood in ver-y deed; For man is of these two combined, And he the

Proper of Season *Corpus Christi*

life that shall not end In our true na- tive land with thee. A- men.
℣. He maketh peace in thy borders, alleluia.
℟. And filleth thee with the flour of wheat, alleluia.

Ben. Ant. I am † the living bread, which came down from heaven: if any man eat of this bread, he shall live for ever, alleluia.

II Evensong

¶ The Office Hymn & Versicle are of I Evensong, with the following Antiphon.

Mag. Ant. O sacred banquet, † wherein Christ is received, the memory of his Passion is renewed; the soul with grace is filled, and a pledge of future glory is bestowed, alleluia.

Divine Compassion   **Proper of Season**

Sunday in the Octave of Corpus Christi

(First Sunday after Trinity)

¶ The Hymns are of the Feast of the Holy Body of Christ (p. 402), with the following Versicles & Antiphons.

℣. He fed them with the finest wheat flour, alleluia.

℟. And with honey out of the stony rock did he satisfy them, alleluia.

Mag. Ant. The child Samuel † ministered unto the Lord before Eli, and the word of the Lord was precious in his sight.

℣. He gave them bread from heaven, alleluia.

℟. So man did eat angels' food, alleluia.

Ben. Ant. Father Abraham, † have mercy on me, and send Lazarus, that he may dip the tip of his finger in water, and cool my tongue.

℣. He fed them with the finest wheat flour, alleluia.

℟. And with honey out of the stony rock did he satisfy them, alleluia.

Mag. Ant. Son, remember † that thou in thy lifetime receivedst thy good things, and likewise Lazarus evil things.

Compassion of Our Lord Jesus Christ

I Evensong

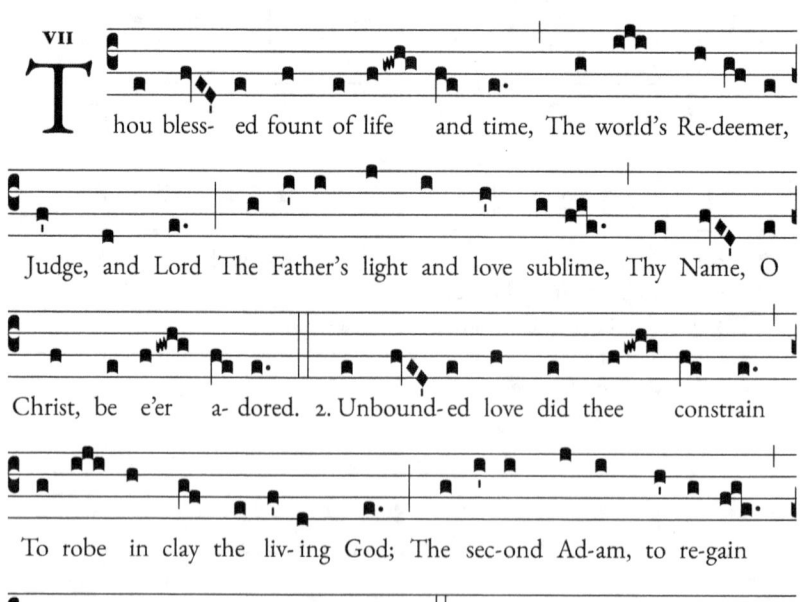

Thou bless-ed fount of life and time, The world's Re-deemer, Judge, and Lord The Father's light and love sublime, Thy Name, O Christ, be e'er a-dored. 2. Unbound-ed love did thee constrain To robe in clay the liv-ing God; The sec-ond Ad-am, to re-gain The prize the first had lost by fraud. 3. All mer-cy thou, O Mak-

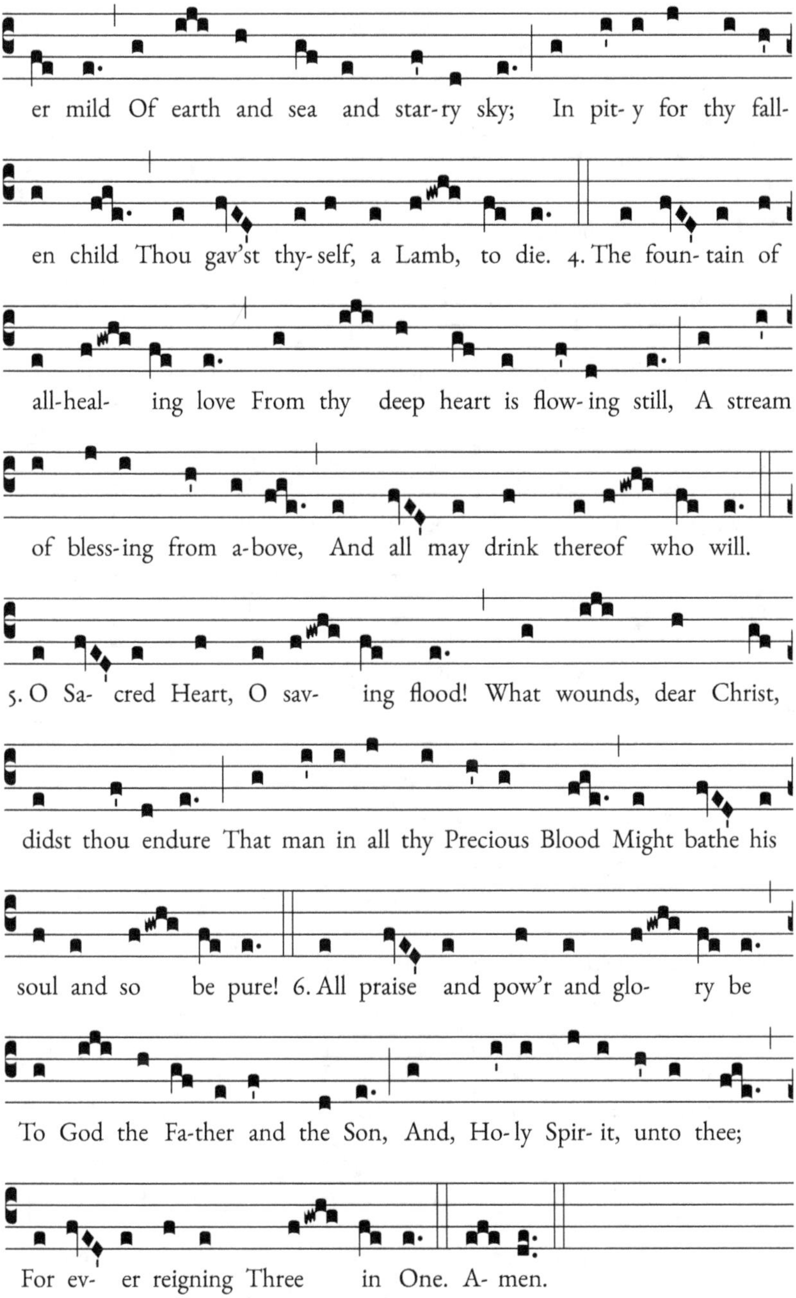

Proper of Season   *Divine Compassion*

er mild Of earth and sea and star-ry sky; In pit-y for thy fall-en child Thou gav'st thy-self, a Lamb, to die. 4. The foun-tain of all-heal-ing love From thy deep heart is flow-ing still, A stream of bless-ing from a-bove, And all may drink thereof who will.

5. O Sa-cred Heart, O sav-ing flood! What wounds, dear Christ, didst thou endure That man in all thy Precious Blood Might bathe his soul and so be pure! 6. All praise and pow'r and glo-ry be To God the Fa-ther and the Son, And, Ho-ly Spir-it, unto thee; For ev-er reigning Three in One. A-men.

℣. I am come to send fire on the earth.

℟. And what will I, if it be already kindled?

Mag. Ant. Thy rebuke † hath broken my heart; I am full of heaviness: I looked for some to have pity on me, but there was no man; neither found I any to comfort me.

Divine Compassion # Proper of Season

Mattins

Invitatory Hymn

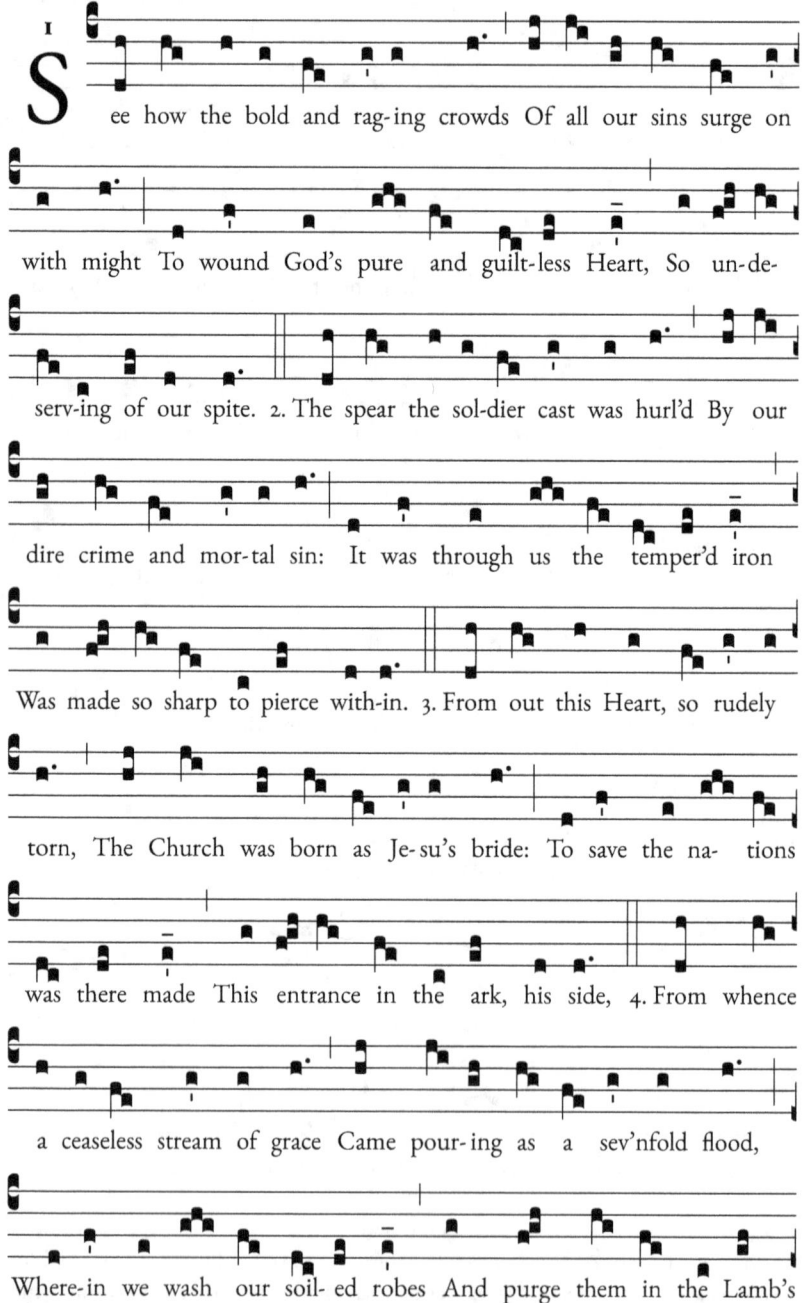

See how the bold and raging crowds Of all our sins surge on with might To wound God's pure and guiltless Heart, So undeserving of our spite. 2. The spear the soldier cast was hurl'd By our dire crime and mortal sin: It was through us the temper'd iron Was made so sharp to pierce within. 3. From out this Heart, so rudely torn, The Church was born as Jesu's bride: To save the nations was there made This entrance in the ark, his side, 4. From whence a ceaseless stream of grace Came pouring as a sev'nfold flood, Wherein we wash our soiled robes And purge them in the Lamb's

Proper of Season *Divine Compassion*

own blood 5. To wound a-gain that bless-ed Heart By sin re-new'd would be dire shame; But let us strive to love in turn That Heart's re- veal- ed lov-ing flame. 6. All glo- ry, Lord, to thee we pay, Who from thy Heart thy grace didst pour; With Father and with Ho- ly Ghost Throughout all ag- es ev-ermore. A- men.

Office Hymn

O Heart of Je- sus, ho- ly ark That holds the lat- ter law di- vine, Not as of old, a ser-vice dark, But mer- cy, grace, and love be-nign; 2. Thou art indeed the dwell-ing-place Of God's mild law and tender might, The temple of outpour-ing grace That rad- iates all the world with light. 3. E- ter-nal mer-cy will'd the blow That gave the

Divine Compassion   # Proper of Season

wounds, O Heart, to thee; That man should ever feel and know The love that suffer'd on the Tree. 4. For Christ, eternal Priest and Lord, Offers his love by holy sign Upon the Cross and at the Board, The twofold Sacrifice divine. 5. We love thee, Jesus, Lord most high, We lift our hearts to thee above, And to thy sacred bosom fly, The everlasting home of love. 6. All praise and pow'r and glory be To God the Father and the Son, And, Holy Spirit, unto thee; For ever reigning Three in One. Amen.

℣. Surely he hath borne our griefs.

℟. And carried our sorrows.

Ben. Ant. He was wounded † for our transgressions he was bruised for our iniquities: the chastisement of our peace was upon him, and with his stripes we are healed.

Proper of Season *Trinitytide*

II Evensong

¶ The Office Hymn is as in I Evensong, with the following Versicle & Antiphon.

℣. With joy shall ye draw water.
℟. Out of the wells of salvation.
Mag. Ant. But when they came to Jesus, † and saw that he was dead already, they brake not his legs: but one of the soldiers with a spear pierced his side, and forthwith came there out blood and water.

Sundays after Trinity

Second Sunday after Trinity

Mag. Ant. And all Israel knew † from Dan even to Beersheba, that Samuel was established to be a prophet of the Lord.
Ben. Ant. A certain man † made a great supper, and bade many; and sent his servants at supper time to say to them that were bidden, Come; for all things are now ready, alleluia.
Mag. Ant. Go out quickly † into the streets and lanes of the city, and compel them to come in; the poor and the maimed, the halt and the blind, that my house may be filled, alleluia.

Third Sunday after Trinity

Mag. Ant. So David prevailed † over the Philistine with a sling and a stone, in the Name of the Lord.
Ben. Ant. What man of you, † having an hundred sheep, if he lose one of them, doth not leave the ninety and nine in the wilderness, and go after that which is lost, until he find it? Alleluia.
Mag. Ant. What woman, † having ten pieces of silver, if she lose one piece, doth not light a candle, and sweep the house, and seek diligently until she find it?

Fourth Sunday after Trinity

Mag. Ant. Ye mountains † of Gilboa, let there be neither dew nor rain upon you; for there the shield of the mighty is vilely cast away, the shield of Saul, as though he had not been anointed with oil. How are the mighty fallen in the midst of the battle! Jonathan was slain upon thy high places! Saul and Jonathan were lovely and exceeding pleasant in their lives, and in their death they were not divided.
Ben. Ant. Be ye therefore † merciful, as your Father also is merciful, saith the Lord.
Mag. Ant. Judge not, † that ye be not judged: for with what judgment ye judge, ye shall be judged, saith the Lord.

Fifth Sunday after Trinity

Mag. Ant. O Lord, I beseech thee, † do away the iniquity of thy servant, for I have done very foolishly.
Ben. Ant. And Jesus entered † into a ship, and sat down, and taught the people, alleluia.
Mag. Ant. Master, † we have toiled all the night, and have taken nothing: nevertheless, at thy word I will let down the net.

Sixth Sunday after Trinity

Mag. Ant. Zadok the priest † and Nathan the prophet anointed Solomon king in Gihon: and the people came up rejoicing and said, Let the king live for ever.

Ben. Ant. Ye have heard that it was said † by them of old time, Thou shalt not kill, and whosoever shall kill, shall be in danger of the judgment.

Mag. Ant. If thou bring † thy gift to the altar, and there rememberest that thy brother hath ought against thee; leave there thy gift before the altar and go thy way; first be reconciled to thy brother, and then come and offer thy gift, alleluia.

Seventh Sunday after Trinity

Mag. Ant. Thou hast heard, O Lord, † the supplication of thy servant, that I might build a temple to thy Name.

Ben. Ant. The multitude being very great, † and having nothing to eat, Jesus called his disciples unto him, and saith unto them, I have compassion on the multitude, because they have now been with me three days, and have nothing to eat, alleluia.

Mag. Ant. I have compassion † on the multitude, because they have now been with me three days, and have nothing to eat: and if I send them away fasting, they will faint by the way, alleluia.

Eighth Sunday after Trinity

Mag. Ant. When the Lord took up Elijah † by a whirlwind into heaven, Elisha cried, saying: My father, the chariot of Israel and the horses thereof.

Ben. Ant. Beware † of false prophets, which come to you in sheep's clothing, but inwardly they are ravening wolves. Ye shall know them by their fruits, alleluia.

Mag. Ant. A good tree † cannot bring forth evil fruit, neither can a corrupt tree bring forth good fruit: every tree that bringeth not forth good fruit is hewn down, and cast into the fire, alleluia.

Ninth Sunday after Trinity

Mag. Ant. Jehoash † did that which was right in the sight of the Lord all his days, wherein Jehoiada the priest instructed him.

Ben. Ant. The lord said † unto the steward, How is it that I hear this of thee? Give an account of thy stewardship, alleluia.

Mag. Ant. What shall I do? † for my lord taketh away from me the stewardship: I cannot dig; to beg I am ashamed: I am resolved what to do, that, when I am put out of the stewardship, they may receive me into their houses.

Tenth Sunday after Trinity

Mag. Ant. I beseech thee, O Lord, † remember now how I have walked before thee in truth and with a perfect heart, and have done that which is good in thy sight.

Ben. Ant. When the Lord was come near to Jerusalem, † he beheld the city, and wept over it, saying: If thou hadst known, even thou! For the days shall come upon thee, that thine enemies shall cast a trench about thee, that thine enemies shall cast a trench about thee, and compass thee round, and keep thee in on every side, and shall lay thee even with the ground; because thou knewest not the time of thy visitation, alleluia.

Mag. Ant. Is it not written, † Mine house shall be called an house of prayer for all people? but ye have made it a den of robbers. And he was daily with them, teaching int he temple.

Proper of Season *Trinitytide*

Eleventh Sunday after Trinity

Ben. Ant. And the publican, † standing afar off, would not lift up so much as his eyes unto heaven, but smote upon his breast, saying, God be merciful to me a sinner.
Mag. Ant. This man went down † to his house justified rather than the other: for every one that exalteth himself shall be abased; and he that humbleth himself shall be exalted.

Twelfth Sunday after Trinity

Ben. Ant. When the Lord had passed † through the coasts of Tyre, he made the deaf to hear and the dumb to speak.
Mag. Ant. He hath done all things well: † he maketh both the deaf to hear, and the dumb to speak.

Thirteenth Sunday after Trinity

Ben. Ant. Master, † what shall I do to inherit eternal life? He said unto him, What is written in the law? how readest thou? Thou shalt love the Lord thy God with all thy heart, alleluia.
Mag. Ant. A certain man † went down from Jerusalem to Jericho, and fell among thieves, which stripped him of his raiment, and wounded him, and departed, leaving him half dead.

Fourteenth Sunday after Trinity

Ben. Ant. As Jesus passed through † a certain village, there met him ten men that were lepers, which stood afar off: and they lifted up their voices, and said, Jesus, Master, have mercy on us.
Mag. Ant. And one of them, † when he saw that he was healed, turned back, and with a loud voice glorified God, alleluia.

Fifteenth Sunday after Trinity

Ben. Ant. Be not therefore anxious, † saying, What shall we eat? or What shall we drink? for your heavenly Father knoweth that ye have need of all these things, alleluia.
Mag. Ant. Seek ye first † the kingdom of God, and his righteousness; and all these things shall be added unto you, alleluia.

Sixteenth Sunday after Trinity

Ben. Ant. Jesus went into a city † called Nain; and behold, there was a dead man carried out, the only son of his mother.
Mag. Ant. A great prophet † is risen up among us: and God hath visited his people.

Seventeenth Sunday after Trinity

Ben. Ant. And Jesus went † into the house of one of the the chief Pharisees to eat bread on the sabbath day, behold there was a certain man before him which had the dropsy; and he took him, and healed him, and let him go.
Mag. Ant. When thou art bidden to † a wedding, sit down in the lowest place; that he that bade thee may say unto thee, Friend, go up higher; then shalt thou have worship in the presence of them that sit at meat with thee, alleluia.

Eighteenth Sunday after Trinity

Ben. Ant. Master, † which is the great commandment in the law? Jesus said unto him, Thou shalt love the Lord thy God with all thy heart, alleluia.
Mag. Ant. What think ye of Christ? † whose son is he? They say unto him, The son of David. Jesus saith unto them, How then doth David in spirit call him

Trinitytide # Proper of Season

Lord, saying, The Lord said unto my Lord, Sit thou on my right hand?

Nineteenth Sunday after Trinity

Ben. Ant. The Lord said † unto the sick of the palsy, Son, be of good cheer, thy sins be forgiven thee.
Mag. Ant. The sick of the palsy † therefore took up his bed whereon he lay, glorifying God: and all the people, when they saw it, give praise unto God.

Twentieth Sunday after Trinity

Ben. Ant. Tell them which are bidden, † Behold, I have prepared my dinner; come unto the marriage, alleluia.
Mag. Ant. And when the king came in † to see the guests, he saw there a man which had not on a wedding garment: and he said unto him, Friend, how camest thou in hither not having a wedding garment?

Twenty-First Sunday after Trinity

Ben. Ant. There was a certain nobleman, † whose son was sick at Capernaum: when he heard that Jesus was come out of Judæa into Galilee, he besought him that he would heal his son.
Mag. Ant. So the father knew † that it was at the same hour in the which Jesus said, Thy son liveth: and himself believed, and his whole house.

Twenty-Second Sunday after Trinity

Ben. Ant. Then said the lord † unto the servant, Pay me that thou owest. The servant therefore fell down and worshipped him, saying, Lord, have patience with me, and I will pay thee all.
Mag. Ant. Thou wicked servant, † I forgave thee all that debt, because thou desiredst me: shouldest not thou also have had compassion on thy fellow-servant, even as I had pity on thee, alleluia.

Twenty-Third Sunday after Trinity

Ben. Ant. Master, † we know that thou art true, and teachest the way of God in truth, alleluia.
Mag. Ant. Render therefore † unto Caesar the things which are Caesar's: and unto God the things that are God's, alleluia.

Twenty-Fourth Sunday after Trinity

Ben. Ant. For she said within herself, † If I may but touch the hem of his garment, I shall be whole.
Mag. Ant. But Jesus turned him about, † and when he saw her, he said, Daughter, be of good comfort; thy faith hath made thee whole, alleluia.

Sunday Next before Advent

Ben. Ant. When Jesus then † lifted up his eyes, and saw a great company come unto him, he saith unto Philip, Whence shall we buy bread, that these may eat? And this he said to prove him: for he himself knew what he would do.
Mag. Ant. Then those men, † when they had seen the miracle that Jesus did, said among themselves, This is of a truth that prophet that should come into the world.

Proper of Season — *Trinitytide Antiphons*

Magnificat Antiphons for Sundays in Trinitytide

Sunday within 29 July - 4 August

Wisdom hath builded her house, † she hath hewn out her seven pillars: she hath subdued the nations, and in her own might hath she trodden under the necks of the proud and lofty.

Sunday within 5 - 11 August

I dwell † in high places, and my throne is in a cloudy pillar.

Sunday within 12 - 18 August

All wisdom † cometh from the Lord, and is with him for ever; and is before the ages.

Sunday within 19 - 25 August

Wisdom crieth † aloud in the broad places: Whosoever loveth wisdom, let him turn in hither, and he shall find her; and when he hath found her, happy is he if he hold her fast.

Sunday within 26 - 28 August

My son † keep thy father's commandment, and forsake not the law of thy mother: bind them continually upon thine heart.

Sunday within 29 August - 4 September

Now when Job had heard † the words of the messengers, he endured with patience, saying, Shall we receive good at the Lord's hand, and shall we not receive evil also? In all this Job sinned not with his lips, neither charged God foolishly.

Sunday within 5 - 11 September

In all this † Job sinned not with his lips, neither charged God foolishly.

Sunday within 12 - 18 September

Remember not, † Lord, our offences, nor the offences of our forefathers; neither take thou vengeance of our sins.

Sunday within 19 - 25 September

Adonai, † Lord God Almighty, great and wonderful, who hast given salvation by the hand of a woman; hear, we beseech thee, the prayers of thy servants.

Sunday within 26 - 27 September

O Lord, † the King Almighty, the whole world is in thy power, and there is no man that can gainsay thee.

Sunday within 28 September - 4 October

The Lord open your hearts † in his law and commandments; and may the Lord our God send you peace.

Sunday within 5 - 11 October

The sun shone † upon the shields of gold, and the mountains glistered therewith: and yet the forces of the heathen were discomfited.

Sunday within 12 - 18 October

But Israel mourned Judas, † and made great lamentation for him, saying: How art thou fallen, valiant in battle, that didst deliver the people of the Lord.

Sunday within 19 - 25 October

God be gracious unto you, † and hear your prayers, and be at one with you: and the Lord our God never forsake you in time of trouble.

Sunday within 26 - 28 October

Thine is the power, O Lord, † and thine is the kingdom: thou art high above all nations: give peace in our time, O Lord our God.

Sunday within 29 October - 4 November

I saw the Lord also, † sitting upon a throne, high and lifted up, and his train filled the temple: the whole earth was full of the majesty of his glory.

Trinitytide Antiphons # Proper of Season

Sunday on 5 November

Behold, O Lord, † how the city is become desolate that was full of precious treasure; she sitteth sorrowful that was great among the nations: none can comfort her but only thou, O our God.

Sunday within 6 - 12 November

Encompass us, † O Lord, with thine impregnable wall: and with the arms of thy power defend us alway, O our God.

Sunday within 13 - 19 November

Thou that upholdest † the throne of the heavens and beholdest the depths, O Lord, King of kings; that weighest the mountains and holdest the earth in the hollow of thine hand: give ear, O Lord, unto us, in the midst of our groanings.

Sunday within 20 - 26 November

I have set watchmen † upon thy walls, O Jerusalem, which shall never hold their peace day nor night, praising the Name of the Lord.

| 29 November | **Proper of Saints** | *St. Andrew Vigil* |

¶ Propers for Feast Days in the Book of Common Prayer are indicated by brackets: [].
Propers for Memorials are indicated by parentheses: (), with the relevant Common simply
mentioned.

29 NOVEMBER. VIGIL OF ST. ANDREW

Vigil

¶ If to-day be Saturday, the anticipated Vigil of St. Andrew is kept, but the commemoration of St. Saturninus is omitted, in which case the 2nd is of St. Mary (p. BCP 541) and the 3rd Against the persecutors of the Church (p. BCP 543) or for the Chief Bishop (p. BCP 543).

Introit

THE Lord, walking by the sea of Galilee, saw two brethren, Peter and Andrew, and he called them, saying: Follow me: I will make you fishers of men. *Ps.* The heavens declare the glory of God: and the firmament sheweth his handy-work.

Collect

WE beseech thee, Almighty God: that the blessed Apostle Andrew, whose festival we prevent, may implore thy help for us; that we, being absolved from our offences, may likewise be delivered from all dangers. Through.

¶ In Advent, 2nd Collect of the Feria, 3rd of St. Saturninus (p. 421).

¶ Outside of Advent, 2nd Collect of St. Saturninus (p. 421), 3rd of St. Mary in Eastertide (p. BCP 542).

Epistle. Ecclesiasticus 44:22

IN Isaac did the Lord establish, for Abraham his father's sake, The blessing of all men, and the covenant: And he made it rest upon the head of Jacob; He acknowledged him in his blessings, And gave to him by inheritance, And divided his portions; Among twelve tribes did he part them. And he brought out of him a man of mercy, Which found favour in the sight of all flesh; A man beloved of God and men, even Moses, Whose memorial is blessed. He made him like to the glory of the saints, And magnified him in the fears of his enemies. By his words he caused the wonders to cease; He glorified him in the sight of kings; He gave him commandment for his people, And shewed him part of his glory. He sanctified him in his faithfulness and meekness; He chose him out of all flesh. He made him to hear his voice, And led him into the thick darkness, And gave him commandments face to face, Even the law of life and knowledge, That he might teach Jacob the covenant, And Israel his judgments. He exalted Aaron, a holy man like unto him, Even his brother, of the tribe of Levi. He established for him an everlasting covenant, And gave him the priesthood of the people; He beautified him with comely ornaments, And girded him about with a robe of glory.

St. Andrew Vigil — **Proper of Saints** — 29 November

Gradual. Right honourable are thy friends, O God: right well is their princedom established. ℣. If I tell them: they are more in number than the sand.

Gospel. John 1:35

AT THAT TIME: John stood, and two of his disciples; And looking upon Jesus as he walked, he saith, Behold the Lamb of God! And the two disciples heard him speak, and they followed Jesus. Then Jesus turned, and saw them following, and saith unto them, What seek ye? They said unto him, Rabbi, (which is to say, being interpreted, Master,) where dwellest thou? He saith unto them, Come and see. They came and saw where he dwelt, and abode with him that day: for it was about the tenth hour. One of the two which heard John speak, and followed him, was Andrew, Simon Peter's brother. He first findeth his own brother Simon, and saith unto him, We have found the Messias, which is, being interpreted, the Christ. And he brought him to Jesus. And when Jesus beheld him, he said, Thou art Simon the son of Jona: thou shalt be called Cephas, which is by interpretation, A stone. The day following Jesus would go forth into Galilee, and findeth Philip, and saith unto him, Follow me. Now Philip was of Bethsaida, the city of Andrew and Peter. Philip findeth Nathanael, and saith unto him, We have found him, of whom Moses in the law, and the prophets, did write, Jesus of Nazareth, the son of Joseph. And Nathanael said unto him, Can there any good thing come out of Nazareth? Philip saith unto him, Come and see. Jesus saw Nathanael coming to him, and saith of him, Behold an Israelite indeed, in whom is no guile! Nathanael saith unto him, Whence knowest thou me? Jesus answered and said unto him, Before that Philip called thee, when thou wast under the fig tree, I saw thee. Nathanael answered and saith unto him, Rabbi, thou art the Son of God; thou art the King of Israel. Jesus answered and said unto him, Because I said unto thee, I saw thee under the fig tree, believest thou? thou shalt see greater things than these. And he saith unto him, Verily, verily, I say unto you, Hereafter ye shall see heaven open, and the angels of God ascending and descending upon the Son of man.

Offertory. Thou hast crowned him with glory and worship: thou hast made him to have dominion of the works of thy hands, O Lord.

Secret

WE offer, O Lord, this gift to be hallowed unto thee: whereby, recalling the festival of thy blessed Apostle Andrew, we likewise implore the purification of our souls. Through.

¶ In Advent, 2nd Secret of the Feria, 3rd of St. Saturninus (p. 421).

¶ Outside of Advent, 2nd Secret of St. Saturninus (p. 421), 3rd of St. Mary in Eastertide (p. BCP 542).

Communion. Andrew saith to Simon his brother: We have found the Messias, which is called the Christ: and he brought him to Jesus.

Proper of Saints

30 November — St. Andrew

Postcommunion

LORD, who hast bestowed on us these sacraments, we humbly beseech thee: that, at the intercession of thy blessed Apostle Andrew, the mysteries which we offer for his venerable passion may be profitable for our healing. Through.

❧ In Advent, 2nd Postcommunion of the Feria, 3rd of St. Saturninus (p. 421).

❧ Outside of Advent, 2nd Postcommunion of St. Saturninus (p. 421), 3rd of St. Mary in Eastertide (p. BCP 542).

(29 NOVEMBER. ST. SATURNINUS)

❧ The Second Common of a Martyr not a Bishop (p. 690), except for the following.

Collect

GOD, who vouchsafest unto us to rejoice in the birthday of thy blessed Martyr Saturninus: grant, we pray thee; that we may be succoured by his merits. Through.

Secret

ANCTIFY, O Lord, we beseech thee, the offerings which we dedicate unto thee: and at the intercession of blessed Saturninus, thy Martyr, for their sake graciously regard us. Through.

Postcommunion

E beseech thee, O Lord, that we, being sanctified by the receiving of thy sacrament: may, at the intercession of thy Saints, be thereby rendered acceptable unto thee. Through.

[30 NOVEMBER. ST. ANDREW]

❧ The Hymns and Versicles are of the Common of Apostles (p. 673), with the Antiphons as followeth.

Mag. Ant. One of the two † which followed the Lord was Andrew, Simon Peter's brother, alleluia.
Ben. Ant. Yield up to us † a man so righteous, restore to us a man so holy: destroy not a man so dear to God, righteous, dutiful, and gentle.
Mag. Ant. When blessed Andrew † came to the place where the Cross had been prepared, he cried out and said: O goodly Cross, so long desired, and now made ready for my eager spirit; fearless and joyful do I come to thee: therefore do thou also receive me gladly, as his disciple, who did hang upon thee.

2 December. St. Peter Chrysologus

Double

¶ The propers are from the Common of Doctors (p. 723), except for the following.

¶ Note, Commemoration of St. Bibiana and of the Advent Feria.

Collect

O GOD, who by divine foreshewing wast pleased to choose blessed Peter Chrysologus thy illustrious Doctor to rule and instruct thy Church: grant, we beseech thee; that, as we have had him for a Doctor of life on earth, so we may be found worthy to have him for an intercessor in heaven. Through.

Gradual. Behold a great priest, who in his days pleased God. ℣. There was none found like unto him, who kept the law of the Most High.

Communion. Lord. thou deliveredst unto me five talents: behold, I have gained beside them five talents more. Well done, thou good and faithful servant, thou hast been faithful over a few things, I will make thee ruler over many things, enter thou into the joy of thy lord.

(2 December. St. Bibiana)

¶ The Second Common of a Virgin Martyress (p. 738), except for the following.

Collect

O GOD, the giver of all good gifts, who in thy handmaid Bibiana didst unite the palm of martyrdom with the flower of virginity: unite by her intercession our hearts in charity with thee; that all perils being done away, we may attain unto everlasting rewards. Through.

Secret

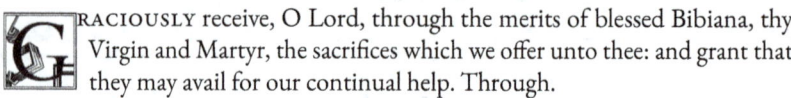
GRACIOUSLY receive, O Lord, through the merits of blessed Bibiana, thy Virgin and Martyr, the sacrifices which we offer unto thee: and grant that they may avail for our continual help. Through.

Postcommunion

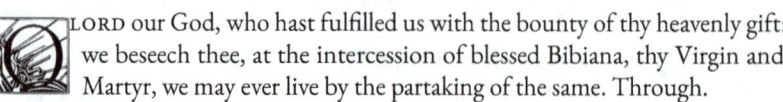
O LORD our God, who hast fulfilled us with the bounty of thy heavenly gift: we beseech thee, at the intercession of blessed Bibiana, thy Virgin and Martyr, we may ever live by the partaking of the same. Through.

6 December · **Proper of Saints** · *St. Nicholas*

(4 December. St. Barbara)

¶ The First Common of a Virgin Martyress (p. 733).

(5 December. St. Sabbas of Judæa)

¶ The Common of Abbots (p. 732).

¶ If today be Saturday, the Mass is of St. Mary on Saturday with 2nd Collect of the Feria & 3rd of St. Sabbas.

6 December. St. Nicholas

Double

¶ The Daily Office propers are from the First Common of a Confessor Bishop (p. 715).

Introit

THE Lord hath established a covenant of peace with him, and made him a prince: that he should have the dignity of the priesthood for ever. *Ps.* Lord, remember David: and all his trouble.

Collect

O GOD, who didst adorn thy blessed Bishop Nicholas with innumerable miracles: grant, we beseech thee; that by his merits and prayers we may be delivered from the fires of hell. Through.

¶ Commemoration is of the Feria, unless it be Saturday.

Epistle. Hebrews 13:7

BRETHREN: Remember them which have the rule over you, who have spoken unto you the word of God: whose faith follow, considering the end of their conversation. Jesus Christ the same yesterday, and to day, and for ever. Be not carried about with divers and strange doctrines. For it is a good thing that the heart be established with grace; not with meats, which have not profited them that have been occupied therein. We have an altar, whereof they have no right to eat which serve the tabernacle. For the bodies of those beasts, whose blood is brought into the sanctuary by the high priest for sin, are burned without the camp. Wherefore Jesus also, that he might sanctify the people with his own blood, suffered without the gate. Let us go forth therefore unto him without the camp, bearing his reproach. For here have we no continuing city, but we seek one to come. By him therefore let us offer the sacrifice of praise to God continually, that is, the fruit of our lips giving thanks to his name. But to do good and to communicate forget not: for with such sacrifices God is well pleased. Obey them that have the rule over you, and submit yourselves: for they watch for your souls, as they that must give account.

St. Nicholas — **Proper of Saints** — 6 December

Gradual. I have found David my servant, with my holy oil have I anointed him: my hand shall hold him fast, and my arm shall strengthen him. ℣. The enemy shall not be able to do him violence, the son of wickedness shall not hurt him.

Alleluia. Alleluia, alleluia. ℣. The righteous shall flourish like a palm-tree: and shall spread abroad like a cedar in Libanus. Alleluia.

Gospel. Matthew 25:14

AT THAT TIME: Jesus spake this parable to his disciples: A man travelling into a far country, who called his own servants, and delivered unto them his goods. And unto one he gave five talents, to another two, and to another one; to every man according to his several ability; and straightway took his journey. Then he that had received the five talents went and traded with the same, and made them other five talents. And likewise he that had received two, he also gained other two. But he that had received one went and digged in the earth, and hid his lord's money. After a long time the lord of those servants cometh, and reckoneth with them. And so he that had received five talents came and brought other five talents, saying, Lord, thou deliveredst unto me five talents: behold, I have gained beside them five talents more. His lord said unto him, Well done, thou good and faithful servant: thou hast been faithful over a few things, I will make thee ruler over many things: enter thou into the joy of thy lord. He also that had received two talents came and said, Lord, thou deliveredst unto me two talents: behold, I have gained two other talents beside them. His lord said unto him, Well done, good and faithful servant; thou hast been faithful over a few things, I will make thee ruler over many things: enter thou into the joy of thy lord.

Offertory. My truth and my mercy shall be with him: and in my name shall his horn be exalted.

Secret

SANCTIFY, we besecch thee, O Lord God, these gifts which we offer on the solemnity of thy holy Bishop Nicholas: that our life may ever thereby be directed both in prosperity and in adversity. Through.

℟ Commemoration is of the Feria, unless it be Saturday.

Communion. I have sworn once by my holiness: His seed shall endure for ever, and his seat is like as the sun before me, he shall stand fast for evermore as the moon, and as the faithful witness in heaven.

Postcommunion

MAY the sacrifices which we have received, O Lord, for the solemnity of thy holy Bishop Nicholas, preserve us by their everlasting protection. Through.

℟ Commemoration is of the Feria, unless it be Saturday.

7 December. St. Ambrose

Greater Double

¶ The Daily Office propers are from the Common of a Confessor Bishop (p. 715).

Introit

IN the midst of the Church he opened his mouth: and the Lord filled him with the spirit of wisdom and of understanding: he clothed him with a robe of glory. *Ps.* It is a good thing to give thanks unto the Lord: and to sing praises unto thy name, O most Highest.

Collect

O GOD, who didst give blessed Ambrose unto thy people to be a minister of everlasting salvation: grant, we beseech thee; that as we have learned of him the doctrine of life on earth, so we may be found worthy to have him for our advocate in heaven. Through.

¶ Commemoration is of the Feria.

¶ The Epistle is from the Common of Doctors (p. 723).

Gradual. Behold a great priest, who in his days pleased God. ℣. There was none foun like unto him, who kept the law of the Most High.

Alleluia. Alleluia, alleluia. ℣. The Lord sware, and will not repent: Thou art a priest for ever after the order of Melchisedech.

¶ In Septuagesimatide or Lent, replacing the Alleluia:

Tract. Blessed is the man that feareth the Lord: he hath great delight in his commandments. ℣. His seed shall be mighty upon earth: the generation of the faithful shall be blessed. ℣. Riches and plenteousness shall be in his house: and his righteousness endureth for ever.

¶ In Eastertide, replacing the Lesser Alleluia:

Alleluia. Alleluia, alleluia. ℣. The Lord loved him, and adorned him: and clothed him with a robe of glory. Alleluia. ℣. The righteous shall grow as the lily and flourish for ever before the Lord. Alleluia.

¶ The Gospel is from the Common of Doctors (p. 723).

Offertory. My truth and my mercy shall be with him: and in my name shall his horn be exalted.

Secret

ALMIGHTY and everlasting God, grant, that the gifts which we present unto thy Majesty, may through the intercession of blessed Ambrose, thy Confessor and Bishop, be profitable unto us for everlasting salvation. Through.

¶ Commemoration is of the Feria.

Communion. I have sworn once by my holiness: His seed shall endure for ever, and his seat is like as the sun before me, he shall stand fast for evermore as the moon, and as the faithful witness in heaven.

Postcommunion

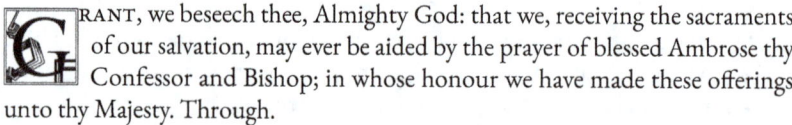RANT, we beseech thee, Almighty God: that we, receiving the sacraments of our salvation, may ever be aided by the prayer of blessed Ambrose thy Confessor and Bishop; in whose honour we have made these offerings unto thy Majesty. Through.

¶ Commemoration is of the Feria. In Lent, the Last Gospel is of the Feria.

[8 December. Conception of the Blessed Virgin Mary]

¶ The Hymns are from the Common of the Blessed Virgin Mary (p. 760) with the following Versicle and Antiphons.

℣. To-day is the Conception of the holy Virgin Mary.
℟. Whose glorious life illumineth all the churches.

Mag. Ant. All generations † shall call me blessed: for he that is mighty hath magnified me, alleluia.

Ben. Ant. The Lord God said † unto the serpent, I will put enmity between thee and the woman, and between thy seed and her seed; it shall bruise thy head, alleluia.

Mag. Ant. Let us celebrate † the worshipful Conception of the blessed and glorious Virgin Mary, whose lowliness the Lord regarded when at the word of an Angel she conceived the world's Redeemer, alleluia.

(10 December. St. Melchiades)

¶ The First Common of a Martyr Bishop (p. 682).

(11 December. St. Damasus)

Introit

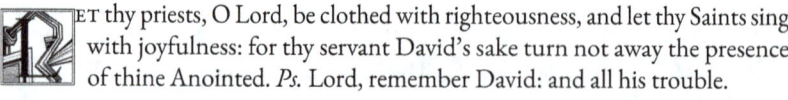ET thy priests, O Lord, be clothed with righteousness, and let thy Saints sing with joyfulness: for thy servant David's sake turn not away the presence of thine Anointed. *Ps.* Lord, remember David: and all his trouble.

Collect

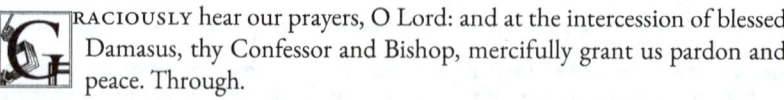RACIOUSLY hear our prayers, O Lord: and at the intercession of blessed Damasus, thy Confessor and Bishop, mercifully grant us pardon and peace. Through.

¶ Commemoration is of the Octave & Feria.

Proper of Saints

<small>13 December — St. Lucy</small>

¶ The Epistle is from the Second Common of a Confessor Bishop (p. 720).

Gradual. Behold a great priest who in his days pleased God. ℣. There was none found like unto him, who kept the law of the Most High.

Alleluia. Alleluia, alleluia. ℣. Thou art a priest for ever after the order of Melchisedech. Alleluia.

¶ The Gospel is from the Second Common of a Confessor Bishop (p. 720).

Communion. I have found David my servant, with my holy oil have I anointed him: my hand shall hold him fast, and my arm shall strengthen him.

Secret

GRANT, O Lord, that like as thy dedicated people do acknowledge that in tribulation they have been succoured by the merits of thy Saints: so this oblation, which they offer unto thee in honour of the same, may be acceptable in thy sight. Through.

¶ Commemoration is of the Octave & Feria.

Communion. Lord, thou deliveredst unto me five talents, behold I have gained beside them five talents more. Well done, thou good and faithful servant, thou hast been faithful over a few things, I will make thee ruler over many things, enter thou into the joy of thy Lord.

Postcommunion

GRANT, we beseech thee, O Lord, that thy faithful people may ever rejoice in the veneration of thy saints: and be defended by their perpetual supplication. Through.

¶ Commemoration is of the Octave & Feria.

13 December. St. Lucy

Greater Double

¶ The Daily Office propers are from the Common of Virgins (p. 742), except for the following.

Mag. Ant. In thy patience † thou didst possess thy soul, O Lucy, spouse of Christ: thou didst hate the things which are in the world, and thou shinest among the Angels: resisting unto blood, thou didst vanquish the enemy.

Ben. Ant. A pillar art thou † that may not be moved, O Lucy, spouse of Christ: and all the people are waiting until thou receive the crown of life, alleluia.

℣. Full of grace are thy lips.
℟. Because God hath blessed thee for ever.

Mag. Ant. With such gravity † was she endued by the Holy Spirit, that the virgin of the Lord remained unmoved.

St. Lucy   **Proper of Saints**   13 December

Introit

THOU hast loved righteousness, and hated iniquity: wherefore God, even thy God, hath anointed thee with the oil of gladness above thy fellows. *Ps.* My heart is inditing of a good matter: I speak of the things which I have made unto the King.

Collect

GRACIOUSLY hear us, O God of our salvation: that, like as we do rejoice in the festival of blessed Lucy thy Virgin; so we may be instructed in all godly and devout affection. Through.

¶ Commemoration is of the Octave & Feria.

¶ The Epistle is from the First Common of a Virgin (p. 742).

Gradual. Thou hast loved righteousness, and hated iniquity. ℣. Wherefore God, even thy God, hath anointed thee with the oil of gladness.

Alleluia. Alleluia, alleluia. ℣. Full of grace are thy lips: because God hath blessed thee for ever. Alleluia.

¶ In Votive Masses after Septuagesima, the Tract, and in Eastertide, the Alleluia, is from the First Common of a Virgin (p. 742).

Gospel. Matthew 13:44

AT THAT TIME: Jesus spake this parable unto his disciples: The kingdom of heaven is like unto treasure hid in a field; the which when a man hath found, he hideth, and for joy thereof goeth and selleth all that he hath, and buyeth that field. Again, the kingdom of heaven is like unto a merchant man, seeking goodly pearls: Who, when he had found one pearl of great price, went and sold all that he had, and bought it. Again, the kingdom of heaven is like unto a net, that was cast into the sea, and gathered of every kind: Which, when it was full, they drew to shore, and sat down, and gathered the good into vessels, but cast the bad away. So shall it be at the end of the world: the angels shall come forth, and sever the wicked from among the just, And shall cast them into the furnace of fire: there shall be wailing and gnashing of teeth. Jesus saith unto them, Have ye understood all these things? They say unto him, Yea, Lord. Then said he unto them, Therefore every scribe which is instructed unto the kingdom of heaven is like unto a man that is an householder, which bringeth forth out of his treasure things new and old.

Offertory. The Virgins that be her fellows shall be brought unto the King: they that bear her company shall be brought unto thee with joy and gladness: and shall enter into the palace of the Lord the King.

Secret

GRANT, O Lord, that like as thy dedicated people do acknowledge that in tribulation they have been succoured by the merits of thy Saints: so this oblation, which they offer unto thee in honour of the same, may be acceptable in thy sight. Through.

¶ Commemoration is of the Octave & Feria.

Communion. Princes have persecuted me without a cause, but my heart standeth in awe of thy word: I am as glad of thy word, as one that findeth great spoils.

Postcommunion

O LORD, who hast satisfied thy family with sacred gifts: we beseech thee; that we may at all times be comforted by the intercession of her whose festival we celebrate. Through.

¶ Commemoration is of the Octave & Feria.

(13 December. St. Herman of Alaska)

¶ The First Common of a Confessor not Bishop (p. 725).

14 December. Day VII within the Octave of the Conception

Semidouble

¶ Of the Octave, as on December 9. But if Ember Wednesday fall on this day, of the Ember Day, with a Commemoration of the Octave. The Mass is with the 3rd Prayer of the Holy Ghost.

¶ If an Ember Day occur on any of the following Feasts, the Commemoration of the Feria is omitted.

15 December. Octave Day of the Conception of the Blessed Virgin Mary

Greater Double

¶ Hymn, Versicle, Antiphon, & Mass as on the Feast, with Commemoration of the Feria.

(16 December. St. Eusebius of Vercelli)

¶ The Second Common of a Martyr Bishop (p. 686), with commemoration of the Feria and the Collect of St. Mary.

18 December. Expectation of the Blessed Virgin Mary

Double

Opening Sentence. Send ye the lamb to the ruler of the land from Sela to the wilderness, unto the mount of the daughter of Zion. (Is. 16:1)

¶ Note, The Magnificat Antiphons are of the 'O' Antiphons (p. 314).

I Evensong

℣. Hail Mary, full of grace.
℟. The Lord is with thee.

¶ The Office Hymns are from the First Sunday of Advent (p. 308).

Mattins

℣. The Holy Ghost shall come upon thee.
℟. And the power of the Highest shall overshadow thee.

Ben. Ant. He shall sit upon the throne of David, † and of his kingdom, for ever.

¶ II Evensong as in I Evensong.

¶ The Mass propers are from the Common of the Blessed Virgin Mary (p. 760), except for the Collect as followeth.

Collect

GOD, who wast pleased that thy Word should take flesh of the womb of the Blessed Virgin Mary at the message of an Angel: grant to thy humble servants; that we who believe her to be truly the Mother of God may be aided by her intercession in thy sight. Through the same.

20 December. Vigil of St. Thomas

Vigil

¶ If today be Sunday, in the Ember Saturday Mass, Commemoration is made of the anticipated Vigil of St. Thomas and the last Gospel of the Vigil is read at the end, the 3rd Collect is of St. Mary.

¶ The Mass propers are from the Vigil of Apostles (p. 672), with Commemoration of the Feria of Advent and the 3rd Collect of St. Mary. But if an Ember Day occur, Commemoration is made of the Vigil in the Mass of the Feria.

10 January — **Proper of Saints** — *St. Paul Hermit*

[21 December. St. Thomas]

¶ The Office Hymn and Versicle are from the Common of Apostles (p. 673), with the following Antiphon.

Mag. & Ben. Ant. Because thou hast seen me, † Thomas, thou hast believed: blessed are they that have not seen, and yet have believed, alleluia.

(10 January. St. Paul the First Hermit)

Introit

THE just shall flourish like a palm-tree: and shall spread abroad like a cedar in Libanus: planted in the house of the Lord: in the courts of the house of our God. *Ps.* It is a good thing to give thanks unto the Lord: and to sing praises unto thy name, O Most Highest.

Collect

O GOD, who makest us glad with the yearly solemnity of blessed Paul, thy Confessor: mercifully grant; that, as we now celebrate his birthday, so we may follow the example of his life. Through.

¶ The Epistle is from the Common of Abbots (p. 732).

Gradual. The just shall flourish like a palm-tree: and shall spread abroad like a cedar in Libanus in the house of the Lord. ℣. To tell of thy loving-kindness early in the morning, and of thy truth in the night-season.

Alleluia. Alleluia, alleluia. ℣. The just shall grow as the lily: and flourish for ever before the Lord. Alleluia.

Gospel. Matthew 11:25

AT THAT TIME: Jesus answered and said: I thank thee, O Father, Lord of heaven and earth, because thou hast hid these things from the wise and prudent, and hast revealed them unto babes. Even so, Father: for so it seemed good in thy sight. All things are delivered unto me of my Father: and no man knoweth the Son, but the Father; neither knoweth any man the Father, save the Son, and he to whomsoever the Son will reveal him. Come unto me, all ye that labour and are heavy laden, and I will give you rest. Take my yoke upon you, and learn of me; for I am meek and lowly in heart: and ye shall find rest unto your souls. For my yoke is easy, and my burden is light.

Offertory. The just shall rejoice in thy strength, O Lord: exceeding glad shall he be of thy salvation: thou hast given him his heart's desire.

Secret

RANT, we beseech thee, O Lord, that we who, trusting in this our sacrifice of praise, do offer it before thee to the honour of thy Saints: may by the same be delivered from all evils both in this life and that which is to come. Through.

Communion. The just shall rejoice in the Lord, and put his trust in him: and all they that are true of heart shall be glad.

Postcommunion

LORD, our God, who hast refreshed us with heavenly meat and drink, we humbly beseech thee: that we may be defended by the prayers of him in whose memory we have received the same. Through.

(11 January. St. Hyginus of Rome)

¶ The First Common of a Martyr not a Bishop (p. 688).

(12 January. St. Benedict Biscop)

¶ The Common of Abbots (p. 732), except for the following.

Collect

GOD, by whose gift the blessed Abbot Benedict left all things that he might be made perfect: grant unto all those who have entered upon the path of evangelical perfection, that they may neither look back nor linger in the way; but hastening to thee without stumbling, may lay hold upon eternal life. Through.

Secret

E beseech thee, O Lord, that thy holy Abbot Benedict, may may intercede for us: that this sacrifice which we offer and present upon thy holy altar may be profitable unto us for our salvation. Through.

Postcommunion

ET thy sacrament, O Lord, which we have now received and the prayers of the blessed Abbot Benedict, effectually defend us: that we may both imitate the example of his conversion, and receive the succour of his intercession. Through.

14 January. St. Hilary

Double

¶ The propers are from the Common of Doctors (p. 723).
NOTE, Commemoration of St. Felix, with the Prayers from the Mass below.

(14 January. St. Felix)

¶ The Second Common of a Martyr not a Bishop (p. 690), except for the following.

Collect

RANT, we beseech thee, Almighty God, that the examples of thy Saints may provoke us to a better life: that as we celebrate their festival so we may imitate their actions. Through.

Secret

E beseech thee, O Lord, mercifully to accept this our sacrifice, which we offer unto thee, pleading the merits of blessed Felix, thy Martyr: that the same may avail for our perpetual succour. Through.

Postcommunion

LORD, who hast fulfilled us with saving mysteries: we beseech thee that we may be aided by the prayers of blessed Felix thy Martyr, whose festival we celebrate. Through.

15 January. St. Maurus

Greater Double

I Evensong

Defender, leader true, thine own companions deem'd
Thy splendour half divine, since all were less esteem'd:
For thy most worthy deeds, Maurus, accept the lays
Wherewith we celebrate thy praise.

Born of a noble stock, great honour was his due,
But palaces he spurn'd, and from the world withdrew;
Delights he trampl'd down, estates and robes unpric'd,
To undergo the yoke of Christ.

The holy Abbot's grace, before his eyes display'd,
By deeds of equal worth he eagerly portray'd;

St. Maurus   **Proper of Saints**   15 January

The pattern of the life monastic shone in truth
From every action of the youth.

Sternly, with sackcloth rough, self-mastery he wrought,
And by the curb of law, unbroken silence sought;
The ever-watchful nights in fervent prayer he spent;
Whole days of fasting underwent

Right speedily he flew to do the father's hest,
Dry-shod, the waters deep with fearless feet he press'd;
And safely he return'd with Placidus, set free
Like Peter walking on the sea.

To thee, O Trinity, high praise and honour be,
Whose countenance desir'd the heaven-dwellers see:
Grant that the Holy Rule may be our pathway plain
The prize of Maurus to attain. Amen.

℣. The Lord loved him and adorned him.
℟. He clothed him with a robe of glory.

Mag. Ant. O most blessed of men! † who, rejecting this world, bore the yoke of Holy Rule from tender years so lovingly; and being made obedient even unto death, he denied himself, that he might wholly cling to Christ his Master, alleluia.

Mattins

Invitatory Hymn

In childhood Placidus was by his father giv'n;
Thus offer'd, he himself did freely yield to God.
Since first he came, he ever shone with wondrous grace,
A pattern to all zealous souls.

His Abbot sent him forth to fill an earthen crock,
He dips it in the lake, unwary, slips and falls,
A wave then carries him a bow-shot from the shore,
Out in the deep drowning is nigh.

But Maurus, what is this, that hast'ning to the lake,
Thou runnest o'er the waves as though thou wast on land?
Wont to obey, 'tis thus thy holy father's voice
Doth lead thee to a miracle.

Straightway the lake restores Placidus safe again,
But whose the merit? Did his Nursian father draw
Him from the swirling depths, or was it Maurus' act?

15 January   **Proper of Saints**   *St. Maurus*

The child resolves their questioning.

O Holy Trinity, through prayers of Placidus,
Grant to thy monks that by the narrow path of Rule
They may at length attain unto the courts of heav'n,
And mingle with celestial choirs. Amen.

Office Hymn

¶ The Office Hymn & Versicle are from the First Common of a Confessor not a Bishop (p. 725), with the Antiphon from I Evensong.

II Evensong

¶ The Office Hymn is of I Evensong, with the Versicle & Antiphon as followeth.

℣. The Lord guided the righteous in right paths.
℟. And shewed him the kingdom of God.

Mag. Ant. To-day holy Maurus, † lying upon a goat-skin, died happily before the altar; to-day the first-begotten disciple of blessed Benedict, through the guiding of the Holy Rule, came up to Christ, rising untroubled, accompanied by choirs of Angels; today the obedient man, telling his victories, was worthy to be crowned by the Lord, alleluia.

Introit

THY way is in the sea, and thy paths in the great waters: and thy footsteps are not known. Thou leddest thy people like sheep. *Ps.* The waters saw thee, O God, the waters saw thee, and were afraid: the depths also were troubled.

Collect

O GOD, who for a pattern of obedience didst cause blessed Maurus to walk dry-shod upon the waters: grant that we may both follow perfectly the example of his virtues, and also be worthy to share in his reward. Through.

Epistle. Ecclesiasticus 51:13

WHEN I was yet young, Or ever I went abroad, I sought wisdom openly in my prayer. Before the temple I asked for her, And I will seek her out even to the end. From her flower as from the ripening grape my heart delighted in her: My foot trod in uprightness, From my youth I tracked her out. I bowed down mine ear a little, and received her, And found for myself much instruction. I profited in her: Unto him that giveth me wisdom I will give glory. For I purposed to practice her, And I was zealous for that which is good; And I shall never be put to shame. My soul hath wrestled in her, And in my doing I was exact: I spread forth my hands to the heaven above, And bewailed my ignorances of her. I set my soul aright unto her, And in pureness I found her. I gat me a heart joined with her from the beginning: Therefore shall I not be forsaken. My inward part also was troubled to seek her: Therefore have I gotten a good possession. The Lord gave me a tongue for my reward; And I will praise him therewith.

Draw near unto me, ye unlearned, And lodge in the house of instruction. Say, wherefore are ye lacking in these things, And your souls are very thirsty? I opened my mouth, and spake, Get her for yourselves without money. Put your neck under the yoke, And let your soul receive instruction: She is hard at hand to find. Behold with your eyes, How that I laboured but a little, And found for myself much rest. Get you instruction with a great sum of silver, And gain much gold by her. May your soul rejoice in his mercy, And may ye not be put to shame in praising him. Work your work before the time cometh, And in his time he will give you your reward.

Gradual. I will bring thy seed from the east, and gather thee from the west. ℣. When thou passest through the waters, I will be with thee; and through the rivers, they shall not overflow thee.

Alleluia. Alleluia, alleluia. ℣. An obedient man shall speak of victory; Wealth and riches shall be in his house. Alleluia.

¶ In Septuagesimatide & Lent, the Alleluia is omitted and the Tract is said instead.

Tract. Blessed is the man that feareth the Lord: he hath great delight in his commandments. ℣. His seed shall be mighty upon earth: the generation of the faithful shall be blessed. ℣. Riches and plenteousness shall be in his house: and his righteousness endureth for ever.

Gospel. Matthew 14:28

T THAT TIME: Peter answered Jesus and said, Lord, if it be thou, bid me come unto thee on the water. And he said, Come. And when Peter was come down out of the ship, he walked on the water, to go to Jesus. But when he saw the wind boisterous, he was afraid; and beginning to sink, he cried, saying, Lord, save me. And immediately Jesus stretched forth his hand, and caught him, and said unto him, O thou of little faith, wherefore didst thou doubt? And when they were come into the ship, the wind ceased. Then they that were in the ship came and worshipped him, saying, Of a truth thou art the Son of God.

Offertory. And the places that have been desolate for ages shall be built in thee: thou shalt raise up the foundations of generation and generation: turning the paths into rest. And I will feed thee with the inheritance of thy Father.

Secret

AY the sacrifices we offer ascend unto thee, O Lord, as an odour of sweetness; and may the intercession of blessed Maurus, Abbot, intervene for us, that thy propitious power may descend upon us. Through.

Communion. I have chosen you, and ordained you, that ye should go and bring forth fruit, and that your fruit should remain: that whatsoever ye shall ask of the Father in my name, he may give it you.

Postcommunion

WE implore thy mercy, O Lord our God, that having received the pledges of our salvation and giving thanks for thy help; thou may accept our offerings unto our salvation; sending upon us thy grace to support us; that the celestial blessing, which thou hast brought us by the patronage of blessed Maurus, Abbot, may be perfected by continuing in imitation of him. Through.

(16 January. St. Marcellus)

Introit

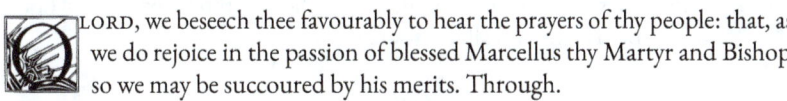

THE Lord hath established a covenant of peace with him, and made him a prince: that he should have the dignity of the priesthood for ever. *Ps.* Lord, remember David: and all his trouble.

Collect

O LORD, we beseech thee favourably to hear the prayers of thy people: that, as we do rejoice in the passion of blessed Marcellus thy Martyr and Bishop, so we may be succoured by his merits. Through.

¶ The Epistle is from the Second Common of a Martyr Bishop (p. 686).

Gradual. I have found David my servant, with my holy oil have I anointed him: my hand shall hold him fast, and my arm shall strengthen him. ℣. The enemy shall not be able to do him violence, the son of wickedness shall not hurt him.

Alleluia. Alleluia, alleluia. ℣. Thou art a priest for ever, after the order of Melchisedech. Alleluia.

¶ The Gospel is from the Second Common of a Martyr Bishop (p. 686).

Offertory. My truth and my mercy shall be with him: and in my name shall his horn be exalted.

Secret

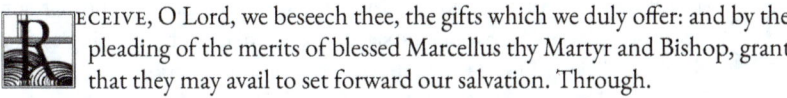

RECEIVE, O Lord, we beseech thee, the gifts which we duly offer: and by the pleading of the merits of blessed Marcellus thy Martyr and Bishop, grant that they may avail to set forward our salvation. Through.

Communion. Lord, thou deliveredst unto me five talents: behold, I have gained beside them five talents more. Well done, thou good and faithful servant, thou hast been faithful over a few things, I will make thee ruler over many things, enter thou into the joy of thy lord.

Postcommunion

LORD, who hast satisfied thy family with sacred gifts: we beseech thee; that we may at all times be comforted by the intercession of him whose festival we celebrate. Through.

17 JANUARY. ST. ANTHONY

Double

¶ The propers are from the Common of Abbots (p. 732), except for the Gospel which is from the First Common of a Confessor not a Bishop (p. 725).

18 JANUARY. CHAIR OF ST. PETER AT ROME

Greater Double

¶ The Daily Office propers are from the Chair of St. Peter at Antioch (p. 465).

Introit

THE Lord hath established a covenant of peace with him, and made him a prince: that he should have the dignity of the priesthood for ever. *Ps.* Lord, remember David: and all his trouble.

Collect

GOD, who didst bestow upon thy blessed Apostle Peter the keys of the kingdom of heaven, and didst appoint unto him the high priesthood of binding and loosing: vouchsafe; that by the help of his intercession we may be delivered from the bonds of our iniquities. Who livest and reignest.

GOD, who by the preaching of the blessed Apostle Paul didst teach the multitude of the Gentiles: grant to us, we beseech thee; that we who celebrate his commemoration may know him to be our advocate with thee. (Through.)

¶ Commemoration of St. Prisca of Rome (p. 440).

Epistle. 1 Peter 1:1

PETER, an apostle of Jesus Christ, to the strangers scattered throughout Pontus, Galatia, Cappadocia, Asia, and Bithynia, elect according to the foreknowledge of God the Father, through sanctification of the Spirit, unto obedience and sprinkling of the blood of Jesus Christ: Grace unto you, and peace, be multiplied. Blessed be the God and Father of our Lord Jesus Christ, which according to his abundant mercy hath begotten us again unto a lively hope by the resurrection of Jesus Christ from the dead, to an inheritance incorruptible, and undefiled, and that fadeth not away, reserved in heaven for you, who are kept by the power of God through faith unto salvation ready to be revealed in the last time. Wherein ye greatly rejoice, though now for a season, if need be, ye are in heaviness through manifold temptations: that the trial of your faith, being much more precious than of gold that perisheth, though it be tried with fire, might be found unto praise and honour and glory at the appearing of Jesus Christ our Lord.

Gradual. Let them exalt him in the congregation of the people: and praise him in the seat of the elders. ℣. O that men would praise the Lord for his goodness, and declare the wonders that he doeth for the children of men.

Alleluia. Alleluia, alleluia. ℣. Thou art Peter, and upon this rock I will build my Church. Alleluia.

¶ In Septuagesimatide & Lent, the Alleluia is replaced with the following.

Tract. Thou art Peter, and upon this rock I will build my Church. ℣. And the gates of hell shall not prevail against it: and I will give unto thee the keys of the kingdom of heaven. ℣. Whatsoever thou shalt bind on earth shall be bound in heaven. ℣. And whatsoever thou shalt loose on earth shall be loosed in heaven.

¶ In Eastertide, the Alleluia is replaced with the following.

Alleluia. Alleluia, alleluia. ℣. O that men would praise the Lord for his goodness, and declare the wonders that he doeth for the children of men. Alleluia. ℣. Thou art Peter, and upon this rock I will build my Church. Alleluia.

Gospel. Matthew 16:13

AT THAT TIME: When Jesus came into the coasts of Cæsarea Philippi, he asked his disciples, saying, Whom do men say that I the Son of man am? And they said, Some say that thou art John the Baptist: some, Elias; and others, Jeremias, or one of the prophets. He saith unto them, But whom say ye that I am? And Simon Peter answered and said, Thou art the Christ, the Son of the living God. And Jesus answered and said unto him, Blessed art thou, Simon Bar-jona: for flesh and blood hath not revealed it unto thee, but my Father which is in heaven. And I say also unto thee, That thou art Peter, and upon this rock I will build my church; and the gates of hell shall not prevail against it. And I will give unto thee the keys of the kingdom of heaven: and whatsoever thou shalt bind on earth shall be bound in heaven: and whatsoever thou shalt loose on earth shall be loosed in heaven.

Offertory. Thou art Peter, and upon this rock I will build my Church: and the gates of hell shall not prevail against it: and I will give unto thee the keys of the kingdom of heaven.

St. Prisca Rome   **Proper of Saints**   18 January

Secret

WE beseech thee, O Lord, that the intercession of blessed Peter the Apostle may commend unto thee the prayers and sacrifices of thy Church: that those things which we celebrate for his glory may avail for our pardon. Through.

SANCTIFY, O Lord, through the prayers of thine Apostle Paul, the gifts of thy people: that those things, which by thine institution are pleasing unto thee, may be made more pleasing by his prayer and advocacy. (Through.)

¶ Commemoration of St. Prisca of Rome (p. 440).

Communion. Thou art Peter, and upon this rock I will build my Church.

Postcommunion

MAY the gift, O Lord, which we have offered, make us to rejoice: that as we proclaim thy wonders in thine Apostle Peter; so through him we may receive the abundance of thy loving-kindness. Through.

O LORD, who hast sanctified us with this saving mystery: we beseech thee; that he whom thou hast given to be our advocate and guide may never fail in prayer for us. (Through.)

¶ Commemoration of St. Prisca of Rome (p. 440).

(18 January. St. Prisca of Rome)

¶ The Second Common of a Virgin Martyress (p. 738), except for the following.

Collect

GRANT, we beseech thee, Almighty God: that we who celebrate the heavenly birthday of blessed Prisca, thy Virgin and Martyr; may both rejoice in her yearly solemnity, and profit by the example of so great a faith. Through.

Secret

WE beseech thee, O Lord, that this sacrifice which we offer in remembrance of the birthday of thy Saints may both loose us from the bonds of our iniquity, and obtain for us the gifts of thy mercy. Through.

Postcommunion

O LORD, who hast fulfilled us with saving mysteries: we beseech thee that we may be aided by the prayers of her whose festival we celebrate. Through.

(19 January. Sts. Marius, Martha, Audifax, & Abachum)

Introit

ET the righteous be glad and rejoice before God: let them also be merry and joyful. *Ps.* Let God arise, and let his enemies be scattered: let them also that hate him flee before him.

Collect

RACIOUSLY hear thy people, O Lord, who call upon thee with the advocacy of thy Saints: and grant us both to rejoice in peace in this temporal life; and to find succour unto life everlasting. Through.

¶ Commemoration of St. Mark of Ephesus (p. 442) and of St. Mary in Epiphanytide (p. BCP 541).

¶ The Epistle is from the Third Common of Many Martyrs (p. 700).

Gradual. The souls of the just are in the hand of God: and there shall no torment of malice touch them. ℣. In the sight of the unwise they seemed to die: but they are in peace.

Alleluia. Alleluia, alleluia. ℣. Our God is wonderful in his Saints. Alleluia.

¶ In Septuagesimatide & Lent, the Alleluia is replaced with the Tract from the Third Common of Many Martyrs (p. 700).

¶ The Gospel is from the first additional Gospel of the Third Common of Many Martyrs (p. 703).

Offertory. Our soul is escaped, even as a bird out of the snare of the fowler: the snare is broken, and we are delivered.

Secret

EGARD, O Lord, the prayers and oblations of thy faithful people: that they may be acceptable unto thee for the festival of thy Saints, and bestow on us the succour of thy mercy. Through.

¶ Commemoration of St. Mark of Ephesus (p. 442) and of St. Mary in Epiphanytide (p. BCP 541).

Communion. I say unto you, my friends: Be not afraid of them that persecute you.

Postcommunion

RANT, we beseech thee, that the intercession of thy Saints may make us acceptable unto thee: that those things which we perform in this temporal celebration we may receive unto eternal salvation. Through.

¶ Commemoration of St. Mark of Ephesus (p. 442) and of St. Mary in Epiphanytide (p. BCP 541).

(19 January. St. Mark of Ephesus)

⁋ The Second Common of a Confessor Bishop (p. 720), except for the following.
Yet to be approved.

Mag. Ant. O blessed Mark † clothed with invincible armour, thou didst cast down rebellious pride.
Ben. Ant. Thou didst serve † as the instrument of the Paraclete, and shone forth as the champion of Orthodoxy.
Mag. Ant. Rejoice, Mark, † the boast of the Orthodox and joy to all true Catholics!

Collect

O LORD Jesu Christ, the only Shepherd and Bishop of our souls; we beseech thee to keep us in thy truth, preserve us by thy grace, and govern us according to thy loving-kindness. That as we imitate the good example of blessed Mark thy Confessor and Bishop, we may grow in love for thy Word and service of thy Church. Who with.

Secret

RECEIVE, O most holy Father, these gifts now offered unto thee in memory of Saint Mark. That as he was a bulwark and defender of the Catholic Faith, so we may, by these gifts, be given the same firm love of thee. Through.

Postcommunion

ABIDE in us, O divine Comforter, who have here received thine holy Sacraments. That just as thy faithful servant Mark did contend for the unity of the Body of Christ, so we may be cleansed and knit together by the same. Who with the Father, from whom alone thou dost proceed, and the Son, who sendeth thy power upon us, liveth and reigneth, God, world without end. Amen.

20 January. Sts. Fabian & Sebastian

Double

¶ The Daily Office propers are from the First Common of Many Martyrs (p. 692).

Introit

LET the sorrowful sighing of the prisoners, O Lord, come before thee, reward thou our neighbours seven-fold into their bosom: avenge thou the blood of thy Saints that is shed. *Ps.* O God, the heathen are come into thine inheritance: thy holy temple have they defiled: and made Jerusalem an heap of stones.

Collect

ALMIGHTY God, mercifully look upon our infirmities: that whereas we are oppressed by the burden of our sins, the glorious intercession of thy blessed Martyrs Fabian and Sebastian may be our succour and defence. Through.

¶ The Epistle is the fifth additional Epistle of the Third Common of Many Martyrs (p. 702).

Gradual. God is glorious in his holy ones: fearful in praises, doing wonders. ℣. Thy right hand, O Lord, is become glorious in power: thy right hand hath dashed in pieces the enemy.

Alleluia. Alleluia, alleluia. ℣. Thy Saints give thanks unto thee, O Lord: they shew the glory of thy kingdom. Alleluia.

¶ In Septuagesimatide & Lent, the Alleluia is replaced with the following.

Tract. They that sow in tears, shall reap in joy. ℣. He that now goeth on his way weeping, and beareth forth good seed. ℣. Shall doubtless come again with joy, and bring his sheaves with him.

Gospel. Luke 6:17

AT THAT TIME: Jesus came down from the mountain, and stood in the plain, and the company of his disciples, and a great multitude of people out of all Judæa and Jerusalem, and from the sea coast of Tyre and Sidon, which came to hear him, and to be healed of their diseases; and they that were vexed with unclean spirits: and they were healed. And the whole multitude sought to touch him: for there went virtue out of him, and healed them all. And he lifted up his eyes on his disciples, and said, Blessed be ye poor: for yours is the kingdom of God. Blessed are ye that hunger now: for ye shall be filled. Blessed are ye that weep now: for ye shall laugh. Blessed are ye, when men shall hate you, and when they shall separate you from their company, and shall reproach you, and cast out your name as evil, for the Son of man's sake. Rejoice ye in that day, and leap for joy: for, behold, your reward is great in heaven.

Offertory. Be glad, O ye righteous, and rejoice in the Lord: and be joyful, all ye that are true of heart.

Secret

WE beseech thee, O Lord, mercifully to accept this our sacrifice which we offer unto thee, pleading the merits of thy blessed Martyrs Fabian and Sebastian: that the same may avail for our perpetual succour. Through.

Communion. A multitude of sick folk, and they that were vexed with unclean spirits came to him: for there went virtue out of him, and healed them all.

Postcommunion

WE beseech thee, O Lord our God, that like as we whom thou hast refreshed by the partaking of thy sacred gift do offer unto thee our worship: so, by the intercession of thy holy Martyrs Fabian and Sebastian, we may perceive the benefit of the same. Through.

21 January. St. Agnes of Rome

Greater Double

¶ The Daily Office propers are from the Common of a Virgin (p. 742), except for that which followeth.

Mag. Ant. Blessed Agnes, † in the midst of the flames, stretched out her hands and prayed: I call on thee, O Father transcendent, august, and dread; for by thy holy Son's protection I have escaped the threats of an impious tyrant, and passed unscathed through the foulness of fleshly pollution: and behold, I come to thee, whom I have loved, whom I have sought, whom I have alway desired.

Ben. Ant. Lo, that which I desired, † now I see; that for which I hoped, I now possess; I am united in heaven unto him, whom on earth I loved with a perfect devotion.

℣. Full of grace are thy lips.
℟. Because God hath blessed thee for ever.

Mag. Ant. While the blessed Agnes † was standing in the midst of the flames, she stretched out her hands, and prayed unto God: Almighty Lord, worthy of all adoration, fear, and worship: I bless thy holy Name, and I glorify thee for ever and ever.

Introit

THE ungodly wait for me to destroy me: O Lord, I will consider thy testimonies: I see that all things come to an end: but thy commandment is exceeding broad. *Ps.* Blessed are those that are undefiled in the way: and walk in the law of the Lord.

21 January **Proper of Saints** *St. Agnes Rome*

Collect

LMIGHTY and everlasting God, who dost choose the weak things of the world to confound those things that are strong: mercifully grant; that we who keep the feast of blessed Agnes thy Virgin and Martyr may feel the succour of her intercession in thy sight. Through.

Epistle. Ecclesiasticus 51:1

I WILL give thanks unto thee, O Lord, O King, And will praise thee, O God my Saviour: I do give thanks unto thy name: For thou wast my protector and helper, And didst deliver my body out of destruction, And out of the snare of a slanderous tongue, From lips that forge lies, And wast my helper before them that stood by; And didst deliver me, according to the abundance of thy mercy, and greatness of thy name, From the gnashings of teeth ready to devour, Out of the hand of such as sought my life, Out of the manifold afflictions which I had; From the choking of a fire on every side, And out of the midst of fire which I kindled not; Out of the depth of the belly of the grave, And from an unclean tongue, And from lying words, The slander of an unrighteous tongue unto the king. My soul drew near even unto death, And my life was near to the grave beneath. They compassed me on every side, And there was none to help me. I was looking for the succour of men, And it was not. And I remembered thy mercy, O Lord, And thy working which hath been from everlasting, How thou deliverest them that wait for thee, And savest them out of the hand of the enemies, O Lord our God.

Gradual. Full of grace are thy lips: because God hath blessed thee for ever. ℣. Because of the word of truth, of meekness, and righteousness: and thy right hand shall teach thee terrible things.

Alleluia. Alleluia, alleluia. ℣. The five wise virgins took oil in their vessels with their lamps: and at midnight there was a cry made: Behold, the bridegroom cometh: go ye out to meet Christ the Lord. Alleluia.

¶ In Septuagesimatide or Lent, replacing the Alleluia:

Tract. Come, Spouse of Christ, receive the crown which the Lord hath prepared for thee for ever: for love of whom thou didst shed thy blood. ℣. Thou hast loved righteousness and hated iniquity: wherefore God, even thy God, hath anointed thee with the oil of gladness above thy fellows. ℣. In thy comeliness and in thy beauty go forth, ride prosperously, and reign.

Gospel. Matthew 25:1

AT THAT TIME: Jesus spake this parable unto his disciples: The kingdom of heaven shall be likened unto ten virgins, which took their lamps, and went forth to meet the bridegroom. And five of them were wise, and five were foolish. They that were foolish took their lamps, and took no oil with them: But the wise took oil in their vessels with their lamps. While the bridegroom tarried, they all slumbered and slept. And at midnight there was a cry made, Behold, the bridegroom cometh; go ye out to meet him. Then all those virgins arose, and trimmed their lamps. And the foolish said unto the wise, Give us of your oil; for our lamps are gone out. But the wise answered, saying, Not so; lest there be not enough for us and you: but go ye rather to them that sell, and buy for yourselves. And while they went to buy, the bridegroom came; and they that were ready went in with him to the marriage: and the door was shut. Afterward came also the other virgins, saying, Lord, Lord, open to us. But he answered and said, Verily I say unto you, I know you not. Watch therefore, for ye know neither the day nor the hour wherein the Son of man cometh.

Offertory. The Virgins that be her fellows shall be brought unto the King: they that bear her company shall be brought unto thee with joy and gladness: and shall enter into the palace of the Lord the King.

Secret

LORD, mercifully regard the sacrifices which we offer unto thee: and at the intercession of blessed Agnes, thy Virgin and Martyr, absolve us from the bonds of our sins. Through.

Communion. The five wise virgins took oil in their vessels with their lamps: and at midnight there was a cry made: Behold, the bridegroom cometh: go ye out to meet Christ the Lord.

Postcommunion

LORD, our God, who hast refreshed us with heavenly meat and drink, we humbly beseech thee: that we may be defended by the prayers of her in whose memory we have received the same. Through.

(22 January. Sts. Vincent & Anastasius)

❧ The First Common of Many Martyrs (p. 692).

(23 January. St. Emerentiana)

❧ The Second Common of a Virgin and Martyr (p. 738).

Proper of Saints

25 January — *St. Paul's Conversion*

24 January. St. Timothy

Double

¶ The propers come from the First Common of a Bishop and Martyr (p. 682), except for the Epistle, as below.

Epistle. 1 Timothy 6:11

DEARLY BELOVED: Follow after righteousness, godliness, faith, love, patience, meekness. Fight the good fight of faith, lay hold on eternal life, whereunto thou art also called, and hast professed a good profession before many witnesses. I give thee charge in the sight of God, who quickeneth all things, and before Christ Jesus, who before Pontius Pilate witnessed a good confession; That thou keep this commandment without spot, unrebukeable, until the appearing of our Lord Jesus Christ: Which in his times he shall shew, who is the blessed and only Potentate, the King of kings, and Lord of lords; Who only hath immortality, dwelling in the light which no man can approach unto; whom no man hath seen, nor can see: to whom be honour and power everlasting. Amen.

[25 January. Conversion of St. Paul the Apostle]

I Evensong

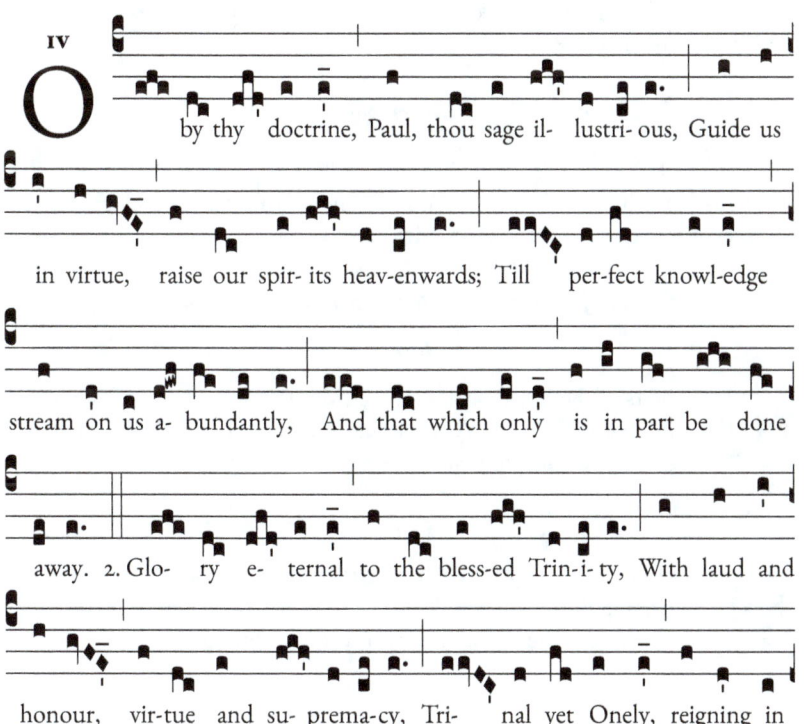

O by thy doctrine, Paul, thou sage illustrious, Guide us in virtue, raise our spirits heav'nwards; Till perfect knowledge stream on us abundantly, And that which only is in part be done away. 2. Glory eternal to the blessed Trinity, With laud and honour, virtue and supremacy, Trinal yet Onely, reigning in

his maj-es-ty Both now and ev-er, through the ag-es in-fi-nite.

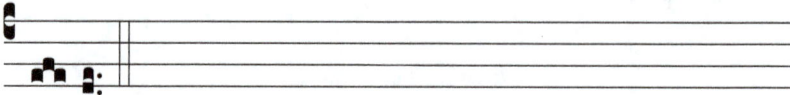

A-men.

℣. Thou art a chosen vessel, holy Apostle Paul.
℞. A preacher of the truth throughout all the world.

Mag. Ant. Go forth, Ananias, † and enquire for Saul, for behold, he prayeth: for he is a chosen vessel unto me, to bear my Name before the Gentiles, and Kings, and the children of Israel.

Mattins

¶ The Invitatory Hymn is as in I Evensong.

¶ The Office Hymn is from the Common of the Apostles (p. 673), with the following Versicle & Antiphon.

℣. Thou art a chosen vessel, holy Apostle Paul.
℞. A preacher of the truth throughout all the world.

Ben. Ant. Ye which have followed me † shall sit upon twelve thrones, judging the twelve tribes of Israel, saith the Lord.

II Evensong

¶ The Office Hymn & Versicle are as in I Evensong, with the following Antiphon.

Mag. Ant. O holy Apostle Paul, † thou preacher of the truth and Doctor of the Gentiles, intercede for us unto God, who hath chosen thee.

(26 January. St. Polycarp of Smyrna)

Introit

YE priests of the Lord, bless ye the Lord: O ye holy and humble men of heart, bless ye the Lord. *Ps.* O all ye works of the Lord, bless ye the Lord: praise him, and magnify him for ever.

Collect

GOD, who makest us glad with the yearly solemnity of blessed Polycarp, thy Martyr and Bishop: mercifully grant; that, as we now cebrate his birthday, so we may likewise rejoice in his protection. Through.

26 January — **Proper of Saints** — *St. Polycarp Smyrna*

Epistle. 1 John 3:10

DEARLY BELOVED: Whosoever doeth not righteousness is not of God, neither he that loveth not his brother. For this is the message that ye heard from the beginning, that we should love one another. Not as Cain, who was of that wicked one, and slew his brother. And wherefore slew he him? Because his own works were evil, and his brother's righteous. Marvel not, my brethren, if the world hate you. We know that we have passed from death unto life, because we love the brethren. He that loveth not his brother abideth in death. Whosoever hateth his brother is a murderer: and ye know that no murderer hath eternal life abiding in him. Hereby perceive we the love of God, because he laid down his life for us: and we ought to lay down our lives for the brethren.

Gradual. Thou hast crowned him with glory and worship. ℣. Thou hast made him to have dominion of the works of thy hands, O Lord.

Alleluia. Alleluia, alleluia. ℣. This is a priest whom the Lord hath crowned. Alleluia.

¶ In Septuagesimatide or Lent, replacing the Alleluia:

Tract. Blessed is the man that feareth the Lord: he hath great delight in his commandments. ℣. His seed shall be mighty upon earth: the generation of the faithful shall be blessed. ℣. Riches and plenteousness shall be in his house: and his righteousness endureth for ever.

Gospel. Matthew 10:26

AT THAT TIME: Jesus said to his disciples: There is nothing covered, that shall not be revealed; and hid, that shall not be known. What I tell you in darkness, that speak ye in light: and what ye hear in the ear, that preach ye upon the housetops. And fear not them which kill the body, but are not able to kill the soul: but rather fear him which is able to destroy both soul and body in hell. Are not two sparrows sold for a farthing? and one of them shall not fall on the ground without your Father. But the very hairs of your head are all numbered. Fear ye not therefore, ye are of more value than many sparrows. Whosoever therefore shall confess me before men, him will I confess also before my Father which is in heaven.

Offertory. I have found David my servant, with my holy oil have I anointed him: my hand shall hold him fast, and my arm shall strengthen him.

Secret

SANCTIFY, O Lord, the gifts which we dedicate to thee: that at the intercession of blessed Polycarp, thy Martyr and Bishop, they may obtain for us thy gracious favour. Through.

Communion. Thou hast set, O Lord, a crown of pure gold upon his head.

St. John Chrysostom   **Proper of Saints**   27 January

Postcommunion

WE beseech thee, O Lord our God, that like as we, whom thou hast refreshed by the partaking of thy sacred gift, do offer unto thee our worship: so, by the intercession of blessed Polycarp, thy Martyr and Bishop, we may perceive the benefit of the same. Through.

27 January. St. John Chrysostom

Double

¶ The propers are from the Common of Doctors (p. 723), except for that which followeth.

Collect

MULTIPLY, we beseech thee, O Lord, thy Church with thy heavenly grace: even as thou didst vouchsafe to enlighten her with the glorious merits and doctrine of blessed John Chrysostom, thy Confessor and Bishop. Through.

Gradual. Behold a great priest, who in his days pleased God. ℣. There was none found like unto him, who kept the law of the Most High.

Alleluia. Alleluia, alleluia. ℣. Blessed is the man that endureth temptation: for when he is tried, he shall receive the crown of life, alleluia.

¶ In Septuagesimatide or Lent, replacing the Alleluia:

Tract. Blessed is the man that feareth the Lord: he hath great delight in his commandments. ℣. His seed shall be mighty upon earth: the generation of the faithful shall be blessed. ℣. Riches and plenteousness shall be in his house: and his righteousness remaineth for ever.

Secret

MAY the devout prayers of Saint John Chrysostom thy Bishop and Doctor, never fail to succour us, O Lord: that they may render our oblations acceptable in thy sight; and may ever obtain for us thy merciful pardon. Through.

Postcommunion

WE beseech thee, O Lord, that blessed John Chrysostom, thy Bishop and illustrious Doctor; may stand before thee as our advocate: that these thy sacrifices may avail for our salvation. Through.

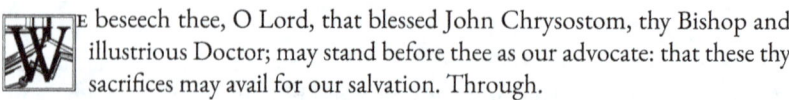

28 January. St. Cyril of Alexandria

Double

¶ The propers are from the Common of Doctors (p. 723), except for that which followeth.

Collect

O GOD, who didst make blessed Cyril, thy Confessor and Bishop, an invincible defender of the divine Motherhood of the most blessed Virgin Mary: grant, by his intercession; that we, who believe her to be indeed the Mother of God, may be saved through her maternal protection. Through the same.

¶ Commemoration of St. Agnes (p. 451).

Secret

ALMIGHTY God, graciously look upon our gifts: and at the intercession of blessed Cyril vouchsafe; that we may be found meet worthily to receive in our hearts thine only-begotten Son, Jesus Christ our Lord, co-eternal with thee in thy glory. Who liveth and reigneth with thee.

¶ Commemoration of St. Agnes (p. 452).

Postcommunion

O LORD, who hast refreshed us with divine mysteries, we humbly beseech thee: that, being aided by the example and merits of the blessed Bishop Cyril, we may be enabled worthily to serve the most holy Mother of thine only-begotten Son. Who liveth and reigneth with thee.

¶ Commemoration of St. Agnes (p. 452).

(28 January. The Second Feast of St. Agnes)

Introit

ALL the rich among the people shall make their supplication before thee: the Virgins that be her fellows shall be brought unto the King: they that bear her company shall be brought unto thee with joy and gladness. *Ps.* My heart is inditing of a good matter: I speak of the things which I have made unto the King.

Collect

O GOD, who makest us glad with the yearly solemnity of blessed Agnes, thy Virgin and Martyr: grant, we beseech thee; that as we venerate her in our service, so we may follow the example of her godly conversation. Through.

¶ The Epistle is from the First Common of a Virgin (p. 742).

¶ The Gradual & Alleluia are from the First Common of a Virgin (p. 742).

Gospel. Matthew 13:44

AT THAT TIME: Jesus spake this parable unto his disciples: The kingdom of heaven is like unto treasure hid in a field; the which when a man hath found, he hideth, and for joy thereof goeth and selleth all that he hath, and buyeth that field. Again, the kingdom of heaven is like unto a merchant man, seeking goodly pearls: Who, when he had found one pearl of great price, went and sold all that he had, and bought it. Again, the kingdom of heaven is like unto a net, that was cast into the sea, and gathered of every kind: Which, when it was full, they drew to shore, and sat down, and gathered the good into vessels, but cast the bad away. So shall it be at the end of the world: the angels shall come forth, and sever the wicked from among the just, And shall cast them into the furnace of fire: there shall be wailing and gnashing of teeth. Jesus saith unto them, Have ye understood all these things? They say unto him, Yea, Lord. Then said he unto them, Therefore every scribe which is instructed unto the kingdom of heaven is like unto a man that is an householder, which bringeth forth out of his treasure things new and old.

Offertory. Full of grace are thy lips, because God hath blessed thee for ever and ever.

Secret

LET thy plenteous benediction, we beseech thee, O Lord, come down upon these sacrifices: that it may mercifully work out our sanctification, and make us to rejoice in the solemnity of thy Martyrs. Through.

Communion. The kingdom of heaven is like unto a merchant man, seeking goodly pearls: who when he had found one pearl of great price, gave all that he had, and bought it.

Postcommunion

GRANT, we beseech thee, O Lord, that the sacrament which we have received in our observance of this yearly festival: may bestow on us thy healing; both in this temporal life and unto life eternal. Through.

(30 January. St. Martina)

¶ The First Common of a Virgin and Martyr (p.733).

Proper of Saints

1 February — *St. Ignatius Antioch*

1 February. St. Ignatius of Antioch

Double

¶ The Daily Office propers are from the First Common of Martyr Bishops (p. 682).

Introit

UT God forbid that I should glory, save in the Cross of our Lord Jesus Christ: by whom the world is crucified unto me, and I unto the world. *Ps.* Lord, remember David: and all his trouble.

Collect

LMIGHTY God, mercifully look upon our infirmities; that whereas we are oppressed by the burden of our sins, the glorious intercession of blessed Ignatius thy Martyr and Bishop may be our succour and defence. Through.

¶ Commemoration of St. Bridget of Ireland, from the First Common of a Virgin (p. 742).

Epistle. Romans 8:35

BRETHREN: Who shall separate us from the love of Christ? shall tribulation, or distress, or persecution, or famine, or nakedness, or peril, or sword? As it is written, For thy sake we are killed all the day long; we are accounted as sheep for the slaughter. Nay, in all these things we are more than conquerors through him that loved us. For I am persuaded, that neither death, nor life, nor angels, nor principalities, nor powers, nor things present, nor things to come, Nor height, nor depth, nor any other creature, shall be able to separate us from the love of God, which is in Christ Jesus our Lord.

Gradual. Behold a great priest, who in his days pleased God. ℣. There was none found like unto him, who kept the law of the Most High.

Alleluia. Alleluia, alleluia. ℣. I am crucifed with Christ: I live, yet not I, but Christ liveth in me. Alleluia.

¶ In Septuagesimatide or Lent, replacing the Alleluia:

Tract. Thou hast given him his heart's desire: and hast not denied him the request of his lips. ℣. For thou hast prevented him with the blessings of goodness. ℣. Thou hast set a crown of pure gold upon his head.

Gospel. John 12:24

AT THAT TIME: Jesus said unto his disciples: Verily, verily, I say unto you, Except a corn of wheat fall into the ground and die, it abideth alone: but if it die, it bringeth forth much fruit. He that loveth his life shall lose it; and he that hateth his life in this world shall keep it unto life eternal. If any man serve me, let him follow me; and where I am, there shall also my servant be: if any man serve me, him will my Father honour.

Offertory. Thou hast crowned him with glory and worship: and hast made him to have dominion of the works of thy hands, O Lord.

Secret

E beseech thee, O Lord, mercifully to accept this our sacrifice which we offer unto thee, pleading the merits of blessed Ignatius thy Martyr and Bishop: that the same may avail for our perpetual succour. Through.

¶ Commemoration of St. Bridget of Ireland, from the First Common of a Virgin (p. 742).

Communion. I am the wheat of Christ: let me be ground by the teeth of beasts, that I may be found pure bread.

Postcommunion

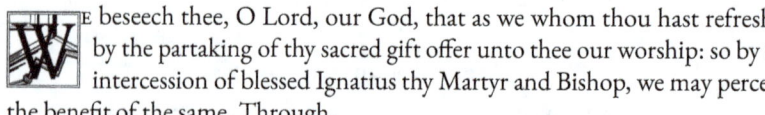E beseech thee, O Lord, our God, that as we whom thou hast refreshed by the partaking of thy sacred gift offer unto thee our worship: so by the intercession of blessed Ignatius thy Martyr and Bishop, we may perceive the benefit of the same. Through.

¶ Commemoration of St. Bridget of Ireland, from the First Common of a Virgin (p. 742).

(1 February. St. Bridget of Ireland)

¶ The First Common of a Virgin (p. 742).

[2 February. Purification of the Blessed Virgin Mary]

¶ The Office Hymn and Versicle are from the Common of the Blessed Virgin Mary (p. 760), except for the Evensong Versicles and the Antiphons as followeth.

℣. It was revealed unto Simeon by the Holy Ghost.
℟. That he should not see death before he had seen the Lord's Christ.

Mag. Ant. The ancient † carried the Infant, but the Infant governed the ancient: he whom a Virgin bare, and after bearing, remained virgin, the same was worshipped by her who bare him.

Ben. Ant. And when the parents † brought in the Child Jesus, then Simeon took him up in his arms, and blessed God, saying: Lord, now lettest thou thy servant depart in peace.

Mag. Ant. To-day † the blessed Virgin Mary presented the Child Jesus in the temple; and Simeon, filled with the Holy Spirit, received him into his arms, and blessed God for ever.

(3 February. St. Blaise)

¶ The Second Common of a Martyr Bishop (p. 686).

(4 February. St. Joseph of Aleppo)

¶ The First Common of a Martyr not a Bishop (p. 688).

¶ Commemoration of the New Martyrs of Russia, from the Prayers in the First Common of Many Martyrs (p. 692).

(4 February. The New Martyrs of Russia)

¶ The First Common of Many Martyrs (p. 692).

5 February. St. Agatha

Greater Double

¶ The Office Hymns and Versicles are from the First Common of a Virgin Martyress (p. 733), except for the II Evensong Versicle as below.

Mag. Ant. The blessed Agatha, † standing in the midst of the prison, with outstretched hands entreated the Lord: O Lord Jesus Christ, my gracious Master, I give thanks unto thee, who hast enabled me to overcome the torments of the executioner: bid me now, O Lord, joyfully to enter into thine unfading glory.

Ben. Ant. The multitude † of the heathen, fleeing to the tomb of the virgin, took thence her veil to defend them from the fire: that the Lord might shew himself a deliverer from the burning, for the merits of Agatha his blessed Martyr.

℣. Full of grace are thy lips.
℞. Because God hath blessed thee for ever.

Mag. Ant. The blessed Agatha, † standing in the midst of the prison, with outstretched hands entreated the Lord: O Lord Jesus Christ, my gracious Master, I give thanks unto thee, who hast enabled me to overcome the torments of the executioner: bid me now, O Lord, joyfully to enter into thine unfading glory.

Introit

REJOICE we all in the Lord, keeping feast day in honour of blessed Agatha, the Virgin and Martyr: in whose passion the Angels rejoice, and glorify the Son of God. *Ps.* My heart is inditing of a good matter: I speak of the things which I have made unto the King.

St. Agatha — **Proper of Saints** — 5 February

Collect

GOD, who among the manifold works of thy power hast bestowed even upon the weakness of women the victory of martyrdom: mercifully grant; that we, who celebrate the birthday of blessed Agatha, thy Virgin and Martyr, may by her example be drawn nearer unto thee. Through.

Epistle. 1 Corinthians 1:26

RETHREN: Ye see your calling: how that not many wise men after the flesh, not many mighty, not many noble, are called: But God hath chosen the foolish things of the world to confound the wise; and God hath chosen the weak things of the world to confound the things which are mighty; And base things of the world, and things which are despised, hath God chosen, yea, and things which are not, to bring to nought things that are: That no flesh should glory in his presence. But of him are ye in Christ Jesus, who of God is made unto us wisdom, and righteousness, and sanctification, and redemption: That, according as it is written, He that glorieth, let him glory in the Lord.

Gradual. God shall help her with his countenance: God is in the midst of her, therefore shall she not be removed. ℣. The rivers of the flood thereof shall make glad the city of God: the holy place of the tabernacle of the Most Highest.

Alleluia. Alleluia, alleluia. ℣. I will speak of thy testimonies even before kings: and will not be ashamed. Alleluia.

¶ In Septuagesimatide or Lent, replacing the Alleluia:

Tract. They that sow in tears, shall reap in joy. ℣. They that now go on their way weeping, and bear forth good seed. ℣. Shall doubtless come again with joy, and bring their sheaves with them.

Gospel. Matthew 19:3

T THAT TIME: The Pharisees came unto Jesus, tempting him, and saying unto him: Is it lawful for a man to put away his wife for every cause? And he answered and said unto them, Have ye not read, that he which made them at the beginning made them male and female, And said, For this cause shall a man leave father and mother, and shall cleave to his wife: and they twain shall be one flesh? Wherefore they are no more twain, but one flesh. What therefore God hath joined together, let not man put asunder. They say unto him, Why did Moses then command to give a writing of divorcement, and to put her away? He saith unto them, Moses because of the hardness of your hearts suffered you to put away your wives: but from the beginning it was not so. And I say unto you, Whosoever shall put away his wife, except it be for fornication, and shall marry another, committeth adultery: and whoso marrieth her which is put away doth commit adultery. His disciples say unto him, If the case of the man be so with his wife, it is not good to marry. But he said unto them, All men cannot receive this saying, save they to whom it is given. For there are some eunuchs, which were so born from their mother's womb: and there are some eunuchs, which were made eunuchs of men: and there be eunuchs, which have made themselves eunuchs for the kingdom of heaven's sake. He that is able to receive it, let him receive it.

Offertory. The Virgins that be her fellows shall be brought unto the King: they that bear her company shall be brought unto thee.

Secret

ECEIVE, O Lord, the gifts which we offer on the solemnity of blessed Agatha, thy Virgin and Martyr, through whose advocacy we trust to be delivered. Through.

Communion. He who deigned to heal my every wound, and to restore my breast unto my body, on him do I call, the living God.

Postcommunion

AY the mysteries which we have received be for our succour, O Lord: and at the intercession of blessed Agatha, thy Virgin and Martyr, cause us to rejoice in thy continual protection. Through.

(6 FEBRUARY. ST. DOROTHEA)

¶ The Second Common of a Virgin Martyress (p. 738), except for the following.

Collect

E beseech thee, O Lord, that as blessed Dorothea, thy Virgin and Martyr, was ever found pleasing unto thee, both by the merit of her chastity, and by her confession of thy power: so she may implore for us thy pardon. Through.

Secret

RACIOUSLY receive, O Lord, through the merits of bressed Dorotnea thy Virgin and Martyr, the sacrifices which we offer unto thee and grant that they may avail for our continual help. Through.

Postcommunion

LORD our God, who hast fulfilled us with the bounty of thy heavenly gift: we beseech thee that, at the intercession of blessed Dorothea thy Virgin and Martyr, we may ever live by the partaking of the same. Through.

7 FEBRUARY. ST. ROMUALD

Double

¶ The propers are from the Common of Abbots (p. 732).

(9 FEBRUARY. ST. APOLLONIA OF ALEXANDRIA)

¶ The First Common of a Virgin Martyress (p. 733), except for the following.

Collect

O GOD who among the manifold works of thy power hast bestowed even upon the weakness of women the victory of martyrdom mercifully grant; that we, who celebrate the birthday of blessed Apollonia thy Virgin and Martyr, may by her example be drawn nearer unto thee. Through.

Secret

RECEIVE, O Lord, the gifts which we offer on the solemnity of blessed Apollonia thy Virgin and Martyr: through whose advocacy we trust to be delivered. Through.

Postcommunion

MAY the mysteries which we have received be for our succour, O Lord: and at the intercession of blessed Apollonia thy Virgin and Martyr, cause us to rejoice in thy continual protection. Through.

[10 FEBRUARY. ST. SCHOLASTICA]

I Evensong

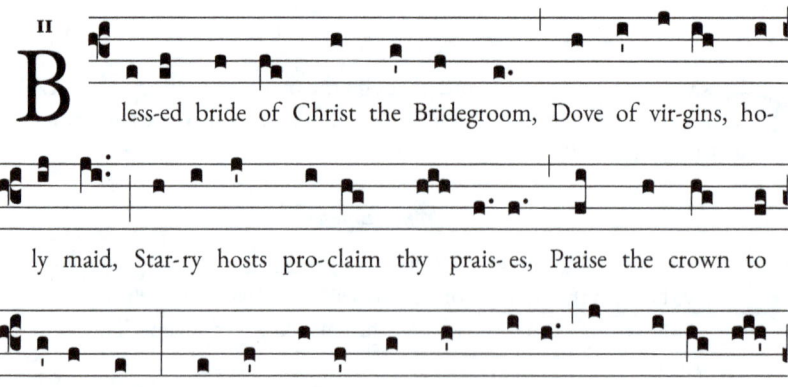

Bless-ed bride of Christ the Bridegroom, Dove of vir-gins, ho-ly maid, Star-ry hosts pro-claim thy prais-es, Praise the crown to virtue paid, While our joy-ful hearts and voic-es Join the anthem

10 February — Proper of Saints — St. Scholastica

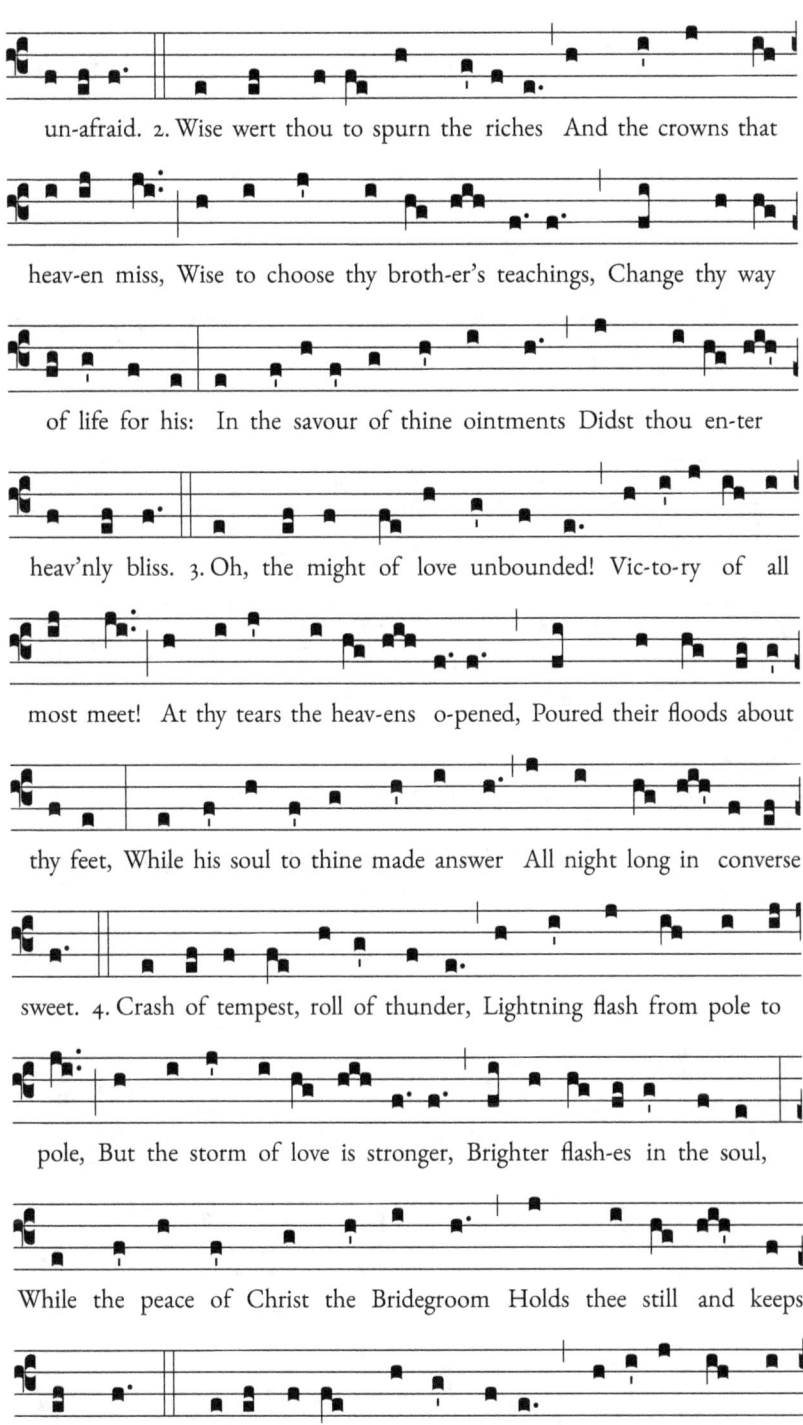

un-afraid. 2. Wise wert thou to spurn the riches And the crowns that heav-en miss, Wise to choose thy broth-er's teachings, Change thy way of life for his: In the savour of thine ointments Didst thou en-ter heav'nly bliss. 3. Oh, the might of love unbounded! Vic-to-ry of all most meet! At thy tears the heav-ens o-pened, Poured their floods about thy feet, While his soul to thine made answer All night long in converse sweet. 4. Crash of tempest, roll of thunder, Lightning flash from pole to pole, But the storm of love is stronger, Brighter flash-es in the soul, While the peace of Christ the Bridegroom Holds thee still and keeps thee whole. 5. Now a gleaming cloud in heav-en, Now a sun with gold-

St. Scholastica   **Proper of Saints**   10 February

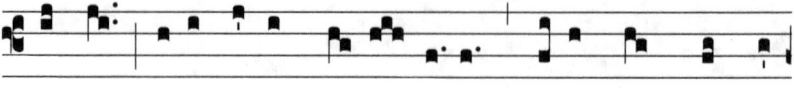
en rays, Nev-er darkling, nev- er fad-ing, Shin-ing still through all

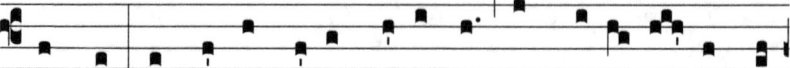
our days, Fill the hearts of all the faithful With the joy of heav'nly

lays. 6. Glo-ry to the Father sing we, Glo-ry to the only Son;

To the Par-a-clete in glo-ry, Equal trib-ute be be-gun, At whose

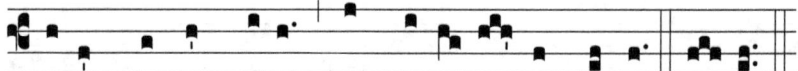
pleas-ure made and gov-ern'd All the ag-es' course is run. A-men.

℣. Who is this that flieth as a cloud?

℟. And as a dove to her windows?

Mag. Ant. Let all the multitude † of the faithful exult in the glory of the gracious virgin Scholastica: and chiefly let the company of virgins be joyful, celebrating her Solemnity; for she besought the Lord, pouring forth her tears, and of him received greater power, because her love was greater.

Mattins

Invitatory Hymn

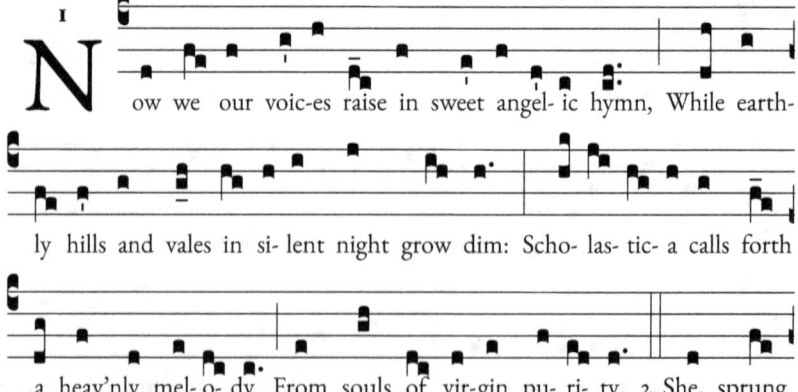
Now we our voic-es raise in sweet angel-ic hymn, While earth-ly hills and vales in si-lent night grow dim: Scho-las-tic-a calls forth a heav'nly mel-o-dy From souls of vir-gin pu-ri-ty. 2. She, sprung

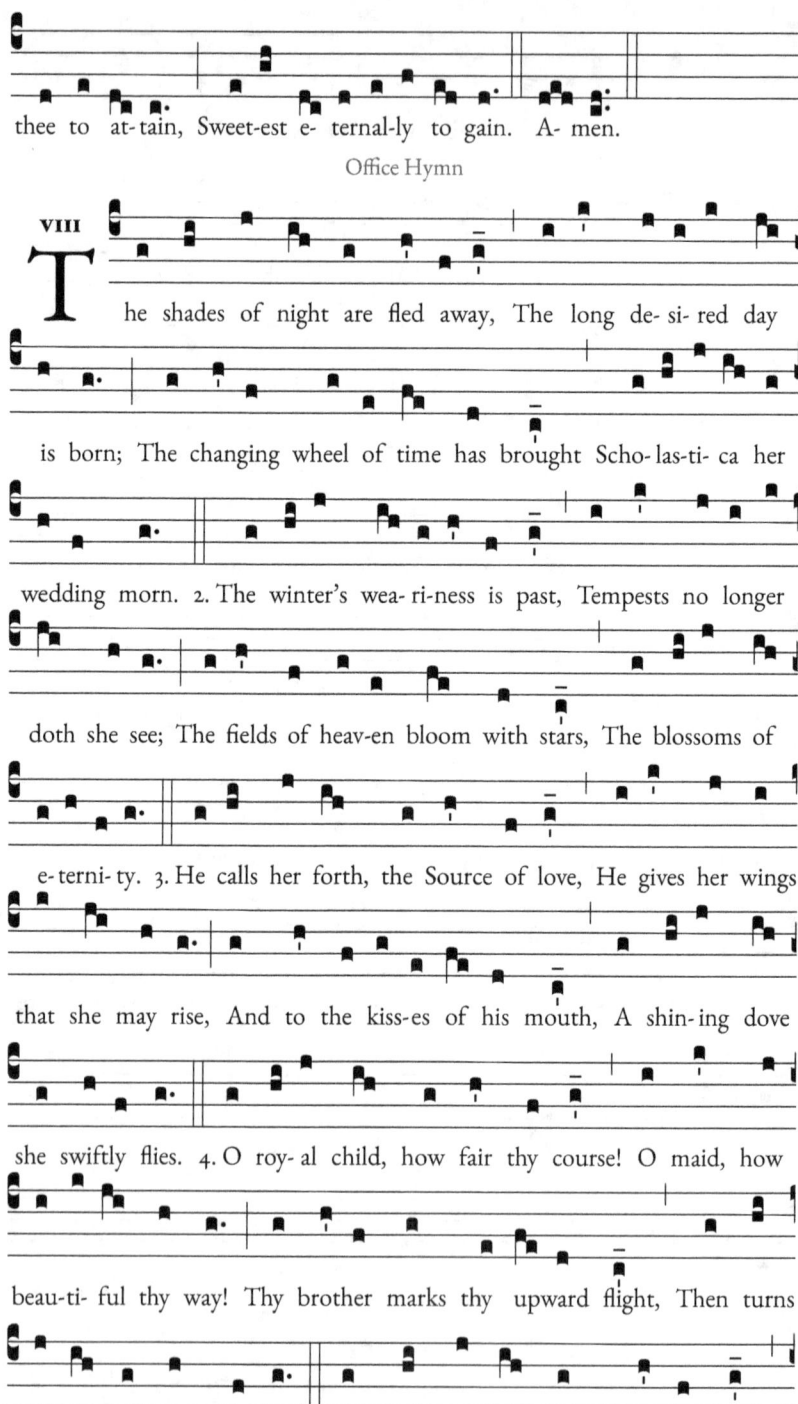

11 February   **Proper of Saints**   *Pope St. Gregory II*

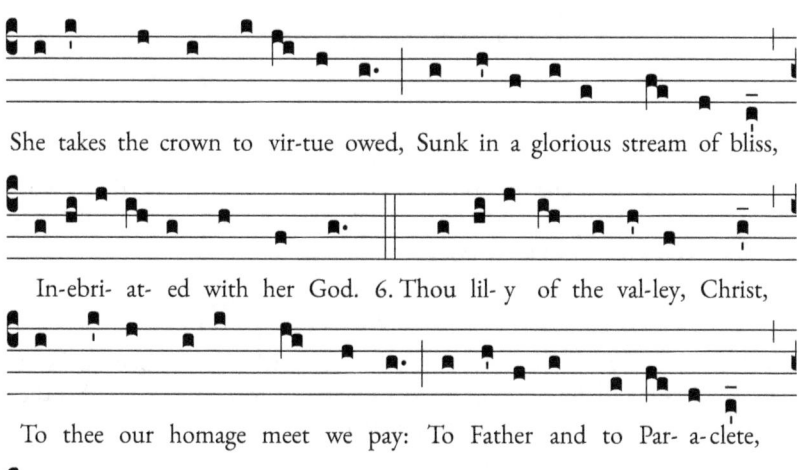

She takes the crown to vir-tue owed, Sunk in a glorious stream of bliss, In-ebri-at-ed with her God. 6. Thou lil-y of the val-ley, Christ, To thee our homage meet we pay: To Father and to Par-a-clete, While endless ag-es roll away. A-men.

℣. Behold, thou art fair, my love.

℟. Behold, thou art fair; thou hast dove's eyes.

Ben. Ant. O how illustrious † are the merits of blessed Scholastica! O how great the power of her tears! through which the renowned virgin, out of sunny clearness, drew down from the air a mighty flood of rain.

II Evensong

¶ The Office Hymn & Versicle are of I Evensong, with the following Antiphon.

Mag. Ant. To-day † the holy virgin Scholastica, in the likeness of a dove, went forth with all gladness to the heavenly places: to-day she was found worthy to enjoy for ever the bliss of celestial life beside her brother.

(11 February. Pope St. Gregory II)

¶ The First Common of a Confessor Bishop (p. 715).

(14 February. St. Valentine)

¶ The First Common of a Martyr not a Bishop (p. 688), except for the following.

Collect

RANT, we beseech thee, Almighty God: that we who observe the birthday of blessed Valentine thy Martyr may by his intercession be delivered from all evils that beset us. Through.

Secret

ECEIVE, O Lord, we beseech thee, the gifts which we duly offer: and by the pleading of the merits of blessed Valentine thy Martyr, grant; that they may avail to set forward our salvation. Through.

Postcommunion

AY this heavenly mystery, O Lord, renew us in soul and body: that as we offer unto thee our worship, so by the intercession of blessed Valentine thy Martyr, we may perceive the benefit of the same. Through.

(15 February. Sts. Faustinus and Jovita)

¶ The Third Common of Many Martyrs (p. 700), except for the following.

Collect

 GOD, who makest us glad with the yearly solemnity of thy holy Martyrs Faustinus and Jovita: mercifully grant; that as we rejoice in their merits, so we may be enkindled by their example. Through.

Secret

SSIST us mercifully, O Lord, in these our supplications which we make before thee in remembrance of thy Saints: that we who trust not in our own righteousness may be succoured by the merits of them that have found favour in thy sight. Through.

Postcommunion

LORD, who hast fulfilled us with saving mysteries, we beseech thee: that we may be aided by the prayers of those whose festival we celebrate. Through.

(18 February. St. Simeon of Jerusalem)

¶ The First Common of a Martyr Bishop (p. 682).

Proper of Saints

Chair St. Peter Antioch

[22 February. Chair of St. Peter at Antioch]

I Evensong

Quodcúmque vinclis super terram strínxeris, Erit in astris religátum fórtiter: Et quod resólvis in terris arbítrio, Erit solútum super cæli rádium: In fine mundi judex eris sǽculi. Glória Patri per imménsa sǽcula; Sit tibi, Nate, decus et impérium; Honor, potéstas, Sanctóque Spirítui: Sit Trinitáti salus indivídua, Per infiníta sæculórum sǽcula. Amen.

℣. Thou art Peter.
℟. And upon this rock I will build my Church.
Mag. Ant. Thou art the shepherd of the sheep, † Prince of the Apostles, unto thee were given the keys of the kingdom of heaven.

Chair St. Peter Antioch — **Proper of Saints** — 22 February

Mattins

¶ The Invitatory Hymn is as in I Evensong.

Office Hymn

Peter, good shepherd, may thy ceaseless orisons, For us prevailing, break the bands of wickedness: For thou of old time didst receive authority The gates to open, or to close, of Paradise. 2. Glory eternal to the blessèd Trinity, With laud and honour, virtue and supremacy, Trinal yet Onely, reigning in his majesty Both now and ever, through the ages infinite. A-men.

℣. Thou art Peter.

℟. And upon this rock I will build my Church.

Ben. Ant. Whatsoever † thou shalt bind on earth shall be bound in heaven: and whatsoever thou shalt loose on earth shall be loosed in heaven, saith the Lord unto Simon Peter.

II Evensong

¶ II Evensong as in I Evensong, except for the Antiphon, as followeth.

Mag. Ant. Whilst he was chief Bishop, he feared nothing on earth, but ascended gloriously to the heavenly kingdoms.

23/24 February. Vigil of St. Matthias

Vigil

¶ The propers are from the Common of Vigils of the Apostles (p. 672).

[24/25 February. St. Matthias]

¶ The Daily Office propers are of the Common of Apostles (p. 673).

(25/26 February. St. Walburga of Heidenheim)

¶ The Common of a Virgin (p. 742), except for the following.

Collect

GOD, who among the manifold gifts of thy grace dost also work great wonders even in the weaker sex: mercifully grant that we may feel the help of the intercession of blessed Walburga, thy Virgin, whose example of chastity doth enlighten us, and whose glory in miracles doth gladden us. Through.

¶ In Lent, Commemoration of the Feria.

Secret

E beseech thee, O Lord, that the prayer of blessed Walburga thy Virgin may render this sacrifice, which we devoutly offer unto thee in her venerable commemoration, acceptable unto thy Majesty. Through.

¶ In Lent, Commemoration of the Feria.

Postcommunion

GRANT, O Lord, that by the intercession of blessed Walburga, thy Virgin, we may obtain the grace of thy blessing: that as we proclaim her venerable glory, she may aid us in all our necessities. Through.

¶ In Lent, Commemoration & Last Gospel of the Feria.

(26/27 February. Pope St. Alexander of Alexandria)

¶ The First Common of a Confessor Bishop (p. 715).

¶ In Lent, Commemoration & Last Gospel of the Feria.

Proper of Saints

27/28 FEBRUARY. ST. RAPHAEL OF BROOKLYN
Greater Double

※ In Lent, Commemoration only.
※ The propers are from the First Common of a Confessor Bishop (p. 715).
※ In Lent, Commemoration & Last Gospel of the Feria.

(1 MARCH. ST. DAVID OF WALES)

※ The First Common of a Confessor Bishop (p. 715), except for the following.

Collect

GRANT to us, Almighty God: that the loving intercession of blessed David, thy Confessor and Bishop, may protect us; that while we celebrate his festival we may imitate his steadfastness in the defence of the Catholic faith. Through.

※ In Lent, Commemoration of the Feria.

Secret

WE beseech thee, O Lord: that we, remembering with gladness the merits of thy Saints, may in all places feel the succour of their intercession. Through.

※ In Lent, Commemoration of the Feria.

Postcommunion

GRANT, we beseech thee, Almighty God: that we, shewing forth our thankfulness for the gifts which we have received, may, at the intercession of blessed David, thy Confessor and Bishop, obtain yet more abundant mercies. Through.

※ In Lent, Commemoration & Last Gospel of the Feria.

(2 MARCH. ST. CHAD)

※ The Second Common of a Confessor Bishop (p. 720), except for the following.

Collect

ALMIGHTY and everlasting God, who on this day dost gladden us by the festival of blessed Chad, thy Confessor and Bishop: we humbly beseech thy mercy; that we, who devoutly observe and venerate his festival, may by his loving advocacy obtain the reward of everlasting life. Through.

※ In Lent, Commemoration of the Feria.

Secret

WE beseech thee, O Lord, mercifully to have respect unto our supplications: and at the intercession of blessed Chad thy Confessor and Bishop on our behalf, grant that we who minister thy heavenly sacraments may be free from all sin; that through thy purifying grace we may be cleansed by those same mysteries which we serve. Through.

℟ In Lent, Commemoration of the Feria.

Postcommunion

GRANT, we beseech thee, O Lord our God: that, at the intercession of blessed Chad, thy Confessor and Bishop, we who have tasted of holy things, being cleansed by divine mysteries, may attain to the fulness of this heavenly sacrament. Through.

℟ In Lent, Commemoration & Last Gospel of the Feria.

(4 March. Pope St. Lucius I)

℟ The Second Common of a Martyr Bishop (p. 686), except for the following.

Collect

O GOD, who makest us glad with the yearly solemnity of blessed Lucius thy Martyr and Bishop: mercifully grant; that, as we now celebrate his birthday, so we may likewise rejoice in his protection. Through.

℟ In Lent, Commemoration of the Feria.

Secret

WE beseech thee, O Lord, mercifully to accept this our sacrifice, which we offer unto thee, pleading the merits of blessed Lucius, thy Martyr and Bishop: that the same may avail for our perpetual succour. Through.

℟ In Lent, Commemoration of the Feria.

Postcommunion

WE beseech thee, O Lord our God, that like as we whom thou hast refreshed by the partaking of thy sacred gift do offer unto thee our worship: so, by the intercession of blessed Lucius thy Martyr and Bishop, we may perceive the benefit of the same. Through.

℟ In Lent, Commemoration & Last Gospel of the Feria.

6 March. Sts. Perpetua and Felicitas

Double

❡ In Lent, Commemoration only.

❡ The propers are from the Common of a Martyress not a Virgin (p. 746), except for that which followeth.

Collect

GRANT, we beseech thee, O Lord our God, that we may at all times so devoutly honour the triumphs of thy holy Martyrs Perpetua and Felicitas: that, although we cannot worthily shew forth their praises, yet we may continually honour them with lowly service. Through.

❡ In Lent, Commemoration of the Feria.

Secret

LORD, we beseech thee, look down upon these gifts, which we offer on thine altars on this festival of thy holy Martyrs Perpetua and Felicitas: that as by these blessed mysteries thou hast bestowed glory upon them, so likewise of thy bounty thou wouldest vouchsafe to us thy pardon. Through.

❡ In Lent, Commemoration of the Feria.

Postcommunion

LORD, who hast fulfilled us with mystic gifts and joys: grant, we beseech thee; that by the intercession of thy holy Martyrs, Perpetua and Felicitas, we may spiritually attain to those things which we temporally perform. Through.

❡ In Lent, Commemoration & Last Gospel of the Feria.

(9 March. St. Gregory of Nyssa)

❡ The Common of Doctors (p. 723).

❡ In Lent, Commemoration & Last Gospel of the Feria.

(10 March. The Forty Holy Martyrs)

Introit

HE just cry, and the Lord heareth them: and delivereth them out of all their troubles. *Ps.* I will alway give thanks unto the Lord; his praise shall ever be in my mouth.

Collect

RANT we beseech thee, Almighty God: that, like as we have known thy glorious Martyrs to be constant in their confession, so we may perceive their loving intercession for us with thee. Through.

¶ In Lent, Commemoration of the Feria.

¶ The Epistle is the fifth additional Epistle of the Third Common of Many Martyrs (p. 702).

Gradual. Behold, how good and joyful a thing it is, brethren, to dwell together in unity! ℣. It is like the precious ointment upon the head, that ran down unto the beard, even unto Aaron's beard.

Tract. They that sow in tears, shall reap in joy. ℣. They that now go on their way weeping, and bear forth good seed. ℣. Shall doubtless come again with joy, and bring their sheaves with them.

¶ The Gospel is from the Second Common of Many Martyrs (p. 699).

Offertory. Be glad, O ye righteous, and rejoice in the Lord: and be joyful, all ye that are true of heart.

Secret

EGARD, O Lord, the prayers and oblations of thy faithful people: that they may be acceptable unto thee for the festival of thy Saints, and bestow on us the succour of thy mercy. Through.

¶ In Lent, Commemoration of the Feria.

Communion. Whosoever shall do the will of my Father which is in heaven: the same is my brother, and sister, and mother, saith the Lord.

Postcommunion

RANT, O Lord, we beseech thee, that the intercession of thy Saints may make us acceptable unto thee: that those things which we perform in this temporal celebration we may receive unto eternal salvation. Through.

¶ In Lent, Commemoration & Last Gospel of the Feria.

Proper of Saints

Pope St. Gregory — 12 March

[12 March. Pope St. Gregory the Great]

I Evensong

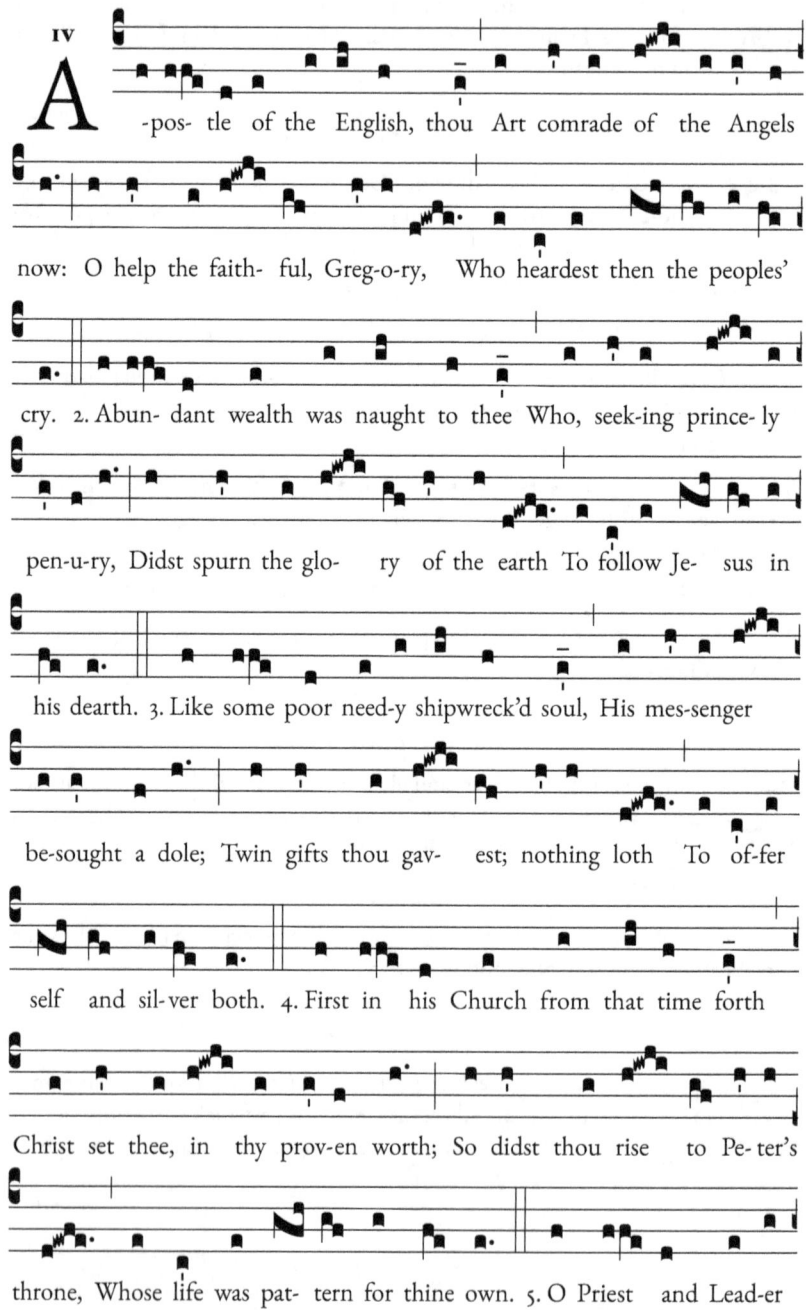

A-pos-tle of the English, thou Art comrade of the Angels now: O help the faith-ful, Greg-o-ry, Who heardest then the peoples' cry. 2. Abun-dant wealth was naught to thee Who, seek-ing prince-ly pen-u-ry, Didst spurn the glo-ry of the earth To follow Je-sus in his dearth. 3. Like some poor need-y shipwreck'd soul, His mes-senger be-sought a dole; Twin gifts thou gav-est; nothing loth To of-fer self and sil-ver both. 4. First in his Church from that time forth Christ set thee, in thy prov-en worth; So didst thou rise to Pe-ter's throne, Whose life was pat-tern for thine own. 5. O Priest and Lead-er

12 March — **Proper of Saints** — *Pope St. Gregory*

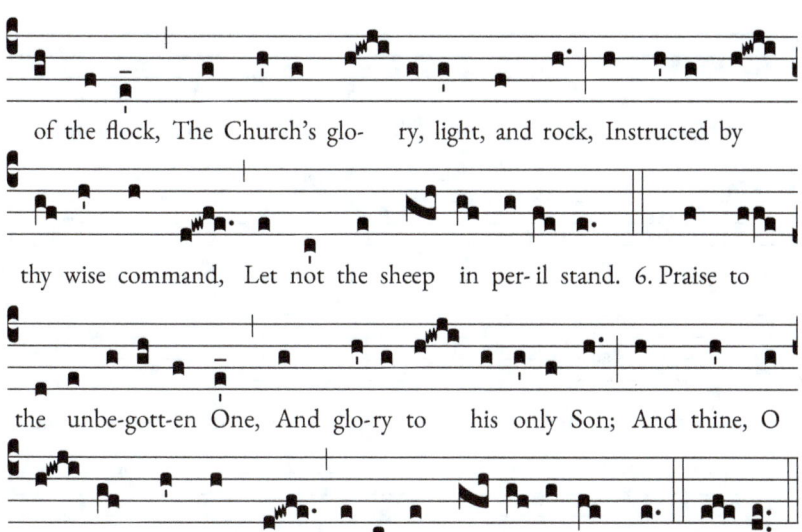

of the flock, The Church's glo- ry, light, and rock, Instructed by thy wise command, Let not the sheep in per- il stand. 6. Praise to the unbe-gott-en One, And glo-ry to his only Son; And thine, O Spir- it, Breath of God, Be equal maj- es- ty and laud. A- men.

℣. The Lord loved him and adorned him.
℟. He clothed him with a robe of glory.

Mag. Ant. O Teacher right excellent, † O light of Holy Church, O blessed Gregory, lover of the divine law: intercede for us unto the Son of God.

Mattins

❡ The Invitatory Hymn is as in I Evensong.

Office Hymn

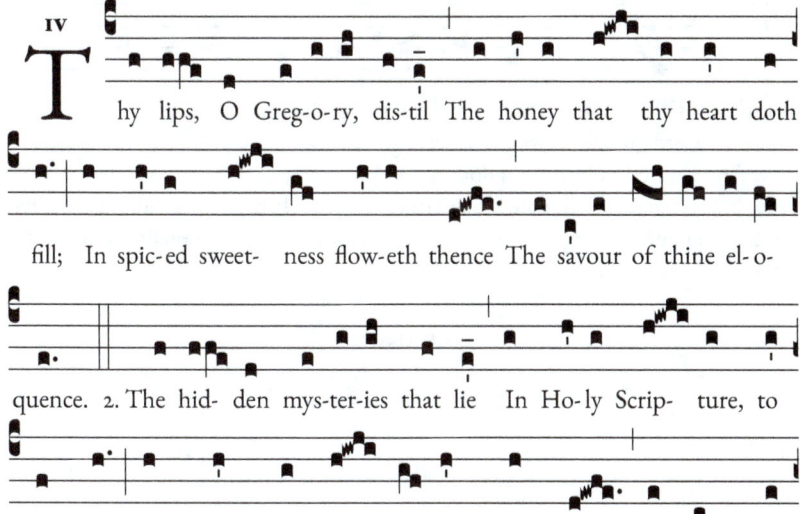

Thy lips, O Greg-o-ry, dis-til The honey that thy heart doth fill; In spic-ed sweet- ness flow-eth thence The savour of thine el-o-quence. 2. The hid- den mys-ter-ies that lie In Ho-ly Scrip- ture, to thine eye Are plain; the Truth himself draws near To make their

Pope St. Gregory — **Proper of Saints** — 12 March

sub- tle se-crets clear. 3. At once the Ap-ostol- ic throne And maj- es-ty be-come thine own: O free us from sin's binding chain That heav'nly man- sions we may gain. 4. O Priest and Lead-er of the flock, The Church's glo- ry, light, and rock, Instructed by thy wise command, Let not the sheep in per- il stand. 5. Praise to the unbe-gott-en One, And glo-ry to his only Son; And thine, O Spir- it, Breath of God, Be equal maj- es- ty and laud. A- men.

℣. The Lord guided the righteous in right paths.
℟. And shewed him the kingdom of God.

Ben. Ant. Gregory, † when he looked upon the youthful Angles, said: They have the countenance of Angels, and such as these should be of the fellowship of the Angels in heaven.

II Evensong

¶ The Office Hymn & Antiphon are of I Evensong, with the Versicle from Mattins.

17 March. St. Patrick

Double

❡ In Lent, Commemoration only.

❡ The propers are from the First Common of a Confessor Bishop (p. 715), except for that which followeth.

Collect

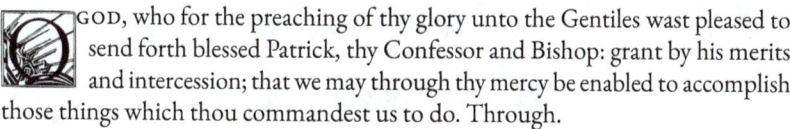O GOD, who for the preaching of thy glory unto the Gentiles wast pleased to send forth blessed Patrick, thy Confessor and Bishop: grant by his merits and intercession; that we may through thy mercy be enabled to accomplish those things which thou commandest us to do. Through.

❡ Commemoration of St. Joseph of Arimathea (p. 476).

❡ In Lent, Commemoration & Last Gospel of the Feria.

Secret

WE beseech thee, O Lord, that we remembering with gladness the merits of thy Saints, may in all places feel the succour of their intercession. Through.

❡ Commemoration of St. Joseph of Arimathea, from the Second Common of a Confessor not a Bishop (p. 729)

❡ In Lent, Commemoration & Last Gospel of the Feria.

Postcommunion

GRANT, we beseech thee, Almighty God: that we, shewing forth our thankfulness for the gifts which we have received, may at the intercession of blessed Patrick, thy Confessor and Bishop, obtain yet more abundant mercies. Through.

❡ Commemoration of St. Joseph of Arimathea, from the Second Common of a Confessor not a Bishop (p. 729)

❡ In Lent, Commemoration & Last Gospel of the Feria.

(17 March. St. Joseph of Arimathea)

¶ The Second Common of a Confessor not a Bishop (p. 729), except for the following.

¶ In Lent, Commemoration & Last Gospel of the Feria.

Collect

O GOD, who didst give such grace unto thy servant Joseph that he boldly craved the body of Jesus, and with great reverence laid him in the rock-hewn sepulchre: grant, we beseech thee, that we likewise may be so emboldened for thee, as to do works meet for thy Kingdom. Through the same.

18 March. St. Cyril of Jerusalem

Double

¶ In Lent, Commemoration only.

¶ The Daily propers are from the Common of Doctors (p. 723), except for that which followeth.

Introit

IN the midst of the Church he opened his mouth: and the Lord filled him with the spirit of wisdom and of understanding: he clothed him with a robe of glory. *Ps.* It is a good thing to give thanks unto the Lord: and to sing praises unto thy name, O most Highest.

Collect

GRANT to us, we beseech thee, Almighty God, at the intercession of the blessed Bishop Cyril: so to know thee, the only true God, and Jesus Christ whom thou hast sent; that we may be found worthy to be numbered for evermore among the sheep who hear his voice. Through the same.

¶ Commemoration of St. Edward (p. 478).

¶ In Lent, Commemoration of the Feria.

¶ The Epistle is from the additional Epistle of the Common of Doctors (p. 723).

Gradual. The mouth of the righteous is exercised in wisdom, and his tongue will be talking of judgement. ℣. The law of his God is in his heart: and his goings shall not slide.

Tract. Blessed is the man that feareth the Lord: he hath great delight in his commandments. ℣. His seed shall be mighty upon earth: the generation of the faithful shall be blessed. ℣. Riches and plenteousness shall be in his house: and his righteousness endureth for ever.

18 March   Proper of Saints   *St. Cyril Jerusalem*

Gospel. Matthew 10:23

T THAT TIME: Jesus said unto his disciples: When they persecute you in this city, flee ye into another: for verily I say unto you, Ye shall not have gone over the cities of Israel, till the Son of man be come. The disciple is not above his master, nor the servant above his lord. It is enough for the disciple that he be as his master, and the servant as his lord. If they have called the master of the house Beelzebub, how much more shall they call them of his household? Fear them not therefore: for there is nothing covered, that shall not be revealed; and hid, that shall not be known. What I tell you in darkness, that speak ye in light: and what ye hear in the ear, that preach ye upon the housetops. And fear not them which kill the body, but are not able to kill the soul: but rather fear him which is able to destroy both soul and body in hell.

Offertory. The righteous shall flourish like a palm-tree: and shall spread abroad like a cedar in Libanus.

Secret

OOK down, O Lord, upon the spotless victim which we offer unto thee: and grant; that by the merits of thy blessed Bishop and Confessor Cyril we may endeavour ourselves to receive it with clean hearts. Through.

❡ Commemoration of St. Edward (p. 478).

❡ In Lent, Commemoration of the Feria.

Communion. A faithful and wise servant, whom the Lord hath made ruler over his household: to give them their portion of meat in due season.

Postcommunion

LORD Jesu Christ, may the sacraments of thy Body and Blood, which we have received: sanctify our minds and hearts through the prayers of the blessed Bishop Cyril; that we may be worthy to be made partakers of the divine nature. Who livest.

❡ Commemoration of St. Edward (p. 478).

❡ In Lent, Commemoration & Last Gospel of the Feria.

St. Joseph Spouse # Proper of Saints 19 March

(18 March. St. Edward)

¶ The First Common of a Martyr not a Bishop (p. 688), except for the following.

Collect

GOD, the triumphant ruler of an everlasting kingdom, mercifully behold this thy family who celebrate the memory of blessed Edward, thy King and Martyr; and, by his merits and intercession, vouchsafe; that they, who glory in his triumph, may also attain unto his rewards. Through.

¶ Commemoration of St. Cyril (p. 476).

¶ In Lent, Commemoration of the Feria.

Secret

GRANT, O Lord, that this our bounden service may be acceptable in thy sight: that these our oblations may, by the prayers of him on whose solemnity they are offered, be made profitable unto our salvation. Through.

¶ Commemoration of St. Cyril (p. 477).

¶ In Lent, Commemoration of the Feria.

Postcommunion

WE beseech thee, O Lord our God, that like as we, whom thou hast refreshed by the partaking of thy sacred gift, do offer unto thee our worship: so by the intercession of blessed Edward thy Martyr, we may perceive the benefit of the same. Through.

¶ Commemoration of St. Cyril (p. 477).

¶ In Lent, Commemoration & Last Gospel of the Feria.

[19 March. St. Joseph, Spouse of the Blessed Virgin Mary]

I Evensong

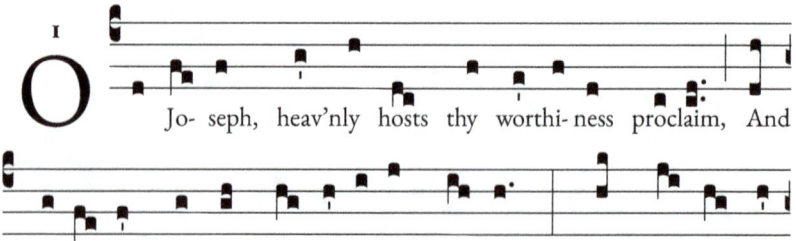

O Joseph, heav'nly hosts thy worthiness proclaim, And Christendom conspires to celebrate thy fame, Thou who in pur-

19 March — Proper of Saints — St. Joseph Spouse

est bonds wert to the Virgin bound; How glorious is thy name renown'd. 2. Thou, when thou didst behold thy Spouse about to bear, Wert sore oppress'd with doubt, wert fill'd with wondering care; At length the Angel's word thy anxious heart reliev'd: She by the Spirit hath conceiv'd. 3. Thou with thy new-born Lord didst seek far Egypt's land, As wand'ring pilgrims, ye fled o'er the desert sand; That Lord, when lost, by thee is in the temple found, While tears are shed, and joys abound. 4. Not till death's hour is past do other men obtain The meed of holiness, and glorious rest attain; Thou, like to Angels made, in life completely blest, Dost clasp thy God unto thy breast.

St. Joseph Spouse   **Proper of Saints**   19 March

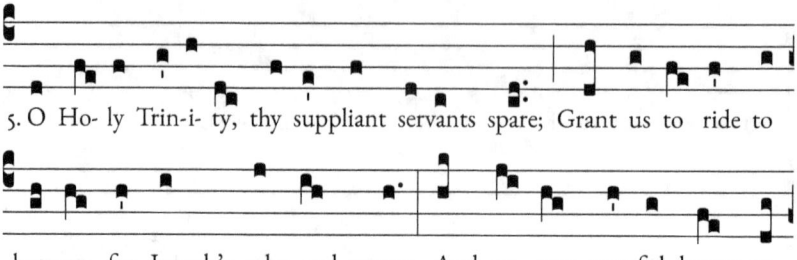

5. O Holy Trinity, thy suppliant servants spare; Grant us to ride to heaven, for Joseph's sake and prayer, And so our grateful hearts to thee shall ever raise Exulting canticles of praise. Amen.

℣. He made him lord of his house.

℟. And ruler of all his substance.

Mag. Ant. Then Joseph, † being raised from sleep, did as the Angel of the Lord had bidden him, and took unto him his wife.

Mattins

Invitatory Hymn

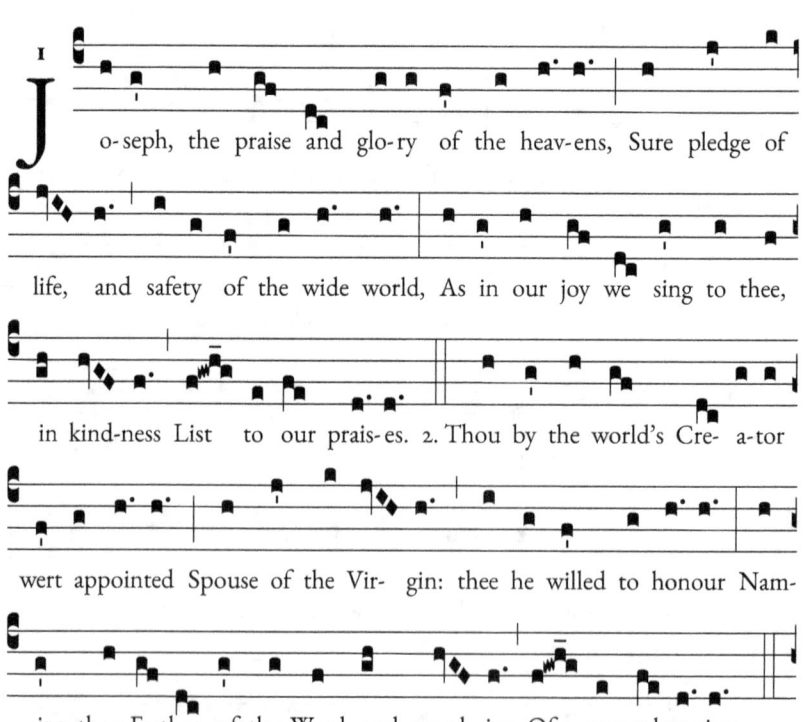

1. Joseph, the praise and glory of the heavens, Sure pledge of life, and safety of the wide world, As in our joy we sing to thee, in kindness List to our praises. 2. Thou by the world's Creator wert appointed Spouse of the Virgin: thee he willed to honour Naming thee Father of the Word, and guardian Of our salvation.

Proper of Saints

19 March — St. Joseph Spouse

3. Thou thy Redeemer, lying in a stable, Whom long ago foretold the choir of prophets, Sawest rejoicing, and thy God adoredst Humble in childhood. 4. God, King of Kings, and Governor of the ages, He at whose word the pow'rs of hell do tremble, He whom the adoring heav'ns ever worship Called thee protector. 5. Praise to the Triune Godhead everlasting, Who with such honour mightily hath blest thee; O may he grant us at thy blest petition Joys everlasting. Amen.

Office Hymn

He, whom the faithful joyously do honor, Singing his praises with devout affection, Won on this feast day, in eternal glory

St. Joseph Spouse — Proper of Saints — 19 March

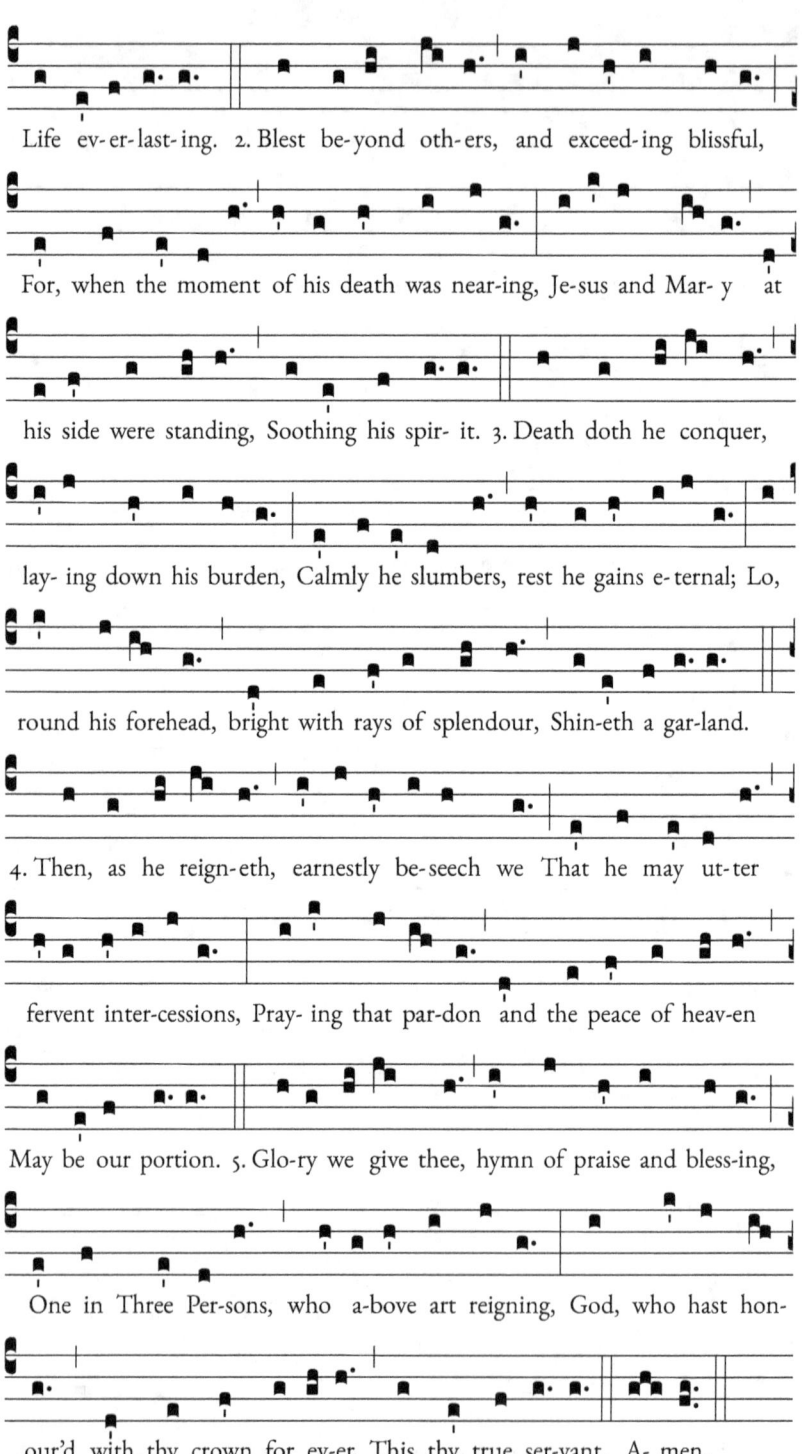

Life ev-er-last-ing. 2. Blest be-yond oth-ers, and exceed-ing blissful, For, when the moment of his death was near-ing, Je-sus and Mar-y at his side were standing, Soothing his spir-it. 3. Death doth he conquer, lay-ing down his burden, Calmly he slumbers, rest he gains e-ternal; Lo, round his forehead, bright with rays of splendour, Shin-eth a gar-land. 4. Then, as he reign-eth, earnestly be-seech we That he may ut-ter fervent inter-cessions, Pray-ing that par-don and the peace of heav-en May be our portion. 5. Glo-ry we give thee, hymn of praise and bless-ing, One in Three Per-sons, who a-bove art reigning, God, who hast hon-our'd with thy crown for ev-er This thy true ser-vant. A-men.

℣. The mouth of the righteous is exercised in wisdom.
℟. And his tongue will be talking of judgement.
Ben. Ant. Jesus himself † began to be about thirty years of age, being, as was supposed, the son of Joseph.

II Evensong

¶ The Office Hymn is of I Evensong, with the following Versicle & Antiphon.

℣. Riches and plenteousness shall be in his house.
℟. And his righteousness endureth for ever.
Mag. Ant. Behold a faithful † and wise servant, whom his Lord hath made ruler over his household.

20 March. St. Cuthbert

Double

¶ In Lent, Commemoration only.

¶ The propers are from the Second Common of a Bishop Confessor (p. 720), except for that which followeth.

Collect

O GOD, who dost make thy Saints glorious by the inestimable gift of thy grace: grant, we beseech thee; that at the intercession of blessed Cuthbert, thy Confessor and Bishop, we may be found worthy to attain to the perfection of all virtue. Through.

¶ In Lent, Commemoration of the Feria.

Secret

ACCEPT, we beseech thee, O Lord, the sacrifice of man's redemption: and at the intercession of blessed Cuthbert, thy Confessor and Bishop, mercifully grant us health of mind and of body. Through.

¶ In Lent, Commemoration of the Feria.

Postcommunion

WE beseech thee, O Lord, that thy holy things which we have received may protect us by their power: and at the intercession of blessed Cuthbert, thy Confessor and Bishop, whose life shone forth in glory, guard us in peace and holiness. Through.

¶ In Lent, Commemoration & Last Gospel of the Feria.

Proper of Saints

St. Benedict — 21 March

[21 March. St. Benedict]

I Evensong

1. Shout, all ye people! Let your meas-ur'd prais-es Ring through the churches sol-emnly and sweet-ly: On this his feast day, Ben-e-dict as-cended Heav-en's high summit. 2. He, when his youthful joy-ous years were blooming, Yet in his boyhood, left his na-tive dwell-ing, Seek-ing conceal-ment hid with-in a cav-ern Lone-ly and si-lent.

3. There a-mid nettles, rig-id thorns, and bri-ars Won he the bat-tle o-ver youth's entice-ment, Nurse of pol-lu-tion: then he wrote a Ho-ly Rule of blest liv-ing. 4. Thy bra-zen im-age, infamous A-pol-lo, Soon hath he smit-ten; burnt the grove of Ve-nus; Then to the

21 March — Proper of Saints — *St. Benedict*

Bap-tist, on the sa-cred mountain Stab-lish'd a chap-el. 5. Now doth he wit-ness happi-ly in heav-en Ser-aphim, lead-ing throngs of shin-ing An-gels, While he re-fresh-es faithful hearts who need him With liv-ing wa-ters. 6. Praise to the Fa-ther, to the Sole-be-got-ten, And to thee, al-way with the Twain co-e-qual, Fos-ter-ing Spir-it; one and on-ly Godhead Through all the ag-es. A-men.

℣. The Lord loved him and adorned him.
℟. He clothed him with a robe of glory.

Mag. Ant. Let all the multitude † of the faithful exult in the glory of the gracious Father Benedict: and chiefly let the company of monks be joyful, celebrating his festival on earth, in whose goodly fellowship the Saints rejoice in heaven.

Mattins

Invitatory Hymn

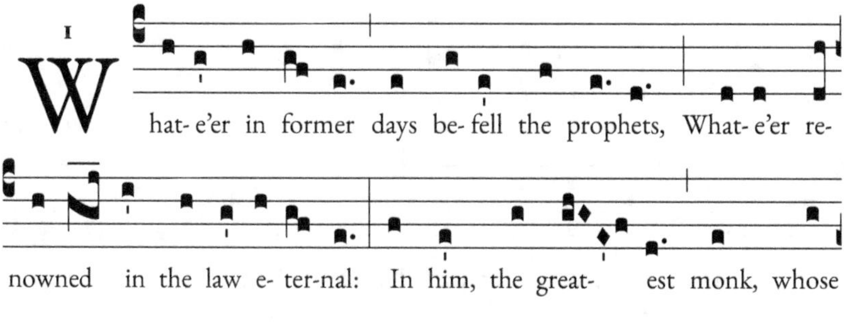

What-e'er in former days be-fell the prophets, What-e'er re-nowned in the law e-ter-nal: In him, the great-est monk, whose

St. Benedict   **Proper of Saints**   21 March

feast we hon-our, All is contain-ed. 2. Virtue of Mo- ses issued forth in mer-cy; Wondrous the offspring unto Abram giv- en; Righteous and stern, the rul- ing of his par- ent Bride gained for I- saac. 3. Ben-e-dict lad- en loft-i- ly with vir-tues: Higher were those our Pa-tri- arch had gath-er'd, Mer- its of I- saac, Abra-ham and Mo- ses One breast con-tain-eth. 4. Those by the world's blows o-vercome he lift-ed, Meekness es-tab-lish'd in the place of an-ger, Peace where it was not, rest he made to well up From midst of ter-ror. 5. Praise to the Fa-ther, to the Sole-be-got-ten, And to thee, alway with the Twain co- e-qual, Fos-ter-ing Spir- it; one and only Godhead Through all the ag- es. A- men.

21 March   **Proper of Saints**   *St. Benedict*

Office Hymn

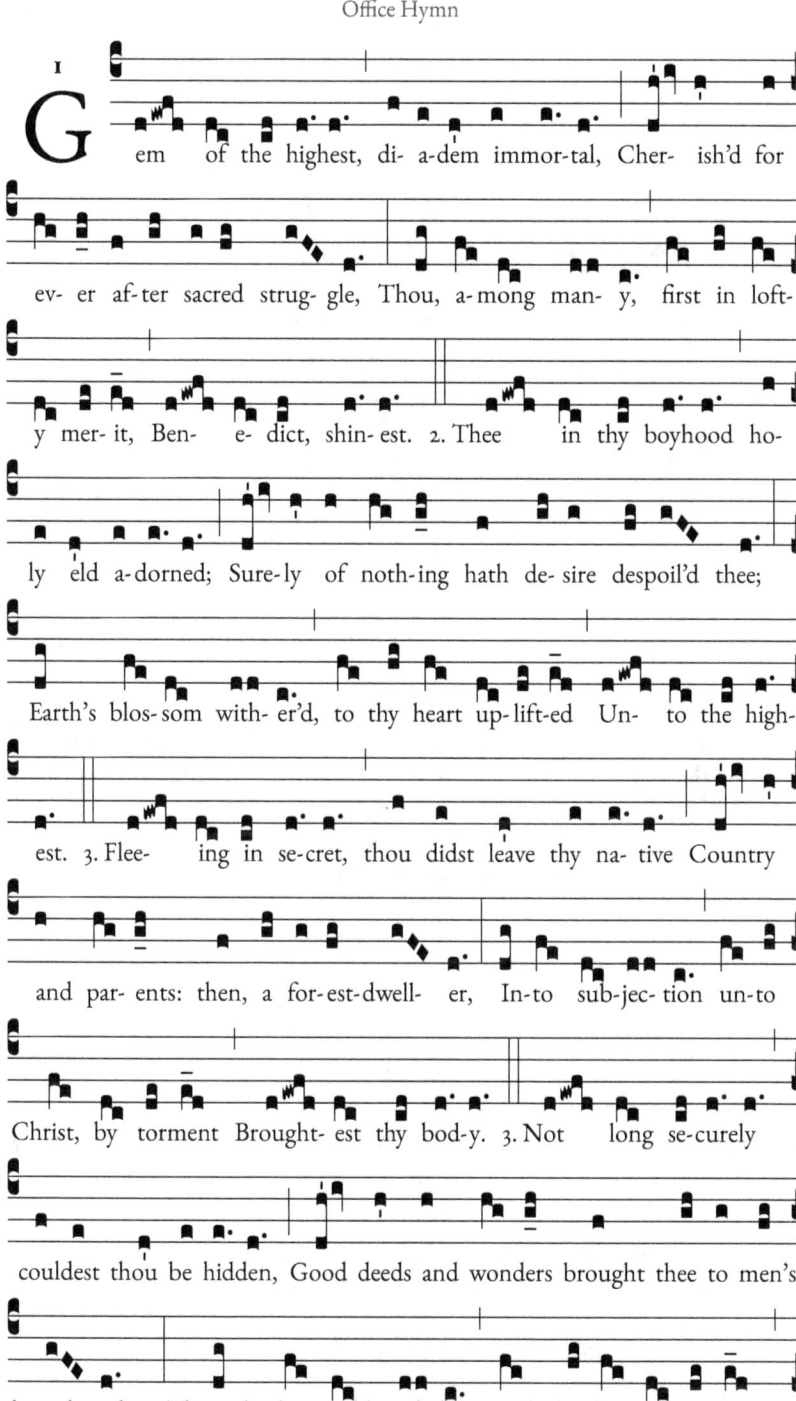

St. Gabriel Archangel   **Proper of Saints**   24 March

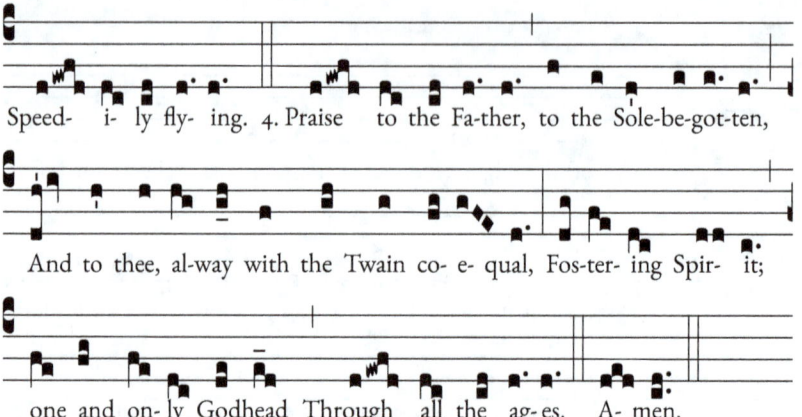

Speed-i-ly fly-ing. 4. Praise to the Fa-ther, to the Sole-be-got-ten, And to thee, al-way with the Twain co-e-qual, Fos-ter-ing Spir-it; one and on-ly Godhead Through all the ag-es. A-men.

℣. The Lord guided the righteous in right paths.
℟. And shewed him the kingdom of God.

Ben. Ant. Benedict, † thou father and guide of monks, thou most holy Confessor of the Lord, intercede for us all and for our salvation.

II Evensong

❡ The Office Hymn is of I Evensong, with the Versicle from Mattins and the following Antiphon.

Mag. Ant. To-day † holy Benedict, while his disciples beheld it, ascending by way of the East on a straight pathway to heaven: to-day with hands uplifted, he died between the words of his supplication: to-day he was received into glory by the Angels.

24 March. St. Gabriel

Greater Double

❡ Commemoration only is made, unless a Votive Mass of St. Gabriel is said outside of Lent or as a patronal Feast Day.

❡ I Evensong: Psalms 9, 11, & 15. Daniel 8:15-19. Revelation 8:1-5.
   Mattins: Psalms 30, 34, & 77. Daniel 9:20-26. Luke 1:5-17
   II Evensong: Psalms 97, 99, & 103. Isaiah 7:10-14. Luke 1:26-38.

Opening Sentence. I saw another angel come down from heaven, having great power; and the earth was lightened with his glory.

I Evensong	Mattins
Christ, the fair glory of the holy Angels,	O Christ, Redeemer of us all,
Thou who hast made us, thou who o'er us rulest,	Protect thy servants when they call, And hear with reconciling care
Grant of thy mercy unto us thy servants Steps up to heaven.	The blessed Virgin's holy prayer.
	Be ever present, Angel high

24 March   # Proper of Saints   *St. Gabriel Archangel*

Send thy Archangel, Gabriel, the mighty,
Herald of heaven; may he from us mortals
Spurn the old serpent, watching o'er the temples
Where thou art worshipp'd.

May the blest Mother of our God and Saviour,
May the assembly of the Saints in glory,
May the celestial companies of Angels
Ever assist us.

This he vouchsafe us, God for ever blessed
Father eternal, Son, and Holy Spirit,
Whose is the glory which through all creation.
Ever resoundeth. Amen.

℣. An Angel stood at the altar of the temple.
℟. Having in his hand a golden censer.
Mag. Ant. The Angel Gabriel † came in unto Mary and said, Hail, thou that art full of grace, the Lord is with thee; blessed art thou among women.

Whose name 'God's might' doth signify:
To all the weak new strength impart,
And solace to the sad of heart.

And ye, O ever blissful throng
Of heav'nly Spirits, guardians strong,
Our past and present ills dispel,
From future peril shield us well.

From lands wherein thy faithful dwell
Drive far away the infidel;
So we to Christ due hymns of praise
Henceforth with eager hearts may raise.

To thee, O Father, born of none,
And thee, O sole-begotten Son,
One with the Holy Paraclete,
Be glory ever, as is meet. Amen.

℣. An Angel stood at the altar of the temple.
℟. Having in his hand a golden censer.
Ben. Ant. The Angel Gabriel † descended to Zacharias, and said unto him: Thy wife shall bear thee a son, and thou shalt call his name John; and many shall rejoice at his birth; for he shall go before the face of the Lord, to prepare his ways.

¶ In II Evensong, the Office Hymn is of I Evensong, with the following Versicle & Antiphon.

℣. In the presence of the Angels I will sing praise unto thee, O my God.
℟. I will worship toward thy holy temple, and praise thy Name.
Mag. Ant. The Archangel Gabriel † said unto Mary: With God nothing shall be impossible. And Mary said, Behold the handmaid of the Lord: be it unto me according to thy word. And the Angel departed from her.

Introit

PRAISE the Lord, ye Angels of his, ye that excel in strength: ye that fulfil his commandment, and hearken unto the voice of his words. *Ps.* Praise the Lord, O my soul: and all that is within me praise his holy name.

Proper of Saints

St. Gabriel Archangel — 24 March

Collect

O GOD, who from the company of Angels didst choose the Archangel Gabriel to proclaim the mystery of thine Incarnation: mercifully grant; that we who celebrate his festival (commemoration) on earth, may perceive his advocacy in heaven. Who livest.

¶ Commemoration is made of the Feria.

Epistle. Daniel 9:21

IN THOSE DAYS: Behold the man Gabriel, whom I had seen in the vision at the beginning, being caused to fly swiftly, touched me about the time of the evening oblation. And he informed me, and talked with me, and said, O Daniel, I am now come forth to give thee skill and understanding. At the beginning of thy supplications the commandment came forth, and I am come to shew thee; for thou art greatly beloved: therefore understand the matter, and consider the vision. Seventy weeks are determined upon thy people and upon thy holy city, to finish the transgression, and to make an end of sins, and to make reconciliation for iniquity, and to bring in everlasting righteousness, and to seal up the vision and prophecy, and to anoint the most Holy. Know therefore and understand, that from the going forth of the commandment to restore and to build Jerusalem unto the Messiah the Prince shall be seven weeks, and threescore and two weeks: the street shall be built again, and the wall, even in troublous times. And after threescore and two weeks shall Messiah be cut off, but not for himself: and the people of the prince that shall come shall destroy the city and the sanctuary; and the end thereof shall be with a flood, and unto the end of the war desolations are determined.

Gradual. O praise the Lord, ye Angels of his, ye that excel in strength, ye that fulfil his commandment. ℣. Praise the Lord, O my soul, and all that is within me praise his holy name.

Tract. Hail, Mary, full of grace; the Lord is with thee. ℣. Blessed art thou among women: and blessed is the fruit of thy womb. ℣. Behold, thou shalt conceive, and bring forth a Son, and shalt call his name Emmanuel. ℣. The Holy Ghost shall come upon thee, and the power of the Highest shall overshadow thee. ℣. Therefore also that Holy Thing which shall be born of thee, shall be called the Son of God.

¶ In Votive Masses before Septuagesima or after Pentecost, the Gradual as above, but in place of the Tract is said:

Alleluia. Alleluia, alleluia. ℣. O praise the Lord, all ye his hosts: ye servants of his that do his pleasure. Alleluia.

¶ In Votive Masses in Eastertide, replacing the Gradual & Tract:

Alleluia. Alleluia, alleluia. ℣. Who maketh his Angels spirits: and his ministers a flaming fire. Alleluia. ℣. Hail, Mary, full of grace; the Lord is with thee: blessed art thou among women. Alleluia.

24 March — **Proper of Saints** — *St. Gabriel Archangel*

Gospel. Luke 1:26

AT THAT TIME: The Angel Gabriel was sent from God unto a city of Galilee named Nazareth, to a virgin espoused to a man whose name was Joseph, of the house of David; and the virgin's name was Mary. And the angel came in unto her, and said, Hail, thou that art highly favoured, the Lord is with thee: blessed art thou among women. And when she saw him, she was troubled at his saying, and cast in her mind what manner of salutation this should be. And the angel said unto her, Fear not, Mary: for thou hast found favour with God. And, behold, thou shalt conceive in thy womb, and bring forth a son, and shalt call his name JESUS. He shall be great, and shall be called the Son of the Highest: and the Lord God shall give unto him the throne of his father David: and he shall reign over the house of Jacob for ever; and of his kingdom there shall be no end. Then said Mary unto the angel, How shall this be, seeing I know not a man? And the angel answered and said unto her, The Holy Ghost shall come upon thee, and the power of the Highest shall overshadow thee: therefore also that holy thing which shall be born of thee shall be called the Son of God. And, behold, thy cousin Elisabeth, she hath also conceived a son in her old age: and this is the sixth month with her, who was called barren. For with God nothing shall be impossible. And Mary said, Behold the handmaid of the Lord; be it unto me according to thy word.

Offertory. An Angel stood at the altar of the temple, having a golden censer in his hand; and there was given unto him much incense: and the smoke of the incense ascended up before God.

Secret

AY the offering of our service, and the prayer of blessed Gabriel the Archangel, be accepted in thy sight, O Lord: that he, who is venerated by us on earth, may be an advocate for us with thee in heaven. Through.

❧ Commemoration of the Feria.

Communion. O all ye Angels of the Lord, bless ye the Lord: sing ye praises, and magnify him above all for ever.

Postcommunion

HAVING received the mysteries of thy Body and Blood, we entreat thy loving kindness, O Lord our God: that, as we have known thine Incarnation by the message of Gabriel, so we may through his help obtain the benefits of that Incarnation. Who livest.

❧ Commemoration & Last Gospel of the Feria.

[25 March. Annunciation of the Blessed Virgin Mary]

¶ The Hymns are from the Common of the Blessed Virgin Mary (p. 760), with the following Versicles & Antiphons.

℣. Hail Mary, full of grace.
℟. The Lord is with thee.

Mag. Ant. The Holy Ghost † shall come upon thee, Mary: and the power of the Highest shall overshadow thee.

℣. Hail Mary, full of grace.
℟. The Lord is with thee.

Ben. Ant. How shall this be, † O Angel of God, seeing I know not a man? Hearken, O Virgin Mary: The Holy Ghost shall come upon thee, and the power of the Highest shall overshadow thee.

℣. Hail Mary, full of grace.
℟. The Lord is with thee.

Mag. Ant. The Angel Gabriel † spake unto Mary, saying: Hail, thou that art full of grace, the Lord is with thee; blessed art thou among women.

27 March. St. John Damascene

Double

¶ Commemoration only.

¶ The Daily Office propers are from the Common of Doctors (p. 723).

Introit

THOU hast holden me by my right hand: thou shalt guide me with thy counsel, and after that receive me with glory. *Ps.* Truly God is loving unto Israel, even unto such as are of a clean heart!

Collect

ALMIGHTY and everlasting God, who, for the defence of the veneration of sacred images, didst endue blessed John with heavenly doctrine and wondrous strength of spirit: grant unto us by his intercession and example; that we may imitate the virtues and perceive the advocacy of those whose images we venerate. Through.

¶ Commemoration of the Feria.

27 March   **Proper of Saints**   *St. John Damascene*

Epistle. Wisdom 10:10

WISDOM guided him in straight paths; She shewed him God's kingdom, and gave him knowledge of holy things; She prospered him in his toils, and multiplied the fruits of his labour; When in their covetousness men dealt hardly with him, She stood by him and made him rich; She guarded him from enemies, And from those that lay in wait she kept him safe, And over his sore conflict she watched as judge, That he might know that godliness is more powerful than all. When a righteous man was sold, wisdom forsook him not, But from sin she delivered him; She went down with him into a dungeon, And in bonds she left him not, Till she brought him the sceptre of a kingdom, And authority over those that dealt tyrannously with him; She shewed them also to be false that had mockingly accused him, And gave him eternal glory. Wisdom delivered a holy people and a blameless seed from a nation of oppressors. She entered into the soul of a servant of the Lord, And withstood terrible kings in wonders and signs. She rendered unto holy men a reward of their toils.

Gradual. It is God that girdeth me with strength of war: and maketh my way perfect, ℣. He teacheth mine hands to fight: and mine arms shall break even a bow of steel.

Tract. I will follow upon mine enemies, and overtake them. ℣. I will smite them that they shall not be able to stand: but fall under my feet. ℣. For this cause will I give thanks unto thee, O Lord, among the Gentiles, and sing praises unto thy name.

Gospel. Luke 6:6

AT THAT TIME: It came to pass on another sabbath, that Jesus entered into the synagogue and taught. And there was a man whose right hand was withered. And the scribes and Pharisees watched him, whether he would heal on the sabbath day; that they might find an accusation against him. But he knew their thoughts, and said to the man which had the withered hand, Rise up, and stand forth in the midst. And he arose and stood forth. Then said Jesus unto them, I will ask you one thing; Is it lawful on the sabbath days to do good, or to do evil? to save life, or to destroy it? And looking round about upon them all, he said unto the man, Stretch forth thy hand. And he did so: and his hand was restored whole as the other. And they were filled with madness; and communed one with another what they might do to Jesus.

Offertory. There is hope of a tree, if it be cut down, that it will sprout again, and that the tender branch thereof will not cease.

Secret

O LORD, let the devout intercession of blessed John and of the Saints, who through his labours are set forth in the temples for our veneration, avail to render the gifts which we offer acceptable in thy sight. Through.

℟ Commemoration of the Feria.

Communion. The arms of the ungodly shall be broken, and the Lord upholdeth the righteous.

Postcommunion

WE beseech thee, O Lord, that the gifts which we have received may shield us with heavenly armour: and that the advocacy of blessed John, together with the united intercession of the Saints, the veneration of whose images in the Church be victoriously upheld, be our defence. Through.

¶ Commemoration & Last Gospel of the Feria.

(30 March. St. John Climacus)

¶ The Common of Abbots (p. 732).

¶ Commemoration & Last Gospel of the Feria.

(31 March. St. Innocent of Alaska)

¶ The Second Common of a Confessor Bishop (p. 720).

¶ Commemoration & Last Gospel of the Feria.

4 April. St. Isidore of Seville

Double

¶ In Lent or Easter Week, Commemoration only.

¶ The propers are from the Common of Doctors (p. 723).

¶ In Lent, Commemoration & Last Gospel of the Feria.

[7 April. St. Tikhon of Moscow]

¶ The Daily Office propers are from the First Common of a Bishop Confessor (p. 715).

¶ In Lent, Commemoration & Last Gospel of the Feria.

11 April. Pope St. Leo the Great

Double

¶ In Lent or Easter Week, Commemoration only.

¶ The Daily Office propers are from the Common of Doctors (p. 723).

Introit

IN the midst of the Church he opened his mouth: and the Lord filled him with the spirit of wisdom and of understanding: he clothed him with a robe of glory. (Alleluia, alleluia.) *Ps.* It is a good thing to give thanks unto the Lord: and to sing praises unto thy name, O Most Highest.

Collect

WE beseech thee, O Lord, graciously to hear the prayers which we offer unto thee on the solemnity of blessed Leo, thy Confessor and Bishop: that, like as he was found worthy to do thee faithful service, so by his merits and intercession we may be absolved from all our sins. Through.

¶ In Lent, Commemoration of the Feria.

¶ The Epistle is the additional Epistle of the Common of Doctors (p. 725).

Gradual. The mouth of the righteous is exercised in wisdom, and his tongue will be talking of judgement. ℣. The law of his God is in his heart: and his goings shall not slide.

Tract. Blessed is the man that feareth the Lord: he hath great delight in his commandments. ℣. His seed shall be mighty upon earth: the generation of the faithful shall be blessed. ℣. Riches and plenteousness shall be in his house: and his righteousness endureth for ever.

¶ In Eastertide, the following Alleluia Verse replaces the Gradual & Tract.

Alleluia. Alleluia, alleluia. ℣. The Lord loved him, and adorned him: he clothed him with a robe of glory. Alleluia. ℣. The righteous shall grow as the lily: and flourish for ever before the Lord. Alleluia.

Gospel. Matthew 16:13

AT THAT TIME: When Jesus came into the coasts of Caesarea Philippi, he asked his disciples, saying, Whom do men say that I the Son of man am? And they said, Some say that thou art John the Baptist: some, Elias; and others, Jeremias, or one of the prophets. He saith unto them, But whom say ye that I am? And Simon Peter answered and said, Thou art the Christ, the Son of the living God. And Jesus answered and said unto him, Blessed art thou, Simon Barjona: for flesh and blood hath not revealed it unto thee, but my Father which is in heaven. And I say also unto thee, That thou art Peter, and upon this rock I will build my church; and the gates of hell shall not prevail against it. And I will give unto thee the keys of the kingdom of heaven: and whatsoever thou shalt bind on earth shall be bound in heaven: and whatsoever thou shalt loose on earth shall be loosed in heaven.

Offertory. I have found David my servant, with my holy oil have I anointed him: my hand shall hold him fast, and my arm shall strengthen him. (Alleluia.)

Secret

WE beseech thee, O Lord, that our devout observance of the yearly solemnity of Saint Leo, thy Confessor and Bishop, may render us acceptable unto thy loving kindness: that this service of propitiation, which we duly offer, may be profitable unto him for the reward of blessed-ness, and obtain for us the gifts of thy grace. Through.

¶ In Lent, Commemoration of the Feria.

Communion. Blessed is the servant, whom the lord when he cometh shall find watching: verily I say unto you, that he shall make him ruler over all his goods. (Alleluia.)

Postcommunion

O GOD, who rewardest the souls of them that put their trust in thee: vouchsafe; that we who keep the solemn festival of blessed Leo, thy Confessor and Bishop, may by his prayers obtain thy merciful pardon. Through.

¶ In Lent, Commemoration & Last Gospel of the Feria.

(13 April. St. Hermengild)

¶ In Lent, the First Common of a Martyr not a Bishop (p. 688), except for the following. And Commemoration & Last Gospel of the Feria.

¶ In Eastertide, the Common of Martyrs in Eastertide (p. 711), except for the following.

Collect

O GOD, who didst teach blessed Hermengild, thy Martyr, to lay down an earthly for a heavenly kingdom: grant to us, we beseech thee; by his example to despise things temporal, and to seek after things eternal. Through.

Gospel. Luke 14:26

AT THAT TIME: Jesus said unto the multitudes: If any man come to me, and hate not his father, and mother, and wife, and children, and brethren, and sisters, yea, and his own life also, he cannot be my disciple. And whosoever doth not bear his cross, and come after me, cannot be my disciple. For which of you, intending to build a tower, sitteth not down first, and counteth the cost, whether

14 April   **Proper of Saints**   *St. Justin*

he have sufficient to finish it? Lest haply, after he hath laid the foundation, and is not able to finish it, all that behold it begin to mock him, Saying, This man began to build, and was not able to finish. Or what king, going to make war against another king, sitteth not down first, and consulteth whether he be able with ten thousand to meet him that cometh against him with twenty thousand? Or else, while the other is yet a great way off, he sendeth an ambassage, and desireth conditions of peace. So likewise, whosoever he be of you that forsaketh not all that he hath, he cannot be my disciple.

Secret

E beseech thee, O Lord, to accept our prayers and oblations: and graciously hearken unto us, whom thou dost cleanse by thy heavenly mysteries. Through.

Postcommunion

RANT, we beseech thee, O Lord our God: that like as we in this life do gladly honour the memory of thy Saints; so we may rejoice to behold them for ever. Through.

(14 April. St. Justin)

Introit

HE proud have digged pits for me, which are not after thy law: I will speak of thy testimonies also, even before kings, and will not be ashamed. (Alleluia, alleluia.) *Ps.* Blessed are those that are undefiled in the way: and walk in the law of the Lord.

Collect

GOD, who through the foolishness of the Cross didst wondrously teach blessed Justin Martyr the excellent knowledge of Jesus Christ: grant to us through his intercession; that we, driving away the errors that beset us, may attain unto steadfastness of faith. Through the same.

¶ Commemoration of Sts. Tiburtius, Valerian, & Maximus (p. 499).

¶ In Lent, Commemoration of the Feria.

Epistle. 1 Corinthians 1:18

BRETHREN: The preaching of the cross is to them that perish foolishness; but unto us which are saved it is the power of God. For it is written, I will destroy the wisdom of the wise, and will bring to nothing the understanding of the prudent. Where is the wise? where is the scribe? where is the disputer of this world? hath not God made foolish the wisdom of this world? For after that

St. Justin   **Proper of Saints**   14 April

in the wisdom of God the world by wisdom knew not God, it pleased God by the foolishness of preaching to save them that believe. For the Jews require a sign, and the Greeks seek after wisdom: But we preach Christ crucified, unto the Jews a stumblingblock, and unto the Greeks foolishness; But unto them which are called, both Jews and Greeks, Christ the power of God, and the wisdom of God. Because the foolishness of God is wiser than men; and the weakness of God is stronger than men. For ye see your calling, brethren, how that not many wise men after the flesh, not many mighty, not many noble, are called: But God hath chosen the foolish things of the world to confound the wise; and God hath chosen the weak things of the world to confound the things which are mighty; And base things of the world, and things which are despised, hath God chosen, yea, and things which are not, to bring to nought things that are: That no flesh should glory in his presence. But of him are ye in Christ Jesus, who of God is made unto us wisdom, and righteousness, and sanctification, and redemption.

Gradual. The wisdom of this world is foolishness with God, for it is written: The Lord knoweth the thoughts of the wise, that they are vain. ℣. I will destroy the wisdom of the wise, and will bring to nothing the understanding of the prudent.

Tract. I determined not to know any thing among you, save Jesus Christ, and him crucified. ℣. We speak the wisdom of God in a mystery, even the hidden wisdom, which God ordained before the world unto our glory. ℣. Which none of the princes of this world knew. For had they known it, they would not have crucified the Lord of glory.

Alleluia. Alleluia, alleluia. ℣. The wisdom of this world is foolishness with God: for it is written: The Lord knoweth the thoughts of the wise, that they are vain. Alleluia. ℣. Yea doubtless, and I count all things but loss for the excellency of the knowledge of Christ Jesus my Lord. Alleluia.

¶ In Votive Masses before Septuagesima or after Pentecost, the Gradual is said, as above, but, the Tract being omitted, there is added

Alleluia. Alleluia, alleluia. ℣. Yea doubtless, and I count all things but loss for the excellency of the knowledge of Christ Jesus my Lord. Alleluia.

Gospel. Luke 12:2

AT THAT TIME: Jesus said to his disciples: There is nothing covered, that shall not be revealed; neither hid, that shall not be known. Therefore whatsoever ye have spoken in darkness shall be heard in the light; and that which ye have spoken in the ear in closets shall be proclaimed upon the housetops. And I say unto you my friends, Be not afraid of them that kill the body, and after that have no more that they can do. But I will forewarn you whom ye shall fear: Fear him, which after he hath killed hath power to cast into hell; yea, I say unto you, Fear him. Are not five sparrows sold for two farthings, and not one of them is forgotten before God? But even the very hairs of your head are all numbered. Fear not therefore: ye are of more value than many sparrows. Also I say unto you,

14 April   **Proper of Saints**   *Sts. Tiburtius &c.*

Whosoever shall confess me before men, him shall the Son of man also confess before the angels of God.

Secret

LORD God, graciously receive our gifts: the wondrous mystery whereof the holy Martyr Justin did manfully defend against the slanders of the ungodly. Through.

¶ Commemoration of Sts. Tiburtius, Valerian, & Maximus (p. 499).

¶ In Lent, Commemoration of the Feria.

Communion. There is laid up for me a crown of righteousness, which the Lord, the righteous judge, shall give me at that day. (Alleluia.)

Postcommunion

LORD, who hast refreshed us with heavenly food, we humbly beseech thee: that following the counsels of blessed Justin, thy Martyr; we may ever continue in thanksgiving for the gifts which we have received. Through.

¶ Commemoration of Sts. Tiburtius, Valerian, & Maximus (p. 499).

¶ In Lent, Commemoration & Last Gospel of the Feria.

(14 April. Sts. Tiburtius, Valerian, and Maximus)

¶ Outside of Eastertide, the Second Common of Many Martyrs (p. 699), except for the following.

¶ In Eastertide, the propers are from the Common of Many Martyrs in Eastertide (p. 711), with the Epistle and Gospel from the Common of a Martyr in Eastertide (p. 705), with the Prayers following.

Collect

RANT, we beseech thee, Almighty God: that we, who celebrate the festival of thy holy Martyrs, Tiburtius, Valerian, and Maximus; may also imitate their virtues. Through.

Secret

E beseech thee, O Lord, that this oblation, which we offer unto thee in commemoration of the birthday of thy holy Martyrs: may both loose the bonds of our iniquity, and obtain for us the gifts of thy mercy. Through.

Postcommunion

LORD, who hast satisfied us with this sacred gift, we humbly beseech thee: that the mysteries, which we celebrate in this service of our bounden duty, we may know to be an increase of thy salvation. Though.

Proper of Saints

(17 April. St. Anicetus)

¶ Outside of Eastertide, the Second Common of a Martyr Bishop outside of Eastertide (p. 686).

¶ In Eastertide, the Common of a Martyr in Eastertide (p. 705), using the Second Prayers for a Martyr Bishop, with the additional Gospel from the Common of Many Martyrs in Eastertide (p. 715).

(22 April. Sts. Soter and Caius)

¶ Outside of Eastertide, the First Common of Many Martyrs outside of Eastertide (p. 692).

¶ In Eastertide, the Common of Many Martyrs in Eastertide (p. 711), with the additional Epistle (p. 714).

[23 April. St. George]

¶ Outside of Eastertide, the Daily Office propers are from the First Common of a Martyr not a Bishop out of Eastertide (p. 688).

¶ In Eastertide, the Daily Office propers are from the Common of a Martyr in Eastertide (p. 705).

[25 April. St. Mark]

¶ Outside of Eastertide, the Daily Office propers are from the Common of Apostles (p. 673).

¶ In Eastertide, the Daily Office propers are from the Common of Apostles in Eastertide (p. 678).

(26 April. Sts. Cletus and Marcellinus)

¶ Outside of Eastertide, the First Common of Many Martyrs out of Eastertide (p. 692), except for the following.

¶ In Eastertide, the Common of Many Martyrs in Eastertide (p. 711), except for the following.

Collect

O LORD, let the precious confession of thy blessed Martyrs and Bishops Cletus and Marcellinus be our defence: and let their loving intercession be a continual defence. Through.

Secret

ASSIST us mercifully, O Lord, in these our supplications, which we make before thee in remembrance of thy Saints: that we who trust not in our own righteousness may be succoured by the merits of them that have found favour in thy sight. Through.

Postcommunion

LORD, who hast fulfilled us with saving mysteries: we beseech thee that we may be aided by the prayers of those whose festival we celebrate. Through.

(28 April. St. Vitalis)

¶ Outside of Eastertide, the First Common of a Martyr not a Bishop out of Eastertide (p. 688).

¶ In Eastertide, the Common of a Martyr in Eastertide (p. 705), using the first Prayers for a Martyr not a Bishop

[1 May. Sts. Philip & James]

¶ The Daily Office propers are from the Common of Apostles in Eastertide (p. 678), except for the following.

Mag. Ant. Let not your heart † be troubled, neither let it be afraid; ye believe in God, believe also in me: in my Father's house are many mansions, alleluia, alleluia.

Ben. Ant. I am the way, † the truth, and the life: no man cometh unto the Father, but by me, alleluia.

℣. Right dear in the sight of the Lord, alleluia.
℟. Is the death of his Saints, alleluia.

Mag. Ant. If ye abide in me, † and my words abide in you, ye shall ask what ye will, and it shall be done unto you, alleluia, alleluia, alleluia.

2 May. St. Athanasius

Double

¶ The Daily Office propers are from the Common of Doctors (p. 723).

Introit

IN the midst of the Church he opened his mouth: and the Lord filled him with the spirit of wisdom and of understanding: he clothed him with a robe of glory, alleluia, alleluia. *Ps.* It is a good thing to give thanks unto the Lord: and to sing praise unto thy name, O Most Highest.

Collect

WE beseech thee, O Lord, graciously to hear the prayers which we offer unto thee on the solemnity of blessed Athanasius, thy Confessor and Bishop: that, like as he was found worthy to do thee faithful service, so by his merits and intercession we may be absolved from all our sins. Through.

St. Athanasius **Proper of Saints** 2 May

Epistle. 2 Corinthians 4:5

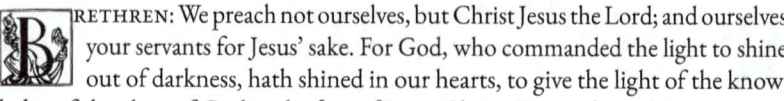RETHREN: We preach not ourselves, but Christ Jesus the Lord; and ourselves your servants for Jesus' sake. For God, who commanded the light to shine out of darkness, hath shined in our hearts, to give the light of the knowledge of the glory of God in the face of Jesus Christ. But we have this treasure in earthen vessels, that the excellency of the power may be of God, and not of us. We are troubled on every side, yet not distressed; we are perplexed, but not in despair; Persecuted, but not forsaken; cast down, but not destroyed; Always bearing about in the body the dying of the Lord Jesus, that the life also of Jesus might be made manifest in our body. For we which live are alway delivered unto death for Jesus' sake, that the life also of Jesus might be made manifest in our mortal flesh. So then death worketh in us, but life in you. We having the same spirit of faith, according as it is written, I believed, and therefore have I spoken; we also believe, and therefore speak; Knowing that he which raised up the Lord Jesus shall raise up us also by Jesus, and shall present us with you.

Alleluia. Alleluia, alleluia. ℣. Thou art a priest for ever, after the order of Melchisedech. Alleluia. ℣. Blessed is the man that endureth temptation: for when he is tried, he shall receive the crown of life. Alleluia.

¶ Outside of Eastertide, the following Gradual & Lesser Alleluia replaces the Greater Alleluia.

Gradual. Behold a great priest who in his days pleased God. ℣. There was none found like unto him who kept the law of the Most High.

Alleluia. Alleluia, alleluia. ℣. Blessed is the man that endureth temptation: for when he is tried, he shall receive the crown of life. Alleluia.

Gospel. Matthew 10:23

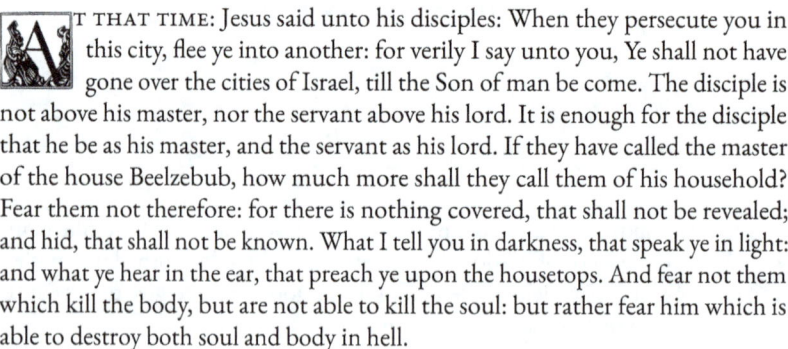T THAT TIME: Jesus said unto his disciples: When they persecute you in this city, flee ye into another: for verily I say unto you, Ye shall not have gone over the cities of Israel, till the Son of man be come. The disciple is not above his master, nor the servant above his lord. It is enough for the disciple that he be as his master, and the servant as his lord. If they have called the master of the house Beelzebub, how much more shall they call them of his household? Fear them not therefore: for there is nothing covered, that shall not be revealed; and hid, that shall not be known. What I tell you in darkness, that speak ye in light: and what ye hear in the ear, that preach ye upon the housetops. And fear not them which kill the body, but are not able to kill the soul: but rather fear him which is able to destroy both soul and body in hell.

Offertory. I have found David my servant, with my holy oil have I anointed him: my hand shall hold him fast, and my arm shall strengthen him, alleluia.

3 May   **Proper of Saints**   *Invention of the Cross*

Secret

WE beseech thee, O Lord, that our devout observance of the yearly solemnity of Saint Athanasius, thy Confessor and Bishop, may render us acceptable unto thy loving kindness: that this service of propitiation, which we duly offer, may be profitable unto him for the reward of blessed-ness, and obtain for us the gifts of thy grace. Through.

Communion. What I tell you in darkness that speak ye in light, saith the Lord: and what ye hear in the ear, that preach ye upon the housetops, alleluia.

Postcommunion

GOD, who rewardest the souls of them that put their trust in thee: vouchsafe; that we who keep the solemn festival of blessed Athanasius, thy Confessor and Bishop, may by his prayers obtain thy merciful pardon. Through.

[3 MAY. INVENTION OF THE HOLY CROSS]

I Evensong

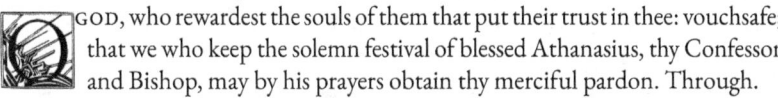

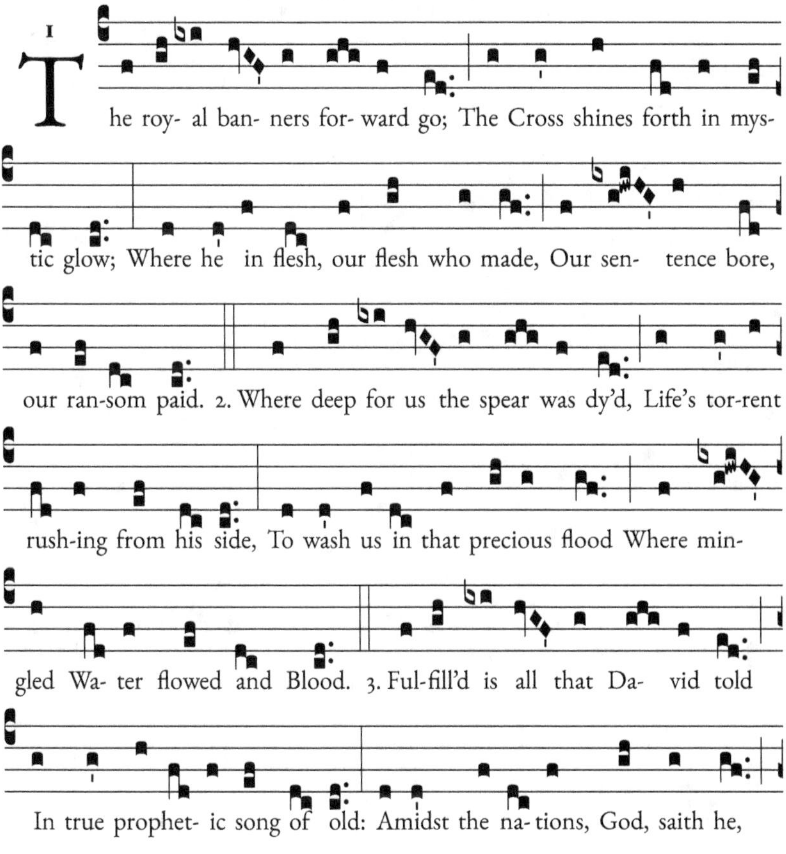

The roy-al ban-ners for-ward go; The Cross shines forth in mys-tic glow; Where he in flesh, our flesh who made, Our sen-tence bore, our ran-som paid. 2. Where deep for us the spear was dy'd, Life's tor-rent rush-ing from his side, To wash us in that precious flood Where min-gled Wa-ter flowed and Blood. 3. Ful-fill'd is all that Da-vid told In true prophet-ic song of old: Amidst the na-tions, God, saith he,

Invention of the Cross   **Proper of Saints**   3 May

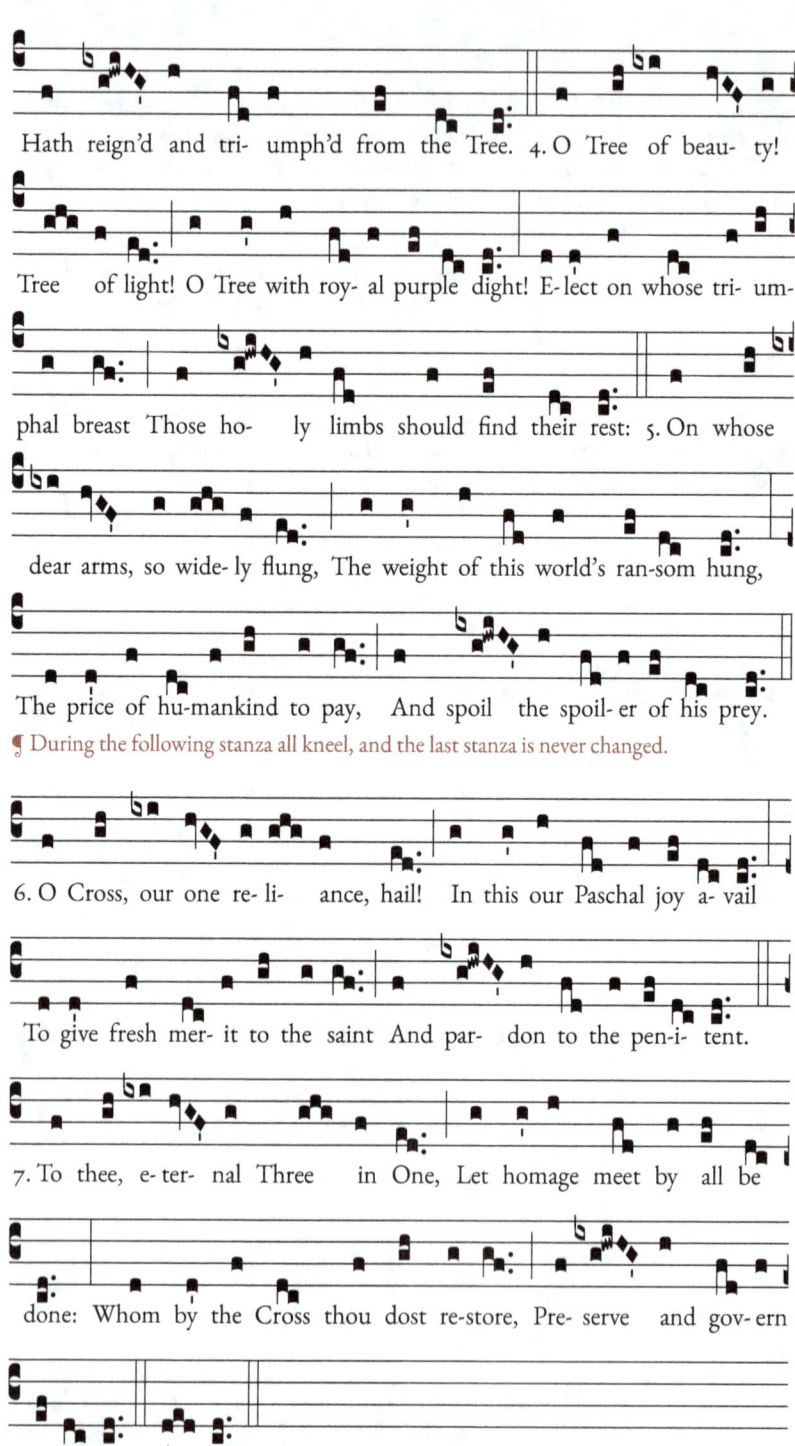

Hath reign'd and tri- umph'd from the Tree. 4. O Tree of beau- ty! Tree of light! O Tree with roy- al purple dight! E-lect on whose tri- umphal breast Those ho- ly limbs should find their rest: 5. On whose dear arms, so wide- ly flung, The weight of this world's ran-som hung, The price of hu-mankind to pay, And spoil the spoil- er of his prey.

℣ During the following stanza all kneel, and the last stanza is never changed.

6. O Cross, our one re- li- ance, hail! In this our Paschal joy a- vail To give fresh mer- it to the saint And par- don to the pen-i- tent.

7. To thee, e- ter- nal Three in One, Let homage meet by all be done: Whom by the Cross thou dost re-store, Pre- serve and gov- ern ev-ermore. A- men.

3 May **Proper of Saints** *Invention of the Cross*

℣. This sign of the Cross shall be in heaven, alleluia.
℟. When the Lord shall come to judgement, alleluia.
Mag. Ant. O Cross, † surpassing all the stars in splendour, world renowned, exceeding dear unto the hearts of men, holier than all things: thou only wert counted worthy to uphold the world's random. Sweet the wood, sweet the iron, bearing so sweet a burden: bring aid to this congregation, who are here assembled to celebrate thy praises, alleluia, alleluia.

Mattins

Invitatory Hymn

Sing, my tongue, the glorious bat-tle Sing the last, the dread af-fray; O'er the Cross, the vic-tor's trophy, Sound the high tri-umphal lay: Tell how Christ, the world's Re-deemer, As a vic-tim won the day. 2. God, our Mak-er, sorely griev-ing That the first-made Ad-am fell, When he ate the fruit of sorrow, Whose re-ward was death and hell, Not-ed then this Wood, the ru-in Of the an-cient wood to quell. 3. For the work of our sal-va-tion Needs would have his or-der

3 May — **Proper of Saints** — *Invention of the Cross*

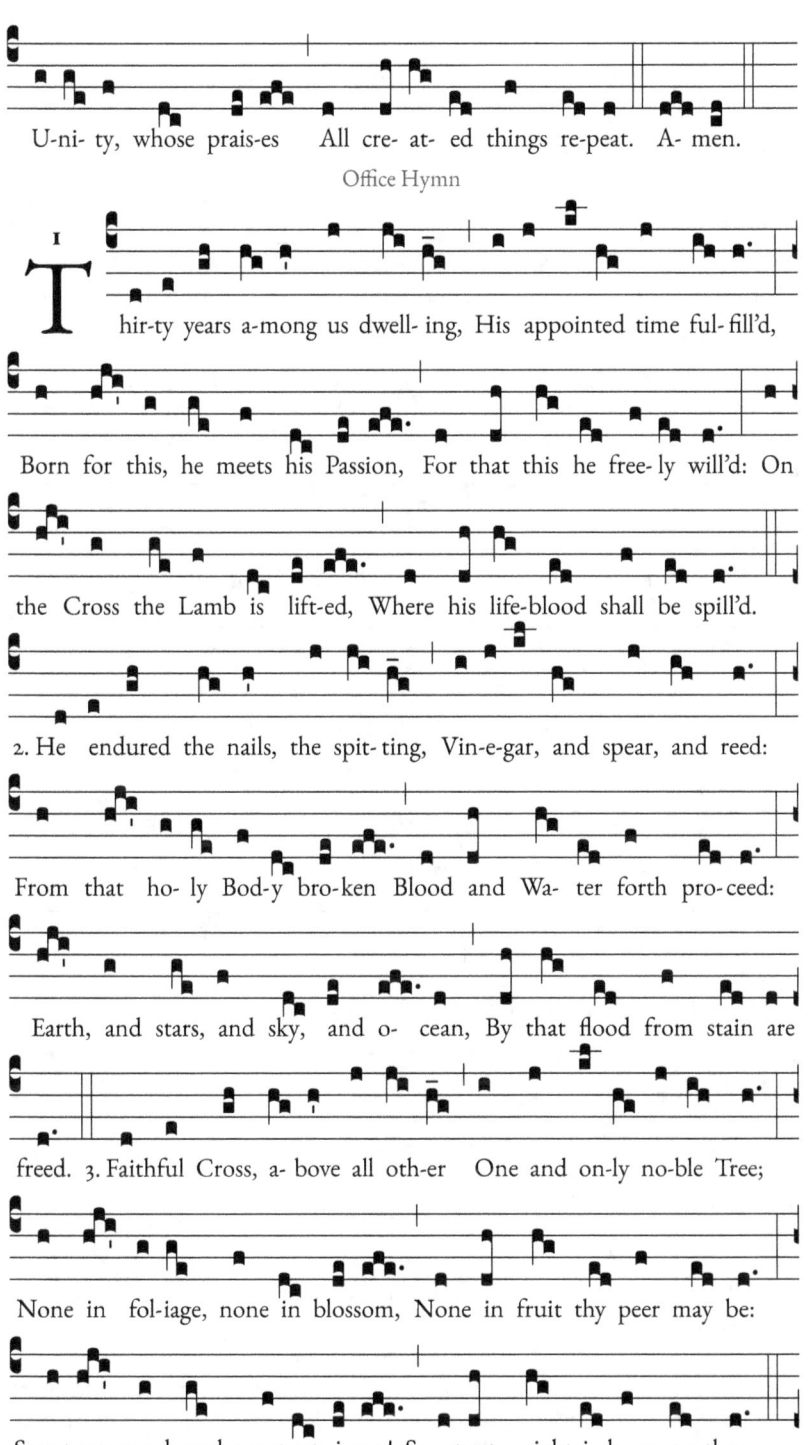

U-ni- ty, whose prais-es All cre- at- ed things re-peat. A- men.

Office Hymn

Thir-ty years a-mong us dwell- ing, His appointed time ful- fill'd, Born for this, he meets his Passion, For that this he free- ly will'd: On the Cross the Lamb is lift-ed, Where his life-blood shall be spill'd.

2. He endured the nails, the spit-ting, Vin-e-gar, and spear, and reed: From that ho- ly Bod-y bro-ken Blood and Wa- ter forth pro-ceed: Earth, and stars, and sky, and o- cean, By that flood from stain are freed.

3. Faithful Cross, a- bove all oth-er One and on-ly no-ble Tree; None in fol-iage, none in blossom, None in fruit thy peer may be: Sweet-est wood, and sweet-est i- ron! Sweet-est weight is hung on thee.

Invention of the Cross — **Proper of Saints** — 3 May

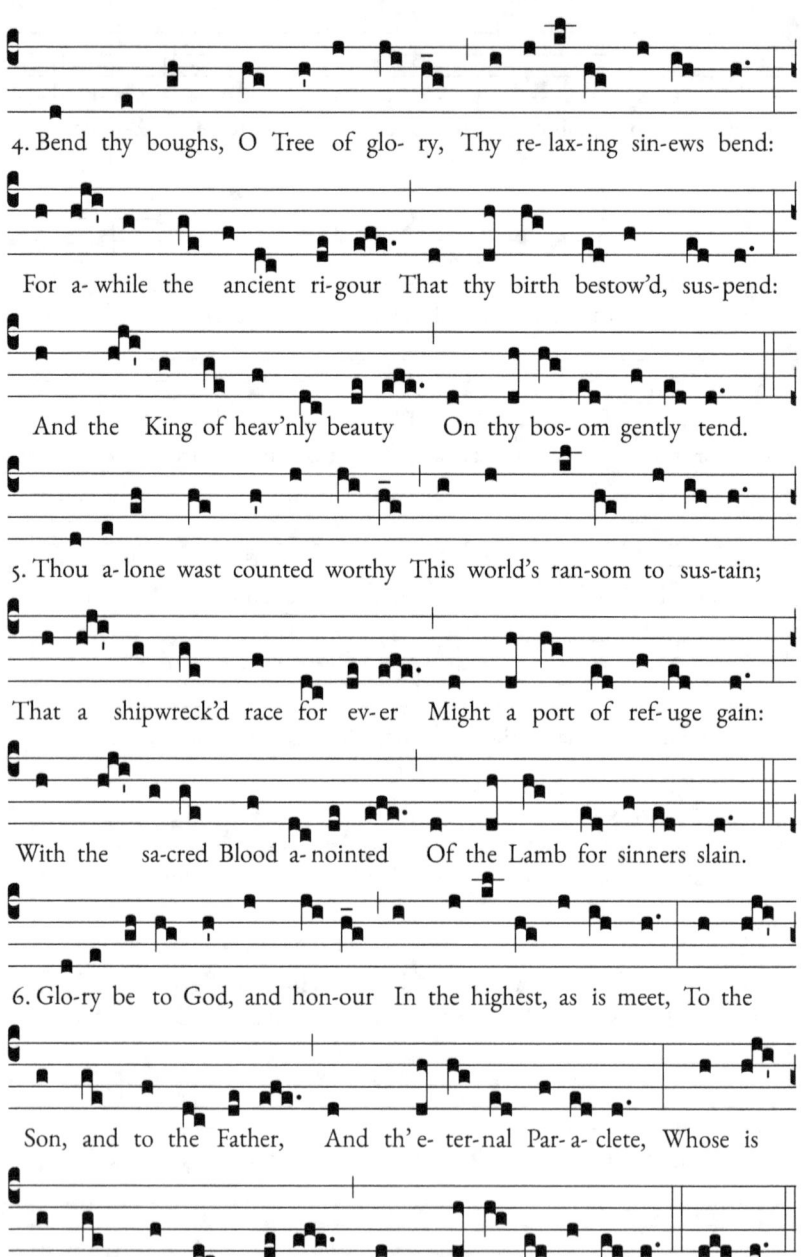

4. Bend thy boughs, O Tree of glo- ry, Thy re- lax- ing sin- ews bend:

For a- while the ancient ri- gour That thy birth bestow'd, sus- pend:

And the King of heav'n- ly beauty On thy bos- om gently tend.

5. Thou a- lone wast counted worthy This world's ran- som to sus- tain;

That a shipwreck'd race for ev- er Might a port of ref- uge gain:

With the sa- cred Blood a- nointed Of the Lamb for sinners slain.

6. Glo- ry be to God, and hon- our In the highest, as is meet, To the

Son, and to the Father, And th'e- ter- nal Par- a- clete, Whose is

boundless praise and pow- er Through the ag- es in- fi- nite. A- men.

℣. We adore thee, O Christ, and we bless thee, alleluia.

℟. Because by thy Cross thou hast redeemed the world, alleluia.

Ben. Ant. Thou alone † excellest in stature all the cedars of Lebanon: for on thee the Life of the world was hanged, on thee was Christ victorious, and death over death did for ever triumph, alleluia.

Proper of Saints

4 May — St. Monica

II Evensong

¶ II Evensong as in I Evensong, with the following Versicle & Antiphon.

℣. This sign of the Cross shall be in heaven, alleluia.
℟. When the Lord shall come to judgement, alleluia.
Mag. Ant. He the holy Cross endured, † Burst the gates of hell in twain: Begirt with might and majesty, On Easter morn he rose again, alleluia.

(3 May. Sts. Alexander, Eventius, Theodulus, and Juvenalis)

¶ The Common of Many Martyrs in Eastertide (p. 711), except for the following.

Collect

RANT, we beseech thee, Almighty God: that we, who devoutly celebrate the birthday of thy Saints Alexander, Eventius, Theodulus, and Juvenal; may, by their intercession, be delivered from all evils that beset us. Through.

Secret

ET thy plenteous benediction, we beseech thee, O Lord, come down upon these sacrifices: that it may mercifully work out our sanctification, and make us to rejoice in the solemnity of thy Saints. Through.

Postcommunion

E beseech thee, O Lord our God, that like as we whom thou hast refreshed by the partaking of thy sacred gift do offer unto thee our worship: so, by the intercession of thy Saints, Alexander, Eventius, Theodulus, and Juvenal, we may perceive the benefit of the same. Through.

(4 May. St. Monica)

¶ The Common of a Holy Matron (p. 751), except for the following.

Collect

O GOD, the comforter of them that mourn, and the salvation of them that hope in thee, who didst mercifully receive the loving tears of blessed Monica for the conversion of Augustine her son: grant to us by the intercession of them both; that we may bewail our sins, and obtain the pardon of thy grace. Through.

¶ The Epistle is the additional Epistle from the same Common (p. 753).

St. Michael Apparition **Proper of Saints** 8 May

Gospel. Luke 7:11

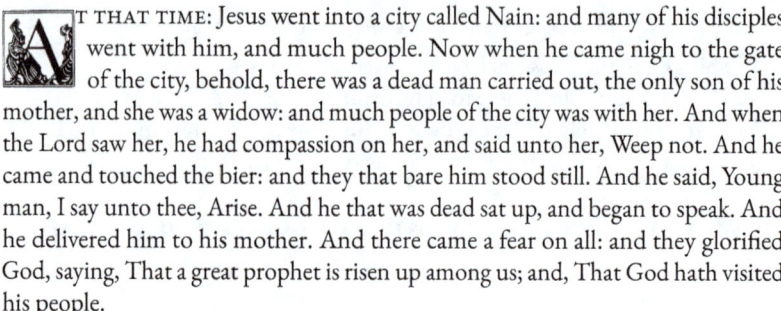T THAT TIME: Jesus went into a city called Nain: and many of his disciples went with him, and much people. Now when he came nigh to the gate of the city, behold, there was a dead man carried out, the only son of his mother, and she was a widow: and much people of the city was with her. And when the Lord saw her, he had compassion on her, and said unto her, Weep not. And he came and touched the bier: and they that bare him stood still. And he said, Young man, I say unto thee, Arise. And he that was dead sat up, and began to speak. And he delivered him to his mother. And there came a fear on all: and they glorified God, saying, That a great prophet is risen up among us; and, That God hath visited his people.

Secret

RANT, O Lord, that like as thy faithful people do acknowledge that in tribulation they have been succoured by the merits of thy Saints: so this oblation, which they here do offer unto thee in honour of the same, may be acceptable in thy sight. Through.

Postcommunion

LORD, who satisfied thy family with sacred gifts: we beseech thee that we may at all times be comforted by the intercession of her whose festival we celebrate. Through.

[6 May. St. John before the Latin Gate]

¶ The Daily Office propers are from the Common of Apostles in Easter (p. 678), with the following Antiphon for both Evensongs.

Mag. Ant. John the Apostle, † being cast into a caldron of boiling oil, by virtue of protecting grace came forth unharmed, alleluia.

(7 May. St. Alexis Toth)

¶ The First Common of a Confessor not a Bishop (p. 725).

8 May. The Apparition of St. Michael the Archangel

Greater Double

Introit

PRAISE the Lord, all ye Angels of his: ye that excel in strength ye that fulfil his commandment, and hearken unto the voice of his words. *Ps.* Praise the Lord, O my soul; and all that is within me praise his holy name

8 May   **Proper of Saints**   *St. Michael Apparition*

Collect

O EVERLASTING God, who hast ordained and constituted the services of Angels and men in a wonderful order; Mercifully grant that, as thy holy Angels always do thee service in heaven, so, by thy appointment, they may succour and defend us on earth. Through.

Epistle. Revelation 1:1

IN THOSE DAYS: God shewed the things which must shortly come to pass, and he sent and. signified it by his Angel unto his servant John, Who bare record of the word of God, and of the testimony of Jesus Christ, and of all things that he saw. Blessed is he that readeth, and they that hear the words of this prophecy, and keep those things which are written therein: for the time is at hand. John to the seven churches which are in Asia: Grace be unto you, and peace, from him which is, and which was, and which is to come; and from the seven Spirits which are before his throne; And from Jesus Christ, who is the faithful witness, and the first begotten of the dead, and the prince of the kings of the earth. Unto him that loved us, and washed us from our sins in his own blood.

Alleluia. Alleluia, alleluia. ℣. Holy Archangel Michael, defend us in the battle; that we perish not in the dreadful judgement. Alleluia. ℣. The sea was shaken, and the earth trembled, when the Archangel Michael came down from heaven. Alleluia.

Gospel. Matthew 18:1

AT THAT TIME: The disciples came unto Jesus, saying, Who is the greatest in the kingdom of heaven? And Jesus called a little child unto him, and set him in the midst of them, And said, Verily I say unto you, Except ye be converted, and become as little children, ye shall not enter into the kingdom of heaven. Whosoever therefore shall humble himself as this little child, the same is greatest in the kingdom of heaven. And whoso shall receive one such little child in my name receiveth me. But whoso shall offend one of these little ones which believe in me, it were better for him that a millstone were hanged about his neck, and that he were drowned in the depth of the sea. Woe unto the world because of offences! for it must needs be that offences come; but woe to that man by whom the offence cometh! Wherefore if thy hand or thy foot offend thee, cut them off, and cast them from thee: it is better for thee to enter into life halt or maimed, rather than having two hands or two feet to be cast into everlasting fire. And if thine eye offend thee, pluck it out, and cast it from thee: it is better for thee to enter into life with one eye, rather than having two eyes to be cast into hell fire. Take heed that ye despise not one of these little ones; for I say unto you, That in heaven their angels do always behold the face of my Father which is in heaven.

Sts. Gordian & Epimachus   # Proper of Saints   10 May

Secret

E offer thee, O Lord, sacrifices of praise, humbly beseeching thee: that by the prayers of the Angels interceding for us, thou wouldest both graciously accept the same, and grant that they may avail to our salvation. Through.

Communion. O all ye Angels of the Lord, bless ye the Lord: sing ye praises, and magnify him above all for ever.

Postcommunion

LORD, forasmuch as we put our trust in the intercession of thy blessed Archangel Michael; we humbly beseech thee; that those things which we touch with our lips we may likewise receive into our hearts. Through.

℟ If it be a Sunday, the Gospel of this Feast is read at the end.

(8 May. Pope St. Boniface IV)

℟ The First Common of a Confessor Bishop (p. 715).

9 May. St. Gregory Nazianzen

Double

℟ The propers are from the Common of Doctors (p. 723), using the additional Epistle.

(10 May. Sts. Gordian & Epimachus)

℟ The Common of Many Martyrs in Eastertide (p. 711), with the additional Epistle (p. 714), except for the following.

Collect

RANT, we beseech thee, Almighty God: that we, who celebrate the festival of thy blessed Martyrs Gordian and Epimachus, may be aided by their intercession with thee. Through.

Secret

E beseech thee, O Lord, mercifully to accept this our sacrifice, which we offer unto thee, pleading the merits of thy blessed Martyrs Gordian and Epimachus: that the same may effectually avail for our perpetual succour. Through.

Postcommunion

E beseech thee, Almighty God: that we, who have received this heavenly food, may at the intercession of thy blessed Martyrs, Gordian and Epimachus, be thereby defended against all adversities. Through.

(12 May. Sts. Nereus, Achilles, Domitilla, and Pancras)

Introit

BEHOLD, the eye of the Lord is upon them that fear him, and put their trust in his mercy, alleluia: to deliver their soul from death: for he is our help and our shield, alleluia, alleluia. *Ps.* Rejoice in the Lord, O ye righteous: for it becometh well the just to be thankful.

Collect

WE beseech thee, O Lord, that the blessed solemnity of thy Martyrs, Nereus, Achilles, Domitilla, and Pancras, may ever protect us: and render us worthy of thy service. Through.

¶ The Epistle is from the Common of a Martyr in Eastertide (p. 705).

Alleluia. Alleluia, alleluia. ℣. This is the true brotherhood which overcame the wickedness of the world: which followed Christ, gaining heaven's glorious realms. Alleluia. ℣. The noble army of Martyrs praise thee, O Lord. Alleluia.

Gospel. John 4:46

AT THAT TIME: There was a certain nobleman, whose son was sick at Capernaum. When he heard that Jesus was come out of Judaea into Galilee, he went unto him, and besought him that he would come down, and heal his son: for he was at the point of death. Then said Jesus unto him, Except ye see signs and wonders, ye will not believe. The nobleman saith unto him, Sir, come down ere my child die. Jesus saith unto him, Go thy way; thy son liveth. And the man believed the word that Jesus had spoken unto him, and he went his way. And as he was now going down, his servants met him, and told him, saying, Thy son liveth. Then enquired he of them the hour when he began to amend. And they said unto him, Yesterday at the seventh hour the fever left him. So the father knew that it was at the same hour, in the which Jesus said unto him, Thy son liveth: and himself believed, and his whole house.

Offertory. O Lord, the very heavens shall praise thy wondrous works: and thy truth in the congregation of the saints, alleluia, alleluia.

Secret

WE beseech thee, O Lord, that the confession of thy holy Martyrs Nereus, Achilles, Domitilla and Pancras may be pleasing unto thee: that it may both commend our gifts, and ever implore for us thy pardon. Through.

Communion. Rejoice in the Lord, O ye righteous, alleluia: for it becometh well the just to be thankful, alleluia.

St. Venantius — Proper of Saints — 18 May

Postcommunion

E beseech thee, O Lord: that by the prayers of thy blessed Martyrs Nereus, Achilles, Domitilla and Pancras, the holy sacraments which we have received may profit us to the increase of thy merciful pardon. Though.

(14 May. St. Boniface of Tarsus)

¶ The propers are from the Common of a Martyr in Eastertide (p. 705), except for the following.

Collect

RANT, we beseech thee, Almighty God: that we, who celebrate the festival of blessed Boniface thy Martyr, may be aided by his intercession with thee. Through.

Secret

E beseech thee, O Lord, to accept our prayers and oblations: and graciously hearken unto us whom thou dost cleanse by thy heavenly mysteries. Through.

Postcommunion

E beseech thee, O Lord our God, that like as we, whom thou hast refreshed by the partaking of thy sacred gift, do offer unto thee our worship: so by the intercession of blessed Boniface, thy Martyr, we may perceive the benefits of the same. Through.

18 May. St. Venantius

Double

¶ The propers are from the Common of a Martyr in Eastertide (p. 705), with the Prayers as followeth.

Collect

GOD, who hast hallowed this day by the triumph of blessed Venantius, thy Martyr: graciously hear the prayers of thy people, and grant; that we who venerate his merits may imitate the constancy of his faith. Through.

Secret

LMIGHTY God, let the merits of blessed Venantius render this oblation acceptable unto thee: that we, being succoured by his assistance, may be made partakers of his glory. Through.

Proper of Saints — *St. Augustine Canterbury* — 26 May

Postcommunion

E have received, O Lord, the sacraments of everlasting life, humbly beseeching thee: that through the prayers of blessed Venantius thy Martyr on our behalf, they may obtain for us both pardon and grace. Through.

(19 May. St. Pudentiana)

¶ The First Common of a Virgin (p. 742).

(22 May. St. Romanus)

¶ The Common of Abbots (p. 732).

(24 May. St. Vincent of Lerins)

¶ The First Common of a Confessor not a Bishop (p. 725).

(25 May. Pope St. Urban I)

¶ The First Common of a Martyr Bishop (p. 682).

26 May. St. Augustine of Canterbury

Double

¶ The Daily Office propers are from the First Common of a Confessor Bishop (p. 715).

Introit

ET thy priests, O Lord, be clothed with righteousness: and let thy saints sing with joyfulness: for thy servant David's sake, turn not away the presence of thine Anointed. Alleluia, alleluia. *Ps.* Lord, remember David: and all his trouble.

Collect

O GOD, who didst give the blessed Bishop Augustine to be the first Teacher of the English people: grant us, we beseech thee; that we who proclaim his merits on earth may perceive his intercession in heaven. Through.

¶ Commemoration of St. Eleutherius (p. 517).

St. Augustine Canterbury **Proper of Saints** 26 May

Epistle. Hebrews 7:23

BRETHREN: They were many priests, because they were not suffered to continue by reason of death: But this man, because he continueth ever, hath an unchangeable priesthood. Wherefore he is able also to save them to the uttermost that come unto God by him, seeing he ever liveth to make intercession for them. For such an high priest became us, who is holy, harmless, undefiled, separate from sinners, and made higher than the heavens; Who needeth not daily, as those high priests, to offer up sacrifice, first for his own sins, and then for the people's: for this he did once, when he offered up himself, Jesus Christ our Lord.

Alleluia. Alleluia, alleluia. ℣. The Lord sware, and will not repent: Thou art a priest for ever after the order of Melchisedech. Alleluia. ℣. The Lord loved him, and adorned him: he clothed him with a robe of glory. Alleluia.

Gospel. Luke 10:1

AT THAT TIME: The Lord appointed other seventy also, and sent them two and two before his face into every city and place, whither he himself would come. Therefore said he unto them, The harvest truly is great, but the labourers are few: pray ye therefore the Lord of the harvest, that he would send forth labourers into his harvest. Go your ways: behold, I send you forth as lambs among wolves. Carry neither purse, nor scrip, nor shoes: and salute no man by the way. And into whatsoever house ye enter, first say, Peace be to this house. And if the son of peace be there, your peace shall rest upon it: if not, it shall turn to you again. And in the same house remain, eating and drinking such things as they give: for the labourer is worthy of his hire. Go not from house to house. And into whatsoever city ye enter, and they receive you, eat such things as are set before you: And heal the sick that are therein, and say unto them, The kingdom of God is come nigh unto you.

Offertory. My truth and my mercy shall be with him: and in my name shall his horn be exalted. Alleluia.

Secret

WE beseech thee, O Lord, that the gifts which we offer may be acceptable unto thee: whereby we venerate the merits of blessed Augustine, thy Confessor and Bishop, and likewise call to remembrance the pledges of our life and freedom. Through.

¶ Commemoration of St. Eleutherius (p. 517).

Communion. Blessed is the servant, whom the lord when he cometh shall find watching: verily I say unto you, He shall make him ruler over all his goods. Alleluia.

26 May   **Proper of Saints**   *Pope St. Eleutherius*

Postcommunion

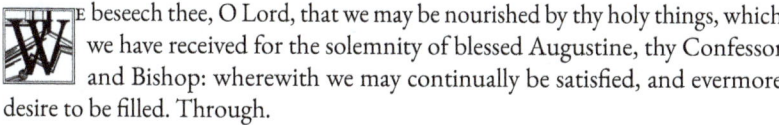E beseech thee, O Lord, that we may be nourished by thy holy things, which we have received for the solemnity of blessed Augustine, thy Confessor and Bishop: wherewith we may continually be satisfied, and evermore desire to be filled. Through.

℣ Commemoration of St. Eleutherius (p. 517).

(26 May. Pope St. Eleutherius)

℣ The Common of a Martyr in Eastertide (p. 705), except for the following.

Collect

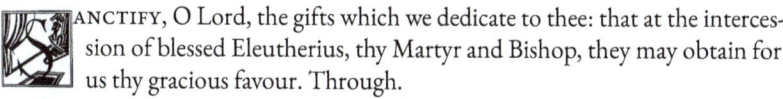LMIGHTY God, mercifully look upon our infirmities: that, whereas we are oppressed by the burden of our sins, the glorious intercession of blessed Eleutherius, thy Martyr and Bishop, may be our succour and defence. Through.

Secret

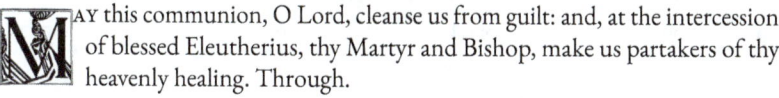ANCTIFY, O Lord, the gifts which we dedicate to thee: that at the intercession of blessed Eleutherius, thy Martyr and Bishop, they may obtain for us thy gracious favour. Through.

Postcommunion

AY this communion, O Lord, cleanse us from guilt: and, at the intercession of blessed Eleutherius, thy Martyr and Bishop, make us partakers of thy heavenly healing. Through.

Proper of Saints

27 May. St. Bede the Venerable

Double

℣ The propers are from the Common of Doctors (p. 723), with the following Prayers.

Collect

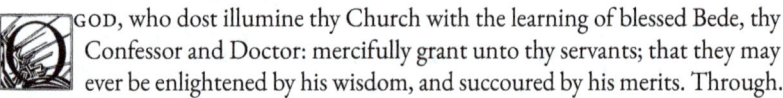GOD, who dost illumine thy Church with the learning of blessed Bede, thy Confessor and Doctor: mercifully grant unto thy servants; that they may ever be enlightened by his wisdom, and succoured by his merits. Through.

℣ Commemoration of Pope St. John I, from the Second Collect of the Common of a Martyr in Eastertide (p. 705).

Secret

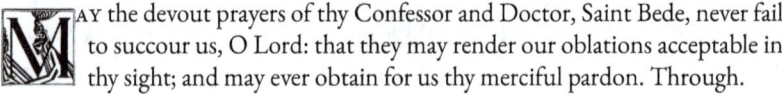AY the devout prayers of thy Confessor and Doctor, Saint Bede, never fail to succour us, O Lord: that they may render our oblations acceptable in thy sight; and may ever obtain for us thy merciful pardon. Through.

℣ Commemoration of Pope St. John I, from the Second Secret of the Common of a Martyr in Eastertide (p. 705).

Postcommunion

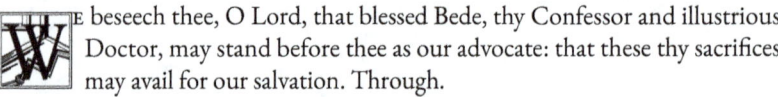E beseech thee, O Lord, that blessed Bede, thy Confessor and illustrious Doctor, may stand before thee as our advocate: that these thy sacrifices may avail for our salvation. Through.

℣ Commemoration of Pope St. John I, from the Second Postcommunion of the Common of a Martyr in Eastertide (p. 705).

(27 May. Pope St. John I)

℣ The Common of a Martyr in Eastertide (p. 705), using the Second Prayers.

(30 May. Pope St. Felix I)

℣ In Eastertide, the Common of a Martyr in Eastertide (p. 705), with the First Collect and the Second Secret and Postcommunion.

℣ Outside of Eastertide, the First Common of a Martyr Bishop (p. 682).

(31 May. St. Petronilla)

℣ The Second Common of a Virgin (p. 744).

(2 June. Sts. Marcellinus, Peter, & Erasmus)

※ Outside of Eastertide, the propers are as followeth.

※ In Eastertide, the Common of Many Martyrs in Eastertide (p. 711) with the Prayers and Epistle as followeth.

Introit

HE righteous cry, and the Lord heareth them: and delivereth them out of all their troubles. *Ps.* I will alway give thanks unto the Lord: his praise shall ever be in my mouth.

Collect

GOD, who makest us glad with the yearly solemnity of thy blessed Martyrs, Marcellinus, Peter, and Erasmus: grant, we beseech thee; that, as we rejoice in their merits, so we may be enkindled by their example. Through.

※ The Epistle is from the third additional Epistle of the Third Common of Many Martyrs (p. 702).

Gradual. The righteous cry, and the Lord heareth them: and delivereth them out of all their troubles. ℣. The Lord is nigh unto them that are of a contrite heart: and will save such as be of an humble spirit.

Alleluia. Alleluia, alleluia. ℣. I have chosen you out of the world that ye should go and bring forth fruit; and that your fruit should remain. Alleluia.

※ In Eastertide, the following Alleluia Verse replaces the Gradual & Lesser Alleluia.

Alleluia. Alleluia, alleluia. ℣. I have chosen you out of the world, that ye should go and bring forth fruit; and that your fruit should remain. Alleluia. ℣. Right dear in the sight of the Lord is the death of his saints. Alleluia.

※ The Gospel is from the First Common of Many Martyrs (p. 692).

Offertory. Be glad, ye righteous, and rejoice in the Lord: and be joyful, all ye that are true of heart.

Secret

E beseech thee, O Lord, that this sacrifice which we offer in remembrance of the birthday of thy holy Martyrs: may both loose the bonds of our iniquity, and obtain for us the gifts of thy mercy. Through.

Communion. The souls of the just are in the hand of God, and there shall no torment of malice touch them: in the sight of the unwise they seemed to die, but they are in peace.

Proper of Saints

Postcommunion

LORD, who hast satisfied us with this sacred gift, we humbly beseech thee: that in the mysteries which we celebrate in this service of our bounden duty, we may perceive the increase of thy saving grace. Through.

5 June. St. Boniface

Double

¶ The Daily Office propers are from the First Common of a Martyr Bishop (p. 682).

Introit

I WILL rejoice in Jerusalem and joy in my people: and the voice of weeping shall be no more heard in her, nor the voice of crying. Mine elect shall not labour in vain, nor bring forth for trouble: for they are the seed of the blessed of the Lord, and their offspring with them. (Alleluia, alleluia.) *Ps.* We have heard with our ears, O God: our fathers have told us, what thou hast done in their time of old.

Collect

GOD, who by the zeal of blessed Boniface, thy Martyr and Bishop, didst vouchsafe to call a multitude of peoples to the knowledge of thy name: mercifully grant; that we who celebrate his festival may likewise perceive his advocacy. Through.

Epistle. Ecclesiasticus 44:1

LET us now praise famous men, And our fathers that begat us. The Lord manifested in them great glory, Even his mighty power from the beginning. Such as did bear rule in their kingdoms, And were men renowned for their power, Giving counsel by their understanding, Such as have brought tidings in prophecies: Leaders of the people by their counsels, And by their understanding men of learning for the people; Wise were their words in their instruction: Such as sought out musical tunes, And set forth verses in writing: Rich men furnished with ability, Living peaceably in their habitations: All these were honoured in their generations, And were a glory in their days. There be of them, that have left a name behind them, To declare their praises. And some there be, which have no memorial; Who are perished as though they had not been, And are become as though they had not been born; And their children after them. But these were men of mercy, Whose righteous deeds have not been forgotten. With their seed shall remain continually a good inheritance; Their children are within the covenants. Their seed standeth fast, And their children for their sakes. Their seed shall remain for ever, And their glory shall not be blotted out. Their bodies were buried in peace, And their name liveth to all generations. Peoples will declare their wisdom, And the congregation telleth out their praise.

Gradual. Rejoice, inasmuch as ye are partakers of Christ's sufferings, that, when his glory shall be revealed, ye may be glad also with exceeding joy. ℣. If ye be reproached for the name of Christ, happy are ye: for the spirit of glory and of God resteth upon you.

Alleluia. Alleluia, alleluia. ℣. I will extend peace to her like a river, and glory like a flowing stream. Alleluia.

¶ In Eastertide, the following Alleluia Verse replaces the Gradual & Lesser Alleluia.

Alleluia. Alleluia, alleluia. ℣. Rejoice ye with Jerusalem, and be glad with her, all ye that love the Lord. Alleluia. ℣. When ye see this, your heart shall rejoice: and the hand of the Lord shall be known toward his servants. Alleluia.

Gospel. Matthew 5:1

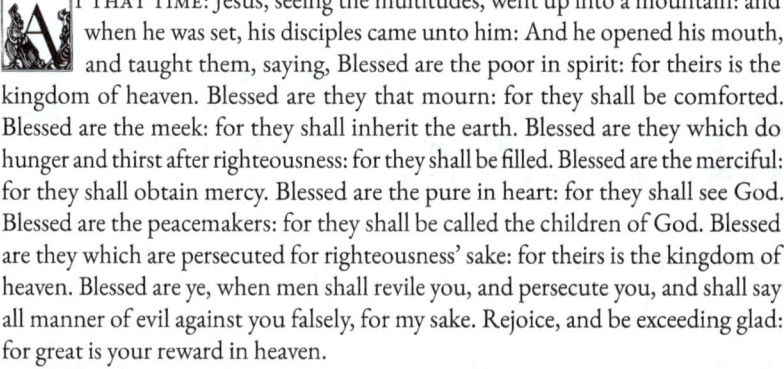AT THAT TIME: Jesus, seeing the multitudes, went up into a mountain: and when he was set, his disciples came unto him: And he opened his mouth, and taught them, saying, Blessed are the poor in spirit: for theirs is the kingdom of heaven. Blessed are they that mourn: for they shall be comforted. Blessed are the meek: for they shall inherit the earth. Blessed are they which do hunger and thirst after righteousness: for they shall be filled. Blessed are the merciful: for they shall obtain mercy. Blessed are the pure in heart: for they shall see God. Blessed are the peacemakers: for they shall be called the children of God. Blessed are they which are persecuted for righteousness' sake: for theirs is the kingdom of heaven. Blessed are ye, when men shall revile you, and persecute you, and shall say all manner of evil against you falsely, for my sake. Rejoice, and be exceeding glad: for great is your reward in heaven.

Offertory. I will thank the Lord for giving me warning: I have set God always before me, for he is on my right hand, therefore I shall not fall. (Alleluia.)

Secret

LET thy plenteous benediction, we beseech thee, O Lord, come down upon these sacrifices: that it may mercifully work out our sanctification; and make us to rejoice in the solemnity of holy Boniface, thy Martyr and Bishop. Through.

Communion. To him that overcometh will I grant to sit with me in my throne: even as I also overcame, and am set down with my Father in his throne. (Alleluia.)

Postcommunion

O LORD, who hast sanctified us with this saving mystery: we beseech thee; that holy Boniface thy Martyr and Bishop, whom thou hast given to be our advocate and guide, may never fail devoutly to pray for us. Through.

Sts. Primus & Felician   **Proper of Saints**   9 June

9 June. St. Columba of Iona

Double

¶ The propers are from the Common of Abbots (p. 732), with Commemoration of Sts. Primus & Felician.

(9 June. Sts. Primus & Felician)

¶ Outside of Eastertide, the propers are as followeth.

¶ In Eastertide, the Common of Many Martyrs in Eastertide (p. 711, with the Prayers, Greater Alleluia, and Gospel as followeth.

Introit

ET the people tell of the wisdom of the Saints, and let the church shew forth their praise: their names shall live for evermore. *Ps.* Rejoice in the Lord, O ye righteous: for it becometh well the just to be thankful.

Collect

LORD, we beseech thee, make us ever to rejoice in the festival of thy holy Martyrs Primus and Felician: that by their prayers we may perceive the gifts of thy protection. Through.

¶ The Epistle is from the Second Common of Many Martyrs (p. 699).

Gradual. O Lord, the very heavens shall praise thy wondrous works: and thy truth in the congregation of the saints. ℣. My song shall be alway of the loving-kindness of the Lord: from one generation to another.

Alleluia. Alleluia, alleluia. ℣. This is the true brotherhood, which overcame the wickedness of the world: which followed Christ, gaining heaven's glorious realms. Alleluia.

¶ In Eastertide, the following Alleluia Verse replaces the Gradual & Lesser Alleluia.

Alleluia. Alleluia, alleluia. ℣. This is the true brotherhood which overcame the wickedness of the world: which followed Christ, gaining heaven's glorious realms. Alleluia. ℣. The noble army of Martyrs praise thee, O Lord. Alleluia.

Gospel. Matthew 11:25

T THAT TIME: Jesus answered and said: I thank thee, O Father, Lord of heaven and earth, because thou hast hid these things from the wise and prudent, and hast revealed them unto babes. Even so, Father: for so it seemed good in thy sight. All things are delivered unto me of my Father: and no man knoweth the Son, but the Father; neither knoweth any man the Father, save the Son, and he to whomsoever the Son will reveal him. Come unto me, all ye that labour and are heavy laden, and I will give you rest. Take my yoke upon you, and learn of me; for I am meek and lowly in heart: and ye shall find rest unto your souls. For my yoke is easy, and my burden is light.

Offertory. God is wonderful in his holy ones: even the God of Israel, he will give strength and power unto his people: blessed be God, alleluia.

Secret

E beseech thee, O Lord, that the oblation to be consecrated on the day of the precious death of thy Martyrs may be acceptable unto thee: for the cleansing of our sins, and for the commending to thee of the prayers of thy servants. Through.

Communion. I have chosen you out of the world, that ye should go and bring forth fruit, and that your fruit should remain.

Postcommunion

E beseech thee, Almighty God: that the solemnity of thy holy Martyrs Primus and Felician, which we have celebrated with heavenly mysteries, may obtain for us thy merciful pardon. Through.

(10 June. St. Margaret of Scotland)

¶ The Common of a Holy Matron (p. 751), except for the following.

Collect

GOD, who didst render the blessed Queen Margaret wondrous by reason of her eminent charity towards the poor: grant; that, by her intercession and example, thy charity may continually increase in our hearts. Through.

Secret

RANT, O Lord, that like as thy faithful people do acknowledge that in tribulation they have been succoured by the merits of thy Saints: so this oblation, which they here do offer unto thee in honour of the same, may be acceptable in thy sight. Through.

Postcommunion

LORD, who hast satisfied thy family with sacred gifts: we beseech thee that we may at all times be comforted by the intercession of her whose festival we celebrate. Through.

Sts. Basilides &c. — # Proper of Saints — 12 June

[11 June. St. Barnabas]

¶ The Daily Office propers are from the Common of Apostles (p. 673).

¶ In Eastertide, the Daily Office propers are from the Common of Apostles in Eastertide (p. 678).

(12 June. Sts. Basilides, Cyrinus, Nabor, and Nazarius)

¶ Outside of Eastertide, the propers are as followeth.

¶ In Eastertide, the propers are from the Common of Many Martyrs in Eastertide (p. 711), with the following Prayers.

Introit

LET the sorrowful sighing of the prisoners, O Lord, come before thee: reward thou our neighbours sevenfold into their bosom: avenge thou the blood of thy Saints, that is shed. *Ps.* O God, the heathen are come into thine inheritance: thy holy temple have they defiled: and made Jerusalem an heap of stones.

Collect

WE beseech thee, O Lord, that the observance of the birthday of thy holy Martyrs Basilides, Cyrinus, Nabor, and Nazarius may shine brightly upon us: that the everlasting excellence which they have obtained may increase by the fruits of our devotion. Through.

¶ The Epistle is from the Third Common of Many Martyrs (p. 700).

Gradual. Avenge thou, O Lord, the blood of thy Saints that is shed. ℣. The dead bodies of thy servants have they given to be meat unto the fowls of the air: and the flesh of thy saints unto the beasts of the land

Alleluia. Alleluia, alleluia. ℣. The bodies of the Saints are buried in peace: but their name liveth for evermore. Alleluia.

¶ The Gospel is from the first additional Gospel from the Third Common of Many Martyrs (p. 703).

Offertory. Let the Saints be joyful with glory, let them rejoice in their beds: let the praises of God be in their mouth.

Secret

WE solemnly offer unto thee, O Lord, these sacrifices, rehearsing thy wondrous works, in honour of the blood of thy Saints Basilides, Cyrinus, Nabor, and Nazarius: whereby their glorious victory was made perfect. Through.

Communion. The dead bodies of thy servants, O Lord, have they given to be meat unto the fowls of the air, and the flesh of thy saints unto the beasts of the land: according to the greatness of thy power, preserve thou those that are appointed to die.

Postcommunion

RANT, we beseech thee, O Lord: that we, ever celebrating the festival of thy holy Martyrs Basilides, Cyrinus, Nabor, and Nazarius; may continually perceive their advocacy. Through.

14 June. St. Basil the Great

Greater Double

¶ The Daily Office propers are from the Common of Doctors (p. 723).

Introit

N the midst of the Church he opened his mouth: and the Lord filled him with the spirit of wisdom and of understanding: he clothed him with a robe of glory. *Ps.* It is a good thing to give thanks unto the Lord: and to sing praises unto thy name, O Most Highest.

Collect

E beseech thee, O Lord, graciously to hear the prayers which we offer unto thee on the solemnity of blessed Basil, thy Confessor and Bishop: that, like as he was found worthy to do thee faithful service, so by his merits and intercession we may be absolved from all our sins. Through.

¶ The Epistle is from the Common of Doctors (p. 723).

Gradual. The mouth of the righteous is exercised in wisdom, and his tongue will be talking of judgment. ℣. The law of his God is in his heart: and his goings shall not slide.

Alleluia. Alleluia, alleluia. ℣. I have found David my servant, with my holy oil have I anointed him. Alleluia.

Gospel. Luke 14:26

T THAT TIME: Jesus said unto the multitudes: If any man come to me, and hate not his father, and mother, and wife, and children, and brethren, and sisters, yea, and his own life also, he cannot be my disciple. And whosoever doth not bear his cross, and come after me, cannot be my disciple. For which of you, intending to build a tower, sitteth not down first, and counteth the cost, whether he have sufficient to finish it? Lest haply, after he hath laid the foundation, and is not able to finish it, all that behold it begin to mock him, Saying, This man began to build, and was not able to finish. Or what king, going to make war against another king, sitteth not down first, and consulteth whether he be able with ten thousand to meet him that cometh against him with twenty thousand? Or else, while the other is yet a great way off, he sendeth an ambassage, and desireth conditions of peace. So likewise, whosoever he be of you that forsaketh not all that he hath, he cannot be my disciple. Salt is good: but if the salt have lost his savour, wherewith shall it be seasoned? It is neither fit for the land, nor yet for the dunghill; but men cast it out. He that hath ears to hear, let him hear.

Offertory. My truth and my mercy shall be with him: and in my name shall his horn be exalted.

Secret

E beseech thee, O Lord, that our devout observance of the yearly solemnity of Saint Basil, thy Confessor and Bishop, may render us acceptable unto thy loving kindness: that this service of propitiation, which we duly offer, may be profitable unto him for the reward of blessedness, and obtain for us the gifts of thy grace. Through.

Communion. A faithful and wise servant, whom the lord hath made ruler over his household: to give them their portion of meat in due season.

Postcommunion

GOD, who rewardest the souls of them that put their trust in thee: vouchsafe; that we who keep the solemn festival of blessed Basil, thy Confessor and Bishop, may by his prayers obtain thy merciful pardon. Through.

(15 June. Sts. Vitus, Modestus, and Crescentia)

¶ Outside of Eastertide, the propers are as followeth.

¶ In Eastertide, the Common of Many Martyrs in Eastertide (p. 711), with Prayers and Gospel as followeth.

Introit

REAT are the troubles of the righteous, but the Lord delivereth him out of all: the Lord keepeth all his bones: so that not one of them is broken. *Ps.* I will alway give thanks unto the Lord: his praise shall ever be in my mouth.

Collect

GRANT, O Lord, we beseech thee, that, at the intercession of thy holy Martyrs, Vitus, Modestus, and Crescentia, thy Church may learn not to be highminded, but to grow in such lowliness as is acceptable unto thee: that, despising things evil, she may with bounteous charity perform those things that be right. Through.

18 June   **Proper of Saints**   *St. Ephrem Syrian*

¶ The Epistle is from First Common of Many Martyrs (p. 697).

Gradual. Let the Saints be joyful with glory: let them rejoice in their beds. ℣. O sing unto the Lord a new song: let the congregation of saints praise him.

Alleluia. Alleluia, alleluia. ℣. Thy Saints shall give thanks unto thee, O Lord: they shew the glory of thy kingdom. Alleluia.

Gospel. Luke 10:16

T THAT TIME: Jesus said unto his disciples: He that heareth you heareth me; and he that despiseth you despiseth me; and he that despiseth me despiseth him that sent me. And the seventy returned again with joy, saying, Lord, even the devils are subject unto us through thy name. And he said unto them, I beheld Satan as lightning fall from heaven. Behold, I give unto you power to tread on serpents and scorpions, and over all the power of the enemy: and nothing shall by any means hurt you. Notwithstanding in this rejoice not, that the spirits are subject unto you; but rather rejoice, because your names are written in heaven.

Secret

LORD, forasmuch as the gifts which we offer for thy Saints do shew forth the glory of thy divine power: so may they achieve in us the effects of thy salvation. Through.

Communion. The souls of the just are in the hand of God, and there shall no torment of malice touch them: in the sight of the unwise they seemed to die: but they are in peace.

Postcommunion

LORD, who hast fulfilled us with thy solemn benediction: we beseech thee; that through the intercession of thy holy Martyrs Vitus, Modestus, and Crescentia, the healing of this sacrament may be profitable both for our bodies and our souls. Through.

18 June. St. Ephrem the Syrian

Double

¶ The propers are from the Common of Doctors (p. 723), with the Prayers as followeth.

Collect

GOD, who wast pleased to adorn thy Church with the wondrous learning and glorious merits of the life of blessed Ephram, thy Confessor and Doctor: we humbly entreat thee; that at his intercession thou wouldest defend her with thy continual power against the snares of error and wickedness. Through.

¶ Commemoration of Sts. Marcus & Marcellianus (p. 528).

Sts. Marcus &c. **Proper of Saints** 18 June

Secret

AY the devout prayers of Saint Ephrem, thy Confessor and Doctor, never fail to succour us, O Lord: that they may render our oblations acceptable in thy sight; and may ever obtain for us thy merciful pardon. Through.

¶ Commemoration of Sts. Marcus & Marcellianus (p. 529).

Postcommunion

E beseech thee, O Lord, that blessed Ephrem, thy Confessor and illustrious Doctor, may stand before thee as our advocate: that these thy sacrifices may avail for our salvation. Through.

¶ Commemoration of Sts. Marcus & Marcellianus (p. 529).

(18 June. Sts. Marcus and Marcellianus)

¶ Outside Eastertide, the propers are as followeth.

¶ In Eastertide, the Common of Many Martyrs in Eastertide (p. 711), with the Prayers and Gospel as followeth.

Introit

UT the salvation of the righteous cometh of the Lord: who is also their strength in the time of trouble. *Ps.* Fret not thyself because of the ungodly: neither be thou envious against the evil-doers.

Collect

RANT, we beseech thee, Almighty God: that we who devoutly celebrate the birthday of thy holy Martyrs Marcus and Marcellianus; may, by their intercession, be delivered from all evils that beset us. Through.

¶ The Epistle is from the second additional Epistle from the Third Common of Many Martyrs (p. 702).

Gradual. The souls of the just are in the hand of God: and there shall no torment of malice touch them. ℣. In the eyes of the unwise they seemed to die: but they are in peace.

Alleluia. Alleluia, alleluia. ℣. This is the true brotherhood which no conflict could sunder: they who, shedding their blood, followed the Lord. Alleluía.

¶ In Eastertide, the following Alleluia Verse replaces the Gradual & Lesser Alleluia.

Alleluia. Alleluia, alleluia. ℣. This is the true brotherhood which no conflict could sunder: they who, shedding their blood, followed the Lord. Alleluia. ℣. The noble army of Martyrs praise thee, O Lord. Alleluia.

¶ The Gospel is from the fourth additional Gospel from the Third Common of Many Martyrs (p. 704).

19 June   **Proper of Saints**   *Sts. Gervase & Protase*

Offertory. Our soul is escaped even as a bird out of the snare of the fowler: the snare is broken, and we are delivered.

Secret

ANCTIFY, O Lord, the gifts which we dedicate unto thee: that, at the intercession of thy holy Martyrs Marcus and Marcellianus, they may obtain for us thy gracious favour. Through.

Communion. Verily I say unto you, whatsoever ye have done unto one of the least of mine, ye have done it unto me: come, ye blessed of my Father, inherit the kingdom prepared for you from the foundation of the world.

Postcommunion

LORD, who hast satisfied us with the gift of thy salvation, we humbly beseech thee: that as we joyfully taste thereof, so at the intercession of thy holy Martyrs Marcus and Marcellianus, we may effectually be renewed by the same. Through.

(19 June. Sts. Gervase and Protase)

¶ Outside of Eastertide, the propers are as followeth.

¶ In Eastertide, the Common of Many Martyrs in Eastertide (p. 711), with the Prayers as followeth and the Greater Alleluia from the Feast of Sts. Primus & Felician (p. 522).

Introit

HE Lord shall speak peace unto his people: and to his saints, that they turn not again. *Ps.* Lord, thou art become gracious unto thy land, thou hast turned away the captivity of Jacob.

Collect

GOD, who makest us glad with the yearly solemnity of thy holy Martyrs Gervase and Protase: mercifully grant; that as we do rejoice in their merits, so we may be enkindled by their example. Through.

¶ The Epistle is from the second additional Epistle from the Second Common of a Martyr not a Bishop (p. 692).

Gradual. God is glorious in his holy ones: fearful in praises, doing wonders. ℣. Thy right hand, O Lord, is become glorious in power: thy right hand hath dashed in pieces the enemy.

Alleluia. Alleluia, alleluia. ℣. This is the true brotherhood, which overcame the wickedness of the world: which followed Christ, gaining heaven's glorious realms. Alleluia.

¶ Note, In Eastertide, the Greater Alleluia is of the the Feast of Sts. Primus & Felician (p. 522).

¶ The Gospel is from the Second Common of Many Martyrs (p. 699).

Offertory. Be glad, O ye righteous, and rejoice in the Lord: and be joyful, all ye that are true of heart.

Secret

E beseech thee, O Lord, mercifully to accept these our oblations: that, at the intercession of thy holy Martyrs Gervase and Protase, we may be defended against all adversities. Through.

Communion. The dead bodies of thy servants, O Lord, have they given to be meat unto the fowls of the air, and the flesh of thy Saints unto the beasts of the land: according to the greatness of thy power, preserve thou those that are appointed to die.

Postcommunion

AY this communion, O Lord, cleanse us from guilt: and at the intercession of thy holy Martyrs Gervase and Protase, make us partakers of thy heavenly healing. Through.

(20 June. St. Silverius)

¶ The First Common of a Martyr Bishop (p. 682), with the Epistle as followeth.

Epistle. Jude 17

DEARLY BELOVED: Remember ye the words which were spoken before of the apostles of our Lord Jesus Christ; How that they told you there should be mockers in the last time, who should walk after their own ungodly lusts. These be they who separate themselves, sensual, having not the Spirit. But ye, beloved, building up yourselves on your most holy faith, praying in the Holy Ghost, Keep yourselves in the love of God, looking for the mercy of our Lord Jesus Christ unto eternal life.

22 June. St. Alban

Double

¶ The Daily Office propers are from the First Common of a Martyr not a Bishop (p. 688).

Introit

THE just shall rejoice in thy strength, O Lord: exceeding glad shall he be of thy salvation: thou hast given him his heart's desire. *Ps.* For thou hast prevented him with the blessings of goodness: thou hast set a crown of pure gold upon his head.

22 June   **Proper of Saints**   *St. Alban*

Collect

GOD, who hast hallowed this day by the martyrdom of blessed Alban: grant, we beseech thee; that as year by year we rejoice to pay him honour, so we may be defended by his continual help. Through.

¶ Commemoration of St. Paulinus (p. 532).

Epistle. Wisdom 10:10

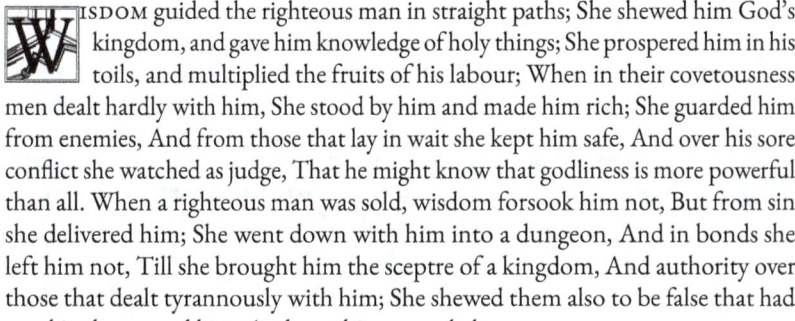ISDOM guided the righteous man in straight paths; She shewed him God's kingdom, and gave him knowledge of holy things; She prospered him in his toils, and multiplied the fruits of his labour; When in their covetousness men dealt hardly with him, She stood by him and made him rich; She guarded him from enemies, And from those that lay in wait she kept him safe, And over his sore conflict she watched as judge, That he might know that godliness is more powerful than all. When a righteous man was sold, wisdom forsook him not, But from sin she delivered him; She went down with him into a dungeon, And in bonds she left him not, Till she brought him the sceptre of a kingdom, And authority over those that dealt tyrannously with him; She shewed them also to be false that had mockingly accused him, And gave him eternal glory.

Gradual. Blessed is the man that feareth the Lord: he hath great delight in his commandments. ℣. His seed shall be mighty upon earth: the generation of the faithful shall be blessed.

Alleluia. Alleluia, alleluia. ℣. Thou hast set, O Lord, a crown of pure gold upon his head. Alleluia.

Gospel. Matthew 16:24

T THAT TIME: Jesus said unto his disciples: If any man will come after me, let him deny himself, and take up his cross, and follow me. For whosoever will save his life shall lose it: and whosoever will lose his life for my sake shall find it. For what is a man profited, if he shall gain the whole world, and lose his own soul? or what shall a man give in exchange for his soul? For the Son of man shall come in the glory of his Father with his angels; and then he shall reward every man according to his works.

Offertory. Thou hast crowned him with glory and worship, and hast made him to have dominion of the works of thy hands, O Lord.

Secret

E beseech thee, O Lord, that like as in the veneration of blessed Alban, thy Martyr, we do shew forth thy wonders: so through this bounden service of propitiation he may be a faithful intercessor for us in the sight of thy mercy. Through.

¶ Commemoration of St. Paulinus (p. 533).

Communion. If any man will come after me, let him deny himself, and take up his cross and follow me.

Postcommunion

ET blessed Alban, thy Martyr, we beseech thee, O Lord, ever implore thy holy Majesty: that these thy sacraments may cleanse us from guilt, and preserve in us the fervour of thy charity. Through.

¶ Commemoration of St. Paulinus (p. 533).

(22 June. St. Paulinus)

Introit

ET thy priests, O Lord, be clothed with righteousness, and let thy saints sing with joyfulness: for thy servant David's sake, turn not away the presence of thine anointed. *Ps.* Lord, remember David, and all his trouble.

Collect

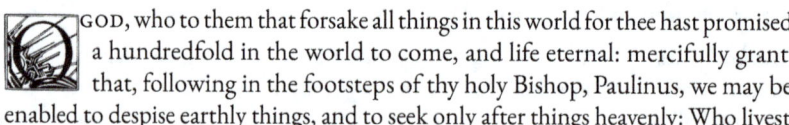GOD, who to them that forsake all things in this world for thee hast promised a hundredfold in the world to come, and life eternal: mercifully grant; that, following in the footsteps of thy holy Bishop, Paulinus, we may be enabled to despise earthly things, and to seek only after things heavenly: Who livest.

¶ If to-day be Saturday, a Commemoration is made of the anticipated Vigil of St. John Baptist, as below.

Epistle. 2 Corinthians 8:9

BRETHREN: Ye know the grace of our Lord Jesus Christ, that, though he was rich, yet for your sakes he became poor, that ye through his poverty might be rich. And herein I give my advice: for this is expedient for you, who have begun before, not only to do, but also to be forward a year ago. Now therefore perform the doing of it; that as there was a readiness to will, so there may be a performance also out of that which ye have. For if there be first a willing mind, it is accepted according to that a man hath, and not according to that he hath not. For I mean not that other men be eased, and ye burdened: But by an equality, that now at this time your abundance may be a supply for their want, that their abundance also may be a supply for your want: that there may be equality: As it is written, He that had gathered much had nothing over; and he that had gathered little had no lack.

Gradual. Behold a great priest who in his days pleased God. ℣. There was none found like unto him, who kept the law of the Most High.

Alleluia. Alleluia, alleluia. ℣. Thou art a priest for ever after the order of Melchisedech. Alleluia.

23 June   **Proper of Saints**   *St. John Baptist Vigil*

¶ The Gospel is from the Second Common of a Confessor not a Bishop (p. 729).

Offertory. I have found David my servant, with my holy oil have I anointed him: my hand shall hold him fast, and my arm shall strengthen him.

Secret

RANT, O Lord, that, after the example of thy holy Bishop Paulinus, we may join the sacrifice of perfect charity to the oblation of the altar: and by zeal in well-doing be found worthy of thine everlasting mercy. Through.

Communion. A faithful and wise servant whom the lord hath made ruler over his household, to give them their portion of meat in due season.

Postcommunion

RANT us, O Lord, through these holy things that love of piety and humility which thy holy Bishop Paulinus drew from this divine fountain: and by his intercession graciously pour forth on all who entreat thee the riches of thy grace. Through.

23 June. Vigil of St. John Baptist

Vigil

Introit

FEAR not, Zacharias, thy prayer is heard: and thy wife Elisabeth shall bear thee a son, and thou shalt call his name John: he shall be great in the sight of the Lord: and shall be filled with the Holy Ghost, even from his mother's womb: and many shall rejoice at his birth. *Ps.* The king shall rejoice in thy strength, O Lord: exceeding glad shall he be of thy salvation.

Collect

GRANT, we beseech thee, Almighty God: that thy family may walk in the way of salvation; and, following the teachings of blessed John the Forerunner, may attain in safety unto him whom he fore-told, Jesus Christ thy Son, our Lord: Who liveth.

¶ 2nd Collect of St. Mary (p. BCP 542) and 3rd Against the Persecutors of the Church (p. BCP 543) or for the Chief Bishop (p. BCP 543).

Epistle. Jeremiah 1:4

N those days: The word of the LORD came unto me, saying, Before I formed thee in the belly I knew thee; and before thou camest forth out of the womb I sanctified thee, and I ordained thee a prophet unto the nations. Then said I, Ah, Lord GOD! behold, I cannot speak: for I am a child. But

St. John Baptist Vigil **Proper of Saints** 23 June

the LORD said unto me, Say not, I am a child: for thou shalt go to all that I shall send thee, and whatsoever I command thee thou shalt speak. Be not afraid of their faces: for I am with thee to deliver thee, saith the LORD. Then the LORD put forth his hand, and touched my mouth. And the LORD said unto me, Behold, I have put my words in thy mouth. See, I have this day set thee over the nations and over the kingdoms, to root out, and to pull down, and to destroy, and to throw down, to build, and to plant: saith the Lord almighty.

Gradual. There was a man sent from God, whose name was John. ℣. The same came to bear witness of the light, to make ready a people prepared for the Lord.

Gospel. Luke 1:5

THERE was in the days of Herod, the king of Judaea, a certain priest named Zacharias, of the course of Abia: and his wife was of the daughters of Aaron, and her name was Elisabeth. And they were both righteous before God, walking in all the commandments and ordinances of the Lord blameless. And they had no child, because that Elisabeth was barren, and they both were now well stricken in years. And it came to pass, that while he executed the priest's office before God in the order of his course, According to the custom of the priest's office, his lot was to burn incense when he went into the temple of the Lord. And the whole multitude of the people were praying without at the time of incense. And there appeared unto him an angel of the Lord standing on the right side of the altar of incense. And when Zacharias saw him, he was troubled, and fear fell upon him. But the angel said unto him, Fear not, Zacharias: for thy prayer is heard; and thy wife Elisabeth shall bear thee a son, and thou shalt call his name John. And thou shalt have joy and gladness; and many shall rejoice at his birth. For he shall be great in the sight of the Lord, and shall drink neither wine nor strong drink; and he shall be filled with the Holy Ghost, even from his mother's womb. And many of the children of Israel shall he turn to the Lord their God. And he shall go before him in the spirit and power of Elias, to turn the hearts of the fathers to the children, and the disobedient to the wisdom of the just; to make ready a people prepared for the Lord.

Offertory. Thou hast crowned him with glory and worship: thou hast made him to have dominion of the works of thy hands, O Lord.

Secret

SANCTIFY, O Lord, the gifts which we offer: and, at the intercession of blessed John Baptist, cleanse us thereby from the defilements of our iniquities. Through.

¶ 2nd Secret of St. Mary (p. BCP 542) and 3rd Against the Persecutors of the Church (p. BCP 543) or for the Chief Bishop (p. BCP 543).

Communion. His honour is great in thy salvation: glory and great worship shalt thou lay upon him, O Lord.

Postcommunion

LORD, let the glorious prayer of blessed John Baptist ever be with us: and may he implore for us the mercy of him, whose coming he fore-told, Jesus Christ thy Son our Lord: Who liveth.

¶ 2nd Postcommunion of St. Mary (p. BCP 542) and 3rd Against the Persecutors of the Church (p. BCP 543) or for the Chief Bishop (p. BCP 543).

(23 JUNE. ST. ETHELDREDA)

¶ The First Common of a Virgin (p. 742), with the Collect as followeth.

Collect

GOD, who makest us glad with the yearly solemnity of blessed Etheldreda, thy Virgin: mercifully grant; that as we are enlightened by the example of her purity, so we may be succoured by her prayers. Through.

[24 JUNE. ST. JOHN BAPTIST]

I Evensong

O for thy spir-it, ho-ly John, to chas-ten Lips sin-pol-lut-ed, fet-ter'd tongues to loos-en; So by thy children might thy deeds of wonder Meet-ly be chant-ed. 2. Lo! a swift her-ald, from the skies de-scending, Bears to thy fa-ther promise of thy greatness; How he shall name thee, what thy fu-ture sto-ry, Du-ly re-veal-ing.

St. John Baptist — Proper of Saints — 24 June

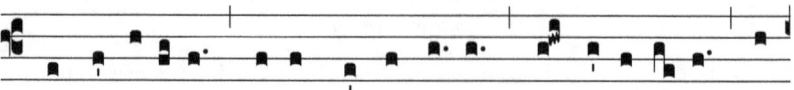
3. Scarcely be-liev-ing mes-sage so transcendent, Him for a sea-son pow'r

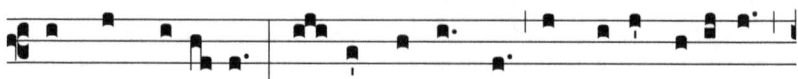
of speech for-sa-keth, Till, at thy wondrous birth, a-gain re-turneth

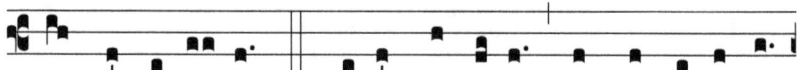
Voice to the voice-less. 4. Thou, in thy mother's womb all darkly cra-

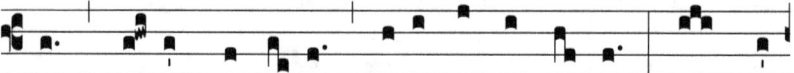
dled, Knew-est thy Mon-arch, bid-ing in his chamber; Whence the

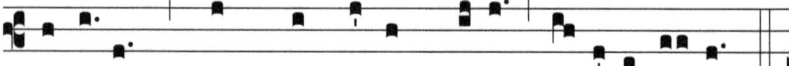
two par-ents, through their children's mer-its, Mys-ter-ies ut-ter'd.

5. Praise to the Father, to the Sole-be-got-ten, And to thee, alway with

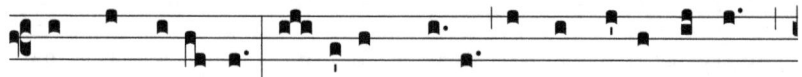
the Twain co-e-qual, Fos-ter-ing Spir-it; one and only Godhead

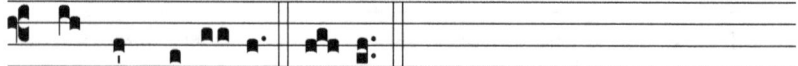
Through all the ag-es. A-men.

℣. There was a man sent from God.
℟. Whose name was John.

Mag. Ant. When Zacharias † went into the temple, there appeared unto him the Angel Gabriel, standing on the right side of the altar of incense.

24 June   **Proper of Saints**   *St. John Baptist*

Mattins

Invitatory Hymn

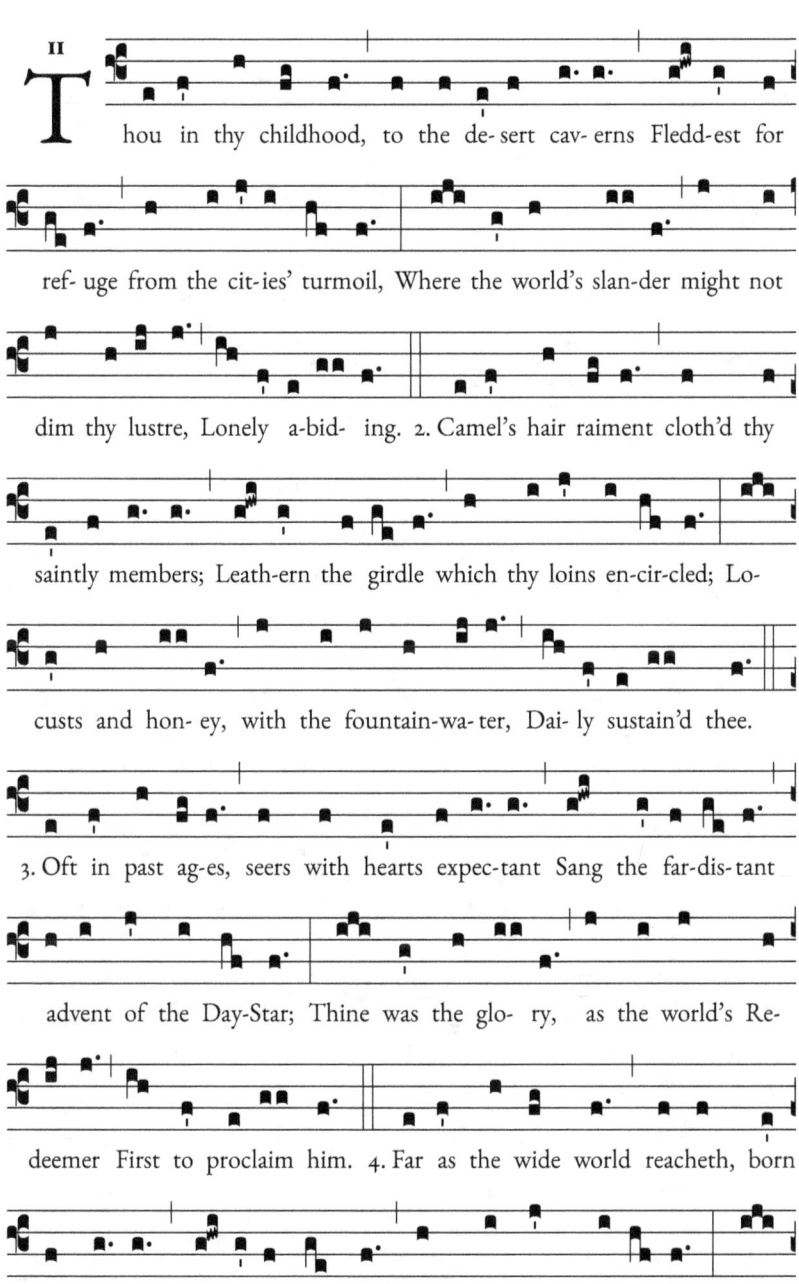

1. Thou in thy childhood, to the desert caverns Fledd-est for refuge from the cities' turmoil, Where the world's slander might not dim thy lustre, Lonely abiding. 2. Camel's hair raiment cloth'd thy saintly members; Leathern the girdle which thy loins encircled; Locusts and honey, with the fountain-water, Daily sustain'd thee. 3. Oft in past ages, seers with hearts expectant Sang the far-distant advent of the Day-Star; Thine was the glory, as the world's Redeemer First to proclaim him. 4. Far as the wide world reacheth, born of woman, Holier was there none than John the Baptist; Meet-

St. John Baptist — Proper of Saints — 24 June

ly in wa- ter lav-ing him who cleanseth Man from pol-lu- tion.

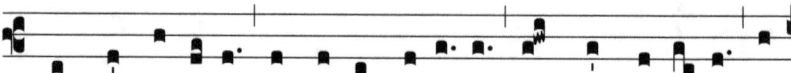

5. Praise to the Father, to the Sole-be-got-ten, And to thee, alway with

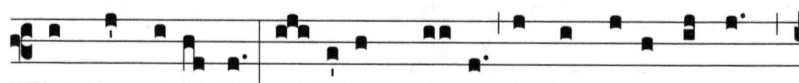

the Twain co- e-qual, Fos- ter- ing Spir- it; one and only Godhead

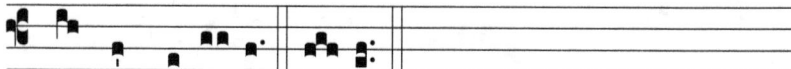

Through all the ag- es. A- men.

Office Hymn

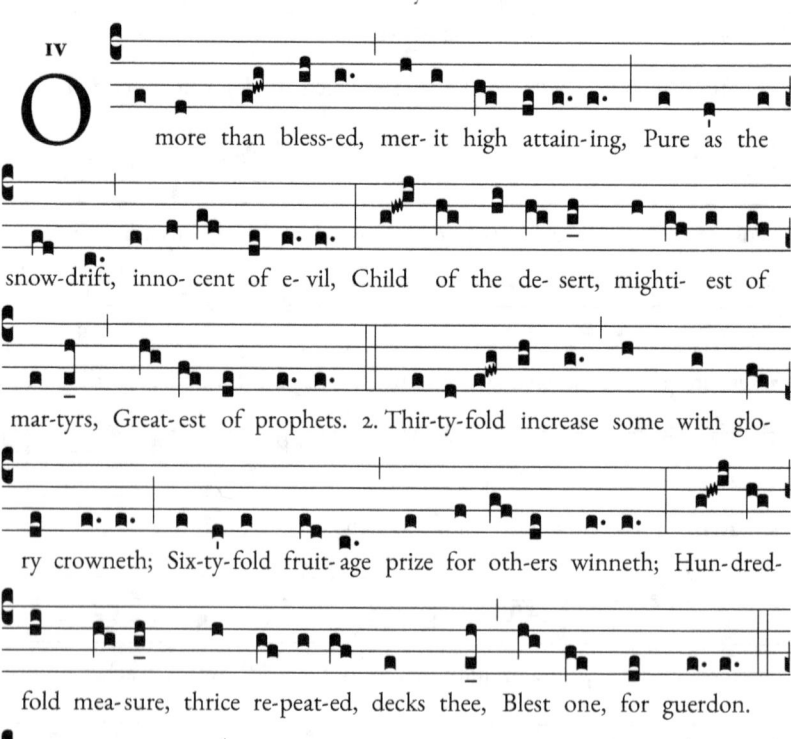

IV

O more than bless-ed, mer- it high attain-ing, Pure as the snow-drift, inno- cent of e- vil, Child of the de- sert, mighti- est of mar-tyrs, Great-est of prophets. 2. Thir-ty-fold increase some with glo- ry crowneth; Six-ty-fold fruit-age prize for oth-ers winneth; Hun-dred-fold mea-sure, thrice re-peat-ed, decks thee, Blest one, for guerdon.

3. O may the virtue of thine in-ter-ces-sion, All ston-y hardness from our

24 June   **Proper of Saints**   *St. John Baptist*

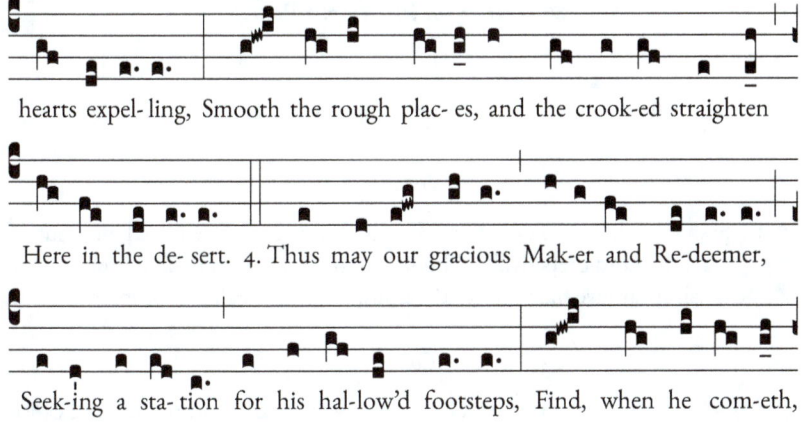

hearts expel-ling, Smooth the rough plac-es, and the crook-ed straighten

Here in the de-sert. 4. Thus may our gracious Mak-er and Re-deemer,

Seek-ing a sta-tion for his hal-low'd footsteps, Find, when he com-eth,

temples unde-fi-led, Meet to re-ceive him. 5. Now as the Angels cel-

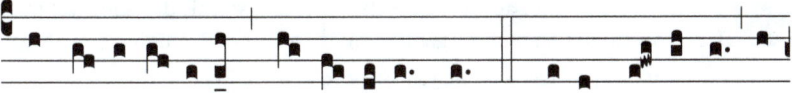

e-brate thy prais-es, Godhead es-sential, Trin-i-ty co-equal; Spare thy

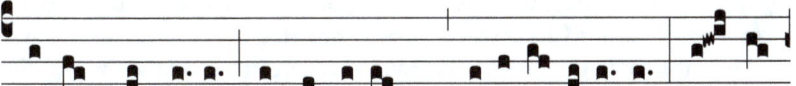

re-deem'd ones, as they bow be-fore thee, Par-don implor-ing. A-men.

℣. This child shall be great in the sight of the Lord.

℟. For the hand of the Lord is with him.

Ben. Ant. The mouth of Zacharias † was opened, and he prophesied, saying: Blessed be the God of Israel.

II Evensong

¶ The Office Hymn is of I Evensong, with the following Versicle & Antiphon.

℣. This child shall be great in the sight of the Lord.

℟. For the hand of the Lord is with him.

Mag. Ant. The child † that is born unto us is more than a prophet; for this is he of whom the Saviour saith: Among them that are born of women, there hath not risen a greater than John the Baptist.

26 June. Sts. John and Paul

Double

⁋ The Daily Office propers are from the First Common of Many Martyrs (p. 692).

Introit

REAT are the troubles of the righteous, but the Lord delivereth him out of all: the Lord keepeth all his bones: so that not one of them is broken. *Ps.* I will alway give thanks unto the Lord: his praise shall ever be in my mouth.

Collect

E beseech thee, Almighty God: that, as their faith and passion did cause blessed John and Paul to be brothers indeed; so this day's festival may bestow upon us a twofold gladness in their glory. Through.

⁋ Commemoration of the Octave of St. John Baptist, as followeth.

LMIGHTY God, by whose providence thy servant John Baptist was wonderfully born, and sent to prepare the way of thy Son our Saviour by preaching repentance; Make us so to follow his doctrine and holy life, that we may truly repent according to his preaching; and after his example constantly speak the truth, boldly rebuke vice, and patiently suffer for the truth's sake. Through the same.

Epistle. Ecclesiasticus 44:10

THESE were men of mercy, Whose righteous deeds have not been forgotten. With their seed shall remain continually a good inheritance; Their children are within the covenants. Their seed standeth fast, And their children for their sakes. Their seed shall remain for ever, And their glory shall not be blotted out. Their bodies were buried in peace, And their name liveth to all generations. Peoples will declare their wisdom, And the congregation telleth out their praise.

Gradual. Behold, how good and joyful a thing it is, brethren, to dwell together in unity! ℣. It is like the precious ointment upon the head, that ran down unto the beard, even Aaron's beard.

Alleluia. Alleluia, alleluia. ℣. This is the true brotherhood, which overcame the wickedness of the world: which followed Christ, gaining heaven's glorious realms. Alleluia.

⁋ The Gospel is from the Third Common of Many Martyrs (p. 700).

Offertory. They that love thy name shall be joyful in thee, for thou, Lord, wilt give thy blessing unto the righteous: and with thy favourable kindness wilt thou defend him as with a shield, O Lord.

28 June   **Proper of Saints**   *Sts. Peter & Paul Vigil*

Secret

E beseech thee, O Lord, mercifully to accept this our sacrifice which we offer unto thee, pleading the merits of thy holy Martyrs John and Paul: that the same may avail for our perpetual succour. Through.

¶ Commemoration of the Octave of St. John Baptist, as followeth.

E set upon thine altars, O Lord, these gifts: celebrating with due honour the nativity of him, who sang of the coming and proclaimed the presence of the Saviour of the world, Jesus Christ thy Son our Lord. Who liveth.

Communion. Though they be punished in the sight of men, God proved them: as gold in the furnace hath he tried them, and received them as a burnt-offering.

Postcommunion

RANT, we beseech thee, O Lord: that we who have received these heavenly sacraments, in celebration of the festival of thy holy Martyrs John and Paul; may attain in everlasting joys the fulfilment of our service in this life. Through.

¶ Commemoration of the Octave of St. John Baptist, as followeth.

ET thy Church, O God, rejoice at the birth of blessed John Baptist: through whom she hath known the author of her new birth, Jesus Christ thy Son our Lord. Who liveth.

28 June. Vigil of Sts. Peter and Paul

Vigil

Introit

HE Lord saith unto Peter: When thou wast young, thou girdedst thyself, and walkedst whither thou wouldest: but when thou shalt be old, thou shalt stretch forth thy hands, and another shall gird thee, and carry thee whither thou wouldest not: this spake he, signifying by what death he should glorify God. *Ps.* The heavens declare the glory of God: and the firmament sheweth his handy-work.

Collect

RANT, we beseech thee, Almighty God: that as thou hast stablished us on the rock of the apostolic confession; so thou wouldest not suffer us to be troubled by any adversities. Through.

Sts. Peter & Paul Vigil   # Proper of Saints   28 June

Epistle. Acts 3:1

IN THOSE DAYS: Peter and John went up together into the temple at the hour of prayer, being the ninth hour. And a certain man lame from his mother's womb was carried, whom they laid daily at the gate of the temple which is called Beautiful, to ask alms of them that entered into the temple; Who seeing Peter and John about to go into the temple asked an alms. And Peter, fastening his eyes upon him with John, said, Look on us. And he gave heed unto them, expecting to receive something of them. Then Peter said, Silver and gold have I none; but such as I have give I thee: In the name of Jesus Christ of Nazareth rise up and walk. And he took him by the right hand, and lifted him up: and immediately his feet and ankle bones received strength. And he leaping up stood, and walked, and entered with them into the temple, walking, and leaping, and praising God. And all the people saw him walking and praising God: And they knew that it was he which sat for alms at the Beautiful gate of the temple: and they were filled with wonder and amazement at that which had happened unto him.

Gradual. Their sound is gone out into all lands: and their words into the ends of the world. ℣. The heavens declare the glory of God: and the firmament sheweth his handy-work.

Gospel. John 21:15

AT THAT TIME: Jesus said unto Simon Peter: Simon, son of John, lovest thou me more than these? He saith unto him, Yea, Lord; thou knowest that I love thee. He saith unto him, Feed my lambs. He saith to him again a second time, Simon, son of John, lovest thou me? He saith unto him, Yea, Lord; thou knowest that I love thee. He saith unto him, Tend my sheep. He saith unto him the third time, Simon, son of John, lovest thou me? Peter was grieved because he said unto him the third time, Lovest thou me? And he said unto him, Lord, thou knowest all things; thou knowest that I love thee. Jesus saith unto him, Feed my sheep. Verily, verily, I say unto thee, When thou wast young, thou girdedst thyself, and walkedst whither thou wouldest: but when thou shalt be old, thou shalt stretch forth thy hands, and another shall gird thee, and carry thee whither thou wouldest not. Now this he spake, signifying by what manner of death he should glorify God.

Offertory. Right honourable are thy friends unto me, O God: right well is their princedom established.

Secret

SANCTIFY, the gift of thy people, we beseech thee, O Lord, by the intercession of thine Apostles: and cleanse us from the defilements of our iniquities. Through.

Communion. Simon, son of Jonas, lovest thou me more than these? Lord, thou knowest all things: thou knowest, Lord, that I love thee.

29 June   **Proper of Saints**   *Sts. Peter & Paul*

Postcommunion

LORD, who hast satisfied us with heavenly food: defend us by the intercession of thine Apostles against all adversity. Through.

(28 June. Pope St. Leo II)

¶ The First Common of a Confessor Bishop (p. 715).

[29 June. Sts. Peter and Paul]

I Evensong

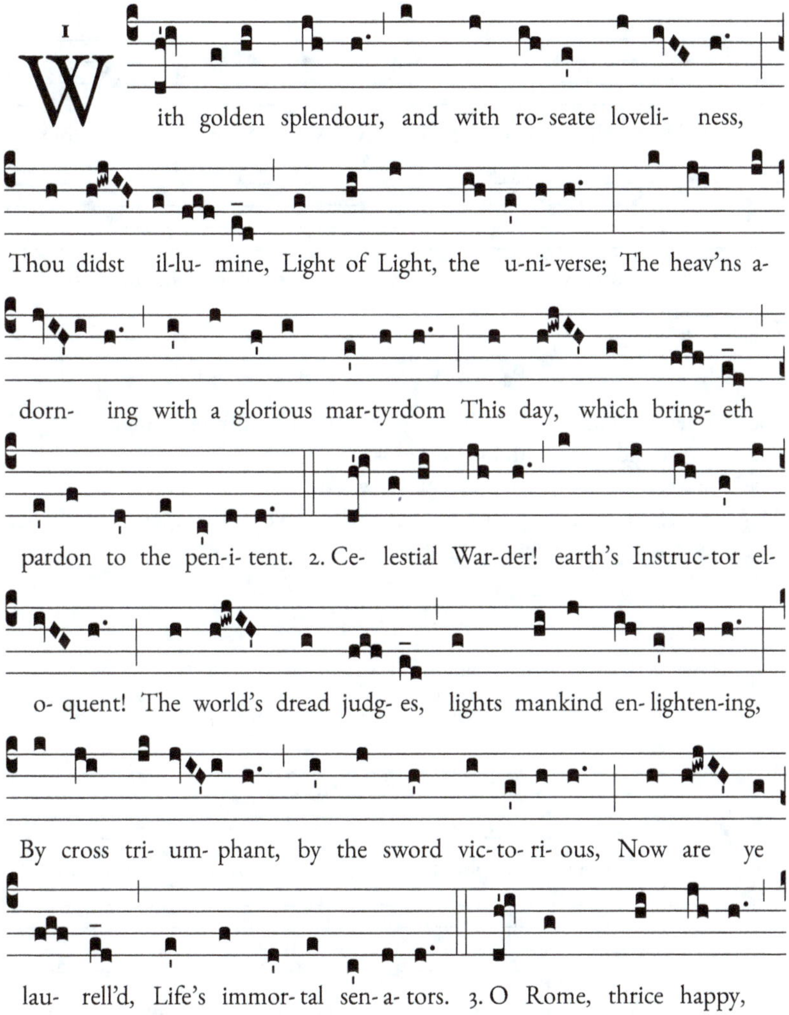

1. With golden splendour, and with roseate loveliness, Thou didst illumine, Light of Light, the universe; The heav'ns adorning with a glorious martyrdom This day, which bringeth pardon to the penitent. 2. Celestial Warder! earth's Instructor eloquent! The world's dread judges, lights mankind enlightening, By cross triumphant, by the sword victorious, Now are ye laurell'd, Life's immortal senators. 3. O Rome, thrice happy,

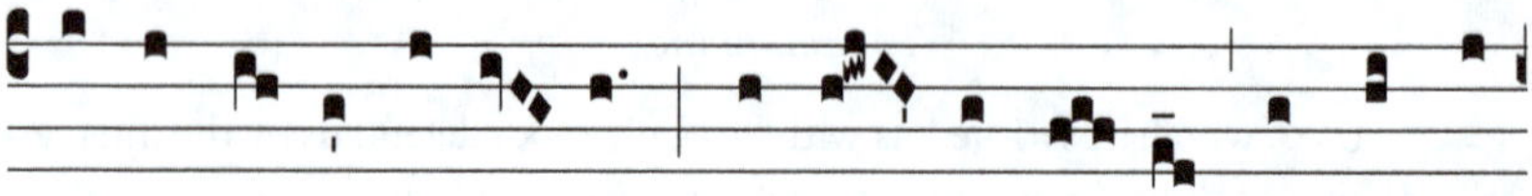

Sts. Peter & Paul — **Proper of Saints** — 29 June

that so great a mar-tyr-dom Thy walls, empur-pled with rich life-blood, hallow-eth! Not thine the mer- it; by thy Princes' excel-lence Thou shin- est fair- er than the world's magnif-i-cence. 4. Glo-ry e-ter-nal to the Bless-ed Trin-i- ty, With laud and hon- our, virtue and su-prema-cy, Tri- nal yet One- ly, reigning in his maj-es-ty Both now and ev- er, through the ag-es in-fi-nite. A- men.

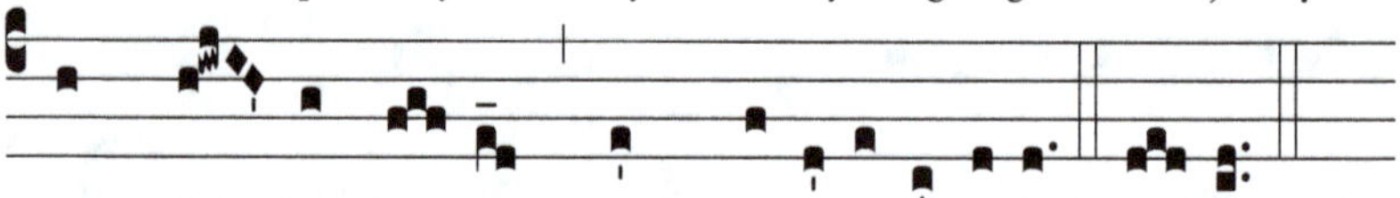

℣. Their sound is gone out into all lands.
℟. And their words into the ends of the world.

Mag. Ant. Thou art the shepherd of the sheep, † O chief of the Apostles: unto thee were given the keys of the kingdom of heaven.

Mattins

¶ The Invitatory Hymn is of the Common of Apostles (p. 673).

Office Hymn

IV

Pe- ter, good shepherd, may thy ceaseless or-i-sons, For us pre-vail- ing, break the bands of wickedness: For thou of old time

29 June — **Proper of Saints** — *Sts. Peter & Paul*

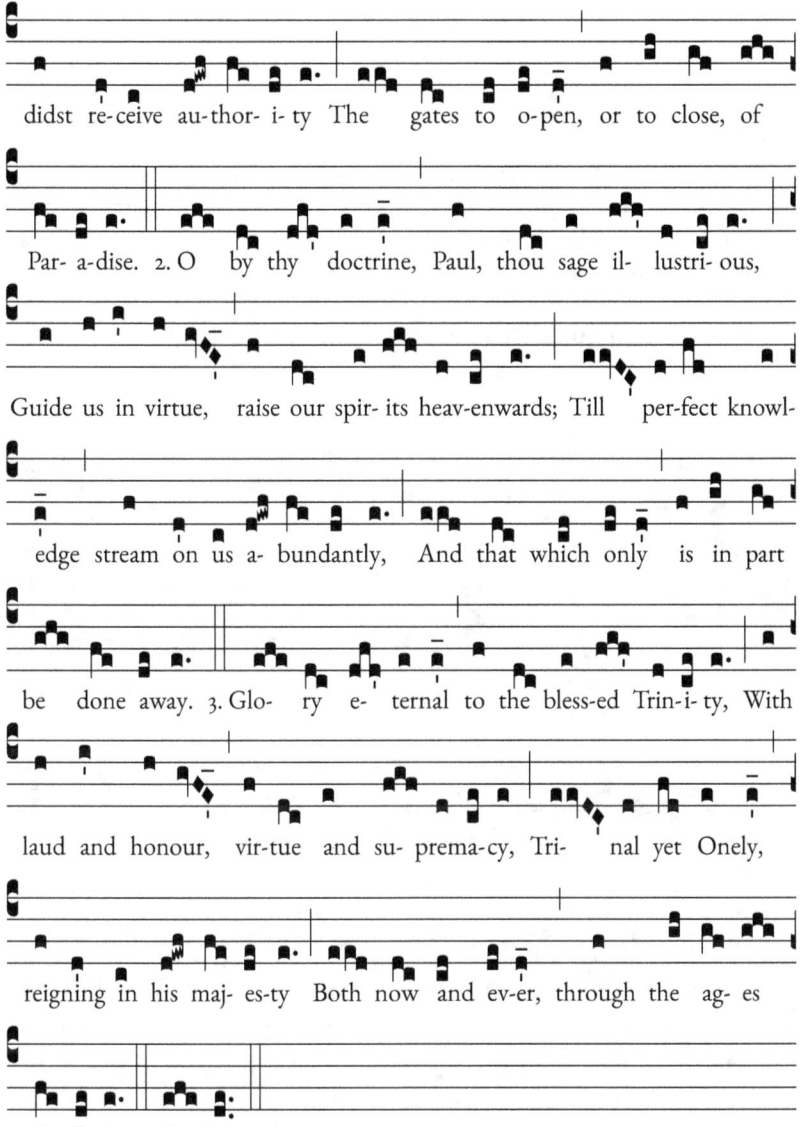

didst re-ceive au-thor-i-ty The gates to o-pen, or to close, of Par-a-dise. 2. O by thy doctrine, Paul, thou sage il-lustri-ous, Guide us in virtue, raise our spir-its heav-enwards; Till per-fect knowl-edge stream on us a-bundantly, And that which only is in part be done away. 3. Glo- ry e-ternal to the bless-ed Trin-i-ty, With laud and honour, vir-tue and su-prema-cy, Tri- nal yet Onely, reigning in his maj-es-ty Both now and ev-er, through the ag- es in-fi-nite. A-men.

℣. They declared the work of God.

℞. And wisely considered of his doing.

Ben. Ant. Whatsoever † thou shalt bind on earth shall be bound in heaven: and whatsoever thou shalt loose on earth shall be loosed in heaven: saith the Lord unto Simon Peter.

St. Paul Commemoration **Proper of Saints** 30 June

II Evensong

¶ The Office Hymn is of I Evensong, with the following Versicle & Antiphon.

℣. They declared the work of God.
℟. And wisely considered of his doing.

Mag. Ant. To-day † Simon Peter ascended the gibbet of the cross, alleluia: to-day the Key-Bearer of the Kingdom joyfully departed to Christ: to-day Paul the Apostle, the light of the whole world, bowed down his head; and for the Name of Christ, received the crown of martyrdom, alleluia.

[30 June. Commemoration of St. Paul]

I Evensong

O by thy doctrine, Paul, thou sage illustrious, Guide us in virtue, raise our spirits heavenwards; Till perfect knowledge stream on us abundantly, And that which only is in part be done away. 2. Glory eternal to the blessed Trinity, With laud and honour, virtue and supremacy, Trinal yet Onely, reigning in his majesty Both now and ever, through the ages infinite.

A-men.

1 July   **Proper of Saints**   *Precious Blood*

℣. Thou art a chosen vessel, holy Apostle Paul.

℟. A preacher of the truth throughout all the world.

Mag. Ant. O holy Apostle Paul, † thou preacher of the truth and Doctor of the Gentiles, intercede for us unto God, who hath chosen thee.

Mattins

¶ The Invitatory Hymn is as in I Evensong.

¶ The Office Hymn is as in the Common of Apostles (p. 673).

¶ In Eastertide, the Office Hymn is as in the Common of Apostles in Eastertide (p. 678).

℣. Thou art a chosen vessel, holy Apostle Paul.

℟. A preacher of the truth throughout all the world.

Ben. Ant. Ye which have followed me † shall sit upon twelve thrones, judging the twelve tribes of Israel, saith the Lord.

II Evensong

¶ II Evensong is as in I Evensong.

[1 JULY. MOST PRECIOUS BLOOD OF OUR LORD JESUS CHRIST]

I Evensong

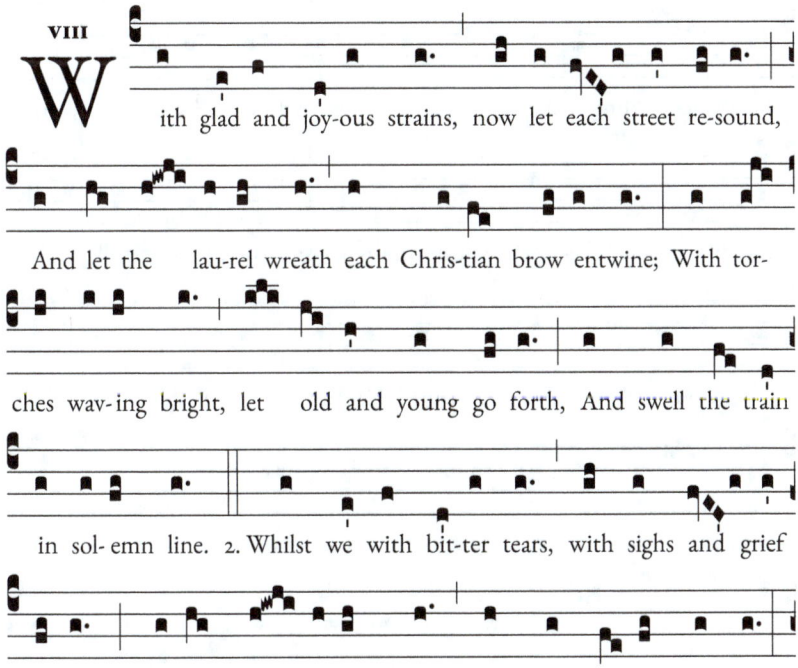

With glad and joy-ous strains, now let each street re-sound, And let the lau-rel wreath each Chris-tian brow entwine; With tor-ches wav-ing bright, let old and young go forth, And swell the train in sol-emn line. 2. Whilst we with bit-ter tears, with sighs and grief pro-found, Wail o'er the sav-ing Blood, pour'd forth up-on the Tree,

Precious Blood   Proper of Saints   1 July

Oh, deep-ly let us muse, and count the heav-y price Which Christ hath paid to make us free. 3. The pri-mal man of old, who fell by serpent's guile, Brought death and man-y woes up-on his fall-en race; But our New Ad-am, Christ, new life unto us gave, And brought to all ne'er-end-ing grace. 4. To heav-en's highest height, the wail-ing cry went up Of him who hung in pain, God's own e-ternal Son; His sav-ing, price-less Blood, his Fa-ther's wrath appeas'd, And for his sons full pardon won. 5. Who-e'er in that pure Blood his guilt-y soul shall wash, Shall from his stains be freed, be made as ros-es bright; Shall vie with An-gels pure, shall please his King and Lord, And pre-cious shine in his glad

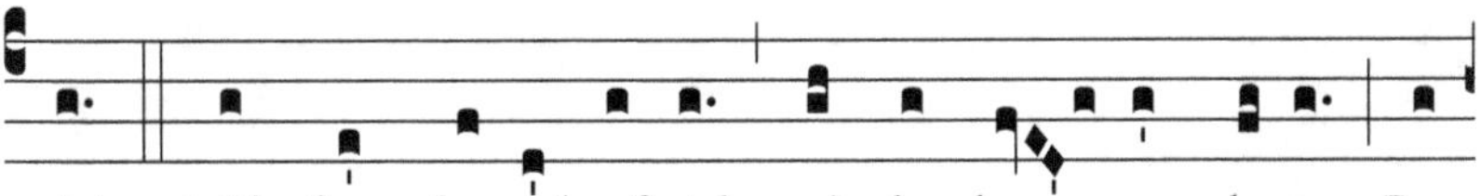

1 July — **Proper of Saints** — *Precious Blood*

sight. 6. Oh, from the path of right ne'er let thy steps de-part, But haste thee to the goal in vir-tue's peaceful ways; Thy God who reigns on high will e'er di-rect thy steps, And crown thy deeds with blissful days. 7. Father of all things made, to us pro-pi-tious be, For whom thy own dear Son his sav-ing Blood did spill; O Ho-ly Spir-it, grant the souls by thee re-fresh'd E-ter-nal bliss may ev-er fill. A-men.

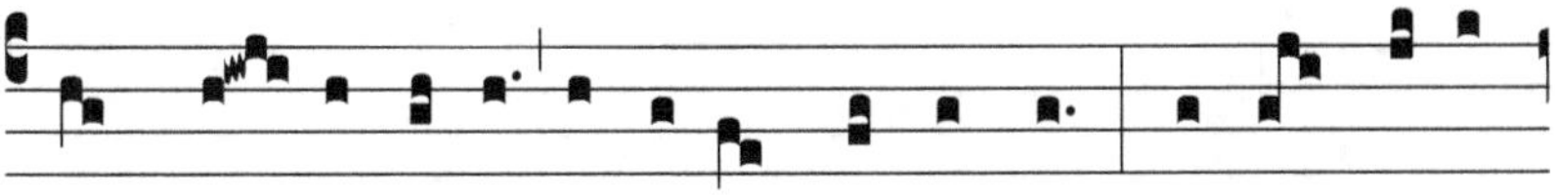

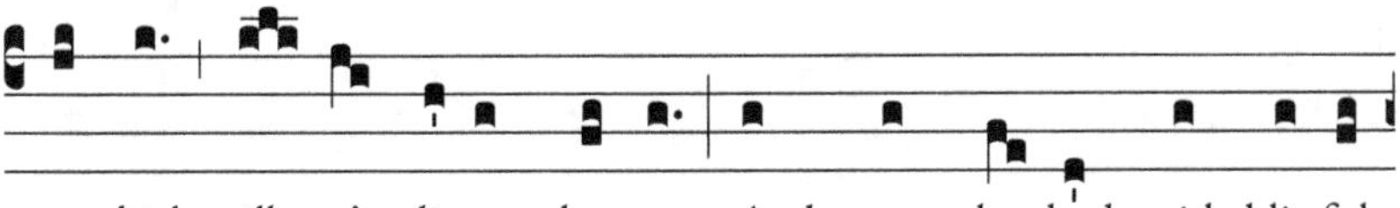

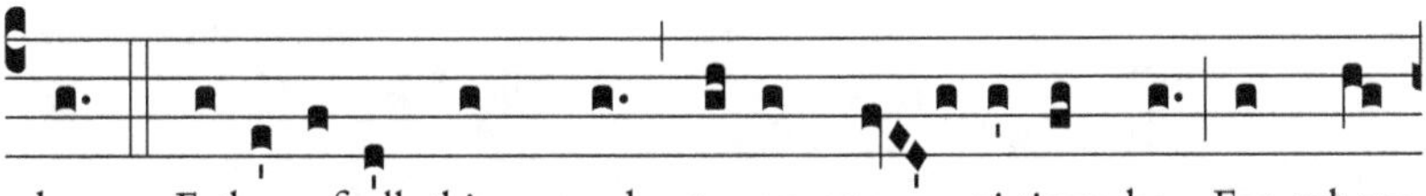

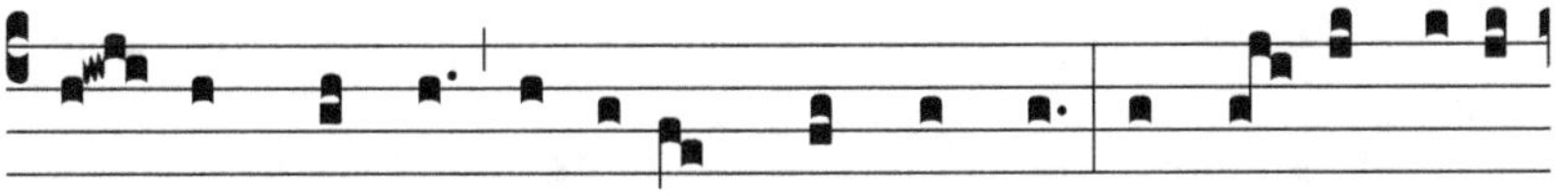

℣. Thou hast redeemed us, O Lord, by thy Blood.

℟. And hast made us unto our God a kingdom.

Mag. Ant. But ye are come † unto mount Sion and unto the city of the living God, the heavenly Jerusalem, and to Jesus, the mediator of the new covenant, and to the Blood of sprinkling, that speaketh better things than that of Abel.

Mattins

Invitatory Hymn

Righteous anger of our Mak-er Pour'd his vengeance in the 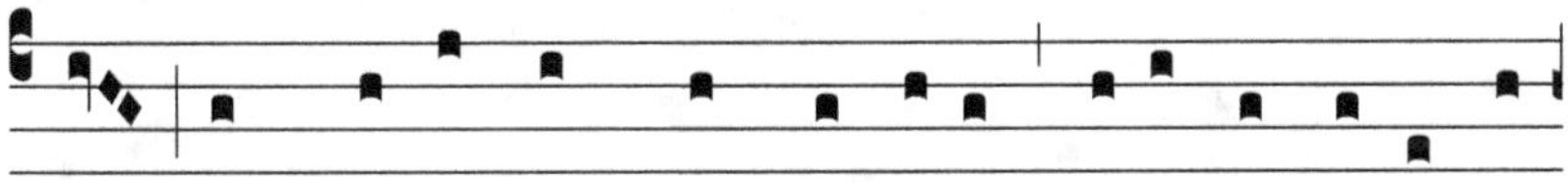 Flood, And the crime-filled world submerged; No-ah sav'd in ark of

Precious Blood   **Proper of Saints**   1 July

wood. Then he came with love stu-pendous, Wash'd the world in Pre-cious Blood. 2. So the happy earth and healthful, Wa-ter'd by such sav-ing show'rs, Though once sown with thorns and trouble, Now sprouts forth with ti-ny flow'rs: All the bit-ter plants of wormwood Change to flow-ing nec-tar's dow'rs. 3. Straightway ceas'd the serpent's ven-om, All its poi-son laid a-side; And the wild beasts' rag-ing ended While their cru-el fierceness died; For the gentle Lamb and wounded Won the vict'ry glo-ri-fi'd. 4. O su-per-nal, wondrous Knowl-edge High ex-alt-ed, heights unknown! O how sweet thy lov-ing-kindness To the weak and sinful shown, That the King of kings, all Goodness, Should for guilt-y slaves a-

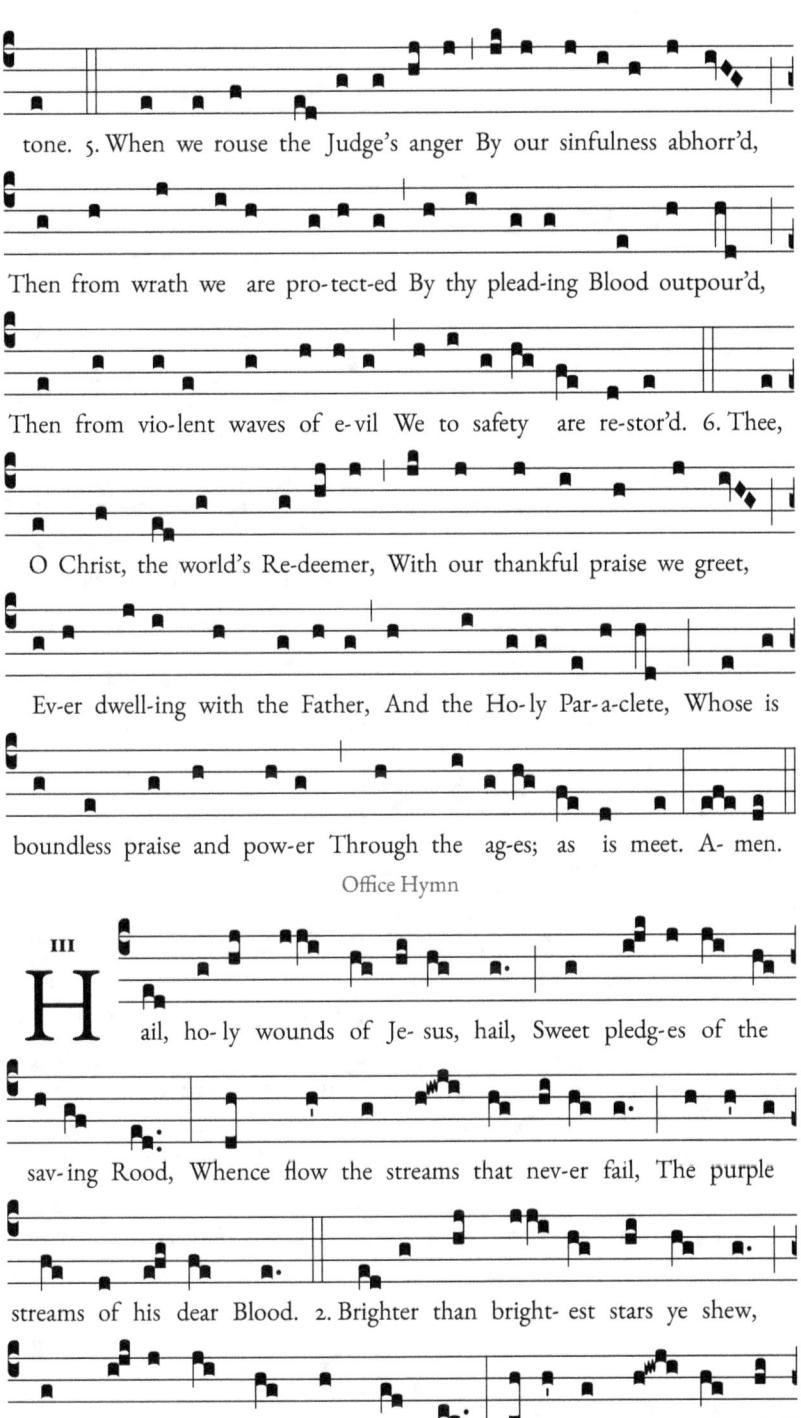

Precious Blood   **Proper of Saints**   1 July

your glow, No honey's taste with yours compare. 3. Por-tals ye are
to that dear home Where-in our wea-ried souls may hide, Whereto
no an-gry foe can come, The Heart of Je-sus cru-ci-fied. 4. What
countless stripes our Je-sus bore, All na-ked left in Pi-late's hall! From
his torn flesh how red a show'r Did round his sa-cred per-son fall!
5. His beauteous brow, oh, shame and grief, By the sharp thorn-y crown
is riv'n; Through hands and feet, without re-lief, The cru-el nails
are rude-ly driv'n. 6. But when for our poor sakes he died, A will-ing
Priest by love subdued, The soldier's lance transfix'd his side, Forth flow'd
the Wa-ter and the Blood. 7. In full a-tone-ment of our guilt, Careless

1 July • **Proper of Saints** • *Precious Blood*

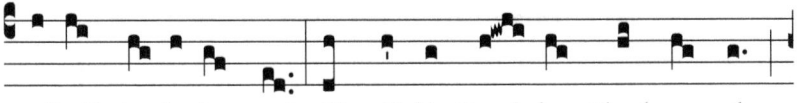
of self, the Saviour trod, E'en till his Heart's best Blood was spilt,

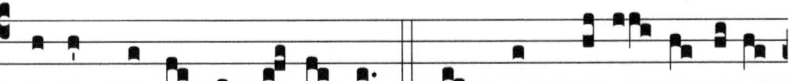
The wine-press of the wrath of God. 8. Come, bathe you in the healing

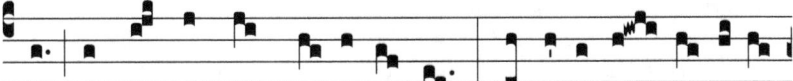
flood, All ye who mourn, by sin oppress'd, Your only hope is Jesus'

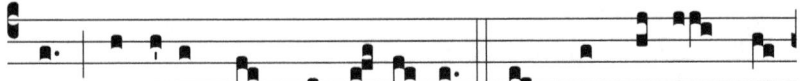
Blood, His sacred Heart your only rest. 9. All praise to him, th' E-

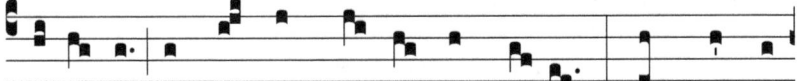
ternal Son, At God's right hand enthroned above, Whose Blood our

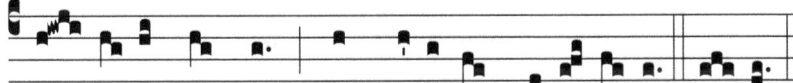
full redemption won, Whose Spirit seals the gift of love. A- men.

℣. Being justified by the Blood of Christ.

℟. We shall be saved from wrath through him.

Ben. Ant. The Blood of the Lamb † shall be to you for a token, saith the Lord: and when I see the Blood, I will pass over you, and the plague shall not be upon you to destroy you.

II Evensong

¶ II Evensong is as in I Evensong, except the following Antiphon.

Mag. Ant. And this day † shall be unto you for a memorial: and ye shall keep it a feast to the Lord throughout your generations by an ordinance for ever.

[2 July. Visitation of the Blessed Virgin Mary]

℣ The Hymns are as in the Common of the Blessed Virgin Mary (p. 760), with the following Versicles & Antiphons.

℣. Blessed art thou amongst women.
℟. And blessed is the fruit of thy womb.

Mag. Ant. Blessed art thou, † O Mary, for thou hast believed: and there shall be a performance in thee of those things which were told thee from the Lord, alleluia.

℣. Blessed art thou amongst women.
℟. And blessed is the fruit of thy womb.

Ben. Ant. When Elisabeth † heard the salutation of Mary, she spake out with a loud voice, and said: Whence is this to me, that the mother of my Lord should come to me? Alleluia.

℣. Blessed art thou amongst women.
℟. And blessed is the fruit of thy womb.

Mag. Ant. All generations † shall call me blessed: for God hath regarded the lowliness of his handmaiden, alleluia.

(2 July. St. John of San Francisco)

℣ The Second Common of a Confessor Bishop (p. 720).

(2 July. Sts. Processus and Martinian)

℣ The Second Common of Many Martyrs (p. 699), except for the following.

Collect

GOD, who dost encompass and protect us by the glorious confession of thy holy Martyrs Processus and Martinian: grant us both to profit by their example, and to rejoice in their intercession. Through.

Secret

ECEIVE, O Lord, our prayers and gifts: and that they may be worthy in thy sight, may we be aided by the prayers of thy Saints. Through.

Postcommunion

LORD our God, who hast fulfilled us with the partaking of the sacred Body and the precious Blood, we beseech thee: that those things which we perform with godly devotion we may attain in the assurance of our redemption. Through the same.

Proper of Saints — Sts. Peter & Paul Octave

3 July. St. Irenæus of Lyon

Double

¶ The propers are from the First Common of a Martyr Bishop (p. 682), except for the following Collect.

Collect

O GOD, who gavest grace to blessed Irenæus thy Martyr and Bishop to overcome false doctrine by the truth of his teaching, and favourably to establish peace in thy Church: give thy people, we beseech thee, constancy in holy religion, and grant us thy peace all the days of our life. Through.

6 July. Octave Day of Sts. Peter and Paul

Greater Double

¶ The Daily Office propers are as on the Feast.

Introit

LET the people tell of the wisdom of the Saints, and let the Church shew forth their praise: their names shall live for evermore. *Ps.* Rejoice in the Lord. O ye righteous: for it becometh well the just to be thankful.

Collect

O GOD, whose right hand upheld blessed Peter lest he should sink when walking on the waves, and thrice from the depths of the sea delivered his fellow-Apostle Paul when suffering shipwreck: graciously hear us and grant; that, through the merits of them both, we may obtain the glory of everlasting life: Who livest.

Epistle. Ecclesiasticus 44:10

THESE were men of mercy, Whose righteous deeds have not been forgotten. With their seed shall remain continually a good inheritance; Their children are within the covenants. Their seed standeth fast, And their children for their sakes. Their seed shall remain for ever, And their glory shall not be blotted out. Their bodies were buried in peace, And their name liveth to all generations. Peoples will declare their wisdom, And the congregation telleth out their praise.

Gradual. The souls of the just are in the hand of God: and there shall no torment of malice touch them. ℣. In the sight of the unwise they seemed to die: but they are in peace.

Alleluia. Alleluia, alleluia. ℣. Ye are they which have continued with me in my temptations: and I appoint unto you a kingdom, that ye may sit on thrones, judging the twelve tribes of Israel. Alleluia.

Sts. Peter & Paul Octave **Proper of Saints** 6 July

Gospel. Matthew 14:22

T THAT TIME: Jesus constrained his disciples to get into a ship, and to go before him unto the other side, while he sent the multitudes away. And when he had sent the multitudes away, he went up into a mountain apart to pray: and when the evening was come, he was there alone. But the ship was now in the midst of the sea, tossed with waves: for the wind was contrary. And in the fourth watch of the night Jesus went unto them, walking on the sea. And when the disciples saw him walking on the sea, they were troubled, saying, It is a spirit; and they cried out for fear. But straightway Jesus spake unto them, saying, Be of good cheer; it is I; be not afraid. And Peter answered him and said, Lord, if it be thou, bid me come unto thee on the water. And he said, Come. And when Peter was come down out of the ship, he walked on the water, to go to Jesus. But when he saw the wind boisterous, he was afraid; and beginning to sink, he cried, saying, Lord, save me. And immediately Jesus stretched forth his hand, and caught him, and said unto him, O thou of little faith, wherefore didst thou doubt? And when they were come into the ship, the wind ceased. Then they that were in the ship came and worshipped him, saying, Of a truth thou art the Son of God.

Offertory. Let the Saints be joyful with glory, let them rejoice in their beds: let the praises of God be in their mouth.

Secret

E offer thee, O Lord, our prayers and gifts: and that they may be acceptable in thy sight, grant that we may aided by the prayers of thine Apostles Peter and Paul. Through.

Communion. The souls of the just are in the hand of God, and there shall no torment of malice touch them: in the sight of the unwise they seemed to die: but they are in peace.

Postcommunion

EFEND, O Lord, thy people: and preserve with thy continual protection those who trust in the advocacy of thine Apostles Peter and Paul. Through.

7 July. Sts. Cyril and Methodius

Double

❧ The propers are from the Second Common of a Confessor Bishop (p. 720), except for the following.

Collect

ALMIGHTY and everlasting God, who by thy blessed Confessors and Bishops, Cyril and Methodius, didst suffer the peoples of Slavonia to come to the knowledge of thy name: vouchsafe; that we, who glory in their festival may be joined unto their fellowship. Through.

Gospel. Luke 10:1

AT THAT TIME: the Lord appointed other seventy also: and sent them two and two before his face into every city and place, whither he himself would come. Therefore said he unto them, The harvest truly is great, but the labourers are few: pray ye therefore the Lord of the harvest, that he would send forth labourers into his harvest. Go your ways: behold, I send you forth as lambs among wolves. Carry neither purse, nor scrip, nor shoes: and salute no man by the way. And into whatsoever house ye enter, first say, Peace be to this house. And if the son of peace be there, your peace shall rest upon it: if not, it shall turn to you again. And in the same house remain, eating and drinking such things as they give: for the labourer is worthy of his hire. Go not from house to house. And into whatsoever city ye enter, and they receive you, eat such things as are set before you: And heal the sick that are therein, and say unto them, The kingdom of God is come nigh unto you.

Offertory. God is wonderful in his holy ones: even the God of Israel, he will give strength and power unto his people: blessed be God.

Secret

WE beseech thee, O Lord, to have respect unto the prayers and oblations of thy faithful people: that they may be acceptable unto thee on this festival of thy Saints, and effectually bestow on us the assistance of thy mercy. Through.

Communion. What I tell you in darkness, that speak ye in light, saith the Lord: and what ye hear in the ear, that preach ye upon the house-tops.

Postcommunion

WE beseech thee, Almighty God: that as thou dost vouchsafe to bestow upon us heavenly gifts, so, at the intercession of thy Saints Cyril and Methodius, thou wouldest grant unto us to despise things earthly. Through.

Proper of Saints

(10 July. Seven Holy Brothers, with Sts. Rufina and Secunda)

Introit

RAISE the Lord, ye servants, O praise the name of the Lord: who maketh the barren woman to keep house, and to be a joyful mother of children. *Ps.* Blessed be the name of the Lord: from this time forth for evermore.

Collect

RANT, we beseech thee, Almighty God: that, like as we have known thy glorious Martyrs to be constant in their confession, so we may perceive their loving intercession. Through.

¶ The Epistle is from the Common of a Holy Matron (p. 751).

Gradual. Our soul is escaped, even as a bird out of the snare of the fowler. ℣. The snare is broken, and we are delivered : our help is in the name of the Lord, who hath made heaven and earth.

Alleluia. Alleluia, alleluia. ℣. This is the true brotherhood, which overcame the wickedness of the world: which followed Christ, gaining heaven's glorious realms. Alleluia.

Gospel. Matthew 12:46

T THAT TIME: While Jesus spake to the multitudes, behold his Mother and brethren stood without, desiring to speak with him. Then one said unto him, Behold, thy mother and thy brethren stand without, desiring to speak with thee. But he answered and said unto him that told him, Who is my mother? and who are my brethren? And he stretched forth his hand toward his disciples, and said, Behold my mother and my brethren! For whosoever shall do the will of my Father which is in heaven, the same is my brother, and sister, and mother.

Offertory. Our soul is escaped, even as a bird out of the snare of the fowler: the snare is broken, and we are delivered.

Secret

E beseech thee, O Lord, mercifully to have respect unto these our sacrifices: that through the intercession of thy Saints, they may increase our devotion, and set forward our salvation. Through.

Communion. Whosoever shall do the will of my Father which is in heaven: the same is my brother, and sister, and mother, saith the Lord.

Postcommunion

E beseech thee, Almighty God: that as in these holy mysteries we have received the pledge of our salvation, so at the intercession of thy Saints, we may be brought unto the fulfilment of the same. Through.

Proper of Saints

(10 July. St. Joseph of Damascus and Companions)

¶ The Third Common of Many Martyrs (p. 700).

(11 July. Pope St. Pius I)

¶ The First Common of a Martyr Bishop (p. 682).

(12 July. Sts. Nabor and Felix)

¶ The Third Common of Many Martyrs (p. 700), except for the following.

Collect

RANT, we beseech thee, O Lord: that as the birthday of thy holy Martyrs, Nabor and Felix, faileth not to return for our observance; so they may continually assist us by their prayers. Through.

Secret

E beseech thee, O Lord, that the gifts of thy people may, by the prayers of thy holy Martyrs, Nabor and Felix, be made acceptable unto thee: that, as they are offered for their triumph to thy name, so by their merits they may be rendered worthy in thy sight. Through.

Postcommunion

LORD, who on the birthday of thy Saints hast quickened us with the gift of thy sacrament: we beseech thee; that, as by thy grace we now receive the comfort of thy blessings, so we may be brought to the everlasting fruition of the same. Through.

(13 July. St. Anacletus)

¶ The Second Common of a Martyr Bishop (p. 686), with the Gospel from the First Common of a Martyr Bishop (p. 682).

15 July. St. Vladimir of Kiev

Double

¶ The propers are from the First Common of a Confessor not a Bishop (p. 725).

(16 July. Sts. Nicholas and Habib Khasha)

¶ The Second Common of Many Martyrs (p. 699).

(17 July. St. Alexius)

❡ The First Common of a Confessor not a Bishop (p. 725), except for the following.

Epistle. 1 Timothy 6:6

DEARLY BELOVED: Godliness with contentment is great gain. For we brought nothing into this world, and it is certain we can carry nothing out. And having food and raiment let us be therewith content. But they that will be rich fall into temptation and a snare, and into many foolish and hurtful lusts, which drown men in destruction and perdition. For the love of money is the root of all evil: which while some coveted after, they have erred from the faith, and pierced themselves through with many sorrows. But thou, O man of God, flee these things; and follow after righteousness, godliness, faith, love, patience, meekness. Fight the good fight of faith, lay hold on eternal life.

Gospel. Matthew 19:27

AT THAT TIME: Peter said unto Jesus: Behold, we have forsaken all, and followed thee; what shall we have therefore? And Jesus said unto them, Verily I say unto you, That ye which have followed me, in the regeneration when the Son of man shall sit in the throne of his glory, ye also shall sit upon twelve thrones, judging the twelve tribes of Israel. And every one that hath forsaken houses, or brethren, or sisters, or father, or mother, or wife, or children, or lands, for my name's sake, shall receive an hundredfold, and shall inherit everlasting life.

18 July. Translation of St. Raphael of Brooklyn

Double

❡ The propers are from the First Common of a Confessor Bishop (p. 715).

(18 July. St. Sergius of Radonezh)

❡ The Common of Abbots (p. 732).

(18 July. Sts. Symphorosa and Her Seven Sons)

Introit

THE just cry, and the Lord heareth them: and delivereth them out of all their troubles. *Ps.* I will alway give thanks unto the Lord; his praise shall ever be in my mouth.

Collect

GOD, who vouchsafest unto us to keep the heavenly birthday of thy holy Martyrs Symphorosa and her sons: grant, we beseech thee; that we may rejoice in the perpetual felicity of their friendship. Through.

20 July   **Proper of Saints**   *St. Elias Prophet*

¶ The Epistle is the fifth additional Epistle of the Third Common of Many Martyrs (p. 702).

Gradual. Behold, how good and joyful a thing it is, brethren, to dwell together in unity! ℣. It is like the precious ointment upon the head, that ran down unto the beard, even unto Aaron's beard.

Alleluia. Alleluia, alleluia. ℣. This is the true brotherhood which overcame the wickedness of the world: which followed Christ, gaining heaven's glorious realms. Alleluia.

¶ The Gospel is from the Third Common of Many Martyrs (p. 700).

Offertory. Be glad, O ye righteous, and rejoice in the Lord: and be joyful, all ye that are true of heart.

Secret

E beseech thee, O Lord, that the gifts which we offer unto thee of our bounden duty and service may be acceptable unto thee for the honour of thy Saints: and by thy mercy profitable unto us for our salvation. Through.

¶ In Lent, Commemoration of the Feria.

Communion. Whosoever shall do the will of my Father which is in heaven: the same is my brother, and sister, and mother, saith the Lord.

Postcommunion

RANT, we beseech thee, Almighty God: that, at the intercession of thy holy Martyrs Symphorosa and her sons, we, who with our outward lips have partaken of this Sacrament, may inwardly receive the same in purity of heart. Through.

(19 July. St. Seraphim of Sarov)

¶ The First Common of a Confessor not a Bishop (p. 725).

20 July. St. Elias the Prophet

Double

Opening Sentence. Then stood up Elias the prophet as fire, and his word burned like a lamp, alleluia.

I Evensong	Mattins Invitatory Hymn
The lofty peaks of Carmel	Creator of the universe, our grateful
With tuneful praises ring,	hearts rejoice,
The anthems of Elias	Exalting thee in this, the mighty
'Tis our delight to sing.	Thesbite of thy choice;
The glory of our Churches,	Whose zeal for thy great glory, enkindled

St. Elias Prophet   **Proper of Saints**   20 July

Our leader, prop, and stay,
From east to west his offspring
Increaseth day by day.

When sorely press'd with famine,
A raven serv'd him bread,
With meal and cruse unfailing,
The widow'd hearth was fed.

The boy from death delivered
Is to his home restor'd,
And light so much desir'd,
In radiant flood is pour'd.

Behold the Heaven closeth,
To open at his voice,
And copious welcome showers
The thirsty lands rejoice.

To Father, Son, and Spirit,
Be equal power and praise,
All glory and dominion
Henceforth for endless days. Amen.

℣. By the word of the Lord he shut up the heaven.
℟. And he brought down fire from heaven thrice.
Mag. Ant. Behold, I † will send you Elias the prophet before the coming of the great and dreadful day of the Lord: And he shall turn the heart of the fathers to the children, and the heart of the children to their fathers

Mattins Office Hymn

Come, blest companions, let our joy resounding
Extol to heav'n the leader of our line.
'Tis meet the mem'ry of his deeds abounding
Should waken ceaseless canticles divine.

He knows the gentle breathing of the Spirit
as a flame,
Defied the impious Prophets, and slew them in thy name.

His holocaust ascendeth, for thy fire may never fail,
While scorn and deep derision mock the clamorous priests of Baal.

The baneful rage of Jezabel he flieth in his dread,
And sleeping 'neath a juniper is by an angel fed.

Empowered by the vision, with new courage he hath trod
Unto the heights of Horeb, unto the Mount of God.

O virtue of this bread divine, imparted by the Lord!
Full forty days he fasteth in the strength it doth afford.

All glory be to thee, O Father, Son, and Paraclete,
O undivided Trinity, thy praise all hearts repeat. Amen.

II Evensong

Thou prop of our Churches, thou pride of our race,
Let thy praises resound far and near,
Let sea and the land and the air give them place,
Rehearsing in gladness thy glory and grace,
Till the earth and the heav'ns give ear.

20 July — **Proper of Saints** — *St. Elias Prophet*

Cloth'd in the whistling murmur of the air,
By God's command the chastisements they merit
Proud Jezebel and Ahab justly share.

The caverns green of Carmel form his dwelling,
With leathern tunic is he rudely clad,
To impious Ahaziah his foretelling
Gives portent of a dissolution sad.

Twice at his pray'r the fire from Heav'n descending
Consumeth trembling soldiers in its flame,
The flowing wat'rs met with his mantle rending,
Dry shod he passeth safely through the same.

O Father, let thy help and thy protection
Be o'er thy children as they humbly plead,
Entreat the Spirit, by his sweet election,
To multiply his graces in their need.

O unbegotten Father, we adore thee,
O Son begotten, rev'rence be to thee,
O glorious Spirit, bow we low before thee,
Thou simple undivided Trinity. Amen.

℣. Elias was covered with the whirlwind.

℟. And his spirit was filled up in Eliseus.

Ben. Ant. Elias was a man † subject to like passions as we are, and he prayed earnestly that it might not rain: and it rained not on the earth by the space of three years and six months. And he prayed again, and the heaven gave rain, and the earth brought forth her fruit.

O sun of the heavens, how lovely thy rays!
What power thy wonders unfold,
How fruitful in merits the length of thy days,
Commission'd by God in His manifold ways,
For noble endeavours of old!

To regions celestial, in power and might,
Triumphant thy chariot speeds;
Uplifted by angels to marvellous height,
While shining in splendour and dazzling with light,
Thou guidest the fiery steeds.

As witness to men of his Sonship divine,
With Jesus thy glory we view;
The Father hath call'd thee on Tabor to shine,
Companion to Moses, and with him to sign
A testament faithful and true.

Protect us we pray, 'neath thy powerful shield,
Incline to our aid from above,
Let thy fost'ring guidance be ever reveal'd
To thy children of Carmel, whose bosoms are seal'd
With the strength of thy fath'rly love

All power, dominion, all glory and praise,
Be given to Father and Son,
To thee, Holy Spirit, for numberless days
Our homage eternal we equally raise
All glory to God, Three in One. Amen.

℣. Blessed are they that saw thee.

℟. And were honoured with thy friendship.

St. Elias Prophet   **Proper of Saints**   20 July

Mag. Ant. And Elias took † his mantle, and wrapped it together, and smote the waters of the Jordan, and they were divided hither and thither, so that he and Eliseus went over on dry ground. As they still went on, behold, there appeared a chariot of fire, and horses of fire, and parted them both asunder; and Elias went up by a whirlwind into heaven, and Eliseus saw him no more.

Introit

I HAVE been very zealous for the Lord God of hosts: for the children of Israel have forsaken thy covenant, thrown down thine altars, and slain thy prophets with the sword; and I, even I only, am left; and they seek my life, to take it away. *Ps.* I will magnify thee, O Lord, for thou hast set me up: and not made my foes to triumph over me.

Collect

GRANT, we beseech thee, Almighty God: that we who believe that thou didst marvellously lift up thy Prophet Elias in a fiery chariot, while yet in this life; may at his intercession, while still alive, be raised to spiritual heights and rejoice in the resurrection of the just. Through.

¶ Commemoration of St. Margaret of Antioch, from the Second Common of a Virgin Martyress (p. 738).

Epistle. Ecclesiasticus 48:1

THERE arose Elijah the prophet as fire, And his word burned like a torch: Who brought a famine upon them, And by his zeal made them few in number. By the word of the Lord he shut up the heaven: Thrice did he thus bring down fire. How wast thou glorified, O Elijah, in thy wondrous deeds! And who shall glory like unto thee? Who did raise up a dead man from death, And from the place of the dead, by the word of the Most High: Who brought down kings to destruction, And honourable men from their bed: Who heard rebuke in Sinai, And judgements of vengeance in Horeb: Who anointed kings for retribution, And prophets to succeed after him: Who was taken up in a tempest of fire, In a chariot of fiery horses: Who was recorded for reproofs in their seasons, To pacify anger, before it brake forth into wrath; To turn the heart of the father unto the son, And to restore the tribes of Jacob.

Gradual. It came to pass, when the Lord would take up Elias into heaven by a whirlwind, that Elias went with Eliseus from Gilgal. ℣. And it came to pass, as they still went on, that, behold, there appeared a chariot of fire, and horses of fire, and parted them both asunder; and Elias went up by a whirlwind into heaven.

20 July — **Proper of Saints** — *St. Elias Prophet*

Alleluia. Alleluia, alleluia. ℣. Elias, while he was full of zeal for the law, was taken up into heaven. Alleluia.

Gospel. Luke 9:28

AT THAT TIME: It came to pass about an eight days after these sayings, Jesus took Peter and John and James, and went up into a mountain to pray. And as he prayed, the fashion of his countenance was altered, and his raiment was white and glistering. And, behold, there talked with him two men, which were Moses and Elias: Who appeared in glory, and spake of his decease which he should accomplish at Jerusalem. But Peter and they that were with him were heavy with sleep: and when they were awake, they saw his glory, and the two men that stood with him. And it came to pass, as they departed from him, Peter said unto Jesus, Master, it is good for us to be here: and let us make three tabernacles; one for thee, and one for Moses, and one for Elias: not knowing what he said. While he thus spake, there came a cloud, and overshadowed them: and they feared as they entered into the cloud. And there came a voice out of the cloud, saying, This is my beloved Son: hear him. And when the voice was past, Jesus was found alone. And they kept it close, and told no man in those days any of those things which they had seen.

Offertory. Elias was a man subject to like passions as we are: and he prayed earnestly that it might not rain, and it rained not on the earth for the space of three years and six months: and he prayed again, and the heaven gave rain, and the earth brought forth her fruit.

Secret

E offer unto thee, O Lord, this sacrifice of praise in honour of thy Prophet Elias: that, as thou didst accept his burnt-offering, so thou wouldest vouchsafe to accept our own sacrifice; that through it we may be made worthy to attain unto everlasting gladness. Through.

¶ Commemoration of **St. Margaret of Antioch,** from the Second Common of a Virgin Martyress (p. 738).

Preface

ND that we, with glad hearts, should praise, bless, and glorify thee in the Solemnity of blessed Elias thy Prophet: Who at thy word stood up like fire; shut the heavens and raised the dead; smote tyrants and slew the blasphemous; and laid the foundation of the monastic profession: Who, being fed with meat and drink served by Angels, walked in the strength of that food, even to the holy mountain: Who, being raised up from earth in a fiery chariot, will return to us as the Forerunner of the second Coming of Jesus Christ our Lord. Therefore.

Communion. Behold, I will send you Elias the Prophet before the coming of the great and terrible day of the Lord: and he shall turn the hearts of the fathers to the children, and the hearts of the children to their fathers.

Postcommunion

GOD, who by thy holy Angel didst give meat and drink to blessed Elias thy Prophet: grant, by his intercession, that what we have received of thy heavenly table, we may keep undefiled in purity of mind. Through.

¶ Commemoration of St. Margaret of Antioch, from the Second Common of a Virgin Martyress (p. 738).

(20 July. St. Margaret of Antioch)

¶ The Second Common of a Virgin Martyress (p. 738).

(21 July. St. Praxedes)

¶ The Second Common of a Virgin (p. 744), except for the following.

Introit

I WILL speak of thy testimonies even before kings, and will not be ashamed: and my delight shall be in thy commandments, which I have loved exceedingly. *Ps.* Blessed are those that are undefiled in the way: and walk in the law of the Lord.

Gradual. Thou hast loved righteousness, and hated iniquity. ℣. Wherefore God, even thy God, hath anointed thee with the oil of gladness.

Alleluia. Alleluia, alleluia. ℣. In thy comeliness and in thy beauty, go forth, proceed prosperously, and reign. Alleluia.

Gospel. Matthew 13:44

AT THAT TIME: Jesus spake this parable unto his disciples: The kingdom of heaven is like unto treasure hid in a field; the which when a man hath found, he hideth, and for joy thereof goeth and selleth all that he hath, and buyeth that field. Again, the kingdom of heaven is like unto a merchant man, seeking goodly pearls: Who, when he had found one pearl of great price, went and sold all that he had, and bought it. Again, the kingdom of heaven is like unto a net, that was cast into the sea, and gathered of every kind: Which, when it was full, they drew to shore, and sat down, and gathered the good into vessels, but cast the bad away. So shall it be at the end of the world: the angels shall come forth, and sever the wicked from among the just, And shall cast them into the furnace of fire: there shall be wailing and gnashing of teeth. Jesus saith unto them, Have ye understood all these things? They say unto him, Yea, Lord. Then said he unto them, Therefore every scribe which is instructed unto the kingdom of heaven is like unto a man that is an householder, which bringeth forth out of his treasure things new and old.

Offertory. Full of grace are thy lips, because God hath blessed thee for ever and ever.

Communion. The kingdom of heaven is like unto a merchant man, seeking goodly pearls: who when he had found one pearl of great price, gave all that he had, and bought it.

[22 July. St. Mary Magdalene, Penitent]

I Evensong

O Father of ce-lest-ial rays, When thou on Magda-lene dost gaze, The flame of burning love appears, Her i-cy heart dis-solves in tears. 2. Wounded by love, she has-tens o'er The feet of Christ her tears to pour, Anoints them, wipes them with her hair, And prints a-dor-ing kiss-es there. 3. Fearless, the Cross she will not leave: And griev-ing, to the Tomb doth cleave: No ruthless soldiers cause her dread: For from her love all fear hath fled. 4. O Christ, true Char-i-ty thou art;

St. Mary Magdalene   Proper of Saints   22 July

Purge thou the foulness of our heart, Fill every soul with grace and love, And give us thy re-wards a-bove. 5. All laud to God the Father be; All praise, e-ternal Son, to thee; All glo-ry, as is ev-er meet, To God the Ho-ly Par-a-clete. A-men.

℣. Mary hath chosen that good part.

℞. Which shall not be taken away from her.

Mag. Ant. A woman † in the city which was a sinner, when she knew that Jesus sat at meat in the house of Simon the leper, brought an alabaster box of ointment, and stood behind at the feet of Jesus, and began to wash his feet with tears, and did wipe them with the hairs of her head, and kissed his feet, and anointed them with the ointment.

Mattins

Invitatory Hymn

The Lord's dear feet did Mar-y lave With her own tears; her hair she gave To wipe them dry; and then she pour'd The precious ointment, and a-dor'd. To God the Fa-ther, God the Son, And God

22 July — Proper of Saints — *St. Mary Magdalene*

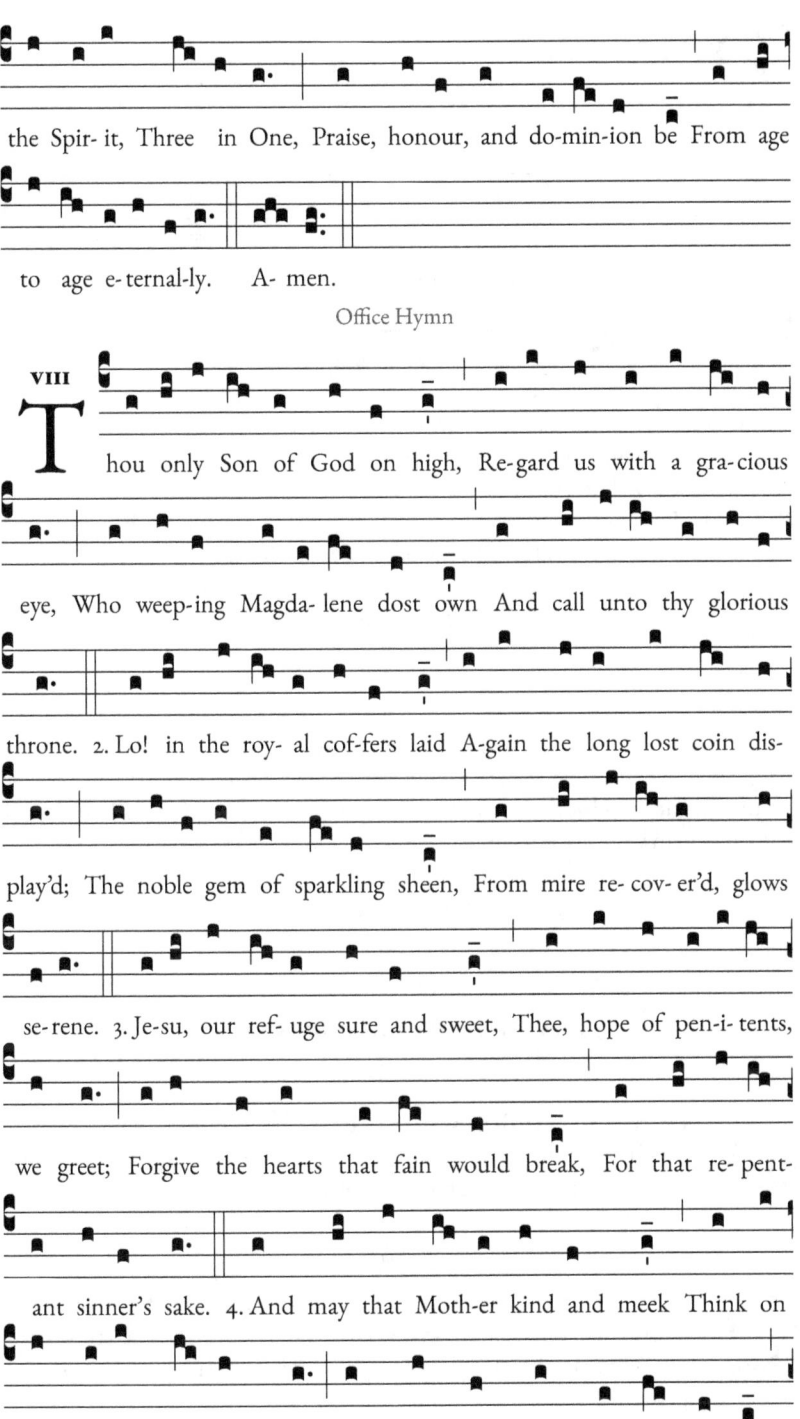

the Spir- it, Three in One, Praise, honour, and do-min-ion be From age to age e- ternal-ly. A- men.

Office Hymn

VIII

Thou only Son of God on high, Re-gard us with a gra-cious eye, Who weep-ing Magda- lene dost own And call unto thy glorious throne. 2. Lo! in the roy- al cof-fers laid A-gain the long lost coin dis-play'd; The noble gem of sparkling sheen, From mire re- cov- er'd, glows se- rene. 3. Je-su, our ref- uge sure and sweet, Thee, hope of pen-i- tents, we greet; Forgive the hearts that fain would break, For that re- pent-ant sinner's sake. 4. And may that Moth-er kind and meek Think on our na-ture frail and weak, And raise her prayer that we may gain

St. Apollinaris Ravenna **Proper of Saints** 23 July

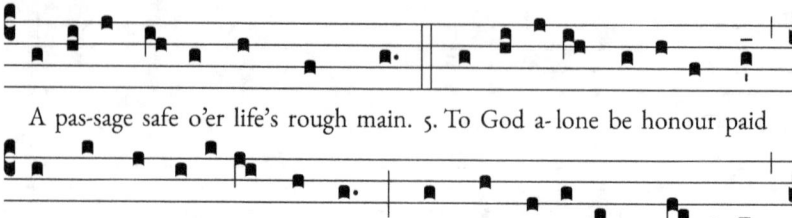

A pas-sage safe o'er life's rough main. 5. To God a-lone be honour paid

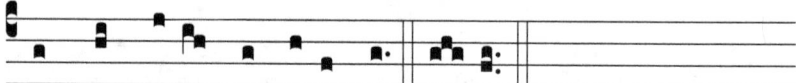

For grace so man-i-fold displayed: Their guilt he pardons who re-pent,

And gives re-ward for pun-ishment. A-men.
℣. Her sins, which are many, are forgiven.
℟. For she loved much.
Ben. Ant. Mary therefore † anointed the feet of Jesus, and wiped them with her hair, and the house was filled with the odour of the ointment.

II Evensong

¶ The Office Hymn is of I Evensong with the following Versicle & Antiphon.

℣. God hath chosen her and preferred her.
℟. He hath made her to dwell in his tabernacle.
Mag. Ant. A woman † in the city which was a sinner, brought an alabaster box of ointment, and stood at the Lord's feet, and began to wash his feet with tears, and did wipe them with the hairs of her head.

(23 July. St. John Cassian)

¶ The Common of Abbots (p. 732).

(23 July. St. Apollinaris of Ravenna)

Introit

YE priests of the Lord, bless ye the Lord: O ye holy and humble men of heart, bless ye the Lord. *Cant.* O all ye works of the Lord, bless ye the Lord: praise him and magnify him for ever.

Collect

GOD, the rewarder of faithful souls, who hast hallowed this day by the martyrdom of blessed Apollinaris, thy Priest: grant, we beseech thee, unto us thy servants; that we who keep his solemn festival may by his prayers obtain thy pardon. Through.

23 July   **Proper of Saints**   *St. Apollinaris Ravenna*

Epistle. 1 Peter 5:1

EARLY BELOVED: The elders which are among you I exhort, who am also an elder, and a witness of the sufferings of Christ, and also a partaker of the glory that shall be revealed: Feed the flock of God which is among you, taking the oversight thereof, not by constraint, but willingly; not for filthy lucre, but of a ready mind; Neither as being lords over God's heritage, but being ensamples to the flock. And when the chief Shepherd shall appear, ye shall receive a crown of glory that fadeth not away. Likewise, ye younger, submit yourselves unto the elder. Yea, all of you be subject one to another, and be clothed with humility: for God resisteth the proud, and giveth grace to the humble. Humble yourselves therefore under the mighty hand of God, that he may exalt you in due time: Casting all your care upon him; for he careth for you. Be sober, be vigilant; because your adversary the devil, as a roaring lion, walketh about, seeking whom he may devour: Whom resist stedfast in the faith, knowing that the same afflictions are accomplished in your brethren that are in the world. But the God of all grace, who hath called us unto his eternal glory by Christ Jesus, after that ye have suffered a while, make you perfect, stablish, strengthen, settle you. To him be glory and dominion for ever and ever. Amen.

Gradual. I have found David my servant, with my holy oil have I anointed him: my hand shall hold him fast, and my arm shall strengthen him. ℣. The enemy shall not be able to do him violence, the son of wickedness shall not hurt him.

Alleluia. Alleluia, alleluia. ℣. The Lord sware, and will not repent: Thou art a priest for ever, after the order of Melchisedech. Alleluia.

Gospel. Luke 22:24

T THAT TIME: There was a strife among the disciples, which of them should be accounted the greatest. And he said unto them, The kings of the Gentiles exercise lordship over them; and they that exercise authority upon them are called benefactors. But ye shall not be so: but he that is greatest among you, let him be as the younger; and he that is chief, as he that doth serve. For whether is greater, he that sitteth at meat, or he that serveth? is not he that sitteth at meat? but I am among you as he that serveth. Ye are they which have continued with me in my temptations. And I appoint unto you a kingdom, as my Father hath appointed unto me; That ye may eat and drink at my table in my kingdom, and sit on thrones judging the twelve tribes of Israel.

Offertory. My truth and my mercy shall be with him: and in my name shall his horn be exalted.

Secret

RACIOUSLY look, O Lord, upon these gifts: which in remembrance of blessed Apollinaris, thy Priest and Martyr, we lay before thee, and offer up for our offences. Through.

Communion. Lord, thou deliveredst unto me five talents, behold, I have gained beside them five talents more. Well done, thou good and faithful servant, thou hast been faithful over a few things, I will make thee ruler over many things, enter thou into the joy of thy Lord.

Postcommunion

WE who have received thy holy things, beseech thee, O Lord, that the protection of blessed Apollinaris may continually defend us: forasmuch as thou failest not to look with mercy on those to whom thou dost grant the succour of his assistance. *Through.*

(23 July. St. Liborius)

¶ The First Common of a Confessor Bishop (p. 715).

24 July. Vigil of St. James

Vigil

¶ The propers are from the Common of Vigils of the Apostles (p. 672), with commemoration of St. Christina from the Second Common of a Virgin Martyress (p. 738), and the 3rd Collect of St. Mary in Eastertide (p. BCP 542).

(24 July. St. Christina)

¶ The Second Common of a Virgin Martyress (p. 738).

[25 July. St. James]

¶ The Daily Office propers are of the Common of Apostles (p. 673).

(25 July. St. Christopher)

¶ The First Common of a Martyr not a Bishop (p. 688).

[26 July. St. Anne]

I Evensong

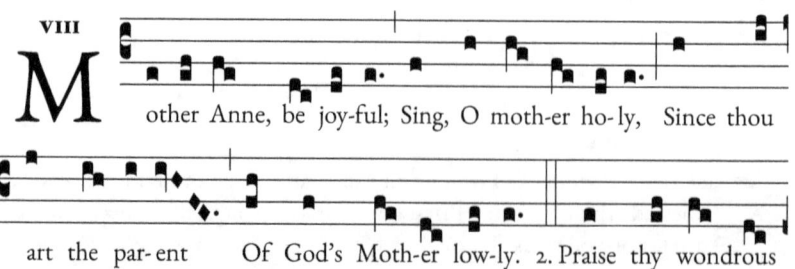

Mother Anne, be joyful; Sing, O mother holy, Since thou art the parent Of God's Mother lowly. 2. Praise thy wondrous

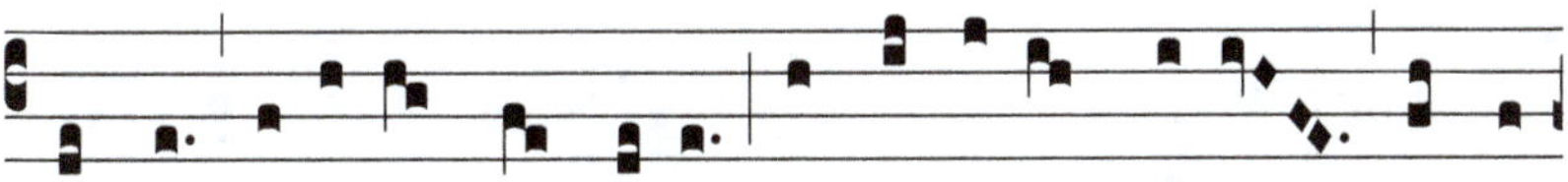

26 July — **Proper of Saints** — *St. Anne*

daughter; Joachim, too, raises To the Virgin Mary His paternal praises. 3. For in her our planet First hath benediction Which in hapless Eva Suffer'd malediction. 4. Therefore take the praises Joyous hearts are paying; And from all defilement Cleanse us by thy praying. 5. Father, Son eternal, Holy Ghost supernal, With one praise we bless thee, Three in One confess thee. Amen.

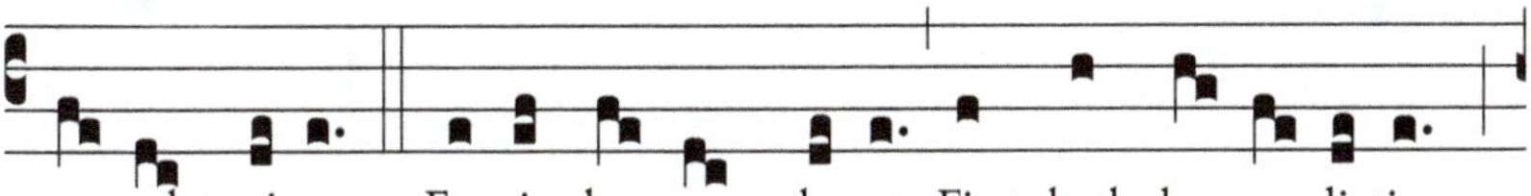

℣. Be glad, O ye righteous and rejoice in the Lord.

℞. And be joyful, all ye that are true of heart.

Mag. Ant. The kingdom of heaven † is likened unto a merchantman seeking goodly pearls; who, when he had found one pearl of great price, went and sold all that he had, and bought it.

Mattins

¶ The Invitatory Hymn is as in I Evensong.

Office Hymn

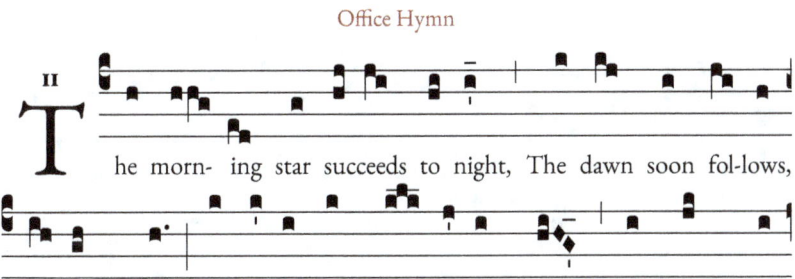

The morning star succeeds to night, The dawn soon follows, growing white To herald in the sunrise bright That floods the

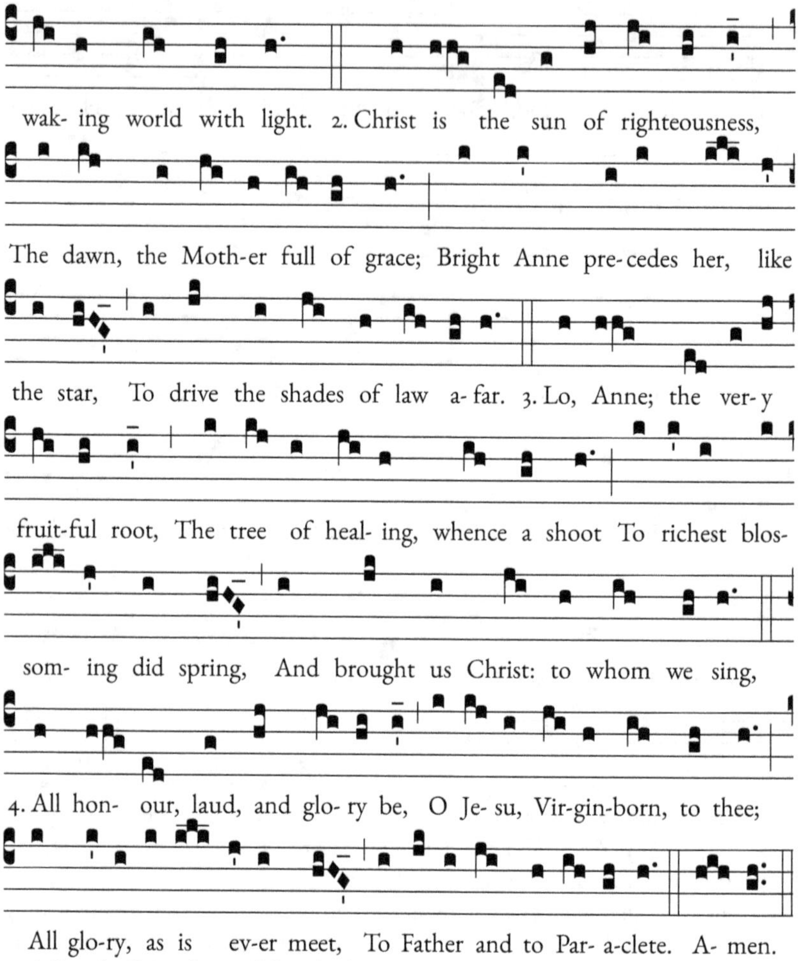

St. Anne — **Proper of Saints** — 26 July

wak- ing world with light. 2. Christ is the sun of righteousness,

The dawn, the Moth-er full of grace; Bright Anne pre-cedes her, like

the star, To drive the shades of law a- far. 3. Lo, Anne; the ver- y

fruit-ful root, The tree of heal- ing, whence a shoot To richest blos-

som- ing did spring, And brought us Christ: to whom we sing,

4. All hon- our, laud, and glo- ry be, O Je- su, Vir-gin-born, to thee;

All glo-ry, as is ev-er meet, To Father and to Par- a-clete. A- men.

℣. Let the Saints be joyful with glory.

℟. Let them rejoice in their beds.

Ben. Ant. Give her † of the fruit of her hands; and let her own works praise her in the gates.

II Evensong

Let all the Saints in concert sing, The moth-er of that Maid

to laud By whose unstain-ed Childbear-ing Sal-va-tion came to men

26 July — **Proper of Saints** — *St. Anne*

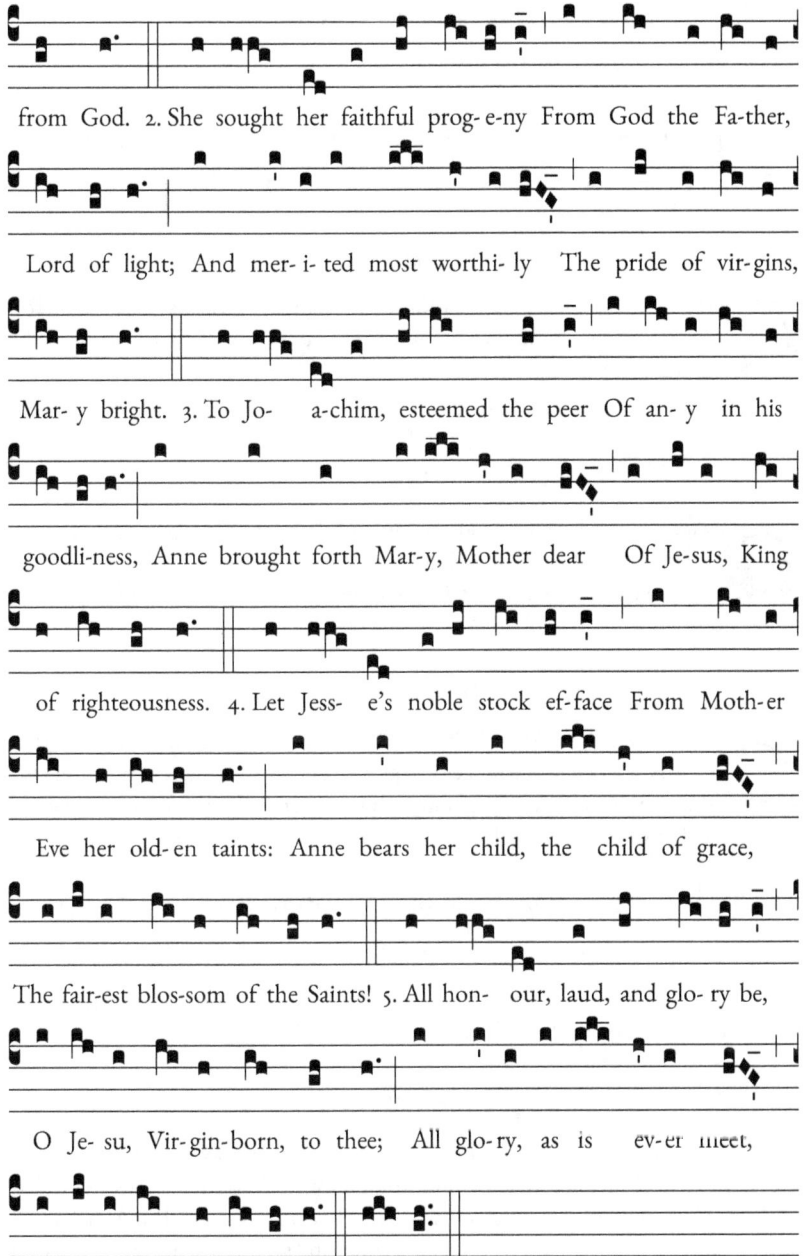

from God. 2. She sought her faithful prog-e-ny From God the Fa-ther, Lord of light; And mer-i-ted most worthi-ly The pride of vir-gins, Mar-y bright. 3. To Jo- a-chim, esteemed the peer Of an-y in his goodli-ness, Anne brought forth Mar-y, Mother dear Of Je-sus, King of righteousness. 4. Let Jess- e's noble stock ef-face From Moth-er Eve her old-en taints: Anne bears her child, the child of grace, The fair-est blos-som of the Saints! 5. All hon- our, laud, and glo-ry be, O Je-su, Vir-gin-born, to thee; All glo-ry, as is ev-er meet, To Father and to Par-a-clete. A-men.

℣. Let the Saints be joyful with glory.

℟. Let them rejoice in their beds.

Mag. Ant. She stretched out † her hand to the poor; yea, she reacheth forth her hands to the needy; she eateth not the bread of idleness.

(27 July. St. Pantaleon)

¶ The Second Common of a Martyr not a Bishop (p. 690).

(28 July. Sts. Nazarius, Celsus, Victor, and Innocent)

¶ The First Common of Many Martyrs (p. 692), except for the following.

Collect

O Lord, let the blessed confession of thy Saints, Nazarius, Celsus, Victor, and Innocent, strengthen us: and obtain for our frailty the succour of thy goodness. Through.

¶ The Epistle is the first additional Epistle of the Third Common of Many Martyrs (p. 701).

Secret

Grant to us, Almighty God: that we, who present these gifts unto thee to the honour of thy Saints, Nazarius, Celsus, Victor, and Innocent, may propitiate thee by the offering, and be quickened by the receiving of the same. Through.

Postcommunion

Grant, O Lord, we beseech thee, that the intercession of thy Saints Nazarius, Celsus, Victor, and Innocent, may so make us acceptable unto thee: that those things which we perform in this temporal celebration we may receive unto eternal salvation. Through.

29 July. St. Martha of Bethany

Double

¶ The propers are from the First Common of a Virgin (p. 742), except for the following, with a Commemoration of Sts. Felix, etc.

Gospel. Luke 10:38

At that time: Jesus entered into a certain village: and a certain woman named Martha received him into her house. And she had a sister called Mary, which also sat at Jesus' feet, and heard his word. But Martha was cumbered about much serving, and came to him, and said, Lord, dost thou not care that my sister hath left me to serve alone? bid her therefore that she help me. And Jesus answered and said unto her, Martha, Martha, thou art careful and troubled about many things: But one thing is needful: and Mary hath chosen that good part, which shall not be taken away from her.

Proper of Saints

30 July — Sts. Abdon & Sennen

(29 July. Sts. Felix II, Simplicius, Faustinus, and Beatrice)

¶ The Second Common of Many Martyrs (p. 699), except for the following.

Collect

GRANT, we beseech thee, O Lord: that as thy Christian people rejoice in the temporal solemnity of thy Martyrs, Felix, Simplicius, Faustinus, and Beatrice, so they may eternally enjoy the same; that those things which they devoutly celebrate, they may effectually obtain. Through.

Secret

WE offer our sacrifices unto thee, O Lord, in commemoration of thy Holy Martyrs Felix, Simplicius, Faustinus, and Beatrice: humbly entreating thee; that they may bestow on us both pardon and salvation. Through.

Postcommunion

GRANT, we beseech thee, Almighty God: that the solemnity of thy holy Martyrs Felix, Simplicius, Faustinus, and Beatrice: which we have celebrated in these heavenly mysteries, may obtain for us merciful pardon. Through.

(30 July. Sts. Abdon and Sennen)

Introit

LET the sorrowful sighing of the prisoners, O Lord, come before thee: reward thou our neighbours sevenfold in their bosom: avenge thou the blood of thy Saints that is shed. *Ps.* O God, the heathen are come into thine inheritance: thy holy temple have they defiled: and made Jerusalem an heap of stones.

Collect

O GOD, who on thy Saints Abdon and Sennen didst bestow the bounteous gift of grace to attain unto thy glory: grant unto thy servants the remission of their sins; that, by the intercession of the merits of thy Saints, they may be found worthy to be delivered from all adversities. Through.

¶ The Epistle is the fourth additional Epistle of the Third Common of Many Martyrs (p. 702).

Gradual. God is glorious in his holy ones, fearful in praises, doing wonders. ℣. Thy right hand, O Lord, is become glorious in power: thy right hand hath dashed in pieces the enemy.

Alleluia. Alleluia, alleluia. ℣. The souls of the just are in the hand of God, and there shall no torment of malice touch them. Alleluia.

Lammas   # Proper of Saints   1 August

Gospel. Matthew 5:1

AT THAT TIME: Jesus, seeing the multitudes, went up into a mountain, and when he was set, his disciples came unto him: And he opened his mouth, and taught them, saying, Blessed are the poor in spirit: for theirs is the kingdom of heaven. Blessed are they that mourn: for they shall be comforted. Blessed are the meek: for they shall inherit the earth. Blessed are they which do hunger and thirst after righteousness: for they shall be filled. Blessed are the merciful: for they shall obtain mercy. Blessed are the pure in heart: for they shall see God. Blessed are the peacemakers: for they shall be called the children of God. Blessed are they which are persecuted for righteousness' sake: for theirs is the kingdom of heaven. Blessed are ye, when men shall revile you, and persecute you, and shall say all manner of evil against you falsely, for my sake. Rejoice, and be exceeding glad: for great is your reward in heaven:

Offertory. God is wonderful in his holy ones: even the God of Israel, he will give strength and power unto his people: blessed be God.

Secret

E beseech thee, O Lord, that the sacrifice, which we offer in remembrance of the birthday of thy holy Martyrs, may both loose the bonds of our iniquity, and obtain for us the gifts of thy mercy. Through.

Communion. The dead bodies of thy servants, O Lord, have they given to be meat unto the fowls of the air, and the flesh of thy Saints unto the beasts of the land: according to the greatness of thy power preserve thou those that are appointed to die.

Postcommunion

AY the operation of this mystery, O Lord, both cleanse our sins: and, at the intercession of thy holy Martyrs Abdon and Sennen, obtain the fulfilment of our rightful desires. Through.

[1 August. Chains of St. Peter]

I Evensong

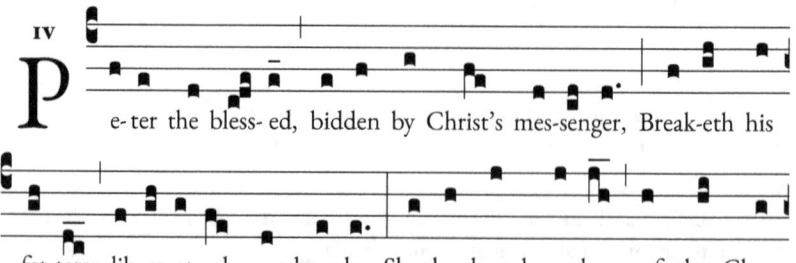

Pe-ter the bless-ed, bidden by Christ's mes-senger, Break-eth his fet-ters, lib-er-at-ed wondrously; Shepherd and teacher of the Chur-

1 August   **Proper of Saints**   *Lammas*

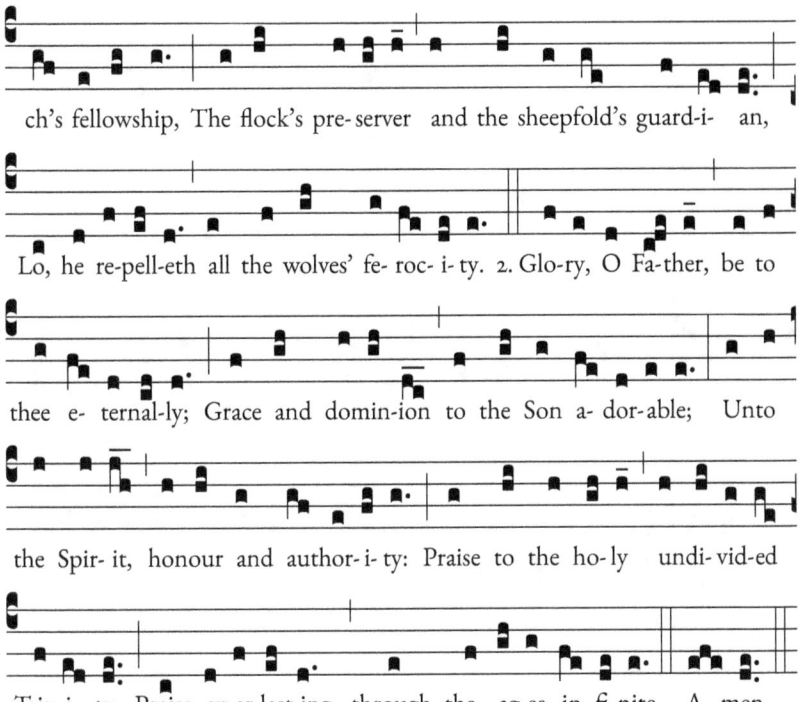

ch's fellowship, The flock's pre-server and the sheepfold's guard-i- an, Lo, he re-pell-eth all the wolves' fe- roc- i- ty. 2. Glo-ry, O Fa-ther, be to thee e- ternal-ly; Grace and domin-ion to the Son a- dor-able; Unto the Spir- it, honour and author-i-ty: Praise to the ho-ly undi-vid-ed Trin-i- ty, Praise ev-er-last-ing, through the ag-es in- fi-nite. A- men.

℣. Thou art Peter.

℟. And upon this rock I will build my Church.

Mag. Ant. Thou art the shepherd of the sheep, † O chief of the Apostles: unto thee were given the keys of the kingdom of heaven.

Mattins

Invitatory Hymn

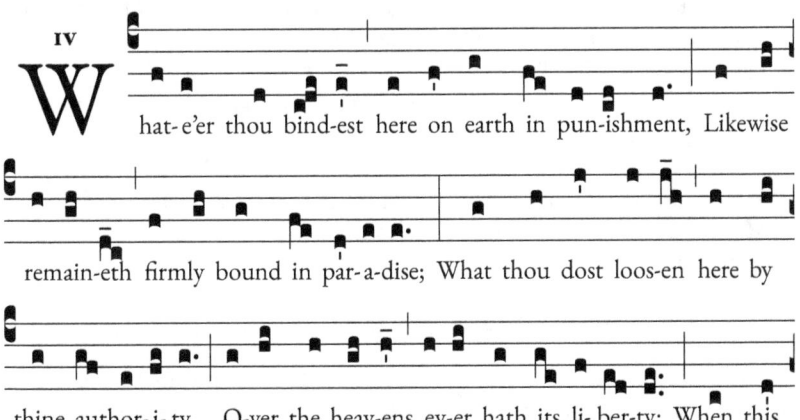

What-e'er thou bind-est here on earth in pun-ishment, Likewise remain-eth firmly bound in par-a-dise; What thou dost loos-en here by thine author-i-ty O-ver the heav-ens ev-er hath its li-ber-ty: When this

Holy Maccabees — **Proper of Saints** — 1 August

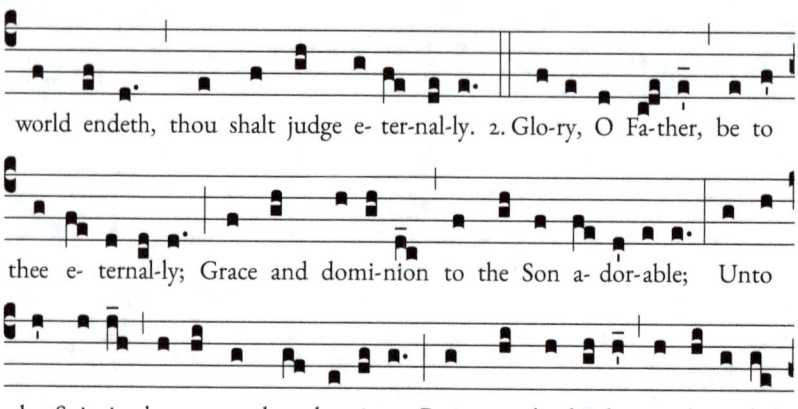

world endeth, thou shalt judge e-ter-nal-ly. 2. Glo-ry, O Fa-ther, be to thee e-ternal-ly; Grace and domi-nion to the Son a-dor-able; Unto the Spir-it, honour and author-i-ty; Praise to the ho-ly undi-vi-ded Tri-ni-ty Praise ev-er-last-ing through the ag-es in-fi-nite. A-men.

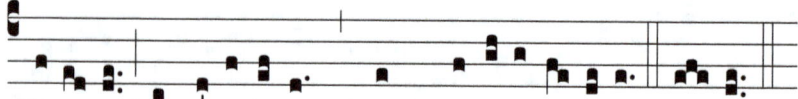

Office Hymn

¶ The Office Hymn is from the Feast of the Chair of St. Peter at Antioch, 22 February (p. 466), with the following Versicle & Antiphon.

℣. Thou art Peter.

℟. And upon this rock I will build my Church.

Ben. Ant. Whatsoever † thou shalt bind on earth shall be bound in heaven: and whatsoever thou shalt loose on earth shall be loosed in heaven: saith the Lord unto Simon Peter.

II Evensong

¶ The Office Hymn & Versicle are as in I Evensong, with the following Antiphon.

Mag. Ant. Loosen these earthly fetters † at the command of God, O Peter; and let the kingdom of heaven be opened unto the blessed.

(1 August. Holy Maccabees)

Introit

THE just cry, and the Lord heareth them: and delivereth them out of all their troubles. *Ps.* I will alway give thanks unto the Lord; his praise shall ever be in my mouth.

Collect

O LORD, let the crown of the brethren, thy Martyrs, cause us to rejoice: that we may thereby be strengthened and increased in our faith; and comforted by their manifold intercession. Through.

2 August — **Proper of Saints** — *Pope St. Stephen*

❧ The Epistle is the fifth additional Epistle of the Third Common of Many Martyrs (p. 702).

Gradual. Behold, how good and joyful a thing it is, brethren, to dwell together in unity! ℣. It is like the precious ointment upon the head, that ran down unto the beard, even unto Aaron's beard.

Alleluia. Alleluia, alleluia. ℣. This is the true brotherhood, which overcame the wickedness of the world: which followed Christ, gaining heaven's glorious realms. Alleluia.

❧ The Gospel is from the Third Common of Many Martyrs (p. 700).

Offertory. Let the Saints be joyful with glory: let them rejoice in their beds: let the praises of God be in their mouth, alleluia.

Secret

RANT, O Lord, that we may with devout hearts celebrate thy mysteries in honour of thy holy Martyrs: and thereby obtain an increase both of protection and joy. Through.

Communion. And I say unto you, my friends: Be not afraid of them that persecute you.

Postcommunion

RANT, we beseech thee, Almighty God: that growing in virtue we may follow the faith of them whose memory we recall by the partaking of this sacrament. Through.

(2 August. Pope St. Stephen)

❧ The Second Common of a Martyr Bishop (p. 686), except for the following.

Introit

 WILL deck her priests with health, and her saints shall rejoice and sing. *Ps.* Lord, remember David: and all his trouble.

Epistle. Acts 20:17

IN THOSE DAYS: From Miletus Paul sent to Ephesus, and called the elders of the church. And when they were come to him, he said unto them, Ye know, from the first day that I came into Asia, after what manner I have been with you at all seasons, serving the Lord with all humility of mind, and with many tears, and temptations, which befell me by the lying in wait of the Jews: and how I kept back nothing that was profitable unto you, but have shewed you, and have taught you publickly, and from house to house, testifying both to the Jews, and also to the Greeks, repentance toward God, and faith toward our Lord Jesus Christ.

Invention of St. Stephen **Proper of Saints** 3 August

Gradual. Behold, a great priest, who in his days pleased God. ℣. There was none found like unto him, who kept the law of the Most High.

Alleluia. Alleluia, alleluia. ℣. Thou art a priest for ever, after the order of Melchisedech. Alleluia.

Communion. Lord, thou deliveredst unto me five talents: behold, I have gained beside them five talents more. Well done, thou good and faithful servant, thou hast been faithful over a few things. I will make thee ruler over many things, enter thou into the joy of thy Lord.

3 August. Invention of St. Stephen

Double

¶ The Office & Mass as on 26 December, except for the following.

¶ Note, The Creed is not said.

Collect

GRANT us, we beseech thee, O Lord, so to imitate that which we revere: that we may learn to love even our enemies; forasmuch as we celebrate the Finding of him, who was able to pray even for his persecutors to our Lord Jesus Christ thy Son. Who liveth.

Epistle. Acts 6:8

IN THOSE DAYS: Stephen, full of faith and power, did great wonders and miracles among the people. Then there arose certain of the synagogue, which is called the synagogue of the Libertines, and Cyrenians, and Alexandrians, and of them of Cilicia and of Asia, disputing with Stephen. And they were not able to resist the wisdom and the spirit by which he spake. When they heard these things, they were cut to the heart, and they gnashed on him with their teeth. But he, being full of the Holy Ghost, looked up stedfastly into heaven, and saw the glory of God, and Jesus standing on the right hand of God, and said, Behold, I see the heavens opened, and the Son of man standing on the right hand of God. Then they cried out with a loud voice, and stopped their ears, and ran upon him with one accord, and cast him out of the city, and stoned him: and the witnesses laid down their clothes at a young man's feet, whose name was Saul. And they stoned Stephen, calling upon God, and saying, Lord Jesus, receive my spirit. And he kneeled down, and cried with a loud voice, Lord, lay not this sin to their charge. And when he had said this, he fell asleep in the Lord.

5 August. Dedication of Our Lady of the Snows

Greater Double

⁋ The Office and Mass are from the Common of the Blessed Virgin Mary (p. 760), with Commemoration of St. Oswald, from the First Common of a Martyr not a Bishop (p. 688).

⁋ Note, The Creed is said and the Preface of the B.V.M. And that in the Festivity.

5 August. St. Oswald

Double

⁋ The propers are from the First Common of a Martyr not a Bishop (p. 688), except for the following.

Collect

ALMIGHTY and everlasting God, who by the martyrdom of the blessed King Oswald hast hallowed this day with holy joy and gladness: grant unto our hearts the increase of thy charity; that we, who honour his glorious battle for the faith, may imitate his constancy even unto death. Through.

Epistle. Wisdom 4:7

BUT a righteous man, though he die before his time, shall be at rest. (For honourable old age is not that which standeth in length of time, Nor is its measure given by number of years: But understanding is gray hairs unto men, And an unspotted life is ripe old age.) Being found well-pleasing unto God he was beloved of him, And while living among sinners he was translated: He was caught away, lest wickedness should change his understanding, Or guile deceive his soul. (For the bewitching of naughtiness bedimmeth the things which are good, And the giddy whirl of desire perverteth an innocent mind.) Being made perfect in a little while, he fulfilled long years; For his soul was pleasing unto the Lord: Therefore hasted he out of the midst of wickedness. But as for the peoples, seeing and understanding not, Neither laying this to heart, That grace and mercy are with his chosen, And that he visiteth his holy ones.

Gospel. Matthew 16:24

AT THAT TIME: Jesus said unto his disciples: If any man will come after me, let him deny himself, and take up his cross, and follow me. For whosoever will save his life shall lose it: and whosoever will lose his life for my sake shall find it. For what is a man profited, if he shall gain the whole world, and lose his own soul? or what shall a man give in exchange for his soul? For the Son of man shall come in the glory of his Father with his angels; and then he shall reward every man according to his works.

Transfiguration   **Proper of Saints**   6 August

[6 August. Transfiguration of Our Lord Jesus Christ]

I Evensong

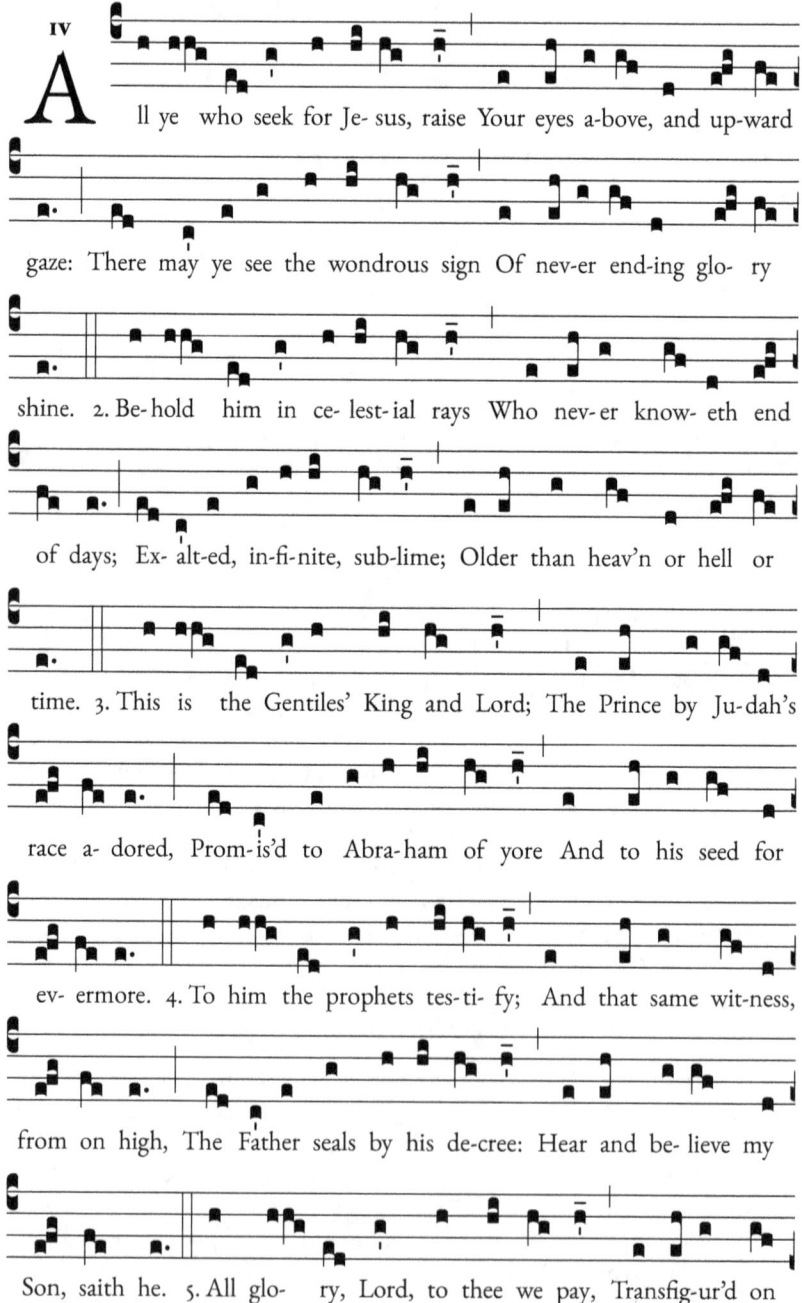

All ye who seek for Je- sus, raise Your eyes a- bove, and up- ward gaze: There may ye see the wondrous sign Of nev- er end- ing glo- ry shine. 2. Be- hold him in ce- lest- ial rays Who nev- er know- eth end of days; Ex- alt- ed, in- fi- nite, sub- lime; Older than heav'n or hell or time. 3. This is the Gentiles' King and Lord; The Prince by Ju- dah's race a- dored, Prom- is'd to Abra- ham of yore And to his seed for ev- ermore. 4. To him the prophets tes- ti- fy; And that same wit- ness, from on high, The Father seals by his de- cree: Hear and be- lieve my Son, saith he. 5. All glo- ry, Lord, to thee we pay, Transfig- ur'd on

6 August — **Proper of Saints** — *Transfiguration*

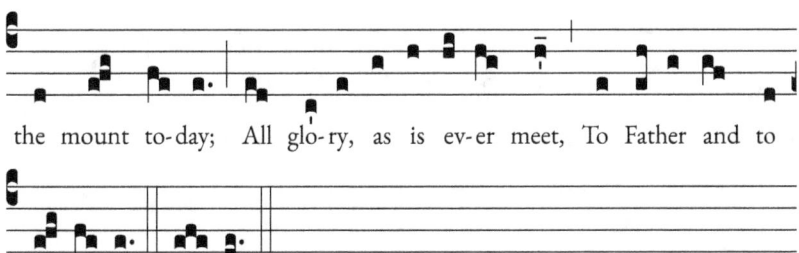

the mount to-day; All glo-ry, as is ev-er meet, To Father and to Par-a-clete. A-men.

℣. Glorious didst thou appear in the sight of the Lord.
℟. Because the Lord hath clothed thee with majesty.

Mag. Ant. Christ Jesus, † the brightness of the Father and the express image of his person, who upholdeth all things by the word of his power, while he was by himself purging away our sins, vouchsafed on this day to shew himself in glory upon an high mountain.

Mattins

¶ The Invitatory Hymn is as in I Evensong.

Office Hymn

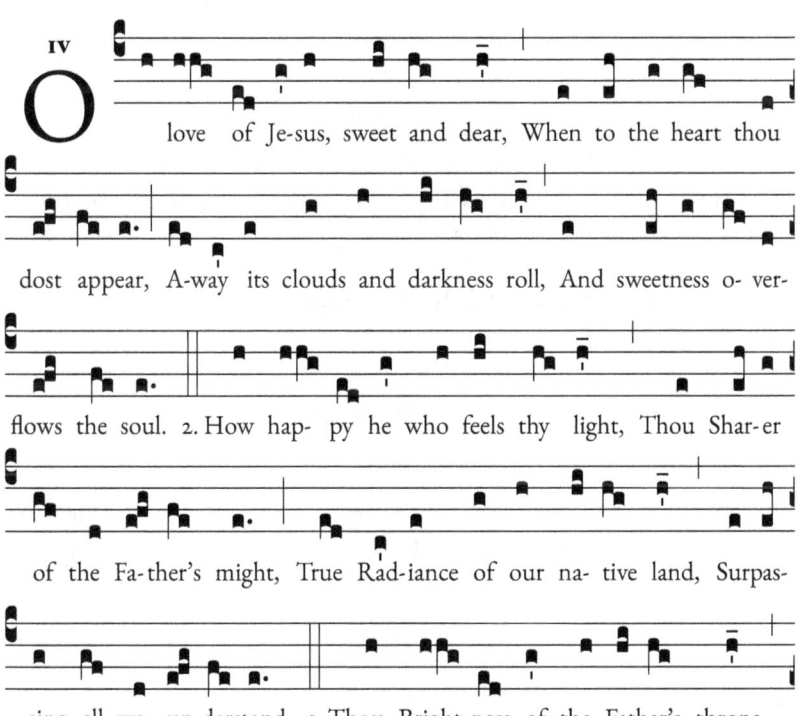

O love of Je-sus, sweet and dear, When to the heart thou dost appear, A-way its clouds and darkness roll, And sweetness o-ver-flows the soul. 2. How hap-py he who feels thy light, Thou Shar-er of the Fa-ther's might, True Rad-iance of our na-tive land, Surpas-sing all we un-derstand. 3. Thou Bright-ness of the Father's throne,

St. Donatus # Proper of Saints 7 August

Goodness that nev- er can be known, The fulness of thy love impart by thy true Pres- ence in the heart. 4. All glo- ry, Lord, to thee we pay, Transfig-ur'd on the mount to-day; All glo-ry, as is ev-er meet, To Father and to Par- a- clete. A- men.

℣. A crown of gold is upon his head.
℟. A visible sign of holiness, glory, and honour.

Ben. Ant. And behold a voice † out of the cloud, which said, This is my beloved Son, in whom I am well pleased; hear ye him, alleluia.

II Evensong

¶ The Office Hymn & Versicle are of I Evensong, with the following Antiphon.

Mag. Ant. And when the disciples heard it, † they fell on their face, and were sore afraid: and Jesus came and touched them, and said, Arise, and be not afraid, alleluia.

(6 August. Sts. Sixtus II, Felicissimus, and Agapitus)

¶ The Second Common of Many Martyrs (p. 699).

(7 August. St. Donatus)

Introit

YE priest of the Lord, bless ye the Lord: O ye holy and humble men of heart, bless ye the Lord. *Cant.* O all ye works of the Lord, bless ye the Lord: praise him and magnify him for ever.

Collect

GOD, the glory of thy priests: grant, we beseech thee; that we may perceive the succour of thy holy Martyr and Bishop Donatus, whose festival we celebrate. Through.

| 8 August | **Proper of Saints** | *Sts. Cyriacus &c.* |

¶ The Epistle is the first additional Epistle from the Second Common of a Martyr not a Bishop (p. 691).

Gradual. The mouth of the just is exercised in wisdom, and his tongue will be talking of judgment. ℣. The law of his God is in his heart: and his goings shall not slide.

Alleluia. Alleluia, alleluia. ℣. The just shall not be moved, for the Lord strengtheneth his hand. Alleluia.

¶ The Gospel is the second additional Gospel from the Second Common of a Confessor Bishop (p. 722).

Offertory. I have found David my servant, with my holy oil have I anointed him: my hand shall hold him fast, and my arm shall strengthen him.

Secret

GRANT, we beseech thee, O Lord: that, as by these gifts which we offer to the praise of thy name, we render honour to thy holy Martyr and Bishop Donatus, so by his intercession we may receive the reward of this our bounden service. Through.

Communion. A faithful and wise servant, whom the lord hath made ruler over his household: to give them their portion of meat in due season.

Postcommunion

ALMIGHTY and merciful God, who makest us alike partakers and ministers of thy sacraments: grant, we beseech thee; that at the intercession of blessed Donatus, thy Martyr and Bishop, we, sharing in his faith and worthily serving thee, may be profited by the same. Through.

(8 August. Sts. Cyriacus, Largus, and Smaragdus)

Introit

O FEAR the Lord, ye that are his saints, for they that fear him lack nothing: the lions do lack, and suffer hunger: but they who seek the Lord shall want no manner of thing that is good. *Ps.* I will alway give thanks unto the Lord: his praise shall ever be in my mouth.

Collect

O GOD, who makest us glad with the yearly solemnity of thy holy Martyrs Cyriacus, Largus, and Smaragdus: mercifully grant; that as we now celebrate their birthday, so we may imitate their constancy in suffering. Through.

¶ If today be Saturday, Commemoration is made of the anticipated Vigil of St. Lawrence, as on the following day; the 3rd Collect of St. Mary (p. BCP 542), and the Last Gospel of the Vigil.

Proper of Saints

Sts. Cyriacus &c. — 8 August

Epistle. 1 Thessalonians 2:13

BRETHREN: We thank God without ceasing, because, when ye received the word of God which ye heard of us, ye received it not as the word of men, but as it is in truth, the word of God, which effectually worketh also in you that believe. For ye, brethren, became followers of the churches of God which in Judæa are in Christ Jesus: for ye also have suffered like things of your own countrymen, even as they have of the Jews: who both killed the Lord Jesus, and their own prophets, and have persecuted us; and they please not God, and are contrary to all men: forbidding us to speak to the Gentiles that they might be saved, to fill up their sins alway: for the wrath is come upon them to the uttermost.

Gradual. O fear the Lord, ye that are his saints: for they that fear him lack nothing. ℣. But they who seek the Lord, shall want no manner of thing that is good.

Alleluia. Alleluia, alleluia. ℣. The righteous shall shine, and run to and fro like sparks among the stubble for ever. Alleluia.

Gospel. Mark 16:15

AT THAT TIME: Jesus said to his disciples: Go ye into all the world, and preach the gospel to every creature. He that believeth and is baptized shall be saved; but he that believeth not shall be damned. And these signs shall follow them that believe; In my name shall they cast out devils; they shall speak with new tongues; they shall take up serpents; and if they drink any deadly thing, it shall not hurt them; they shall lay hands on the sick, and they shall recover.

Offertory. Be glad, O ye righteous, and rejoice in the Lord: and be joyful, all ye that are true of heart.

Secret

GRANT, O Lord, that this our bounden service may be acceptable in thy sight: that these our oblations may, by the prayers of those on whose solemnity they are offered, be made profitable unto our salvation. Through.

Communion. These signs shall follow them that believe in me: they shall cast out devils: they shall lay hands on the sick, and they shall recover.

Postcommunion

WE beseech thee, O Lord our God, that like as we, whom thou hast refreshed by the partaking of thy sacred gift, do offer unto thee our worship: so by the intercession of thy holy Martyrs, Cyriacus, Largus and Smaragdus, we may perceive the benefit of the same. Through.

9 August. Vigil of St. Lawrence

Vigil

Introit

E hath dispersed abroad, and given to the poor: his righteousness remaineth for ever: his horn shall be exalted with honour. *Ps.* Blessed is the man that feareth the Lord: he hath great delight in his commandments.

¶ Gloria in excelsis is not said.

Collect

SSIST us, O Lord, in these our supplications: and at the intercession of thy blessed Martyr Lawrence, whose festival we prevent, graciously bestow upon us thy perpetual mercy. Through.

¶ Commemoration of St. Romanus (p. 590).

Epistle. Ecclesiasticus 51:1

 WILL give thanks unto thee, O Lord, O King, And will praise thee, O God my Saviour: I do give thanks unto thy name: For thou wast my protector and helper, And didst deliver my body out of destruction, And out of the snare of a slanderous tongue, From lips that forge lies, And wast my helper before them that stood by; And didst deliver me, according to the abundance of thy mercy, and greatness of thy name, From the gnashings of teeth ready to devour, Out of the hand of such as sought my life, Out of the manifold afflictions which I had; From the choking of a fire on every side, And out of the midst of fire which I kindled not; Out of the depth of the belly of the grave, And from an unclean tongue, And from lying words, The slander of an unrighteous tongue unto the king. My soul drew near even unto death, And my life was near to the grave beneath. They compassed me on every side, And there was none to help me. I was looking for the succour of men, And it was not. And I remembered thy mercy, O Lord, And thy working which hath been from everlasting, How thou deliverest them that wait for thee, And savest them out of the hand of the enemies, O Lord our God.

Gradual. He hath dispersed abroad, and given to the poor: and his righteousness remaineth for ever. ℣. His seed shall be mighty upon earth: the generation of the faithful shall be blessed.

Gospel. Matthew 16:24

AT THAT TIME: Jesus said unto his disciples: If any man will come after me, let him deny himself, and take up his cross, and follow me. For whosoever will save his life shall lose it: and whosoever will lose his life for my sake shall find it. For what is a man profited, if he shall gain the whole world, and lose his own soul? or what shall a man give in exchange for his soul? For the Son of man shall come in the glory of his Father with his angels; and then he shall reward every man according to his works.

Offertory. My prayer is pure: and therefore I ask that a place be given to my voice in heaven: for my witness is in heaven, and my record is on high: let my prayer ascend to the Lord.

Secret

LORD, mercifully regard the sacrifices which we offer unto thee: and at the intercession of blessed Lawrence, thy Martyr, absolve us from the bonds of our sins. Through.

¶ Commemoration of St. Romanus (p. 590).

Communion. He that will come after me, let him deny himself, and take up his cross, and follow me.

Postcommunion

RANT, we beseech thee, O Lord, our God: that like as we in this life do gladly honour the memory of blessed Lawrence, thy Martyr; so we may rejoice to behold him for ever. Through.

¶ Commemoration of St. Romanus (p. 590).

(9 August. St. Romanus)

¶ The Second Common of a Martyr not a Bishop (p. 690), except for the following.

Collect

RANT, we beseech thee, Almighty God: that, at the intercession of blessed Romanus, thy Martyr, we may both be delivered from all adversities which may happen to the body, and from all evil thoughts which may assault and hurt the soul. Through.

Secret

E beseech thee, O Lord, to accept our prayers and oblations: and graciously hearken unto us, whom thou dost cleanse by thy heavenly mysteries. Through.

Postcommunion

WE beseech thee, Almighty God: that we, who have received this heavenly food, may, at the intercession of blessed Romanus, thy Martyr, be thereby defended against all adversities. Through.

Proper of Saints *Sts. Tiburtius & Susanna*

[10 August. St. Lawrence]

❡ The Daily Office propers are of the First Common of a Martyr Bishop (p. 682), except for the following.

Mag. Ant. Lawrence the Deacon † hath wrought a pious work; who by the sign of the Cross enlightened the blind: and distributed to the poor the Church's treasures.

℣. He hath dispersed abroad and given to the poor.
℟. And his righteousness remaineth for ever.

Ben. Ant. On the iron grate, † O God, I denied thee not; and when fire was kindled beneath me, O Christ, I confessed thee: thou hast proved my heart and hast visited me in the night season; thou hast tried me with fire, and hast found no wickedness in me.

℣. Laurence the Deacon hath wrought a pious work.
℟. Who by the sign of the Cross enlightened the blind.

Mag. Ant. Blessed Lawrence, † when laid and burning on the iron grating, spake to the impious tyrant, saying: The feast is ready, turn and eat; but the Church's treasures, which thou claimest, have been garnered up in heaven, by the hands of the poor and needy.

(11 August. Sts. Tiburtius and Susanna)

❡ The Third Common of Many Martyrs (p. 700), except for the following.

Collect

O LORD, let the protection of thy holy Martyrs Tiburtius and Susanna continually defend us: forasmuch as thou failest not to look with mercy on those to whom thou dost grant the succour of their assistance. Through.

❡ The Epistle is from the third additional epistle of the Third Common of Many Martyrs (p. 702).

Secret

ASSIST, O Lord, the prayers of thy people, assist their oblations: that those things which are offered in these sacred mysteries may, by the intercession of thy Saints, be acceptable unto thee. Through.

Postcommunion

O LORD, through whom we have received the pledge of eternal redemption: we beseech thee that at the intercession of thy holy Martyrs, it may avail for our succour both in this life and that which is to come. Through.

Assumption B.V.M. Vigil # Proper of Saints   14 August

13 August. St. Maximus of Constantinople

Double

❡ The propers are from the Second Common of a Confessor not a Bishop (p. 729), with Commemoration of Sts. Hippolytus & Cassian.

(13 August. Sts. Hippolytus and Cassian)

❡ The Third Common of Many Martyrs (p. 700), except for the following.

Collect

RANT, we beseech thee, Almighty God: that the venerable solemnity of thy blessed Martyrs, Hippolytus and Cassian, may increase our devotion and set forward our salvation. Through.

Secret

EGARD, O Lord, the gifts of thy people, which we offer on the festival of thy Saints: and let this confession of thy truth be profitable for our salvation. Through.

Postcommunion

AY the communion of thy sacraments, O Lord, which we have received, avail for our salvation: stablish us in the light of thy truth. Through.

❡ If today be Saturday, the anticipated Vigil of the Assumption of the B.V. Mary is kept, as is noted on the following day, but with Commemoration of Sts. Hippolytus and Cassian, instead of St. Eusebius.

14 August. Vigil of the Assumption of the Blessed Virgin Mary

Vigil

Introit

AIL, Holy Mother, who didst bring forth the King who ruleth over heaven and earth for ever and ever. *Gospel.* Blessed art thou among women, and blessed is the fruit of thy womb.

14 August   **Proper of Saints** *Assumption B.V.M. Vigil*

Collect

O GOD, who didst vouchsafe to choose the virgin womb of blessed Mary wherein to make thy dwelling: grant, we beseech thee; that, being defended by her protection, we may by thee be enabled to attain with gladness to her festival. Who livest.

❡ Commemoration of St. Eusebius (p. 594) & 3rd Collect of the Holy Ghost (p. BCP 544).

Epistle. Ecclesiasticus 24:9

HE created me from the beginning before the world; And to the end I shall not fail. In the holy tabernacle I ministered before him; And so was I established in Sion. In the beloved city likewise he gave me rest; And in Jerusalem was my authority. And I took root in a people that was glorified, Even in the portion of the Lord's own inheritance.

Gradual. Blessed and venerable art thou, O Virgin Mary: who without spot wast found the Mother of the Saviour. ℣. Virgin, Mother of God, he whom the whole world containeth not, being made man lay hid in thy womb.

Gospel. Luke 11:27

AT THAT TIME: As Jesus spake to the multitudes, a certain woman of the company lifted up her voice, and said unto him, Blessed is the womb that bare thee, and the paps which thou hast sucked. But he said, Yea rather, blessed are they that hear the word of God, and keep it.

Offertory. Happy art thou, O holy Virgin Mary, and most worthy of all praise, for from thee sprang the Sun of Righteousness, Christ our God. ℣. Blessed art thou, Virgin Mary, who didst bear the Lord, didst give birth to the Creator of the world, Who made thee, and ever remainest Virgin.

Secret

O LORD, who didst translate the Mother of God from this present life, to the intent that she might faithfully intercede before thee for our sins: grant that her prayers may render these our oblations acceptable in the sight of thy mercy. Through the same.

❡ Commemoration of St. Eusebius (p. 595).

❡ 3rd Secret of the Holy Ghost (p. BCP 544).

Communion. Gentle Mother of God, succour all that pray; we, too, with them, humbly entreat that by the aid of thy prayers we may sing praises unto the Trinity.

Proper of Saints

Postcommunion

E beseech thee, O merciful God, to strengthen our frailty, that we who keep the requiem of the Holy Virgin Mother of God, may by her intercession rise again from our iniquities. Through.

¶ Commemoration of St. Eusebius (p. 595).

¶ 3rd Postcommunion of the Holy Ghost (p. BCP 544).

(14 August. St. Eusebius)

Introit

HE just shall flourish like a palm-tree: and shall spread abroad like a cedar in Libanus: planted in the house of the Lord: in the courts of the house of our God. *Ps.* It is a good thing to give thanks unto the Lord: and to sing praises unto thy name, O Most Highest.

Collect

GOD, who makest us glad with the yearly solemnity of blessed Eusebius thy Confessor: mercifully grant; that we, who celebrate his birthday, may by his example, be drawn nearer unto thee. Through.

¶ The Epistle is additional Epistle from the Second Common of a Confessor not a Bishop (p. 731).

Gradual. The just shall flourish like a palm-tree: and shall spread abroad like a cedar in Libanus in the house of the Lord. ℣. To tell of thy loving-kindness early in the morning, and of thy truth in the night-season.

Alleluia. Alleluia, alleluia. ℣. The just shall grow as the lily: and flourish for ever before the Lord. Alleluia.

Gospel. Matthew 11:25

AT THAT TIME: Jesus answered and said: I thank thee, O Father, Lord of heaven and earth, because thou hast hid these things from the wise and prudent, and hast revealed them unto babes. Even so, Father: for so it seemed good in thy sight. All things are delivered unto me of my Father: and no man knoweth the Son, but the Father; neither knoweth any man the Father, save the Son, and he to whomsoever the Son will reveal him. Come unto me, all ye that labour and are heavy laden, and I will give you rest. Take my yoke upon you, and learn of me; for I am meek and lowly in heart: and ye shall find rest unto your souls. For my yoke is easy, and my burden is light.

Offertory. The just shall rejoice in strength, O Lord: exceeding glad shall he be of thy salvation: thou hast given him his heart's desire.

Secret

RANT, we beseech thee, O Lord, that we who, trusting in this our sacrifice of praise, do offer it before thee to the honour of thy Saints: may by the same be delivered from all evils both in this life and in that which is to come. Through.

Communion. The just shall rejoice in the Lord, and put his trust in him: and all they that are true of heart shall be glad.

Postcommunion

O LORD, our God, who hast refreshed us with heavenly meat and drink, we humbly beseech thee: that we may be defended by the prayers of him in whose memory we have received the same. Through.

[15 AUGUST. ASSUMPTION OF THE BLESSED VIRGIN MARY]

¶ The Daily Office propers are of the Common of the Blessed Virgin Mary (p. 760), except for the following.

¶ NOTE, the following Office Hymn may be said during Evensong.

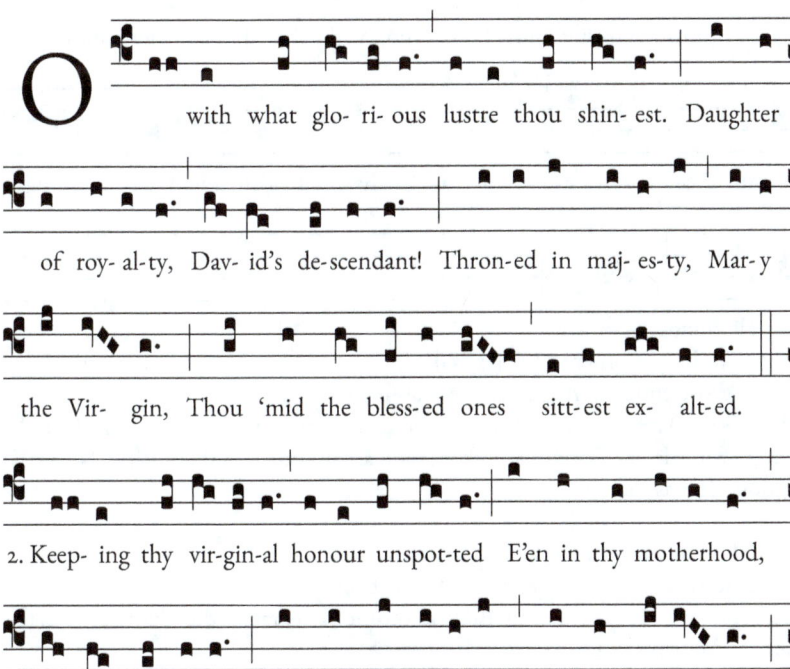

O with what glorious lustre thou shinest. Daughter of royalty, David's descendant! Throned in majesty, Mary the Virgin, Thou 'mid the blessed ones sittest exalted.

2. Keeping thy virginal honour unspotted E'en in thy motherhood, chastely thou gav'est Shrine for the Holy One, Lord of the Angels;

Assumption   **Proper of Saints**   15 August

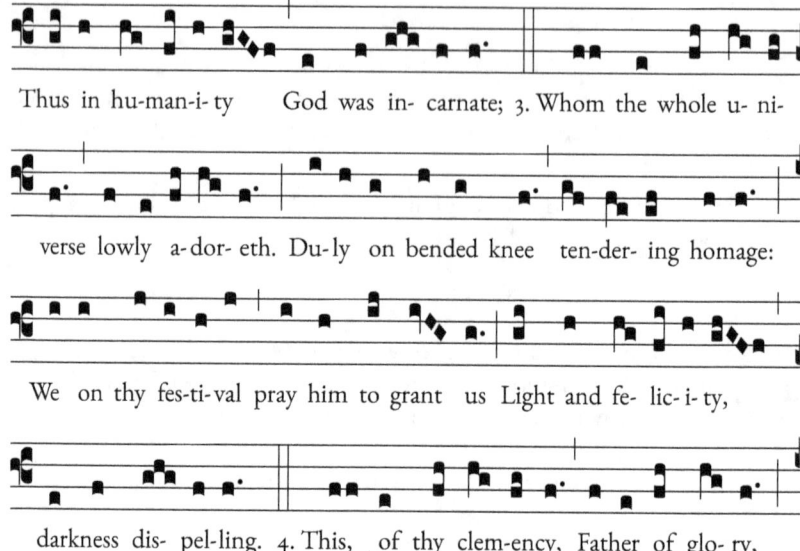

Thus in humanity God was incarnate; 3. Whom the whole universe lowly adoreth. Duly on bended knee tendering homage: We on thy festival pray him to grant us Light and felicity, darkness dispelling. 4. This, of thy clemency, Father of glory, Grant through thine only Son, who, with the Spirit, Evermore one with thee liveth and reigneth In the bright firmament, ordering all things. Amen.

℣. The holy Mother of God is exalted.
℟. Above choirs of Angels to the heavenly kingdom.

Mag. Ant. O most prudent Virgin, † whither goest thou, shining resplendent like the glowing dawn? Daughter of Sion, thou art all comely and beautiful, fair as the moon, clear as the sun.

℣. The holy Mother of God is exalted.
℟. Above choirs of Angels to the heavenly kingdom.

Ben. Ant. Who is she † that riseth up as the morning, fair as the moon, clear as the sun, and terrible as an army with banners?

¶ II Evensong is as in I Evensong, except the following Antiphon.

Mag. Ant. On this day † the Virgin Mary went up into heaven: rejoice, because she reigneth with Christ for ever and ever.

17 August   **Proper of Saints**   *St. Lawrence Octave Day*

[16 August. St. Joachim]

¶ The Daily Office propers are of the First Common of a Confessor not a Bishop (p. 725), except for the following Versicle & Antiphon used for I Evensong and Mattins.

℣. His seed shall be mighty upon earth.
℟. The generation of the faithful shall be blessed.

Mag. & Ben. Ant. Let us praise a man famous † in his generation, with whom the Lord established the blessing of all nations, and the covenant, and made it rest upon his head.

17 August. Octave Day of St. Lawrence

Simple

Introit

THOU hast proved and visited mine heart, O Lord, in the night-season: thou hast tried me with fire, and hast found no wickedness in me. *Ps.* Hear the right, O Lord: consider my complaint.

Collect

STIR up, O Lord, in thy Church that Spirit whom the blessed Levite Lawrence served: that we, being filled with the same, may study to love that which he loved, and to perform in deed that which he taught. Through . . . in the unity of the same Holy Spirit.

Epistle. 2 Corinthians 9:6

BRETHREN: He which soweth sparingly shall reap also sparingly; and he which soweth bountifully shall reap also bountifully. Every man according as he purposeth in his heart, so let him give; not grudgingly, or of necessity: for God loveth a cheerful giver. And God is able to make all grace abound toward you; that ye, always having all sufficiency in all things, may abound to every good work: (As it is written, He hath dispersed abroad; he hath given to the poor: his righteousness remaineth for ever. Now he that ministereth seed to the sower both minister bread for your food, and multiply your seed sown, and increase the fruits of your righteousness;)

Gradual. Thou hast crowned him with glory and worship, O Lord. ℣. And hast made him to have dominion of the works of thy hands.

Alleluia. Alleluia, alleluia. ℣. The Levite Lawrence wrought a good work: who by the sign of the cross gave light to the blind. Alleluia.

Gospel. John 12:24

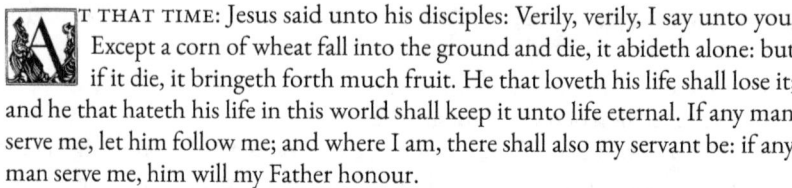T THAT TIME: Jesus said unto his disciples: Verily, verily, I say unto you, Except a corn of wheat fall into the ground and die, it abideth alone: but if it die, it bringeth forth much fruit. He that loveth his life shall lose it; and he that hateth his life in this world shall keep it unto life eternal. If any man serve me, let him follow me; and where I am, there shall also my servant be: if any man serve me, him will my Father honour.

Offertory. The just shall rejoice in thy strength, O Lord: exceeding glad shall he be of thy salvation: thou hast given him his heart's desire.

Secret

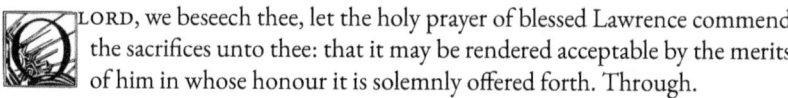LORD, we beseech thee, let the holy prayer of blessed Lawrence commend the sacrifices unto thee: that it may be rendered acceptable by the merits of him in whose honour it is solemnly offered forth. Through.

Communion. He that will come after me, let him deny himself, and take up his cross, and follow me.

Postcommunion

E humbly beseech thee, Almighty God: that we, whom thou hast fulfilled with heavenly gifts, may, at the intercession of blessed Lawrence thy Martyr, be defended by thy continual protection. Through.

(18 August. St. Helen)

Introit

UT God forbid that I should glory, save in the Cross of our Lord Jesus Christ: by whom the world is crucified unto me, and I unto the world. *Ps.* Thy rod and thy staff comfort me.

Collect

O LORD Jesu Christ, who didst reveal unto blessed Helen the place where thy Cross lay hid, that through her thou mightest enrich thy Church with this precious treasure: grant unto us at her intercession; that by the ransom of the life-giving tree we may attain unto the rewards of everlasting life. Who livest.

Epistle. Proverbs 31:10

WHO can find a virtuous woman? for her price is far above rubies. The heart of her husband doth safely trust in her, so that he shall have no need of spoil. She will do him good and not evil all the days of her life. She seeketh wool, and flax, and worketh willingly with her hands. She is like the merchants' ships; she bringeth her food from afar. She riseth also while it is yet night, and giveth meat to her household, and a portion to her maidens. She considereth a field, and buyeth it: with the fruit of her hands she planteth a vineyard. She girdeth her loins with strength, and strengtheneth her arms. She perceiveth that her merchandise is good: her candle goeth not out by night. She layeth her hands to the spindle, and her hands hold the distaff. She stretcheth out her hand to the poor; yea, she reacheth forth her hands to the needy. She is not afraid of the snow for her household: for all her household are clothed with scarlet. She maketh herself coverings of tapestry; her clothing is silk and purple. Her husband is known in the gates, when he sitteth among the elders of the land. She maketh fine linen, and selleth it; and delivereth girdles unto the merchant. Strength and honour are her clothing; and she shall rejoice in time to come. She openeth her mouth with wisdom; and in her tongue is the law of kindness. She looketh well to the ways of her household, and eateth not the bread of idleness. Her children arise up, and call her blessed; her husband also, and he praiseth her. Many daughters have done virtuously, but thou excellest them all. Favour is deceitful, and beauty is vain: but a woman that feareth the LORD, she shall be praised. Give her of the fruit of her hands; and let her own works praise her in the gates.

Gradual. Like as the rich also among the people shall make their supplication before thee. Kings' daughters were among thy honourable women. ℣. She shall be brought unto the King in raiment of needle-work: the virgins that be her fellows shall bear her company, and shall be brought unto thee. With joy and gladness shall they be brought: and shall enter into the King's palace.

Alleluia. Alleluia, alleluia. ℣. He hath dispersed abroad, and given to the poor : and his righteousness remaineth for ever. Alleluia.

Gospel. Matthew 13:44

AT THAT TIME: Jesus spake this parable to his disciples: The kingdom of heaven is like unto treasure hid in a field; the which when a man hath found, he hideth, and for joy thereof goeth and selleth all that he hath, and buyeth that field. Again, the kingdom of heaven is like unto a merchant man, seeking goodly pearls: Who, when he had found one pearl of great price, went and sold all that he had, and bought it. Again, the kingdom of heaven is like unto a net, that was cast into the sea, and gathered of every kind: Which, when it was full, they drew to shore, and sat down, and gathered the good into vessels, but cast the bad away. So shall it be at the end of the world: the angels shall come forth, and sever the wicked from among the just, And shall cast them into the furnace of fire: there shall be wailing and gnashing of teeth. Jesus saith unto them, Have ye understood all these things? They say unto him, Yea, Lord. Then said he unto them, Therefore every scribe which is instructed unto the kingdom of heaven is like unto a man that is an householder, which bringeth forth out of his treasure things new and old.

Offertory. For I determined not to know any thing, save Jesus Christ, and him crucified.

St. Agapitus   **Proper of Saints**   18 August

Secret

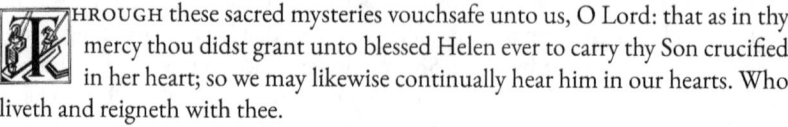THROUGH these sacred mysteries vouchsafe unto us, O Lord: that as in thy mercy thou didst grant unto blessed Helen ever to carry thy Son crucified in her heart; so we may likewise continually hear him in our hearts. Who liveth and reigneth with thee.

Communion. I will go up to the palm tree, I will take hold of the boughs thereof.

Postcommunion

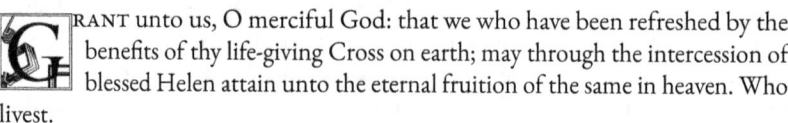RANT unto us, O merciful God: that we who have been refreshed by the benefits of thy life-giving Cross on earth; may through the intercession of blessed Helen attain unto the eternal fruition of the same in heaven. Who livest.

(18 August. St. Agapitus)

¶ The Second Common of a Martyr not a Bishop (p. 690), except for the following.

Collect

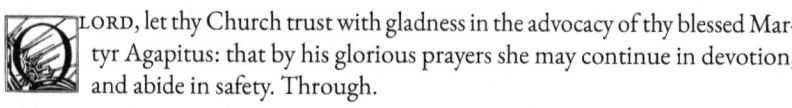LORD, let thy Church trust with gladness in the advocacy of thy blessed Martyr Agapitus: that by his glorious prayers she may continue in devotion, and abide in safety. Through.

Gospel. John 12:24

AT THAT TIME: Jesus said unto his disciples: Verily, verily, I say unto you, Except a corn of wheat fall into the ground and die, it abideth alone: but if it die, it bringeth forth much fruit. He that loveth his life shall lose it; and he that hateth his life in this world shall keep it unto life eternal. If any man serve me, let him follow me; and where I am, there shall also my servant be: if any man serve me, him will my Father honour.

Secret

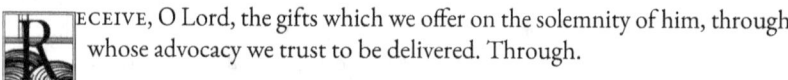ECEIVE, O Lord, the gifts which we offer on the solemnity of him, through whose advocacy we trust to be delivered. Through.

Postcommunion

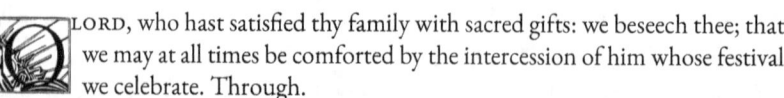LORD, who hast satisfied thy family with sacred gifts: we beseech thee; that we may at all times be comforted by the intercession of him whose festival we celebrate. Through.

Proper of Saints

23 August — *St. Bartholomew Vigil*

22 August. Octave Day of the Assumption of the Blessed Virgin Mary

Greater Double

℣ Mass as on the Feast with commemoration of Sts. Timothy, Hippolytus, & Symphorian, as in the following Mass.

℣ If today be Saturday, the anticipated Vigil of St. Bartholomew is kept, as is noted on the following day.

(22 August. Sts. Timothy, Hippolytus, and Symphorian)

℣ The Third Common of Many Martyrs (p. 700), except for the following.

Collect

E beseech thee, O Lord, graciously to impart unto us thy help: and, at the intercession of thy blessed Martyrs Timothy, Hippolytus, and Symphorian, stretch forth upon us the right hand of thy mercy. Through.

Secret

RANT, O Lord, that like as thy dedicated people do acknowledge that in tribulation they have been succoured by the merits of thy Saints: so this oblation, which they offer unto thee in honour of the same, may be acceptable in thy sight. Through.

Postcommunion

LORD our God, who hast fulfilled us with the bounty of thy heavenly gift: we beseech thee, that, at the intercession of thy holy Martyrs, Timothy, Hippolytus, and Symphorian, we may ever live by the partaking of the same. Through.

23 August. Vigil of St. Bartholomew

Vigil

℣ The propers come from the Common of the Vigil of Apostles (p. 672).

  Note, 2nd Collect of St. Mary in Eastertide (p. BCP 542) & 3rd Against the Persecutors of the Church (p. BCP 543) or for the Chief Bishop (p. BCP 543).

Proper of Saints

[24 August. St. Bartholomew]

¶ The Daily Office propers are from the Common of Apostles (p. 673), with the following Antiphons.

Mag. Ant. They will deliver you up † to the councils, and they will scourge you in their synagogues; and ye shall be brought before governors and kings for my sake, for a testimony against them and the Gentiles.

Ben. Ant. Ye which have forsaken all, † and followed me, shall receive an hundredfold, and shall inherit everlasting life.

Mag. Ant. Be ye valiant in warfare, † and contend ye with the old serpent: and ye shall receive an eternal kingdom, alleluia.

(26 August. St. Zephyrinus)

¶ The Second Common of a Martyr Bishop out of Eastertide (p. 686), except for the following.

Collect

RANT, we beseech thee, Almighty God: that we who rejoice in the merits of blessed Zephyrinus, thy Martyr and Bishop, may be instructed by his example. Through.

Secret

ANCTIFY, O Lord, the gifts which we dedicate to thee: that at the intercession of blessed Zephyrinus thy Martyr and Bishop they may obtain for us thy gracious favour. Through.

Postcommunion

AY this communion, O Lord, cleanse us from guilt: and, at the intercession of blessed Zephyrinus, thy Martyr and Bishop, make us partakers of thy heavenly healing. Through.

28 August. St. Augustine of Hippo

Greater Double

¶ The propers are from the Common of Doctors (p. 723), except for that which followeth.

Introit

IN the midst of the Church he opened his mouth: and the Lord filled him with the spirit of wisdom and of understanding: he clothed him with a robe of glory. *Ps.* It is a good thing to give thanks unto the Lord: and to sing praises unto thy name, O most Highest.

28 August — *St. Hermes*

Proper of Saints

Collect

ASSIST us, Almighty God, in these our supplications: that as thou dost suffer us to put our trust and confidence in thy mercy, so, at the intercession of blessed Augustine thy Confessor and Bishop, thou wouldest graciously vouchsafe unto us the wonted effects of thy compassion. Through.

℣ Commemoration of St. Hermes (p. 603).

Gradual. The mouth of the righteous is exercised in wisdom, and his tongue will be talking judgment. ℣. The law of his God is in his heart: and his goings shall not slide.

Alleluia. Alleluia, alleluia. ℣. I have found David my servant, with my holy oil have I anointed him. Alleluia.

Offertory. The righteous shall flourish like a palm-tree: and shall spread abroad like a cedar in Libanus.

Secret

MAY the devout prayers of thy Bishop and Doctor, Saint Augustine, never fail to succour us, O Lord: that they may render our oblations acceptable in thy sight; and may ever obtain for us thy merciful pardon. Through.

℣ Commemoration of St. Hermes (p. 604).

Communion. A faithful and wise servant, whom the lord hath made ruler over his household: to give them their portion of meat in due season.

Postcommunion

WE beseech thee, O Lord, that blessed Augustine, thy Bishop and illustrious Doctor, may stand before thee as our advocate: that these thy sacrifices may avail for our salvation. Through.

℣ Commemoration of St. Hermes (p. 604).

(28 August. St. Hermes)

℣ The Second Common of a Martyr not a Bishop (p. 690), except for the following.

Collect

O GOD, who didst strengthen blessed Hermes thy Martyr with the virtue of constancy in his passion: Grant unto us by his example; to despise for love of thee the prosperity of the world, and to fear none of its adversities. Through.

Proper of Saints

Sts. Felix & Adauctus — 30 August

Secret

E offer unto thee, O Lord, this sacrifice of praise in commemoration of thy Saints: grant, we beseech thee; that as it hath bestowed glory on them, so may it avail for our salvation. Through.

Postcommunion

LORD, who hast fulfilled us with thy heavenly benediction, we beseech thy mercy: that, at the intercession of thy blessed Martyr Hermes, this service of our lowliness may avail for the comforting of our souls. Through.

[29 August. Decollation of St. John Baptist]

¶ The Hymns and Versicle are from the Common of Apostles (p. 673), with the Antiphons as followeth.

Mag. & Ben. Ant. Herod sent † an executioner, and commanded him to behead John in the prison: and when his disciples heard of it, they came, and took up his body, and laid it in a tomb.

Mag. Ant. The king, the unbeliever, † sent his detestable servants, and commanded them to behead John the Baptist.

(29 August. St. Sabina)

¶ The Common of a Martyress not a Virgin (p. 746).

(30 August. Sts. Felix and Adauctus)

Introit

ET the people tell of the wisdom of the Saints, and let the church shew forth their praise: their names shall live for evermore. *Ps.* Rejoice in the Lord, O ye righteous: for it becometh well the just to be thankful.

Collect

LORD, we humbly entreat thy Majesty: that, like as thou dost continually gladden us with the commemoration of thy Saints; so thou wouldest evermore defend us with their supplication. Through.

¶ The Epistle is the third additional Epistle from the Third Common of Many Martyrs (p. 701).

Gradual. The souls of the just are in the hand of God, and there shall no torment of malice touch them. ℣. In the eyes of the unwise they seemed to die: but they are in peace.

Alleluia. Alleluia, alleluia. ℣. The righteous shall shine forth, and run to and fro like sparks among the stubble for ever. Alleluia.

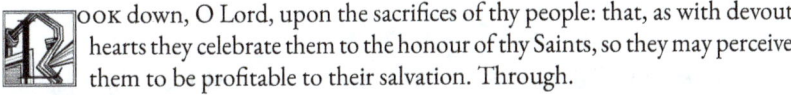

Proper of Saints

1 September — *12 Holy Brothers*

¶ The Gospel is the fifth additional Gospel from the Third Common of Many Martyrs (p. 704).

Offertory. Be glad, O ye righteous, and rejoice in the Lord: and be joyful, all ye that are true of heart.

Secret

OOK down, O Lord, upon the sacrifices of thy people: that, as with devout hearts they celebrate them to the honour of thy Saints, so they may perceive them to be profitable to their salvation. Through.

Communion. What I tell you in darkness, that speak ye in light, saith the Lord: and what ye hear in the ear, that preach ye upon the housetops.

Postcommunion

WE beseech thee, O Lord: that we, being filled with the sacred gifts; may at the intercession of thy Saints ever continue in thanksgiving for the same. Through.

(31 August. St. Aidan of Lindisfarne)

¶ The First Common of a Confessor Bishop (p. 715).

(1 September. St. Giles)

¶ The Common of Abbots (p. 732).

(1 September. Twelve Holy Brothers)

Introit

HE just cry, and the Lord heareth them: and delivereth them out of all their troubles. *Ps.* I will alway give thanks unto the Lord; his praise shall ever be in my mouth.

Collect

LORD, let the crown of the brethren thy Martyrs, cause us to rejoice: that we may thereby be strengthened and increased in our faith; and comforted by their manifold intercession. Through.

¶ The Epistle is the fifth additional Epistle of the Third Common of Many Martyrs (p. 702).

Gradual. Behold, how good and joyful a thing it is, brethren, to dwell together in unity! ℣. It is like the precious ointment upon the head, that ran down unto the beard, even unto Aaron's beard.

St. Stephen Hungary — **Proper of Saints** — 2 September

Alleluia. Alleluia, alleluia. ℣. This is the true brotherhood which overcame the wickedness of the world: which followed Christ, gaining heaven's glorious realms. Alleluia.

℣ The Gospel is from the Third Common of Many Martyrs (p. 699).

Offertory. Be glad, O ye righteous, and rejoice in the Lord: and be joyful, all ye that are true of heart.

Secret

RANT, O Lord, that we may with devout hearts celebrate thy mysteries in honour of thy holy Martyrs: and thereby obtain an increase both of protection and joy. Through.

Communion. Whosoever shall do the will of my Father which is in heaven: the same is my brother, and sister, and mother, saith the Lord.

Postcommunion

RANT, we beseech thee, Almighty God: that growing in virtue we may follow the faith of them whose memory we recall by the partaking of this sacrament. Through.

(2 September. St. Stephen of Hungary)

℣ The First Common of Confessor not Bishop (p. 725), except for the following.

Collect

RANT, we beseech thee, Almighty God unto thy Church: that as thy blessed Confessor Stephen, while he reigned on earth, did spread abroad her faith, so she may be found worthy to have him for her glorious defender in the heavens. Through.

℣ The Gospel is the additional Gospel from the Second Common of a Confessor not a Bishop (p. 731).

Secret

LMIGHTY God, look upon the sacrifices which we offer: and grant; that we, who celebrate the mysteries of the Passion of the Lord, may imitate that which we perform. Through the same.

Postcommunion

GRANT, we beseech thee, Almighty God: that, as thy blessed Confessor Stephen, for the propagation of thy faith, was counted worthy to pass from an earthly kingdom to the glory of the heavenly realm; so we may imitate his faith with due devotion. Through.

4 September. St. Gorazde of Prague

Double

¶ The propers are from the Second Common of a Martyr Bishop (p. 686).

[8 September. Nativity of the Blessed Virgin Mary]

¶ The Hymns are from the Common of the Blessed Virgin Mary (p. 760), with the following Versicles & Antiphons.

℣. To-day is the Nativity of the holy Virgin Mary.
℟. Whose glorious life illumineth all the churches.

Mag. Ant. Let us celebrate † the worshipful Nativity of the blessed and glorious Virgin Mary: for she hath obtained the dignity of Motherhood, and yet lost not her maiden purity.

℣. To-day is the Nativity of the holy Virgin Mary.
℟. Whose glorious life illumineth all the churches.

Ben. Ant. To-day let us celebrate † with due solemnity the Nativity of God's Mother, the ever Virgin Mary: from whom the Son of the Highest proceeded, alleluia.

℣. To-day is the Nativity of the holy Virgin Mary.
℟. Whose glorious life illumineth all the churches.

Mag. Ant. Thy Nativity, † O Virgin Mother of God, hath proclaimed joyful tidings unto all the world: for out of thee hath arisen the Sun of righteousness, even Christ our God: who, taking away the curse, hath bestowed a blessing; and confounding death, hath given unto us life everlasting.

(8 September. St. Hadrian)

¶ The First Common of a Martyr not a Bishop (p. 688).

(9 September. St. Gorgonius)

¶ The Second Common of a Martyr not a Bishop (p. 690), except for the following.

Collect

LET thy Saint Gorgonius, O Lord, gladden us by his intercession; and make us to rejoice in this holy solemnity. Through.

Secret

LORD, let thy holy Martyr Gorgonius so intercede for us: that this oblation of our service may be acceptable unto thee. Through.

Holy Name of Mary   **Proper of Saints**   12 September

Postcommunion

RANT, O God, that thy household may be quickened and refreshed by thine eternal goodness: and in thy Martyr Gorgonius be continually nourished with the sweet savour of Christ, thy Son. Who liveth and reigneth with thee.

(11 September. Sts. Protus and Hyacinth)

¶ The Third Common of Many Martyrs out of Eastertide (p. 700), except for the following.

Collect

LORD, let the meritorious confession of thy blessed Martyrs, Protus and Hyacinth, comfort us; and may their loving intercession ever defend us. Through.

Secret

RANT, we beseech thee, O Lord, that the oblation of our bounden service which we offer unto thee for the commemoration of thy holy Martyrs, Protus and Hyacinth; may effectually avail for our healing unto everlasting salvation. Through.

Postcommunion

E beseech thee, O Lord, that by the supplication of thy blessed Martyrs, Protus and Hyacinth: thy holy mysteries which we have received may avail for our cleansing. Through.

12 September. Most Holy Name of Mary

Greater Double

¶ The Daily Office propers are from the Common of the Blessed Virgin Mary (p. 760), except for the antiphon for I Evensong, as followeth.

Mag. Ant. O holy Mary, † help thou the suffering, strengthen the faint-hearted, comfort the sorrowful; pray for the people, entreat for the clergy, intercede for all womankind vowed unto God: may all acknowledge the help of thy prayer, who celebrate the commemoration of thine holy Name.

Introit

LL the rich among the people shall make their supplication before thee: the Virgins that be her fellows shall be brought unto the King: they that bear her company shall be brought unto thee with joy and gladness. *Ps.* My heart is inditing of a good matter: I speak of the things which I have made unto the King.

12 September   **Proper of Saints**   *Holy Name of Mary*

Collect

GRANT, we beseech thee, Almighty God: that thy faithful people, who rejoice in the Name and protection of the most Holy Virgin Mary; may by her loving intercession be delivered from all evils upon earth, and be found worthy to attain unto everlasting joys in heaven. Through.

Epistle. Ecclesiasticus 24:17

As the vine I put forth grace; And my flowers are the fruit of glory and riches. Come unto me, ye that are desirous of me, And be ye filled with my produce. For my memorial is sweeter than honey, And mine inheritance than the honeycomb. They that eat me shall yet be hungry; And they that drink me shall yet be thirsty. He that obeyeth me shall not be ashamed; And they that work in me shall not do amiss.

Gradual. Blessed and venerable art thou, O Virgin Mary: who without spot wast found the Mother of the Saviour. ℣. Virgin, Mother of God, he whom the world containeth not, being made man lay hid in thy womb.

Alleluia. Alleluia, alleluia. ℣. After child-birth, O Virgin, thou didst remain inviolate: Mother of God, intercede for us. Alleluia.

Gospel. Luke 1:26

AT THAT TIME: The angel Gabriel was sent from God unto a city of Galilee, named Nazareth, to a virgin espoused to a man whose name was Joseph, of the house of David; and the virgin's name was Mary. And the angel came in unto her, and said, Hail, thou that art highly favoured, the Lord is with thee: blessed art thou among women. And when she saw him, she was troubled at his saying, and cast in her mind what manner of salutation this should be. And the angel said unto her, Fear not, Mary: for thou hast found favour with God. And, behold, thou shalt conceive in thy womb, and bring forth a son, and shalt call his name JESUS. He shall be great, and shall be called the Son of the Highest: and the Lord God shall give unto him the throne of his father David: and he shall reign over the house of Jacob for ever; and of his kingdom there shall be no end. Then said Mary unto the angel, How shall this be, seeing I know not a man? And the angel answered and said unto her, The Holy Ghost shall come upon thee, and the power of the Highest shall overshadow thee: therefore also that holy thing which shall be born of thee shall be called the Son of God. And, behold, thy cousin Elisabeth, she hath also conceived a son in her old age: and this is the sixth month with her, who was called barren. For with God nothing shall be impossible. And Mary said, Behold the handmaid of the Lord; be it unto me according to thy word.

Offertory. Hail, Mary, full of grace; the Lord is with thee: blessed art thou among women, and blessed is the fruit of thy womb.

Autumn Ember Saturday Proper of Saints

Secret

THROUGH thy mercy, O Lord, and the intercession of blessed Mary ever Virgin, may this oblation avail for our prosperity and peace, both now and for ever. Through.

Communion. Blessed is the womb of the Virgin Mary, that bore the Son of the everlasting Father.

Postcommunion

RANT, we beseech thee, O Lord: that we, who have received these aids to our salvation, may at all times and in all places be protected through the advocacy of blessed Maty ever Virgin; in whose honour we have made these offerings to thy Majesty. Through.

[14 SEPTEMBER. EXALTATION OF THE HOLY CROSS]

¶ The Daily Office propers are as in the Feast of the Invention of the Holy Cross, 3 May (p. 503), omitting the Alleluia. If II Evensong be said, the following Antiphon is said.

Mag. Ant. O Cross † exceeding blessed, which alone wast counted worthy to bear the Lord, the King of heaven, alleluia.

[EMBER WEDNESDAY IN AUTUMN]

Ben. Ant. This kind † of evil spirit can come forth by nothing but by prayer and fasting.

[EMBER FRIDAY IN AUTUMN]

Ben. Ant. A woman † in the city, which was a sinner, stood at the Lord's feet behind him, and began to wash his feet with tears, and did wipe them with the hairs of her head, and kissed his feet, and anointed them with the ointment.

[EMBER SATURDAY IN AUTUMN]

Ben. Ant. Give light, O Lord, † to them that sit in darkness: and gudie our feet into the way of peace, thou God of Israel.

Proper of Saints

15 September — *Seven Sorrows*

[15 September. Seven Sorrows of the Blessed Virgin Mary]

I Evensong

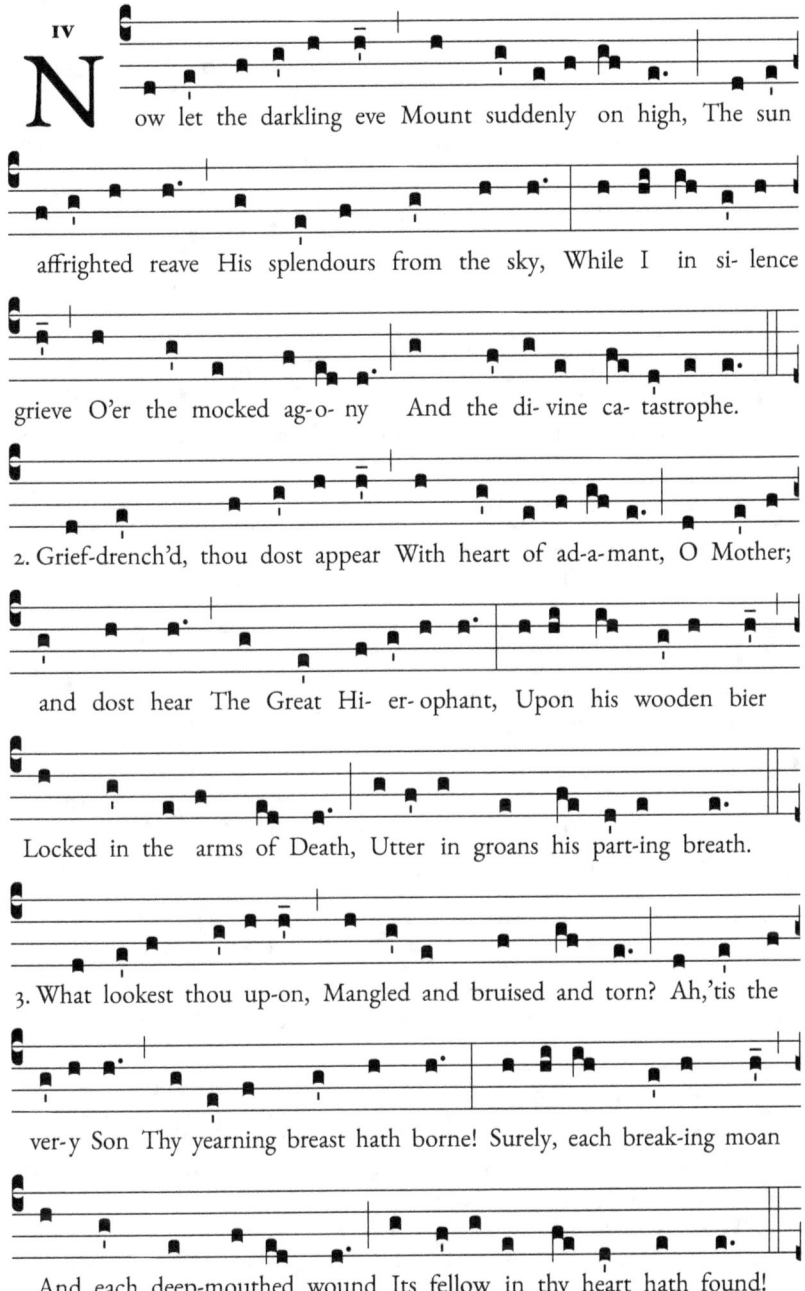

Now let the darkling eve Mount suddenly on high, The sun affrighted reave His splendours from the sky, While I in silence grieve O'er the mocked agony And the divine catastrophe.

2. Grief-drench'd, thou dost appear With heart of adamant, O Mother; and dost hear The Great Hierophant, Upon his wooden bier Locked in the arms of Death, Utter in groans his parting breath.

3. What lookest thou upon, Mangled and bruised and torn? Ah,'tis the very Son Thy yearning breast hath borne! Surely, each breaking moan And each deep-mouthed wound Its fellow in thy heart hath found!

Seven Sorrows — **Proper of Saints** — 15 September

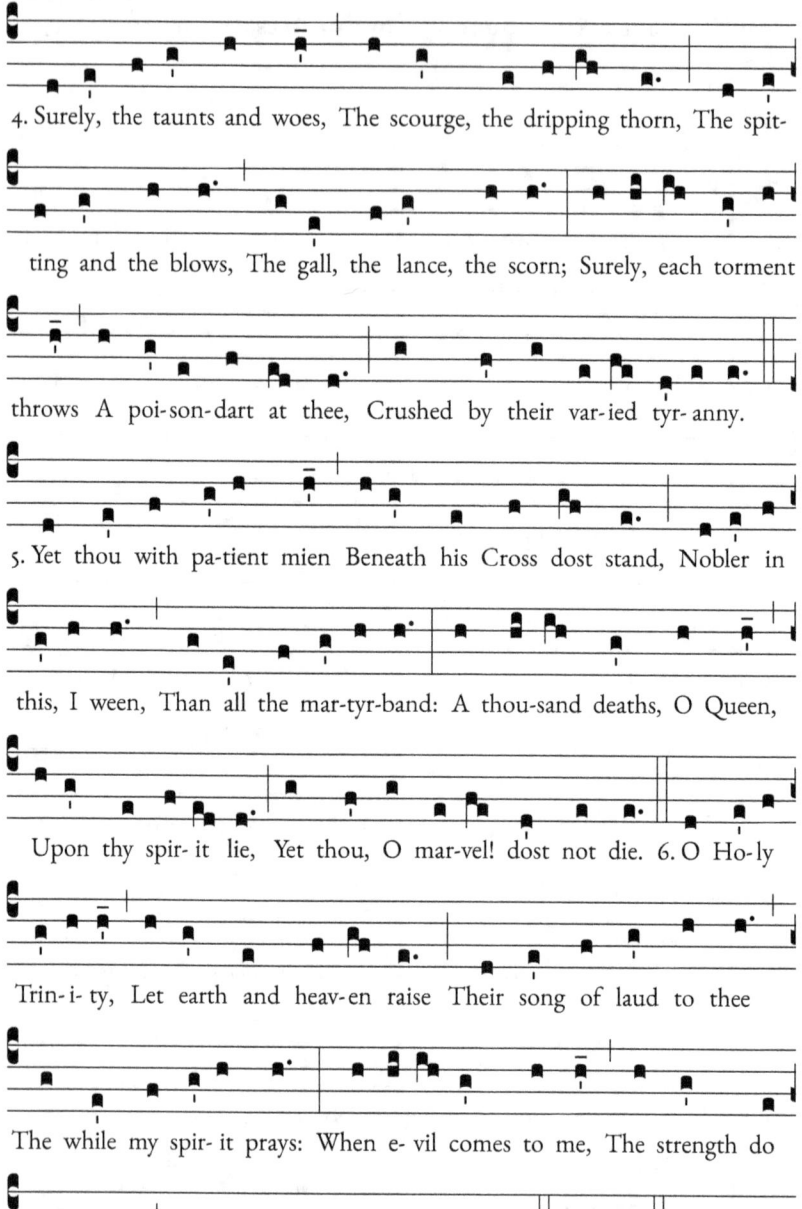

4. Surely, the taunts and woes, The scourge, the dripping thorn, The spitting and the blows, The gall, the lance, the scorn; Surely, each torment throws A poi-son-dart at thee, Crushed by their var-ied tyr-anny.

5. Yet thou with pa-tient mien Beneath his Cross dost stand, Nobler in this, I ween, Than all the mar-tyr-band: A thou-sand deaths, O Queen, Upon thy spir-it lie, Yet thou, O mar-vel! dost not die.

6. O Ho-ly Trin-i-ty, Let earth and heav-en raise Their song of laud to thee The while my spir-it prays: When e-vil comes to me, The strength do thou impart That erst upheld the Vir-gin's heart! A-men.

℣. Pray for us, O Queen of Martyrs.

℟. Who didst stand by the Cross of Jesus.

Mag. Ant. Look not † upon me, because I am black, because the sun hath looked upon me: my mother's children were angry with me.

15 September   **Proper of Saints**   *Seven Sorrows*

Mattins

Invitatory Hymn

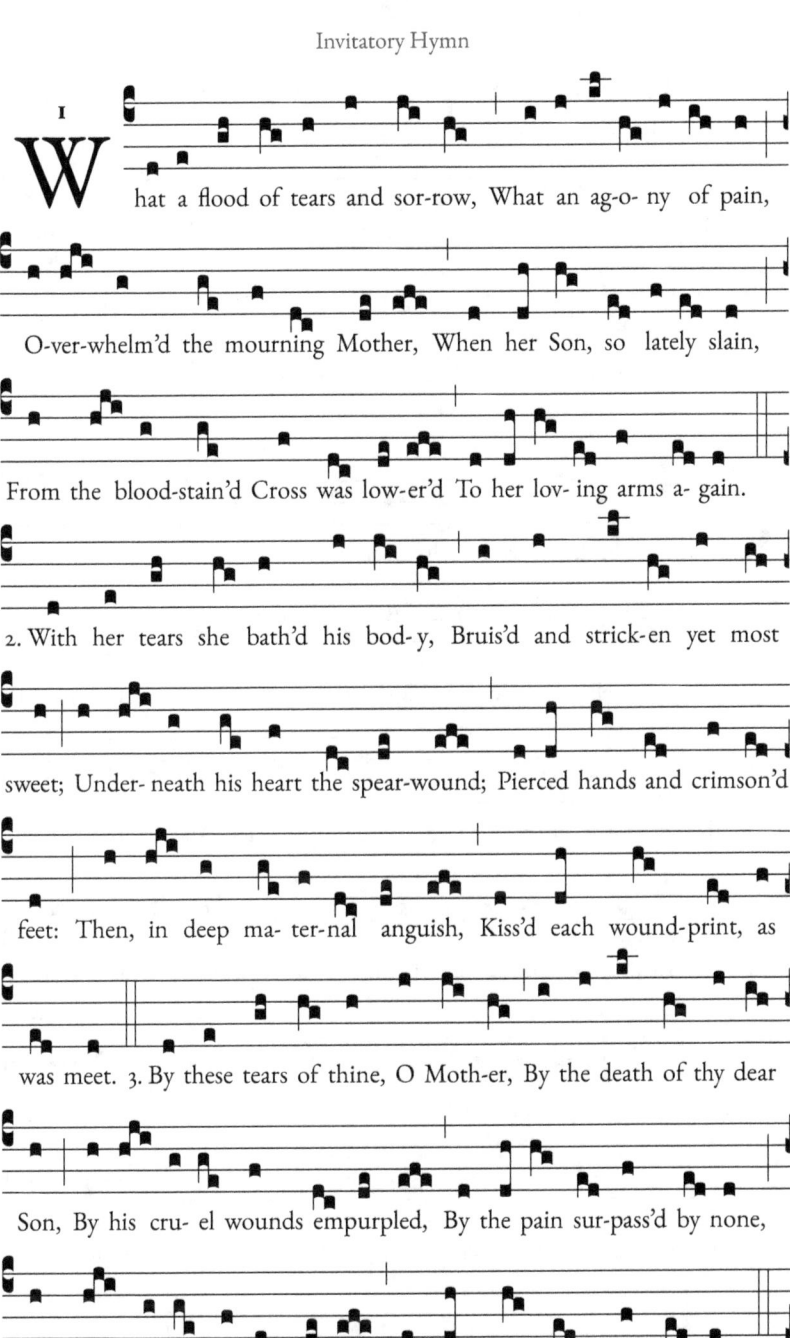

What a flood of tears and sor-row, What an ag-o-ny of pain, O-ver-whelm'd the mourning Mother, When her Son, so lately slain, From the blood-stain'd Cross was low-er'd To her lov-ing arms a-gain.

2. With her tears she bath'd his bod-y, Bruis'd and strick-en yet most sweet; Under-neath his heart the spear-wound; Pierced hands and crimson'd feet: Then, in deep ma-ter-nal anguish, Kiss'd each wound-print, as was meet.

3. By these tears of thine, O Moth-er, By the death of thy dear Son, By his cru-el wounds empurpled, By the pain sur-pass'd by none, Move our spir-its to compassion Till our grief with thine is one.

Seven Sorrows — Proper of Saints — 15 September

4. To the Fa-ther, Son, and Spir-it, To the Trin-i-ty most high, Co-e-ter-nal and co-equal, Ev-er-last-ing glo-ry be; Praise un-ending, hon-our, bless-ing, Now and through e-ter-ni-ty. A-men.

Office Hymn

O God, in whom all grace doth dwell, Grant us the grace to pon-der well The Vir-gin Moth-er's sor-rows sev'n, The cru-el wounds to Je-sus giv'n. 2. O may the tears which Mar-y pour'd Gain for us par-don of the Lord; The ho-ly tears which in their worth Excel all pen-anc-es of earth. 3. And may the con-templa-tion sore Of those five wounds which Je-sus bore. With all the Vir-gin's sor-rows be Our joy throughout e-ter-ni-ty. 4. Glo-ry to thee, O Lord,

15 September   **Proper of Saints**   *St. Nicomedes*

we give, Who died to make thy ser-vants live; Whom with the Fa-ther

we a-dore And Ho-ly Spir-it ev-ermore. A-men.

℣. O Virgin Mary, by thy sorrow's might.
℟. Make us rejoice in heaven's kingdom bright.

Ben. Ant. Come ye, † and let us go up to the mountain of the Lord, and see if there be any sorrow like unto my sorrow.

II Evensong

¶ The Office Hymn & Versicle are as in I Evensong, with the following Antiphon.

Mag. Ant. Sorrow oppresseth me, † my face is swollen with weeping, and on my eyelids is the shadow of death.

(15 September. St. Nicomedes)

¶ The First Common of a Martyr not a Bishop (p. 688), except for the following.

Collect

SSIST, O Lord, thy people: that as they do profit by the glorious merits of blessed Nicomedes thy Martyr, so his advocacy may at all times succour them to the obtaining of thy mercy. Through.

Secret

MERCIFULLY receive, O Lord, the gifts which we offer: and let the prayer of the blessed Martyr Nicomedes commend them unto thy Majesty. Through.

Postcommunion

CLEANSE us, O Lord, by the sacraments which we have received: that through the intercession of blessed Nicomedes, thy Martyr, they may set us free from all our offences. Through.

16 September. Sts. Cornelius and Cyprian

Double

❧ The propers are from the First Common of Many Martyrs out of Eastertide (p. 692), except for the following.

Collect

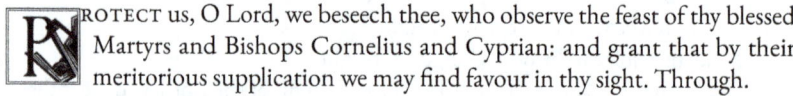ROTECT us, O Lord, we beseech thee, who observe the feast of thy blessed Martyrs and Bishops Cornelius and Cyprian: and grant that by their meritorious supplication we may find favour in thy sight. Through.

❧ Commemoration of Sts. Euphemia, Lucy, and Geminian (p. 616).

Secret

SSIST us mercifully, O Lord, in these our supplications which we make before thee in remembrance of thy Saints: that we who trust not in our own righteousness may be succoured by the merits of them that have found favour in thy sight. Through.

❧ Commemoration of Sts. Euphemia, Lucy, and Geminian (p. 616).

Postcommunion

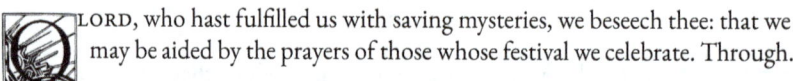LORD, who hast fulfilled us with saving mysteries, we beseech thee: that we may be aided by the prayers of those whose festival we celebrate. Through.

❧ Commemoration of Sts. Euphemia, Lucy, and Geminian (p. 617).

(16 September. Sts. Euphemia, Lucy, and Geminian)

❧ The First Common of Many Martyrs (p. 692), except for the following.

Collect

RANT, O Lord, that our prayers in this time of our rejoicing may be brought to good effect: that as with yearly service we recall the day of the passion of thy holy Martyrs, Euphemia, Lucy, and Geminian, so we may imitate the steadfastness of their faith. Through.

❧ The Gospel is from the Second Common of Many Martyrs (p. 699).

Secret

RACIOUSLY hearken, we beseech thee, O Lord, unto the prayers of thy people: and make us to rejoice in the intercession of those, whose festival thou dost suffer us to celebrate. Through.

Proper of Saints

21 September — St. Matthew

Postcommunion

LORD, graciously hear our prayers: that we, who solemnly observe the feast of thy holy Martyrs, Euphemia, Lucy, and Geminian, may be succoured by their continual help. Through.

19 September. Sts. Januarius and Companions

Double

¶ The propers are from the Third Common of Many Martyrs (p. 700), except for the first additional Gospel of the same Common (p. 703).

¶ Note, Commemoration is make of St. Theodore of Canterbury.

(19 September. St. Theodore of Canterbury)

¶ The First Common of a Confessor Bishop (p. 715).

¶ If today be Saturday, the anticipated Vigil of St. Matthew is kept.

20 September. Sts. Eustace and Companions

Double

¶ The propers are from the Second Common of Many Martyrs (p. 699).

20 September. Vigil of St. Matthew

Vigil

¶ The propers are from the Common of Vigils of the Apostles (p. 672) (with the 2nd Prayers of St. Mary in Eastertide (p. BCP 542) and the 3rd Against the Persecutors of the Church (p. BCP 543) or for the Chief Bishop (p. BCP 543)), except for the following Gospel.

Gospel. Luke 5:27

T THAT TIME: Jesus saw a publican, named Levi, sitting at the receipt of custom: and he said unto him, Follow me. And he left all, rose up, and followed him. And Levi made him a great feast in his own house: and there was a great company of publicans and of others that sat down with them. But their scribes and Pharisees murmured against his disciples, saying, Why do ye eat and drink with publicans and sinners? And Jesus answering said unto them, They that are whole need not a physician; but they that are sick. I came not to call the righteous, but sinners to repentance.

[21 September. St. Matthew]

¶ The Daily Office propers are of the Common of Apostles (p. 673).

Proper of Saints

Pope St. Linus — 23 September

(22 September. Sts. Maurice and Companions)

¶ The First Common of Many Martyrs (p. 692), except for the following.

Collect

RANT, we beseech thee, Almighty God: that the solemn festival of thy holy Martyrs, Maurice and his Companions, may in such wise gladden us: that, as we do lean upon their advocacy, so we may glory in their heavenly birth. Through.

¶ The Epistle is the sixth additional Epistle from the Third Common of Many Martyrs (p. 703).

Secret

EGARD, we beseech thee, O Lord, the gifts which we offer unto thee in commemoration of thy holy Martyrs, Maurice and his Companions: and grant; that through the intercession of them, for whose sake they are acceptable unto thee, they may be profitable unto us for evermore. Through.

Postcommunion

LORD, who hast refreshed us with the gladness of thy heavenly sacraments: we humbly entreat thee; that we may be protected by the succour of them in whose triumphs we glory. Through.

(23 September. Pope St. Linus)

¶ The First Common of a Martyr Bishop (p. 682), except for the following.

Collect

GOD, who makest us glad with the yearly solemnity of blessed Linus thy Martyr and Bishop: mercifully grant; that, as we now celebrate his birthday, so we may likewise rejoice in his protection. Through.

¶ Commemoration of St. Thecla (p. 619).

Secret

ANCTIFY, O Lord, the gifts which we dedicate to thee: that at the intercession of blessed Linus, thy Martyr and Bishop, they may obtain for us thy gracious favour. Through.

¶ Commemoration of St. Thecla (p. 619).

Postcommunion

AY this communion, O Lord, cleanse us from guilt: and, at the intercession of blessed Linus, thy Martyr and Bishop, make us partakers of thy heavenly healing. Through.

¶ Commemoration of St. Thecla (p. 619).

(23 SEPTEMBER. ST. THECLA)

¶ The First Common of a Virgin Martyress (p. 733), except for the following.

Collect

RANT, we beseech thee, Almighty God: that we, who celebrate the birthday of blessed Thecla, thy Virgin and Martyr; may both rejoice in her yearly solemnity, and likewise profit by the example of her faith. Through.

Secret

ECEIVE, O Lord, the gifts which we offer on the solemnity of blessed Thecla, thy Virgin and Martyr: through whose advocacy we trust to be delivered. Through.

Postcommunion

AY the mysteries which we have received be for our succour, O Lord: and at the intercession of blessed Thecla, thy Virgin and Martyr, cause us to rejoice in thy continual protection. Through.

(26 SEPTEMBER. STS. CYPRIAN AND JUSTINA)

¶ The Third Common of Many Martyrs (p. 700), except for the following.

Collect

LORD, let the protection of thy blessed Martyrs, Cyprian and Justina, continually defend us: forasmuch as thou failest not to look with mercy on those to whom thou dost grant the succour of thy assistance. Through.

Secret

E beseech thee, O Lord, that the gifts which we offer unto thee of our bounden duty and service may be acceptable unto thee for the honour of thy Just ones: and by thy mercy profitable unto us for our salvation. Through.

Postcommunion

RANT to us, we beseech thee, O Lord: at the intercession of thy holy Martyrs Cyprian and Justina; that those things which we touch with our mouths we may receive in purity of heart. Through.

(27 SEPTEMBER. STS. COSMAS AND DAMIAN)

Introit

ET the people tell of the wisdom of the Saints, and let the Church shew forth their praise: their names shall live for evermore. *Ps.* Rejoice in the Lord, O ye righteous: for it becometh well the just to be thankful.

Collect

RANT, we beseech thee, Almighty God: that we, who observe the heavenly birthday of thy holy Martyrs, Cosmas and Damian, may by their intercession be delivered from all evils that beset us. Through.

¶ The Epistle is from the Second Common of Many Martyrs (p. 699).

Gradual. The righteous cry, and the Lord heareth them: and delivereth them out of all their troubles. ℣. The Lord is nigh unto them that are of a contrite heart: and will save such as be of an humble spirit.

Alleluia. Alleluia, alleluia. ℣. This is the true brotherhood, which overcame the wickedness of the world: which followed Christ, gaining heaven's glorious realms. Alleluia.

¶ The Gospel is from the Second Common of Many Martyrs (p. 699).

Offertory. All they that love thy Name shall be joyful in thee: for thou, Lord, wilt give thy blessing unto the righteous: and with thy favourable kindness, O Lord, wilt thou defend us as with a shield.

Secret

AY the devout prayers of thy Saints never fail us, O Lord: that they may both render our oblations acceptable, and ever obtain for us thy merciful pardon. Through.

Communion. The dead bodies of thy servants, O Lord, have they given to be meat unto the fowls of the air, and the flesh of thy Saints unto the beasts of the land: according to the greatness of thy power preserve thou those that are appointed to die.

Postcommunion

E beseech thee, O Lord, that thy people may be protected by the prayers which thy Saints do offer, and by this heavenly banquet, whereof thou hast suffered them to be partakers. Through.

29 September   **Proper of Saints**   *St. Michael Archangel*

(28 SEPTEMBER. ST. WENCESLAUS)

¶ The First Common of a Martyr not a Bishop (p. 688), except for the following.

Collect

O GOD, who through the victory of martyrdom didst translate blessed Wenceslas from an earthly principality to the glory of heaven: defend us through his prayers from all adversity; and grant us likewise to rejoice in his fellowship. Through.

[29 SEPTEMBER. ST. MICHAEL]

I Evensong

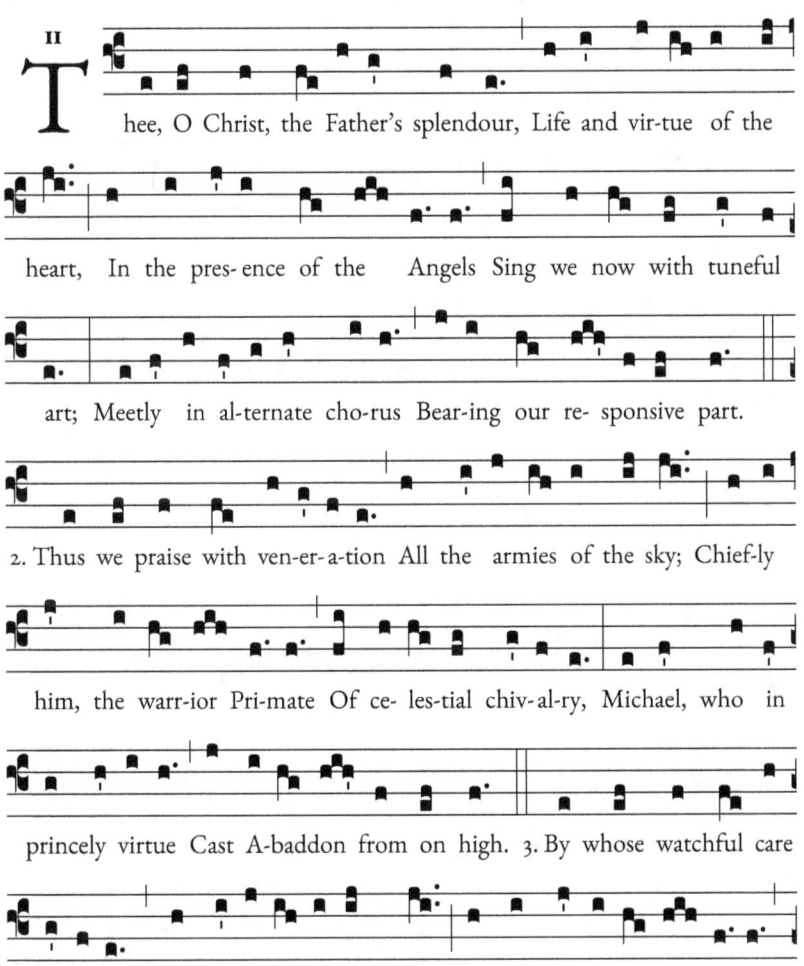

Thee, O Christ, the Father's splendour, Life and vir-tue of the heart, In the pres-ence of the Angels Sing we now with tuneful art; Meetly in al-ternate cho-rus Bear-ing our re-sponsive part.

2. Thus we praise with ven-er-a-tion All the armies of the sky; Chief-ly him, the warr-ior Pri-mate Of ce-les-tial chiv-al-ry, Michael, who in princely virtue Cast A-baddon from on high. 3. By whose watchful care re-pel-ling, King of ev-er-last-ing grace, Every ghostly ad-ver-sar-y,

St. Michael Archangel # Proper of Saints 29 September

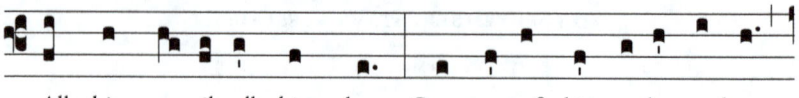
All things e-vil, all things base, Grant us of thine only goodness

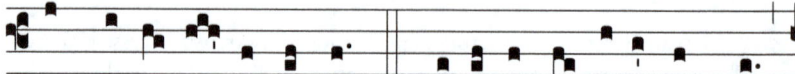
In thy Par-a-dise a place. 4. Glo-ry to the Father sing we

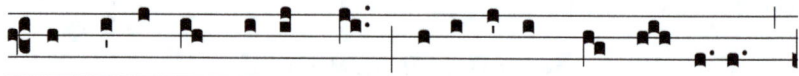
With re-sounding voic-es sweet, Glo-ry unto Christ our Saviour,

Glo-ry to the Par-a-clete: Standing forth, One God and Tri-nal, Ere

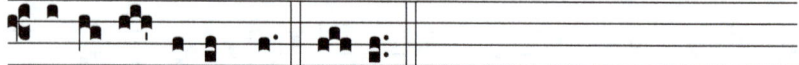
the ag-es; as is meet. A-men.

℣. An Angel stood at the altar of the temple.
℟. Having in his hand a golden censer.

Mag. Ant. While John beheld † the sacred mystery, the Archangel Michael sounded the trumpet: Forgive us, O Lord our God, that openest the book, and loosest the seals thereof, alleluia.

Mattins

¶ The Invitatory Hymn is as in I Evensong.

Office Hymn

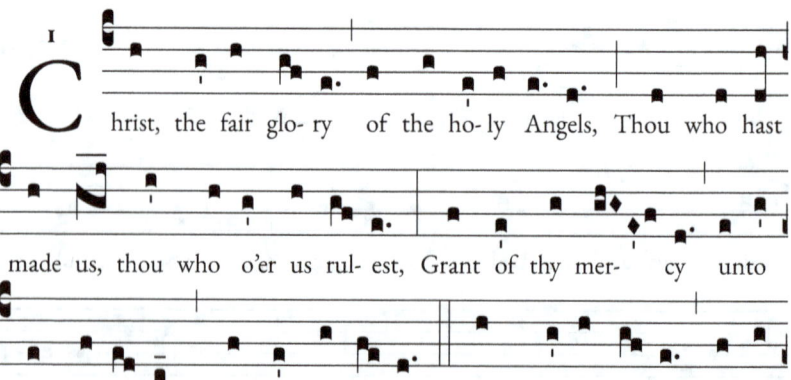
Christ, the fair glo-ry of the ho-ly Angels, Thou who hast made us, thou who o'er us rul-est, Grant of thy mer-cy unto us thy ser-vants Steps up to heav-en. 2. Send thy Archangel, Michael,

29 September **Proper of Saints** *St. Michael Archangel*

to our succour; Peacemak-er bless-ed, may he ban-ish from us Striv-ing and ha- tred, so that for the peaceful All things may pros-per.

3. Send thy Archangel, Gabri- el, the mighty, Her-ald of heav-en; may he from us mor-tals Spurn the old ser- pent, watching o'er the temples Where thou art worshipp'd. 4. Send thy Archangel, Rapha- el, re-stor- er Of the misguid-ed ways of men who wander, Who at thy bid- ding strengthens soul and bod-y With thine a-nointing.

5. May the blest Moth-er of our God and Saviour, May the as-sembly of the Saints in glo- ry, May the ce-les- tial compa-nies of An-gels Ev-er as-sist us. 6. This he vouchsafe us, God for ev-er bless-ed,

St. Jerome   **Proper of Saints**   30 September

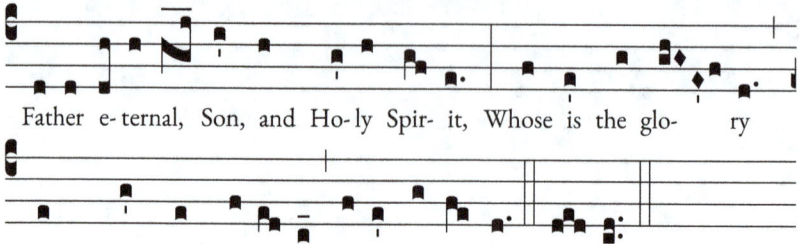

Father eternal, Son, and Holy Spirit, Whose is the glory which through all creation Ever resoundeth. A-men.

℣. An Angel stood at the altar of the temple.
℟. Having in his hand a golden censer.

Ben. Ant. There was silence in heaven † while the dragon waged war: and Michael fought against him, and had the victory, alleluia.

II Evensong

¶ The Office Hymn is as in I Evensong, with the following Versicle & Antiphon.

℣. In the presence of the Angels I will sing praise unto thee, O my God.
℟. I will worship toward thy holy temple, and praise thy Name.

Mag. Ant. O Prince most glorious, † Michael the Archangel, keep us in remembrance: here and everywhere, always, entreat the Son of God for us, alleluia, alleluia.

30 September. St. Jerome

Greater Double

¶ The propers are from the Common of Doctors (p. 723), except for the following.

Collect

GOD, who for the exposition of the sacred Scriptures didst bestow upon thy Church blessed Jerome, thy Confessor and most illustrious Doctor: grant, we beseech thee; that, by the intercession of his merits, we may through thine assistance be enabled to perform those things which he taught both in word and deed. Through.

¶ Commemoration of St. Gregory of Armenia (p. 625).

Secret

GRANT us, we beseech thee, O Lord, through these heavenly gifts to serve thee in freedom of spirit: that the gifts which we offer may, through the mediation of blessed Jerome, thy Confessor, work in us both healing and glory. Through.

¶ Commemoration of St. Gregory of Armenia (p. 625).

Postcommunion

E beseech thee, O Lord, that we whom thou hast fulfilled with heavenly nourishment: may through the mediation of blessed Jerome, thy Confessor, be found worthy to obtain the grace of thy loving-kindness. Through.

℣ Commemoration of St. Gregory of Armenia (p. 625).

(30 September. St. Gregory of Armenia)

℣ The First Common of a Confessor Bishop (p. 715), except for the following.

Collect

GOD, who, through thy blessed Bishop and Confessor Gregory, didst grant that the people and King of Armenia receive the light of true faith: likewise grant unto thy Church to rejoice in such mighty triumphs, and, by the merits and intercession of the same, to be succoured before thee. Through.

Secret

RACIOUSLY receive, O Lord, the sacrifices dedicated unto thee, by the merits of thy blessed Bishop and Confessor Gregory: and grant that they may avail us unto everlasting help. Through.

Postcommunion

RANT, we beseech thee, O Lord our God; that we, having been refreshed by participation in the holy gifts, may experience the fruit of the intercession of blessed Gregory thy Bishop and Confessor, whose festival we now celebrate. Through.

(1 October. St. Remigius)

℣ The First Common of a Confessor Bishop (p. 715).

[2 October. Holy Guardian Angels]

I Evensong

The Guardians of our race, our Angel Guides we hail; Our Father sendeth forth to aid our nature frail These heav'nly friends, lest

Guardian Angels   **Proper of Saints**   2 October

we should suf-fer o-verthrow Through cunning of our subtle foe.

2. For he, who justly lost the honour once his own, The trai-tor an-gel, rues his lost and va-cant throne, With burning envy strives to make them fall a-way Whom God doth call to heav'nly day.

3. Then, watchful Guardian, spread thy wings and cleave the air, Haste hither to our home commit-ted to thy care; Drive thence each noxious ill that might the soul in-fest, Nor suf-fer danger here to rest.

4. Now to the ho-ly Three your praise devout-ly pour; His glorious God-head guides and gov-erns ev-ermore This tri-ple frame: to him ascribe we all our praise Who reigns through ev-er-last-ing days. A-men.

2 October — **Proper of Saints** — *Guardian Angels*

℣. In the presence of the Angels I will sing praise unto thee, O my God.
℞. I will worship toward thy holy temple, and praise thy Name.
Mag. Ant. They are all † ministering spirits, sent forth to minister to them who shall be heirs of salvation.

Mattins

¶ The Invitatory Hymn is as in I Evensong.

Office Hymn

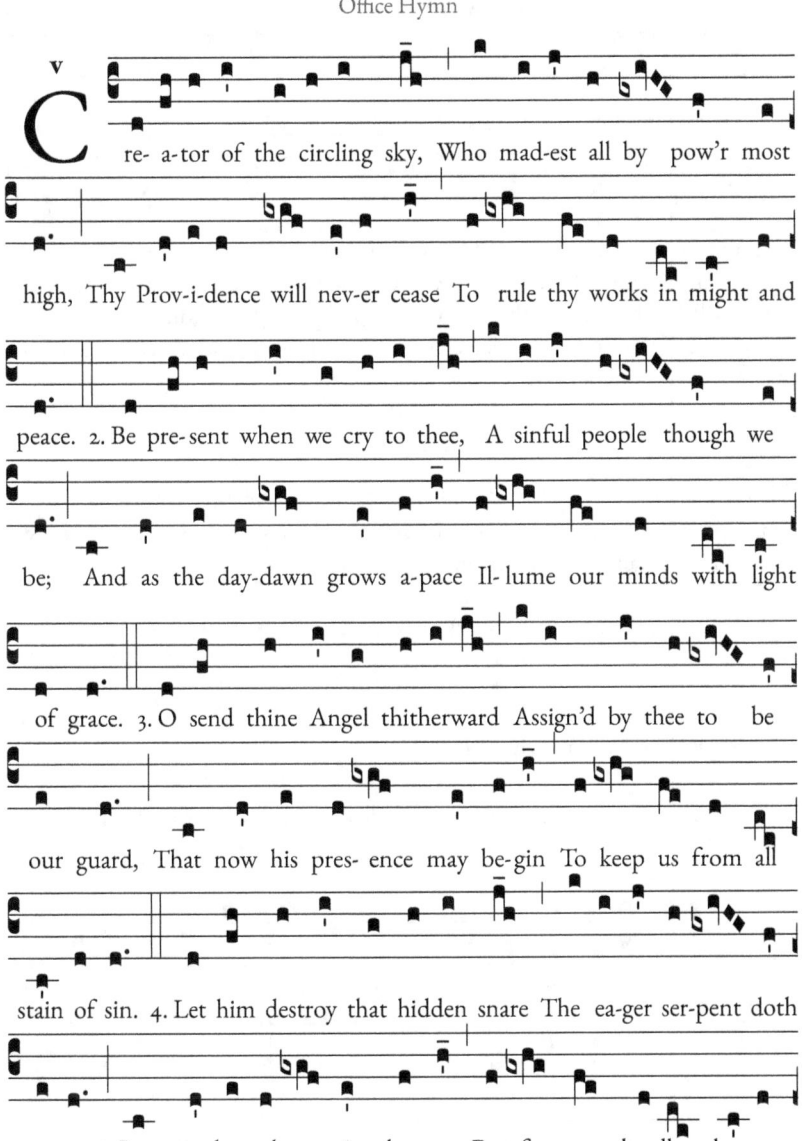

Cre-a-tor of the circling sky, Who mad-est all by pow'r most high, Thy Prov-i-dence will nev-er cease To rule thy works in might and peace. 2. Be pre-sent when we cry to thee, A sinful people though we be; And as the day-dawn grows a-pace Il-lume our minds with light of grace. 3. O send thine Angel thitherward Assign'd by thee to be our guard, That now his pres-ence may be-gin To keep us from all stain of sin. 4. Let him destroy that hidden snare The ea-ger ser-pent doth pre-pare, Lest we be tak-en in the net Be-fore our heedless bos-oms

Holy Rosary   Proper of Saints   7 October

set. 5. At his command let every fear Of hos-tile foemen dis- appear; Let civ- il strife give way to peace, And pes- ti- lence and fam-ine cease. 6. To God the Father glo-ry be; For those the Sav-iour set-teth free, A- nointed by the Ho- ly Ghost, Are guard-ed by the Angel host. A- men.

℣. In the presence of the Angels I will sing praise unto thee, O my God.
℟. I will worship toward thy holy temple, and praise thy Name.

Ben. Ant. And the Angel † that talked with me came again, and waked me, as a man that is wakened out of his sleep.

II Evensong

❡ The Office Hymn & Versicle is as in I Evensong, with the following Antiphon.
Mag. Ant. Ye holy Angels, † our Guardians, defend us in time of battle, lest we perish in the dreadful day of judgment.

5 October. Sts. Placidus and Companions

Double

❡ The propers are from the Third Common of Many Martyrs (p. 700), with the Prayers from the First Common of Many Martyrs (p. 692).

[7 October. Holy Rosary of the Blessed Virgin Mary]

I Evensong

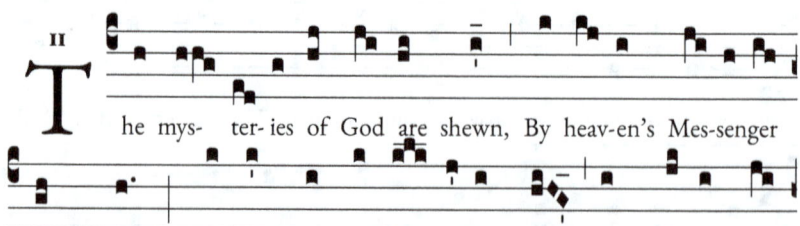

The mys- ter- ies of God are shewn, By heav-en's Mes-senger made known, Who hails the Maid of Da-vid's race, God's Vir-gin Moth-

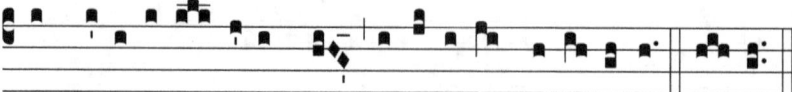

All glo-ry, as is ev-er meet, To Father and to Par-a-clete. A-men.

℣. Queen of the holy Rosary, pray for us.

℟. That we may be made worthy of the promises of Christ.

Mag. Ant. Blessed art thou, † O Virgin Mary, Mother of God, for thou hast believed the Lord: for those things are accomplished in thee which were told thee: intercede for us unto the Lord our God.

Mattins

Invitatory Hymn

The Mount of Ol-ives wit-ness-eth The awful ag-o-ny of  God: His soul is sorrow-ful to death, His sweat of blood be-dews the sod. 2. And now the trai-tor's work is done: The clam'rous crowds a-round him surge; Bound to pil-lar, O God the Son Quiv-ers be-neath the blood-red scourge. 3. Lo! clad in purple soiled and worn, Meekly the Sav-iour wait-eth now While wretches plait the cru-el thorn To crown with shame his roy-al brow. 4. Sweat-ing and sighing, faint

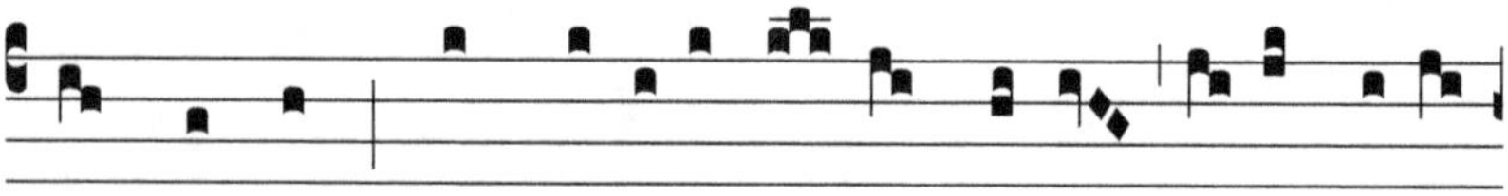

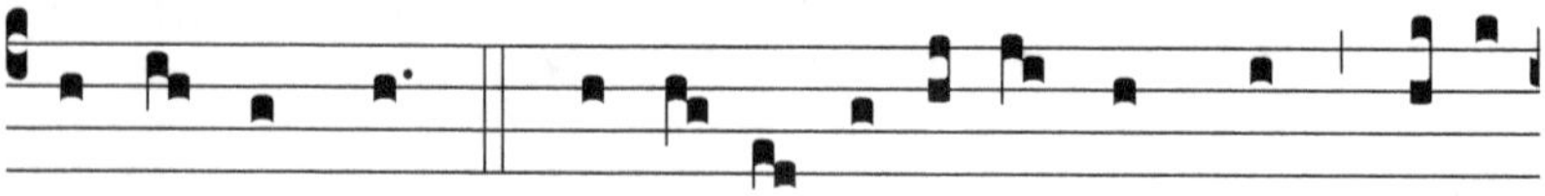

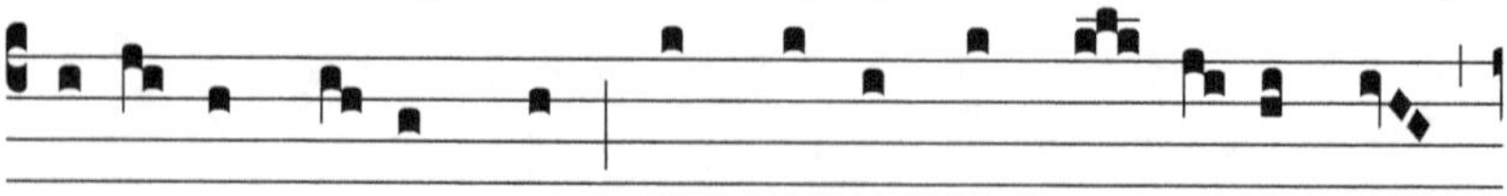

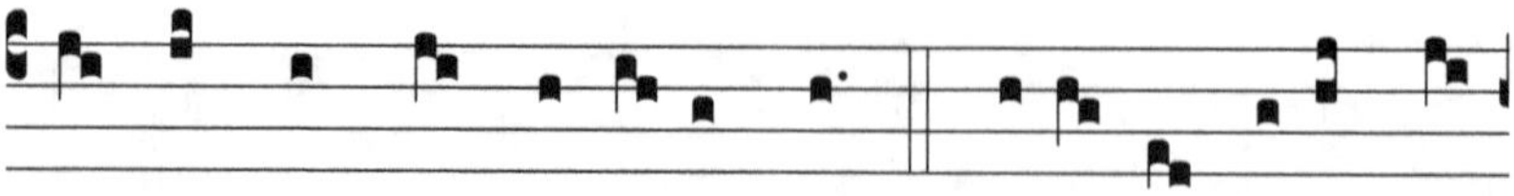

7 October — Proper of Saints — *Holy Rosary*

with loss Of what hath flowed from life's red fount, He bears th' exceed-ing heav-y Cross Up to the verge of Calv'ry's mount. 5. Nail'd to the wood of an-cient curse, Between two thieves the Sin-less One Still pray-ing for his mur-der-ers, Breathes forth his soul, and all is done! 6. Glo-ry to thee, and hon-our meet, Je-su, of Maid-en-Moth-er born, And Father and the Par-a-clete, Through endless ag-es of the morn! A-men.

Office Hymn

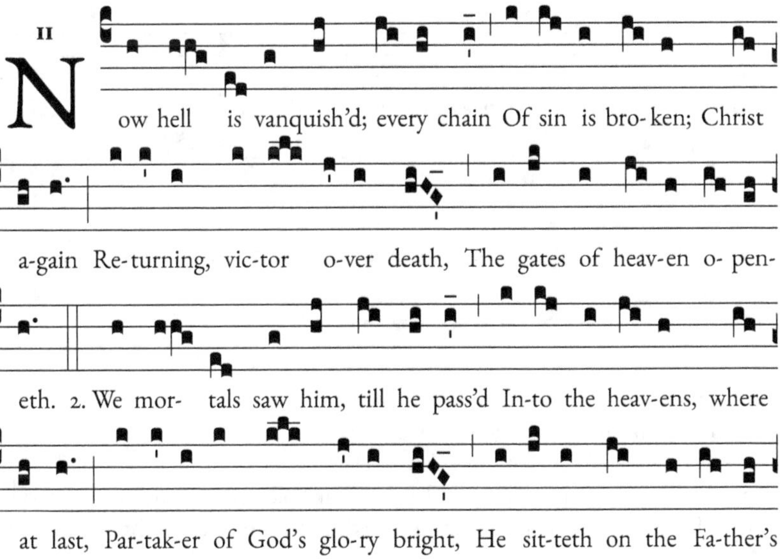

Now hell is vanquish'd; every chain Of sin is bro-ken; Christ a-gain Re-turning, vic-tor o-ver death, The gates of heav-en o-pen-eth. 2. We mor-tals saw him, till he pass'd In-to the heav-ens, where at last, Par-tak-er of God's glo-ry bright, He sit-teth on the Fa-ther's

Holy Rosary — **Proper of Saints** — 7 October

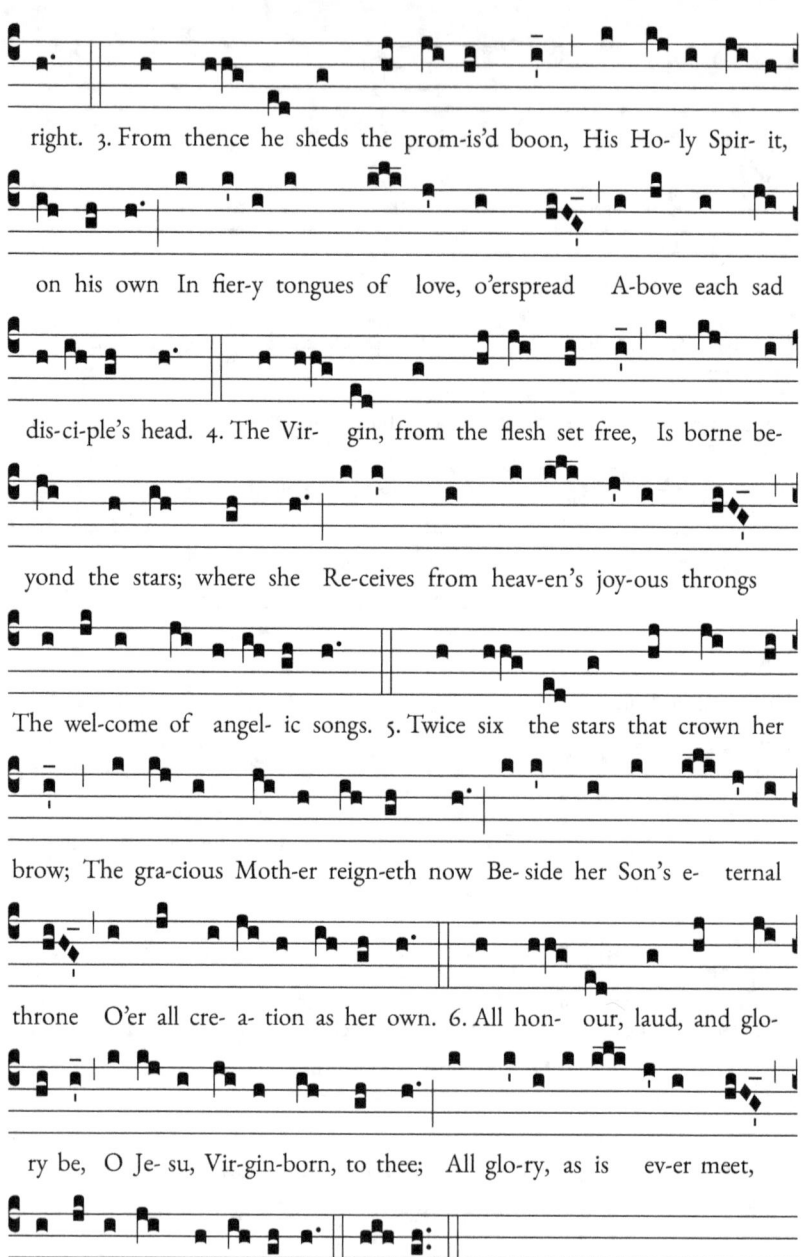

right. 3. From thence he sheds the prom-is'd boon, His Ho- ly Spir- it, on his own In fier-y tongues of love, o'erspread A-bove each sad dis-ci-ple's head. 4. The Vir- gin, from the flesh set free, Is borne be-yond the stars; where she Re-ceives from heav-en's joy-ous throngs The wel-come of angel- ic songs. 5. Twice six the stars that crown her brow; The gra-cious Moth-er reign-eth now Be- side her Son's e- ternal throne O'er all cre- a- tion as her own. 6. All hon- our, laud, and glo-ry be, O Je- su, Vir-gin-born, to thee; All glo-ry, as is ev-er meet, To Father and to Par- a-clete. A- men.

℣. God hath chosen her and preferred her.

℟. He hath made her to dwell in his tabernacle.

Ben. Ant. To-day let us celebrate † devoutly the Solemnity of the holy Rosary of Mary, Mother of God, that she may intercede for us unto Jesus Christ the Lord.

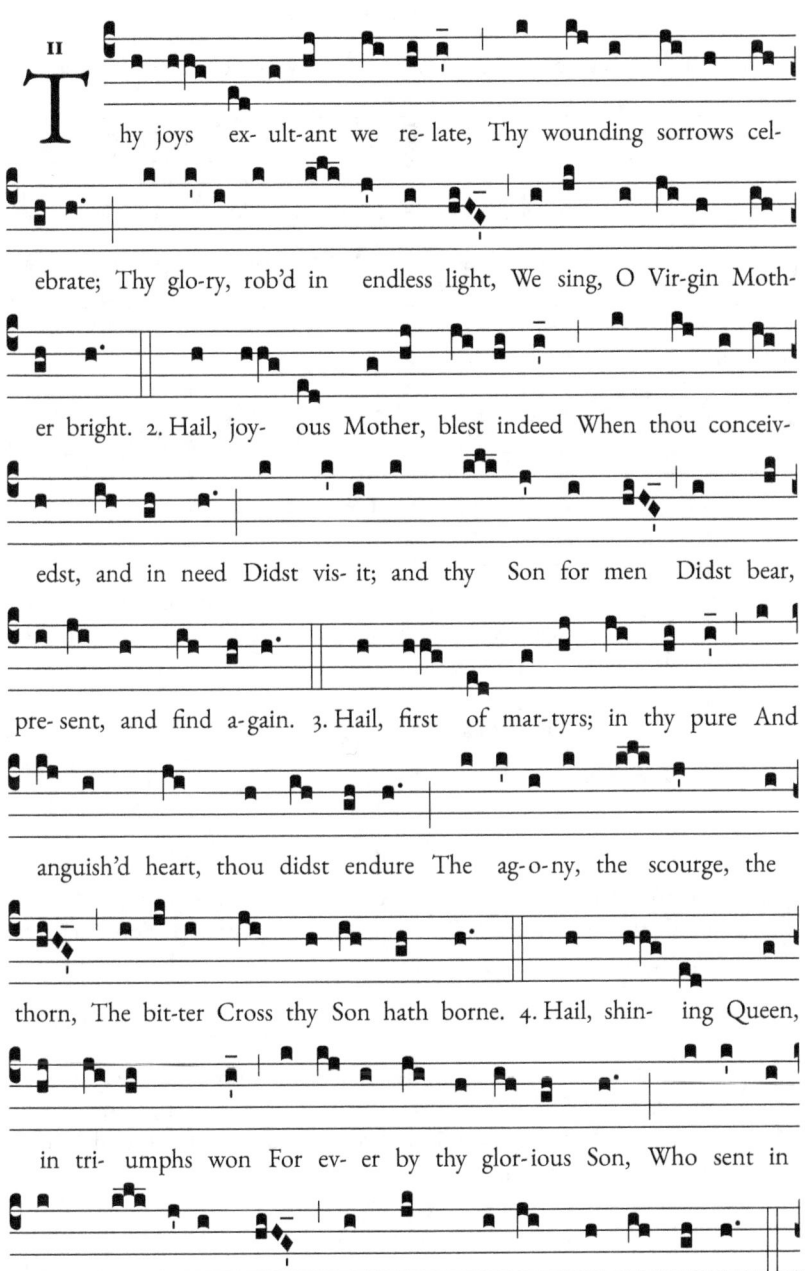

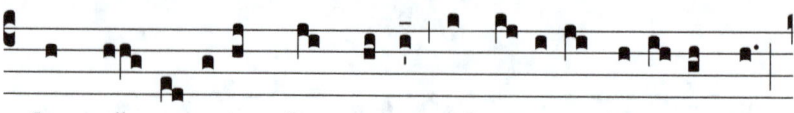

5. Come, all ye na-tions, from this vine Of mys-ter-ies the ros- es twine

In gar-lands for your Queen a-bove, The glorious Moth-er of fair love.

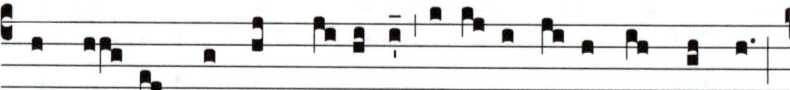

6. All hon- our, laud, and glo- ry be, O Je- su, Vir-gin-born, to thee;

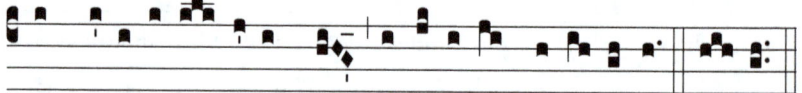

All glo-ry, as is ev-er meet, To Father and to Par- a-clete. A- men.

℣. Queen of the holy Rosary, pray for us.

℟. That we may be made worthy of the promises of Christ.

Mag. Ant. O blessed Mother † and spotless Virgin, thou glorious Queen of the world, may all acknowledge the help of thy prayer who celebrate the solemnity of thy holy Rosary.

(7 October. St. Mark of Rome)

❡ The Second Common of a Confessor Bishop (p. 720), except for the following.

Collect

RACIOUSLY hear our prayers, O Lord: and at the intercession of blessed Mark, thy Confessor and Bishop, mercifully grant us pardon and peace. Through.

Secret

GRANT, O Lord, that like as thy dedicated people do acknowledge that in tribulation they have been succoured by the merits of thy Saints: so this oblation, which they offer unto thee in honour of the same, may be acceptable in thy sight. Through.

Postcommunion

RANT, we beseech thee, O Lord, that thy faithful people may ever rejoice in the veneration of thy Saints: and be defended by their perpetual supplication. Through.

Proper of Saints

9 October — Sts. Denys &c.

(7 October. Sts. Sergius, Bacchus, Marcellus, and Apuleius)

¶ The Second Common of Many Martyrs (p. 699), except for the following.

Collect

MAY the blessed merits of thy holy Martyrs Sergius, Bacchus, Marcellus, and Apuleius uphold us, O Lord: and ever make us fervent in thy love. Through.

Secret

WE beseech thee, O Lord, that, through the meritorious supplication of thy Saints: this sacrifice, which we offer, may obtain for us the favour of thy Majesty. Through.

Postcommunion

GRANT, O Lord, that, being strengthened by the sacraments which we have received: we may, at the intercession of thy holy Martyrs, Sergius, Bacchus, Marcellus, and Apuleius, fight against all iniquity, and be defended by thy heavenly armour. Through.

(9 October. Sts. Denys, Rusticus, and Eleutherius)

Introit

LET the people tell of the wisdom of the Saints, and let the Church shew forth their praise: their names shall live for evermore. *Ps.* Rejoice in the Lord, O ye righteous: for it becometh well the just to be thankful.

Collect

O GOD, who on this day didst strengthen blessed Denys, thy Martyr and Bishop, with the virtue of constancy in his passion, and didst vouchsafe to join unto him Rusticus and Eleutherius for the preaching of thy glory to the Gentiles: grant us, we beseech thee; by their example, to despise for love of thee the prosperity of the world, and to fear none of its adversities. Through.

Epistle. Acts 17:22

IN THOSE DAYS: Paul stood in the midst of Mars' hill, and said: Ye men of Athens, I perceive that in all things ye are too superstitious. For as I passed by, and beheld your devotions, I found an altar with this inscription, To THE UNKNOWN GOD. Whom therefore ye ignorantly worship, him declare I unto you. God that made the world and all things therein, seeing that he is Lord of heaven and earth, dwelleth not in temples made with hands; Neither is worshipped with men's hands, as though he needed any thing, seeing he giveth to all life, and breath, and all things; And hath made of one blood all nations of men for to dwell on all the face of the earth, and hath determined the times before appointed, and the bounds of their habitation; That they should seek the Lord, if haply they might feel after him, and find him, though he be not far from every one of us: For in him we live, and move, and have our being; as certain also of your own poets have said, For we are also his offspring. Forasmuch then as we are the offspring of God, we ought not to think that the Godhead is like unto gold, or silver, or stone, graven by art and man's device. And the times of this ignorance God winked at; but now commandeth all men every where to repent: Because he hath appointed a day, in the which he will judge the world in righteousness by that man whom he hath ordained; whereof he hath given assurance unto all men, in that he hath raised him from the dead. And when they heard of the resurrection of the dead, some mocked: and others said, We will hear thee again of this matter. So Paul departed from among them. Howbeit certain men clave unto him, and believed: among the which was Dionysius the Areopagite, and a woman named Damaris, and others with them.

Gradual. Our soul is escaped even as a bird out of the snare of the fowler. ℣. The snare is broken, and we are delivered: our help is in the name of the Lord, who hath made heaven and earth.

Alleluia. Alleluia, alleluia. ℣. Let the righteous be glad and rejoice before God: let them also be merry and joyful. Alleluia.

Gospel. Luke 12:1

AT THAT TIME: Jesus said unto his disciples: Beware ye of the leaven of the Pharisees, which is hypocrisy. For there is nothing covered, that shall not be revealed; neither hid, that shall not be known. Therefore whatsoever ye have spoken in darkness shall be heard in the light; and that which ye have spoken in the ear in closets shall be proclaimed upon the housetops. And I say unto you my friends, Be not afraid of them that kill the body, and after that have no more that they can do. But I will forewarn you whom ye shall fear: Fear him, which after he hath killed hath power to cast into hell; yea, I say unto you, Fear him. Are not five sparrows sold for two farthings, and not one of them is forgotten before God? But even the very hairs of your head are all numbered. Fear not therefore: ye are of more value than many sparrows. Also I say unto you, Whosoever shall confess me before men, him shall the Son of man also confess before the angels of God.

Offertory. Let the Saints be joyful with glory, let them rejoice in their beds: let the praises of God be in their mouth, alleluia.

Secret

GRACIOUSLY receive, we beseech thee, O Lord, the oblations of thy people, for the honour of thy Saints: and sanctify us by their intercession. Through.

11 October   **Proper of Saints**   *Motherhood*

Communion. And I say unto you, my friends: Be not afraid of them that persecute you.

Postcommunion

E beseech thee, O Lord that we, who have received thy sacraments: may at the intercession of thy blessed Martyrs Denys, Rusticus, and Eleutherius, be profited thereby unto the increase of eternal redemption. Through.

[11 October. Motherhood of the Blessed Virgin Mary]

I Evensong

¶ The Office Hymn is from the Common of the Blessed Virgin Mary (p. 760), with the following Versicle & Antiphon.

℣. Blessed art thou amongst women.
℟. And blessed is the fruit of thy womb.
Mag. Ant. Let us celebrate with joy † the Motherhood of the blessed Mary ever Virgin.

Mattins

Invitatory Hymn

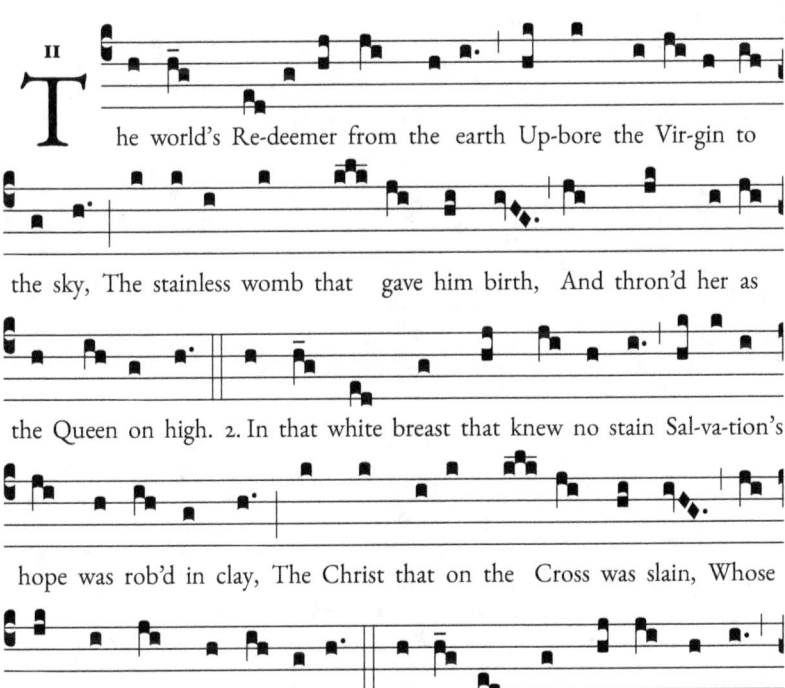

The world's Re-deemer from the earth Up-bore the Vir-gin to the sky, The stainless womb that gave him birth, And thron'd her as the Queen on high. 2. In that white breast that knew no stain Sal-va-tion's hope was rob'd in clay, The Christ that on the Cross was slain, Whose blood has wash'd our sins away. 3. Let joy and hope to man be won,

Motherhood   **Proper of Saints**   11 October

And drive a-way all anxious fears For Mar-y to her pit-ying Son Will sweetly bear our prayers and tears. 4. The moth-er's words her tender Child Will heed and each entreat-y bless; Re-vere and love that moth-er mild, And seek her aid in all distress. 5. Thou Tri-une God, all praise to thee, That to the stain-less bos-om bore The vir-gin-al ma-ter-ni-ty; We sing thy glo-ry ev-ermore. A-men.

Office Hymn

Sweet moth-er of the Lord most high, To thee we bow in humble prayer, To thee from e-vil pow'rs we fly; O shield and keep us in thy care. 2. It was to lift our fall-en race A-bove the curse of A-dam's crime, The King bestow'd on thee his grace And shap'd

11 October — **Proper of Saints** — *Motherhood*

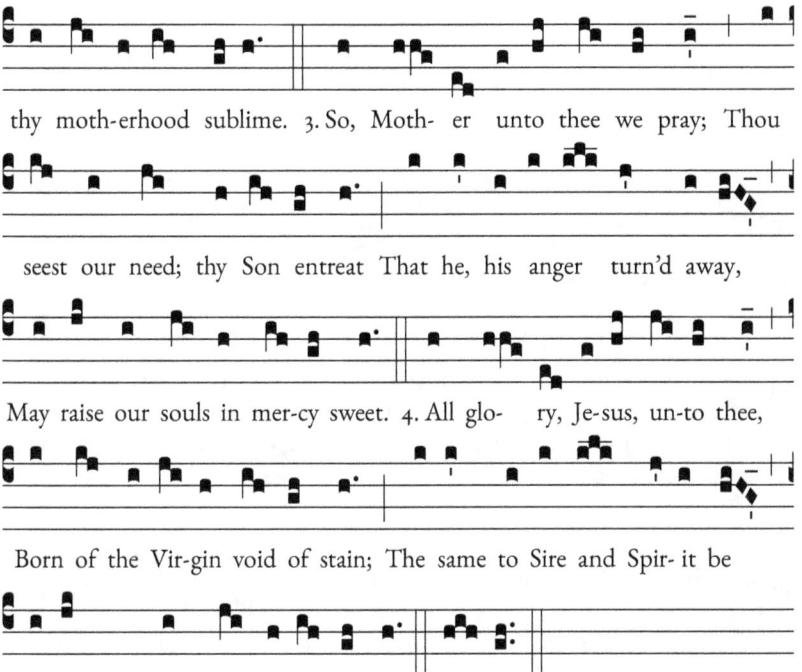

thy moth-erhood sublime. 3. So, Moth- er unto thee we pray; Thou seest our need; thy Son entreat That he, his anger turn'd away, May raise our souls in mer-cy sweet. 4. All glo- ry, Je-sus, un-to thee, Born of the Vir-gin void of stain; The same to Sire and Spir- it be Proclaim'd through one e- ter-nal reign. A- men.

℣. The root of Jesse hath budded forth: a star hath arisen out of Jacob.

℟. The Virgin hath brought forth the Saviour: we praise thee, O our God.

Ben. Ant. O holy Mary, † help thou the suffering, strengthen the faint-hearted, comfort the sorrowful; pray for the people, entreat for the clergy, intercede for all womankind vowed unto God: may all experience thy help, who celebrate thine admirable motherhood.

II Evensong

¶ The Office Hymn is from the Common of the Blessed Virgin Mary (p. 760), with the following Versicle & Antiphon.

℣. Blessed art thou amongst women.

℟. And blessed is the fruit of thy womb.

Mag. Ant. Thy motherhood, O Virgin Birthgiver of God, announces joy unto the whole world: for from thee the Sun of Righteousness hath arisen, Christ our God.

(12 October. St. Wilfred)

¶ The Second Common of a Confessor Bishop (p. 720), except for the following.

Collect

O GOD, by whose grace the blessed Bishop Wilfrid did wondrously shine forth with the glorious tokens of his merits: mercifully grant unto us; that we, who by his doctrine are taught to seek after things heavenly, may ever be defended by his advocacy. *Through.*

Secret

PURIFY, we beseech thee, Almighty God, the hearts of thy family by the enlightening of thy Holy Spirit: that through the intercession of blessed Wilfrid, thy Confessor and Bishop, these gifts of devotion may be rendered acceptable unto thee. *Through . . . in the unity of the same.*

Postcommunion

O LORD, who hast fulfilled us with the food of eternal redemption, we humbly entreat thy mercy: that by the intercession of blessed Wilfrid, thy Confessor and Bishop, we may receive the gifts of everlasting salvation. *Through.*

(13 October. St. Edward)

¶ The First Common of a Confessor not a Bishop (p. 725), except for the following.

Collect

O GOD, who didst bestow upon thy blessed Confessor King Edward the crown of everlasting glory: grant us, we beseech thee; so to venerate him on earth, that we may be enabled to reign with him in heaven. *Through.*

14 October. St. Callistus

Double

¶ The Daily Office propers are from the First Common of a Martyr Bishop (p. 682).

Introit

O YE priests of the Lord, bless ye the Lord: O ye holy and humble men of heart, bless ye the Lord. *Cant.* O all ye works of the Lord, bless ye the Lord: praise him, and magnify him for ever.

Collect

O GOD, who seest that we fail by reason of our infirmity: through the examples of thy Saints mercifully restore us to the love of thee. *Through.*

15 October   **Proper of Saints**   *Walsingham*

Epistle. Hebrews 5:1

RETHREN: Every high priest taken from among men is ordained for men in things pertaining to God, that he may offer both gifts and sacrifices for sins: Who can have compassion on the ignorant, and on them that are out of the way; for that he himself also is compassed with infirmity. And by reason hereof he ought, as for the people, so also for himself, to offer for sins. And no man taketh this honour unto himself, but he that is called of God, as was Aaron.

Gradual. I have found David my servant, with my holy oil have I anointed him: my hand shall hold him fast, and my arm shall strengthen him. ℣. The enemy shall not be able to do him violence: the son of wickedness shall not hurt him.

Alleluia. Alleluia, alleluia. ℣. The Lord loved him, and adorned him: he clothed him with a robe of glory. Alleluia.

¶ The Gospel is of the Second Common of a Martyr not a Bishop (p. 690).

Offertory. My truth and my mercy shall be with him: and in my name shall his horn be exalted.

Secret

LORD, let this mystical oblation be profitable unto us: that it may both deliver us from our offences, and stablish us in everlasting salvation. Through.

Communion. Blessed is the servant whom the lord, when he cometh, shall find watching: verily I say unto you, that he shall make him ruler over all his goods.

Postcommunion

E beseech thee, Almighty God: that the gifts which we have hallowed may cleanse us from our iniquities, and bring forth in us the fruit of godly living. Through.

[15 October. Our Lady of Walsingham]

<table>
<tr><td>I Evensong</td><td>Mattins</td></tr>
<tr><td>Hail Mary, ever blessed,
Of Walsingham the Queen!
Through vision of Richeldis,
Thy favours there were seen.
When England was thy dowry,
There pilgrims bowed the knee.
At morn and noon and even,
They knelt to honour thee.

Hail Mary, ever blessed.
Thy children still delight</td><td>¶ Note, The Invitatory Hymn is the *Salve Regina* (p 75).

When Christ was born in Bethlehem,
The Angels worshipped and adored;
And kings and shepherds bowed the knee
To him their Saviour and their Lord.

For thirty years in Nazareth,
His Mother worshipped at the shrine
Of him who came in human form</td></tr>
</table>

Walsingham   **Proper of Saints**   15 October

To tell abroad thy praises,
Thy miracles, thy might.
Still pilgrim feet are treading
Along the holy way.
Hostess of England's Nazareth,
Receive us home today!

Hail Mary, ever blessed.
The wells of water pure
Which mark thy holy places
Are signs that God doth cure
For sick of soul and body.
E'er since Richeldis' day,
They spring in benediction
Beside the Pilgrims' Way.

Hail Mary, ever blessed.
Thy name is great indeed;
For Jesus Christ our Saviour
Was in thy womb conceived.
Thy name be ever praised,
Increasing in this place,
And loud the angel's greeting:
'Hail Mary, full of grace!'

All glory, laud, and honour be
O Jesu, Virgin-born
Our worship is alone to thee
With Father and the Ghost.
Thou art our Mediator true,
Appealing for our sin;
Send unto us thine own Spirit,
Who makes us thy true kin. Amen.

℣. O Mary, Queen of Heaven and of England, praise ye the Lord.
℟. And bring us unto the majesty of thy Son.
Mag. Ant. O all ye Saints, † come unto the Holy Place of Walsingham, and bless ye the Lord.

To save the world, your Lord and mine.

For thirty years in Nazareth
He lived a hidden life of prayer;
And then went forth to work and die,
And every human sorrow share.

A thousand years have passed away;
Another Nazareth must rise
In England's fair and lovely land,
Beneath those distant northern skies.

So Mary, God's own Mother blest,
Seeks out Richeldis, lady fair;
And bids her build at Walsingham
A second Nazareth of prayer.

Richeldis hastens to obey;
And soon the builder's work is done:
The Shrine of England's Nazareth
Proclaims the Mother and the Son.

But times did come when wicked hands
Were laid upon that holy place;
And men who knew not Mary's love
Did Walsingham's fair Shrine deface.

Four hundred years again have passed;
Once more the Mother of our Lord
Is shrined and honoured where her Son
Upon his Altar is adored.

So when you come to Walsingham,
Remember this, and mark it well:
It is to Nazareth you come,
Where Jesus, Mary, Joseph dwell.

All glory, laud, and honour be
To Jesu, Virgin-born, to thee;
All glory, as is ever meet,
To Father and to Paraclete. Amen.

℣. Blessed is the holy Virgin Mary, and most worthy of all praise.

21 October   **Proper of Saints**   *Sts. Ursula &c.*

℟. Through her hath arisen the Sun of Justice, Christ our God, by whom we are saved and redeemed.

Ben. Ant. Wicked men in their lust defied the Church, † and razed the Shrine of Our Lady.

¶ In II Evensong, the Office Hymn & Versicle are of I Evensong, with the following Antiphon.

Mag. Ant. O God, raise thou up again devotion to thy daughter: † Our blessed Lady of Walsingham.

[18 October. St. Luke]

¶ The Daily Office propers are of the Common of Apostles (p. 673).

(19 October. St. Frideswide)

¶ The First Common of a Virgin (p. 742), except for the following.

Collect

ALMIGHTY and everlasting God, the author of virtue and lover of virginity: grant us, we beseech thee; that, like as thy Virgin Frideswide was pleasing unto thee by the merit of chastity of life; so through her merits we may find favour in thy sight. Through.

Secret

WE offer thee, O Lord, our prayers and gifts with gladness in honour of Saint Frideswide thy Virgin: that we may be enabled worthily to perform the same, and to obtain thine everlasting healing. Through.

Postcommunion

WE beseech thee, O Lord, that the mysteries which we have received may be profitable unto many: through the intercession of thy blessed Virgin Frideswide, may they both deliver us from our sins, and obtain for us thy gracious protection. Through.

(21 October. St. Hilarion)

¶ The Common of Abbots (p. 732).

(21 October. Sts. Ursula and Companions)

¶ The First Common of a Virgin Martyress (p. 733), with the Prayers from the Common of Many Virgin Martyresses (p. 740).

St. Evaristus   # Proper of Saints   26 October

[24 OCTOBER. ST. RAPHAEL]

❡ The Hymns & Versicles are of Michaelmas Day (p. 621), with the following Antiphons.

Mag. & Ben. Ant. I am Raphael † the Angel, that stand before the Holy One: wherefore bless ye God for ever, and confess ye all his great and wonderful doings. *Mag. Ant.* O Prince most glorious, † Raphael the Archangel, keep us in remembrance: here and everywhere, always, entreat the Son of God for us.

(25 OCTOBER. STS. CHRYSANTHUS AND DARIA)

❡ The First Common of Many Martyrs (p. 692), except for the following.

Collect

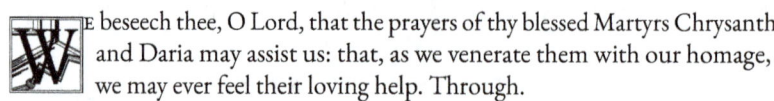E beseech thee, O Lord, that the prayers of thy blessed Martyrs Chrysanthus and Daria may assist us: that, as we venerate them with our homage, so we may ever feel their loving help. Through.

❡ The Epistle is the fourth additional Epistle of the Third Common of Many Martyrs (p. 702).

❡ The Gospel is the fourth additional Gospel of the Third Common of Many Martyrs (p. 704).

Secret

E beseech thee, O Lord, that the sacrifice of thy people, which they solemnly offer on the birthday of thy holy Martyrs Chrysanthus and Daria, may be pleasing unto thee. Through.

Postcommunion

O LORD, who hast fulfilled us with mystic gifts and joys: grant, we beseech thee; that by the intercession of thy holy Martyrs Chrysanthus and Daria, we may spiritually attain to those things which we temporally perform. Through.

(26 OCTOBER. ST. EVARISTUS)

❡ The First Common of a Martyr Bishop (p. 682).

❡ If to-day be Saturday, the anticipated Vigil of Sts. Simon and Jude is kept, as is noted on the following day: but the 2nd Collect is of St. Evaristus, and the 3rd of St. Mary in Eastertide (p. BCP 542).

27 October. Vigil of Sts. Simon and Jude

Vigil

Introit

LET the sorrowful sighing of the prisoners, O Lord, come before thee: reward thou our neighbours sevenfold into their bosom: avenge thou the blood of thy saints that is shed. *Ps.* O God, the heathen are come into thine inheritance: thy holy temple have they defiled: and made Jerusalem an heap of stones.

¶ Gloria in excelsis is not said.

Collect

GRANT, we beseech thee, Almighty God: that as we prevent the glorious birthday of thine Apostles Simon and Jude; so they may prevent us in the sight of thy Majesty, for the obtaining of thy blessings. Through.

¶ 2nd Collect of St. Mary in Eastertide (p. BCP 542). 3rd Against the Persecutors of the Church (BCP 543) or for the Chief Bishop (p. BCP 543).

Epistle. 1 Corinthians 4:9

BRETHREN: We are made a spectacle unto the world, and to Angels, and to men. We are fools for Christ's sake, but ye are wise in Christ; we are weak, but ye are strong; ye are honourable, but we are despised. Even unto this present hour we both hunger, and thirst, and are naked, and are buffeted, and have no certain dwellingplace; And labour, working with our own hands: being reviled, we bless; being persecuted, we suffer it: Being defamed, we intreat: we are made as the filth of the world, and are the offscouring of all things unto this day. I write not these things to shame you, but as my beloved sons I warn you.

Gradual. Avenge thou, O Lord, the blood of thy Saints that is shed. ℣. The dead bodies of thy servants, O Lord, have they given to be meat unto the fowls of the air: and the flesh of thy Saints unto the beasts of the land.

Gospel. John 15:1

AT THAT TIME: Jesus said unto his disciples: I am the true vine, and my Father is the husbandman. Every branch in me that beareth not fruit he taketh away: and every branch that beareth fruit, he purgeth it, that it may bring forth more fruit. Now ye are clean through the word which I have spoken unto you. Abide in me, and I in you. As the branch cannot bear fruit of itself, except it abide in the vine; no more can ye, except ye abide in me. I am the vine, ye are the branches: He that abideth in me, and I in him, the same bringeth forth much fruit: for without me ye can do nothing. If a man abide not in me, he is cast forth as a branch, and is withered; and men gather them, and cast them into the fire, and

Christ the King   **Proper of Saints**

they are burned. If ye abide in me, and my words abide in you, ye shall ask what ye will, and it shall be done unto you.

Offertory. Let the Saints be joyful with glory: let them rejoice in their beds: let the praises of God be in their mouth.

Secret

WE humbly beseech thee, O Lord: that, although our consciences be burdened by reason of our sins: the gifts, wherewith we do prevent the festival of thy holy Apostles Simon and Jude, may through their merits be rendered acceptable in thy sight. Through.

¶ 2nd Secret of St. Mary in Eastertide (p. BCP 542). 3rd Against the Persecutors of the Church (BCP 543) or for the Chief Bishop (p. BCP 543).

Communion. The dead bodies of thy servants, O Lord, have they given to be meat unto the fowls of the air, and the flesh of thy Saints unto the beasts of the land: according to the greatness of thy power, preserve thou those that are appointed to die.

Postcommunion

WE who have received thy sacrament, humbly entreat thee, O Lord: that, by the intercession of thy blessed Apostles Simon and Jude, those things which we temporally perform we may receive unto life eternal. Through.

¶ 2nd Postcommunion of St. Mary in Eastertide (p. BCP 542). 3rd Against the Persecutors of the Church (BCP 543) or for the Chief Bishop (p. BCP 543).

[28 OCTOBER. STS. SIMON AND JUDE]

¶ The Daily Office propers are of the Common of Apostles (p. 673).

[CHRIST THE KING SUNDAY]

I Evensong

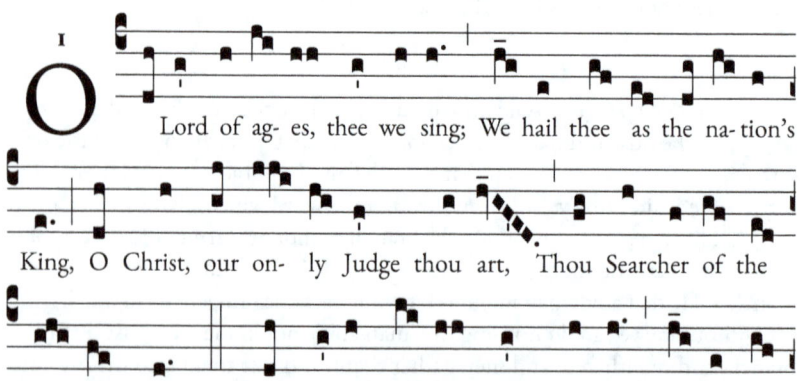

O Lord of ag- es, thee we sing; We hail thee as the na- tion's King, O Christ, our on- ly Judge thou art, Thou Searcher of the mind and heart. 2. Though e-vil shout-ing mobs maintain: We will not

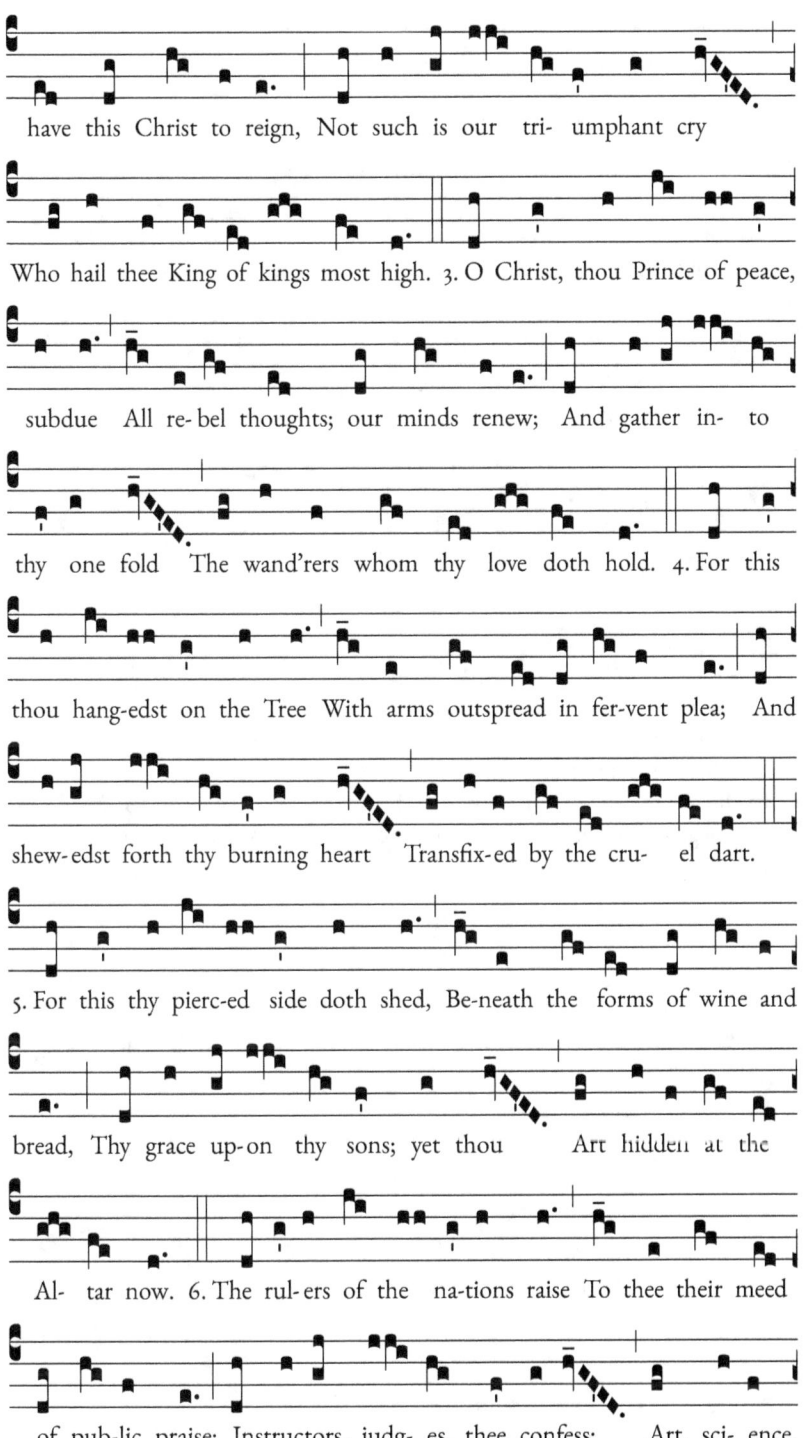

Christ the King   # Proper of Saints

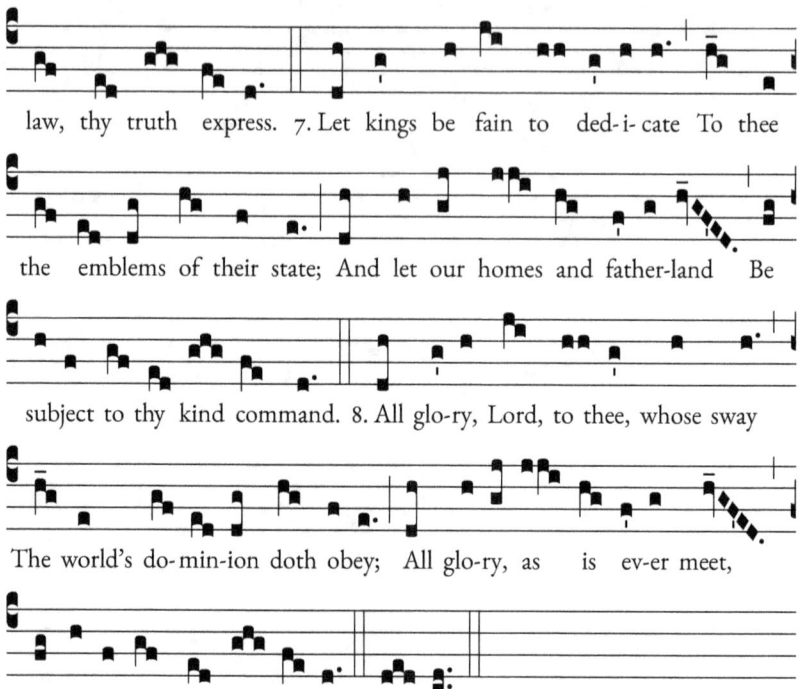

law, thy truth express. 7. Let kings be fain to ded-i-cate To thee the emblems of their state; And let our homes and father-land Be subject to thy kind command. 8. All glo-ry, Lord, to thee, whose sway The world's do-min-ion doth obey; All glo-ry, as is ev-er meet, To Father and to Par- a- clete. A- men.

℣. All power is given unto me.

℟. In heaven and in earth.

Mag. Ant. The Lord God shall give unto him † the throne of his father David: and he shall reign over the house of Jacob for ever; and of his kingdom there shall be no end, alleluia.

Mattins

Invitatory Hymn

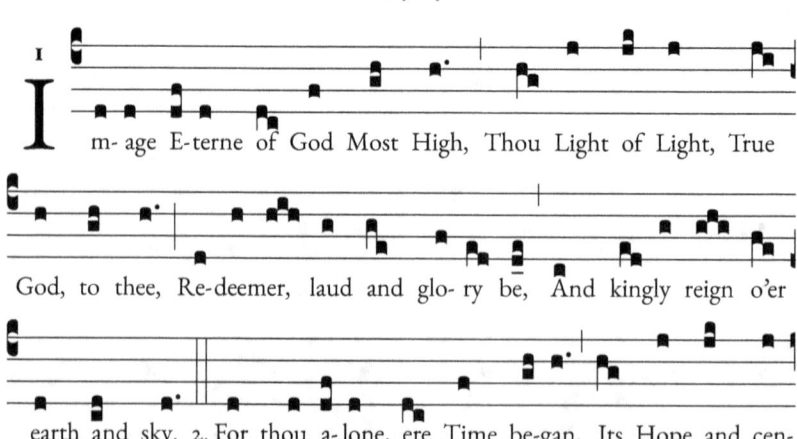

Im-age E-terne of God Most High, Thou Light of Light, True God, to thee, Re-deemer, laud and glo-ry be, And kingly reign o'er earth and sky. 2. For thou a-lone, ere Time be-gan, Its Hope and cen-

Proper of Saints *Christ the King*

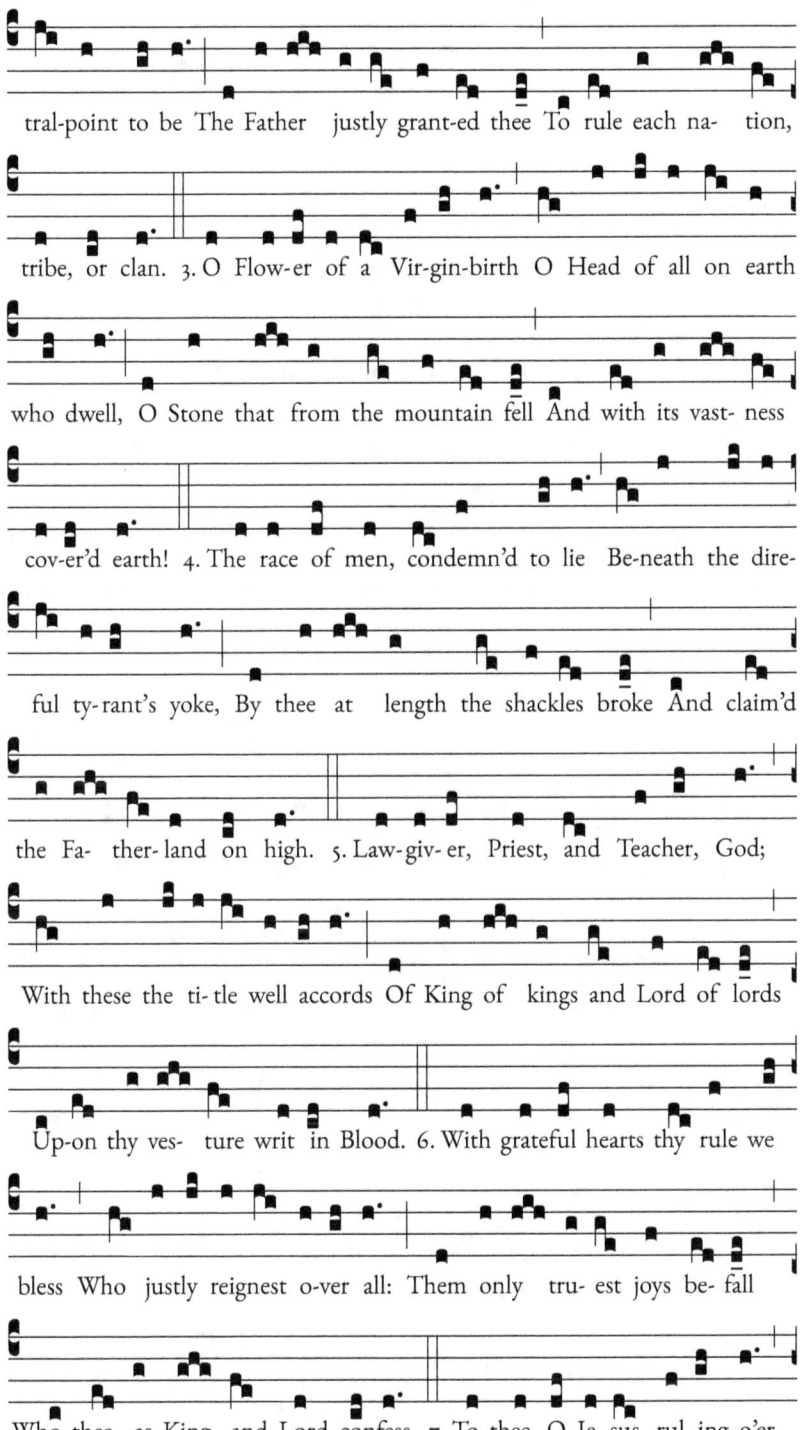

tral-point to be The Father justly grant-ed thee To rule each na- tion, tribe, or clan. 3. O Flow-er of a Vir-gin-birth O Head of all on earth who dwell, O Stone that from the mountain fell And with its vast- ness cov-er'd earth! 4. The race of men, condemn'd to lie Be-neath the dire- ful ty-rant's yoke, By thee at length the shackles broke And claim'd the Fa- ther-land on high. 5. Law-giv- er, Priest, and Teacher, God; With these the ti- tle well accords Of King of kings and Lord of lords Up-on thy ves- ture writ in Blood. 6. With grateful hearts thy rule we bless Who justly reignest o-ver all: Them only tru- est joys be- fall Who thee as King and Lord confess. 7. To thee, O Je- sus, rul- ing o'er

Christ the King   **Proper of Saints**

Earth's rul-ers all, be glo-ry meet, With Father and the Par-a-clete, Throughout the ag-es ev-ermore! A-men.

Office Hymn

1. Now Christ unfurls, in tri-umph high, His glor-ious banner to the sky: Ye suppliant na-tions, kneel and praise The King of kings with joy-ful lays.
2. He hath not won his kingdom here By dev-as-ta-tion, force, or fear; But on the Cross up-lift-ed high By love a-lone draws all men nigh.
3. How trebly bless-ed is the land O-bed-ient un-to Christ's command, Which urges laws that prove the worth Of heav'nly e-dicts here on earth!
4. No arm'd re-bel-lion kindles there, Peace strengthens un-ion everywhere, And concord smiles; up-on

Proper of Saints *Christ the King*

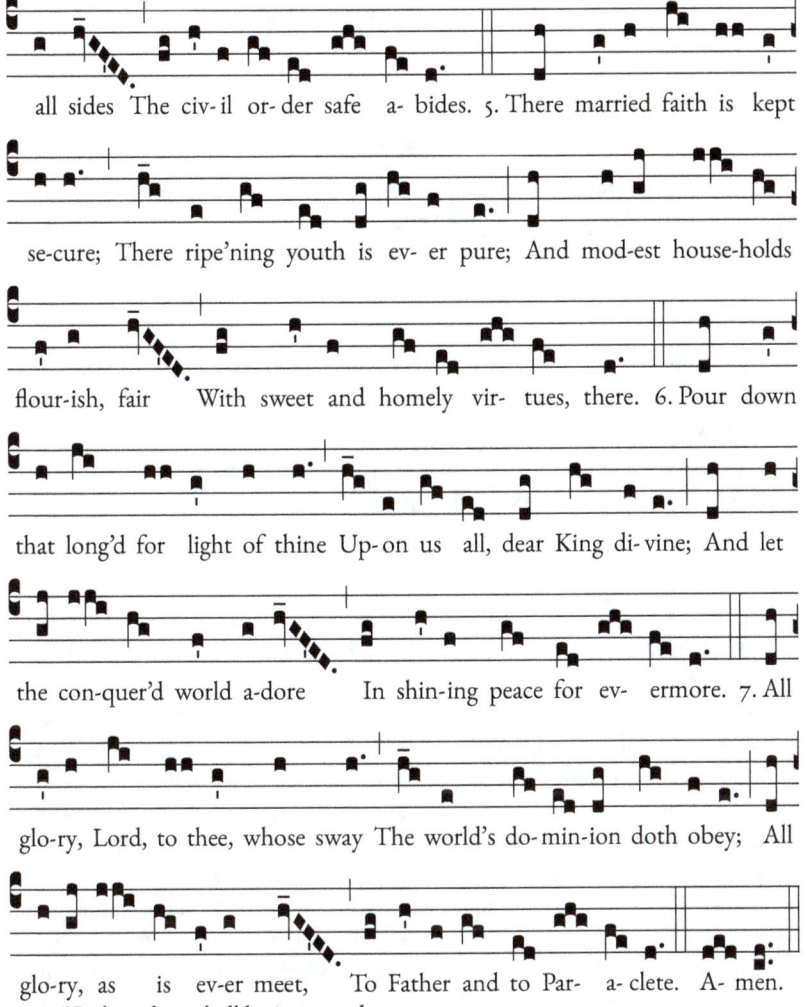

all sides The civ-il or-der safe abides. 5. There married faith is kept

se-cure; There ripe'ning youth is ev-er pure; And mod-est house-holds

flour-ish, fair With sweet and homely vir-tues, there. 6. Pour down

that long'd for light of thine Up-on us all, dear King di-vine; And let

the con-quer'd world a-dore In shin-ing peace for ev-ermore. 7. All

glo-ry, Lord, to thee, whose sway The world's do-min-ion doth obey; All

glo-ry, as is ev-er meet, To Father and to Par-a-clete. A-men.

℣. His kingdom shall be increased.
℟. And of his peace there shall be no end.

Ben. Ant. Unto God and his Father † hath he made us to be a kingdom, who is the first begotten of the dead, and the Prince of the kings of the earth, alleluia.

II Evensong

¶ The Office Hymn is as in I Evensong, with the following Versicle & Antiphon.

℣. His kingdom shall be increased.
℟. And of his peace there shall be no end.

Mag. Ant. He hath on his vesture † and on his thigh a name written, King of kings, and Lord of lords: to him be glory and dominion for ever and ever.

31 October. Vigil of All Hallows

Vigil

Introit

THE Saints and judges of the nations, and have dominion over the people: and the Lord their God shall reign for ever. *Ps.* Rejoice in the Lord, O ye righteous: for it becometh well the just to be thankful.

Collect

O LORD, our God, multiply upon us thy grace: and grant, that by our holy profession we may follow after the gladness of them, whose glorious festival we prevent. Through.

¶ 2nd Collect of the Holy Ghost (p. BCP 544). 3rd Collect Against the Persecutors of the Church (p. BCP 543) or for the Chief Bishop (p. BCP 543).

Epistle. Revelation 5:6

IN THOSE DAYS: Lo, I, John, saw in the midst of the throne and of the four living creatures, and in the midst of the elders, a Lamb standing, as though it had been slain, having seven horns, and seven eyes, which are the seven Spirits of God, sent forth into all the earth. And he came, and he taketh it out of the right hand of him that sat on the throne. And when he had taken the book, the four living creatures and the four and twenty elders fell down before the Lamb, having each one a harp, and golden bowls full of incense, which are the prayers of the saints. And they sing a new song, saying, Worthy art thou to take the book, and to open the seals thereof: for thou wast slain, and didst purchase unto God with thy blood men of every tribe, and tongue, and people, and nation, and madest them to be unto our God a kingdom and priests; and they reign upon the earth. And I saw, and I heard a voice of many angels round about the throne and the living creatures and the elders; and the number of them was ten thousand times ten thousand, and thousands of thousands; saying with a great voice, Worthy is the Lamb that hath been slain to receive the power, and riches, and wisdom, and might, and honour, and glory, and blessing.

Gradual. Let the Saints be joyful with glory: let them rejoice in their beds. ℣. O sing unto the Lord a new song: let the congregation of saints praise him.

Gospel. Luke 6:17

AT THAT TIME: Jesus came down from the mountain, and stood in the plain, and the company of his disciples, and a great multitude of people out of all Judaea and Jerusalem, and from the sea coast of Tyre and Sidon, which came to hear him, and to be healed of their diseases; And they that were vexed with unclean spirits: and they were healed. And the whole multitude sought to touch him: for there went virtue out of him, and healed them all. And he lifted up his eyes on his disciples, and said, Blessed be ye poor: for yours is the kingdom of God. Blessed are ye that hunger now: for ye shall be filled. Blessed are ye that weep now: for ye shall laugh. Blessed are ye, when men shall hate you, and when they shall separate you from their company, and shall reproach you, and cast out your name as evil, for the Son of man's sake. Rejoice ye in that day, and leap for joy: for, behold, your reward is great in heaven.

Offertory. Let the Saints be joyful with glory, let them rejoice in their beds: let the praises of God be in their mouth.

Secret

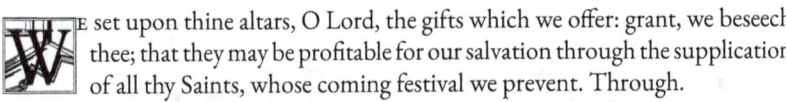E set upon thine altars, O Lord, the gifts which we offer: grant, we beseech thee; that they may be profitable for our salvation through the supplication of all thy Saints, whose coming festival we prevent. Through.

¶ 2nd *Secret* of the Holy Ghost (p. BCP 544). 3rd *Secret* Against the Persecutors of the Church (p. BCP 543) or for the Chief Bishop (p. BCP 543).

Communion. The souls of the righteous are in the hand of God, and there shall no torment of malice touch them: in the sight of the unwise they seemed to die, but they are in peace.

Postcommunion

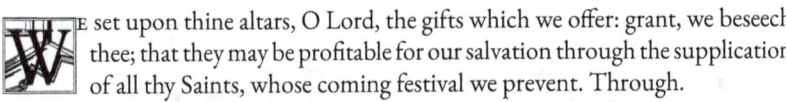E beseech thee, O Lord: that, having accomplished with joy the mysteries of the coming feast; we may be aided by the prayers of them in whose memory they are shewn forth. Through.

¶ 2nd *Postcommunion* of the Holy Ghost (p. BCP 544). 3rd *Postcommunion* Against the Persecutors of the Church (p. BCP 543) or for the Chief Bishop (p. BCP 543).

[1 November. All Hallows]

I Evensong

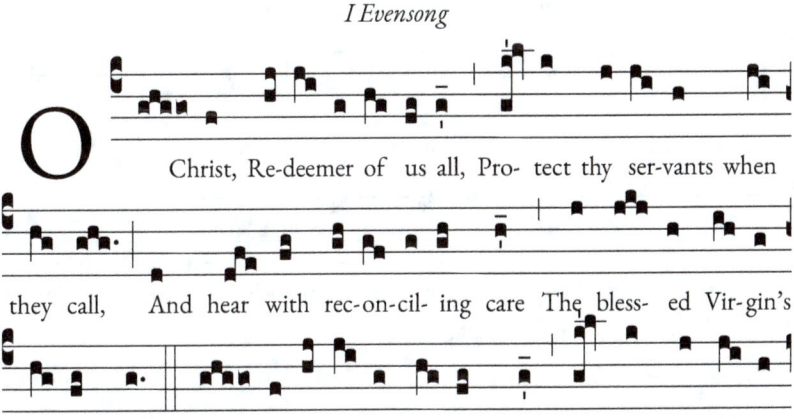

O Christ, Re-deemer of us all, Pro- tect thy ser-vants when they call, And hear with rec-on-cil- ing care The bless- ed Vir-gin's ho- ly prayer. 2. And ye, O ev- er blissful throng Of heav'nly Spir- its,

All Hallows   **Proper of Saints**   1 November

1 November   **Proper of Saints**   *All Hallows*

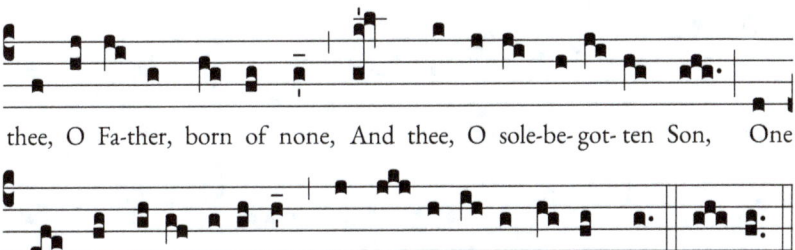

thee, O Fa-ther, born of none, And thee, O sole-be-got-ten Son, One

with the Ho-ly Par-a-clete, Be glo-ry ev-er, as is meet. A-men.

℣. Be glad, O ye righteous, and rejoice in the Lord.

℞. And be joyful, all ye that are true of heart.

Mag. Ant. O ye Angels and Archangels, † O ye Thrones and Dominions, Principalities and Powers, Virtues of the heavens, Cherubim and Seraphim, O ye Patriarchs and Prophets, ye holy Doctors of the law, O all ye Apostles, ye Martyrs of Christ, ye holy Confessors, ye Virgins of the Lord, ye holy Hermits, and all Saints: offer for us your intercessions.

Mattins

¶ The Invitatory Hymn is as in I Evensong.

Office Hymn

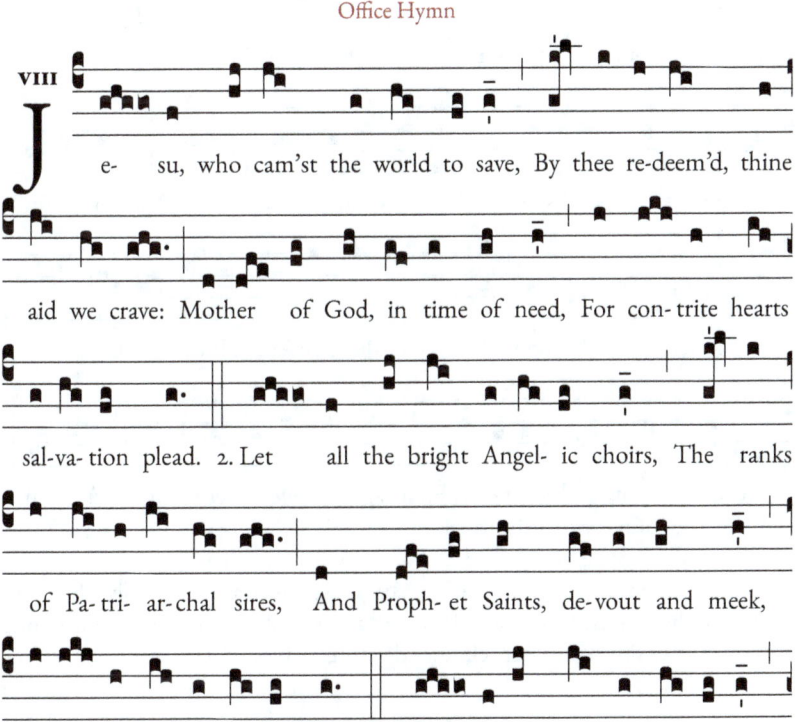

Je-su, who cam'st the world to save, By thee re-deem'd, thine aid we crave: Mother of God, in time of need, For con-trite hearts sal-va-tion plead. 2. Let all the bright Angel-ic choirs, The ranks of Pa-tri-ar-chal sires, And Proph-et Saints, de-vout and meek, Forgive-ness for our er-rors seek. 3. The Baptist, thy great har-binger,

All Hallows   **Proper of Saints**   1 November

With heav'n's appointed Key-bear-er, And all A-pos-tles strive to win From God re-mis-sion of our sin. 4. So may the sa-cred Mar-tyr band, Con-fes-sors, Priests, a-dor-ing stand, And eve-ry Vir-gin chastely pray That he would purge our guilt away. 5. Your suffrag-es, ye Monks, u-nite With all the cit-i-zens of light To speed our vows, combine your pow'rs That life's e-ter-nal prize be ours. 6. To God the Fa-ther, God the Son, And God the Spir-it, Three in One, Laud, hon-our, might, and glo-ry be From age to age e-ter-nal-ly. A-men.

℣. Let the Saints be joyful with glory.

℟. Let them rejoice in their beds.

Ben. Ant. The glorious company † of the Apostles praise thee; the goodly fellowship of the Prophets praise thee; the white-robed army of Martyrs praise thee; with one heart and voice do all the elect acknowledge thee: O blessed Trinity, one only God.

5 November   **Proper of Saints**   *St. Elizabeth*

II Evensong

¶ The Office Hymn is as in I Evensong, with the following Versicle & Antiphon.

℣. Let the Saints be joyful with glory.

℟. Let them rejoice in their beds.

Mag. Ant. O how glorious † is the kingdom wherein all the Saints rejoice with Christ; arrayed in white robes, they follow the Lamb whithersoever he goeth.

¶ The Office is of All Hallows through its Octave, unless there occur a Sunday or Feast Day (Double or higher), any concurring Memorial being commemorated.

[2 November. All Souls]

¶ The Office of the Day is the Office of the Dead.

(3 November. St. Winifred)

¶ The First Common of a Virgin Martyress (p. 733).

(4 November. Sts. Vitalis and Agricola)

¶ The Second Common of Many Martyrs (p. 699), except for the following.

Collect

RANT, we beseech thee, Almighty God: that we, who devoutly celebrate the festival of thy holy Martyrs Vitalis and Agricola, may be aided by their intercession with thee. Through.

¶ The Epistle is from the Third Common of Many Martyrs (p. 700).

¶ The Gospel is from the Second Common of a Martyr Bishop (p. 686).

Secret

E beseech thee, O Lord, mercifully to accept these our oblations: that, at the intercession of thy holy Martyrs Vitalis and Agricola, we may be defended against all adversities. Through.

Postcommunion

AY this communion, O Lord, cleanse us from guilt: and at the intercession of thy holy Martyrs, Vitalis and Agricola, make us partakers of thy heavenly healing. Through.

(5 November. St. Elizabeth)

¶ The Common of a Holy Matron (p. 751).

St. Theodore Tyro   **Proper of Saints**   9 November

(7 November. St. Willibrord)

¶ The First Common of a Confessor Bishop (p. 715).

8 November. Octave Day of All Hallows

Greater Double

¶ The propers as on the Feast, with Commemoration of the Four Crowned Martyrs.

(8 November. Four Crowned Martyrs)

¶ The First Common of Many Martyrs (p. 692), except for the following.
¶ Note, The Epistle and Gospel are of All Hallows' Day (p. BCP 532).

Collect

RANT, we beseech thee, Almighty God: that, like as we have known thy glorious Martyrs to be constant in their confession, so we may perceive their loving intercession for us with thee. Through.

Secret

ET thy plenteous benediction descend, O Lord: and both render our gifts acceptable unto thee at the intercession of thy holy Martyrs, and make them to us a sacrament of redemption. Through.

Postcommunion

LORD, who hast refreshed us with the gladness of thy heavenly sacraments: we humbly entreat thee; that we may be protected by the succour of them in whose triumphs we glory. Through.

9 November. Dedication of the Basilica of St. Saviour

Greater Double

¶ The propers are from the Common of a Dedication of a Church (p. 753).
¶ Note, The Creed is said, and Commemoration of St. Theodore Tyro.

(9 November. St. Theodore Tyro)

¶ The Second Common of a Martyr not a Bishop (p. 690), except for the following.

Collect

GOD, who dost encompass and protect us with the glorious confession of blessed Theodore, thy Martyr: grant us both to profit by his example, and to be supported by his intercession. Through.

10 November   **Proper of Saints**   *Sts. Tryphon &c.*

Secret

CCEPT, O Lord, the prayers of thy faithful people, and the oblations of their sacrifices: and at the intercession of blessed Theodore, thy Martyr, may we through these offices of godly devotion enter into heavenly glory. Through.

Postcommunion

RANT to us, we beseech thee, O Lord: at the intercession of blessed Theodore thy Martyr; that those things which we touch with our lips we may receive in purity of heart. Through.

(10 NOVEMBER. STS. TRYPHON, RESPICIUS, AND NYMPHA)

Introit

HE righteous cry, and the Lord heareth them: and delivereth them out of all their troubles. *Ps.* I will alway give thanks unto the Lord: his praise shall ever be in my mouth.

Collect

RANT, we beseech thee, O Lord, that we, ever keeping the feast of thy holy Martyrs Tryphon, Respicius, and Nympha: may through their intercession enjoy the benefit of thy protection. Through.

¶ The Epistle is the third additional Epistle from the Third Common of Many Martyrs (p. 702).

Gradual. Avenge, O Lord, the blood of thy Saints that is shed. ℣. The dead bodies of thy servants have they given to be meat unto the fowls of the air: the flesh of thy Saints unto the beasts of the land.

Alleluia. Alleluia, alleluia. ℣. Right dear in the sight of the Lord is the death of his Saints. Alleluia.

¶ The Gospel is from the Third Common of Many Martyrs (p. 700).

Offertory. Be glad, O ye righteous, and rejoice in the Lord: and be joyful, all ye that are true of heart.

Secret

E beseech thee, O Lord, that the gifts which we offer unto thee of our bounden duty and service may be acceptable unto thee for honour of thy Just ones: and by thy mercy profitable unto us for our salvation. Through.

Communion. Whosoever shall do the will of my Father who is in heaven: the same is my brother, and sister, and mother, saith the Lord.

St. Martin Tours   **Proper of Saints**   11 November

Postcommunion

RANT to us, we beseech thee, O Lord: at the intercession of thy holy Martyrs Tryphon, Respicius and Nympha; that those things which we touch with our lips we may receive in purity of heart. Through.

11 November. St. Martin of Tours

Greater Double

¶ The Hymns and Versicles are from the First Common of a Confessor Bishop (p. 715), with the following Antiphons.

Mag. & Ben. Ant. O blessed Martin, † whose righteous soul possesseth Paradise; whereat the Angels triumph, the Archangels are jubilant: thee the choir of Saints proclaimeth, the throng of Virgins inviteth, saying, Abide with us for ever.
Mag. Ant. O blessed Bishop, † who with all his heart loved Christ the King, and feared not the dominion of princes! O holy soul, which, although withheld from the persecutor's sword, lacked not the palm of martyrdom!

Introit

HE Lord hath established a covenant of peace with him, and made him a prince: that he should have the dignity of the priesthood for ever. *Ps.* Lord, remember David: and all his trouble.

Collect

GOD, who seest that we stand not in our own strength: mercifully grant; that, by the intercession of blessed Martin, thy Confessor and Bishop, we may be defended against all adversities. Through.

¶ Commemoration of St. Mennas, from the First Common of a Martyr not a Bishop (p. 688).

Epistle. Ecclesiasticus 44:16

ENOCH pleased the Lord, and was translated, Being an example of repentance to all generations. Noah was found perfect and righteous; In the season of wrath he was taken in exchange for the world; Therefore was there left a remnant unto the earth, When the flood came. Everlasting covenants were made with him, That all flesh should no more be blotted out by a flood. Abraham was a great father of a multitude of nations; And there was none found like him in glory; Who kept the law of the Most High, And was taken into covenant with him: In his flesh he established the covenant; And when he was proved, he was found faithful. Therefore he assured him by an oath, That the nations should be blessed in his seed; That he would multiply him as the dust of the earth, And exalt his seed as the stars, And cause them to inherit from sea to sea, And from the River unto the utmost part of the earth. In Isaac also did he establish likewise, for Abraham his father's sake, The blessing of all men, and the covenant: And he made it rest upon the head of Jacob; He acknowledged him in his blessings, And gave to him by inheritance, And divided his portions; Among twelve tribes did he part them. And he brought out of him a man of mercy, Which found favour in the sight of all flesh.

Gradual. Behold a great priest, who in his days pleased God. ℣. There was none found like unto him, who kept the law of the Most High.

Alleluia. Alleluia, alleluia. ℣. The blessed man Saint Martin, Bishop of the city of Tours, entered into rest: whom Angels and Archangels, Thrones, Dominations, and Virtues received. Alleluia.

Gospel. Luke 11:33

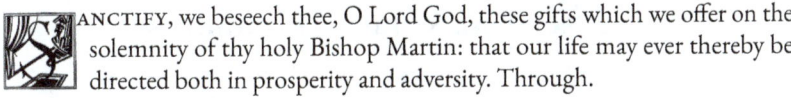

AT THAT TIME: Jesus said unto his disciples: No man, when he hath lighted a candle, putteth it in a secret place, neither under a bushel, but on a candlestick, that they which come in may see the light. The light of the body is the eye: therefore when thine eye is single, thy whole body also is full of light; but when thine eye is evil, thy body also is full of darkness. Take heed therefore that the light which is in thee be not darkness. If thy whole body therefore be full of light, having no part dark, the whole shall be full of light, as when the bright shining of a candle doth give thee light.

Offertory. My truth and my mercy shall be with him: and in my name shall his horn be exalted.

Secret

SANCTIFY, we beseech thee, O Lord God, these gifts which we offer on the solemnity of thy holy Bishop Martin: that our life may ever thereby be directed both in prosperity and adversity. Through.

¶ Commemoration of St. Mennas, from the First Common of a Martyr not a Bishop (p. 688).

Communion. Blessed is the servant, whom the lord when he cometh shall find watching: verily I say unto you, that he shall make him ruler over all his goods.

Postcommunion

GRANT, we beseech thee, O Lord our God: that through the intercession of them, on whose festival they are offered, these sacraments may avail for our salvation. Through.

¶ Commemoration of St. Mennas, from the First Common of a Martyr not a Bishop (p. 688).

(11 November. St. Mennas)

¶ The Second Common of a Martyr not a Bishop (p. 690), with the Prayers from the First Common of a Martyr not a Bishop (p. 688).

(12 November. Pope St. Martin I)

¶ The Second Common of a Martyr Bishop (p. 686), with the second additional Epistle from the Second Common of a Martyr not a Bishop (p. 692) and the Gospel from the First Common of a Martyr Bishop (p. 682).

(13 November. St. Britius of Tours)

¶ The First Common of a Confessor Bishop (p. 715).

(14 November. St. Gregory Palamas)

¶ The First Common of a Bishop Confessor (p. 715).

(17 November. St. Gregory the Wonder-worker)

¶ The First Common of a Bishop Confessor (p. 715), except for the following.

Gospel. Mark 11:22

T THAT TIME: Jesus answering his disciples, saith unto them: Have faith in God. For verily I say unto you, That whosoever shall say unto this mountain, Be thou removed, and be thou cast into the sea; and shall not doubt in his heart, but shall believe that those things which he saith shall come to pass; he shall have whatsoever he saith. Therefore I say unto you, What things soever ye desire, when ye pray, believe that ye receive them, and ye shall have them.

(17 November. St. Hilda of Whitby)

¶ The First Common of a Virgin (p. 742), except for the following.

Collect

GRANT, we beseech thee, Almighty God: that we, who rejoice in the yearly solemnity of blessed Hilda thy Virgin, may by her intercession be led from our old nature to newness of life. Through.

Gradual. Thou hast loved justice and hated iniquity. ℣. Wherefore God, even thy God, hath anointed thee with the oil of gladness.

Alleluia. Alleluia, alleluia. ℣. For I am jealous over you with godly jealousy: for I have espoused you to one husband, that I may present you as a chaste virgin to Christ. Alleluia.

Secret

E bring unto thee, O Lord, our offerings for the sacrifice: that we, being reconciled to thy mercy through the merits of blessed Hilda thy Virgin, may be made thereby a living sacrifice acceptable unto thee. Through.

Postcommunion

O LORD, through whom we have received the benediction of this heavenly banquet, we entreat thee: that as unto us it is thy sacrament, so at the intercession of blessed Hilda thy Virgin, it may effectually avail for our salvation. Through.

18 November. Dedication of the Basilica of the Holy Apostles Peter and Paul

Greater Double

¶ The propers are from the Dedication of a Church (p. 753).

(19 November. Pope St. Pontianus)

¶ The First Common of a Martyr Bishop (p. 682), except for the Gospel from the Second Common of a Martyr not a Bishop (p. 690).

20 November. St. Edmund

Double

¶ The propers are from the First Common of a Martyr not a Bishop (p. 688), except for the following.

Collect

O GOD of unspeakable mercy, who didst give grace to the most blessed King Edmund to overcome the enemy by dying for thy name: mercifully grant unto this thy family; that, by his intercession they may be found worthy to vanquish and destroy in themselves the temptations of their ancient foe. Through.

Secret

WE beseech thee, Almighty God, mercifully regard this sacrifice of our redemption: and at the intercession of blessed Edmund, thy King and Martyr, graciously accept it for this thy family. Through.

Postcommunion

LET the homage of our service be pleasing unto thee, Almighty God: that these holy things which we have received may, at the intercession of blessed Edmund, thy King and Martyr, be profitable unto us for the obtaining of the rewards of everlasting life. Through.

21 November. Presentation of the Blessed Virgin Mary

Greater Double

¶ The Hymns and Versicles are from the Common of the Blessed Virgin Mary (p. 760), except for the following Antiphon for I & II Evensong.

Mag. Ant. O ever blessed Mother of God, † Mary ever Virgin, temple of the Godhead, hallowed shrine of the Holy Spirit: thou only, above all others, wast acceptable to our Lord Jesus Christ, alleluia.

¶ The Mass propers are from the Common of the Blessed Virgin Mary (p. 760), except for the following.

Collect

O GOD, who didst will that blessed Mary ever Virgin, the dwelling-place of Holy Ghost, should this day be presented in the temple: grant, we beseech thee; that through her intercession we may be found worthy to be presented in the temple of thy glory. Through . . . in the unity of the same.

Secret

THROUGH thy mercy, O Lord, and the intercession of blessed Mary ever Virgin, may this oblation avail for our prosperity and peace, both now and for ever. Through.

Postcommunion

GRANT, we beseech thee, O Lord: that we, who have received these aids to our salvation, may at all times and in all places be protected through the advocacy of blessed Mary ever Virgin; in whose honour we have made these offerings to thy Majesty. Through.

¶ When this Feast Day is only commemorated, the following is said for the Last Gospel.

Last Gospel. Luke 11:27

AT THAT TIME: As Jesus spake unto the multitudes, a certain woman of the company lifted up her voice, and said unto him: Blessed is the womb that bare thee, and the paps which thou hast sucked. But he said: Yea rather, blessed are they that hear the word of God, and keep it.

(21 November. St. Gelasius)

¶ The First Common of a Confessor Bishop (p. 715).

(21 November. St. Columbanus)

¶ The Common of Abbots (p. 732).

22 November. St. Cecilia

Greater Double

❡ The Hymns & Versicles are from the First Common of a Virgin Martyress (p. 733), with the following Antiphons.

Mag. Ant. It is secret, † O Valerian, what now I wish to tell thee: I have an Angel of God who loves me, and guards my body with exceeding zeal.

Ben. Ant. When the dawn of day was breaking, † Cecilia the Martyr cried, saying: Forward, soldiers of Christ! Cast off the works of darkness, and put on the armour of light.

Mag. Ant. This noble maiden † alway bare the glorious Gospel of Christ in her bosom: without ceasing, she continued in prayer and supplication, and celestial converse, night and day.

Introit

I WILL speak of thy testimonies, even before kings, and will not be ashamed: and my delight shall be in thy commandments, which I have loved exceedingly. *Ps.* Blessed are those that are undefiled in the way: and walk in the law of the Lord.

Collect

O GOD, who makest us glad with the yearly solemnity of blessed Cecilia thy Virgin and Martyr: grant, that we do venerate her in our service, so we may follow the example of her godly conversation. Through.

Epistle. Ecclesiasticus 51:9

O LORD MY GOD, I lifted up my supplication from the earth, And prayed for deliverance from death. I called upon the Lord, the Father of my Lord, That he would not forsake me in the days of affliction, In the time when there was no help against the proud. I will praise thy name continually, And will sing praise with thanksgiving; And my supplication was heard: For thou savedst me from destruction, And deliveredst me from the evil time: Therefore will I give thanks and praise unto thee, And bless thy name, O Lord our God.

Gradual. Hearken, O daughter, and consider, incline thine ear: so shall the King have pleasure in thy beauty. ℣. In thy comeliness and in thy beauty, go forth, proceed prosperously, and reign.

Alleluia. Alleluia, alleluia. ℣. The five wise virgins took oil in their vessels with their lamps: and at midnight there was a cry made: Behold, the bridegroom cometh: go ye out to meet Christ the Lord. Alleluia.

❡ The Gospel is from the First Common of a Virgin Martyress (p. 733).

Offertory. The Virgins that be her fellow shall be brought unto the King: they that bear her company shall be brought unto thee, with joy and gladness: and shall enter into the palace of the Lord the King.

Secret

E beseech thee, O Lord: that by the intercession of blessed Cecilia, thy Virgin and Martyr, this sacrifice of atonement and praise may ever render us worthy of thy loving-kindness. Through.

Communion. Let the proud be confounded, for they go wickedly about to destroy me: but I will be occupied in thy commandments and in thy statures, that I be not ashamed.

Postcommunion

LORD, who hast satisfied thy family with sacred gifts: we beseech thee, that we may at all times be comforted by the intercession of her whose festival we celebrate. Through.

23 November. St. Clement

Double

¶ The Hymns are from the First Common of Many Martyrs (p. 692), with the following Versicles & Antiphons.

℣. Thou hast crowned him with glory and honour, O Lord.

℟. And madest him to have dominion of the works of thy hands.

Mag. Ant. Let us all pray † to our Lord Jesus Christ, that he would open a fountain for his Confessors.

℣. Let the Saints be joyful with glory.

℟. Let them rejoice in their beds.

Ben. Ant. When he had started going to the sea, † the people cried out with loud voices, O Lord Jesus Christ, save him: and Clement responded, weeping, Heavenly Father, receive my spirit.

℣. Let the Saints be joyful with glory.

℟. Let them rejoice in their beds.

Mag. Ant. In the heavenly kingdom † rejoice the souls of the Blessed, who followed the footsteps of Christ their Master: and since for love of him they poured forth their life-blood, therefore with Christ do they exult for ever.

Introit

HE Lord saith: My words which I have put in thy mouth, shall not depart out of thy mouth: and thy gifts shall be accepted upon mine altar. *Ps.* Blessed is the man that feareth the Lord: he hath great delight in his commandments.

23 November   **Proper of Saints**   *St. Clement*

Collect

GOD, who makest us glad with the yearly solemnity of blessed Clement thy Martyr and Bishop: mercifully grant; that as we now celebrate his birthday, so we may imitate his constancy in suffering. Through.

¶ Commemoration of St. Felicitas (p. 668).

Epistle. Philippians 3:17

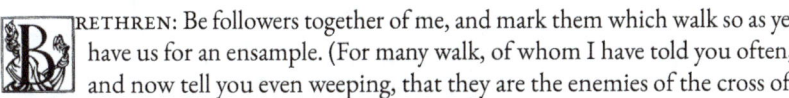Christ: Whose end is destruction, whose God is their belly, and whose glory is in their shame, who mind earthly things.) For our conversation is in heaven; from whence also we look for the Saviour, the Lord Jesus Christ: Who shall change our vile body, that it may be fashioned like unto his glorious body, according to the working whereby he is able even to subdue all things unto himself. Therefore, my brethren dearly beloved and longed for, my joy and crown, so stand fast in the Lord, my dearly beloved. I beseech Euodias, and beseech Syntyche, that they be of the same mind in the Lord. And I intreat thee also, true yokefellow, help those women which laboured with me in the gospel, with Clement also, and with other my fellowlabourers, whose names are in the book of life.

Gradual. The Lord sware, and will not repent: Thou art a priest for ever, after the order of Melchisedech. ℣. The Lord said unto my Lord: Sit thou on my right hand.

Alleluia. Alleluia, alleluia. ℣. This is a priest whom the Lord hath crowned. Alleluia.

¶ The Gospel is of the Second Common of a Confessor Bishop (720).

Offertory. My truth and my mercy shall be with him: and in my name shall his horn be exalted.

Secret

SANCTIFY, O Lord, the gifts which we offer unto thee: and, at the intercession of blessed Clement, thy Martyr and Bishop, cleanse us thereby from the defilement of our sins. Through.

¶ Commemoration of St. Felicitas (p. 668).

Communion. Blessed is the servant, whom the Lord when he cometh shall find watching: verily I say unto you, that he shall make him ruler over all his goods.

Postcommunion

LORD our God, who hast fulfilled us with the partaking of the sacred Body, and the precious Blood, we beseech thee: that those things which we perform with godly devotion, we may at the intercession of blessed Clement, thy Martyr and Bishop, attain in the assurance of our redemption. Through.

¶ Commemoration of St. Felicitas (p. 668).

(23 November. St. Felicitas)

¶ The Common of a Martyress not a Virgin (p. 746), except for the following.

Collect

RANT, we beseech thee, Almighty God: that we, celebrating the festival of blessed Felicitas, thy Martyr, may be protected by her merits and prayers. Through.

Secret

RACIOUSLY hearken, O Lord, to the prayers of thy people: and make us to rejoice in the intercession of her whose festival thou dost grant unto us to celebrate. Through.

Postcommunion

E humbly beseech thee, Almighty God: that by the intercession of thy Saints thou wouldest both multiply in us thy gifts, and likewise dispose our times according to thy will. Through.

(24 November. St. Chrysogonus)

¶ The First Common of a Martyr not a Bishop (p. 688, except for the following.

Collect

SSIST us, O Lord, in these our supplications: that we, who acknowledge ourselves to be guilty by reason of our iniquity, may be delivered by the intercession of thy blessed Martyr Chrysogonus. Through.

Secret

E beseech thee, O Lord, mercifully to accept these our oblations: that at the intercession of thy blessed Martyr Chrysogonus, we may be defended against all perils. Through.

Postcommunion

LORD, let the partaking of thy sacrament both cleanse us from our secret faults, and deliver us from the snares of our enemies. Through.

25 November. St. Catherine of Alexandria

Double

⁋ The propers are from the First Common of a Virgin Martyress (p. 733), except for the following.

Collect

O GOD, who didst give the law to Moses on the height of Mount Sinai, and in the same place didst through thy holy Angels wondrously bestow the body of blessed Catherine, thy Virgin and Martyr: grant, we beseech thee; that by her merits and intercession we may be enabled to attain unto that mount which is Christ. Who liveth.

Secret

RECEIVE, O Lord, the gifts which we offer on the solemnity of blessed Catherine, thy Virgin and Martyr: through whose advocacy we trust to be delivered. Through.

Postcommunion

MAY the mysteries which we have received be for our succour, O Lord: and at the intercession of blessed Catherine, thy Virgin and Martyr, cause us to rejoice in thy continual protection. Through.

(26 November. St. Peter of Alexandria)

⁋ The First Common of a Martyr Bishop (p. 682).

Commons
of the Saints

Apostolic Vigils # Common of Saints

Commons for the Apostles

COMMON OF VIGILS OF THE APOSTLES

Introit

s for me, I am like a green olive-tree in the house of the Lord, my trust is in the tender mercy of my God: and I will hope in thy name, for thy saints like it well. *Ps.* Why boastest thou thyself, thou tyrant: that thou canst do mischief?

Collect

RANT, we beseech thee, Almighty God: that the venerable solemnity of blessed *N.* thine Apostle, which we here prevent, may increase our devotion and set forward our salvation. Through.

¶ If, however, the preceding Collect has already been said in the Mass, or for the commemoration of a Confessor Bishop, then the following is to be said:

E beseech thee, Almighty God: that as we do prevent the festival of blessed *N.* thine Apostle, so he may implore thy mercy for us; that we being delivered from our iniquities, may likewise be defended against all adversities. Through.

¶ 2nd Collect of St. Mary in Eastertide (p. BCP 542) & 3rd Against the Persecutors of the Church (p. BCP 543) or for the Chief Bishop (p. BCP 543).

Epistle. Ecclesiasticus 44:22

IN Isaac did the Lord establish, for Abraham his father's sake, The blessing of all men, and the covenant: And he made it rest upon the head of Jacob; He acknowledged him in his blessings, And gave to him by inheritance, And divided his portions; Among twelve tribes did he part them. And he brought out of him a man of mercy, Which found favour in the sight of all flesh; A man beloved of God and men, even Moses, Whose memorial is blessed. He made him like to the glory of the saints, And magnified him in the fears of his enemies. By his words he caused the wonders to cease; He glorified him in the sight of kings; He gave him commandment for his people, And shewed him part of his glory. He sanctified him in his faithfulness and meekness; He chose him out of all flesh. He made him to hear his voice, And led him into the thick darkness, And gave him commandments face to face, Even the law of life and knowledge, That he might teach Jacob the covenant, And Israel his judgments. He exalted Aaron, a holy man like unto him, Even his brother, of the tribe of Levi. He established for him an everlasting covenant, And gave him the priesthood of the people; He beautified him with comely ornaments, And girded him about with a robe of glory.

Gradual. The righteous shall flourish like a palm-tree: and shall spread abroad like a cedar in Libanus in the house of the Lord. ℣. To tell of thy loving-kindness early in the morning, and of thy truth in the night-season.

Common of Saints *Apostles*

Gospel. John 15:12

AT THAT TIME: Jesus said unto his disciples: This is my commandment, That ye love one another, as I have loved you. Greater love hath no man than this, that a man lay down his life for his friends. Ye are my friends, if ye do whatsoever I command you. Henceforth I call you not servants; for the servant knoweth not what his lord doeth: but I have called you friends; for all things that I have heard of my Father I have made known unto you. Ye have not chosen me, but I have chosen you, and ordained you, that ye should go and bring forth fruit, and that your fruit should remain: that whatsoever ye shall ask of the Father in my name, he may give it you.

Offertory. Thou hast crowned him with glory and worship: thou hast made him to have dominion of the works of thy hands, O Lord.

Secret

O LORD, who didst exalt blessed *N.* to be numbered among thine Apostles: grant that we thy people, who on this day, preventing his heavenly birth, do offer unto thee these holy mysteries, may be assisted by his intercession both in the making of our supplications before thee, and in the obtaining of all that we desire. Through.

¶ 2ⁿᵈ Secret of St. Mary in Eastertide (p. BCP 542) & 3ʳᵈ Against the Persecutors of the Church (p. BCP 543) or for the Chief Bishop (p. BCP 543).

Communion. His honour is great in thy salvation: glory and great worship shalt thou lay upon him, O Lord.

Postcommunion

WE beseech thee, O Lord, mercifully to hear the supplication of thy holy Apostle *N.*: that thou wouldest vouchsafe unto us thy pardon, and grant us thy everlasting healing. Through.

¶ 2ⁿᵈ Postcommunion of St. Mary in Eastertide (p. BCP 542) & 3ʳᵈ Against the Persecutors of the Church (p. BCP 543) or for the Chief Bishop (p. BCP 543).

COMMON OF THE APOSTLES

I Evensong

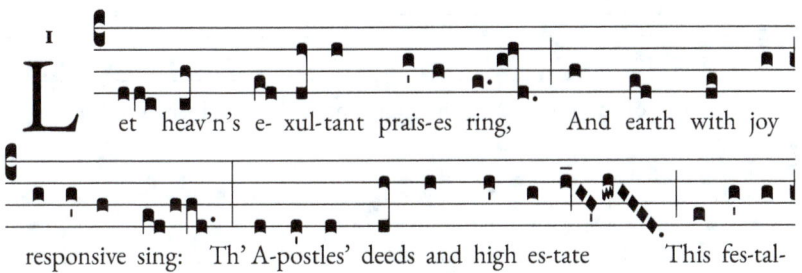

Let heav'n's exultant praises ring, And earth with joy responsive sing: Th' Apostles' deeds and high estate This festal-

Apostles   # Common of Saints

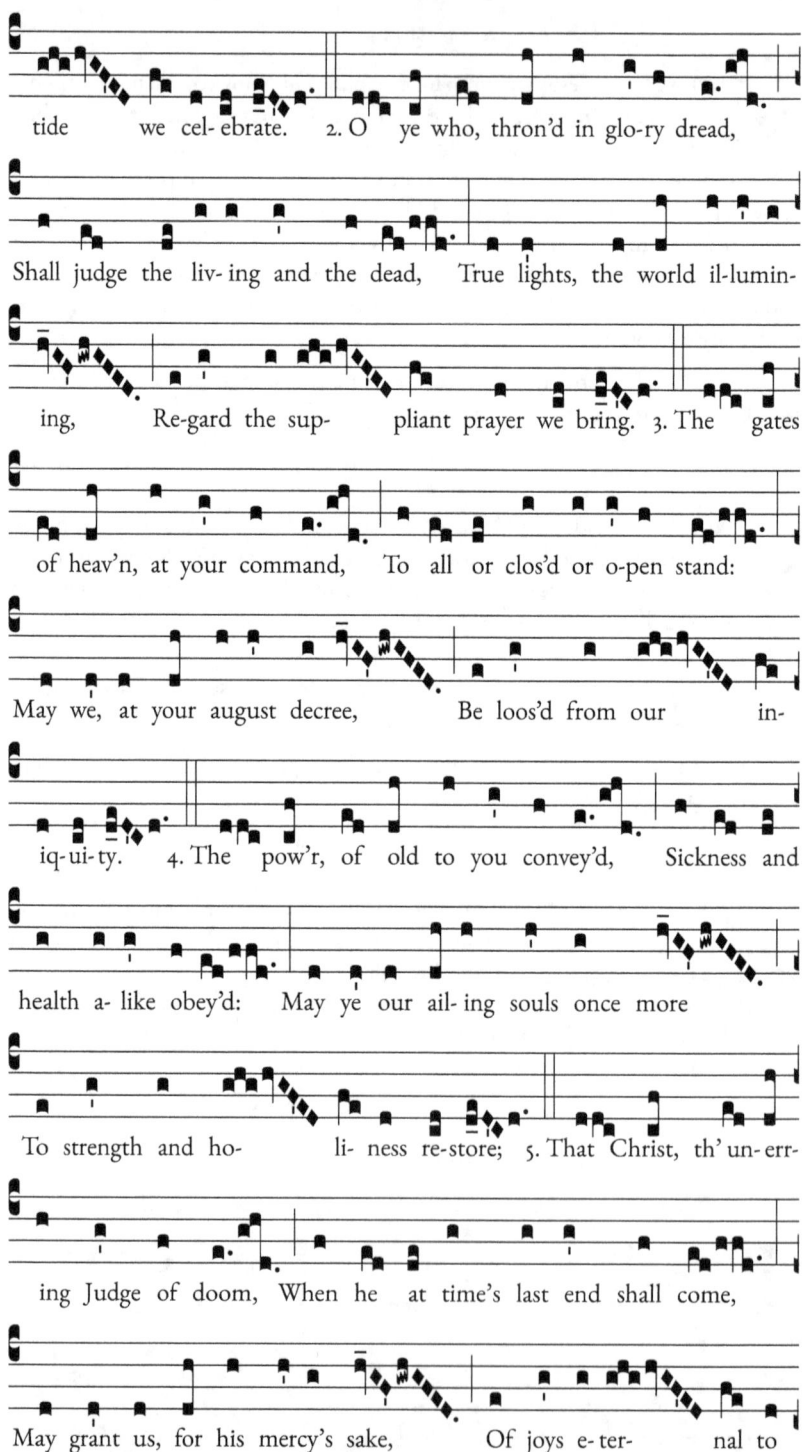

Common of Saints *Apostles*

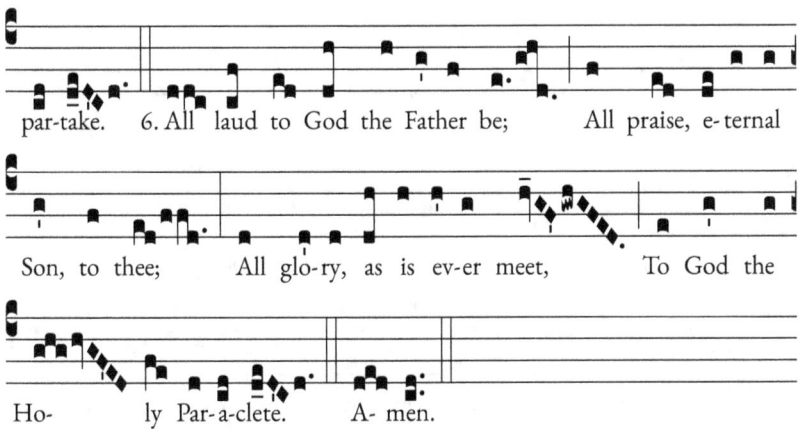

par-take. 6. All laud to God the Father be; All praise, e-ternal Son, to thee; All glo-ry, as is ev-er meet, To God the Ho- ly Par-a-clete. A-men.

℣. Their sound is gone out into all lands.
℟. And their words into the ends of the world.

Mag. Ant. They will deliver you up † to the councils, and they will scourge you in their synagogues; and ye shall be brought before governors and kings for my sake, for a testimony against them and the Gentiles.

Mattins

Invitatory Hymn

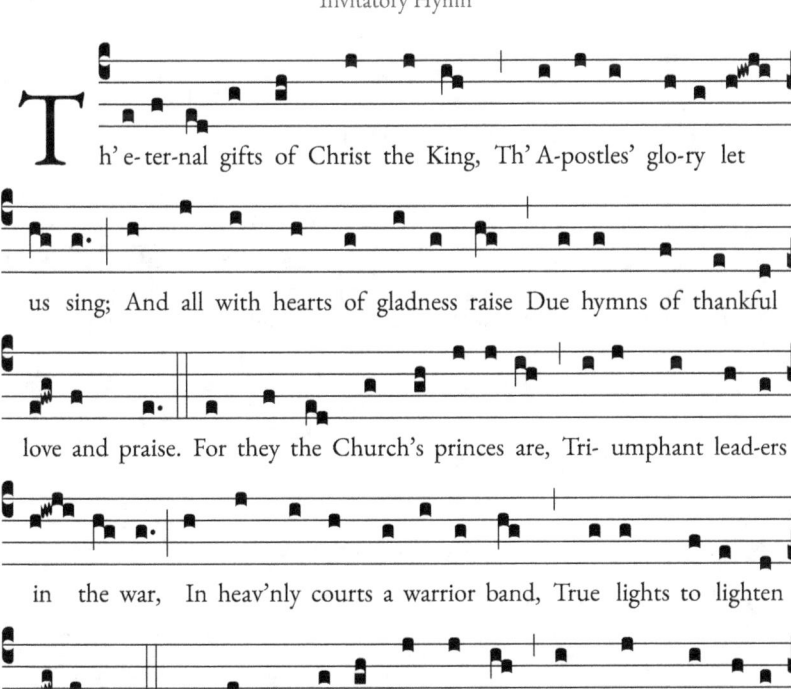

Th' e-ter-nal gifts of Christ the King, Th' A-postles' glo-ry let us sing; And all with hearts of gladness raise Due hymns of thankful love and praise. For they the Church's princes are, Tri-umphant lead-ers in the war, In heav'nly courts a warrior band, True lights to lighten every land. Theirs is the steadfast faith of saints, And hope that nev-er

Apostles

Common of Saints

yields nor faints, The love of Christ in per-fect glow That lays the prince of this world low. In them the Father's glo-ry shone, In them the will of God the Son, In them ex-ults the Ho-ly Ghost, Through them re-joice the heav'nly host. To thee, Re-deemer, now we cry, That thou wouldst join with them on high Thy servants, who this grace implore, For ev-er and for ev-ermore. A-men.

Office Hymn

Let heav'n's e-xul-tant prais-es ring, And earth with joy re-spon-sive sing: Th' A-postles' deeds and high es-tate This fes-tal-tide we cel-ebrate. 2. O ye who, thron'd in glo-ry dread, Shall judge the liv-ing and the dead, True lights, the world il-lu-min-ing, Re-gard the

Common of Saints *Apostles*

suppliant prayer we bring. 3. The gates of heav'n, at your command, To all or clos'd or o-pen stand: May we, at your au-gust de-cree, Be loos'd from our in- iq- ui-ty. 4. The pow'r, of old to you convey'd, Sickness and health a- like o- bey'd: May ye our ail- ing souls once more To strength and ho- li- ness re-store; 5. That Christ, th' un-err- ing Judge of doom, When he at time's last end shall come, May grant us, for his mer-cy's sake, Of joys e- ternal to par-take. 6. All laud to God the Father be; All praise, e- ter- nal Son, to thee; All glo-ry, as is ev-er meet, To God the Ho-ly Par- a-clete. A- men.

℣. They declared the work of God.

℟. And wisely considered of his doing.

Ben. Ant. Ye which have forsaken all, † and followed me, shall receive an hundredfold, and shall inherit everlasting life.

Apostles Easter # Common of Saints

II Evensong

¶ The Office Hymn & Versicle are of I Evensong with the following Antiphon.

Mag. Ant. Be ye valiant in warfare, † and contend ye with the old serpent: and ye shall receive an eternal kingdom, alleluia.

COMMON OF THE APOSTLES IN EASTERTIDE

I Evensong

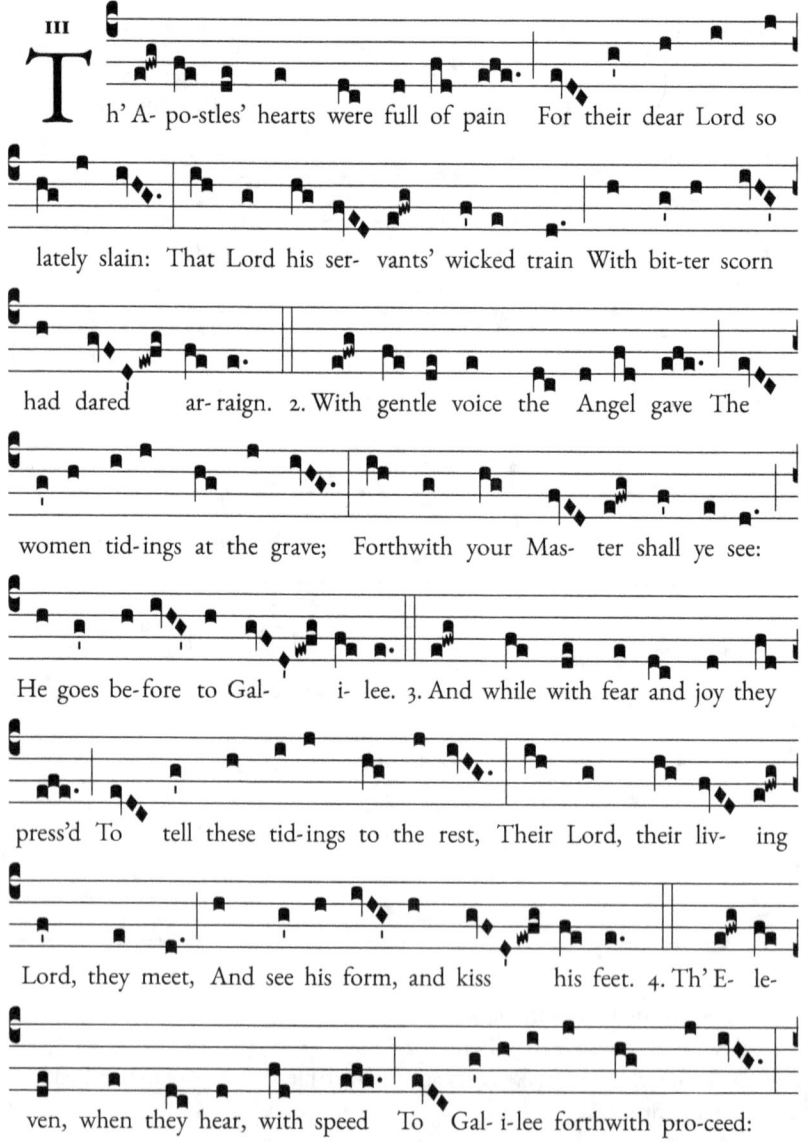

Th' A-postles' hearts were full of pain For their dear Lord so lately slain: That Lord his ser-vants' wicked train With bit-ter scorn had dared ar-raign. 2. With gentle voice the Angel gave The women tid-ings at the grave; Forthwith your Mas-ter shall ye see: He goes be-fore to Gal-i-lee. 3. And while with fear and joy they press'd To tell these tid-ings to the rest, Their Lord, their liv-ing Lord, they meet, And see his form, and kiss his feet. 4. Th' E-le-ven, when they hear, with speed To Gal-i-lee forthwith pro-ceed:

Common of Saints *Apostles Easter*

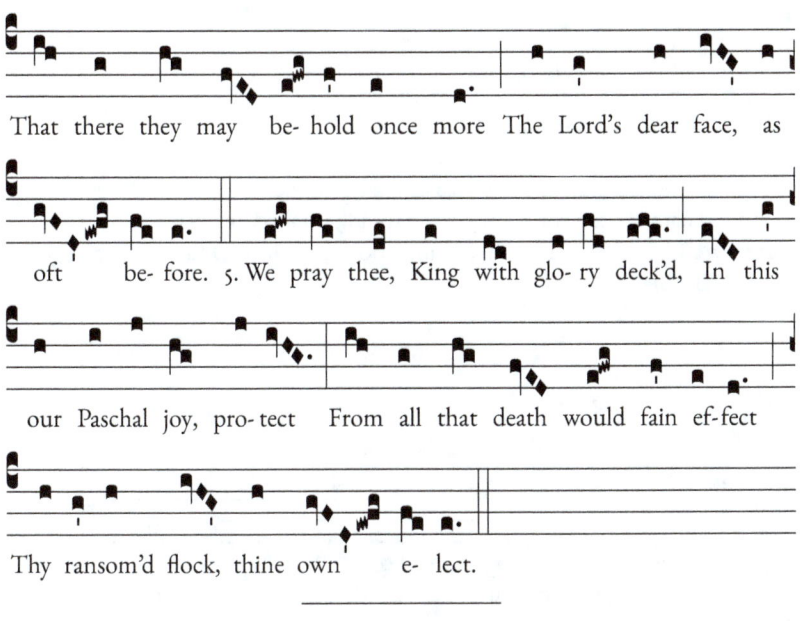

That there they may behold once more The Lord's dear face, as oft before. 5. We pray thee, King with glory deck'd, In this our Paschal joy, protect From all that death would fain effect Thy ransom'd flock, thine own elect.

¶ From Low Sunday, exclusive, until Ascension Thursday, exclusive:

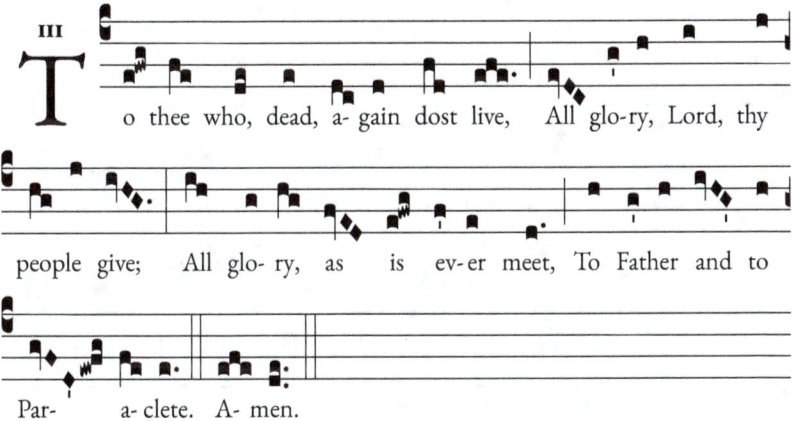

To thee who, dead, again dost live, All glory, Lord, thy people give; All glory, as is ever meet, To Father and to Paraclete. Amen.

¶ From Ascension Thursday, inclusive, until Whitsunday, inclusive:

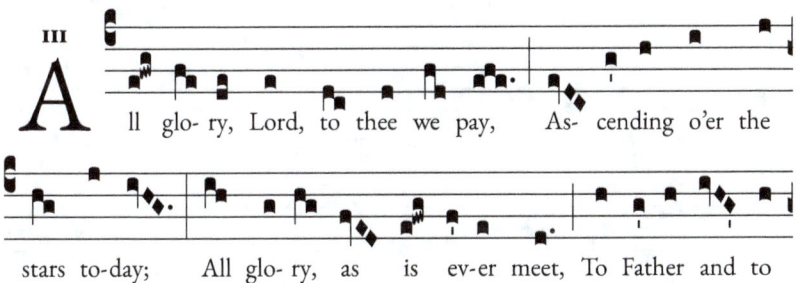

All glory, Lord, to thee we pay, Ascending o'er the stars to-day; All glory, as is ever meet, To Father and to

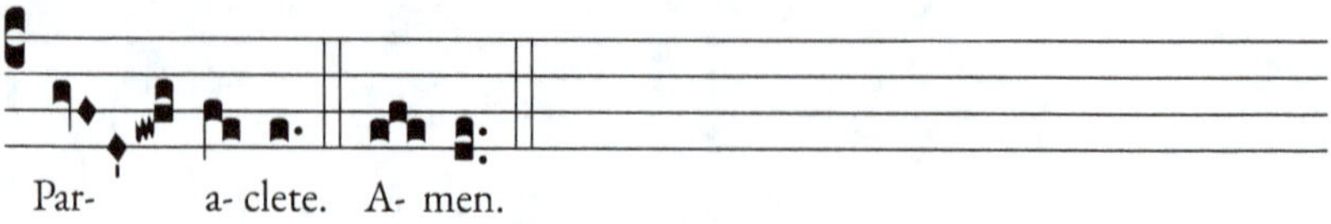

Apostles Easter

Common of Saints

Par- a- clete. A- men.

℣. O ye holy and righteous, rejoice in the Lord, alleluia.
℟. God hath chosen you to him to be his inheritance, alleluia.
Mag. Ant. Light perpetual † shall shine upon thy Saints, O Lord; and an ageless eternity, alleluia.

Mattins

¶ The Invitatory Hymn is of I Evensong.

Office Hymn

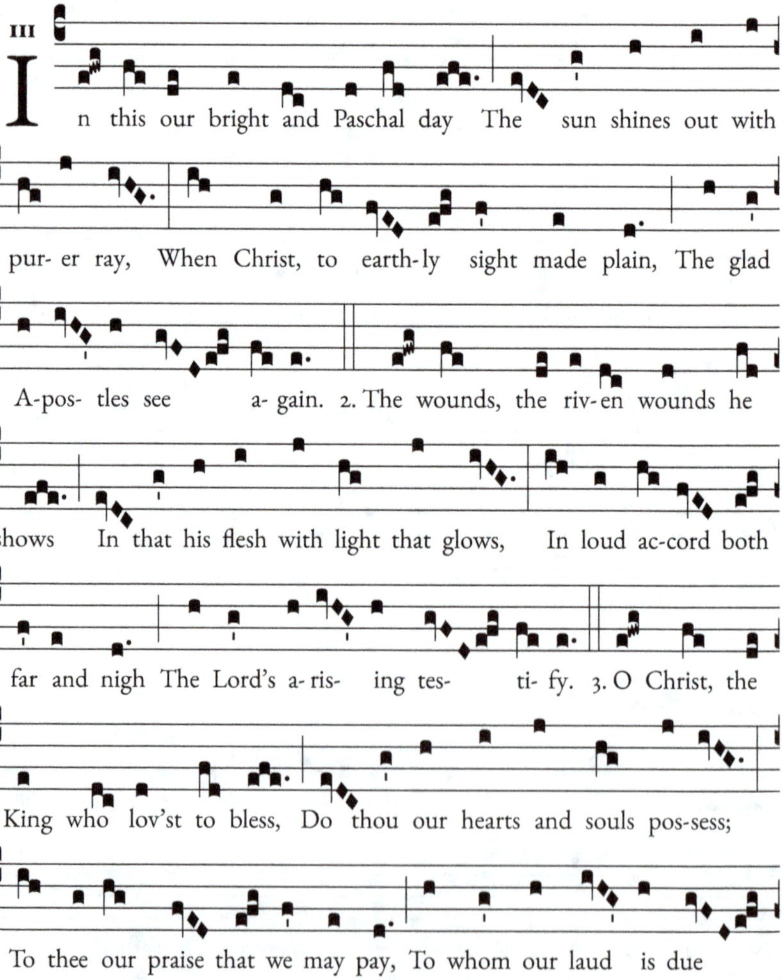

In this our bright and Paschal day The sun shines out with pur- er ray, When Christ, to earth- ly sight made plain, The glad A- pos- tles see a- gain. 2. The wounds, the riv- en wounds he shows In that his flesh with light that glows, In loud ac-cord both far and nigh The Lord's a- ris- ing tes- ti- fy. 3. O Christ, the King who lov'st to bless, Do thou our hearts and souls pos-sess; To thee our praise that we may pay, To whom our laud is due

Common of Saints   *Apostles Easter*

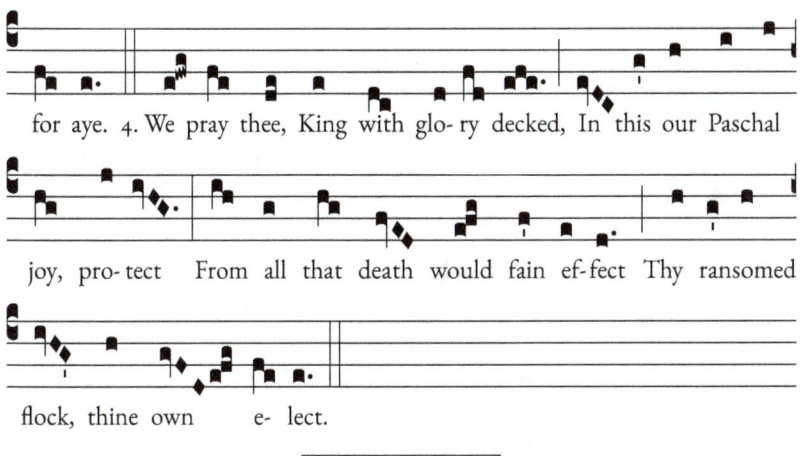

for aye. 4. We pray thee, King with glo- ry decked, In this our Paschal joy, pro- tect From all that death would fain ef-fect Thy ransomed flock, thine own e- lect.

℣ From Low Sunday, exclusive, until Ascension Thursday, exclusive:

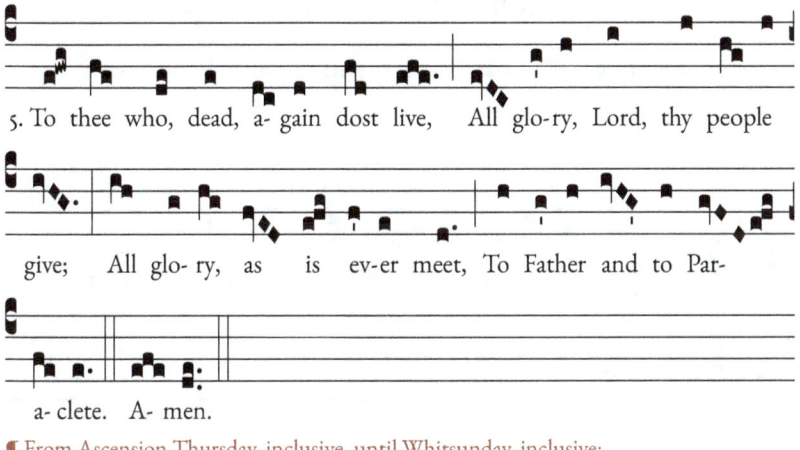

5. To thee who, dead, a- gain dost live, All glo- ry, Lord, thy people give; All glo- ry, as is ev-er meet, To Father and to Par- a- clete. A- men.

℣ From Ascension Thursday, inclusive, until Whitsunday, inclusive:

5. All glo- ry, Lord, to thee we pay, As- cending o'er the stars to- day; All glo- ry, as is ev-er meet, To Father and to Par- a- clete. A- men.

Martyr Bishop I   # Common of Saints

℣. Right dear in the sight of the Lord, alleluia.
℟. Is the death of his Saints, alleluia.
Ben. Ant. Daughters of Jerusalem, † come forth and behold the Martyrs with the diadems wherewith the Lord hath crowned them in the day of solemnity and rejoicing, alleluia, alleluia.

II Evensong

¶ The Office Hymn is of I Evensong with the following Versicle & Antiphon.

℣. Right dear in the sight of the Lord, alleluia.
℟. Is the death of his Saints, alleluia.
Mag. Ant. O ye holy and righteous, † rejoice in the Lord, alleluia: God hath chosen you to him to be his inheritance, alleluia.

Commons for a Martyr Bishop

I: Common of One Martyr Bishop out of Eastertide

I Evensong

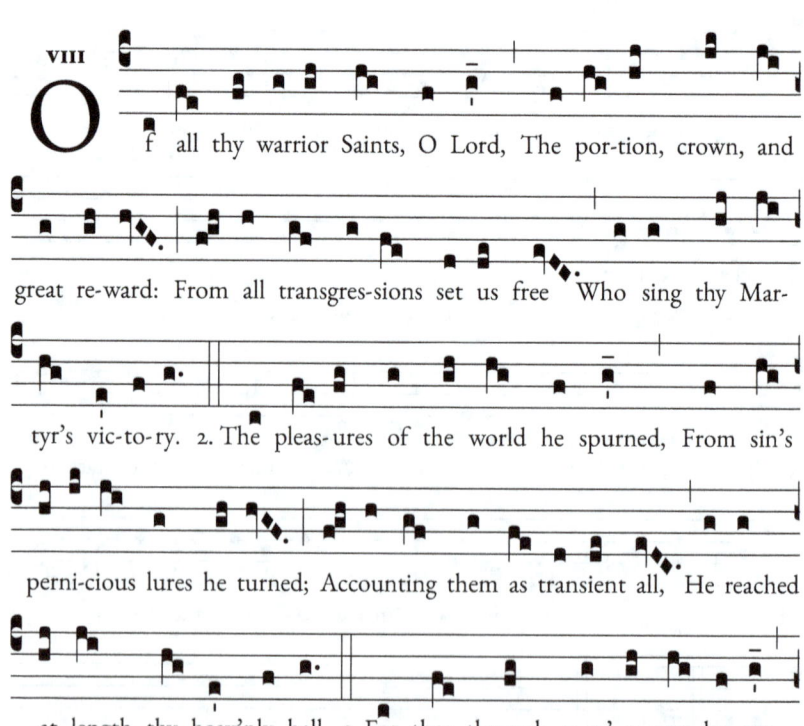

VIII. Of all thy warrior Saints, O Lord, The por-tion, crown, and great re-ward: From all transgres-sions set us free Who sing thy Mar-tyr's vic-to-ry. 2. The pleas-ures of the world he spurned, From sin's perni-cious lures he turned; Accounting them as transient all, He reached at length thy heav'nly hall. 3. For thee through man' a woe he ran,

Common of Saints *Martyr Bishop I*

In man' a fight he played the man; For thee his blood he dared to pour, And thence hath joy for ev-ermore. 4. *We therefore pray thee, full of love, Re- gard us from thy throne a-bove: On this thy Mar-tyr's tri- umph day, Wash every stain of sin away.* 5. *Endur- ing laud and praise be done To God the Fa-ther, and the Son, And to the Ho- ly Par- a-clete, For endless ag- es, as is meet. A- men.*

℣. Thou hast crowned him with glory and honour, O Lord.
℟. And madest him to have dominion of the works of thy hands.

Mag. Ant. This is a Martyr † who strove for his Master's precepts, even unto death: and feared not the words of evil men, forasmuch as he was stablished on a sure foundation.

Mattins

¶ The Invitatory Hymn is of I Evensong.

Office Hymn

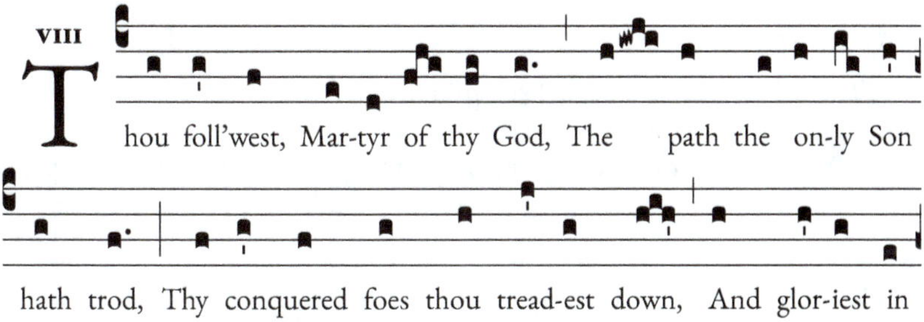

VIII

Thou foll'west, Mar-tyr of thy God, The path the on-ly Son hath trod, Thy conquered foes thou tread-est down, And glor-iest in

683

Martyr Bishop I ## Common of Saints

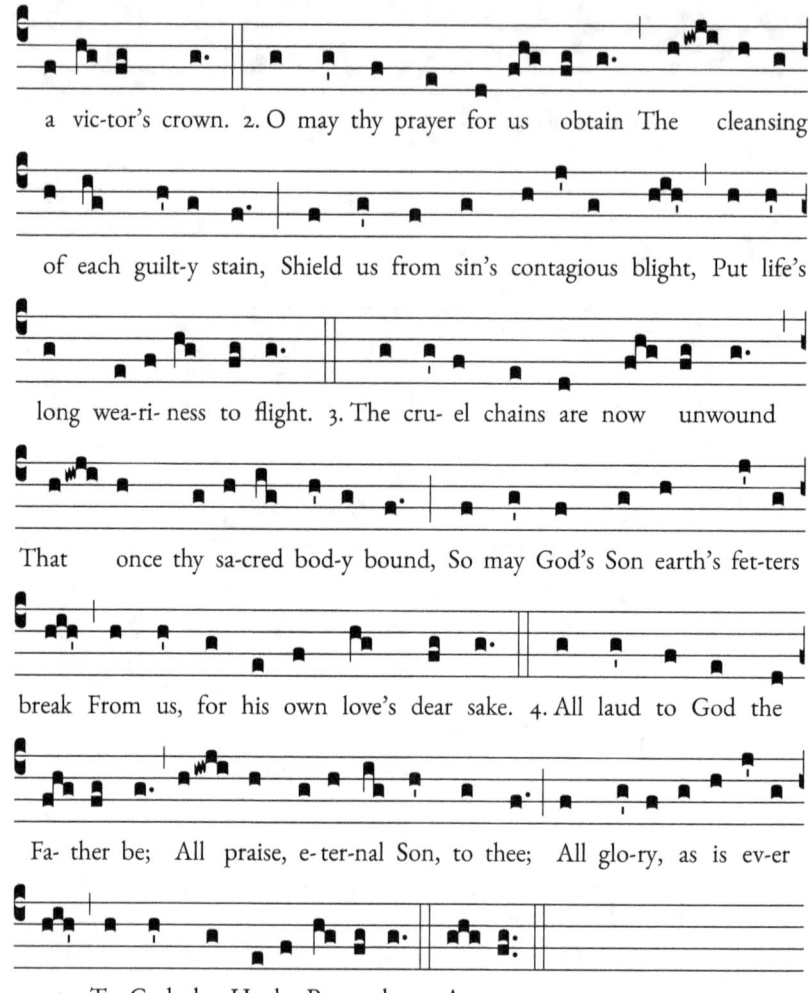

a vic-tor's crown. 2. O may thy prayer for us obtain The cleansing of each guilt-y stain, Shield us from sin's contagious blight, Put life's long wea-ri-ness to flight. 3. The cru-el chains are now unwound That once thy sa-cred bod-y bound, So may God's Son earth's fet-ters break From us, for his own love's dear sake. 4. All laud to God the Fa-ther be; All praise, e-ter-nal Son, to thee; All glo-ry, as is ev-er meet, To God the Ho-ly Par-a-clete. A-men.

℣. The righteous shall flourish like a palm-tree.
℞. And shall spread abroad like a cedar in Libanus.
Ben. Ant. He that hateth his life † in this world shall keep it unto life eternal.

II Evensong

¶ The Office Hymn is of I Evensong with the following Versicle & Antiphon.

℣. The righteous shall flourish like a palm-tree.
℞. And shall spread abroad like a cedar in Libanus.
Mag. Ant. Whosoever will come after me, † let him deny himself, and take up his cross, and follow me.

Common of Saints *Martyr Bishop I*

Introit

HE Lord hath established a covenant of peace with him, and made him a prince: that he should have the dignity of the priesthood for ever. *Ps.* Lord, remember David: and all his trouble.

Collect

LMIGHTY God, mercifully look upon our infirmities: that whereas we are oppressed by the burden of our sins, the glorious intercession of blessed *N.* thy Martyr and Bishop may be our succour and defence. Through.

Epistle. James 1:12

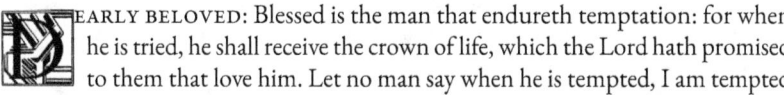EARLY BELOVED: Blessed is the man that endureth temptation: for when he is tried, he shall receive the crown of life, which the Lord hath promised to them that love him. Let no man say when he is tempted, I am tempted of God: for God cannot be tempted with evil, neither tempteth he any man: but every man is tempted, when he is drawn away of his own lust, and enticed. Then when lust hath conceived, it bringeth forth sin: and sin, when it is finished, bringeth forth death. Do not err, my beloved brethren. Every good gift and every perfect gift is from above, and cometh down from the Father of lights, with whom is no variableness, neither shadow of turning. Of his own will begat he us with the word of truth, that we should be a kind of firstfruits of his creatures.

Gradual. I have found David my servant, with my holy oil have I anointed him: my hand shall hold him fast, and my arm shall strengthen him. ℣. The enemy shall not be able to do him violence, the son of wickedness shall not hurt him.

Alleluia. Alleluia, alleluia. ℣. Thou art a priest for ever, after the order of Melchisedech. Alleluia.

¶ In Septuagesimatide or Lent, replacing the Alleluia:

Tract. Thou hast given him his heart's desire: and hast not denied him the request of his lips. ℣. For thou hast prevented him with the blessings of goodness. ℣. And hast set a crown of pure gold upon his head.

Gospel. Luke 14:26

T THAT TIME: Jesus said unto the multitudes: If any man come to me, and hate not his father, and mother, and wife, and children, and brethren, and sisters, yea, and his own life also, he cannot be my disciple. And whosoever doth not bear his cross, and come after me, cannot be my disciple. For which of you, intending to build a tower, sitteth not down first, and counteth the cost, whether he have sufficient to finish it? lest haply, after he hath laid the foundation, and is not able to finish it, all that behold it begin to mock him, saying, This man began to build, and was not able to finish. Or what king, going to make war against another king, sitteth not down first, and consulteth whether he be able with ten thousand to meet him that cometh against him with twenty thousand? Or else, while the other is yet a great way off, he sendeth an ambassage, and desireth conditions of peace. So likewise, whosoever he be of you that forsaketh not all that he hath, he cannot be my disciple.

Offertory. My truth and my mercy shall be with him: and in my name shall his horn be exalted.

Secret

E beseech thee, O Lord, mercifully to accept this our sacrifice which we offer unto thee pleading the merits of blessed *N*. thy Martyr and Bishop: that the same may avail for our perpetual succour. Through.

Communion. I have sworn once by my holiness: His seed shall endure for ever: and his seat is like as the sun before me; he shall stand fast for evermore as the moon, and as the faithful witness in heaven.

Postcommunion

E beseech thee, O Lord our God, that like as we whom thou hast refreshed by the partaking of thy sacred gift do offer unto thee our worship; so, by the intercession of blessed *N*. thy Martyr and Bishop, we may perceive the benefit of the same. Through.

II: Common of One Martyr Bishop out of Eastertide

¶ Daily Office propers as in the First Common of a Martyr Bishop (p. 682).

Introit

YE priests of the Lord, bless ye the Lord: O ye holy and humble men of heart, bless ye the Lord. *Ps.* O all ye works of the Lord, bless ye the Lord: praise him, and magnify him for ever.

Collect

GOD, who makest us glad with the yearly solemnity of blessed *N*. thy Martyr and Bishop: mercifully grant; that, as we now celebrate his birthday, so we may likewise rejoice in his protection. Through.

Epistle. 2 Corinthians 1:3

RETHREN: Blessed be God, even the Father of our Lord Jesus Christ, the Father of mercies, and the God of all comfort; who comforteth us in all our tribulation, that we may be able to comfort them which are in any trouble, by the comfort wherewith we ourselves are comforted of God. For as the sufferings of Christ abound in us, so our consolation also aboundeth by Christ. And whether

Common of Saints — *Martyr Bishop II*

we be afflicted, it is for your consolation and salvation, which is effectual in the enduring of the same sufferings which we also suffer: or whether we be comforted, it is for your consolation and salvation. And our hope of you is stedfast, knowing, that as ye are partakers of the sufferings, so shall ye be also of the consolation: in Christ Jesus our Lord.

Gradual. Thou hast crowned him with glory and worship. ℣. Thou hast made him to have dominion of the works of thy hands, O Lord.

Alleluia. Alleluia, alleluia. ℣. This is a priest whom the Lord hath crowned. Alleluia.

¶ In Septuagesimatide or Lent, replacing the Alleluia:

Tract. Blessed is the man that feareth the Lord: he hath great delight in his commandments. ℣. His seed shall be mighty upon earth: the generation of the faithful shall be blessed. ℣. Riches and plenteousness shall be in his house: and his righteousness endureth for ever.

Gospel. Matthew 16:24

AT THAT TIME: Jesus said unto his disciples: If any man will come after me, let him deny himself, and take up his cross, and follow me. For whosoever will save his life shall lose it: and whosoever will lose his life for my sake shall find it. For what is a man profited, if he shall gain the whole world, and lose his own soul? or what shall a man give in exchange for his soul? For the Son of man shall come in the glory of his Father with his angels; and then he shall reward every man according to his works.

Offertory. I have found David my servant, with my holy oil have I anointed him: my hand shall hold him fast, and my arm shall strengthen him.

Secret

SANCTIFY, O Lord, the gifts which we dedicate to thee: that at the intercession of blessed *N.*, thy Martyr and Bishop, they may obtain for us thy gracious favour. Through.

Communion. Thou hast set, Lord, a crown of pure gold upon his head.

Postcommunion

MAY this communion, O Lord, cleanse us from guilt: and, at the intercession of blessed *N.*, thy Martyr and Bishop, make us partakers of thy heavenly healing. Through.

Martyr not Bishop I   # Common of Saints

Commons for a Martyr

I: Common of One Martyr not a Bishop out of Eastertide

¶ Daily Office propers as in the First Common of a Martyr Bishop (p. 682).

Introit

THE righteous shall rejoice: in thy strength, O Lord: exceeding glad shall he be of thy salvation: thou hast given him his heart's desire. *Ps.* For thou hast prevented him with the blessings of goodness: and hast set a crown of pure gold upon his head.

Collect

GRANT, we beseech thee, Almighty God: that we, who devoutly celebrate the birthday of blessed *N.*, thy Martyr, may by his intercession be stablished in the love of thy name. Through.

Epistle. Wisdom 10:10

WISDOM guided the righteous man in straight paths; She shewed him God's kingdom, and gave him knowledge of holy things; She prospered him in his toils, and multiplied the fruits of his labour; When in their covetousness men dealt hardly with him, She stood by him and made him rich; She guarded him from enemies, And from those that lay in wait she kept him safe, And over his sore conflict she watched as judge, That he might know that godliness is more powerful than all. When a righteous man was sold, wisdom forsook him not, But from sin she delivered him; She went down with him into a dungeon, And in bonds she left him not, Till she brought him the sceptre of a kingdom, And authority over those that dealt tyrannously with him; She shewed them also to be false that had mockingly accused him, And gave him eternal glory.

Gradual. Blessed is the man that feareth the Lord: he hath great delight in his commandments. ℣. His seed shall be mighty upon earth: the generation of the faithful shall be blessed.

Alleluia. Alleluia, alleluia. ℣. Thou hast set, O Lord, a crown of pure gold upon his head. Alleluia.

¶ In Septuagesimatide or Lent, replacing the Alleluia:

Tract. Thou hast given him his heart's desire: and hast not denied him the request of his lips. ℣. For thou hast prevented him with the blessings of goodness. ℣. And hast set a crown of pure gold upon his head.

Common of Saints *Martyr not Bishop I*

Gospel. Matthew 10:34

AT THAT TIME: Jesus said unto his disciples: 34 Think not that I am come to send peace on earth: I came not to send peace, but a sword. For I am come to set a man at variance against his father, and the daughter against her mother, and the daughter in law against her mother in law. And a man's foes shall be they of his own household. He that loveth father or mother more than me is not worthy of me: and he that loveth son or daughter more than me is not worthy of me. And he that taketh not his cross, and followeth after me, is not worthy of me. He that findeth his life shall lose it: and he that loseth his life for my sake shall find it. He that receiveth you receiveth me, and he that receiveth me receiveth him that sent me. He that receiveth a prophet in the name of a prophet shall receive a prophet's reward; and he that receiveth a righteous man in the name of a righteous man shall receive a righteous man's reward. And whosoever shall give to drink unto one of these little ones a cup of cold water only in the name of a disciple, verily I say unto you, he shall in no wise lose his reward.

Offertory. Thou hast crowned him with glory and worship: thou hast made him to have dominion of the works of thy hands, O Lord.

Secret

WE beseech thee, O Lord, to accept our prayers and oblations: and graciously hearken unto us, whom thou dost cleanse by thy heavenly mysteries. Through.

Communion. If any man will come after me, let him deny himself, and take up his cross, and follow me.

Postcommunion

GRANT, we beseech thee, O Lord our God: that like as we in this life do gladly honour the memory of thy saints; so we may rejoice to behold them for ever. Through.

Martyr not Bishop II # Common of Saints

II: Common of One Martyr not a Bishop out of Eastertide

¶ Daily Office propers as in the First Common of a Martyr Bishop (p. 682).

Introit

HE righteous shall rejoice in the Lord, and put his trust in him: and all they that are true of heart shall be glad. *Ps.* Hear my voice, O God, in my prayer: preserve my life from fear of the enemy.

Collect

RANT, we beseech thee, Almighty God: that, at the intercession of blessed *N.*, thy Martyr, we may both be delivered from all adversities which may happen to the body, and from all evil thoughts, which may assault and hurt the soul. Through.

Epistle. 2 Timothy 2:8

EARLY BELOVED: Remember that Jesus Christ of the seed of David was raised from the dead according to my gospel: wherein I suffer trouble, as an evil doer, even unto bonds; but the word of God is not bound. Therefore I endure all things for the elect's sakes, that they may also obtain the salvation which is in Christ Jesus with eternal glory. But thou hast fully known my doctrine, manner of life, purpose, faith, longsuffering, charity, patience, persecutions, afflictions, which came unto me at Antioch, at Iconium, at Lystra; what persecutions I endured: but out of them all the Lord delivered me. Yea, and all that will live godly in Christ Jesus shall suffer persecution.

Gradual. Though the righteous fall, he shall not be cast away: for the Lord upholdeth him with his hand. ℣. He is ever merciful, and lendeth: and his seed is blessed.

Alleluia. Alleluia, alleluia. ℣. He that followeth me shall not walk in darkness: but shall have the light of eternal life. Alleluia.

¶ In Septuagesimatide or Lent, replacing the Alleluia:

Tract. Blessed is the man that feareth the Lord: he hath great delight in his commandments. ℣. His seed shall be mighty upon earth: the generation of the faithful shall be blessed. ℣. Riches and plenteousness shall be in his house: and his righteousness endureth for ever.

Gospel. Matthew 10:26

T THAT TIME: Jesus said unto his disciples: There is nothing covered, that shall not be revealed; and hid, that shall not be known. What I tell you in darkness, that speak ye in light: and what ye hear in the ear, that preach ye

Common of Saints *Martyr not Bishop II*

upon the housetops. And fear not them which kill the body, but are not able to kill the soul: but rather fear him which is able to destroy both soul and body in hell.

Are not two sparrows sold for a farthing? and one of them shall not fall on the ground without your Father. But the very hairs of your head are all numbered. Fear ye not therefore, ye are of more value than many sparrows.

Whosoever therefore shall confess me before men, him will I confess also before my Father which is in heaven.

Offertory. Thou hast set, O Lord, a crown of pure gold upon his head: he asked life of thee, and thou gavest it him, alleluia.

Secret

RANT, O Lord, that this our bounden service may be acceptable in thy sight: that these our oblations may, by the prayers of him on whose solemnity they are offered, be made profitable unto our salvation. Through.

Communion. If any man serve me, let him follow me: and where I am, there shall also my servant be.

Postcommunion

E beseech thee, O Lord our God, that like as we, whom thou hast refreshed by the partaking of thy sacred gift, do offer unto thee our worship: so by the intercession of blessed *N.*, thy Martyr, we may perceive the benefit of the same. Through.

¶ The following Epistles and Gospel may be used instead of the ones provided above.

1. Epistle. James 1:2

EARLY BELOVED: Count it all joy when ye fall into divers temptations; knowing this, that the trying of your faith worketh patience. But let patience have her perfect work, that ye may be perfect and entire, wanting nothing. If any of you lack wisdom, let him ask of God, that giveth to all men liberally, and upbraideth not; and it shall be given him. But let him ask in faith, nothing wavering. For he that wavereth is like a wave of the sea driven with the wind and tossed. For let not that man think that he shall receive any thing of the Lord. A double minded man is unstable in all his ways. Let the brother of low degree rejoice in that he is exalted: but the rich, in that he is made low: because as the flower of the grass he shall pass away. For the sun is no sooner risen with a burning heat, but it withereth the grass, and the flower thereof falleth, and the grace of the fashion of it perisheth: so also shall the rich man fade away in his ways.

Blessed is the man that endureth temptation: for when he is tried, he shall receive the crown of life, which the Lord hath promised to them that love him.

Martyrs I # Common of Saints

2. Epistle. 1 Peter 4:13

DEARLY BELOVED: Rejoice, inasmuch as ye are partakers of Christ's sufferings; that, when his glory shall be revealed, ye may be glad also with exceeding joy. If ye be reproached for the name of Christ, happy are ye; for the spirit of glory and of God resteth upon you: on their part he is evil spoken of, but on your part he is glorified. But let none of you suffer as a murderer, or as a thief, or as an evildoer, or as a busybody in other men's matters. Yet if any man suffer as a Christian, let him not be ashamed; but let him glorify God on this behalf. For the time is come that judgment must begin at the house of God: and if it first begin at us, what shall the end be of them that obey not the gospel of God? And if the righteous scarcely be saved, where shall the ungodly and the sinner appear? Wherefore let them that suffer according to the will of God commit the keeping of their souls to him in well doing, as unto a faithful Creator.

Another Gospel. John 12:24

AT THAT TIME: Jesus said unto his disciples: Verily, verily, I say unto you, Except a corn of wheat fall into the ground and die, it abideth alone: but if it die, it bringeth forth much fruit. He that loveth his life shall lose it; and he that hateth his life in this world shall keep it unto life eternal. If any man serve me, let him follow me; and where I am, there shall also my servant be: if any man serve me, him will my Father honour.

Commons for Many Martyrs

I: COMMON OF MANY MARTYRS OUT OF EASTERTIDE

I Evensong

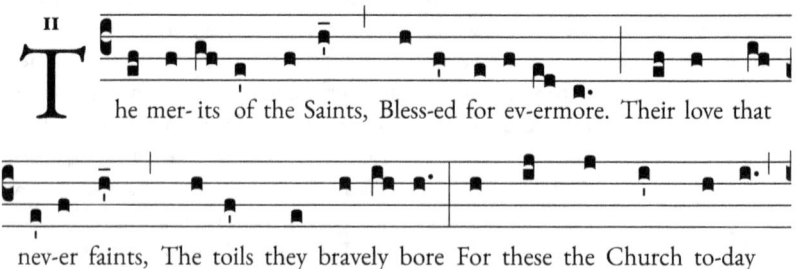

he mer-its of the Saints, Bless-ed for ev-ermore. Their love that nev-er faints, The toils they bravely bore For these the Church to-day

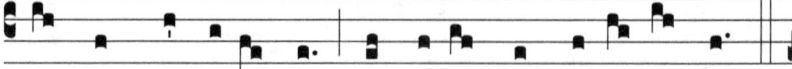

Pours forth her joy-ous lay: These vic-tors win the nobl-est bay.

Common of Saints *Martyrs I*

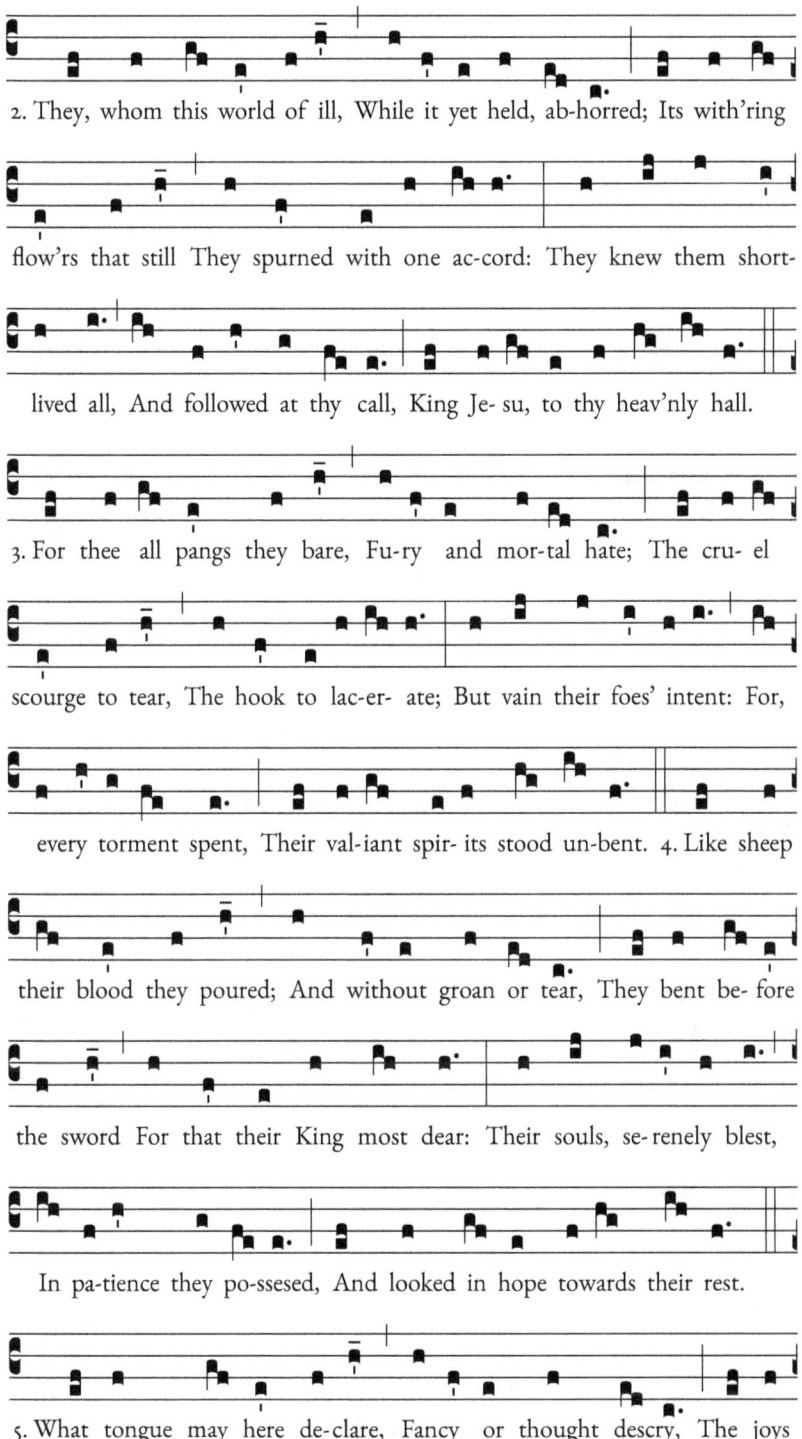

Martyrs I

Common of Saints

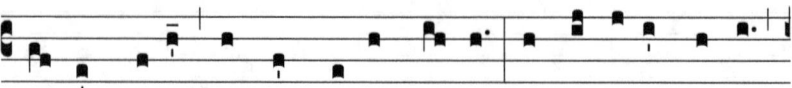

thou dost pre-pare For these thy Saints on high! Empurpled in the flood

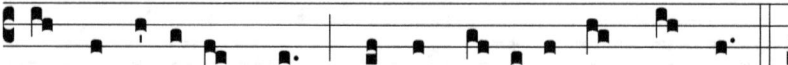

Of their vic-tor-ious blood. They won the lau-rel from their God.

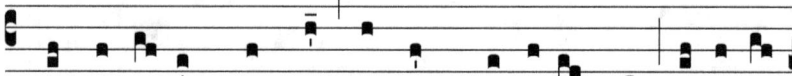

6. To thee, O Lord Most High, One in Three Per-sons still, To par-don

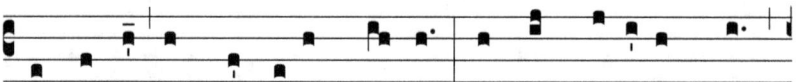

us we cry. And to pre-serve from ill: Here give thy servants peace,

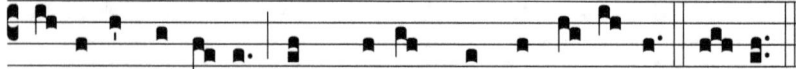

Here-af-ter glad re-lease. And pleas-ures that shall nev-er cease. A-men.

℣. Be glad, O ye righteous, and rejoice in the Lord.

℟. And be joyful, all ye that are true of heart.

Mag. Ant. For theirs is the kingdom of heaven, † who despised worldly living: who have won the rewards of the kingdom, and have washed their robes in the blood of the Lamb.

Mattins

Invitatory Hymn

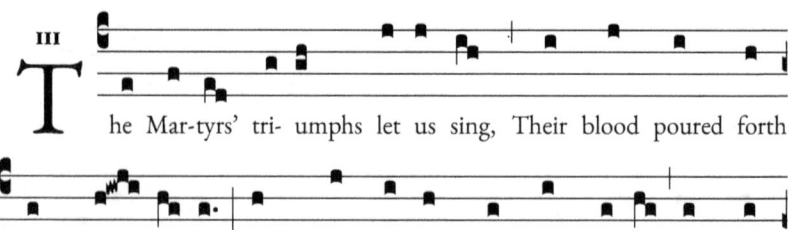

The Mar-tyrs' tri-umphs let us sing, Their blood poured forth

for Christ the King, And while due hymns of praise we pay, Our thank-

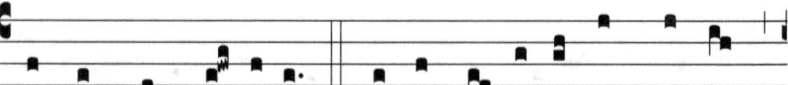

ful hearts cast grief away. 2. The world its ter-rors urged in vain;

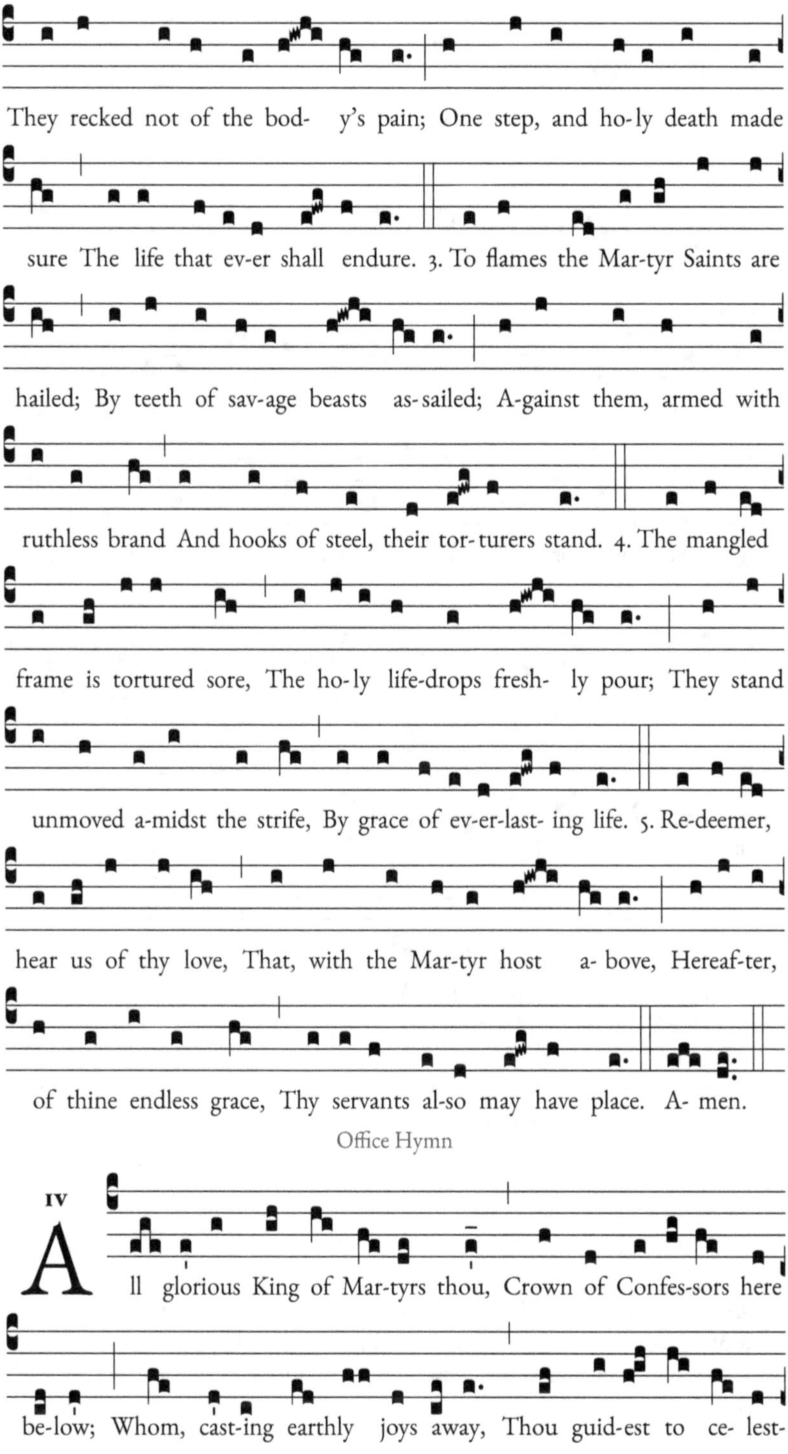

Common of Saints
Martyrs I

They recked not of the bod- y's pain; One step, and ho-ly death made sure The life that ev-er shall endure. 3. To flames the Mar-tyr Saints are hailed; By teeth of sav-age beasts as-sailed; A-gainst them, armed with ruthless brand And hooks of steel, their tor-turers stand. 4. The mangled frame is tortured sore, The ho-ly life-drops fresh-ly pour; They stand unmoved a-midst the strife, By grace of ev-er-last-ing life. 5. Re-deemer, hear us of thy love, That, with the Mar-tyr host a-bove, Hereaf-ter, of thine endless grace, Thy servants al-so may have place. A-men.

Office Hymn

IV

A-ll glorious King of Mar-tyrs thou, Crown of Confes-sors here be-low; Whom, cast-ing earthly joys away, Thou guid-est to ce-lest-

Martyrs I — **Common of Saints**

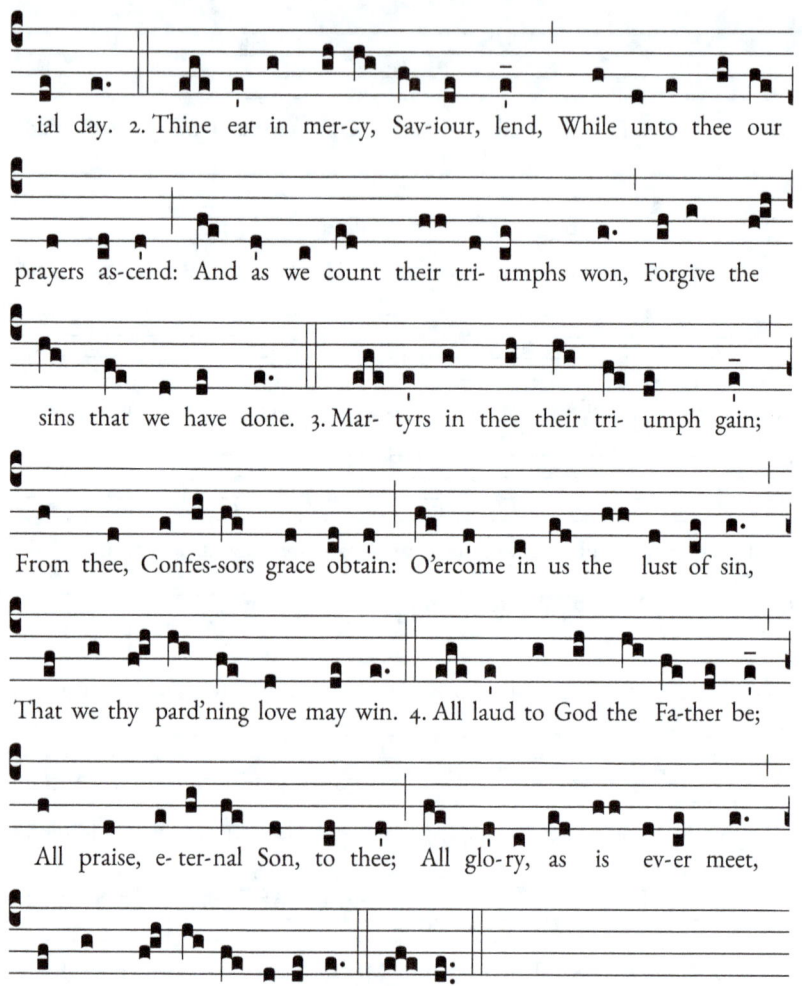

ial day. 2. Thine ear in mer-cy, Sav-iour, lend, While unto thee our prayers as-cend: And as we count their tri- umphs won, Forgive the sins that we have done. 3. Mar- tyrs in thee their tri- umph gain; From thee, Confes-sors grace obtain: O'ercome in us the lust of sin, That we thy pard'ning love may win. 4. All laud to God the Fa-ther be; All praise, e- ter-nal Son, to thee; All glo-ry, as is ev-er meet, To God the Ho- ly Par-a-clete. A- men.

℣. Let the Saints be joyful with glory.

℟. Let them rejoice in their beds.

Ben. Ant. The very hairs of your head † are all numbered: fear ye not therefore, ye are of more value than many sparrows.

II Evensong

¶ The Office Hymn is of I Evensong, and the Versicle is of Mattins, with the following Antiphon.

Mag. Ant. In the heavenly kingdom † rejoice the souls of the Blessed, who followed the footsteps of Christ their Master: and since for love of him they poured forth their life-blood, therefore with Christ do they exult for ever.

Common of Saints — *Martyrs I*

Introit

LET the sorrowful sighing of the prisoners, O Lord, come before thee: reward thou our neighbours seven-fold into their bosom: avenge thou the blood of thy Saints that is shed. *Ps.* O God, the heathen are come into thine inheritance: thy holy temple have they defiled: and made Jerusalem an heap of stones.

Collect

Many Martyrs not Bishops

O GOD, who vouchsafest unto us to celebrate the birthday of thy holy Martyrs *N. and N.*: grant that we may rejoice in the everlasting felicity of their fellowship. Through.

Many Martyrs Bishops

PROTECT us, O Lord, we beseech thee, who observe the feast of thy blessed Martyrs and Bishops *N. and N.*: and grant that by their meritorious supplication we may find favour in thy sight. Through.

Epistle. Wisdom 3:1

THE souls of the righteous are in the hand of God, And no torment shall touch them. In the eyes of the foolish they seemed to have died; And their departure was accounted to be their hurt, And their journeying away from us to be their ruin: But they are in peace. For even if in the sight of men they be punished, Their hope is full of immortality; And having borne a little chastening, they shall receive great good; Because God made trial of them, and found them worthy of himself. As gold in the furnace he proved them, And as a whole burnt offering he accepted them. And in the time of their visitation they shall shine forth, And as sparks among stubble they shall run to and fro. They shall judge nations, and have dominion over peoples; And the Lord shall reign over them for evermore.

Gradual. God is glorious in his holy ones: fearful in praises, doing wonders. ℣. Thy right hand, O Lord, is become glorious in power: thy right hand hath dashed in pieces the enemy.

Alleluia. Alleluia, alleluia. ℣. The bodies of the Saints are buried in peace, but their name liveth for evermore. Alleluia.

¶ In Septuagesimatide or Lent, replacing the Alleluia:

Tract. They that sow in tears, shall reap in joy. ℣. He that now goeth on his way weeping, and beareth forth good seed. ℣. Shall doubtless come again with joy, and bring his sheaves with him.

Gospel. Luke 21:9

AT THAT TIME: Jesus said unto his disciples: When ye shall hear of wars and commotions, be not terrified: for these things must first come to pass; but the end is not by and by. Then said he unto them, Nation shall rise against

Martyrs I   # Common of Saints

nation, and kingdom against kingdom: and great earthquakes shall be in divers places, and famines, and pestilences; and fearful sights and great signs shall there be from heaven. But before all these, they shall lay their hands on you, and persecute you, delivering you up to the synagogues, and into prisons, being brought before kings and rulers for my name's sake. And it shall turn to you for a testimony. Settle it therefore in your hearts, not to meditate before what ye shall answer: for I will give you a mouth and wisdom, which all your adversaries shall not be able to gainsay nor resist. And ye shall be betrayed both by parents, and brethren, and kinsfolks, and friends; and some of you shall they cause to be put to death. And ye shall be hated of all men for my name's sake. But there shall not an hair of your head perish. In your patience possess ye your souls.

¶ After Septuagesima, **Alleluia** at the end of the following Offertory is omitted.

Offertory. God is wonderful in his holy ones: even the God of Israel, he will give strength and power unto his people: blessed be God, alleluia.

Secret

Many Martyrs not Bishops

WE beseech thee, O Lord, that the gifts which we offer unto thee of our bounden duty and service may be acceptable unto thee for the honour of thy Just ones: and by thy mercy profitable unto us for our salvation. Through.

Many Martyrs Bishops

ASSIST us mercifully, O Lord, in these our supplications which we make before thee in remembrance of thy Saints: that we who trust not in our own righteousness may be succoured by the merits of them that have found favour in thy sight. Through.

Communion. Though they be punished in the sight of men, yet hath God proved them: as gold in the furnace hath he tried them, and received them as a burnt offering.

Postcommunion

Many Martyrs not Bishops

GRANT to us, we beseech thee, O Lord: at the intercession of thy holy Martyrs *N.* and *N.*; that those things which we touch with our mouths we may receive in purity of heart. Through.

Many Martyrs Bishops

O LORD, who hast fulfilled us with saving mysteries: we beseech thee that we may be aided by the prayers of those whose festival we celebrate. Through.

Common of Saints *Martyrs II*

II: Common of Many Martyrs out of Eastertide

¶ Daily Office propers as in the First Common of Many Martyrs (p. 692).
¶ The Collect, Secret, & Postcommunion are of the preceding Mass.

Introit

ET the people tell of the wisdom of the Saints, and let the church shew forth their praise: their names shall live for evermore. *Ps.* Rejoice in the Lord, O ye righteous: for it becometh well the just to be thankful.

Epistle. Wisdom 5:15

BUT the righteous live for ever, And in the Lord is their reward, And the care for them with the Most High. Therefore shall they receive the crown of royal dignity And the diadem of beauty from the Lord's hand; Because with his right hand shall he cover them, And with his arm shall he shield them. He shall take his jealousy as complete armour, And shall make the whole creation his weapons for vengeance on his enemies: He shall put on righteousness as a breastplate, And shall array himself with judgement unfeigned as with a helmet; He shall take holiness as an invincible shield.

Gradual. Our soul is escaped even as a bird out of the snare of the fowler. ℣. The snare is broken, and we are delivered: our help standeth in the name of the Lord, who hath made heaven and earth.

Alleluia. Alleluia, alleluia. ℣. Let the righteous be glad and rejoice before God: let them also be merry and joyful. Alleluia.

¶ In Septuagesimatide or Lent, replacing the Alleluia:

Tract. They that sow in tears, shall reap in joy. ℣. He that now goeth on his way weeping, and beareth forth good seed. ℣. Shall doubtless come again with joy, and bring his sheaves with him.

Gospel. Luke 6:17

T THAT TIME: Jesus came down from the mountain, and stood in the plain, and the company of his disciples, and a great multitude of people out of all Judæa and Jerusalem, and from the sea coast of Tyre and Sidon, which came to hear him, and to be healed of their diseases; and they that were vexed with unclean spirits: and they were healed. And the whole multitude sought to touch him: for there went virtue out of him, and healed them all.

And he lifted up his eyes on his disciples, and said, Blessed be ye poor: for yours is the kingdom of God. Blessed are ye that hunger now: for ye shall be filled. Blessed are ye that weep now: for ye shall laugh. Blessed are ye, when men shall hate you, and when they shall separate you from their company, and shall reproach you, and cast out your name as evil, for the Son of man's sake. Rejoice ye in that day, and leap for joy: for, behold, your reward is great in heaven.

Martyrs III # Common of Saints

¶ After Septuagesima, Alleluia at the end of the following Offertory is omitted.

Offertory. Let the saints be joyful with glory, let them rejoice in their beds: let the praises of God be in their mouth, alleluia.

Communion. I say unto you, my friends: Be not afraid of them that persecute you.

III: Common of Many Martyrs out of Eastertide

¶ Daily Office propers as in the First Common of Many Martyrs (p. 692).

Introit

UT the salvation of the righteous cometh of the Lord: who is also their strength in the time of trouble. *Ps.* Fret not thyself because of the ungodly: neither be thou envious against the evil doers.

Collect

 GOD, who makest us glad with the yearly solemnity of thy holy Martyrs *N. and N.*: mercifully grant; that as we do rejoice in their merits, so we may be enkindled by their example. Through.

Epistle. Hebrews 10:32

RETHREN: Call to remembrance the former days, in which, after ye were illuminated, ye endured a great fight of afflictions; partly, whilst ye were made a gazingstock both by reproaches and afflictions; and partly, whilst ye became companions of them that were so used. For ye had compassion of me in my bonds, and took joyfully the spoiling of your goods, knowing in yourselves that ye have in heaven a better and an enduring substance. Cast not away therefore your confidence, which hath great recompence of reward. For ye have need of patience, that, after ye have done the will of God, ye might receive the promise. For yet a little while, and he that shall come will come, and will not tarry. Now the just shall live by faith.

Gradual. The righteous cry, and the Lord heareth them: and delivereth them out of all their troubles. ℣. The Lord is nigh unto them that are of a contrite heart: and will save such as be of an humble spirit.

Alleluia. Alleluia, alleluia. ℣. The noble army of Martyrs praise thee, O Lord. Alleluia.

¶ In Septuagesimatide or Lent, replacing the Alleluia:

Tract. They that sow in tears, shall reap in joy. ℣. He that now goeth on his way weeping, and beareth forth good seed. ℣. Shall doubtless come again with joy, and bring his sheaves with him.

Common of Saints *Martyrs III*

Gospel. Luke 12:1

AT THAT TIME: Jesus said unto his disciples: Beware ye of the leaven of the Pharisees, which is hypocrisy. For there is nothing covered, that shall not be revealed; neither hid, that shall not be known. Therefore whatsoever ye have spoken in darkness shall be heard in the light; and that which ye have spoken in the ear in closets shall be proclaimed upon the housetops. And I say unto you my friends, Be not afraid of them that kill the body, and after that have no more that they can do. But I will forewarn you whom ye shall fear: Fear him, which after he hath killed hath power to cast into hell; yea, I say unto you, Fear him. Are not five sparrows sold for two farthings, and not one of them is forgotten before God? But even the very hairs of your head are all numbered. Fear not therefore: ye are of more value than many sparrows. Also I say unto you, Whosoever shall confess me before men, him shall the Son of man also confess before the angels of God.

¶ After Spetuagesima, Alleluia at the end of the following Offertory is omitted.

Offertory. The souls of the just are in the hand of God, and there shall no torment of malice touch them: in the sight of the unwise they seemed to die: but they are in peace, alleluia.

Secret

E beseech thee mercifully to accept these our oblations: that at the intercession of thy holy Martyrs *N. and N.* we may be defended against all adversities. Through.

Communion. What I tell you in darkness, that speak ye in light, saith the Lord: and what ye hear in the ear, that preach ye upon the housetops.

Postcommunion

AY this communion, O Lord, cleanse us from guilt: and at the intercession of thy holy Martyrs *N. and N.* make us partakers of thy heavenly healing. Through.

¶ The following Epistles and Gospel may be used instead of the ones provided above.

1. Epistle. Wisdom 10:17

WISDOM rendered unto holy men a reward of their toils; She guided them along a marvellous way, And became unto them a covering in the day-time, And a flame of stars through the night. She brought them over the Red sea, And led them through much water; But their enemies she drowned, And out of the bottom of the deep she cast them up. Therefore the righteous spoiled the ungodly; And they sang praise to thy holy name, O Lord, And extolled with one accord thy hand that fought for them, O Lord our God.

Martyrs III   # Common of Saints

2. *Epistle.* Romans 5:1

BRETHREN: Being justified by faith, we have peace with God through our Lord Jesus Christ: by whom also we have access by faith into this grace wherein we stand, and rejoice in hope of the glory of God. And not only so, but we glory in tribulations also: knowing that tribulation worketh patience; and patience, experience; and experience, hope: and hope maketh not ashamed; because the love of God is shed abroad in our hearts by the Holy Ghost which is given unto us.

3. *Epistle.* Romans 8:18

BRETHREN: I reckon that the sufferings of this present time are not worthy to be compared with the glory which shall be revealed in us. For the earnest expectation of the creature waiteth for the manifestation of the sons of God. For the creature was made subject to vanity, not willingly, but by reason of him who hath subjected the same in hope, because the creature itself also shall be delivered from the bondage of corruption into the glorious liberty of the children of God. For we know that the whole creation groaneth and travaileth in pain together until now. And not only they, but ourselves also, which have the firstfruits of the Spirit, even we ourselves groan within ourselves, waiting for the adoption, to wit, the redemption of our body: in Christ Jesus our Lord.

4. *Epistle.* 2 Corinthians 6:4

BRETHREN: Let us approve ourselves as the ministers of God, in much patience, in afflictions, in necessities, in distresses, in stripes, in imprisonments, in tumults, in labours, in watchings, in fastings; by pureness, by knowledge, by longsuffering, by kindness, by the Holy Ghost, by love unfeigned, by the word of truth, by the power of God, by the armour of righteousness on the right hand and on the left, by honour and dishonour, by evil report and good report: as deceivers, and yet true; as unknown, and yet well known; as dying, and, behold, we live; as chastened, and not killed; as sorrowful, yet alway rejoicing; as poor, yet making many rich; as having nothing, and yet possessing all things.

5. *Epistle.* Hebrews 11:33

BRETHREN: The saints through faith subdued kingdoms, wrought righteousness, obtained promises, stopped the mouths of lions, quenched the violence of fire, escaped the edge of the sword, out of weakness were made strong, waxed valiant in fight, turned to flight the armies of the aliens: women received their dead raised to life again: and others were tortured, not accepting deliverance, that they might obtain a better resurrection: and others had trial of cruel mockings and scourgings, yea, moreover of bonds and imprisonment: they were stoned, they were sawn asunder, were tempted, were slain with the sword: they wandered about in sheepskins and goat-skins, being destitute, afflicted, tormented:

Common of Saints — *Martyrs III*

(of whom the world was not worthy;) they wandered in deserts, and ia mountains, and in dens and caves of the earth. And these all obtained a good report through faith, and were found in Christ Jesus our Lord.

6. Epistle. Revelation 7:13

IN THOSE DAYS: One of the elders answered, saying unto me, What are these which are arrayed in white robes? and whence came they? And I said unto him, Sir, thou knowest. And he said to me, These are they which came out of great tribulation, and have washed their robes, and made them white in the blood of the Lamb. Therefore are they before the throne of God, and serve him day and night in his temple: and he that sitteth on the throne shall dwell among them. They shall hunger no more, neither thirst any more; neither shall the sun light on them, nor any heat. For the Lamb which is in the midst of the throne shall feed them, and shall lead them unto living fountains of waters: and God shall wipe away all tears from their eyes.

1. Gospel. Matthew 24:3

AT THAT TIME: As Jesus sat upon the mount of Olives, the disciples came unto him privately, saying: Tell us, when shall these things be? and what shall be the sign of thy coming, and of the end of the world? And Jesus answered and said unto them, Take heed that no man deceive you. For many shall come in my name, saying, I am Christ; and shall deceive many. And ye shall hear of wars and rumours of wars: see that ye be not troubled: for all these things must come to pass, but the end is not yet. For nation shall rise against nation, and kingdom against kingdom: and there shall be famines, and pestilences, and earthquakes, in divers places. All these are the beginning of sorrows.

Then shall they deliver you up to be afflicted, and shall kill you: and ye shall be hated of all nations for my name's sake. And then shall many be offended, and shall betray one another, and shall hate one another. And many false prophets shall rise, and shall deceive many. And because iniquity shall abound, the love of many shall wax cold. But he that shall endure unto the end, the same shall be saved.

2. Gospel. Matthew 5:1

AT THAT TIME: Jesus, seeing the multitudes, went up into a mountain, and when he was set, his disciples came unto him, and he opened mouth, and taught them, saying: Blessed are the poor in spirit: for theirs is the kingdom of heaven. Blessed are they that mourn: for they shall be comforted. Blessed are the meek: for they shall inherit the earth. Blessed are they which do hunger and thirst after righteousness: for they shall be filled. Blessed are the merciful: for they shall obtain mercy. Blessed are the pure in heart: for they shall see God. Blessed are the peacemakers: for they shall be called the children of God. Blessed are they which are persecuted for righteousness' sake: for theirs is the kingdom of heaven. Blessed are ye, when men shall revile you, and persecute you, and shall say all manner of evil against you falsely, for my sake. Rejoice, and be exceeding glad: for great is your reward in heaven.

3. Gospel. Matthew 11:25

At that time: Jesus answered and said: I thank thee, O Father, Lord of heaven and earth, because thou hast hid these things from the wise and prudent, and hast revealed them unto babes. Even so, Father: for so it seemed good in thy sight. All things are delivered unto me of my Father: and no man knoweth the Son, but the Father; neither knoweth any man the Father, save the Son, and he to whomsoever the Son will reveal him.

Come unto me, all ye that labour and are heavy laden, and I will give you rest. Take my yoke upon you, and learn of me; for I am meek and lowly in he art: and ye shall find rest unto your souls. For my yoke is easy, and my burden is light.

4. Gospel. Luke 11:47

At that time: Jesus said unto the scribes and Pharisees: Woe unto you! for ye build the sepulchres of the prophets, and your fathers killed them. Truly ye bear witness that ye allow the deeds of your fathers: for they indeed killed them, and ye build their sepulchres. Therefore also said the wisdom of God, I will send them prophets and apostles, and some of them they shall slay and persecute: that the blood of all the prophets, which was shed from the foundation of the world, may be required of this generation; from the blood of Abel unto the blood of Zacharias, which perished between the altar and the temple: verily I say unto you, It shall be required of this generation.

5. Gospel. Luke 10:16

At that time: Jesus said unto his disciples: He that heareth you heareth me; and he that despiseth you despiseth me; and he that despiseth me despiseth him that sent me. And the seventy returned again with joy, saying, Lord, even the devils are subject unto us through thy name. And he said unto them, I beheld Satan as lightning fall from heaven. Behold, I give unto you power to tread on serpents and scorpions, and over all the power of the enemy: and nothing shall by any means hurt you. Notwithstanding in this rejoice not, that the spirits are subject unto you; but rather rejoice, because your names are written in heaven.

Common of Saints   *Martyr in Easter*

Commons for Martyrs in Eastertide

COMMON OF ONE MARTYR IN EASTERTIDE

¶ Daily Office Antiphons & Versicles as in the Common of Apostles in Eastertide (p. 673), with the following Hymns.

I Evensong

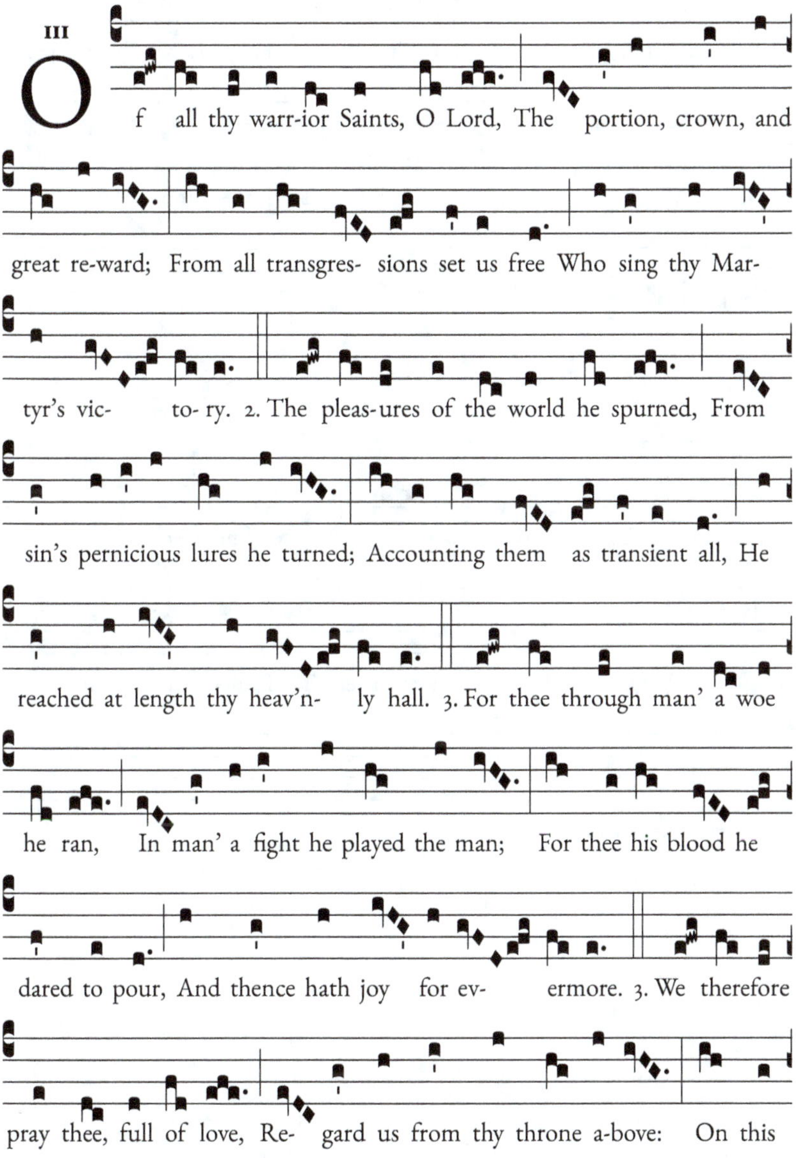

O f all thy warr-ior Saints, O Lord, The portion, crown, and great re-ward; From all transgres- sions set us free Who sing thy Mar- tyr's vic- to- ry. 2. The pleas-ures of the world he spurned, From sin's pernicious lures he turned; Accounting them as transient all, He reached at length thy heav'n- ly hall. 3. For thee through man' a woe he ran, In man' a fight he played the man; For thee his blood he dared to pour, And thence hath joy for ev- ermore. 3. We therefore pray thee, full of love, Re- gard us from thy throne a-bove: On this

Martyr in Easter   # Common of Saints

thy Mar- tyr's tri- umph day, Wash every stain of sin a-way.

¶ From Low Sunday, exclusive, until Ascension Thursday, exclusive:

4. To thee who, dead, a- gain dost live, All glor-y, Lord, thy people give; All glor-y, as is e-ver meet, To Father and to Par- a-clete. A- men.

¶ From Ascension Thursday, inclusive, until Whitsunday, inclusive:

4. All glo- ry, Lord, to thee we pay, As- cending o'er the stars to-day; All glo-ry, as is ev-er meet, To Father and to Par- a-clete. A- men.

Common of Saints *Martyr in Easter*

Mattins

¶ The Invitatory Hymn is of I Evensong.

Office Hymn

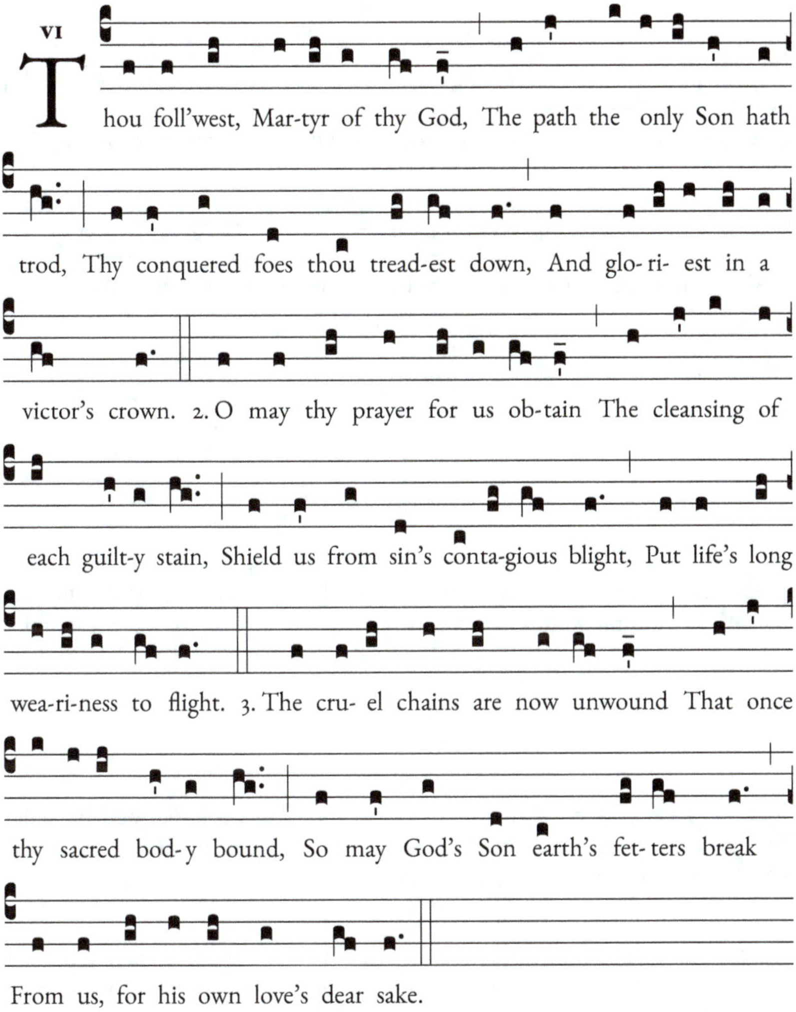

Thou foll'west, Mar-tyr of thy God, The path the only Son hath trod, Thy conquered foes thou tread-est down, And glo-ri-est in a victor's crown. 2. O may thy prayer for us ob-tain The cleansing of each guilt-y stain, Shield us from sin's conta-gious blight, Put life's long wea-ri-ness to flight. 3. The cru-el chains are now unwound That once thy sacred bod-y bound, So may God's Son earth's fet-ters break From us, for his own love's dear sake.

¶ From Low Sunday, exclusive, until Ascension Thursday, exclusive:

4. To thee who, dead, a-gain dost live, All glo-ry, Lord, thy people give;

Martyr in Easter # Common of Saints

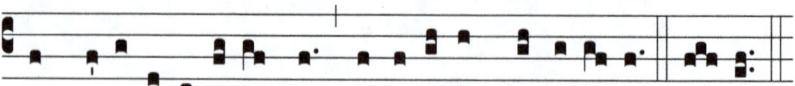

All glo-ry, as is ev-er meet, To Father and to Par-a-clete. A-men.

⁋ From Ascension Thursday, inclusive, until Whitsunday, inclusive:

4. All glo-ry, Lord, to thee we pay, Ascending o'er the stars to-day;

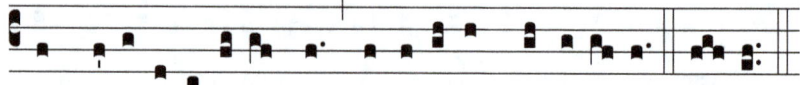

All glo-ry, as is ev-er meet, To Father and to Par-a-clete. A-men.

II Evensong

⁋ The Office Hymn is of I Evensong.

Introit

THOU hast hidden me, O God, from the gathering together of the froward, alleluia: and from the insurrection of the wicked doers, alleluia, alleluia. *Ps.* Hear my voice, O God, in my prayer: preserve my life from fear of the enemy.

Collect

Martyr not Bishop

GRANT, we beseech thee, Almighty God: that we, who devoutly celebrate the birthday of blessed *N.*, thy Martyr; may by his intercession be stablished in the love of thy name. Through.

or

GRANT, we beseech thee, Almighty God: that at the intercession of blessed *N.* thy Martyr, we may both be delivered from all adversities which may happen to the body, and from all evil thoughts which may assault and hurt the soul. Through.

Martyr Bishop

ALMIGHTY God, mercifully look upon our infirmities: that whereas we are oppressed by the burden of our sins, the glorious intercession of blessed *N.* thy Martyr and Bishop may be our succour and defence. Through.

or

Common of Saints *Martyr in Easter*

O GOD, who makest us glad with the yearly solemnity of blessed *N.*, thy Martyr and Bishop: mercifully grant; that as we now devoutly celebrate his birthday, so we may likewise rejoice in his protection. Through.

Epistle. Wisdom 5:1

THE righteous man shall stand in great boldness Before the face of them that afflicted him, And them that make his labours of no account. When they see it, they shall be troubled with terrible fear, And shall be amazed at the marvel of God's salvation. They shall say within themselves repenting, And for distress of spirit shall they groan, This was he whom aforetime we had in derision, And made a parable of reproach: We fools accounted his life madness, And his end without honour: How was he numbered among sons of God? And how is his lot among saints?

¶ The Epistle from the Third Common of One Martyr not a Bishop out of Eastertide (2 Timothy 2:8) may be said instead.

Alleluia. Alleluia, alleluia. ℣. O Lord, the very heavens shall praise thy wondrous works: and thy truth in the congregation of the saints. Alleluia. ℣. Thou hast set, O Lord, a crown of pure gold upon his head. Alleluia.

Gospel. John 15:1

AT THAT TIME: Jesus said unto his disciples: I am the true vine, and my Father is the husbandman. Every branch in me that beareth not fruit he taketh away: and every branch that beareth fruit, he purgeth it, that it may bring forth more fruit. Now ye are clean through the word which I have spoken unto you. Abide in me, and I in you. As the branch cannot bear fruit of itself, except it abide in the vine; no more can ye, except ye abide in me. I am the vine, ye are the branches: He that abideth in me, and I in him, the same bringeth forth much fruit: for without me ye can do nothing. If a man abide not in me, he is cast forth as a branch, and is withered; and men gather them, and cast them into the fire, and they are burned. If ye abide in me, and my words abide in you, ye shall ask what ye will, and it shall be done unto you.

Offertory. O Lord, the very heavens shall praise thy wondrous works: and thy truth in the congregation of the saints, alleluia, alleluia.

Secret

Martyr not Bishop

WE beseech thee, O Lord, accept our prayers and oblations: and graciously hearken unto us whom thou dost cleanse by thy heavenly mysteries. Through.

or

GRANT, O Lord, that our bounden service may be acceptable in thy sight: that these our oblations may, by the prayers of him on whose solemnity they are offered, be made profitable unto our salvation. Through.

Martyr in Easter   # Common of Saints

Martyr Bishop

E beseech thee, O Lord, mercifully to accept this our sacrifice, which we offer unto thee pleading the merits of blessed *N.*, thy Martyr and Bishop: that the same may effectually avail for our perpetual succour. Through.

or

ANCTIFY, O Lord, the gifts which we dedicate to thee: that at the intercession of blessed *N.*, thy Martyr and Bishop, they may obtain for us thy gracious favour. Through,

Communion. The righteous shall rejoice in the Lord, and put his trust in him: and all they that are true of heart shall be glad, alleluia, alleluia.

Postcommunion

Martyr not Bishop

RANT, we beseech thee, O Lord our God: that like as we in this life do gladly honour the memory of thy Saints; so we may rejoice to behold them for ever. Through.

or

E beseech thee, O Lord our God: that like as we, whom thou hast refreshed by the partaking of thy sacred gift, do offer unto thee our worship; so by the intercession of blessed *N.*, thy Martyr, we may perceive the benefit of the same. Through.

Martyr Bishop

E beseech thee, O Lord our God, that like as we, whom thou hast refreshed by the partaking of thy sacred gift, do offer unto thee our worship: so by the intercession of blessed *N.*, thy Martyr and Bishop, we may perceive the benefit of the same. Through.

or

AY this communion, O Lord, cleanse us from guilt: and, at the intercession of blessed *N.*, thy Martyr and Bishop, make us partakers of thy heavenly healing. Through,

¶ The first Epistle and the Gospel of the above Mass may be said also in the following Mass, and those in the following may be said in the above, provided a special Epistle or Gospel is not appointed.

Common of Saints *Martyrs in Easter*

COMMON OF MANY MARTYRS IN EASTERTIDE

¶ Daily Office Antiphons & Versicles as in the Common of Apostles in Eastertide (p. 673), with the following Hymns.

I Evensong

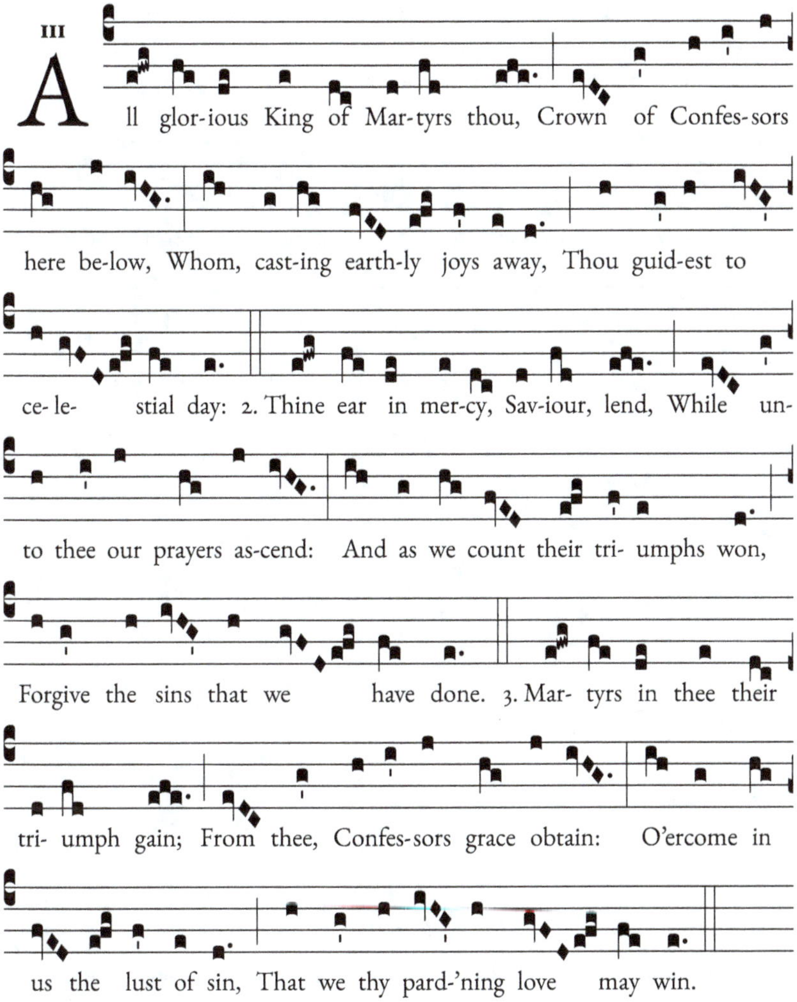

All glorious King of Martyrs thou, Crown of Confessors here below, Whom, casting earthly joys away, Thou guidest to celestial day: 2. Thine ear in mercy, Saviour, lend, While unto thee our prayers ascend: And as we count their triumphs won, Forgive the sins that we have done. 3. Martyrs in thee their triumph gain; From thee, Confessors grace obtain: O'ercome in us the lust of sin, That we thy pard'ning love may win.

¶ From Low Sunday, exclusive, until Ascension Thursday, exclusive:

4. To thee who, dead, again dost live, All glory, Lord, thy people

Martyrs in Easter   # Common of Saints

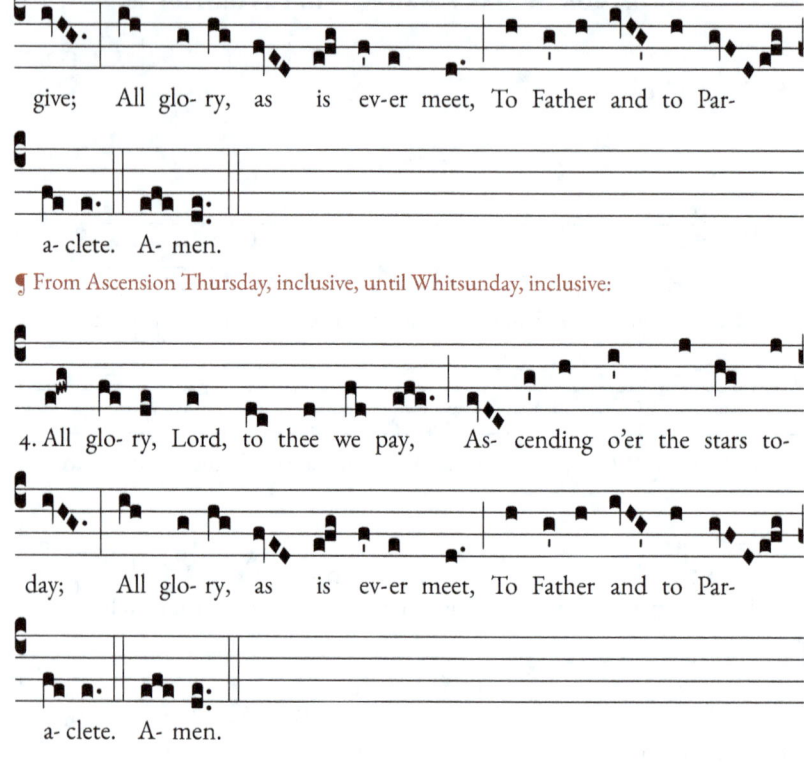

give; All glo-ry, as is ev-er meet, To Father and to Par-a-clete. A-men.

¶ From Ascension Thursday, inclusive, until Whitsunday, inclusive:

4. All glo-ry, Lord, to thee we pay, As-cending o'er the stars to-day; All glo-ry, as is ev-er meet, To Father and to Par-a-clete. A-men.

Mattins

¶ The Invitatory Hymn is from the First Common of Many Martyrs (p. 692).

¶ The Office Hymn is as in I Evensong.

II Evensong

¶ The Office Hymn is as in I Evensong.

Introit

THY saints give thanks unto thee, O Lord: they shew the glory of thy kingdom, alleluia, alleluia. *Ps.* I will magnify thee, O God, my King: and I will praise thy name for ever and ever.

Common of Saints   *Martyrs in Easter*

Collect

Many Martyrs not Bishops

GOD, who vouchsafest unto us to celebrate the birthday of thy holy Martyrs *N. and N.*: grant that we may rejoice in the everlasting felicity of their fellowship. Through.

or

GOD, who makest us glad with the yearly solemnity of thy holy Martyrs *N. and N.*: mercifully grant that as we rejoice in their merits, so we may be enkindled by their example. Through.

Martyrs Bishops

ROTECT us, O Lord, we beseech thee, who observe the feast of thy blessed Martyrs and Bishops *N. and N.*: and grant that by their meritorious supplication we may ever find favour in thy sight. Through.

Epistle. 1 Peter 1:3

LESSED be the God and Father of our Lord Jesus Christ, which according to his abundant mercy hath begotten us again unto a lively hope by the resurrection of Jesus Christ from the dead, to an inheritance incorruptible, and undefiled, and that fadeth not away, reserved in heaven for you, who are kept by the power of God through faith unto salvation ready to be revealed in the last time. Wherein ye greatly rejoice, though now for a season, if need be, ye are in heaviness through manifold temptations: that the trial of your faith, being much more precious than of gold that perisheth, though it be tried with fire, might be found unto praise and honour and glory at the appearing of Jesus Christ our Lord.

Alleluia. Alleluia, alleluia. ℣. Thy saints, O Lord, shall grow as the lily, and as the odour of balsam shall they be before thee. Alleluia. ℣. Right dear in the sight of the Lord is the death of his saints. Alleluia.

Gospel. John 15:5

T THAT TIME: Jesus said unto his disciples: I am the vine, ye are the branches: He that abideth in me, and I in him, the same bringeth forth much fruit: for without me ye can do nothing. If a man abide not in me, he is cast forth as a branch, and is withered; and men gather them, and cast them into the fire, and they are burned. If ye abide in me, and my words abide in you, ye shall ask what ye will, and it shall be done unto you. Herein is my Father glorified, that ye bear much fruit; so shall ye be my disciples. As the Father hath loved me, so have I loved you: continue ye in my love. If ye keep my commandments, ye shall abide in my love; even as I have kept my Father's commandments, and abide in his love. These things have I spoken unto you, that my joy might remain in you, and that your joy might be full.

Offertory. Be glad, O ye righteous, and rejoice in the Lord: and be joyful, all ye that are true of heart, alleluia, alleluia.

Martyrs in Easter # Common of Saints

Secret

Martyrs not Bishops

E beseech thee, O Lord, that the gifts which we offer unto thee of our bounden duty and service may be acceptable unto thee for the honour of thy Just ones: and by thy mercy profitable unto us for our salvation. Through.

or

E beseech thee, O Lord, mercifully to accept these our oblations: that at the intercession of thy holy Martyrs *N. and N.* we may be defended against all adversities. Through.

Martyrs Bishops

SSIST us mercifully, O Lord, in these our supplications, which we make before thee in remembrance of thy Saints: that we who trust not in our own righteousness may be succoured by the merits of them that have found favour in thy sight. Through.

Communion. Rejoice in the Lord, O ye righteous, alleluia: for it becometh well the just to be thankful, alleluia.

Postcommunion

Martyrs not Bishops

RANT to us, we beseech thee, O Lord: at the intercession of thy holy Martyrs *N. and N.*; that those things which we touch with the mouth, we may receive in purity of heart. Through.

or

AY this communion, O Lord, cleanse us from guilt: and, at the intercession of thy holy Martyrs *N. and N.*, make us partakers of thy heavenly healing. Through.

Martyrs Bishops

LORD, who hast fulfilled us with saving mysteries: we beseech thee that we may be aided by the prayers of those whose festival we celebrate. Through.

¶ The following Epistle and Gospel may be used instead of the ones provided above.

Another Epistle. Revelation 19:1

N THOSE DAYS: After these things I, John, heard a great voice of much people in heaven, saying, Alleluia; Salvation, and glory, and honour, and power, unto the Lord our God: for true and righteous are his judgments: for he hath judged the great whore, which did corrupt the earth with her fornication, and hath avenged the blood of his servants at her hand. And again they said, Alleluia. And her smoke rose up for ever and ever. And the four and twenty elders and the

Common of Saints *Confessor Bishop I*

four beasts fell down and worshipped God that sat on the throne, saying, Amen; Alleluia.

And a voice came out of the throne, saying, Praise our God, all ye his servants, and ye that fear him, both small and great. And I heard as it were the voice of a great multitude, and as the voice of many waters, and as the voice of mighty thunderings, saying, Alleluia: for the Lord God omnipotent reigneth. Let us be glad and rejoice, and give honour to him: for the marriage of the Lamb is come, and his wife hath made herself ready. And to her was granted that she should be arrayed in fine linen, clean and white: for the fine linen is the righteousness of saints.

And he saith unto me, Write, Blessed are they which are called unto the marriage supper of the Lamb.

Another Gospel. John 16:20

AT THAT TIME: Jesus said unto his disciples: Verily, verily, I say unto you, That ye shall weep and lament, but the world shall rejoice: and ye shall be sorrowful, but your sorrow shall be turned into joy. A woman when she is in travail hath sorrow, because her hour is come: but as soon as she is delivered of the child, she remembereth no more the anguish, for joy that a man is born into the world. And ye now therefore have sorrow: but I will see you again, and your heart shall rejoice, and your joy no man taketh from you.

¶ In the Common of Confessors, and Virgins, and in other Masses of Eastertide, all is said as in the rest of the year, a double Alleluia being added in the Introit before the Psalm, and at the end of the Offertory and Communion one Alleluia, where it is not given; and the Gradual being omitted, two ℣℣. are said with four Alleluias, as is set down in their places.

Commons for a Confessor Bishop

I: COMMON OF A CONFESSOR BISHOP

I Evensong

This the Confes-sor of the Lord, whose tri- umph Now through the wide world cel- ebrate the faith- ful, Mer- i- ted this day joy-ful-ly to en-ter Heav- en-ly mansions. 2. Saint- ly and pru-

Confessor Bishop I ## Common of Saints

dent, conti-nent and humble, Chaste was he ev- er, peaceable and so-ber, While liv- ing vig- our, cours-ing through his bod-y, Quick- en'd his be- ing. 3. When to his honour'd sep-ulchre, with members Languish-ing sorely, suf-fer-ers re-sort- ed, Oft un- to whole-ness did the Lord re-store them At his pe-ti- tion. 4. Where- fore our cho-rus chanteth in his honour Here, on his feast-day, this most will-ing an-them; That in his mer- its we may have our por-tion Now and for ev-er. 5. His be the glo-ry, pow-er, and sal-va-tion, Who, o'er the heav-ens, dwell-ing in the high- est, Earth's might-y fab-ric rul-eth and di-rect-eth, One-ly and Tri-nal. A- men.

Common of Saints *Confessor Bishop I*

℣. The Lord loved him and adorned him.
℟. He clothed him with a robe of glory.
Mag. Ant. O thou Priest and Bishop, † thou worker of mighty works, thou good shepherd of the people, pray unto the Lord for us.

Mattins

¶ The Invitatory Hymn is from I Evensong.

Office Hymn

IV

Je-su, the world's Re-deemer, hear; Thy Bish-op's fade- less Crown, draw near: Accept with gentl- est love to-day The prayers and prais- es that we pay. 2. This meek Confes-sor of thy Name To-day attain'd a glorious fame; Whose yearly feast, in sol- emn state, Thy faithful peo- ple cel- e- brate. 3. The world and all its boasted good, As vain and pass- ing, he eschew'd; And therefore with An- gel- ic bands In endless joy for ev-er stands. 4. Grant then that we, most gracious God, May follow in the steps he trod: And at his prayer thy servants

Confessor Bishop I   # Common of Saints

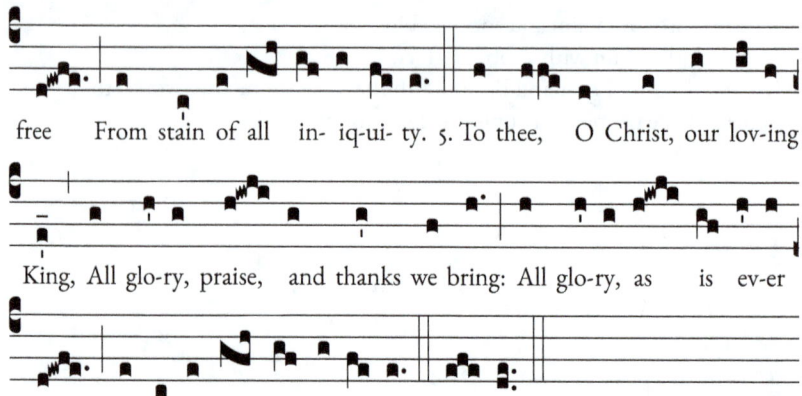

free From stain of all in-iq-ui-ty. 5. To thee, O Christ, our lov-ing King, All glo-ry, praise, and thanks we bring: All glo-ry, as is ev-er meet, To Father and to Par-a-clete. A-men.

℣. The Lord guided the righteous in right paths.
℟. And shewed him the kingdom of God.

Ben. Ant. Well done, † thou good and faithful servant: thou hast been faithful over a few things, I will make thee ruler over many things, saith the Lord.

II Evensong

¶ The Office Hymn is of I Evensong, and the Versicle is of Mattins, with the following Antiphon.

Mag. Ant. I will liken him † unto a wise man, which built his house upon a rock.

Introit

THE Lord hath established a covenant of peace with him, and made him a prince: that he should have the dignity of the priesthood for ever (Alleluia, alleluia). *Ps.* Lord, remember David: and all his trouble.

Collect

GRANT, we beseech thee, Almighty God: that the venerable solemnity of blessed N., thy Confessor and Bishop may increase our devotion and set forward our salvation. Through.

Epistle. Ecclesiasticus 44:16

ENOCH pleased the Lord, and was translated, Being an example of repentance to all generations. Noah was found perfect and righteous; In the season of wrath he was taken in exchange for the world; Therefore was there left a remnant unto the earth, When the flood came. Everlasting covenants were made with him, That all flesh should no more be blotted out by a flood. Abraham was a great father of a multitude of nations; And there was none found like him in glory; Who kept the law of the Most High, And was taken into covenant with him: In his flesh he established the covenant; And when he was proved, he was found faithful.

Common of Saints *Confessor Bishop I*

Therefore he assured him by an oath, That the nations should be blessed in his seed; That he would multiply him as the dust of the earth, And exalt his seed as the stars, And cause them to inherit from sea to sea, And from the River unto the utmost part of the earth. In Isaac also did he establish likewise, for Abraham his father's sake, The blessing of all men, and the covenant: And he made it rest upon the head of Jacob; He acknowledged him in his blessings, And gave to him by inheritance, And divided his portions; Among twelve tribes did he part them. And he brought out of him a man of mercy, Which found favour in the sight of all flesh.

Gradual. Behold, a great priest, who in his days pleased God. ℣. There was none found like unto him who kept the law of the Most High.

Alleluia. Alleluia, alleluia. ℣. Thou art a Priest for ever after the order of Melchisedech. Alleluia.

¶ In Septuagesimatide or Lent, replacing the Alleluia:

Tract. Blessed is the man that feareth the Lord: he hath great delight in his commandments. ℣. His seed shall be mighty upon earth: the generation of the faithful shall be blessed. ℣. Riches and plenteousness shall be in his house: and his righteousness endureth for ever.

¶ In Eastertide, replacing the Lesser Alleluia:

Alleluia. Alleluia, alleluia. ℣. Thou art a priest for ever after the order of Melchisedech, alleluia. ℣. This is a priest whom the Lord hath crowned. Alleluia.

Gospel. Matthew 25:14

AT THAT TIME: Jesus spake this parable unto his disciples: A man travelling into a far country, called his own servants, and delivered unto them his goods. And unto one he gave five talents, to another two, and to another one; to every man according to his several ability; and straightway took his journey. Then he that had received the five talents went and traded with the same, and made them other five talents. And likewise he that had received two, he also gained other two. But he that had received one went and digged in the earth, and hid his lord's money. After a long time the lord of those servants cometh, and reckoneth with them. And so he that had received five talents came and brought other five talents, saying, Lord, thou deliveredst unto me five talents: behold, I have gained beside them five talents more. His lord said unto him, Well done, thou good and faithful servant: thou hast been faithful over a few things, I will make thee ruler over many things: enter thou into the joy of thy lord. He also that had received two talents came and said, Lord, thou deliveredst unto me two talents: behold, I have gained two other talents beside them. His lord said unto him, Well done, good and faithful servant; thou hast been faithful over a few things, I will make thee ruler over many things: enter thou into the joy of thy lord.

Offertory. I have found David my servant, with my holy oil have I anointed him; my hand shall hold him fast, and my arm shall strengthen him (Alleluia).

Confessor Bishop II   # Common of Saints

Secret

E beseech thee, O Lord, that we, remembering with gladness the merits of thy Saints, may in all places feel the succour of their intercession. Through.

Communion. A faithful and wise steward, whom the lord hath made ruler over his household: to give them their portion of meat in due season (Alleluia).

Postcommunion

RANT, we beseech thee, Almighty God: that we, shewing forth our thankfulness for the gifts which we have received, may, at the intercession of blessed *N.*, thy Confessor and Bishop, obtain yet more abundant mercies. Through.

II: Common of a Confessor Bishop

❡ Daily Office propers are as in the First Common of a Confessor Bishop (p. 715).

Introit

ET thy priests, O Lord, be clothed with righteousness, and let thy saints sing with joyfulness: for thy servant David's sake, turn not away the presence of thine Anointed (Alleluia, alleluia). *Ps.* Lord, remember David: and all his trouble.

Collect

E beseech thee, O Lord, graciously to hear the prayers which we offer unto thee on the solemnity of blessed *N.*, thy Confessor and Bishop: that, like as he was found worthy to do thee faithful service, so by his merits and intercession we may be absolved from all our sins. Through.

Epistle. Hebrews 7:23

RETHREN: They were many priests, because they were not suffered to continue by reason of death: but this man, because he continueth ever, hath an unchangeable priesthood. Wherefore he is able also to save them to the uttermost that come unto God by him, seeing he ever liveth to make intercession for them.

    For such an high priest became us, who is holy, harmless, undefiled, separate from sinners, and made higher than the heavens; who needeth not daily, as those high priests, to offer up sacrifice, first for his own sins, and then for the people's: for this he did once, when he offered up himself, Jesus Christ, our Lord.

Common of Saints *Confessor Bishop II*

Gradual. I will deck her priests with health: and her saints shall rejoice and sing. ℣. There shall I make the horn of David to flourish: I have ordained a lantern for mine Anointed.

Alleluia. Alleluia, alleluia. ℣. The Lord sware, and will not repent: Thou art a priest for ever after the order of Melchisedech. Alleluia.

¶ In Septuagesimatide or Lent, replacing the Alleluia:

Tract. Blessed is the man that feareth the Lord: he hath great delight in his commandments. ℣. His seed shall be mighty upon earth: the generation of the faithful shall be blessed. ℣. Riches and plenteousness shall be in his house: and his righteousness endureth for ever.

¶ In Eastertide, replacing the Lesser Alleluia:

Alleluia. Alleluia, alleluia. ℣. The Lord sware, and will not repent: Thou art a priest for ever after the order of Melchisedech. Alleluia. ℣. The Lord loved him, and adorned him: and clothed him with a robe of glory. Alleluia.

Gospel. Matthew 24:42

AT THAT TIME: Jesus said unto his disciples: Watch, for ye know not what hour your Lord doth come. But know this, that if the goodman of the house had known in what watch the thief would come, he would have watched, and would not have suffered his house to be broken up. Therefore be ye also ready: for in such an hour as ye think not the Son of man cometh. Who then is a faithful and wise servant, whom his lord hath made ruler over his household, to give them meat in due season? Blessed is that servant, whom his lord when he cometh shall find so doing. Verily I say unto you, That he shall make him ruler over all his goods.

Offertory. My truth and my mercy shall be with him: and in my name shall his horn be exalted (Alleluia).

Secret

WE beseech thee, O Lord, that our devout observance of the yearly solemnity of blessed N., thy Confessor and Bishop, may render us acceptable unto thy loving-kindness: that this service of propitiation, which we duly offer, may be profitable unto him for the reward of blessedness, and obtain for us the gifts of thy grace. Through.

Communion. Blessed is the servant, whom the lord when he cometh shall find watching: verily I say unto you, He shall make him ruler over all his goods (Alleluia).

Postcommunion

O GOD, who rewardest the souls of them that put their trust in thee: vouchsafe; that we who keep the solemn festival of blessed N., thy Confessor and Bishop, may by his prayers obtain thy merciful pardon. Through.

Confessor Bishop II # Common of Saints

¶ The following Epistles and Gospels may be used instead of the ones provided above.

1. *Epistle.* Hebrews 5:1

BRETHREN: Every high priest taken from among men is ordained for men in things pertaining to God, that he may offer both gifts and sacrifices for sins: who can have compassion on the ignorant, and on them that are out of the way; for that he himself also is compassed with infirmity. And by reason hereof he ought, as for the people, so also for himself, to offer for sins. And no man taketh this honour unto himself, but he that is called of God, as was Aaron.

2. *Epistle.* Hebrews 13:7

BRETHREN: Remember them which have the rule over you, who have spoken unto you the word of God: whose faith follow, considering the end of their conversation. Jesus Christ the same yesterday, and to day, and for ever. Be not carried about with divers and strange doctrines. For it is a good thing that the heart be established with grace; not with meats, which have not profited them that have been occupied therein.

We have an altar, whereof they have no right to eat which serve the tabernacle. For the bodies of those beasts, whose blood is brought into the sanctuary by the high priest for sin, are burned without the camp. Wherefore Jesus also, that he might sanctify the people with his own blood, suffered without the gate. Let us go forth therefore unto him without the camp, bearing his reproach. For here have we no continuing city, but we seek one to come. By him therefore let us offer the sacrifice of praise to God continually, that is, the fruit of our lips giving thanks to his name. But to do good and to communicate forget not: for with such sacrifices God is well pleased. Obey them that have the rule over you, and submit yourselves: for they watch for your souls, as they that must give account.

1. *Gospel.* Luke 11:33

AT THAT TIME: Jesus said unto his disciples: No man, when he hath lighted a candle, putteth it in a secret place, neither under a bushel, but on a candlestick, that they which come in may see the light. The light of the body is the eye: therefore when thine eye is single, thy whole body also is full of light; but when thine eye is evil, thy body also is full of darkness. Take heed therefore that the light which is in thee be not darkness. If thy whole body therefore be full of light, having no part dark, the whole shall be full of light, as when the bright shining of a candle doth give thee light.

2. *Gospel.* Mark 13:33

AT THAT TIME: Jesus said unto his disciples: Take ye heed, watch and pray: for ye know not when the time is. For the Son of man is as a man taking a far journey, who left his house, and gave authority to his servants, and

Common of Saints — *Doctors*

to every man his work, and commanded the porter to watch. Watch ye therefore: for ye know not when the master of the house cometh, at even, or at midnight, or at the cockcrowing, or in the morning: lest coming suddenly he find you sleeping. And what I say unto you I say unto all, Watch.

Common of Doctors

¶ The Daily Office propers are from the closest relevant Common, except for the **Magnificat Antiphon**, as followeth.

Mag. Ant. O Teacher right excellent, † O light of Holy Church, O blessed *N*., lover of the divine law: intercede for us unto the Son of God.

Introit

IN the midst of the Church he opened his mouth: and the Lord filled him with the spirit of wisdom and of understanding: and clothed him with a robe of glory. (Alleluia, alleluia.) *Ps.* It is a good thing to give thanks unto the Lord: and to sing praises unto thy name, O most Highest.

Collect

O GOD, who didst give blessed *N*. unto thy people to be a minister of everlasting salvation: grant, we beseech thee; that as we have learned of him the doctrine of life on earth, so we may be found worthy to have him for our advocate in heaven. Through.

Epistle. 2 Timothy 4:1

DEARLY BELOVED: I charge thee therefore before God, and the Lord Jesus Christ, who shall judge the quick and the dead at his appearing and his kingdom; preach the word; be instant in season, out of season; reprove, rebuke, exhort with all longsuffering and doctrine. For the time will come when they will not endure sound doctrine; but after their own lusts shall they heap to themselves teachers, having itching ears; and they shall turn away their ears from the truth, and shall be turned unto fables. But watch thou in all things, endure afflictions, do the work of an evangelist, make full proof of thy ministry.

For I am now ready to be offered, and the time of my departure is at hand. I have fought a good fight, I have finished my course, I have kept the faith: henceforth there is laid up for me a crown of righteousness, which the Lord, the righteous judge, shall give me at that day: and not to me only, but unto all them also that love his appearing.

Gradual. The mouth of the righteous is exercised in wisdom, and his tongue will be talking of judgment. ℣. The law of his God is in his heart: and his goings shall not slide.

Doctors   # Common of Saints

Alleluia. Alleluia, alleluia. ℣. The Lord loved him, and adorned him: and clothed him with a robe of glory. Alleluia.

¶ In Septuagesimatide or Lent, replacing the Alleluia:

Tract. Blessed is the man that feareth the Lord: he hath great delight in his commandments. ℣. His seed shall be mighty upon earth: the generation of the faithful shall be blessed. ℣. Riches and plenteousness shall be in his house: and his righteousness endureth for ever.

¶ In Eastertide, replacing the Lesser Alleluia:

Alleluia. Alleluia, alleluia. ℣. The Lord loved him, and adorned him: and clothed him with a robe of glory. Alleluia. ℣. The righteous shall grow as the lily; and flourish for ever before the Lord. Alleluia.

Gospel. Matthew 5:13

AT THAT TIME: Jesus said unto his disciples: Ye are the salt of the earth: but if the salt have lost his savour, wherewith shall it be salted? it is thenceforth good for nothing, but to be cast out, and to be trodden under foot of men. Ye are the light of the world. A city that is set on an hill cannot be hid. Neither do men light a candle, and put it under a bushel, but on a candlestick; and it giveth light unto all that are in the house. Let your light so shine before men, that they may see your good works, and glorify your Father which is in heaven.

Think not that I am come to destroy the law, or the prophets: I am not come to destroy, but to fulfil. For verily I say unto you, Till heaven and earth pass, one jot or one tittle shall in no wise pass from the law, till all be fulfilled. Whosoever therefore shall break one of these least commandments, and shall teach men so, he shall be called the least in the kingdom of heaven: but whosoever shall do and teach them, the same shall be called great in the kingdom of heaven.

Offertory. The righteous shall flourish like a palm-tree: and shall spread abroad like a cedar in Libanus (Alleluia).

Secret

Doctor & Bishop

AY the devout prayers of thy Bishop and Doctor, Saint *N.*, never fail to succour us, O Lord: that they may render our oblations acceptable in thy sight; and may ever obtain for us thy merciful pardon. Through.

Doctor not a Bishop

AY the devout prayers of thy Confessor and Doctor, Saint *N.*, never fail to succour us, O Lord: that they may render our oblations acceptable in thy sight; and may ever obtain for us thy merciful pardon. Through.

Communion. A faithful and wise steward, whom his lord hath made ruler over his household: to give them their portion of meat in due season (Alleluia).

Common of Saints *Confessor not Bishop I*

Postcommunion

Doctor & Bishop

E beseech thee, O Lord, that blessed *N.*, thy Bishop and illustrious Doctor, may stand before thee as our advocate: that these thy sacrifices may avail for our salvation. Through.

Doctor not a Bishop

E beseech thee, O Lord, that blessed *N.*, thy Confessor and illustrious Doctor, may stand before thee as our advocate: that these thy sacrifices may avail for our salvation. Through.

¶ The following Epistle may be used instead of the one provided above.

Another Epistle. Ecclesiasticus 39:5

THE just will apply his heart to resort early to the Lord that made him, And will make supplication before the Most High, And will open his mouth in prayer, And will make supplication for his sins. If the great Lord will, He shall be filled with the spirit of understanding: He shall pour forth the words of his wisdom, And in prayer give thanks unto the Lord. He shall direct his counsel and knowledge, And in his secrets shall he meditate. He shall shew forth the instruction which he hath been taught, And shall glory in the law of the covenant of the Lord. Many shall commend his understanding; And so long as the world endureth, it shall not be blotted out: His memorial shall not depart, And his name shall live from generation to generation. Nations shall declare his wisdom, And the congregation shall tell out his praise.

Commons for a Confessor

I: Common of a Confessor not a Bishop

I Evensong

¶ The Hymn is from the First Common of a Confessor Bishop (p. 715), with the following.

℣. The Lord loved him and adorned him.
℟. He clothed him with a robe of glory.
Mag. Ant. I will liken him † unto a wise man, which built his house upon a rock.

Confessor not Bishop I # Common of Saints

Mattins

¶ The Invitatory Hymn is from I Evensong of the First Common of a Confessor Bishop (p. 715)

Office Hymn

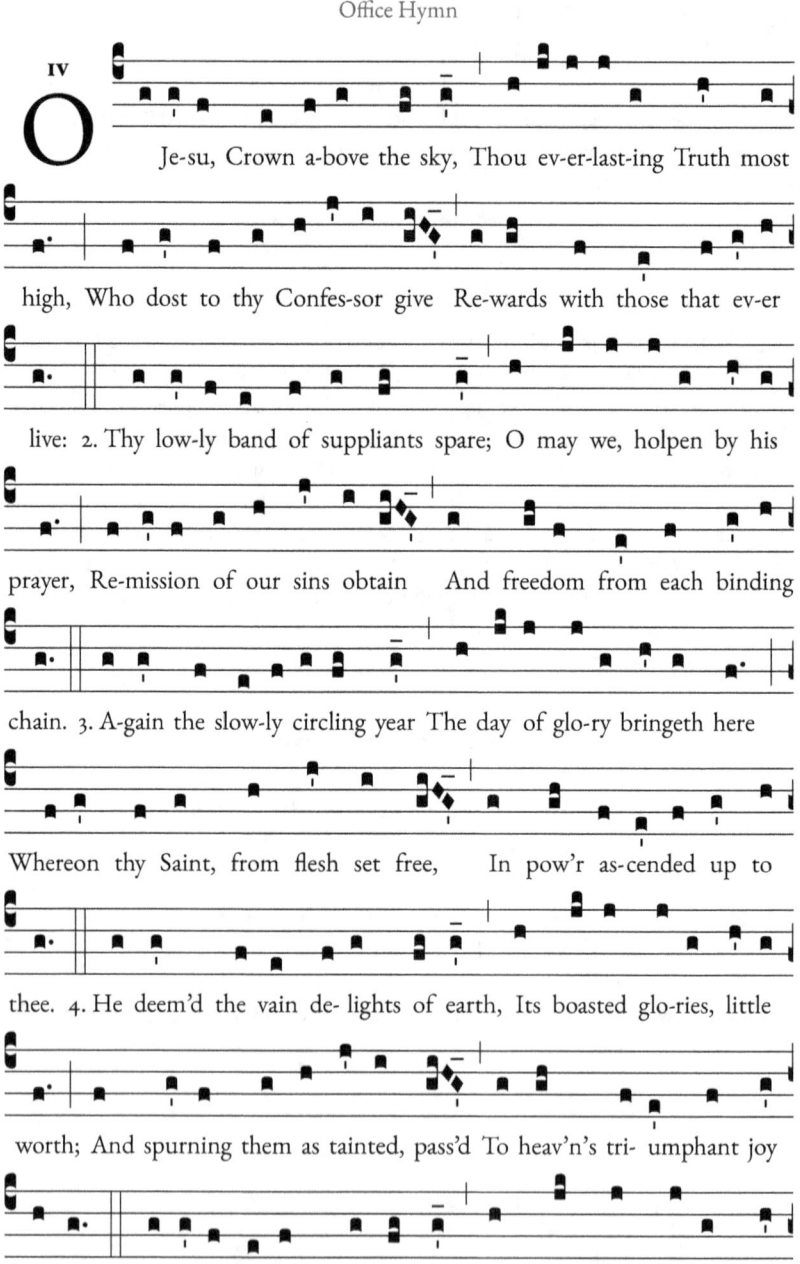

O Je-su, Crown a-bove the sky, Thou ev-er-last-ing Truth most high, Who dost to thy Confes-sor give Re-wards with those that ev-er live: 2. Thy low-ly band of suppliants spare; O may we, holpen by his prayer, Re-mission of our sins obtain And freedom from each binding chain. 3. A-gain the slow-ly circling year The day of glo-ry bringeth here Whereon thy Saint, from flesh set free, In pow'r as-cended up to thee. 4. He deem'd the vain de-lights of earth, Its boasted glo-ries, little worth; And spurning them as tainted, pass'd To heav'n's tri-umphant joy at last. 5. By ev-er owning thee his King, O Christ most gracious, did

Common of Saints *Confessor not Bishop I*

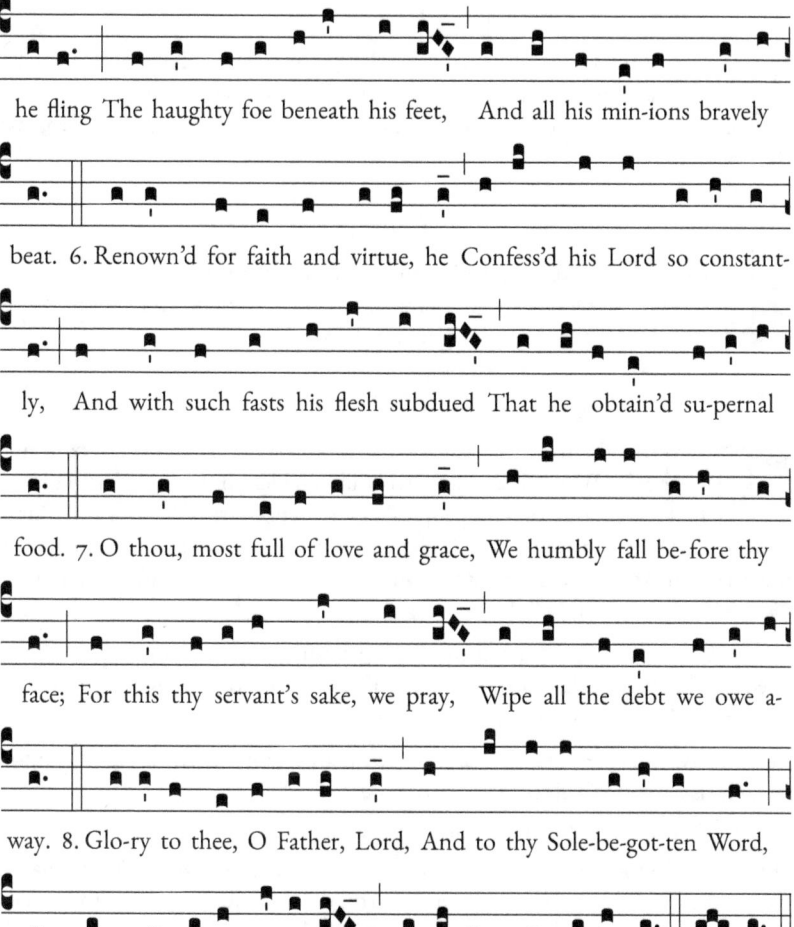

he fling The haughty foe beneath his feet, And all his min-ions bravely beat. 6. Renown'd for faith and virtue, he Confess'd his Lord so constant-ly, And with such fasts his flesh subdued That he obtain'd su-pernal food. 7. O thou, most full of love and grace, We humbly fall be-fore thy face; For this thy servant's sake, we pray, Wipe all the debt we owe a-way. 8. Glo-ry to thee, O Father, Lord, And to thy Sole-be-got-ten Word, Both with the Ho-ly Spir- it One While ev-er-last-ing ag-es run. A- men.

℣. The Lord guided the righteous in right paths.
℟. And shewed him the kingdom of God.

Ben. Ant. Well done, good and faithful servant, † thou hast been faithful over a few things, I will make thee ruler over many things: enter thou into the joy of thy Lord.

II Evensong

¶ The Hymn is from I Evensong of the First Common of a Confessor Bishop (p. 715), with the following.

℣. The Lord guided the righteous in right paths.
℟. And shewed him the kingdom of God.

Mag. Ant. The world, and all things earthly, † this man despised, triumphant: he laid up treasures in heaven by word and deed.

Confessor not Bishop I 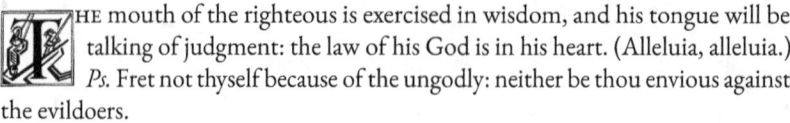 Common of Saints

Introit

THE mouth of the righteous is exercised in wisdom, and his tongue will be talking of judgment: the law of his God is in his heart. (Alleluia, alleluia.) *Ps.* Fret not thyself because of the ungodly: neither be thou envious against the evildoers.

Collect

GOD, who makest us glad with the yearly solemnity of blessed *N.*, thy Confessor: mercifully grant; that, as we now celebrate his birthday, so we may follow the example of his life. Through.

Epistle. Ecclesiasticus 31:8

BLESSED is the man that is found without blemish, And that goeth not after gold. Who is he? and we will call him blessed: For wonderful things hath he done among his people. Who hath been tried thereby, and found perfect? Then let him glory. Who hath had the power to transgress, and hath not transgressed? And to do evil, and hath not done it? His goods shall be made sure, And the congregation shall declare his alms.

Gradual. The righteous shall flourish like a palm-tree: and shall spread abroad like a cedar in Libanus in the house of the Lord. ℣. To tell of thy loving-kindness early in the morning, and of thy truth in the night-season.

Alleluia. Alleluia, alleluia. ℣. Blessed is the man that endureth temptation: for when he is tried, he shall receive the crown of life. Alleluia.

¶ In Septuagesimatide or Lent, replacing the Alleluia:

Tract. Blessed is the man that feareth the Lord: he hath great delight in his commandments. ℣. His seed shall be mighty upon earth: the generation of the faithful shall be blessed. ℣. Riches and plenteousness shall be in his house: and his righteousness endureth for ever.

¶ In Eastertide, replacing the Lesser Alleluia:

Alleluia. Alleluia, alleluia. ℣. Blessed is the man that endureth temptation: for when he is tried, he shall receive the crown of life. Alleluia. ℣. The Lord loved him, and adorned him: and clothed him with a robe of glory. Alleluia.

Gospel. Luke 12:35

AT THAT TIME: Jesus said unto his disciples: Let your loins be girded about, and your lights burning; and ye yourselves like unto men that wait for their lord, when he will return from the wedding; that when he cometh and knocketh, they may open unto him immediately. Blessed are those servants, whom the lord when he cometh shall find watching: verily I say unto you, that he shall gird himself, and make them to sit down to meat, and will come forth and serve them. And if he shall come in the second watch, or come in the third watch,

Common of Saints *Confessor not Bishop II*

and find them so, blessed are those servants. And this know, that if the goodman of the house had known what hour the thief would come, he would have watched, and not have suffered his house to be broken through. Be ye therefore ready also: for the Son of man cometh at an hour when ye think not.

Offertory. My truth and my mercy shall be with him: and in my name shall his horn be exalted (Alleluia).

Secret

GRANT, we beseech thee, O Lord, that we who, trusting in this our sacrifice of praise, do offer it before thee to the honour of thy Saints: may by the same be delivered from all evils both in this life and in that which is to come. Through.

Communion. Blessed is the servant whom the lord when he cometh shall find watching: verily I say unto you, he shall make him ruler over all his goods (Alleluia).

Postcommunion

O LORD, our God, who hast refreshed us with heavenly meat and drink, we humbly beseech thee: that we may be defended by the prayers of him in whose memory we have received the same. Through.

II: Common of a Confessor not a Bishop

¶ Daily Office propers are as in the First Common of a Confessor not a Bishop (p. 725).

Introit

THE just shall flourish like a palm-tree: and shall spread abroad like a cedar in Libanus: planted in the house of the Lord: in the courts of the house of our God. (Alleluia, alleluia.) *Ps.* It is a good thing to give thanks unto the Lord: and to sing praises unto thy name, O most Highest.

Collect

ASSIST us mercifully, O Lord, in these our supplications which we make before thee on the solemnity of blessed *N.*, thy Confessor: that we, who put not our trust in our own righteousness, may be succoured by the prayers of him who found favour in thy sight. Through.

Epistle. 1 Corinthians 4:9

BRETHREN: We are made a spectacle unto the world, and to angels, and to men. We are fools for Christ's sake, but ye are wise in Christ; we are weak, but ye are strong; ye are honourable, but we are despised. Even unto this present hour we both hunger, and thirst, and are naked, and are buffeted, and have

Confessor not Bishop II Common of Saints

no certain dwellingplace; and labour, working with our own hands: being reviled, we bless; being persecuted, we suffer it: being defamed, we intreat: we are made as the filth of the world, and are the offscouring of all things unto this day. I write not these things to shame you, but as my beloved sons I warn you: in Christ Jesus our Lord.

Gradual. The mouth of the righteous is exercised in wisdom, and his tongue will be talking of judgment. ℣. The law of his God is in his heart: and his goings shall not slide.

Alleluia. Alleluia, alleluia. ℣. Blessed is the man that feareth the Lord: he hath great delight in his commandments. Alleluia.

¶ In Septuagesimatide or Lent, replacing the Alleluia:

Tract. Blessed is the man that feareth the Lord: he hath great delight in his commandments. ℣. His seed shall be mighty upon earth: the generation of the faithful shall be blessed. ℣. Riches and plenteousness shall be in his house: and his righteousness endureth for ever.

¶ In Eastertide, replacing the Lesser Alleluia:

Alleluia. Alleluia, alleluia. ℣. Blessed is the man that feareth the Lord: he hath great delight in his commandments. Alleluia. ℣. The righteous shall grow as the lily: and flourish for ever before the Lord. Alleluia.

Gospel. Luke 12:32

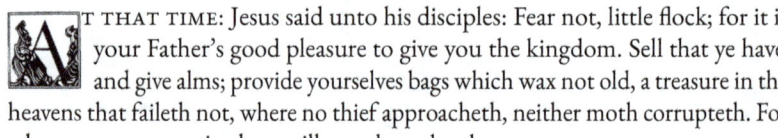T THAT TIME: Jesus said unto his disciples: Fear not, little flock; for it is your Father's good pleasure to give you the kingdom. Sell that ye have, and give alms; provide yourselves bags which wax not old, a treasure in the heavens that faileth not, where no thief approacheth, neither moth corrupteth. For where your treasure is, there will your heart be also.

Offertory. The righteous shall rejoice in thy strength, O Lord, exceeding glad shall he be of thy salvation: thou hast given him his heart's desire (Alleluia).

Secret

RANT to us, we beseech thee, Almighty God: that this oblation of our humble service may be acceptable in thy sight to the honour of thy Saints, and may cleanse us both in body and soul. Through.

Communion. Verily I say unto you: that ye which have forsaken all, and followed me, shall receive an hundredfold, and shall inherit everlasting life (Alleluia).

Postcommunion

E beseech thee, Almighty God: that we, who have received this heavenly food, may at the intercession of blessed *N.*, thy Confessor, be thereby defended against all adversities. Through.

Common of Saints *Confessor not Bishop II*

¶ The following Epistle and Gospel may be used instead of the ones provided above.

Another Epistle. Philippians 3:7

BRETHREN: What things were gain to me, those I counted loss for Christ. Yea doubtless, and I count all things but loss for the excellency of the knowledge of Christ Jesus my Lord: for whom I have suffered the loss of all things, and do count them but dung, that I may win Christ, and be found in him, not having mine own righteousness, which is of the law, but that which is through the faith of Christ, the righteousness which is of God by faith: that I may know him, and the power of his resurrection, and the fellowship of his sufferings, being made conformable unto his death; if by any means I might attain unto the resurrection of the dead. Not as though I had already attained, either were already perfect: but I follow after, if that I may apprehend that for which also I am apprehended of Christ Jesus.

Another Gospel. Luke 19:12

AT THAT TIME: Jesus spake this parable unto his disciples: A certain nobleman went into a far country to receive for himself a kingdom, and to return. And he called his ten servants, and delivered them ten pounds, and said unto them, Occupy till I come. But his citizens hated him, and sent a message after him, saying, We will not have this man to reign over us. And it came to pass, that when he was returned, having received the kingdom, then he commanded these servants to be called unto him, to whom he had given the money, that he might know how much every man had gained by trading. Then came the first, saying, Lord, thy pound hath gained ten pounds. And he said unto him, Well, thou good servant: because thou hast been faithful in a very little, have thou authority over ten cities. And the second came, saying, Lord, thy pound hath gained five pounds. And he said likewise to him, Be thou also over five cities. And another came, saying, Lord, behold, here is thy pound, which I have kept laid up in a napkin: for I feared thee, because thou art an austere man: thou takest up that thou layedst not down, and reapest that thou didst not sow. And he saith unto him, Out of thine own mouth will I judge thee, thou wicked servant. Thou knewest that I was an austere man, taking up that I laid not down, and reaping that I did not sow: wherefore then gavest not thou my money into the bank, that at my coming I might have required mine own with usury? And he said unto them that stood by, Take from him the pound, and give it to him that hath ten pounds. (And they said unto him, Lord, he hath ten pounds.) For I say unto you, That unto every one which hath shall be given; and from him that hath not, even that he hath shall be taken away from him.

Common of Saints

COMMON OF ABBOTS

¶ Daily Office propers are as in the First Common of a Confessor not a Bishop (p. 725).

Introit

THE mouth of the righteous is exercised in wisdom, and his tongue will be talking of judgment: the law of his God is in his heart. (Alleluia, alleluia) *Ps.* Fret not thyself because of the ungodly: neither be thou envious against the evil doers.

Collect

E beseech thee, O Lord, that the prayers of the blessed Abbot, *N.* may commend us unto thee: that by his advocacy thou wouldest vouchsafe unto us those things to which by our own merits we cannot obtain. Through.

Epistle. Ecclesiasticus 45:1

BELOVED of God and men, even Moses, Whose memorial is blessed. He made him like to the glory of the saints, And magnified him in the fears of his enemies. By his words he caused the wonders to cease; He glorified him in the sight of kings; He gave him commandment for his people, And shewed him part of his glory. He sanctified him in his faithfulness and meekness; He chose him out of all flesh. He made him to hear his voice, And led him into the thick darkness, And gave him commandments face to face, Even the law of life and knowledge,

Gradual. Thou hast prevented him, O Lord, with the blessings of goodness: and hast set a crown of pure gold upon his head. ℣. He asked life of thee, and thou gavest him a long life, even for ever and ever.

Alleluia. Alleluia, alleluia. ℣. The righteous shall flourish like a palm-tree: and shall spread abroad like a cedar in Libanus. Alleluia.

¶ In Septuagesimatide or Lent, replacing the Alleluia:

Tract. Blessed is the man that feareth the Lord: he hath great delight in his commandments. ℣. His seed shall be mighty upon earth: the generation of the faithful shall be blessed. ℣. Riches and plenteousness shall be in his house: and his righteousness endureth for ever.

¶ In Eastertide, replacing the Lesser Alleluia:

Alleluia. Alleluia, alleluia. ℣. The righteous shall flourish like a palm-tree: and shall spread abroad like a cedar in Libanus. Alleluia. ℣. The righteous shall grow as the lily: and flourish for ever before the Lord. Alleluia.

Common of Saints *Virgin Martyress I*

Gospel. Matthew 19:27

T THAT TIME: Peter said unto Jesus, Behold, we have forsaken all, and followed thee; what shall we have therefore? And Jesus said unto them, Verily I say unto you, That ye which have followed me, in the regeneration when the Son of man shall sit in the throne of his glory, ye also shall sit upon twelve thrones, judging the twelve tribes of Israel. And every one that hath forsaken houses, or brethren, or sisters, or father, or mother, or wife, or children, or lands, for my name's sake, shall receive an hundredfold, and shall inherit everlasting life.

Offertory. Thou hast given him his heart's desire, O Lord, and hast not denied him the request of his lips: thou hast set a crown of pure gold upon his head. (Alleluia.)

Secret

E beseech thee, O Lord, that thy holy Abbot *N.* may intercede for us: that this sacrifice which we offer and present upon thy holy altar may be profitable unto us for our salvation. Through.

Communion. A faithful and wise steward, whom his lord hath made ruler over his household, to give them their portion of meat in due season (Alleluia.)

Postcommunion

LET thy sacrament, O Lord, which we have now received and the prayers of the blessed Abbot, *N.*, effectually defend us: that we may both imitate the example of his conversation, and receive the succour of his intercession. Through.

Commons for Virgin Martyresses

I: Common of a Virgin Martyress

I Evensong

¶ The Hymn is of Mattins with the following Versicle & Antiphon.

℣. In thy grace and in thy beauty.
℟. Go forth, ride prosperously, and reign.

Mag. Ant. Come thou Bride of Christ, | receive the crown which the Lord hath prepared for thee for ever.

Virgin Martyress I   # Common of Saints

Mattins

Invitatory Hymn

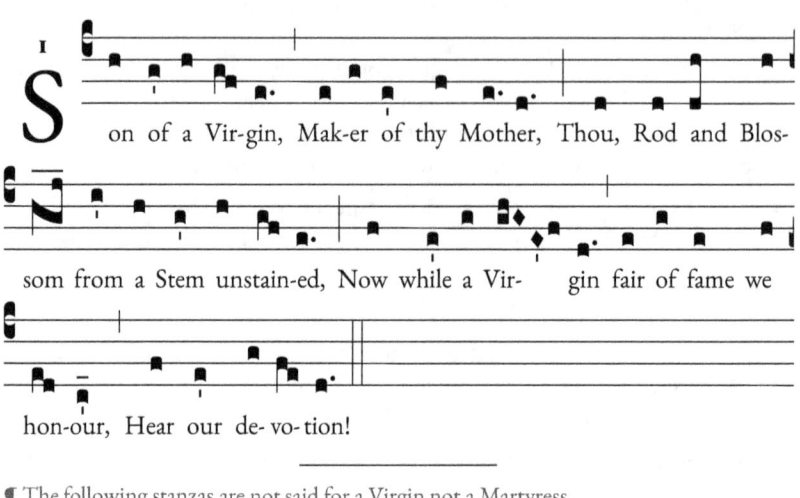

Son of a Virgin, Maker of thy Mother, Thou, Rod and Blossom from a Stem unstained, Now while a Virgin fair of fame we honour, Hear our devotion!

¶ The following stanzas are not said for a Virgin not a Martyress.

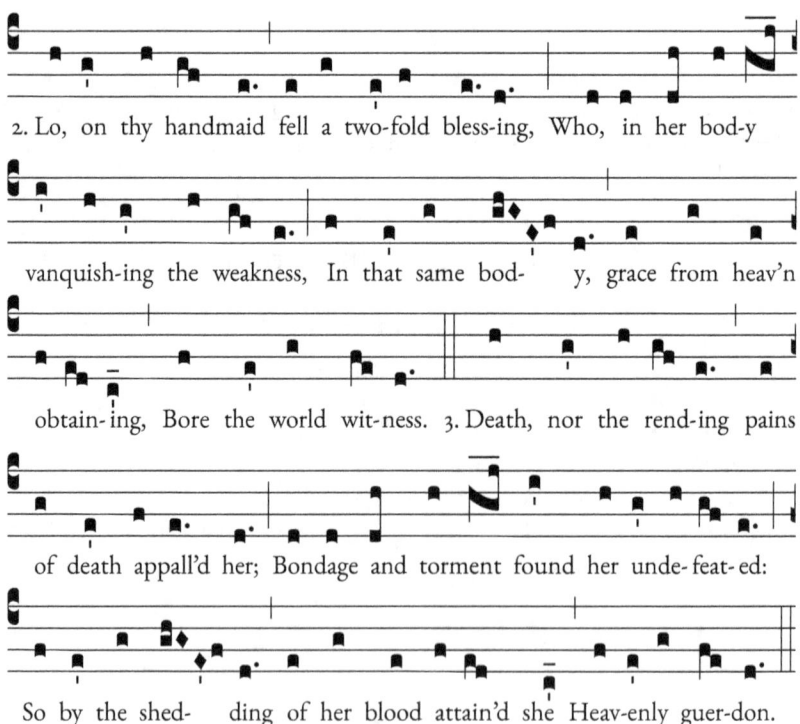

2. Lo, on thy handmaid fell a two-fold blessing, Who, in her body vanquishing the weakness, In that same body, grace from heav'n obtaining, Bore the world witness. 3. Death, nor the rending pains of death appall'd her; Bondage and torment found her undefeated: So by the shedding of her blood attain'd she Heav'nly guerdon.

Common of Saints *Virgin Martyress I*

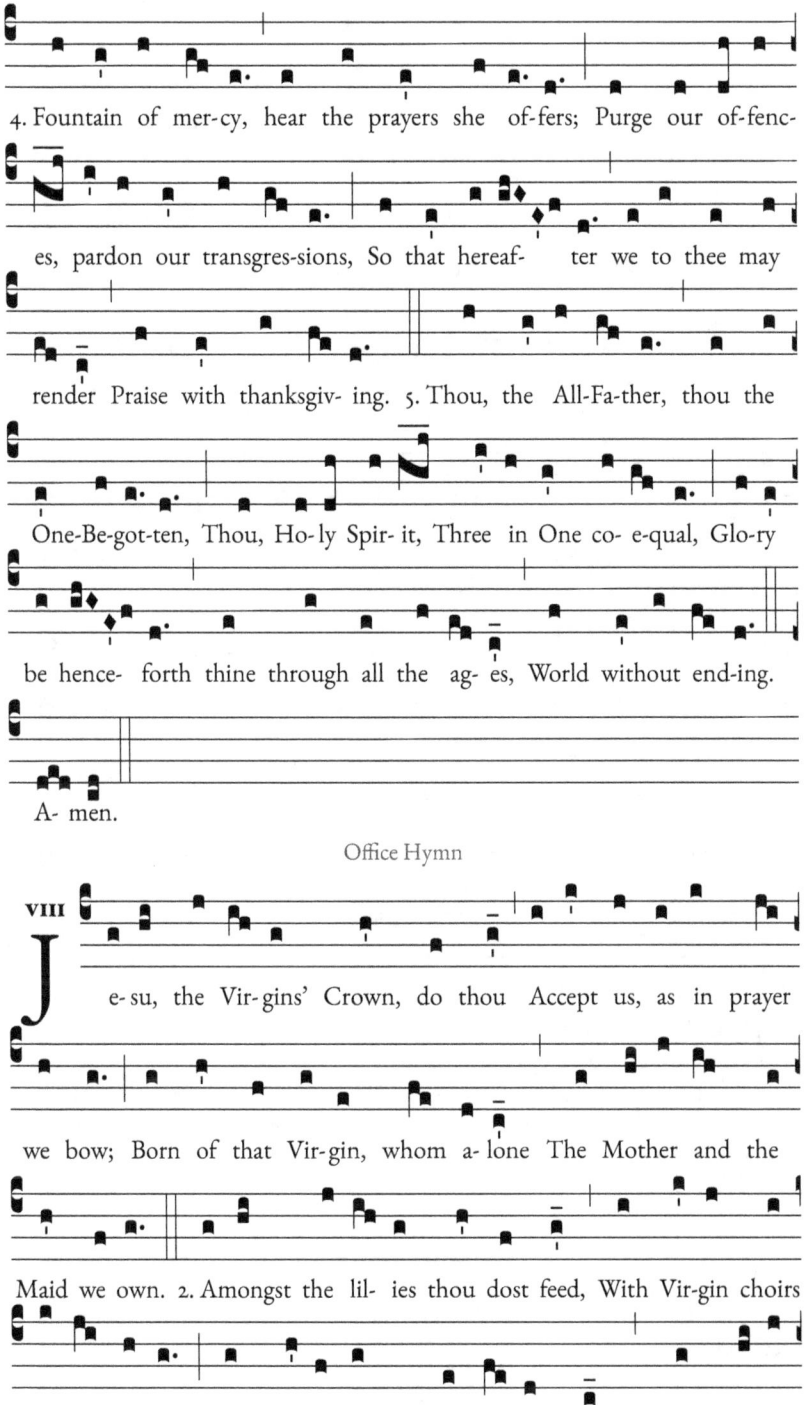

4. Fountain of mer-cy, hear the prayers she of-fers; Purge our of-fenc-es, pardon our transgres-sions, So that hereaf- ter we to thee may render Praise with thanksgiv- ing. 5. Thou, the All-Fa-ther, thou the One-Be-got-ten, Thou, Ho- ly Spir- it, Three in One co- e-qual, Glo-ry be hence- forth thine through all the ag- es, World without end-ing. A- men.

Office Hymn

Je-su, the Vir-gins' Crown, do thou Accept us, as in prayer we bow; Born of that Vir-gin, whom a- lone The Mother and the Maid we own. 2. Amongst the lil- ies thou dost feed, With Vir-gin choirs ac-compa-nied; With glo-ry deck'd, the spot-less brides Whose brid-al

Virgin Martyress I # Common of Saints

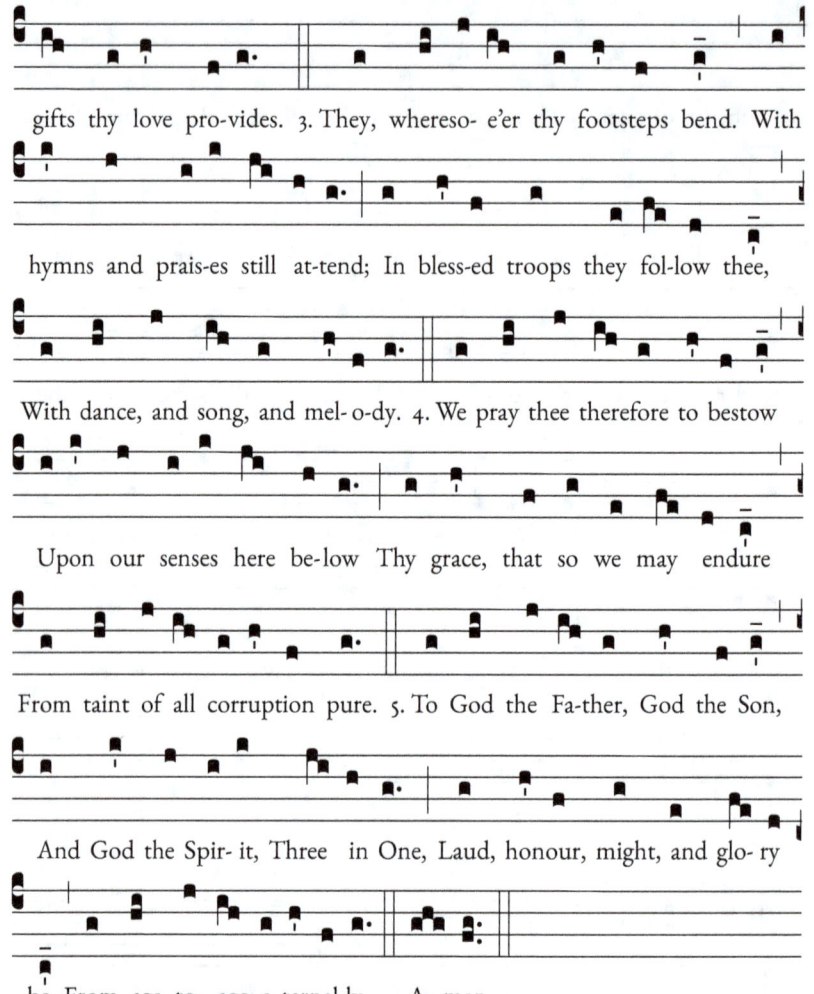

gifts thy love pro-vides. 3. They, whereso- e'er thy footsteps bend. With hymns and prais-es still at-tend; In bless-ed troops they fol-low thee, With dance, and song, and mel- o-dy. 4. We pray thee therefore to bestow Upon our senses here be-low Thy grace, that so we may endure From taint of all corruption pure. 5. To God the Fa-ther, God the Son, And God the Spir- it, Three in One, Laud, honour, might, and glo- ry be From age to age e-ternal-ly. A- men.

℣. Full of grace are thy lips.
℞. Because God hath blessed thee for ever.

Ben. Ant. The kingdom of heaven † is likened unto a merchantman seeking goodly pearls; who, when he had found one pearl of great price, went and sold all that he had, and bought it.

II Evensong

❡ The Hymn & Versicle are of Mattins with the following Antiphon.

Mag. Ant. Come thou Bride of Christ, † receive the crown which the Lord hath prepared for thee for ever.

Common of Saints *Virgin Martyress I*

Introit

I WILL speak of thy testimonies, even before kings, and will not be ashamed: and my delight shall be in thy commandments, which I have loved exceedingly (Alleluia, alleluia). *Ps.* Blessed are those that are undefiled in the way: and walk in the law of the Lord.

Collect

O GOD, who among the manifold works of thy power hast bestowed even upon the weakness of women the victory of martyrdom: mercifully grant; that we, who celebrate the birthday of blessed *N.* thy Virgin and Martyr, may by her example be drawn nearer unto thee. Through.

Epistle. Ecclesiasticus 51:1

I WILL give thanks unto thee, O Lord, O King, And will praise thee, O God my Saviour: I do give thanks unto thy name: For thou wast my protector and helper, And didst deliver my body out of destruction, And out of the snare of a slanderous tongue, From lips that forge lies, And wast my helper before them that stood by; And didst deliver me, according to the abundance of thy mercy, and greatness of thy name, From the gnashings of teeth ready to devour, Out of the hand of such as sought my life, Out of the manifold afflictions which I had; From the choking of a fire on every side, And out of the midst of fire which I kindled not; Out of the depth of the belly of the grave, And from an unclean tongue, And from lying words, The slander of an unrighteous tongue unto the king. My soul drew near even unto death, And my life was near to the grave beneath. They compassed me on every side, And there was none to help me. I was looking for the succour of men, And it was not. And I remembered thy mercy, O Lord, And thy working which hath been from everlasting, How thou deliverest them that wait for thee, And savest them out of the hand of the enemies, O Lord our God.

Gradual. Thou hast loved righteousness, and hated iniquity. ℣. Wherefore God, even thy God, hath anointed thee with the oil of gladness.

Alleluia. Alleluia, alleluia. ℣. The Virgins that be her fellows shall be brought unto the King: they that bear her company shall be brought unto thee with joy. Alleluia.

¶ In Septuagesimatide or Lent, replacing the Alleluia:

Tract. Come, Spouse of Christ, receive the crown, which the Lord hath prepared for thee for ever: for love of whom thou didst shed thy blood. ℣. Thou hast loved righteousness, and hated iniquity: wherefore God, even thy God, hath anointed thee with the oil of gladness above thy fellows. ℣. In thy comeliness and in thy beauty, go forth, proceed prosperously and reign.

¶ In Eastertide, replacing the Lesser Alleluia:

Alleluia. Alleluia, alleluia. ℣. The Virgins that be her fellows shall be brought unto the King: they that bear her company shall be brought unto thee with joy. Alleluia. ℣. In thy comeliness and in thy beauty go forth, proceed prosperously and reign. Alleluia.

Virgin Martyress II 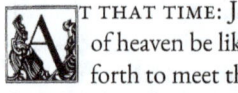 # Common of Saints

Gospel. Matthew 25:1

AT THAT TIME: Jesus spake this parable unto his disciples: The kingdom of heaven be likened unto ten virgins, which took their lamps, and went forth to meet the bridegroom. And five of them were wise, and five were foolish. They that were foolish took their lamps, and took no oil with them: but the wise took oil in their vessels with their lamps. While the bridegroom tarried, they all slumbered and slept. And at midnight there was a cry made, Behold, the bridegroom cometh; go ye out to meet him. Then all those virgins arose, and trimmed their lamps. And the foolish said unto the wise, Give us of your oil; for our lamps are gone out. But the wise answered, saying, Not so; lest there be not enough for us and you: but go ye rather to them that sell, and buy for yourselves. And while they went to buy, the bridegroom came; and they that were ready went in with him to the marriage: and the door was shut. Afterward came also the other virgins, saying, Lord, Lord, open to us. But he answered and said, Verily I say unto you, I know you not. Watch therefore, for ye know neither the day nor the hour.

Offertory. The Virgins that be her fellows shall be brought unto the King: they that bear her company shall be brought unto thee, with joy and gladness: and shall enter into the palace of the Lord the King (Alleluia).

Secret

ECEIVE, O Lord, the gifts which we offer on the solemnity of blessed *N.*, thy Virgin and Martyr: through whose advocacy we trust to be delivered. Through.

Communion. Let the proud be confounded, for they go wickedly about to destroy me: but I will be occupied in thy commandments and in thy statutes, that I be not ashamed (Alleluia).

Postcommunion

AY the mysteries which we have received be for our succour, O Lord: and at the intercession of blessed *N.*, thy Virgin and Martyr, cause us to rejoice in thy continual protection. Through.

II: Common of a Virgin Martyress

¶ Daily Office propers as in the First Common of a Virgin Martyress (p. 733).

Introit

HE ungodly laid wait for me to destroy me: O Lord, I will consider thy testimonies: I see that all things come to an end: but thy commandment is exceeding broad (Alleluia, alleluia). *Ps.* Blessed are those that are undefiled in the way: and walk in the law of the Lord.

Common of Saints *Virgin Martyress II*

Collect

E beseech thee, O Lord, that, like as blessed *N.*, thy Virgin and Martyr, was ever found pleasing unto thee, both by the merit of her chastity, and by her confession of thy power: so she may implore for us thy pardon. Through.

Epistle. Ecclesiasticus 51:9

LORD MY GOD, I lifted up my supplication from the earth, And prayed for deliverance from death. I called upon the Lord, the Father of my Lord, That he would not forsake me in the days of affliction, In the time when there was no help against the proud. I will praise thy name continually, And will sing praise with thanksgiving; And my supplication was heard: For thou savedst me from destruction, And deliveredst me from the evil time: Therefore will I give thanks and praise unto thee, And bless thy name, O Lord our God.

Gradual. God shall help her with his countenance: God is in the midst of her, therefore shall she not be removed. ℣. The rivers of the flood thereof shall make glad the city of God: the holy place of the tabernacle of the Most Highest.

Alleluia. Alleluia, alleluia. ℣. This is a wise Virgin, and one of the number of the prudent. Alleluia.

¶ In Septuagesimatide or Lent, replacing the Alleluia:

Tract. Come, Spouse of Christ, receive the crown which the Lord hath prepared for thee for ever: for love of whom thou didst shed thy blood. ℣. Thou hast loved righteousness, and hated iniquity: wherefore God, even thy God, hath anointed thee with the oil of gladness above thy fellows. ℣. In thy comeliness and in thy beauty go forth, proceed prosperously and reign.

¶ In Eastertide, replacing the Lesser Alleluia:

Alleluia. Alleluia, alleluia. ℣. This is a wise Virgin, and one of the number of the prudent. Alleluia. ℣. O how beautiful is the chaste generation with its glory. Alleluia.

Gospel. Matthew 13:44

T THAT TIME: Jesus spake this parable unto his disciples: The kingdom of heaven is like unto treasure hid in a field; the which when a man hath found, he hideth, and for joy thereof goeth and selleth all that he hath, and buyeth that field.

Again, the kingdom of heaven is like unto a merchant man, seeking goodly pearls: who, when he had found one pearl of great price, went and sold all that he had, and bought it.

Again, the kingdom of heaven is like unto a net, that was cast into the sea, and gathered of every kind: which, when it was full, they drew to shore, and sat down, and gathered the good into vessels, but cast the bad away. So shall it be at the end of the world: the angels shall come forth, and sever the wicked from among the just, and shall cast them into the furnace of fire: there shall be wailing and gnashing of teeth.

Jesus saith unto them, Have ye understood all these things? They say unto him, Yea, Lord. Then said he unto them, Therefore every scribe which is instructed unto the kingdom of heaven is like unto a man that is an householder, which bringeth forth out of his treasure things new and old.

¶ NOTE, The Gospel from the Common of Many Virgin Martyresses (p. 740) may be used instead of the one provided above.

Offertory. Full of grace are thy lips, because God hath blessed thee for ever and ever (Alleluia).

Secret

RACIOUSLY receive, O Lord, through the merits of blessed *N.*, thy Virgin and Martyr, the sacrifices which we offer unto thee: and grant that they may avail for our continual help. Through.

Communion. I deal with the thing that is lawful and right, O Lord, let the proud do me no wrong: I hold straight all thy commandments, and all false ways I utterly abhor (Alleluia).

Postcommunion

LORD our God, who hast fulfilled us with the bounty of thy heavenly gift: we beseech thee, that, at the intercession of blessed *N.*, thy Virgin and Martyr, we may ever live by the partaking of the same. Through.

COMMON OF MANY VIRGIN MARTYRESSES

¶ The Daily Office propers as in the First Common of a Virgin Martyress (p. 738), except for the following.

Mag. Ant. O ye wise Virgins, † arise and trim your lamps: for behold the Bridegroom cometh; go ye out to meet him.

Introit

HE ungodly laid wait for me to destroy me: O Lord, I will consider thy testimonies: I see that all things come to an end: but thy commandment is exceeding broad (Alleluia, alleluia). *Ps.* Blessed are those that are undefiled in the way: and walk in the law of the Lord.

Collect

RANT, we beseech thee, O Lord our God, that we may at all times so devoutly honour the triumphs of thy holy Virgins and Martyrs *N. and N.*: that, although we cannot worthily shew forth their praises, yet we may continually honour them with lowly service. Through.

Common of Saints *Virgin Martyresses*

Epistle. 1 Corinthians 7:25

BRETHREN: Concerning virgins I have no commandment of the Lord: yet I give my judgment, as one that hath obtained mercy of the Lord to be faithful. I suppose therefore that this is good for the present distress, I say, that it is good for a man so to be. Art thou bound unto a wife? seek not to be loosed. Art thou loosed from a wife? seek not a wife. But and if thou marry, thou hast not sinned; and if a virgin marry, she hath not sinned. Nevertheless such shall have trouble in the flesh: but I spare you.

But this I say, brethren, the time is short: it remaineth, that both they that have wives be as though they had none; and they that weep, as though they wept not; and they that rejoice, as though they rejoiced not; and they that buy, as though they possessed not; and they that use this world, as not abusing it: for the fashion of this world passeth away.

But I would have you without carefulness. He that is unmarried careth for the things that belong to the Lord, how he may please the Lord: but he that is married careth for the things that are of the world, how he may please his wife. There is difference also between a wife and a virgin. The unmarried woman careth for the things of the Lord, that she may be holy both in body and in spirit: in Christ Jesus our Lord.

Gospel. Matthew 19:3

AT THAT TIME: The Pharisees came unto Jesus, tempting him, and saying unto him, Is it lawful for a man to put away his wife for every cause? And he answered and said unto them, Have ye not read, that he which made them at the beginning made them male and female, and said, For this cause shall a man leave father and mother, and shall cleave to his wife: and they twain shall be one flesh? Wherefore they are no more twain, but one flesh. What therefore God hath joined together, let not man put asunder. They say unto him, Why did Moses then command to give a writing of divorcement, and to put her away? He saith unto them, Moses because of the hardness of your hearts suffered you to put away your wives: but from the beginning it was not so. And I say unto you, Whosoever shall put away his wife, except it be for fornication, and shall marry another, committeth adultery: and whoso marrieth her which is put away doth commit adultery.

His disciples say unto him, If the case of the man be so with his wife, it is not good to marry. But he said unto them, All men cannot receive this saying, save they to whom it is given. For there are some eunuchs, which were so born from their mother's womb: and there are some eunuchs, which were made eunuchs of men: and there be eunuchs, which have made themselves eunuchs for the kingdom of heaven's sake. He that is able to receive it, let him receive it.

Offertory. Full of grace are thy lips, because God hath blessed thee for ever and ever (Alleluia).

Virgin I # Common of Saints

Secret

O LORD, we beseech thee, look down upon these gifts, which we offer on thine altars on this festival of thy holy Virgins and Martyrs *N. and N.*: that as by these blessed mysteries thou hast bestowed glory upon them; so likewise of thy bounty thou wouldest vouchsafe to us thy pardon. Through.

Postcommunion

G RANT to us, we beseech thee, O Lord, at the intercession of thy holy Virgins and Martyrs, *N. and N.*: that those things which we touch with our lips we may receive in purity of heart. Through.

Commons for a Virgin

I: COMMON OF A VIRGIN ONLY

¶ Daily Office propers as in the First Common of a Virgin Martyress (p. 733).

¶ NOTE, The 2nd and 3rd stanzas of the Invitatory Hymn should be omitted.

Introit

T HOU hast loved righteousness, and hated iniquity: wherefore God, even thy God, hath anointed thee with the oil of gladness above thy fellows (Alleluia, alleluia). *Ps.* My heart is inditing of a good matter: I speak of the things which I have made unto the King.

Collect

G RACIOUSLY hear us, O God of our salvation: that, like as we do rejoice in the festival of blessed *N.*, thy Virgin; so we may be instructed in all godly and devout affection. Through.

Epistle. 2 Corinthians 10:17

B RETHREN: He that glorieth, let him glory in the Lord. For not he that commendeth himself is approved, but whom the Lord commendeth. Would to God ye could bear with me a little in my folly: and indeed bear with me. For I am jealous over you with godly jealousy: for I have espoused you to one husband, that I may present you as a chaste virgin to Christ.

Gradual. In thy comeliness and in thy beauty go forth, proceed prosperously and reign. ℣. Because of the word of truth, of meekness, and righteousness: and thy right hand shall teach thee terrible things.

Alleluia. Alleluia, alleluia. ℣. The Virgins that be her fellows shall be brought unto the King: they that bear her company shall be brought unto thee with joy. Alleluia.

Common of Saints *Virgin I*

¶ In Septuagesimatide or Lent, replacing the Alleluia:

Tract. Hearken, O daughter, and consider, incline thine ear: so shall the King have pleasure in thy beauty. ℣. The rich among the people shall make their supplication before thee: kings' daughters were among thy honourable women. ℣. The Virgins that be her fellows shall be brought unto the King: they that bear her company shall be brought unto thee. ℣. With joy and gladness shall they be brought: and shall enter into the King's palace.

¶ In Eastertide, replacing the Lesser Alleluia:

Alleluia. Alleluia, alleluia. ℣. The Virgins that be her fellows shall be brought unto the King: they that bear her company shall be brought unto them with joy. Alleluia. ℣. In thy comeliness and in thy beauty go forth, proceed prosperously and reign. Alleluia.

Gospel. Matthew 25:1

AT THAT TIME: Jesus spake this parable unto his disciples: the kingdom of heaven shall be likened unto ten virgins, which took their lamps, and went forth to meet the bridegroom. And five of them were wise, and five were foolish. They that were foolish took their lamps, and took no oil with them: but the wise took oil in their vessels with their lamps. While the bridegroom tarried, they all slumbered and slept. And at midnight there was a cry made, Behold, the bridegroom cometh; go ye out to meet him. Then all those virgins arose, and trimmed their lamps. And the foolish said unto the wise, Give us of your oil; for our lamps are gone out. But the wise answered, saying, Not so; lest there be not enough for us and you: but go ye rather to them that sell, and buy for yourselves. And while they went to buy, the bridegroom came; and they that were ready went in with him to the marriage: and the door was shut. Afterward came also the other virgins, saying, Lord, Lord, open to us. But he answered and said, Verily I say unto you, I know you not. Watch therefore, for ye know neither the day nor the hour.

Offertory. Kings' daughters were among thy honourable women, upon thy right hand did stand the queen in a vesture of gold, wrought about with divers colours (Alleluia).

Secret

GRANT, O Lord, that like as thy dedicated people do acknowledge that in tribulation they have been succoured by the merits of thy Saints: so this oblation, which they offer unto thee in honour of the same, may be acceptable in thy sight. Through.

Communion. The five wise virgins took oil in their vessels with their lamps: and at midnight there was a cry made: Behold the bridegroom cometh: go ye out to meet Christ the Lord.

Communion. I deal with the thing that is lawful and right, O Lord, let the proud do me no wrong: I hold straight all thy commandments, and all false ways I utterly abhor (Alleluia).

Postcommunion

LORD, who hast satisfied thy family with sacred gifts: we beseech thee; that we may at all times be comforted by the intercession of her whose festival we celebrate. Through.

II: Common of a Virgin Only

¶ Daily Office propers as in the First Common of a Virgin Martyress (p. 733).

¶ Note, The 2nd and 3rd stanzas of the Invitatory Hymn should be omitted.

Introit

LL the rich among the people shall make their supplication before thee: the Virgins that be her fellows shall be brought unto the King: they that bear her company shall be brought unto thee with joy and gladness (Alleluia, alleluia). *Ps.* My heart is inditing of a good matter: I speak of the things which I have made unto the King.

Collect

RACIOUSLY hear us, O God of our salvation: that, like as we do rejoice in the festival of blessed *N.*, thy Virgin, so we may be instructed in all godly and devout affection. Through.

Epistle. 1 Corinthians 7:25

RETHREN: Concerning virgins I have no commandment of the Lord: yet I give my judgment, as one that hath obtained mercy of the Lord to be faithful. I suppose therefore that this is good for the present distress, I say, that it is good for a man so to be. Art thou bound unto a wife? seek not to be loosed. Art thou loosed from a wife? seek not a wife. But and if thou marry, thou hast not sinned; and if a virgin marry, she hath not sinned. Nevertheless such shall have trouble in the flesh: but I spare you.

But this I say, brethren, the time is short: it remaineth, that both they that have wives be as though they had none; and they that weep, as though they wept not; and they that rejoice, as though they rejoiced not; and they that buy, as though they possessed not; and they that use this world, as not abusing it: for the fashion of this world passeth away.

But I would have you without carefulness. He that is unmarried careth for the things that belong to the Lord, how he may please the Lord: but he that is married careth for the things that are of the world, how he may please his wife. There is difference also between a wife and a virgin. The unmarried woman careth for the things of the Lord, that she may be holy both in body and in spirit: in Christ Jesus our Lord.

Common of Saints — *Virgin II*

Gradual. The King shall have pleasure in thy beauty, for he is thy Lord God. ℣. Hearken, O daughter, and consider, incline thine ear.

Alleluia. Alleluia, alleluia. ℣. This is a wise Virgin, and one of the number of the prudent. Alleluia.

¶ In Septuagesimatide or Lent, replacing the Alleluia:

Tract. The King shall have pleasure in thy beauty. ℣. The rich among the people shall make their supplication before thee: kings' daughters were among thy honourable women. ℣. The Virgins that be her fellows shall be brought unto the King: they that bear her company shall be brought unto thee. ℣. With joy and gladness shall they be brought: and shall enter into the King's palace.

¶ In Eastertide, replacing the Lesser Alleluia:

Alleluia. Alleluia, alleluia. ℣. This is a wise Virgin, and one of the number of the prudent. Alleluia. ℣. O how beautiful is the chaste generation with its glory. Alleluia.

Gospel. Matthew 13:44

AT THAT TIME: Jesus spake this parable unto his disciples: The kingdom of heaven is like unto treasure hid in a field; the which when a man hath found, he hideth, and for joy thereof goeth and selleth all that he hath, and buyeth that field.

Again, the kingdom of heaven is like unto a merchant man, seeking goodly pearls: who, when he had found one pearl of great price, went and sold all that he had, and bought it.

Again, the kingdom of heaven is like unto a net, that was cast into the sea, and gathered of every kind: which, when it was full, they drew to shore, and sat down, and gathered the good into vessels, but cast the bad away. So shall it be at the end of the world: the angels shall come forth, and sever the wicked from among the just, and shall cast them into the furnace of fire: there shall be wailing and gnashing of teeth.

Jesus saith unto them, Have ye understood all these things? They say unto him, Yea, Lord. Then said he unto them, Therefore every scribe which is instructed unto the kingdom of heaven is like unto a man that is an householder, which bringeth forth out of his treasure things new and old.

Offertory. The Virgins that be her fellows shall be brought unto the King: they that bear her company shall be brought unto thee, with joy and gladness: and shall enter into the palace of the Lord the King (Alleluia).

Secret

GRANT, O Lord, that like as thy dedicated people do acknowledge that in tribulation they have been succoured by the merits of thy Saints: so this oblation, which they do offer unto thee in honour of the same, may be acceptable in thy sight. Through.

Martyress not Virgin # Common of Saints

Communion. The kingdom of heaven is like unto a merchant man, seeking goodly pearls: who when he had found one pearl of great price, gave all that he had, and bought it (Alleluia).

Postcommunion

O LORD, who hast satisfied thy family with sacred gifts: we beseech thee, that we may at all times be comforted by the intercession of her whose festival we celebrate. Through.

❧ The following Gospel may be used instead of the one provided above.

Another Gospel. Matthew 25:1

AT THAT TIME: Jesus spake this parable unto his disciples: The kingdom of heaven be likened unto ten virgins, which took their lamps, and went forth to meet the bridegroom. And five of them were wise, and five were foolish. They that were foolish took their lamps, and took no oil with them: but the wise took oil in their vessels with their lamps. While the bridegroom tarried, they all slumbered and slept. And at midnight there was a cry made, Behold, the bridegroom cometh; go ye out to meet him. Then all those virgins arose, and trimmed their lamps. And the foolish said unto the wise, Give us of your oil; for our lamps are gone out. But the wise answered, saying, Not so; lest there be not enough for us and you: but go ye rather to them that sell, and buy for yourselves. And while they went to buy, the bridegroom came; and they that were ready went in with him to the marriage: and the door was shut. Afterward came also the other virgins, saying, Lord, Lord, open to us. But he answered and said, Verily I say unto you, I know you not. Watch therefore, for ye know neither the day nor the hour.

Commons for Holy Women not Virgins

COMMON OF A MARTYRESS NOT A VIRGIN

I Evensong

❧ The Hymn is of Mattins with the following Versicle & Antiphon.

℣. In thy grace and in thy beauty.
℟. Go forth, ride prosperously, and reign.

Mag. Ant. The kingdom of heaven † is likened unto a merchantman seeking goodly pearls; who, when he had found one pearl of great price, went and sold all that he had, and bought it.

Common of Saints *Martyress not Virgin*

Mattins

℣ The Invitatory Hymn is the 4th and 5th stanzas of the Invitatory Hymn from the First Common of a Virgin Martyress (p. 734).

Office Hymn

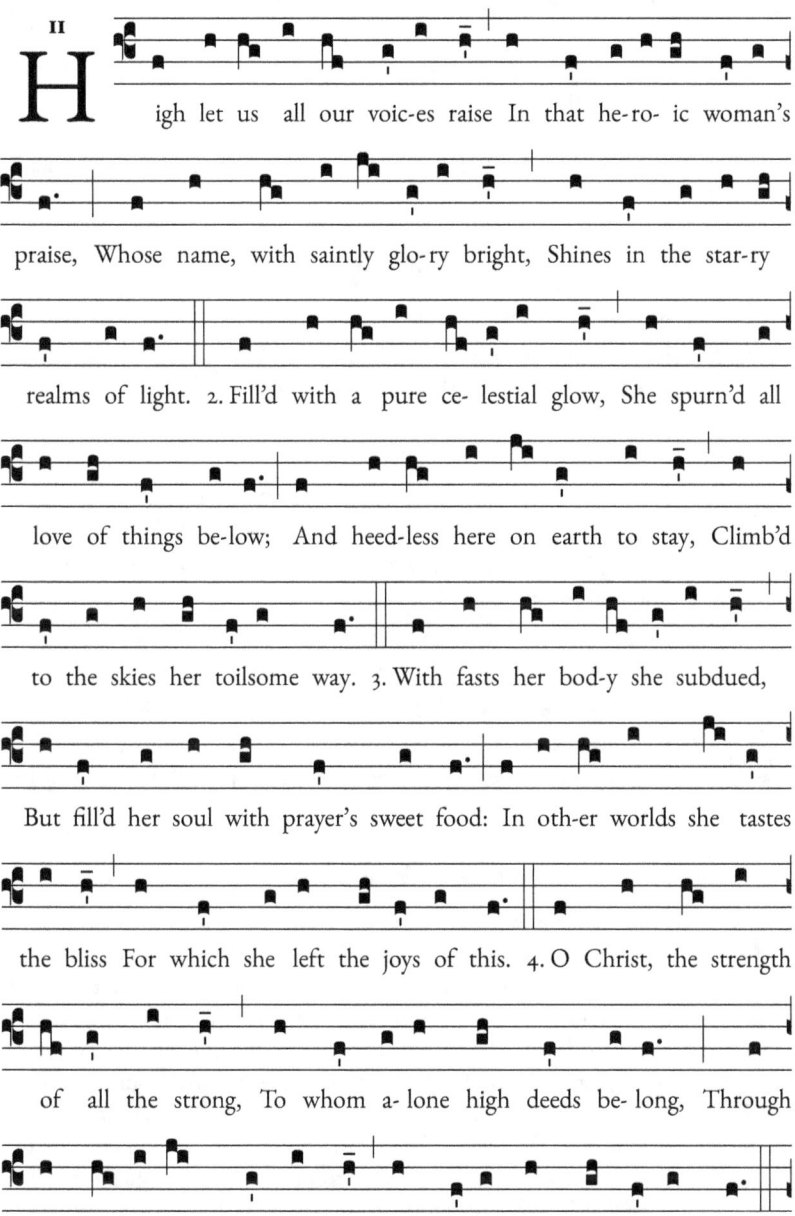

High let us all our voic-es raise In that he-ro-ic woman's praise, Whose name, with saintly glo-ry bright, Shines in the star-ry realms of light. 2. Fill'd with a pure ce-lestial glow, She spurn'd all love of things be-low; And heed-less here on earth to stay, Climb'd to the skies her toilsome way. 3. With fasts her bod-y she subdued, But fill'd her soul with prayer's sweet food: In oth-er worlds she tastes the bliss For which she left the joys of this. 4. O Christ, the strength of all the strong, To whom a-lone high deeds be-long, Through her pre-vail-ing prayer on high In mercy hear thy people's cry.

Martyress not Virgin # Common of Saints

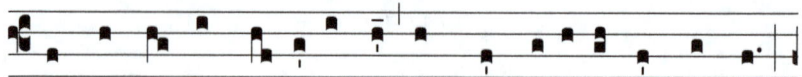

5. All laud to God the Father be; All praise, e- ternal Son, to thee;

All glo- ry, as is ev-er meet, To God the Ho-ly Par-a-clete. A- men.

℣. Full of grace are thy lips.

℟. Because God hath blessed thee for ever.

Ben. Ant. Give her † of the fruit of her hands; and let her own works praise her in the gates.

II Evensong

¶ The Hymn & Versicle are of Mattins with the following Antiphon.

Mag. Ant. She stretched out † her hand to the poor; yea, she reacheth forth her hands to the needy; she eateth not the bread of idleness.

Introit

THE ungodly laid wait for me to destroy me: O Lord, I will consider thy testimonies: I see that all things come to an end: but thy commandment is exceeding broad (Alleluia). *Ps.* Blessed are those that are undefiled in the way: and walk in the law of the Lord.

Collect

O GOD, who among the manifold works of thy power hast bestowed even upon the weakness of women the victory of martyrdom: mercifully grant; that we, who celebrate the birthday of blessed *N.*, thy Martyr, may by her example draw nearer unto thee. *Through.*

Epistle. Ecclesiasticus 51:1

I WILL give thanks unto thee, O Lord, O King, And will praise thee, O God my Saviour: I do give thanks unto thy name: For thou wast my protector and helper, And didst deliver my body out of destruction, And out of the snare of a slanderous tongue, From lips that forge lies, And wast my helper before them that stood by; And didst deliver me, according to the abundance of thy mercy, and greatness of thy name, From the gnashings of teeth ready to devour, Out of the hand of such as sought my life, Out of the manifold afflictions which I had; From the choking of a fire on every side, And out of the midst of fire which I kindled not; Out of the depth of the belly of the grave, And from an unclean tongue, And from lying words, The slander of an unrighteous tongue unto the king. My soul drew near even unto death, And my life was near to the grave beneath. They compassed

Common of Saints *Martyress not Virgin*

me on every side, And there was none to help me. I was looking for the succour of men, And it was not. And I remembered thy mercy, O Lord, And thy working which hath been from everlasting, How thou deliverest them that wait for thee, And savest them out of the hand of the enemies, O Lord our God.

Gradual. Thou hast loved righteousness and hated iniquity. ℣. Wherefore God, even thy God, hath anointed thee with the oil of gladness.

Alleluia. Alleluia, alleluia. ℣. In thy comeliness and in thy beauty go forth, proceed prosperously and reign. Alleluia.

¶ In Septuagesimatide or Lent, replacing the Alleluia:

Tract. Come, Spouse of Christ, receive the crown which the Lord hath prepared for thee for ever: for love of whom thou didst shed thy blood. ℣. Thou hast loved righteousness and hated iniquity: wherefore God, even thy God, hath anointed thee with the oil of gladness, above thy fellows. ℣. In thy comeliness and in thy beauty go forth, proceed prosperously and reign.

¶ In Eastertide, replacing the Lesser Alleluia:

Alleluia. Alleluia, alleluia. ℣. In thy comeliness and in thy beauty, go forth, proceed prosperously and reign. Alleluia. ℣. Because of the word of truth, of meekness, and righteousness: and thy right hand shall teach thee terrible things. Alleluia.

Gospel. Matthew 13:44

AT THAT TIME: Jesus spake this parable unto his disciples: The kingdom of heaven is like unto treasure hid in a field; the which when a man hath found, he hideth, and for joy thereof goeth and selleth all that he hath, and buyeth that field.

Again, the kingdom of heaven is like unto a merchant man, seeking goodly pearls: who, when he had found one pearl of great price, went and sold all that he had, and bought it.

Again, the kingdom of heaven is like unto a net, that was cast into the sea, and gathered of every kind: which, when it was full, they drew to shore, and sat down, and gathered the good into vessels, but cast the bad away. So shall it be at the end of the world: the angels shall come forth, and sever the wicked from among the just, and shall cast them into the furnace of fire: there shall be wailing and gnashing of teeth.

Jesus saith unto them, Have ye understood all these things? They say unto him, Yea, Lord. Then said he unto them, Therefore every scribe which is instructed unto the kingdom of heaven is like unto a man that is an householder, which bringeth forth out of his treasure things new and old.

¶ After Septuagesima the Alleluia at the end of the following Offertory is omitted.

Offertory. Full of grace are thy lips: because God hath blessed thee for ever and ever, alleluia.

Martyresses not Virgins Common of Saints

Secret

ECEIVE, O Lord, the gifts which we offer on the solemnity of blessed *N.*, thy Martyr: through whose advocacy we trust to be delivered. Through.

Communion. Princes have persecuted me without a cause: but my heart standeth in awe of thy word: I am as glad of thy word, as one that findeth great spoils (Alleluia).

Postcommunion

AY the mysteries which we have received, O Lord, be for our succour: and, at the intercession of blessed *N.* thy Martyr, cause us to rejoice in thy continual protection. Through.

COMMON OF MANY MARTYRESSES NOT VIRGINS

¶ The propers as in the Common of a Martyress not a Virgin (p. 746), except for the following.

℣. Thou hast crowned them with glory and honour, O Lord.
℟. And madest them to have dominion of the works of thy hands.
Mag. & Ben. Ant. For theirs is the kingdom of heaven, † who despised worldly living: who have won the rewards of the kingdom, and have washed their robes in the blood of the Lamb.

Collect

RANT, we beseech thee, O Lord our God, that we may at all times so devoutly honour the triumphs of thy holy Martyrs *N. and N.*: that although we cannot worthily shew forth their praises, yet we may continually honour them with lowly service. Through.

Secret

LORD, we beseech thee, look down upon these gifts which we offer on thine altars on this festival of thy holy Martyrs *N. and N.*: that as by these blessed mysteries thou hast bestowed glory upon them; so likewise of thy bounty thou wouldest vouchsafe us thy pardon. Through.

Postcommunion

RANT to us, we beseech thee, O Lord, at the intercession of thy holy Martyrs *N. and N.*: that those things which we touch with our lips, we may receive in purity of heart. Through.

Common of Saints — *Holy Matron*

Common of Holy Matron

¶ Daily Office propers as in the Common of a Martyress not a Virgin (p. 746).

Introit

KNOW, O Lord, that thy judgments are right, and that thou of very faithfulness hast caused me to be troubled: my flesh trembleth for fear of thee, and I am afraid of thy judgments (Alleluia, alleluia). *Ps.* Blessed are those that are undefiled in the way: and walk in the law of the Lord.

Collect

GRACIOUSLY hear us, O God of our salvation: and grant that, like as we do rejoice in the festival of blessed *N.*; so we may be instructed in all godly and devout affection. Through.

Epistle. Proverbs 31:10

WHO can find a virtuous woman? for her price is far above rubies. The heart of her husband doth safely trust in her, so that he shall have no need of spoil. She will do him good and not evil all the days of her life. She seeketh wool, and flax, and worketh willingly with her hands. She is like the merchants' ships; she bringeth her food from afar. She riseth also while it is yet night, and giveth meat to her household, and a portion to her maidens. She considereth a field, and buyeth it: with the fruit of her hands she planteth a vineyard. She girdeth her loins with strength, and strengtheneth her arms. She perceiveth that her merchandise is good: her candle goeth not out by night. She layeth her hands to the spindle, and her hands hold the distaff. She stretcheth out her hand to the poor; yea, she reacheth forth her hands to the needy. She is not afraid of the snow for her household: for all her household are clothed with scarlet. She maketh herself coverings of tapestry; her clothing is silk and purple. Her husband is known in the gates, when he sitteth among the elders of the land. She maketh fine linen, and selleth it; and delivereth girdles unto the merchant. Strength and honour are her clothing; and she shall rejoice in time to come. She openeth her mouth with wisdom; and in her tongue is the law of kindness. She looketh well to the ways of her household, and eateth not the bread of idleness. Her children arise up, and call her blessed; her husband also, and he praiseth her. Many daughters have done virtuously, but thou excellest them all. Favour is deceitful, and beauty is vain: but a woman that feareth the Lord, she shall be praised. Give her of the fruit of her hands; and let her own works praise her in the gates.

Gradual. Full of grace are thy lips: because God hath blessed thee for ever. ℣. Because of the word of truth, of meekness, and righteousness: and thy right hand shall teach thee terrible things.

Alleluia. Alleluia, alleluia. ℣. In thy comeliness and in thy beauty go forth, ride prosperously, and reign. Alleluia.

Holy Matron # Common of Saints

❧ In Septuagesimatide or Lent, replacing the Alleluia:

Tract. Come, Spouse of Christ, receive the crown, which the Lord hath prepared for thee for ever. ℣. Thou hast loved righteousness, and hated iniquity: wherefore God, even thy God, hath anointed thee with the oil of gladness above thy fellows. ℣. In thy comeliness and in thy beauty go forth, ride prosperously, and reign.

❧ In Eastertide, replacing the Lesser Alleluia:

Alleluia. Alleluia, alleluia. ℣. In thy comeliness and in thy beauty, go forth, ride prosperously, and reign. Alleluia. ℣. Because of the word of truth, of meekness, and righteousness: and thy right hand shall teach thee terrible things. Alleluia.

Gospel. Matthew 13:44

AT THAT TIME: Jesus spake this parable unto his disciples: The kingdom of heaven is like unto treasure hid in a field; the which when a man hath found, he hideth, and for joy thereof goeth and selleth all that he hath, and buyeth that field.

Again, the kingdom of heaven is like unto a merchant man, seeking goodly pearls: who, when he had found one pearl of great price, went and sold all that he had, and bought it.

Again, the kingdom of heaven is like unto a net, that was cast into the sea, and gathered of every kind: which, when it was full, they drew to shore, and sat down, and gathered the good into vessels, but cast the bad away. So shall it be at the end of the world: the angels shall come forth, and sever the wicked from among the just, and shall cast them into the furnace of fire: there shall be wailing and gnashing of teeth.

Jesus saith unto them, Have ye understood all these things? They say unto him, Yea, Lord. Then said he unto them, Therefore every scribe which is instructed unto the kingdom of heaven is like unto a man that is an householder, which bringeth forth out of his treasure things new and old.

Offertory. Full of grace are thy lips: because God hath blessed thee for ever and ever (Alleluia).

Secret

GRANT, O Lord, that like as thy faithful people do acknowledge that in tribulation they have been succoured by the merits of thy Saints: so this oblation, which they here do offer unto thee in honour of the same, may be acceptable in thy sight. Through.

Communion. Thou hast loved righteousness, and hated iniquity: wherefore God, even thy God, hath anointed thee with the oil of gladness above thy fellows (Alleluia).

Common of Saints *Church Dedication*

Postcommunion

LORD, who hast satisfied thy family with sacred gifts: we beseech thee that we may at all times be comforted by the intercession of her whose festival we celebrate. Through.

¶ The following Epistle may be used for a Widow instead of the Epistle provided above.

Another Epistle. 1 Timothy 5:3

DEARLY BELOVED: Honour widows that are widows indeed. But if any widow have children or nephews, let them learn first to shew piety at home, and to requite their parents: for that is good and acceptable before God. Now she that is a widow indeed, and desolate, trusteth in God, and continueth in supplications and prayers night and day. But she that liveth in pleasure is dead while she liveth. And these things give in charge, that they may be blameless. But if any provide not for his own, and specially for those of his own house, he hath denied the faith, and is worse than an infidel. Let not a widow be taken into the number under threescore years old, having been the wife of one man, well reported of for good works; if she have brought up children, if she have lodged strangers, if she have washed the saints' feet, if she have relieved the afflicted, if she have diligently followed every good work.

Commons Dear to Christ

COMMON OF THE DEDICATION OF A CHURCH

I Evensong

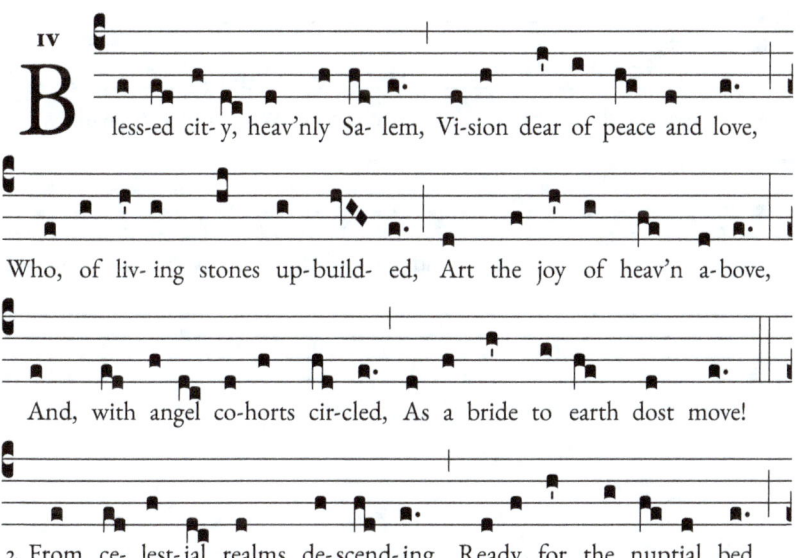

Blessed city, heav'nly Salem, Vision dear of peace and love,
Who, of living stones upbuilded, Art the joy of heav'n above,
And, with angel cohorts circled, As a bride to earth dost move!

2. From celestial realms descending, Ready for the nuptial bed,

Church Dedication   # Common of Saints

To his pres-ence, deck'd with jew- els, By her Lord shall she be led;

All her streets, and all her bulwarks, Of pure gold are fashion-ed.

3. Bright with pearls her por-tal glit-ters, It is o-pen ev- ermore; And, by

virtue of his mer- its, Thither faithful souls may soar, Who for Christ's

dear Name in this world Pain and trib-u- la-tion bore. 4. Man' a blow

and bit-ing sculpture Pol- ish'd well those stones e- lect, In their plac-es

now compact- ed By the heav'nly Archi- tect, Who therewith hath will'd

for ev- er That his pal-ace should be deck'd. 5. Glo- ry be to God, and

hon-our In the highest, as is meet, To the Son and to the Fa- ther,

And th' e-ternal Par- a-clete, Whose is boundless praise and pow- er

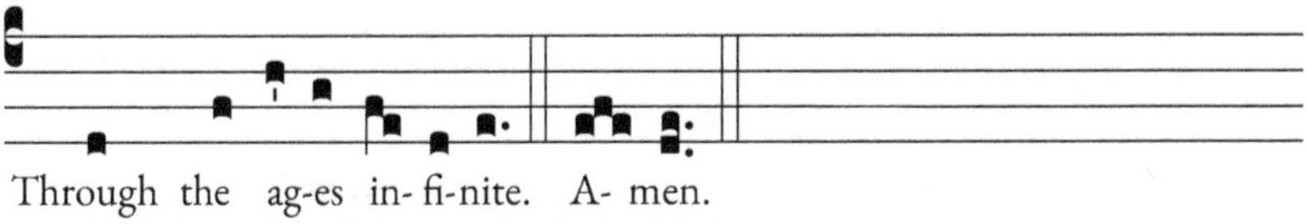

Common of Saints — *Church Dedication*

Through the ag-es in-fi-nite. A-men.
℣. This is the Lord's house, firmly builded.
℟. It is well founded on the solid rock.

Mag. Ant. The Lord hath hallowed † his tabernacle: for this is the house of the Lord, wherein men may call upon his Name; whereof it is written, My Name shall be therein, saith the Lord.

Mattins

¶ The Invitatory Hymn is from I Evensong.

Office Hymn

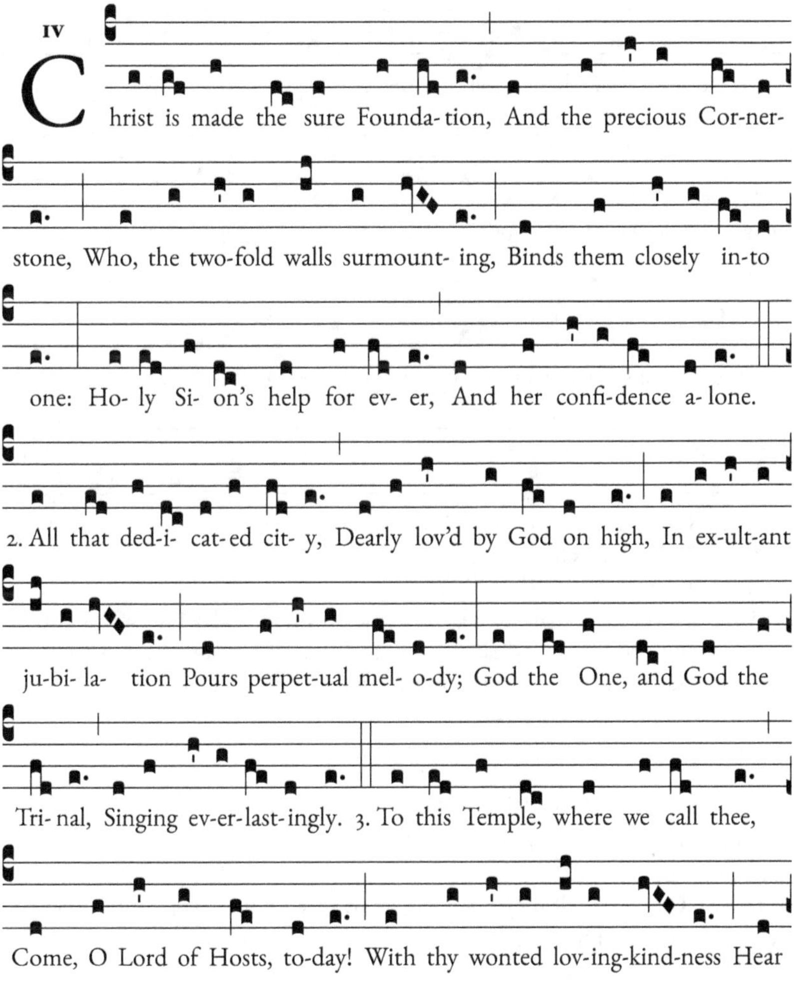

Christ is made the sure Founda-tion, And the precious Cor-ner-stone, Who, the two-fold walls surmount-ing, Binds them closely in-to one: Ho-ly Si-on's help for ev-er, And her confi-dence a-lone.

2. All that ded-i-cat-ed cit-y, Dearly lov'd by God on high, In ex-ult-ant ju-bi-la-tion Pours perpet-ual mel-o-dy; God the One, and God the Tri-nal, Singing ev-er-last-ingly. 3. To this Temple, where we call thee, Come, O Lord of Hosts, to-day! With thy wonted lov-ing-kind-ness Hear

Church Dedication   # Common of Saints

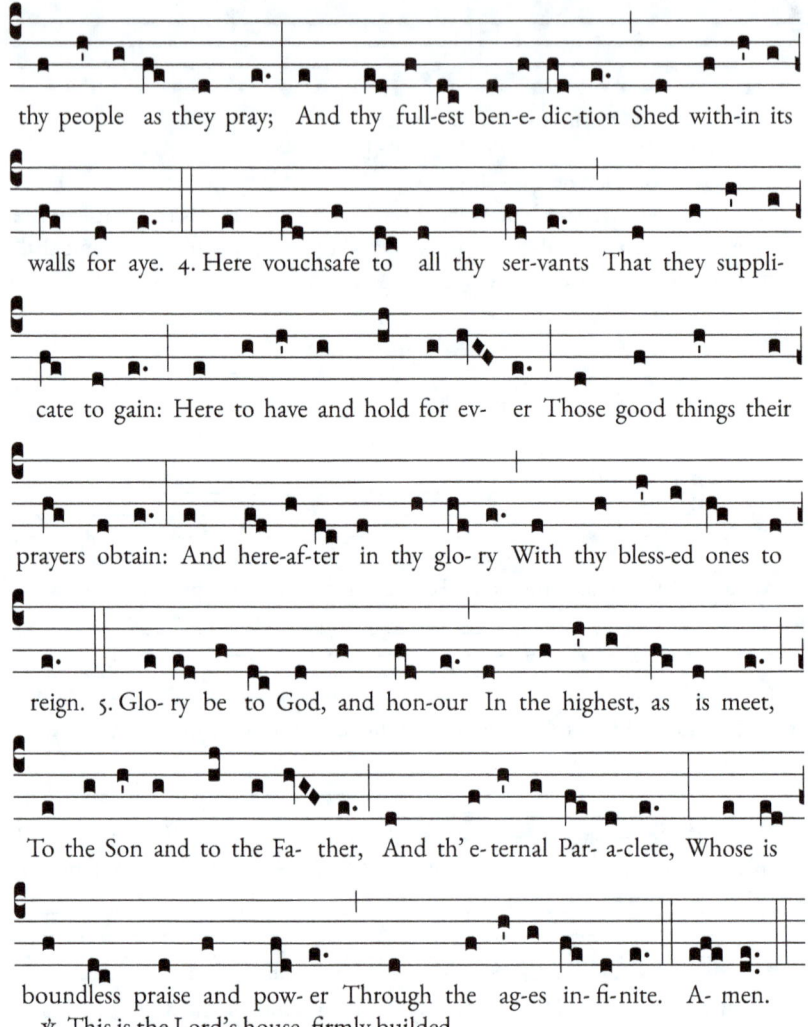

thy people as they pray; And thy full-est ben-e-dic-tion Shed with-in its walls for aye. 4. Here vouchsafe to all thy ser-vants That they suppli-cate to gain: Here to have and hold for ev- er Those good things their prayers obtain: And here-af-ter in thy glo- ry With thy bless-ed ones to reign. 5. Glo- ry be to God, and hon-our In the highest, as is meet, To the Son and to the Fa- ther, And th' e-ternal Par-a-clete, Whose is boundless praise and pow- er Through the ag-es in- fi-nite. A- men.

℣. This is the Lord's house, firmly builded.

℟. It is well founded on the solid rock.

Ben. Ant. Zacchaeus, † make haste, and come down; for today I must abide at thy house: and he made haste, and came down, and received him joyfully into his house. This day is salvation come to this house form the Lord, alleluia.

II Evensong

¶ The Hymn is of I Evensong with the following Versicle & Antiphon.

℣. Holiness becometh thine house, O Lord.

℟. For ever.

Mag. Ant. O how dreadful † is this place! truly this is none other but the house of God, and the gate of heaven.

Common of Saints *Church Dedication*

Introit

How dreadful is this place: this is the house of God, and the gate of heaven: and men shall call it the palace of God (Alleluia, alleluia). *Ps.* O how amiable are thy dwellings, thou Lord of hosts! My soul hath a desire and longing to enter into the courts of the Lord.

Collect

O GOD, who year by year renewest unto us the day of consecration of this thy holy temple, and dost ever bring us again in safety to thy sacred mysteries: graciously hear the prayers of thy people, and grant; that whosoever entereth this temple to ask for blessings may rejoice in the obtaining of all his petitions. Through.

¶ On the day itself of the Dedication of a Church and through the Octave, and when the Collect is to be varied, is said the following.

O GOD, who thyself invisible, containest all things, but dost for the salvation of mankind shew forth visibly the signs of thy power: enlighten this temple with the power of thine in-dwelling, and grant; that all they, who come together here to ask thy mercy, may, in whatsoever tribulation they call upon thee, obtain the blessings of thy consolation. Through.

Epistle. Revelation 21:2

IN THOSE DAYS: I saw the holy city, new Jerusalem, coming down from God out of heaven, prepared as a bride adorned for her husband. And I heard a great voice out of heaven saying, Behold, the tabernacle of God is with men, and he will dwell with them, and they shall be his people, and God himself shall be with them, and be their God. And God shall wipe away all tears from their eyes; and there shall be no more death, neither sorrow, nor crying, neither shall there be any more pain: for the former things are passed away. And he that sat upon the throne said, Behold, I make all things new.

Gradual. This dwelling is God's handywork, it is a mystery beyond all price, that cannot be spoken against. ℣. O God, before whom standeth the choir of Angels, graciously hear the prayers of thy servants.

Alleluia. Alleluia, alleluia. ℣. I will worship toward thy holy temple: and praise thy name. Alleluia.

¶ In Septuagesimatide or Lent, replacing the Alleluia:

Tract. They that put their trust in the Lord shall be even as the mount Sion: which may not be removed, but standeth fast for ever. ℣. The hills stand about Jerusalem, even so standeth the Lord round about his people, from this time forth for evermore.

¶ In Eastertide, replacing the Lesser Alleluia:

Alleluia. Alleluia, alleluia. ℣. I will worship toward thy holy temple: and praise thy name. Alleluia. ℣. The house of the Lord is well founded upon a sure rock. Alleluia.

Church Dedication # Common of Saints

Gospel. Luke 19:1

AT THAT TIME: Jesus entered and passed through Jericho. And, behold, there was a man named Zacchæus, which was the chief among the publicans, and he was rich. And he sought to see Jesus who he was; and could not for the press, because he was little of stature. And he ran before, and climbed up into a sycomore tree to see him: for he was to pass that way. And when Jesus came to the place, he looked up, and saw him, and said unto him, Zacchæus, make haste, and come down; for to day I must abide at thy house. And he made haste, and came down, and received him joyfully. And when they saw it, they all murmured, saying, That he was gone to be guest with a man that is a sinner. And Zacchæus stood, and said unto the Lord; Behold, Lord, the half of my goods I give to the poor; and if I have taken any thing from any man by false accusation, I restore him fourfold. And Jesus said unto him, This day is salvation come to this house, forsomuch as he also is a son of Abraham. For the Son of man is come to seek and to save that which was lost.

¶ After Septuagesima the **Alleluia** at the end of the following Offertory is omitted.

Offertory. O Lord God, in the uprightness of mine heart I have willingly offered all these things; and now I have seen with joy thy people, which are present here: O God of Israel, keep this imagination of their heart, alleluia.

Secret

In the Dedication itself

O LORD, we beseech thee, mercifully hear our prayers: that all we, who are gathered within the precincts of this temple, whose dedication year by year we celebrate, may perfectly serve thee, both in body and soul; that, like as we do here present our offerings unto thee, so we may by thee be enabled to attain unto the rewards of everlasting felicity. Through.

Outside the dedicated Church itself

O LORD, we beseech thee, mercifully hear our prayers: that, like as we do here present our offerings unto thee, so we may by thee be enable to attain unto the rewards of everlasting felicity. Through.

On the day itself of the Dedication of a Church, and through the Octave, and when the secret is to be varied, is said the following.

O GOD, who art the author of the gifts to be consecrated unto thee, pour forth upon this house of prayer thy blessing: that all who shall call upon thy name therein may perceive the succour of thy defence. Through.

¶ The common Preface, even in Lent, although there shall occur some Commemoration or common Octave with a Preface of their own, which are not of some Mystery of our Lord.

Communion. My house shall be called the house of prayer, saith the Lord: in it every one that asketh receiveth; and he that seeketh findeth: and to him that knocketh it shall be opened (Alleluia).

Common of Saints *Church Dedication*

Postcommunion

O GOD, who of elect and living stones dost fashion for thy Majesty an everlasting habitation: assist the supplications of us thy people; that, like as thy Church increaseth in visible habitations, so it may grow and prosper in spiritual advancement. Through.

❡ On the day itself of the Dedication of a Church, and through the Octave, or where the Postcommunion is to be varied, is said the following.

WE beseech thee, Almighty God: that in this place, which we, though unworthy, have dedicated to thy name, thou wouldest incline thy merciful ears to all that call upon thee. Through.

❡ On the day of the Dedication itself, Mass is said as above with the second Prayers; and the Collect of the Mystery or Saint in whose honour the church is dedicated is added to the first under one conclusion.

❡ During the Octave, Mass is said as above; but within the Octave the 2nd Collect is of St. Mary, from the Votive Mass of the Season: 3rd Against the Persecutors of the Church or for the Chief Bishop.

❡ On the day of the Dedication of an Altar, Mass is said as on the Dedication of a Church, except the Prayers following: to which likewise in the case of a fixed Altar the Prayer of the Mystery or Saint in whose honour the Altar is dedicated is added under one conclusion.

Collect

O GOD, who from the whole assembly of thy Saints dost prepare for thyself an everlasting habitation: grant to this building the increase of heavenly grace; that like as we do here venerate with devout affection the relics of thy Saints, so we may ever be aided by their merits. Through.

Secret

WE beseech thee, thy Lord our God, let thy Holy Spirit come down upon this altar: that he may sanctify the gifts of thy people, and graciously cleanse the hearts of them that receive the same. Through . . . in the unity of the same Holy Spirit.

Postcommunion

ALMIGHTY and everlasting God, sanctify with the power of thy heavenly benediction this altar, which we have dedicated to the honour of thy name: and shew forth upon all that put their trust in thee the bounty of thy succour; that they may here obtain the grace of thy sacraments and the fulfilment of their desires. Through.

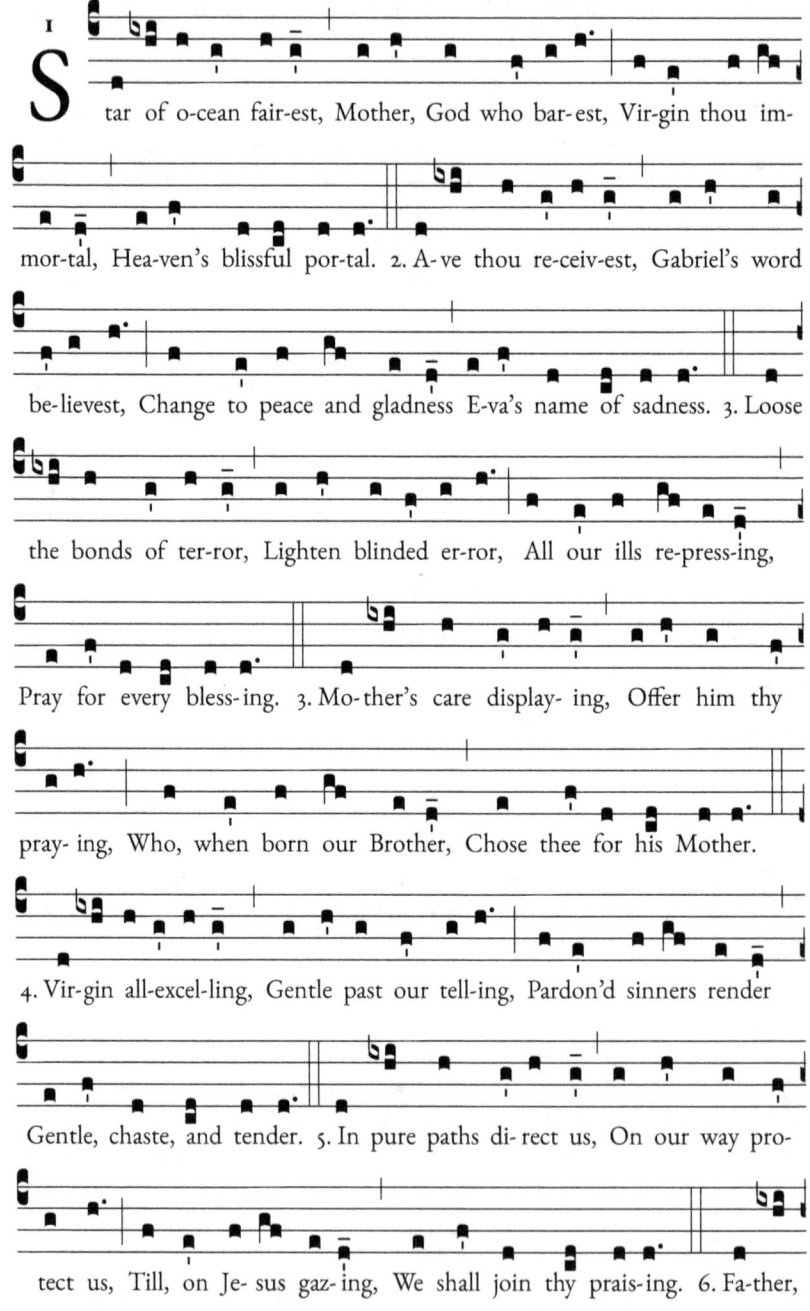

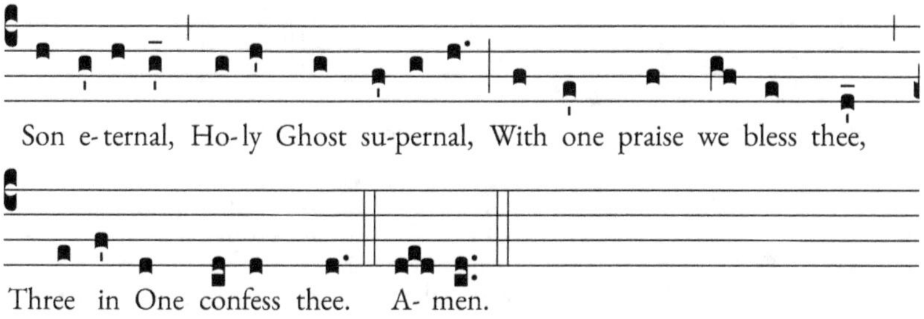

Common of Saints *Blessed Virgin Mary*

Son e-ternal, Ho-ly Ghost su-pernal, With one praise we bless thee, Three in One confess thee. A- men.

℣. Vouchsafe that I may praise thee, O holy Virgin.
℟. Give me strength against thine enemies.

Mag. Ant. O holy Mary, † help thou the suffering, strengthen the faint-hearted, comfort the sorrowful; pray for the people, entreat for the clergy, intercede for all womankind vowed unto God: may all acknowledge the help of thy prayer, who celebrate thy holy festival.

Mattins

Invitatory Hymn

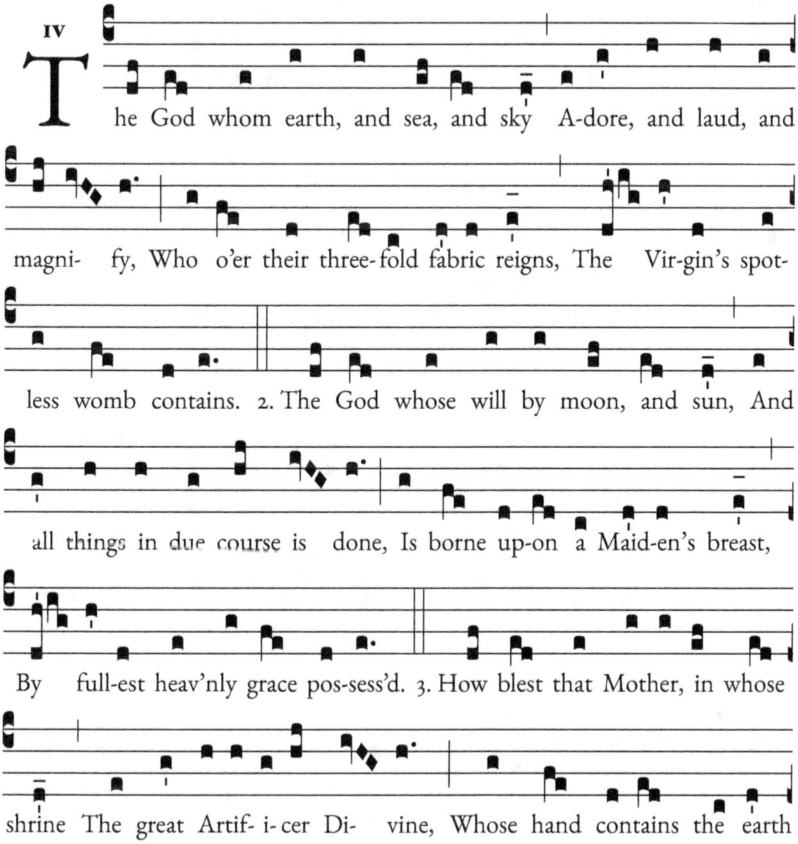

IV

The God whom earth, and sea, and sky A-dore, and laud, and magni- fy, Who o'er their three-fold fabric reigns, The Vir-gin's spot-less womb contains. 2. The God whose will by moon, and sun, And all things in due course is done, Is borne up-on a Maid-en's breast, By full-est heav'nly grace pos-sess'd. 3. How blest that Mother, in whose shrine The great Artif- i- cer Di- vine, Whose hand contains the earth

Blessed Virgin Mary # Common of Saints

and sky, Vouch-saf'd, as in his ark, to lie. 4. Blest, in the message Gabriel brought; Blest, by the work the Spir-it wrought; From whom the great De-sire of earth Took human flesh and hu-man birth. 5. All hon-our, laud, and glo-ry be, O Je-su Vir-gin-born, to thee, Whom with the Fa-ther we a-dore, And Ho-ly Ghost for ev-ermore. A-men.

Office Hymn

O glor-ious La-dy, thron'd in rest, Amidst the star-ry host a-bove, Who gav-est nurture from thy breast To God, with pure ma-ternal love. 2. What we had lost through sin-ful Eve The Blos-som sprung from thee re-stores, And, granting bliss to souls that grieve, Unbars the ev-er-last-ing doors. 3. O Gate, through which hath pass'd

Common of Saints *Blessed Virgin Mary*

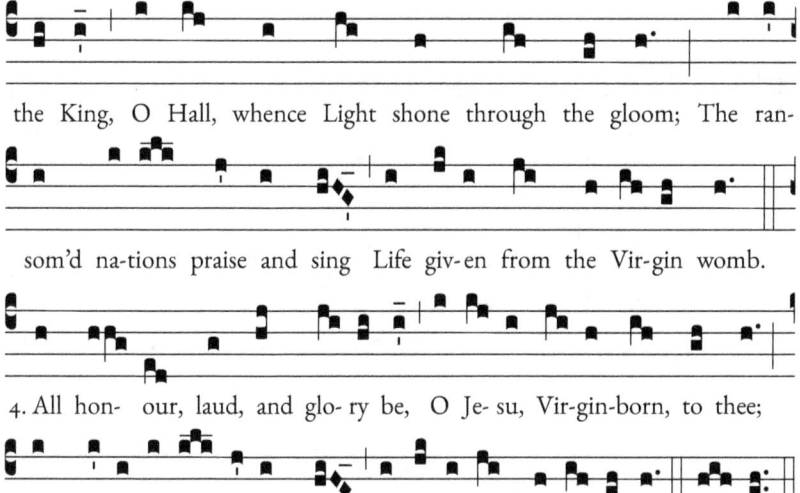

the King, O Hall, whence Light shone through the gloom; The ransom'd nations praise and sing Life given from the Virgin womb.

4. All honour, laud, and glory be, O Jesu, Virgin-born, to thee; All glory, as is ever meet, To Father and to Paraclete. A- men.

℣. Full of grace are thy lips.
℟. Because God hath blessed thee for ever.

Ben. Ant. Blessed art thou, † O Mary, for thou hast believed: and there shall be a performance in thee of those things which were told thee from the Lord, alleluia.

II Evensong

¶ The Hymn & Versicle are of I Evensong with the following Antiphon.

Mag. Ant. All generations † shall call me blessed: for God hath regarded the lowliness of his handmaiden.

Introit

HAIL, O Mother most holy, who in childbirth didst bring forth the Monarch: him who o'er heaven and earth reigneth for ever and ever (Alleluia, alleluia). *Ps.* My heart is inditing of a good matter: I speak of the things which I have made unto the King.

Collect

GRANT, we beseech thee, O Lord God, that we thy servants may enjoy perpetual health of mind and of body: and, at the glorious intercession of blessed Mary ever Virgin, be delivered from present sadness, and rejoice in everlasting gladness. Through.

Blessed Virgin Mary # Common of Saints

Epistle. Ecclesiasticus 24:9

HE created me from the beginning before the world; And to the end I shall not fail. In the holy tabernacle I ministered before him; And so was I established in Sion. In the beloved city likewise he gave me rest; And in Jerusalem was my authority. And I took root in a people that was glorified, Even in the portion of the Lord's own inheritance.

Gradual. Blessed and venerable art thou, O Virgin Mary: who without spot wast found Mother of the Saviour. ℣. Virgin Mother of God, he whom the whole world containeth not, being made man lay hid in thy womb.

Alleluia. Alleluia, alleluia. ℣. After childbirth, O Virgin, thou didst remain inviolate: Mother of God, intercede for us. Alleluia.

❧ In Advent, the following Alleluia Verse replaces the one above.

Alleluia. Alleluia, alleluia. ℣. Hail, Mary, full of grace; the Lord is with thee: blessed art thou among women. Alleluia.

❧ In Septuagesimatide or Lent, replacing the Alleluia:

Tract. Rejoice, O Virgin Mary, alone thou hast destroyed all heresies. ℣. Who didst believe the words of the Archangel Gabriel. ℣. Whilst a Virgin thou didst bring forth him who is God and man: and after childbirth, O Virgin, inviolate didst remain. ℣. Mother of God intercede for us.

❧ In Eastertide, replacing the Lesser Alleluia:

Alleluia. Alleluia, alleluia. ℣. Now hath blossomed Jesse's rod: a Virgin bears both man and God: God restoreth peace to men, high and low are one again. Alleluia. ℣. Hail, Mary, full of grace, the Lord is with thee: blessed art thou among women. Alleluia.

Gospel. Luke 11:27

T THAT TIME: As Jesus spake to the multitudes, a certain woman of the company lifted up her voice, and said unto him: Blessed is the womb that bare thee, and the paps which thou hast sucked. But he said: Yea rather, blessed are they that hear the word of God, and keep it.

Offertory. Hail, Mary, full of grace; the Lord is with thee: blessed art thou among women, and blessed is the fruit of thy womb (Alleluia).

Secret

HROUGH thy mercy, O Lord, and the intercession of blessed Mary ever Virgin, may this oblation avail for our prosperity and peace, both now and for ever. Through.

Communion. Blessed is the womb of the Virgin Mary, that bore the Son of the everlasting Father (Alleluia).

Common of Saints *Saturday BVM*

Postcommunion

GRANT, we beseech thee, O Lord: that we, who have received these aids to our salvation, may at all times and in all places be protected through the advocacy of blessed Mary ever Virgin; in whose honour we have made these offerings to thy Majesty. Through.

Office of Saint Mary on Saturday

¶ The Hymns are as in the Common of the Blessed Virgin Mary (p. 760).

Through the Year

Evensong

℣. Full of grace are thy lips.
℟. Because God hath blessed thee for ever.
Mag. Ant. O blessed Mother † and spotless Virgin, thou glorious Queen of the world, intercede for us to the Lord.

GRANT, we beseech thee, O Lord God, that we thy servants may enjoy perpetual health of mind and of body: and, at the glorious intercession of blessed Mary ever Virgin, be delivered from present sadness, and rejoice in everlasting gladness. Through.

DEFEND us, we beseech thee, O Lord, from all perils of mind and body: and at the intercession of blessed Joseph, of thy blessed Apostles Peter and Paul, of blessed N. and of all Saints, graciously bestow upon us both peace and safety: that all adversity and error being done away, thy Church may serve thee in untroubled freedom. Through.

Mattins

℣. Blessed art thou amongst women.
℟. And blessed is the fruit of thy womb.
Ben. Ant. O ever blessed Mother of God, † Mary ever Virgin, temple of the Godhead, hallowed shrine of the Holy Spirit, thou only, above all others, wast acceptable to our Lord Jesus Christ: pray for the people, entreat for the clergy, intercede for all womankind vowed unto God.

GRANT, we beseech thee, O Lord God, that we thy servants may enjoy perpetual health of mind and of body: and, at the glorious intercession of blessed Mary ever Virgin, be delivered from present sadness, and rejoice in everlasting gladness. Through.

DEFEND us, we beseech thee, O Lord, from all perils of mind and body: and at the intercession of blessed Joseph, of thy blessed Apostles Peter and Paul, of blessed N. and of all Saints, graciously bestow upon us both peace and safety: that all adversity and error being done away, thy Church may serve thee in untroubled freedom. Through.

Saturday BVM # Common of Saints

After Christmas

¶ From Saturday after the Epiphany Octave through Saturday before Purification.

Evensong

℣. Full of grace are thy lips.
℟. Because God hath blessed thee for ever.

Mag. Ant. Great † is the mystery of the inheritance: the womb of her that knew not man is become the temple of the Godhead: by taking flesh of her, he was no way defiled: all the nations shall gather, saying: Glory be to thee, O Lord.

GOD, who by the virgin child-bearing of blessed Mary hast bestowed upon mankind the rewards of eternal salvation: grant, we beseech thee; that we may perceive her intercession for us, through whom we have been counted worthy to receive the author of life, Jesus Christ thy Son, our Lord. Who liveth.

DEFEND us, we beseech thee, O Lord, from all perils of mind and body: and at the intercession of blessed Joseph, of thy blessed Apostles Peter and Paul, of blessed *N.* and of all Saints, graciously bestow upon us both peace and safety: that all adversity and error being done away, thy Church may serve thee in untroubled freedom. Through.

Mattins

℣. Blessed art thou amongst women.
℟. And blessed is the fruit of thy womb.

Ben. Ant. A great and wondrous mystery † is made known to us this day; a new thing is wrought in both natures: God is made man; that which was, remained, and that which was not, he assumed; suffering no confusion, nor yet division.

GOD, who by the virgin child-bearing of blessed Mary hast bestowed upon mankind the rewards of eternal salvation: grant, we beseech thee; that we may perceive her intercession for us, through whom we have been counted worthy to receive the author of life, Jesus Christ thy Son, our Lord. Who liveth.

DEFEND us, we beseech thee, O Lord, from all perils of mind and body: and at the intercession of blessed Joseph, of thy blessed Apostles Peter and Paul, of blessed *N.* and of all Saints, graciously bestow upon us both peace and safety: that all adversity and error being done away, thy Church may serve thee in untroubled freedom. Through.

Common of Saints *Saturday BVM*

Eastertide

Evensong

℣. Full of grace art thy lips, alleluia.
℟. Because God hath blessed thee for ever, alleluia.
Mag. Ant. O Queen of heaven, † be joyful, alleluia; Because he whom so meetly thou barest, alleluia, Hath arisen, as he promised, alleluia: Pray for us to the Father, alleluia.

GRANT, we beseech thee, O Lord God, that we thy servants may enjoy perpetual health of mind and of body: and, at the glorious intercession of blessed Mary ever Virgin, be delivered from present sadness, and rejoice in everlasting gladness. *Through.*

O GOD, who didst will that thy Son should for us undergo the burden of the Cross, that he might deliver us from the power of the enemy: grant unto us thy servants that we may attain unto the joy of his resurrection. *Through the same.*

Mattins

¶ Mattins is as in Evensong.

Hymn Index

First Lines

A great and mighty wonder .... #40
A mighty fortress is our God .... #1
A solis ortu cardine (From lands that see the sun arise) .... p. 319
A thrilling voice by Jordan rings, (*Vox clara ecce intonat*) .... p. 310
Ad coenam Agni providi (The Lamb's high banquet we await) .... p. 368
Aeterna caeli gloria (Eternal glory of the sky) .... p. 27 (Summer), p. 46 (Winter)
Aeterna Christi munera (The eternal gifts of Christ the King) .... p. 675
Aeterna Christi munera et Martyrum (The Martyrs' triumphs let us sing) .... p. 694
Aeterna Imago Altissime (Image Eterne of God Most High) .... p. 648
Aeterne rerum Conditor (Maker of all eternal King) .... p. 32
Aeterne Rex altissime (Eternal Monarch, King most high) .... p. 382
Aeterni Patris Unice (Thou only Son) .... p. 569
Ales diei nuntius (The winged herald of the day) .... p. 19 (Summer), p. 38 (Winter)
All creatures of our God and King .... #2
All glorious King of Martyrs thou (*Rex gloriose Martyrum*) .. p. 711 (Martyrs Evensong in Easter), p. 695 (Martyrs Mattins)
All glory, laud, and honour .... #64
All hail! ye infant martyr flowers (*Salvete flores*) .... p. 326
All praise to Jesus' hallowed Name .... #41
All ye who seek (*Quicumque Christum*) .... p. 584
Alleluia! sing to Jesus! .... #3
Almighty God whose will (*Magnae Deus potentiae*) ..... p. 25 (Summer), p. 44 (Winter)
Amazing grace! How sweet the sound .... #4
Amor Jesu dulcissime (O love of Jesus) .... p. 585
And did those feet in ancient time .... #5
Angels we have heard on high .... #42
Anglorum Jam Apostolus (Apostle of the English) .... p. 472
Angularis fundamentum (Christ is Made the Sure Foundation) .... p. 755
Antra Deserta (Thou in thy childhood) .... p. 537
Apostle of the English (*Anglorum Jam Apostolus*) .... p. 472
As with gladness, men of old .... #56
At the Lamb's high feast we sing .... #69
At this our solemn feast (*Sacris Solemnis*) .... p. 404
Auctor beate saeculi (Thou blessed fount of life and time) .... p. 408
Audi benigne Conditor (O maker of the world, give ear) .... p. 352
Audit tyrannus (The moody tyrant hears aghast) .... p. 325
Aurea luce (With golden splendour) .... p. 543
Aurora jam spargit polum (Dawn sprinkles all the east) ... p. 30 (Summer), p. 48 (Winter)
Aurora lucis rutilat (Light's glittering morn bedecks the sky) .... p. 366
Ave maris stella (Star of ocean fairest) .... p. 760
Away in a manger .... #43
Be thou my Vision .... #6
Beata nobis gaudia (Blest joys for mighty wonders wrought) .... p. 397
Behold the golden dawn arise (*Lux ecce surgit aurea*) ..... p. 24 (Summer), p. 43 (Winter)
Blessed bride of Christ (*Te beata sponsa Christi*) .... p. 458
Blessed City, Heav'nly Salem (*Urbs Jerusalem beata*) .... p. 753

Hymn Index

Blest joys for mighty wonders wrought (*Beata nobis gaudia*) .... p. 397
Brightest and best of the sons of the morning .... #57
Caeli Deus sanctissime (O God whose hand hath spread) . p. 23 (Summer), p. 42 (Winter)
Caelestis aulae Nuntius (The mysteries of God are shewn) .... p. 628
Caelitum Joseph (Joseph, the praise and glory of the heavens) .. p. 375 (Patronage Mattins)
Caelitum, Joseph, decus (Joseph, the praise and glory) .... p. 480 (Joseph Invitatory)
Caelo Redemptor Praetulit (The world's Redeemer from the earth) .... p. 637
Christ is Made the Sure Foundation (*Angularis fundamentum*) .... p. 755
Christ, the fair glory (*Christe sanctorum*) .... p. 622
Christ the Lord is risen today, alleluia .... #70
Christe, Redemptor omnium (Jesu, the Father's only Son) .... p. 317 (Christmas)
Christe, Redemptor omnium (O Christ Redeemer of us all) .... p. 653 (All Hallows')
Christe sanctorum (Christ, the fair glory) .... p. 622
Claro Paschali gaudio (In this our bright and Paschal day) .... p. 680
Come, Holy Ghost, Creator blest (*Veni, Creator Spiritus*) .... p. 393
Come thou Fount of every blessing .... #7
Come, thou long expected Jesus .... #36
Conditor alme siderum (Creator of the stars of night) .... p. 308
Consors paterni (Light of Light, O Dayspring bright) .... p. 7
Cor arca legem continens (O Heart of Jesus, holy ark) .... p. 411
Creator of the circling sky (*Orbis patrator optime*) .... p. 627
Creator of the Earth and Sky (*Deus creator omnium*) .... p. 4
Creator of the stars of night (*Conditor alme siderum*) .... p. 308
Crown him with many crowns .... #8
Custodes hominum (The Guardians of our race) .... p. 625
Dawn sprinkles all the east (*Aurora jam spargit polum*) ... p. 30 (Summer), p. 48 (Winter)
Dear Christians, one and all rejoice .... #9
Defender, leader true (*Qui te, posthabitis*) .... p. 433
Deus creator omnium (Creator of the Earth and Sky) .... p. 4
Deus tuorum militum (Of all thy warrior Saints, O Lord) ... p. 322, p. 682), p. 711 (Martyr Evensong in Easter)
Doctor egregie, Paule (O by thy doctrine) .... p. 546
Drop down, ye heavens, from above (*Rorate Caeli*) .... p. 115
Ecce jam noctis (Lo! the dim shadows) .... p. 14
Earth's mighty Maker whose command (*Telluris ingens Conditor*) . p. 20 (Summer), p. 39 (Winter)
En ut superba (See how the bold and raging crows) .... p. 410
Eternal glory of the sky (*Aeterna caeli gloria*) .... p. 27 (Summer), p. 46 (Winter)
Eternal Monarch, King most high (*Aeterne Rex altissime*) .... p. 382
Ex more docti (The fast, as taught by holy lore) .... p. 354
Exsultet caelum gaudibus (Let heav'n's exultant praises ring) .... p. 324
Exsultet caelum laudibus (Let heav'n's exultant praises ring) p. 673 (Apostles Evensong), p. 676 (Apostles Mattins)
Faith of our fathers .... #10
Father we praise thee now (*Nocte surgentes*) .... p. 2
Festivis Resonent (With glad and joyous strains) .... p. 549
Fortem virili pectore (High let us all our voices raise) .... p. 747
From lands that see the sun arise (*A solis ortu cardine*) .... p. 319
Gaude, mater Anna (Mother Anne be joyful) .... p. 572

Hymn Index

Gem of the highest diadem immortal (*Inter aeternas*) .... p. 488
God the Father, be our Stay .... #79
God rest ye merry gentlemen .... #44
Good King Wenceslas looked out .... #45
Great God of boundless mercy hear (*Summae Deus*) .... p. 12
Hail, holy wounds (*Salvete, Christe vulnera*) .... p. 553
Hail Mary, ever blessed .... p. 641
Hail thee, festival day! .... #71 (Easter), #73 (Ascension), #76 (Whitsun)
Hark! The herald angels sing .... #46
He, whom the faithful (*Iste Quem Laeti*) .... p. 481
Hence night and clouds (*Nox et tenebrae et nubila*) ...... p. 22 (Summer), p. 41 (Winter)
High let us all our voices raise (*Fortem virili pectore*) .... p. 747
High Word of God, who once didst come (*Verbum supernum*) .... p. 309
Holy God, we praise thy Name .... #80
Holy, holy, holy! .... #81
Hostis Herodes (Why, impious Herod, vainly fear) .... p. 337
Hymnis angelicis ora (Now we our voices raise) .... p. 460
I bind unto myself today .... #82
I need thee every hour .... #11
I sing the mighty power of God .... #12
I vow thee, my country .... #13
If God had not been on our side .... #14
Image Eterne of God Most High (*Aeterna Imago Altissime*) .... p. 648
Immaculate Mary! .... #15
Immense caeli Conditor (O great Creator of the sky) ...... p. 18 (Summer), p. 37 (Winter)
Immortal, invisible, God only wise .... #16
In childhood Placidus was by his father given (*Puellus Placidus, quem pater obtulit*) p. 434
In monte Olivis (The Mount of Olives witnesseth) .... p. 630
In the bleak wid-winter .... #47
In this our bright and Paschal day (*Claro Paschali gaudio*) .... p. 680
Inter aeternas (Gem of the highest diadem immortal) .... p. 488
Ira justa Conditoris (Righteous anger of our Maker) .... p. 551
Isaiah, mighty seer, in days of old .... #83
Iste Confessor (This the Confessor of the Lord) .... p. 715
Iste Quem Laeti (He, whom the faithful) .... p. 481
It came upon the midnight clear .... #48
Jam bone pastor (Peter, good shepherd) .. p. 466 (Chair of Peter Antioch Mattins), p. 544 (Peter Mattins)
Jam Christe sol justitiae (Now Christ, thou Sun of righteousness) .... p. 355
Jam Christus astra ascendunt (Now Christ, ascending whence he came) .... p. 395
Jam morte, victor, obruta (Now hell is vanquished) .... p. 631
Jam noctis umbrae concidunt (The shades of night) .... p. 462
Jam toto subitus (Now let the darkling eve) .... p. 611
Jesu corona celsior (O Jesu, Crown above the Sky) .... p. 726
Jesu corona Virginum (Jesu! the Virgins' Crown) .... p. 735
Jesu, decus angelicum (Jesu, the beauty Angels see) .... p. 331
Jesu dulcis memoria (Jesu! the very thought is sweet) .... p. 328
Jesu nostra redemptio (Jesu, Redemption all divine) .... p. 384
Jesu, Redemption all divine (*Jesu nostra redemptio*) .... p. 384

Hymn Index

Jesu Redemptor omnium (Jesu, the world's Redeemer, hear) .... p. 717
Jesu Rex admirabilis (O Jesu, King of wondrous might) .... p. 329
Jesu, Salvator saeculi (Jesu who cam'st the world to save) .... p. 655
Jesu, the beauty Angels see (*Jesu, decus angelicum*) .... p. 331
Jesu, the Father's only Son (*Christe, Redemptor omnium*) .... p. 317
Jesu! the very thought is sweet (*Jesu dulcis memoria*) .... p. 328
Jesu! the Virgins' Crown (*Jesu corona Virginum*) .... p. 735
Jesu, the world's Redeemer, hear (*Jesu Redemptor omnium*) .... p. 717
Jesu who cam'st the world to save (*Jesu, Salvator saeculi*) .... p. 655
Joseph, the praise and glory (*Caelitum, Joseph, decus*) .... p. 480 (Joseph Invitatory)
Joseph, the praise and glory of the heavens (*Caelitum Joseph*) .. p. 375 (Patronage Mattins)
Joy to the world .... #49
Joyful, joyful, we adore thee .... #18
Laudibus cives resonent canoris (Shout all ye people) .... p. 485
Let all mortal flesh keep silence .... #19
Let all the Saints in concert (*Omnis sanctorum concio*) .... p. 574
Let Angels chant thy praise, pure spouse of purest Bride (*Te Joseph celebrent*) ...... p. 373
Let heav'n's exultant praises ring (*Exsultet caelum gaudibus*) .... p. 324
Let heav'n's exultant praises ring (*Exsultet caelum laudibus*) . p. 673 (Apostles Evensong), 676 (Apostles Mattins)
Let the Holy Spirit's Grace .... #77
Lift high the cross .... #20
Light of Light, O Dayspring bright (*Consors paterni*) .... p. 7
Light's glittering morn bedecks the sky (*Aurora lucis rutilat*) .... p. 366
Lo, how a Rose ever blooming .... #50
Lo! the dim shadows (*Ecce jam noctis*) .... p. 14
Look down, O Lord, from heaven behold .... #21
Lord, keep us steadfast in thy Word .... #22
Lord, who at Cana's wedding feast .... #58
Lord, who throughout these forty days .... #65
Lucis Creator optime (O blest Creator of the light) .... p. 15 (Summer), p. 34 (Winter)
Lustris sex qui jam peractis (Thirty years among us dwelling) p. 362 (Passion Sunday), p. 507 (Invention)
Lux ecce surgit aurea (Behold the golden dawn arise) ..... p. 24 (Summer), p. 43 (Winter)
Magnae Deus potentiae (Almighty God whose will) ..... p. 25 (Summer), p. 44 (Winter)
Maker of all eternal King (*Aeterne rerum Conditor*) .... p. 32
Maker of earth, to thee alone .... #60
Maker of men from heav'n (*Plasmator hominis, Deus*) ... p. 28 (Summer), p. 47 (Winter)
Martyr Dei (Thou followest, Martyr of thy God) p. 321 (Stephen Mattins), p. 683 (Martyr Mattins)
Martyr Dei unicum (Thou foll'west, Martyr of thy God) .... p. 707
Mater Alme Numinis (Sweet mother of the Lord most high) .... p. 638
Mella cor obdulcantia (Thy lips, O Gregory) .... p. 473
Mother Anne be joyful (*Gaude, mater Anna*) .... p. 572
Nardo maria Pistico (The Lord's dear feet) .... p. 568
Nocte surgentes (Father we praise thee now) .... p. 2
Now Christ, ascending whence he came (*Jam Christus astra ascenderat*) .... p. 395
Now Christ, thou Sun of righteousness (*Jam Christe sol justitiae*) .... p. 355
Now Christ unfurls (*Vexilla Christus inclyta*) .... p. 650

Hymn Index

Now hell is vanquished (*Jam morte, victor, obruta*) .... p. 631
Now let the darkling eve (*Jam toto subitus*) .... p. 611
Now, my tongue, the Mystery telling (*Pange lingua gloriosi Corporis*) .... p. 402
Now thank we all our God .... #23
Now we our voices raise (*Hymnis angelicis ora*) .... p. 460
Nox atra rerum (The dusky veil of night hath laid) .... p. 10
Nox et tenebrae et nubila (Hence night and clouds) ...... p. 22 (Summer), p. 41 (Winter)
O blest Creator of the light (*Lucis Creator optime*) .... p. 15 (Summer), p. 34
O by thy doctrine (*Doctor egregie, Paule*) .... p. 546
O Christ Redeemer of us all (*Christe, Redemptor omnium*) .... p. 653
O Christ, thou heaven's eternal King (*Rex sempiterne, Domine*) .... p. 365
O come, all ye faithful .... #51
O come, O come Emmanuel .... #37
O Father of celestial rays (*Pater superni luminis*) .... p. 567
O for thy spirit (*Ut queant laxis*) .... p. 535
O gloriosa Domina (O glorious Lady, throned in rest) .... p. 762
O glorious Lady, throned in rest (*O gloriosa Domina*) .... p. 762
O God by whose command is swayed (*Summae Deus clementiae*) .... p. 400
O God, in whom all grace (*Summae Deus clementiae*) .... p. 614
O God whose hand hath spread (*Caeli Deus sanctissime*) . p. 23 (Summer), p. 42 (Winter)
O great Creator of the sky (*Immense caeli Conditor*) ...... p. 18 (Summer), p. 37 (Winter)
O Heart of Jesus, holy ark (*Cor arca legem continens*) .... p. 411
O Jesu, Crown above the Sky (*Jesu corona celsior*) .... p. 726
O Jesu, King of wondrous might (*Jesu Rex admirabilis*) .... p. 329
O Jesus Christ, from thee began .... #66
O Joseph heave'nly hosts (*Te Joseph celebrent*) .... p. 478
O Lord of ages thee (*Te saeculorum Principem*) .... p. 646
O love, how deep, how broad, how high! .... #61
O love of Jesus (*Amor Jesu dulcissime*) .... p. 585
O maker of the world, give ear (*Audi benigne Conditor*) .... p. 352
O more than blessed (*O nimis felix*) .... p. 538
O more than mighty cities known (*O sola*) .... p. 339
O nimis felix (O more than blessed) .... p. 538
O quot undis lacrimarum (What a flood of tears) .... p. 613
O sacred Head, now wounded .... #67
O sola (O more than mighty cities known) .... p. 339
O Trinity of blessed light (*O lux beata Trinitas*) .... p. 31 (Summer), p. 50 (Winter)
O wondrous type! O vision fair .... #86
O Word of God the Father .... #84
Of all thy warrior Saints, O Lord (*Deus tuorum militum*) p. 322 (Stephen Evensong), p. 682)
    (Martyr Evensong), p. 711 (Martyr Evensong in Easter)
Omnis sanctorum concio (Let all the Saints in concert) .... p. 574
On Jordan's bank the Baptist's cry .... #38
Orbis partrator optime (Creator of the circling sky) .... p. 627
Our God, our help in ages past .... #24
Our limbs refreshed with slumber now (*Somno Refectis*) .... p. 6
Out of the deep I cry to thee .... #25
Pange lingua gloriosi Corporis (Now, my tongue, the Mystery telling) .... p. 402

Hymn Index

Pange lingua gloriosi Proelium (Sing, my tongue, the glorious battle) ..... p. 360 (Passion Sunday), p. 505 (Invention)
Pater superni luminis (O Father of celestial rays) .... p. 567
Peter, good shepherd (*Jam bone pastor*) .. p. 466 (Chair of Peter Antioch Mattins), p. 544 (Peter Mattins)
Peter the Blessed (*Petrus beatus catenarum*) .... p. 578
Petrus beatus catenarum (Peter the Blessed) .... p. 578
Plasmator hominis, Deus (Maker of men from heav'n) ... p. 28 (Summer), p. 47 (Winter)
Praise God, from whom all blessings flow .... #26
Praise, my soul, the King of heaven .... #27
Praise to the Holiest in the height .... #62
Praise to the Lord, the Almighty .... #28
Primo dierum (This day the first of days) .... p. 3
Puellus Placidus, quem pater obtulit (In childhood Placidus was by his father given) p. 434
Quem terra, pontus, aethera (The God whom earth, and sea, and sky) .... p. 761
Qui te, posthabitis (Defender, leader true) .... p. 433
Quicumque Christum (All ye who seek) .... p. 584
Quidquid antiqui (Whate'er in former days befell the) .... p. 486
Quodcumque vinclis (Whate'er thou bindest) .... p. 579 (Lammas Invitatory)
Quodcumque vinclis (Whatsoever chain) .. p. 465 (Chair of St. Peter at Antioch Evensong)
Rerum Creator (Who madest all and dost control) .... p. 8
Rex gloriose Martyrum (All glorious King of Martyrs thou) .. p. 711 (Martyrs Evensong in Easter), p. 695 (Martyrs Mattins)
Rex sempiterne, Domine (O Christ, thou heaven's eternal King) .... p. 365
Righteous anger of our Maker (*Ira justa Conditoris*) .... p. 551
Rorate Caeli (Drop down, ye heavens, from above) .... p. 115
Salvete flores (All hail! ye infant martyr flowers) .... p. 326
Sacris Solemnis (At this our solemn feast) .... p. 404
Salvete, Christe vulnera (Hail, holy wounds) .... p. 553
Sanctorum meritis (The merits of the Saints) .... p. 692
Saviour of the nations, come .... #39
See how the bold and raging crows (*En ut superba*) .... p. 410
See, the Lord ascends in triumph .... #74
Shout all ye people (*Laudibus cives resonent canoris*) .... p. 485
Silent night, holy night .... #52
Sing, my tongue, the glorious battle (*Pange lingua gloriosi Proelium*) ...... p. 360 (Passion Sunday), p. 505 (Invention)
Sing we triumphant hymns of praise .... #75
Somno Refectis (Our limbs refreshed with slumber now) .... p. 6
Son of a Virgin (*Virginis Proles*) .... p. 734
Spirit of mercy, truth, and love .... #78
Splendor paternae gloriae (Thou Brightness of the Father's ray) .... p. 35
Star of ocean fairest (*Ave maris stella*) .... p. 760
Succedit nocti lucifer (The morning star succeeds to night) .... p. 573
Summae Deus (Great God of boundless mercy hear) .... p. 12
Summae Deus clementiae (O God, in whom all grace) ..... p. 614 (Seven Sorrows Mattins)
Summae Deus clementiae (O God by whose command is swayed) . p. 400 (Trinity Sunday Invitatory)
Sweet mother of the Lord most high (*Mater Alme Numinis*) .... p. 638

Hymn Index

Te gestientem gaudiis (Thy joys exultant) .... p. 633
Te beata sponsa Christi (Blessed bride of Christ) .... p. 458
Te Joseph celebrent (Let Angels chant thy praise, pure spouse of purest Bride) ...... p. 373 (Patronage of St. Joseph Evensong)
Te Joseph celebrent (O Joseph heave'nly hosts) .... p. 478 (St. Joseph Evensong)
Te saeculorum Principem (O Lord of ages thee) .... p. 646
Telluris ingens Conditor (Earth's mighty Maker whose command) . p. 20 (Summer), p. 39 (Winter)
Th' Apostles' hearts were full of pain (*Tristis erant Apostoli*) .... p. 678
That men a godly life might live .... #29
The Church's one foundation .... #30
The dusky veil of night hath laid (*Nox atra rerum*) .... p. 10
The eternal gifts of Christ the King (*Aeterna Christi munera*) .... p. 675
The fast, as taught by holy lore (*Ex more docti*) .... p. 354
The first Noel .... #53
The God whom earth, and sea, and sky (*Quem terra, pontus, aethera*) .... p. 761
The Guardians of our race (*Custodes hominum*) .... p. 625
The King of love my shepherd is .... #31
The Lamb's high banquet we await (*Ad coenam Agni providi*) .... p. 368
The Lord's dear feet (*Nardo maria Pistico*) .... p. 568
The Martyrs' triumphs let us sing (*Aeterna Christi munera et Martyrum*) .... p. 694
The merits of the Saints (*Sanctorum meritis*) .... p. 692
The moody tyrant hears aghast (*Audit tyrannus*) .... p. 325
The morning star succeeds to night (*Succedit nocti lucifer*) .... p. 573
The Mount of Olives witnesseth (*In monte Olivis*) .... p. 630
The mouth of fools doth God confess .... #32
The mysteries of God are shewn (*Caelestis aulae Nuntius*) .... p. 628
The royal banners forward go (*Vexilla Regis*) . . p. 358 (Passion Sunday), p. 503 (Invention)
The shades of night (*Jam noctis umbrae concidunt*) .... p. 462
The strife is o'er, the battle done .... #72
The winged herald of the day (*Ales diei nuntius*) .... p. 19 (Summer), p. 38 (Winter)
The Word proceeding from above (*Verbum supernum prodiens*) .... p. 406
The world's Redeemer from the earth (*Caelo Redemptor Praetulit*) .... p. 637
Thee, O Christ (*Tibi Christe splendor Patris*) .... p. 621
There is a book who runs may read .... #63
Thirty years among us dwelling (*Lustris sex qui jam peractis*) p. 362 (Passion Sunday), p. 507 (Invention)
This day the first of days (*Primo dierum*) .... p. 3
This the Confessor of the Lord (*Iste Confessor*) .... p. 715
Thou blessed fount of life and time (*Auctor beate saeculi*) .... p. 408
Thou Brightness of the Father's ray (*Splendor paternae gloriae*) .... p. 16 (Summer), p. 35 (Winter)
Thou foll'west, Martyr of thy God (*Martyr Dei unicum*) .... p. 707
Thou followest, Martyr of thy God (*Martyr Dei*) p. 321 (Stephen Mattins), p. 683 (Martyr Mattins)
Thou in thy childhood (*Antra Deserta*) .... p. 537
Thou only Son (*Aeterni Patris Unice*) .... p. 569
Thou Trinity in Unity (*Tu, Trinitatis Unitas*) .... p. 401 (Trinity Mattins)
Though in the midst of life we be .... #33

Hymn Index

Three in One and One in Three (*Tu Trinitatis*) . . . . p. 11 (Friday Invitatory)
Thy joys exultant (*Te gestientem gaudiis*) . . . . p. 633
Thy lips, O Gregory (*Mella cor obdulcantia*) . . . . p. 473
Tibi Christe splendor Patris (Thee, O Christ) . . . . p. 621
Tis good, Lord, to be here . . . . #87
To avert from men God's wrath . . . . #34
To shepherds as they watched by night . . . . #54
Tristis erant Apostoli (Th' Apostles' hearts were full of pain) . . . . p. 678
Tu Trinitatis (Three in One and One in Three) . . . . p. 11 (Friday Invitatory)
Tu, Trinitatis Unitas (Thou Trinity in Unity) . . . . p. 401
Urbs Jerusalem beata (Blessed City, Heav'nly Salem) . . . . p. 753
Ut queant laxis (O for thy spirit) . . . . p. 535
Veni, Creator Spiritus (Come, Holy Ghost, Creator blest) . . . . p. 393
Verbum supernum (High Word of God, who once didst come) . . . . p. 309
Verbum supernum prodiens (The Word proceeding from above) . . . . p. 406
Vexilla Christus inclyta (Now Christ unfurls) . . . . p. 650
Vexilla Regis (The royal banners forward go) . . p. 358 (Passion Sunday), p. 503 (Invention)
Virginis Proles (Son of a Virgin) . . . . p. 734
Vox clara ecce intonat (A thrilling voice by Jordan rings) . . . . p. 310
We all believe in one true God . . . . #85
We three Kings of Orient are . . . . #59
What a flood of tears (*O quot undis lacrimarum*) . . . . p. 613
What Child is this . . . . #55
Whate'er in former days befell the (*Quidquid antiqui*) . . . . p. 486
Whate'er thou bindest (*Quodcumque vinclis*) . . . . p. 579
Whatsoever chain (*Quodcumque vinclis*) . . . . p. 465
When I survey the wondrous cross . . . . #68
When peace like a river . . . . #17
Who madest all and dost control (*Rerum Creator*) . . . . p. 8
With glad and joyous strains (*Festivis Resonent*) . . . . p. 549
With golden splendour (*Aurea luce*) . . . . p. 543
When Christ was born in Bethlehem . . . . p. 641
Why, impious Herod, vainly fear (*Hostis Herodes*) . . . . p. 337
Ye watchers and ye holy ones . . . . #35

Most Holy Trinity, Save Us.
St. Mary Ever-Virgin, Pray for Us.
St. John the Divine, Pray for Us.
St. Alban the Martyr, Pray for Us.
St. Augustine of Canterbury, Pray for Us.
St. Gregory the Great, Pray for Us.
St. Tikhon of Moscow, Pray for Us.
St. John of San Francisco, Pray for Us.
All Ye Holy Angels & Saints, Pray for Us.

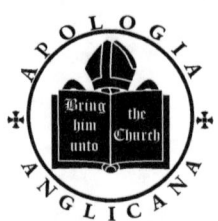

© 2025 Some Rights Reserved (CC-BY-SA-4.0)
Apologia Anglicana, LLC
Boston, MA
www.ApologiaAnglicana.org

www.ingramcontent.com/pod-product-compliance
Lightning Source LLC
Chambersburg PA
CBHW070320010526
44107CB00004B/371